SOCIAL WELFARE

THE NELSON-HALL SERIES IN SOCIAL WORK

Consulting Editor: Charles Zastrow
University of Wisconsin—Whitewater

ABOUT THE AUTHOR

Katherine Stuart van Wormer, a native of New Orleans, is associate professor of social work at University of Northern Iowa, Cedar Falls. The author's international experience includes community work in Catholic areas in Northern Ireland, where she taught English and actively participated in the Irish civil rights movement and campaign for nuclear disarmament. Ultimately becoming a social worker and alcoholism counselor in the United States, Dr. van Wormer was invited to Norway where she was the program director of the Vangseter Treatment Center. Recently, van Wormer initiated a faculty exchange program between University of Northern Iowa and University of Hull, England. A graduate of University of North Carolina, the author holds a graduate degree in education from Queens University, Northern Ireland; a master's degree from Western Kentucky University; a Ph.D. from University of Georgia; and a master's degree in social work from University of Tennessee, Nashville. Dr. van Wormer is the author of *Alcoholism Treatment: A Social Work Perspective* published in 1995 by Nelson-Hall.

SOCIAL WELFARE
A World View

KATHERINE VAN WORMER

University of Northern Iowa

Nelson-Hall Publishers

Chicago

Project Editor: Laura Weber
Production/Design: Tamra Phelps
Typesetter: Fine Print, Ltd.
Printer: The Maple Vail Book Manufacturing Company
Illustrations: Corasue Nicholas
Cover Painting: "The Delivery" by Gay McCarter

Library of Congress Cataloging-in-Publication Data

Van Wormer, Katherine S.
    Social welfare : a world view / Katherine van Wormer.
        p.   cm.
    Includes bibliographical references (p.   ) and index.
    ISBN 0-8304-1435-5
    1. Public welfare. 2. Social service. I. Title.
HV31.V35   1996
361—dc20   96-10556
                                                            CIP

Manufactured in the United States of America

10 9 8 7 6 5 4 3 2

The paper used in this book meets the minimum requirements of American National Standard for Information Sciences—Permanence of Paper for Printed Library Materials, ANSI Z39.48-1984.

DEDICATION

This book is dedicated to people of courage: conscientious objectors of the world, out-of-the-closet gays and lesbians, rape victims (men and women) who take a public stand against rape, and murder victims' families who publicly oppose the death penalty, and above all to the persons who see themselves not as citizens of a particular nation or commonwealth but, rather, as citizens of the world.

CONTENTS

Chapter 4: Historical Foundations of Social Work 159

Chapter 5: Poverty and Social Institutions 241

PART II

CARE THROUGH THE LIFE CYCLE

Chapter 8: Health Care and Housing 407

Chapter 9: Care for the Aged 469

PART III

WORLD POLICY ISSUES

PREFACE

My search for an appropriate textbook for the course, Social Welfare: A World View was unproductive. Various edited volumes contained single chapters on a selection of countries; these did not inspire me. When I consulted fellow instructors at a regional conference, they recommended the use of several small paperbacks, each covering a specialized and unrelated topic. The lack of continuity discouraged me from this plan. The one highly-readable and well-integrated textbook available, was hopelessly out of date due to events in eastern Europe which could not have been foreseen by the author.

At first when the thought occurred to me to write my own book, to present the United States and its social welfare system through international lenses, the task seemed insurmountable. While dismissing the recurring thought, I found myself excitedly collecting material from a magazine here, and a textbook there. From the United Nations and its affiliate, the World Health Organization, I gathered shocking statistics on missing females in Asia, facts on the AIDS epidemic in southeast Asia and Africa, and figures on death through illegal abortion. On a local radio station I heard a commentary on rural Iowa as a Third World Country. I called the radio station and requested a copy.

Why not just do a preliminary chapter outline, I thought, and see if these bits and pieces of knowledge, these disjointed data, fit together somehow? So I did, and they did. How exciting to view policies across the world, and to draw from these policies a sense of the global interconnectedness.

One land's blight, disease, or war spilling over into another's territory, one country's sick economy shaking up the balance of trade elsewhere, one nation's war reflected in a neighbor's refugee crisis: these all demonstrate the interdependence of countries of the world. Industrial pollution, similarly, contaminates earth and water without heed to national boundaries. In short, health, welfare, and environmental problems are becoming increasingly international in scope. There are positive aspects of the global network too: One nation's economic market may create demands for goods or services elsewhere which, in turn, may enhance cultural and technological growth. A communications revolution significantly decreases the sense of distance between places so that knowledge from around the world becomes the new world of knowledge.

This vision of interrelatedness combined with the need to ensure our common future has given shape to what is now this book, *Social Welfare: A World View.*

WHY AN INTERNATIONAL FOCUS

Persons who have lived in another country and been immersed in its folkways and language have a unique advantage in viewing the social welfare system of either their home or host country. They can understand the host country's pattern and identify incongruities. They can quickly pinpoint the customs and values of both the country of origin and the adopted country. Most natives of a particular country do not enjoy this perspective; they do not see the forest for the trees. Nor do they know the variety of trees that may grow there.

A view beyond regional borders reveals problems and solutions in a broader light. New possibilities abound. Indeed, for students of social welfare, merely learning the facts pertaining to one's own national policies (for example, legal stipulations and agency goals such as permanency planning) is less significant in the long run than learning to make connections between the facts to see how the parts belong to the whole. Policies come and go, but a holistic view can serve for all time.

Consistent with social work's focus on the person-in-the-environment, the focus of this book is on the country-in-the-world. The country is the United States, the topic is the social welfare system, and the framework is a holistic or ecosystems approach. The rudiments of this model will be discussed in chapter 1.

The reality of global interdependence extends to everyday social work practice. Increasing numbers of illegal immigrant, refugee, and cross-cultural child welfare cases reflect the growing diversity of the U.S. population. To provide competent service, persons in the helping professions will require familiarity

---

with the values and customs of diversified populations. At the policy-making level, knowledge of other countries' social welfare innovations can contribute to the resolution of domestic problems. While comparative study of other western welfare systems introduces the student to sophisticated social welfare options, recognition of a commonality of social problems between the United States and countries in the eastern and southern hemispheres is crucial to the amelioration of mutual concerns. The ubiquity of organized crime, terrorism, drug abuse, and disease epidemics graphically illustrates the interdependence of nations. Other problems such as high infant mortality, homelessness, and street crime represent the shared failure of nations to meet the needs of all their citizens. In short, for creative, well-informed policy-making on the local, or global level, a multicultural worldview is paramount. The word, *worldview,* is used in a double sense here to denote the perspective of the world as in Germany's worldview, and when used as two words, *world view* refers to a consideration of the whole world.

Accordingly, *Social Welfare: A World View* is designed to challenge, even provoke readers into examining their preconceived notions concerning their country's treatment of the poor, the sick, and the elderly. The comparative approach helps reveal the uniqueness of the United States' ideology regarding human need and suffering. There is much to learn from a study of alternative solutions to common problems.

This volume has been shaped to achieve two often mutually exclusive objectives. The first objective is to critically examine social welfare issues from an international perspective. It is imperative that students of social welfare recognize the bearing of cultural factors on a society's allocation of resources. International material challenges complacency and raises questions concerning traditional policy responses of a given society.

The second objective of this book is to provide a highly useful and comprehensive study which covers in detail the fundamentals of the history and structure of the social welfare system in U.S. society. As a general textbook, the content is organized to follow course outlines for basic, introductory courses which examine social welfare programs, policies, and issues. *Social Welfare* also discusses specific populations which have suffered particular hardships within the broader society. These groups include women, African Americans, Native Americans, Hispanic Americans, gays and lesbians, persons with mental and physical illnesses, and the unemployed. The social, psychological, political, and economic dimensions of the United States' treatment of minority groups are highlighted. The cross-cultural perspective, additionally, should provide a resource for both undergraduate and graduate-level courses concerned with global problems and development.

Due to the vastness of the subject matter and material available, the selection has necessarily been quite limited. Selections for boxed readings are based on human interest, relevance to the chapter's subject matter, and cultural diversity. Readings on environmental destruction in Haiti, homelessness in Japan, and prostitution and slavery worldwide are chosen to parallel similar crises in the United States. Such thought-provoking material from the worldwide press and autobiographical sketches are geared to personalize the presentation of the text.

Based on the knowledge provided in this textbook, students who complete a course in international social welfare should be able to: understand how values may be an aid or hindrance in the provision of social services; grasp how a society's social welfare system is dependent upon the financial and human resources available; be familiar with services or programs available for the dispersion of resources; learn of the structure of the provision of services; realize the social psychology of helping and punishing vulnerable citizens; be familiar with policies pertaining to the provision of social services throughout a person's life cycle (e.g., services for infants, the sick, and the aged); view the social policy issues of the day within the context of the global corporate economy; and recognize the international similarities and differences in social work roles in the development and provision of social services. This textbook offers the following features:

- An ecological, interactionist framework for viewing the personal dimension within the social environment.
- Composite portraits of alternative responses to social problems of global concern in Japan, Mexico, Norway, Canada, and Great Britain, as well as the United States.
- A developmental focus in comparing problems facing impoverished children and families in both industrialized and non-industrialized nations.
- Attention to the physical environment and the interrelationship between the environment and society; emphasis on the need for a sustainable world.
- A multifaceted survey of social welfare subsystems such as child welfare, health care, corrections, and services to the elderly (women's and minority issues will be infused throughout the text as well as dealt with in separate chapters).
- Attention to oppressed populations, including gays and lesbians in various parts of the world.

- Dynamic excerpts from international and popular sources revealing the human side of social issues.
- Summary and review questions at the end of each chapter.
- A comprehensive instructor's manual to accompany the text.

COUNTRIES CHOSEN

The countries singled out for close study in this comparative text are Great Britain, Japan, Mexico, Canada, and Norway/Sweden. Each of these countries should be of special interest to social welfare students for its following attributes:

Great Britain: The roots of the North American social welfare system are in the British Poor Laws which introduced a system of residual assistance for the destitute. The political and economic affairs of the United States and the former mother country have been intertwined over the years.

Japan: A densely populated country of the Far East with relatively few social problems and one of the highest life expectancies in the world, this capitalist society provides a welfare system dependent on employers and women family members. The collectivist thrust contrasts sharply with American individualism. Japan represents a clear political polarity in terms of reliance on the state for social welfare entitlement.

Mexico: A Latin American country undergoing rapid social and economic change due in part to the trade agreement with the United States, this nation is chosen to represent a nation where most welfare comes from family care and yet one in which the national statistics on life expectancy, human rights violation, literacy, crime, and environmental pollution are indicative of a developing nation undergoing rapid change.

Canada: A country often overlooked by internationally oriented American textbooks, Canada offers proximity, a federal system covering a similar expansive territory, historic, and ethnic heritage, yet alternative approaches to health care, poverty, and crime control to those found in the United States. The economic systems of Canada and the United States are intertwined, nevertheless.

Norway/Sweden: Both countries represent the welfare state *par excellence.* Here prevention of problems is given precedence over treatment. These largely homogeneous societies provide universal, cradle-to-grave protection for their citizens. Despite trends toward privatization (especially in Sweden), faith in the government to provide social services is in sharp contrast to the U.S. suspicion of government interference in the private doings of individuals.

Each of these societies selected for study in the chapters to follow represents a different geographical region and tradition, and each has developed its own unique approach to social welfare, embedded in the social fabric of the culture.

To present a complete picture of social welfare internationally, illustrative material is included from various parts of the world. The selections include the slaughter of street children in Brazil, street social work in Hong Kong, care of the elderly and dowry deaths in India, organized crime in Russia, and the human side of marketing alcohol in central Africa. The inclusion of this diverse material is consistent with social work's commitment to resolving issues of global poverty and oppression, and learning from other countries' social welfare innovations.

PLAN OF THE BOOK

This text is divided, like Gaul in the old Latin schoolbooks, into three parts. The five chapters comprising part I concern the functions and structure of social welfare. In order to elucidate the more specific material, chapter 1 provides the theoretical framework of the book and of social work as well, and provides the concepts, definitions, and teachings of other disciplines (psychology, sociology, and anthropology) pertinent to this work. Analysis of social value systems and methods of regulating the poor lays the groundwork for what follows.

Chapter 2 deals with the structure and underlying ideology of social welfare in the United States. In addition, for comparative purposes, alternative social welfare arrangements in Great Britain, Japan, Mexico, Canada, and Norway/Sweden are described, with emphasis on cultural and value systems.

Beginning with the earliest known religious and philosophical traditions, chapter 3 on the foundation of social welfare places the Anglo-American method of providing social help in historical context. International social phenomena of present and past—war, serfdom, and slavery—are viewed in terms of human suffering.

Social work, the profession most closely associated with social welfare, is examined historically and internationally in chapter 4. Unique among the professions, the practice of social work is shaped by economic and political forces: Economics determines the scope of the services offered, politics determines their form. These two factors are often intertwined. Today's notion of the free market economy, for instance, is both economic and political. The recent upsurge in right wing politics throughout the Americas and western Europe has drastic implications for the social work profession. Punishment is in; treatment and rehabilitation are out. This chapter considers the implications from a cross-cultural perspective. While social workers in all societies are committed to improving the social welfare of the people, social work is also marked by diversity in the roles performed. Much of this diversity is related to the economic and political climate of a given society.

Poverty, the subject of chapter 5, is an issue with worldwide implications. On the continents of Asia, Africa, and South America, the majority of people live at near subsistence levels. Due to famine, wars, and overpopulation, the number of poor has increased in urban and rural areas everywhere. Global economic policies can also be shown to bear responsibility for the growing discrepancy between the rich and the poor across the globe.

Whereas part I is concerned with the structural aspects of social welfare, part II presents the human dimension. The organization of this section of the book is in terms of the lifespan or life cycle—the universal human progression associated with chronological age and developmental tasks.

Chapters 6 though 9 will cover the spectrum from birth until death, emphasizing informal as well as formal systems of care. What is the societal response to basic human needs? To child welfare? To work and family welfare? To health care and housing? And to care for the aged? These issues exist in every part of the world. After all, human needs at various parts of the life cycle are the same. Yet every culture deals with life and its progression in its own way—the care of young and old, the protection of families, and the provision for health care and housing. Chapters 6 and 9, therefore, are concerned with contemporary needs and trends in rendering services across the spectrum of age. Facts presented in these chapters sensitize the student to the growing array of client problems, issues that transcend international boundaries, and to compelling human rights issues as well.

Part III surveys social policies in the modern world. The chapters included in this section reveal the extent to which we live in a global village. Nations of the world have become increasingly interdependent. This trend is manifest economically, politically, and technologically. The focus of chapter 10 is on special populations in an international context. The growing diversity of the North

American population is replicated throughout the world as refugees are forced to migrate across borders. The theme of the chapter is the nature of prejudice and its consequences. Treatment of ethnic minorities, women, and gays and lesbians is also considered.

Human rights issues are dealt with in chapter 11. Topics included in this section range from human rights violations in times of war to a comparative study of criminal justice systems across the world. Whether in war or peace, the ability of the state to deprive its citizens of life and freedom represents the ultimate power. The definition of crime and appropriate punishments differs by country and state. Human rights violations, when measured in terms of international standards of justice, are surprisingly widespread. Today, in the West, the fervor to punish is strong; mandatory sentencing and removal of prisoner privileges have become politically popular. Financial resources invested in building prisons are diverted from other social welfare programs.

The connection between the physical and social environment is increasingly recognized by social workers all over the world. The depletion of natural resources is the cause of severe suffering in non-industrialized nations. Pollution from industry is associated with health problems everywhere—a burden carried disporportionately by the poor. The physical environment, a primary global issue for today and the future, is the subject of the concluding chapter titled Sustainable Development. The international economy, through corporate activities and the restructuring requirements of the World Bank, has been associated with the despoilment of the environment, thereby reducing the quality of life in many areas. The air, land, and water have all been affected. Family planning, the resettlement of refugees, and other similar welfare programs necessitate cooperative efforts across national boundaries. The emergence of an impetus for global social policy remedies through the United Nations is a significant development in international social welfare.

Observations of numerous treatment, welfare, and correctional institutions abroad and here in the United States, and familiarity with alcoholism treatment establishments here and in Norway contribute to this text. Case studies, relevant interviews, anecdotes, and international charts and tables enable the reader to witness the various aspects of the welfare apparatus. Where possible, the human element of giving and receiving (or not receiving) welfare benefits, is included. The political is forever personal. One would not want to leave the student merely poring over graphs and tables and, like the William Faulkner character, "unable to listen—too busy with the facts."

During the final stages of production of this book, President Clinton announced his decision to sign into law a sweeping welfare bill designed "to end welfare as we know it." The Personal Responsibility and Work Opportunity Act of 1996 is expected to save the nation $55 billion over six years. Savings will come in the form of drastic cuts in food stamps, cash assistance to poor children, and benefits to legal immigrants, disabled and otherwise. As the United States government ends federal responsibility for welfare and turns it over to the states, the lives of tens of millions of Americans will be drastically altered. Official estimates predict that the new provisions will throw a million more children into poverty. The only question is how much pain, anguish, and misery will it take before we learn once again what happens when society turns on its own? But, alas, that is the subject for a later book, one that will tell a longer and undoubtedly, sadder story.

ACKNOWLEDGMENTS

My thanks and appreciation to the University of Northern Iowa for granting me a professional development leave to pursue writing of this book, and to the graduate college for its generosity in funding travel abroad. Members of the Fem School Collective, a women's community for feminist social work, provided many thoughtful suggestions, personal support, and a wealth of bibliographical material that shaped the course of this project from its earliest stage. Additionally, I am grateful to Carri Fox and JoEllyn Reinertson who typed diligently, uncomplainingly, draft after draft of the original manuscript, and who somehow make the unreadable, readable. And finally, I want to thank Laura Weber, editorial assistant of Nelson-Hall, whose meticulous attention to detail, although it drove me "up the wall" at times ("author: please clarify;" "author: provide a reference;" "author: what is this? Please explain."), thoughtfulness, patience, and good humor brought this lengthy project to fruition.

PART I

SOCIAL WELFARE FUNCTIONS
AND STRUCTURE

1

SOCIAL VALUES:
THE THEORETICAL CONTEXT

There's nothing so practical as good theory.—Kurt Lewin

The basic concerns of social welfare—poverty, disability, disease, and care of the young and old—have been the concerns of society from time immemorial. The world over, common societal needs generate similar institutional responses and national ideologies shape the level of care provided. Despite surface similarities, however, there are vast international differences in the magnitude of the problems encountered and in the nature and pattern of services developed to deal with them. The idea that social welfare is a guarantee of well-being for all citizens is more firmly rooted in some countries (for example, in the northern parts of western Europe) than in others. Countries that value independence, autonomy, and minimal governmental interference, like the United States, are likely to be resistant to sweeping welfare legislation. Countries with strong labor and socialist political parties, on the other hand, are more apt to be amenable to the social service provisions.

How is the wealth in a given country distributed? How much poverty and misery is one state or nation willing to tolerate? Why are there such vast socio-political differences in the provision of services around the world? The answers can be sought in the predominant social values of a people, or the national ethos. The means of ensuring the welfare of a people, in fact, may be determined as much by the national mood—the values and beliefs of the day and

3

the place — as by the economic situation. In the end, it is not the level of a nation's wealth that is important. It is the basis for the distribution of that wealth that matters. Accordingly, this introductory chapter provides the theoretical framework for understanding the close interrelationship between a society's values and its social policies for addressing need. Unlike other chapters in this volume, chapter 1 is largely theoretical: Its purpose is to lay the building blocks for a better understanding of the more factual material that follows.

Following a discussion of relevant terms, we will examine the concept of social values from the following disciplines: psychology, social psychology, sociology, anthropology, and social work. A discussion of American social values completes this chapter.

DEFINITION OF TERMS

Social Welfare

The word *welfare* harks back to the Middle English word for well-being. In German the word used for social welfare is *wohlfahrt* and in Norwegian it is *velferd*. The Spanish word is *bienestar* and in French it's *bien-être;* literally, well-to be. All these meanings are highly positive. These words are related to the English word *benefit,* derived from Latin.

The Social Work Dictionary (Barker, 1995) gives the following definition of *social welfare:*

1. A nation's system of programs, benefits, and services that help people meet those social, economic, educational, and health needs that are fundamental to the maintenance of society.
2. The state of collective well-being of a community or society.

Probably because of its association in the United States with the downtrodden of society, social welfare and welfare work have come to assume negative connotations. Persons "on welfare" are stigmatized by the wider society; the welfare system itself and its workers are stigmatized also. The fragmentation of issues encourages the ubiquitous complaint that our social welfare efforts are a "crazy quilt" of overlapping and conflicting programs that create waste (Marmor et al., 1990). Karger and Stoesz (1990: 353) define *social welfare policy* as:

The regulation of the provision of benefits to people who require assistance meeting basic needs in living, such as employment, income, food, health care, and relationships.

Welfare State

Much more confusing in its usage is the term *welfare state*. To writers such as Gould (1993), welfare state is a term that should be reserved for those countries that are committed to a policy of full employment and in which the state is responsible for the provision of comprehensive services, such as in northern Europe. Bryson's concern (1992) is that what is left of the welfare state, a term originating from Germany in the 1930s, is quickly being eroded in Germany and elsewhere by a counterreaction. Bryson's definition of *welfare state* is fairly inclusive and refers to the achievement of a minimum level of aid for citizens. The problem is in determining the meaning of minimum. The National Association of Social Workers' (NASW) definition (Barker, 1995) of welfare state is less ambiguous:

> A nation or society that considers itself responsible for meeting the basic educational, health care, economic, and social security needs of its people.

Because of its clarity, this is the definition that will be used in this text. According to this definition, one could say that the capitalist countries of Japan and the United States have weak forms of the welfare state in contrast to Scandinavian countries.

Social Work

The profession most closely related to the provision of social welfare services is social work. Social work is the professional occupation of graduates of accredited schools of social work who help individuals, groups, or communities enhance their social functioning. The term social worker is restricted to persons who are professionally trained in the skills and ethics of social work practice. Incorrect usage of the term sometimes occurs as, for instance, when the mass media refer to any person who distributes food stamps as a social worker. The worker at a social welfare office may or may not be a member of the profession.

Whereas psychiatrists rely primarily on the strengths of their biological training in medicating and treating individuals, and psychologists rely heavily on their psychological testing instruments in assessing their patients, social workers are trained in macro- as well as micro-level intervention (Morales and Sheafor, 1995). The growth and development of the social work profession are chronicled in chapter 3 which surveys social work in an international context.

Developing Country

In collaboration with the International Committee of the Council on Social Work Education (CSWE), a curriculum manual was produced by Healy (1992) for the purpose of providing teaching modules with international content for use by social work educators. This manual uses the term *developing country* to contrast the lower-income, less industrialized countries of the world with the more industrialized, higher-income countries labeled as *developed* countries. There are two major drawbacks to the use of these terms. First, the differentiation between developing and developed is pejorative. Second, the implication that economic growth necessarily breeds progress for the majority of people is faulty. Quite often progress exists only for the wealthy elite. In contrast to these notions, social development theory includes the meeting of common human needs (Healy, 1992). A newer term, *sustainable development*, refers to the achievement of social progress while preserving available resources for use by future generations.

The difficulty still persists in finding a term to adequately differentiate technologically advanced countries from others. Over the past decade the terms *First World, Second World,* and *Third World* have gained currency. The origin of the terms is provided by Healy (1992: 20):

> *Third World:* A term used to describe the poorer nonindustrialized countries of the world. Related concepts are the *First World* (the industrialized nations), and the *Second World* (the Soviet Union and its satellites). The term originated from the French, *Tiers Monde,* labeled from the parallel between the poorer countries and the *Tiers État,* or Third Estate in the French

Revolution. Usage is now controversial, as it is interpreted by some to put poorer countries last in importance.

Other objections include the obsolescence of the Second World with the dissolution of the Soviet Union, and the fact that some countries that are considered Third World due to the level of poverty represent great accumulation of capital at the higher echelons. Accordingly, the Third World concept will only be used in this book in quotes and selections from other sources.

Because of the limitations of present terminology, general terms will have to suffice. Thus geographical terms such as North/South, countries of the South, the Western Hemisphere, and so on, and descriptive terms such as overpopulated nations, or technologically advanced countries, or the non-industrialized world will be used to highlight differences in standards of living. Where possible, specific regions of the world will be named as, for example, Latin America, sub-Saharan Africa, and Northern Europe.

What does the news story, "Elderly Couple Who Shoplifted Find Compassion Instead of Court," in box 1.1 say about American society? How could one explain to a foreign visitor that in the midst of harshness there is kindness, and in the midst of impersonal policies there is personal generosity? How does one explain the social values of a nation when the contradictions may be more evident than the generalities? How does one single out social values at all?

We will return to the news story at the end of the chapter. In order to define the predominant social values of the United States or in any other country, we will draw upon the wealth of knowledge from the social and behavioral sciences.

A logical starting point for discussion of the values on which the social welfare system is based is with the concept of common social needs. The formal or informal help that a society provides is tied to the society's definition of needs and to the importance attached to these needs. Social welfare, in fact, can be considered the institutional expression of society's interest in meeting human needs. One of the disciplines most closely associated with the study of human needs is psychology.

PSYCHOLOGY OF SOCIAL VALUES

Psychology examines human behavior from the viewpoint of the individual. Emphasis is placed on learning, drives, and motivation. Sigmund Freud, the

BOX 1.1

ELDERLY COUPLE WHO SHOPLIFTED FIND COMPASSION INSTEAD OF COURT

Deborah Wiley

An elderly Clinton couple arrested last month for shoplifting a package of cheese and a bag of peanuts have found mercy in the courts of law and public opinion.

David Tiesman, 72, and his wife, Alice Tiesman, 66, admitted they slipped the items, worth just more than $3, into her purse Sept. 23 because they needed food but couldn't afford to pay for it.

By Friday, charges had been dismissed in court and word about their situation had resulted in an outpouring of food and other donations.

David Tiesman said he was grateful for the help, because about $500 of the couple's combined $800 monthly Social Security income is used to cover medications for Alice Tiesman's heart condition and diabetes.

When caught at the Eagle Supermarket in Clinton, he said, he tried to rectify the situation.

"I just went and took a cheese and they caught me at it," said Tiesman, who had about $2 at the time. "I told them I'd pay for it." Instead, the couple was arrested and charged.

When vacationing store manager Bob Davis returned to work, he gave about $150 worth of groceries to the couple and said he'd drop the charges, Tiesman said.

Davis refused to comment about the incident Friday.

Others who heard of the couple's plight offered meat, potatoes, apples, chicken and other goods, enough to last about two months, Tiesman said. Some of the donated goods will have to be eaten by David Tiesman alone, because they contain salt or sugar, which Alice Tiesman can't have, he said.

"People have come up who I have never met in my life," said Tiesman. "We got a lot of help."

And a local barber extended another helping hand: "I didn't know the guy, but he's just around the corner from where I live," said Tiesman. "He said, 'You come up and get your hair cut the rest of your life.'"

Source: Des Moines Register, October 3, 1992, p. 1. Reprinted with permission of the *Des Moines Register.*

father of psychoanalysis, pinpointed love and work as indispensable to happiness. Psychologist Abraham Maslow (1970) provided a fuller paradigm of needs, taking into account a range of variables. Maslow's hierarchy of needs includes the primary or physiological needs which have to be fulfilled before higher needs can be met. As shown in figure 1.1, the basic physical needs of human survival must be met first before higher levels of needs — safety, belongingness and love, esteem, and self-actualization — are realized. Self-actualization refers to a person achieving his or her highest potential as a human being. Because each person in Maslow's conceptualization tries to satisfy these needs in ascending order, high self-esteem is not likely to occur in the absence of love, or self-actualization without a certain degree of financial security. Nor is the stage of self-actualization permanent. Given the uncertainties in life, one may lose his or her balance at any moment and be reduced to the lowest rung of the ladder, struggling at the level of mere survival.

This theory is psychological in its emphasis on an individual driven by impulses toward an identifiable goal. The concepts of esteem and self-actualization are not aggregate concepts, certainly. Strength comes from one's own inner resources, not from rootedness in the community. Because of its relevance to social welfare, however, Maslow's conceptualization of human needs is commonly cited in social work literature. With slight modification (such as linking self actualization to generativity — giving to others and posterity) the hierarchy-of-needs construct offers a guide for comparative evaluation. The

FIGURE 1.1
Maslow's Hierarchy of Needs

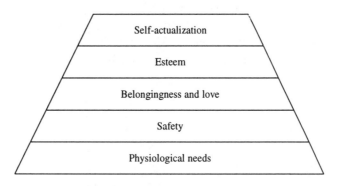

Source: Formulation of Maslow, A. (1970). *Motivation and Personality.* New York: Harper & Row.

connection between social values and common human needs is reflected in a society's priorities. Does the society meet the needs of all its people or of only those determined to be deserving on the basis of strictly determined criteria?

SOCIOLOGICAL FRAMEWORK

To the traditional sociologist, social values are essential as organizing principles for the integration of individual and group goals. Values are internalized by members of society through the process of socialization (Abercrombie et al., 1988). In a homogeneous society, values are relatively tangible and easy to define. In a heterogeneous society, however, there may be a contradiction in values held by different parts of the society during different periods of time. The contrast between the social values of homogeneous Iceland and of the diversified United States illustrates this point.

Social Institutions

In sociological terminology, roles that are standardized become social institutions. The social roles and norms comprising the social institution define proper and expected behavior oriented to the fulfillment of a particular social need (Theodorson and Theodorson, 1969). Like the family, religion, and education, social welfare is a social institution with a distinct function to perform and structures that enable it to do so (Federico, 1990). Social welfare institutions exist for the purpose of ensuring the well-being of individuals, groups, and communities. The nature and extent of social welfare activities are shaped by the values of society. The values determine who is to be helped and the extent of the assistance that is offered.

Functionalism

Borrowed originally from biology, the functionalist perspective focused solely on the structure of an organism. However, the functionalist perspective in sociology provides for the viewing of social phenomena in terms of structure and function. Functionalist analysis asks the question, how is a given phenomenon functional for society? Or alternatively, how is it dysfunctional? A sociologist, for example, might analyze the functions and dysfunctions of deviant behavior. Related concepts are manifest and latent functions of a social phenomenon. Manifest functions are the obvious, stated reasons for an activity while the latent functions are the secondary, sometimes unintended, often hidden motives behind its existence. Whereas Robert K. Merton (1949) in his classic definition of latent functions defined them as neither intended nor recognized, we will rely on the dictionary definition of latent as "lying hidden or underdeveloped within a person or thing, derivation is from the Latin verb, to be hidden" (*Webster's New World Dictionary,* 1991). See table 1.1 for examples of manifest and latent functions.

Functional analysis is a useful technique utilized in sociology and anthropology to reveal the community value of a cultural trait or institution (such as religious rituals). Viewing a cultural norm (for example, punishing those who shirk responsibility) in terms of manifest and latent functions, and dysfunctions leads to new ways of thinking about social phenomena. This approach will be used as a means of explaining a number of concepts (for example, social welfare and poverty) that will be discussed in subsequent chapters of this book.

TABLE 1.1
Manifest and Latent Functions

Item or Activity	Manifest Functions	Latent Functions
Car	Transportation	Status
Higher education	Job preparation	Keeping people off job market
Military hair-cut	For neatness, cleanliness	Creating a new identity
Funeral	Bury the dead	Grieving, funeral home business
Prisons	Protect society	Getting revenge
War	Free a country	Economic interests
New Deal	Alleviate poverty	Preventing riots and Marxism
Welfare benefits	Provide for well-being	Controlling the poor

Regulating the Poor

Piven and Cloward (1993), following the functional analysis definition of Merton, viewed the social welfare system as a societal device for "regulating the poor" in the interests of capitalism. This is the latent function of social welfare. Creating consensus and encouraging social altruism—the rationales that figure so largely in traditional histories of social welfare—are the manifest functions of the social welfare system (Piven and Cloward, 1993). Chapters 3 and 5, which tackle the foundations of social welfare and poverty, will examine the "regulating the poor" thesis in greater depth. Of relevance to social values is the fact that the degree to which social control over the poor is exercised is a reflection of the values of the dominant groups in the society.

Social Needs and Power

Unlike the approach of the psychologist, the sociologist looks at needs subjectively and collectively. Needs are real if people perceive them to be real (Horton and Hunt, 1976). Real or imagined, needs may stimulate innovation, social change, and the manufacturing of new products. The marketing of products creates a sense of need, where heretofore, there was none. Conversely, although living conditions may be quite low, there may be no perception of need. Mexican social workers, for instance, might see family strengths where visiting Americans might only see the lack of electricity and running water. At the same time, Mexican social workers will go beyond the giving of charity to individuals and also address the *causes* of social inequities (Bibus, 1995).

Over the centuries, out of sheer ignorance, the root causes of problems have often been overlooked. For instance, in cities sickness and death resulted from water contamination and personal filth. Today, similarly, failure to recognize a need for birth control in some parts of the world is associated with mass misery and starvation. When a nation's rulers value military might over health and housing, the social welfare system is diminished accordingly. People in need are left to fend for themselves. Social values shift over time and are influenced by the vested interests in the society.

Whether or not cultural values differ according to social class is one of the enduring controversies within the fields of sociology and criminology.

Sociologists generally agree that some American cultural values such as materialism and achieving status are universal, and that other values such as delaying gratification and obeying the social norms vary from class to class (Macionis, 1994). The middle classes are considered more scrupulous than persons at the top or bottom. *Power* is a sociological concept of relevance to both social class and the possession of values. In the tradition of Max Weber, power can be defined as the ability to get people to do what you want even against their will (Abercrombie et al., 1988). Perhaps the key issue of interest to social welfare is who in the society has the power to get his or her perceived needs met and who does not. A related issue is who in society can meet these ends without violating the norms of society. For example, who can achieve wealth and status through conventional means and who must use illegitimate means to achieve the same?

From another angle, those with power ("the power elites") can shape a society according to the principles they value. In a real sense they control the flow of knowledge as well as the knowledge itself. For instance, corporations and companies advertising in the local newspaper may have an inhibiting effect on news reporting of various sorts because newspapers don't want to lose their funding. Information imparted in a political campaign, similarly, is apt to be influenced by the giant contributors to that campaign. The burgeoning political influence of conservative think tanks on the mass media is described in the following chapter.

SOCIAL PSYCHOLOGICAL CONCEPTS

Interaction

The discipline of social psychology falls midway between psychology and sociology in terms of the size of the population being studied. Social psychology studies the individual interacting with the group, and the group as internalized within the individual. In other words, as C.H. Cooley (1909) eloquently stated, "Self and society are twin born." Interactionism, reciprocity, internalization of norms—these are fundamental concepts of social psychology that have clear relevance for social values. They are also concepts widely used in social work. Like social psychology, social work views individuals in constant interaction with other individuals and with the environment.

As the theoretical frameworks for later chapters of this book concern issues such as special populations and oppression, and crime and punishment, we will draw upon two classics from social psychology—Gordon Allport's *The Nature of Prejudice* (1981/1954) and Erving Goffman's *Asylums* (1961). Allport's discussion of the theory of displaced aggression—the redirecting of anger from one source onto a vulnerable person or group—is highly informative. Unemployed persons may scapegoat other oppressed groups, for example. Goffman's analysis of punishment rituals is equally compelling. An individual who, through whatever cruel circumstance, comes to acquire a role, the role of prisoner, say, may internalize that role to the point of undergoing observable behavior change. Labeling theory from sociology is a related concept. The individual receives a label from society (for example, juvenile delinquent) and then through a self-fulfilling prophecy he or she becomes the image of that label. This process involves the development of a distinctive self identity, which is quite often a negative one.

The social psychology of values posits that through the interaction with significant others, we come to see ourselves as others see us and we take on their values. This is the process of socialization. Social psychologists have studied social value orientations in small groups (Baron and Graziano, 1991). Personal values of cooperation, altruism, competitiveness, and individualism are revealed in problem-solving laboratory situations. Cooperators are more inclined to make prosocial, mutually beneficial choices than individualists or competitors are. Generalizing from the microcosm to society, it can be seen that the socialization into the norms of helpfulness and cooperation is congruent with the dominant value orientations that support the welfare of the group or community.

Prejudice

Prejudice, which we can define as a preconceived and unjustified negative attitude, is a widely studied phenomenon. Before turning to the social psychology of prejudice, let us consider the cultural dimensions. Prejudice against others who are different is largely learned through others' comments, attitudes, and possibly a negative experience with members of the disfavored group. A history of war, territorial disputes, persecutions, and economic exploitation exacerbates prejudice in the exploiters who must justify their group's deeds. Those who are exploited, quite naturally, will be prejudiced as well. Once ethnic or racial hatred is entrenched, the tendency is for it to escalate. As people become defined as enemies, their misdeeds are remembered and dwelled upon. Thus in the former Yugoslavia as in Azerbajan and in Northern Ireland, William Faulkner's description of the postbellum South is hauntingly apt, "the past is not dead; it's not even past."

To ask the classic sociological question—what are the functions of prejudice? Prejudice solidifies the group and encourages internal bonding. By scapegoating an outgroup, the powers-that-be in a society are protected. For example, during periods of economic depression in the South, the poor whites targeted blacks. In the United States today, with the working class effectively divided along racial lines, the power elites can rule without opposition. Each of these functions listed can be construed, of course, as dysfunctions. Chapter 10 on marginalized populations chronicles some of the pain associated with oppression related to prejudice.

The social psychology of prejudice is more complex, but also more intriguing. Bogardus' social distance scale devised in 1928, and used by generations of college students across the years, provides a measure of acceptance of various designated groups. The particular groups selected vary with geographical location and concerns of the day. This familiar technique asks respondents to indicate which steps on the following scale they would admit members of various ethnic, religious, and racial groups: 1. To live in my country; 2. To employment in my occupation; 3. To my neighborhood; 4. To my club as personal friends; 5. To close kinship by marriage.

Generally, the closer the contact, the greater the reluctance to accept persons who are different from ourselves. In his definitive study, *The Nature of Prejudice,* Allport (1954) was struck by the generalization of outgroup prejudice, or the tendency for an individual to be intolerant of all forms of diversity. Prejudice is basically a trait of personality, claims Allport, one that is correlated with hostility and fear. Social psychologists, in fact, are inclined to regard such generalized prejudice as a symptom of a particular type of personality.

Empirical support for the existence of a personality dimension in prejudice was provided during the 1940s by a team of researchers who carried out an in-depth investigation into the dynamics of anti-Semitism. The study was inspired by events that had occurred in Nazi Germany. Adorno et al. (1950) devised an F-Scale to measure fascist or authoritarian tendencies. Among items included in this scale are the following:

- Obedience and respect for authority are the most important virtues children should learn.
- There is hardly anything lower than a person who does not feel great love, gratitude, and respect for his parents.
- Sexual offenders ought to be publicly whipped or worse.
- The businessman and the manufacturer are much more important to society than the artist and the professor.

Findings were that scores on the F-Scale correlated quite strongly with scores on scales of anti-Semitism, general ethnocentrism, and political conservatism (also dogmatic communism as revealed in a later study). To explain the development of authoritarianism, Adorno and his associates looked at early child-rearing practices. Employing arbitrary and harsh methods of discipline, authoritarian parents may produce children whose feelings of frustration are repressed. This hostility may be displaced and directed instead toward powerless groups in society.

Other social psychologists have studied the role of intergroup competition for scarce resources in promoting prejudice. Experiments with twelve-year-old summer campers revealed that conditions of extreme competition produced conflict and hostility between rival groups. When a situation was set up, however, where all opposing teams united to achieve superordinate goals, feelings of harmony and trust prevailed (Sherif et al., 1961). The findings of such small group experiments are relevant to situations experienced on the larger scale such as keen competition over well-paying jobs.

How can ethnic and racial prejudice be prevented or offset? The basic remedies range from societal to individual efforts. Although media campaigns against racial and ethnic hatred have had limited success, the inclusion for members of diverse groups in advertisements reinforces the notion of an integrated society. Legal remedies such as outlawing hate crimes and segregation practices can change attitudes as citizens are forced to comply with the law. Group therapy with individuals from varied backgrounds can enhance communication and the recognition of the universality of problems and feelings. Individual therapy can be of value in teaching empathy skills and in focusing on underlying problems that perhaps indirectly are related to intolerance. Finally, exposure to films and books depicting the lives of persons who have had to overcome prejudice may go a long way toward breaking our sense of dissimilarity with members of that particular population. The more we come to identify with others, the more we realize how much we have in common.

Blaming the Victim

A concept derived from psychologists of the social psychological school, victim blaming refers to a fundamental tendency in American culture (Zastrow, 1996). This tendency occurs when the downtrodden or underdogs of society are held responsible for creating their own distress. Because of the reciprocity involved, the victim tends to internalize the blame attached to his or her condition (the self talk is "I have failed"), and the negativity may become a self-fulfilling prophecy (the self talk becomes "I will never amount to anything").

In an article astutely titled, "All the World Loathes a Loser," Lerner (1971) indicates our vulnerability to the suffering of other people. We are only vulnerable, however, to the suffering of a hero. Condemning the victim (of crime, disease, a relationship) is a response we create privately without awareness so as to maintain our sense of justice in the world. The seemingly natural tendency is to believe that the unfortunate victim somehow merited his or her fate.

Pervasive in the American psyche, the phenomenon of blaming the victim is a generic process applied to almost every social problem in the United States (Ryan, 1976). As a traditional ideology related to the work ethic, intellectual, scientific, and religious forces have all historically fed the mythology. As noted by Dolgoff et al. (1993), the growth of industrialism, the development of the Protestant ethic and social Darwinism each contributed to blaming the victim. In chapter 3, we discuss these historical currents. Even today, new formulations of blaming are constantly appearing. Internal (genetic) differences among individuals once again have been paraded out as the rationale for social inequality (Herrnstein and Murray, 1994). New support has been lent to the old suspicion that social welfare programs cause more problems than they solve. Chapter 5 considers the blaming-the-victim ideology in terms of the social implications relating to poverty.

What is the opposite of victim blaming? Is it tolerance? Or support? In the helping professions, the opposite of blaming is *empathy*. Empathy is the ability to identify with another person and through a leap of the imagination momentarily to view the world through the other's eyes. The Sioux prayer reveals the difficulty in acquiring this virtue, "Oh Great Spirit keep me from judging a man until I've walked a mile in his moccasins." And in the words of the black gospel hymn, "Do not accuse, condemn, or abuse, til you've walked in my shoes."

These theoretical concepts of social psychology offer explanatory knowledge which helps us understand and predict human behavior. Seemingly bizarre aspects of human behavior are often normal reactions to abnormal situations. Such explanatory knowledge guides the practitioner in addressing several "why" questions: Why is a rape victim often blamed for her or his own victimization? Why do prison populations rise and fall with the national mood? Why are gays and lesbians subject to attack? Throughout, *Social Welfare: A World View* is concerned with the relationships among value orientations, worldviews, and social policy prescriptions. This book is concerned with the impact of the dominant values of the society and policies on various classes and categories of people. Internalization of values is a chief relevant concept from social psychology. Through interaction, the individual develops a self-perception, an image of himself or herself reflected from the broader society. The introjected sense of one's group membership, in turn, is reflected back onto society. One can understand hatred breeding hatred, violence breeding violence, and love breeding love accordingly.

ANTHROPOLOGICAL CONCEPTS

Cultural anthropology (in contrast to physical anthropology) is the study of human differences and variations in behavior pertaining to culture (Encyclopaedia Britannica, 1993). Different cultures may have many specific patterns that are similar, but within each culture there is an organization or configuration that renders it an integrated whole. Anthropologists look at culture as an adaptive mechanism, or a body of solutions for dealing with turbulence in the environment and with the vicissitudes of life.

Culture

The concept of culture is central to anthropology. Culture is social heredity, or a way of thinking, feeling, and believing that sets one group apart from another. Culture is traditional knowledge that is passed down from one generation to the next (Podolefsky and Brown, 1994). The individual's behavior is controlled by his or her culture in many deep and pervasive ways. Even what we think of as personality is culturally determined. Culture can be considered the mold in which the individual figure is cast.

Because of the close relationship between personality and culture, members of one nation or tribe (or sex) appear homogeneous to outsiders. A group member absorbs the essential content of a culture by means of socialization.

Language shapes and is shaped by culture. In Mexico, for example, where there is a complete reliance on the family to provide care, a visiting American social worker had difficulty translating the sentence, "My mother-in-law is in a nursing home" into Spanish (Bibus, 1995). In Mexico, according to Bibus, the meaning of life is the family. In the United States, the meaning of life is work. These differences in values are reflected in the spoken vocabulary.

Anthropologists study other cultures; many believe this is the best means of understanding ourselves (de Roche, 1989). Our notions of love, freedom, justice, and the like are highly culturally bound. The principles and practices by which we live are not always self evident. In working with persons from other cultural backgrounds understanding the native culture or point of view is essential. This includes worldviews and value orientations. Beginning with the client perspective and through ecological studies, anthropology has developed a systematic approach to knowing how the many different parts of whole cultural systems work together (Esber, 1989).

Systems Theory

The view of culture as an integrated whole borrows a concept from the biological sciences in which the organs of the body complement each other in remarkable ways to comprise a functioning system. Like an organism, culture has form and pattern. There is a degree of order and a system that is greater than the sum of its parts. To the anthropologist, the related patterns of the environment, the resources available for exploration within it, the organization of people to utilize the resources, their beliefs about what they do and the relationships between the larger group and themselves are all part of the system out of which individuals structure their behaviors (Esber, 1989).

Once a sense of a culture and its values is acquired, the social scientist can analyze the values in a systematic fashion. Is there internal consistency between ascribed values and practices? Which values are conducive to smooth functioning of the society and which are obstacles to smooth functioning? (Berger et al., 1991). In Northern Ireland, for instance, the dominant cultural values and beliefs favor school segregation for Catholics and Protestants. How is this arrangement conducive to harmony? How might it lead to conflict? What changes might one predict? In Japan, similarly, traditional values are being examined (see box 1.2 for a portrait of family life in Japan).

Ethnocentrism

According to Podolefsky and Brown (1994) the paradox of culture is that as we humans learn to accept our own cultural beliefs and values, we unconsciously learn to reject those of other people. Sumner (1906: 13) called the outlook that one's group is superior to other groups *ethnocentrism,* and defined it as "that view of things in which one's own group is the center of everything and all others are scaled and related with reference to it." Immigration provides an example of potential conflict as disparate value systems exist side by side. Boundaries between groups can become increasingly thick and exclusionary. Neighborhoods are affected by an influx of immigrants; the workplace is affected also as newcomers flock to accept jobs that locals would find undesirable. Such a complex set of potential problems must be addressed by the social welfare system; a holistic, non-ethnocentric approach to the delivery of services is essential. Awareness of one's own culture's peculiarities is the first place to start. We must learn about our own culture, according to Nakanishi and Rittner (1992) before we can learn about other cultures. The reverse is true also; we must have an appreciation for other cultures and their values before we can come to appreciate or even grasp our own. We are like the introspective hero of *Absalom, Absalom!* (Faulkner, 1936: 174) who must leave the South before he can answer questions regarding the South such as, "What's it like there. What do they do there?"

Margaret Mead, in her autobiography *Blackberry Winter* (1972: 275), provides this approach to unraveling the intricacies of a new culture. The goal is to: "Understand a myriad of acts, words, glances, and silences as they are integrated into a pattern one had no way of working out as yet, and finally, to 'get' the structure of the whole culture."

BOX 1.2

JAPAN'S MISSING CHILDREN

Like much of Asia, Japan boasts strong family values. Its divorce rate, though higher than it used to be, remains well below that of other rich countries: last year there were 1.53 divorces per 1,000 people, around a third of the American rate. On other measures, however, Japan's families are not so exemplary. For the past two decades they have not produced enough children to replace the parents' generation. Japan's total fertility rate, which is the number of children the average woman has by the end of her life, has fallen even further than elsewhere in the developed world.

This is a puzzle, for the Japanese love children. A screaming baby on a bus attracts sympathy, not disapproving stares. According to opinion surveys, nearly all young couples claim to want at least two children. What makes children scarce, according to Yasuhiko Yuzawa, of Ochanomizu University in Tokyo, is that Japan's young women are in no hurry to become the servants of men.

Two decades ago most Japanese women were married in their early to middle 20s; in 1970, for example, just 18% of women aged 25–29 were still single. By 1990, however, that proportion had doubled to 40%. In the end, women do succumb to marriage: by the age of 40–44, only 5.8% are single. But later marriages leave less time for having children.

Why put marriage off? Not for the sake of romantic adventure: a 1987 survey found that two out of five women aged 18–34 were not dating anybody. Instead, those in their 20s shun marriage because it means giving up both their jobs and their comforts. While they are single, most women work and live at home with their parents. This gives them plenty of spare cash. A 1991 survey in Tokyo found that 76% of unmarried women in their 20s lived with their parents; few did any housework or contributed to the household budget.

Once married, however, life gets tough. Only 13.5% of mothers with infants manage to carry on in full-time work. A 1991 survey found that only one working man in 30 did anything resembling housework on weekdays. On Sundays men are not much more helpful: even those married to women with full-time jobs spend an average of 26 minutes on housework and 12 minutes playing with their children.

Men's negligence reflects the attitude of companies. When long commutes are counted in, about one working man in two is away from home for 12 or more hours a day. Some get sent on compulsory postings so inconvenient that they abandon their families for a few years; in 1992 some 480,000 married men were living away from home

(Continued on next page)

BOX 1.2 (Continued)

Reluctant wives

Japanese fertility rate*

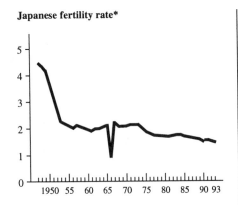

International fertility rates*

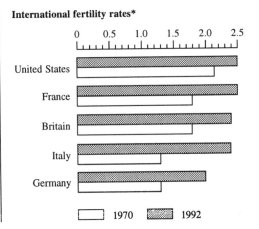

1970   1992

---

*Average number of children who would be born alive to a woman in her lifetime.
Source: Japan's Ministry of Health and Welfare: World Bank.

because of their work, 14.8% more than five years earlier.

Excluded from jobs and abandoned by their spouses, Japanese mothers concentrate on education for their offspring. Classes have sprung up for pregnant women to teach their unborn children English: mum intones vocabulary into a tube, which is attached to a funnel strapped to her belly. Fully 42% of pre-school children are shepherded off to special lessons (mainly sports or music); by the early teens the ratio hits 69% (mainly because of cram-school lessons). A 1992 survey in Tokyo found that more than one in five children in their early teens had no time on weekdays to talk to mother. Small wonder that women think twice before devoting their lives to them.

Source: The Economist, November 12, 1994, p. 46.

Margaret Mead's daughter, Mary Catherine Bateson (1984: 202–203) uses the metaphor of finding four-leaf clovers to describe the anthropological task. "A four-leaf clover," writes Bateson, "is a break in pattern, a light dissonance, that can only be seen against an awareness of the orderly configuration in the grass." Approaching an unfamiliar culture, one seeks regularity in behavior. Over time, the details that seem so chaotic at first do hang together. "Often a dissonance," says Bateson, "the interruption is one pattern you have learned to expect, is the key to a larger pattern" (204).

McMahon (1994) sees fear of the unknown as a natural part of ethnocentrism. Before understanding or appreciating other cultures, according to McMahon, an individual must strive to achieve multiculturalism. *Multiculturalism* is the state of feeling comfortable and communicating effectively with persons of diverse cultural backgrounds and outlooks.

AMERICAN SOCIAL VALUES

In confronting what Wilensky and Lebeaux (1958) termed "the reluctant welfare state," our first task is to come to terms with our ideological heritage. The basis of this heritage is found in a people's social values. Values are defined by Podolefsky and Brown as "the ideals of a culture that are concerned with appropriate goals and behavior" (1994: 284). Building on sociologist Robin Williams' (1979) classic array of crucial American values, Tropman (1989) has delineated seven fundamental value dimensions of clear relevance to the social welfare system. These seven value dimensions are: work, mobility, status, independence, individualism, moralism, and ascription.

Because the United States is a pluralistic society, there is much conflict among the various values and within each dimension itself. Consensus, as Federico (1990) indicates, is difficult to achieve in a large, heterogenous society composed of many different cultural groups, each with its own predominant values.

Well aware of the cultural contradictions and policy contradictions in the welfare state, Tropman (1989) discusses each value dimension in terms of both consistencies and dilemmas. Drawing on Tropman's framework, we will view each of the classic American values as singled out in Tropman's *American Values and Social Welfare*. The emphasis will be on the relationship between values and welfare. The underlying assumption of this discussion, consistent with systems theory is the notion of the general interconnectedness of values, attitudes, behavior (in this case, social welfare activities), and the political-economic structure.

WORK. A focal point of American culture is work and preparation for work. Through one's occupation or profession, an individual gains status and a sense of self importance. Equality of incomes from work is seen as undesirable because of the feared deleterious effects on work incentives and because of the detraction from the social esteem which high pay engenders (George and Wilding, 1976). The work ethic is a highly valued attribute in the United States; leisure time for workers is probably the least in the industrialized world. New workfare requirements are being tacked on to welfare benefits to ensure that only the "worthy" poor receive aid.

MOBILITY. A value related to work is the desire to "get ahead," to move upward and onward. A significant proportion of Americans are geographically mobile as well, moving their households every five years. The American ideology promotes a belief in progress; workers are expected to climb the corporate ladder and to be willing to relocate if necessary for career advancement; persons receiving government aid are expected to get training and to quickly gain their independence. Because the United States had been a land of unparalleled resources and opportunity, people who are downwardly mobile or who remain at the bottom are often held responsible for their lowly status. According to Dolgoff et al. (1993) the mentality continues to be that the problem somehow is in the psyche or the culture of the poor themselves rather than in the social conditions of the society.

STATUS. Status is one's position in society and is determined, according to Tropman, in terms of class (money), education, occupation, power, and prestige. The notion of achievement is closely related to status, a much admired attribute in American society. Recipients of social welfare benefits are often lumped together and given a common status. The belief that this is a just society is an important value in U.S. society. The counterpart of this is blaming the poor for the low standard of living in which they exist.

INDEPENDENCE. Within the family as well as society, Americans strive for independence. The word, *codependency,* which signifies a too-close emotional dependence, has taken on extremely negative connotations. Parents train their children to be independent and to one day leave the "nest." The myth of independence suggests that each individual is independently in control of his or her own destiny, according to Tropman. As people age, they fight to hang on to their independence as long as possible. The value of independence has important implications for social welfare. Prolonged dependence on government help is actively discouraged and many Americans refuse to accept benefits because of personal pride.

INDIVIDUALISM. In the 1830s, the French social philosopher and most renowned commentator on the American psyche, Alexis de Tocqueville (1966, orig. 1835) characterized the people on this continent as individualists. The risk to the American character, said de Tocqueville, was that in the future, isolation might prevail. The primary value dimension that sums up the cultural climate in the United States today is still this trait of individualism. Individualism is defined by George and Wilding (1976) as a composite creed dominated by the belief that people must be as free as possible to pursue their interests and to bear the consequences of their actions. The opposite trait of individualism is collective consciousness, the sense of "we" instead of "I."

On this side of the Atlantic, welfare programs are geared to specific individuals or groups who are functioning poorly. (In Europe the focus is more on the population as a whole.) In the United States social welfare programs that focus on changing the internal person, rather than the external system, have been favored. This is not to say that a collective spirit has not prevailed at various key periods in American history. Kaplan and Kaplan (1993) provide careful documentation to show that public opinion in the post-war era favored strong government intervention; surveys of that time reveal that a substantial portion of the population thought in collectivist terms. Again for a short period in the mid-sixties, the national fervor was for social and economic equity (chapters 2 and 3 will expound on this argument further).

MORALISM. Perhaps a carryover from Puritanism, moralism is one of the singular features of American society. Tropman defines moralism as the tendency to be judgmental about affairs and events. So pervasive is this notion to Americans that poverty becomes a moral issue, and money becomes the focus of moral judgment, according to Tropman. Time and again, the issues of responsibility and fault have been major concerns in addressing social problems. These themes generate one of the central social welfare conflicts—punishment versus compassion. Today, the construction of new jails and prisons is expanding exponentially. Meanwhile, clients are being forcibly removed from the welfare rolls.

ASCRIPTION. Ascription is the process of assigning attributes on the basis of inborn or cultural characteristics such as race, gender, disability, or ethnicity. Ascription involves a division in the society based on such characteristics. The opposite of ascription is a division based on achieved or earned qualities such as education and occupation. Most societies categorize people according to a combination of ascribed and achieved attributes.

Although modern, industrialized societies such as the United States are built on incentives of achievement rather than ascription, Tropman includes ascription as a major value dimension in light of the racism, sexism, and ageism in American society. Sometimes who you are seems to carry more weight than what you can do.

Because the lower class is composed of minority groups who are discriminated against on the basis of sex, age, race, ethnic background, or disability, society often judges its members harshly. Although it is not fashionable in most circles to be prejudiced, it is fashionable to crack the whip on welfare recipients (and also on prisoners). Illegitimacy, laziness, freeloading, irresponsibility— labels such as these are bandied about in a society built on a creed of independence, individualism, and inequality. Because the social work profession is associated with advocacy and programming for the down-and-outs, the stigma accorded this population has generalized into the helpers. The social work profession will be discussed shortly.

Katz (1985) has produced a paradigm of dominant U.S. white cultural values and beliefs. This list of European-American values, which are roughly comparable to Tropman's configuration, is reproduced in table 1.2.

Let's turn back to the news story presented earlier in the chapter. The example of a destitute, elderly couple who fell through the cracks of the health care system and resorted to theft, pinpoints the ambivalence which society feels toward

TABLE 1.2
The Components of White Culture: Values and Beliefs

Rugged individualism:
Individual is primary unit
Individual has primary responsibility
Independence and autonomy highly valued
and rewarded
Individual can control environment

Competition:
Winning is everything
Win/lose dichotomy

Action orientation:
Must master and control nature
Must always do something about a situation
Pragmatic/utilitarian view of life

Decision making:
Majority rule when whites have power
Hierarchical
Pyramid structure

Communication:
Standard English
Written tradition
Direct eye contact
Limited physical contact
Control emotions

Time:
Adherence to rigid time schedules
Time is viewed as a commodity

Holidays:
Based on Christian religion
Based on white history and male leaders

History:
Based on European immigrants' experience in
the United States
Romanticize war

Protestant work ethic:
Working hard brings success

Progress and future orientation:
Plan for future
Delayed gratification
Value continual improvement and progress

Emphasis on scientific method:
Objective, rational, linear thinking
Cause and effect relationships
Quantitative emphasis
Dualistic thinking

Status and power:
Measured by economic possessions
Credentials, titles, and positions
Believe "own" system
Believe better than other systems
Owning goods, space, property

Family structure:
Nuclear family is the ideal social unit
Male is breadwinner and the head of the
household
Female is homemaker and subordinate to the
husband
Patriarchal structure

Aesthetics:
Music and art based on European cultures
Women's beauty based on blonde, blue-eyed,
thin, young
Men's attractiveness based on athletic ability,
power, economic status

Religion:
Belief in Christianity
No tolerance for deviation from single god
concept

Source: Katz, J. (1985). The Sociopolitical Nature of Counseling. *The Counseling Psychologist,* 13: 615–624. Reprinted with permission of Sage: Thousand Oaks, CA.

the poor. A system set up to reward the rich and punish the poor—the U.S. social system—is simultaneously able to provide compassion. Put another way, medical needs were not met; the law was harsh; yet in the midst of harshness there is kindness, and in the midst of despair there is hope.

To Tropman's formulation of dominant American values I would add one more—charity. For those designated as the "worthy poor" an outpouring of generosity in an isolated case may ensue. The source of the charity is private, and the recipient is expected to convey gratitude. Unlike providers of formal welfare, the charity donors or philanthropists receive public acclaim. Like the welfare recipients, however, those who receive charity often experience a sense of shame.

SOCIAL WORK

In assisting persons to cope with their situations and maximize their social functioning, social work is the formalized activity that corresponds to society's interest in meeting common needs. Social workers are the practitioners in the welfare state (Cox, 1994).

The social work profession originally developed in response to international crises stemming from the Industrial Revolution and reflected at the local level. Over the years, the focus of American social work has shifted from the community, to the inner-psyche, to the person-in-the-environment—a happy middle ground between the first and second stages of professional development. And once again, social work is involved in helping to resolve problems brought on by international crises, this time related to forces in the global market.

Ecosystems Model

Ecosystems theory is interactive and concentrates on the effects of one person on another, and of one system on another, rather than on internal dynamics. Linear, cause and effect explanations are avoided. Although dichotomies or divisions into *either/or* categories (for example, "you are either for me or against me") may be employed for didactic purposes, *both/and* formulations (for example, you are both for me and against me) are preferred. For social action, the emphasis is on changing the environment rather than on molding the individual to the environment. Clients and their worlds are treated as systems in dynamic interaction with other systems.

Systems theory can be used to study the distinctiveness and interdependence of actions and to analyze and compare welfare policies and services (McMahon, 1994). Systems theory, moreover, can be employed to view the world in global context. The delicate balance of earth's biological life forms is in danger of being irrevocably altered by use of pesticides, industrial pollution, and destruction of natural resources. Cutting down rain forests in South America and Africa and Canada depletes the production of oxygen in the atmosphere affecting all life forms in one way or another. Fish and other aquatic life die from chemicals in the water; the food supply is irrevocably altered. As shown in these examples, any change in one part of a system has an impact on all other parts. A system can be visualized as a series of smaller units in constant interaction with each other comprising a whole which is more than the sum of the individual parts.

The current social work framework draws on an ecosystems orientation to practice that involves the application of ecology (the study of relationship between organisms and their environment) and general systems theory to the promotion of individual and social welfare. Locke's (1992) paradigm of multicultural understanding provides a solid foundation for explaining how ethnic differences among people impinge upon the social system with positive and/or negative consequences. Five levels of analysis are included in this model—individual, family, community, (dominant) culture, and global. Awareness of self and of one's cultural heritage to Locke is the key to understanding others' cultural values and traditions.

Tester (1994) has adopted an ecosystems model for social work practice in an ecological age. As figure 1.2 indicates, history, the economy, and culture are strong determinants in shaping the physical environment which, in turn, shapes the economy and culture. At the dawn of the twenty-first century, depletion and pollution of the physical environment threaten to become major influences on the social welfare of individuals and whole societies. Therefore, the *physical* environment is as much an issue for the social work profession as is the traditional focus on the social environment (Hoff, 1994). Social work's unique method of multidimensional and multilevel intervention and person-in-the-environment configuration render this profession ideally suited to address the relationship between people and their physical environment.

The environmental crisis is affecting present day life. Increasingly, our physical health, employment, recreation and leisure, the health of our children, the quality of work environments, and the level of stress and anxiety can be directly related to manipulations of the physical environment (Tester, 1994). Cultural values promoting extreme individualism, militarism, and competition to the neglect of care of the earth are at the heart of our destructiveness of natural resources. Yet the human needs of all people are dependent on natural resources — clean air and water, tillable soil, safe food, and adequate shelter. Tester (1994) provides a model for environmental social practice which encapsulates the emerging social work theory for sustainable living (see figure 1.2).

The Biopsychosocial Whole

At the individual level, the first level of analysis in Locke's multicultural scheme, the focus is on the biopsychosocial endowment each person possesses. The rapid expansion in the *biological* component of the biopsychosocial framework has generated the acquisition and use of new knowledge about genetic and biochemical links to individual problems (McMahon, 1994). For social work practice geared toward the biological side of human behavior, the practitioner must have knowledge of psychopathology, substance abuse, mental illness, the impact of illness on individuals and families, and psychotropic medications. The society's definition of the situation (the disease, disability, etc.) and of the causes give it meaning. Old age and death thus are regarded differently in various cultural settings.

Social work's focus of helping extends well beyond the individual to groups, families, and communities. Communities where people of color and low-income live at the economic margin, and subsistence-level societies, are highly susceptible to environmental pollution and the destruction of their regional habitats (see chapter 12 for a discussion of environmental racism). Biologically, humans benefit from a healthy atmosphere — clean air and water, noncontaminated and abundant plant and marine life. Human physical health problems emanate from environmental abuses; among them are birth defects, cancer, respiratory problems, and lead and radiation poisoning. It is imperative that social welfare professionals be guided by sustainable social development concepts to contribute to policy decisions needed in this time of unprecedented global challenge.

FIGURE 1.2
Model for an Environmental Social Practice

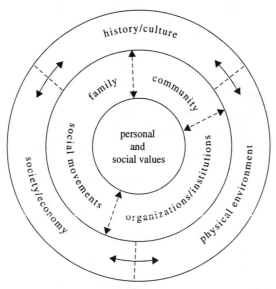

Broken arrows indicate "mediated through;" solid arrows indicate "mutual influence upon."
Source: Frank Tester (1994). In an "Age of Ecology: Limits to Voluntarism and Traditional Theory in Social Work Practice." In M. Hoff and J. McNutt (eds.), *The Global Environment Crisis: Implications for Social Welfare and Social Work.* Aldershot, England: Avebury, 75–99.

Interventions aimed at the *psychological* dimension of human behavior look at the thinking-feeling component, not only at the situation itself but at one's perception of the situation. (For example, persons traumatized through early childhood experiences or war may blame themselves, be fatalistic, or conversely, cope in a positive way). Psychological belief systems are related to values in that they, like values, spring from society. Understanding human behavior necessitates attention to the role that culture plays in one's thinking, feeling, and acting. Five components of culture presented by Steward (1972) provide a framework which social workers can employ in relating to the cultural dimension of personality. The five components address:

1. *Activity:* What are the goals of life?
2. *Definition of social relations:* How are roles defined?

3. *Motivation:* Is cooperation or competition emphasized?
4. *Perception of the world:* What is the predominant worldview?
5. *Perception of self and the individual:* What are the boundaries between self and other?

When helping an individual with *social* adjustment, the social worker may work with the family unit, seeking to enhance the family functioning and communication. Alternatively, social workers may define the problem as having political or economic origins, and intervention may have to take place at the community level or above. Advocacy for legislative changes may be involved, for instance, to establish a half-way house for alcoholic mothers. At the national level a society's organization of social workers may advocate their government to sign an international document such as the *United Nations Convention on the Rights of the Child.* This structural change orientation focuses on systemic change rather than on individual adjustment. The biopsychosocial approach allows the social worker to view the person holistically, as both an individual with inner biological drives and as a social and cultural being. Each component in the system — whether biological, psychological, or social — is intertwined with every other component. The biopsychosocial framework itself can be viewed as part and parcel of ecosystems theory. It reminds social workers that even in individual micro-level intervention, a holistic, environmental approach will enhance understanding.

SOCIAL WORK VALUES

Despite significant changes that have taken place in the practice of social work, social workers have continually embraced a set of values central to the profession (Reamer, 1994). A profession that emerged out of a socio-religious ethos with a goal of helping society's vulnerable people, social work has promoted values that generally reflect a more compassionate stance than that of many other professional groups. A commitment to human welfare, social justice, and individual dignity is an enduring characteristic of the social work profession. A further commitment to the tradition of social and political activism has characterized the field since the days when the founders worked for women's suffrage, children's and minorities' rights, and universal peace.

What, then, are the commonly held social work values? In 1984, NASW identified a core of values central to social work practice at any level of intervention. The basic U.S. social work values according to NASW are:

1. Commitment to the primary importance of the individual in society.
2. Commitment to social change to meet social recognized needs.
3. Commitment to social justice and the economic, physical, and mental well-being of all in society.
4. Respect and appreciation for individual and group differences.
5. Commitment to developing clients' ability to help themselves.
6. Willingness to transmit knowledge and skills to others.
7. Willingness to keep personal feelings and needs separate from professional relationships.
8. Respect for the confidentiality of relationships with clients.
9. Willingness to persist in efforts on behalf of clients despite frustration.
10. Commitment to a high standard of personal and professional conduct.

Especially pertinent to social welfare considerations are values two through seven. These values are codified in the NASW Code of Ethics with which all U.S. social workers should be thoroughly familiar. A serious omission from this somewhat cumbersome list (revised in 1990) is a commitment to a sustainable environment and global social welfare. The Code of Ethics presently is under revision (the 1990 version is presented in chapter 5). Of special significance to the readers of *Social Welfare: A World View* is the International Code of Ethics for professional social work which was adopted by the International Federation of Social Workers (IFSW) at Sri Lanka, 1994. This document is remarkable in its success in introducing universal social work ethics as guidelines for members of the fifty-six professional associations across the world. The International Code of Ethics is reproduced in box 1.3 at the conclusion of this chapter.

Development education is a term used in the NASW curriculum manual (Healy, 1992) to refer to education for a world undergoing rapid development and social change. The overriding value emphasis of such education is on promoting justice and equity. Other key values are:

1. Respect for different cultures.
2. Sense of personal responsibility for development.
3. Acceptance of global interdependence as an irrefutable fact of life.
4. Values clarification in relation to world hunger and poverty.
5. Appreciation of cooperation as a means to increased global security.

Development education focuses on preventing poverty, hunger, and inequality. A major goal for internationally-oriented social workers is to develop the competence to influence public policy on issues relevant to development. This development is not the sort of corporate economic growth benefiting only the ruling classes in a country. Rather it is enhancement of the living conditions for all the nation's people.

Estes (1992) takes this model one step further and introduces a "new world order" model which is oriented toward fundamental restructuring of the global, social, political, economic, and ecological order. Similar to the social development model, the social action goal is pursued through mobilizing people "to think globally, act locally." The focus here is on social change.

SOCIAL POLICY AND U.S. VALUES

A variety of historical, cultural, and political forces shape social welfare policy. Barker provides a definition of *social policy* in *The Social Work Dictionary* (1995):

> the activities and principles of a society that guide the way it intervenes in and regulates relationships between individuals, groups, communities, and social institutions. These principles and activities are the result of the society's values and customs and largely determine the distribution of resources and the level of well-being of its people. Thus, social policy includes plans and programs in education, health care, crime and corrections, economic security, and social welfare made by governments, voluntary organizations, and the people in general. It also includes social perspectives that result in society's rewards and constraints.

Turning to Tropman's delineation of American value constructs, the work ethic emerges as one of the most enduring themes in social welfare history. Generally, programs which require work or are work-related (unemployment benefits and social security) have more political clout than programs which are not work-related (aid to families in need). The most vigorously challenged programs involve aid to able-bodied people.

Because mobility is a basic tenet in U.S. society, workers are expected to be willing to relocate in search of work. Those unwilling to do so are not highly regarded. The emphasis on status or achievement urges citizens to strive for success. Those who fall behind are thought somehow to be deserving of their fate. Hence, a rather punitive treatment is accorded persons who take handouts. Programs designed to equalize the distribution of wealth thus become generally unacceptable in a competitive social structure.

The stress on independence and individualism militates against the provision of "cradle to grave" social services. Moralism dictates that persons dependent on welfare suffer certain discomforts. Criminals are punished harshly in a society built on a puritan creed. When discrimination (on the basis of ascription) against minorities, women, the aged, and the disabled becomes played out as discrimination against the poor, or non-achievers in the society, it is hard for the social welfare system to get the public support to expand substantially. In the United States, as Tropman indicates, there is no political movement of the poor, and no labor political party with strong working class allegiance.

As the tides of political change come and go, and as the public mood shifts, so do the social policies. Once ingrained, they tend to reinforce the social values. The cycle is complete with values shaping policies and policies, values. For instance, one could make the case that the value of equality led to racial integration while the policy of integration greatly furthered the belief in equality. Figure 1.3 presents the value-policy configuration. The arrow drawn between values and policies is a two-headed arrow. This denotes a reciprocal, not causal, relationship. The two-headed arrows between values and economics, and between economics and policies indicate reciprocity also. For example, religious belief in hard work and frugality can promote economic investment and growth; economic growth can reinforce the Protestant work ethic. Simultaneously, the religious value of compassion can influence a willingness to pay more taxes (economic consequences) in order to introduce programs to provide shelters for the homeless.

Not only do values play into policies, but policies play into values. For instance, American means-tested programs associated with the poor and minorities generate more opposition than support. As Piven and Cloward (1993) correctly note, the effects are far-reaching—dampening support for other welfare state programs. Citizens resent paying taxes for services from which they themselves receive no benefits. The value of providing social welfare is thus altered when fragmented programs reach only narrowly defined groups. Some affirmative action programs, limited as they are in magnitude, have created resentment and hostility.

FIGURE 1.3
Contemporary Value-policy Configuration

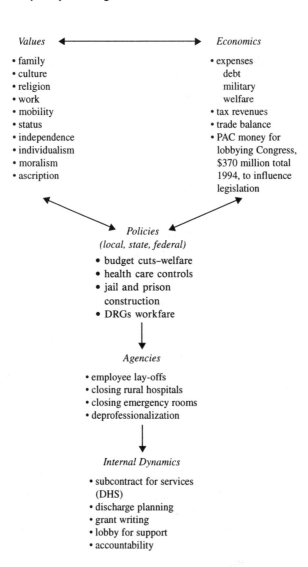

Values

- family
- culture
- religion
- work
- mobility
- status
- independence
- individualism
- moralism
- ascription

Economics

- expenses
  debt
  military
  welfare
- tax revenues
- trade balance
- PAC money for
  lobbying Congress,
  $370 million total
  1994, to influence
  legislation

Policies
(local, state, federal)

- budget cuts–welfare
- health care controls
- jail and prison
  construction
- DRGs workfare

Agencies

- employee lay-offs
- closing rural hospitals
- closing emergency rooms
- deprofessionalization

Internal Dynamics

- subcontract for services
  (DHS)
- discharge planning
- grant writing
- lobby for support
- accountability

The theory that social policy is influenced by values on one hand, and by economic structure on the other is hypothesized in figure 1.3. The arrows in the diagram indicate the flow and direction of influence and examples of each factor such as family, religion, and culture are given. As indicated in the diagram, social welfare programs are products of their time. Policies swing back and forth in cycles: first, tough, stringent requirements and cutbacks, then a relaxation of restrictions and rules, to be replaced once again by a constrictive period. Often the punitive and compassionate forces wrestle against each other with contradictory results. In the United States the fragmentation of services and differences in state laws, policies, and tax structures complicates addressing people's needs.

As practitioners in the welfare state, social workers must learn the process of policy development, and be prepared to shape as well as carry out the social policies which define their work.

CONCLUSION AND SUMMARY

The purpose of this introductory chapter has been to provide the vocabulary and theoretical context for viewing social welfare internationally and multidimensionally. The subject of the chapter is social values. People act in accordance with values, and therefore, it is the task of the social sciences to understand these values and how they play into the development and support of the social welfare state. To understand the American welfare state is to know the psychology of human needs; the sociology of social values (including frameworks for viewing human phenomena within the context of social structure); the social psychology of interactionism; and the anthropology of systems theory. There is a vast knowledge base relevant to grasping the psychological, political, and social dimensions in the conceptualization of social welfare. Social work, the ultimate applied social science, embraces an interdisciplinary knowledge base under the rubric of ecosystems theory. Drawing upon the terminology of the ecosystems perspective, the American welfare state can be viewed both within the context of a seeming jumble of contradictory goals and also against the backdrop of a more or less cohesive set of enduring cultural values. These values are invested in the social institutions. The overarching institutional commitment in the United States has been to limited government and individual and local

BOX 1.3

INTERNATIONAL FEDERATION OF SOCIAL WORKERS: ETHICS OF SOCIAL WORK— PRINCIPLES AND STANDARDS

I. Background

Ethical awareness is a necessary part of the professional practice of any social worker. His or her ability to act ethically is an essential aspect of the quality of the service offered to clients.

The purpose of IFSW's work on ethics is to promote ethical debate and reflection in the member associations and among the providers of social work in member countries.

The basis for the further development of IFSW's work on ethics is to be found in *"Ethics of Social Work—Principles and Standards,"* which consists of two documents, *"International Declaration of Ethical Principles of Social Work"* and *"International Ethical Standards for Social Workers."* These documents present the basic ethical principles of the social work profession, recommend procedure when the work presents ethical dilemmas, and deal with the profession's and the individual social worker's relation to clients, colleagues, and others in the field. The documents are components in a continuing process of use, review and revision.

2. International Declaration of Ethical Principles of Social Work

2.1 Introduction

The IFSW recognises the need for a declaration of ethical principles for guidance in dealing with ethical problems in social work.

The purposes of the **International Declaration of Ethical Principles** *are:*

1. to formulate a set of basic principles for social work, which can be adapted to cultural and social settings.
2. to identify ethical problem areas in the practice of social work (below referred to as 'problem areas'), and
3. to provide guidance as to the choice of methods for dealing with ethical issues/problems (below referred to as 'methods for addressing ethical issues/problems').

Compliance

The *International Declaration of Ethical Principles* assumes that both member associations

(Continued on next page)

BOX 1.3 (Continued)

of the IFSW and their constituent members adhere to the principles formulated therein. The IFSW expects each member association to assist its members in identifying and dealing with ethical issues/problems in the practice of their profession.

Member associates of the IFSW and individual members of these can report any member association to the Executive Committee of the IFSW should it neglect to adhere to these principles. National Associations who experience difficulties adopting these principles should notify the Executive Committee of IFSW. The Executive Committee may impose the stipulations and intentions of the Declaration of Ethical Principles on an association which neglects to comply. Should this not be sufficient the Executive Committee can, as a following measure, suggest suspension or exclusion of the association.

The *International Declaration of Ethical Principles* should be made publicly known. This would enable clients, employers, professionals from other disciplines, and the general public to have expectations in accordance with the ethical foundations of social work.

We acknowledge that a detailed set of ethical standards for the member associations would be unrealistic due to legal, cultural and government differences among the member countries.

2.2 The Principles

Social workers serve the development of human beings through adherence to the following basic principles:

2.2.1. Every human being has a unique value, which justifies moral consideration for that person.

2.2.2. Each individual has the right to self-fulfillment to the extent that it does not encroach upon the same right of others, and has an obligation to contribute to the well-being of society.

2.2.3. Each society, regardless of its form, should function to provide the maximum benefits for all of its members.

2.2.4. Social workers have a commitment to principles of social justice.

2.2.5. Social workers have the responsibility to devote objective and disciplined knowledge and skill to aid individuals, groups, communities, and societies in their development and resolution of personal-societal conflicts and their consequences.

2.2.6. Social workers are expected to provide the best possible assistance to anybody seeking their help and advice, without unfair discrimination on the basis of gender, age, disability, colour, social class, race, religion, language, political beliefs, or sexual orientation.

(Continued on next page)

BOX 1.3 (Continued)

2.2.7. Social workers respect the basic human rights of individuals and groups as expressed in the *United Nations Universal Declaration of Human Rights* and other international conventions derived from that Declaration.

2.2.8. Social workers pay regard to the principles of privacy, confidentiality, and responsible use of information in their professional work. Social workers respect justified confidentiality even when their country's legislation is in conflict with this demand.

2.2.9. Social workers are expected to work in full collaboration with their clients, working for the best interests of the clients but paying due regard to the interests of others involved. Clients are encouraged to participate as much as possible, and should be informed of risks and likely benefits of proposed courses of action.

2.2.10. Social workers generally expect clients to take responsibility in collaboration with them, for determining courses of action affecting their lives. Compulsion which might be necessary to solve one party's problems at the expense of the interests of others involved should only take place after careful explicit evaluation of the claims of the conflicting parties. Social workers should mimimise the use of legal compulsion.

2.2.11. Social work is inconsistent with direct or indirect support of individuals, groups, political forces or power-structures suppressing their fellow human beings by employing terrorism, torture or similar brutal means.

2.2.12. Social workers make ethically justified decisions, and stand by them, paying due regard to the *IFSW International Declaration of Ethical Principles,* and to the *"International Ethical Standards for Social Workers"* adopted by their national professional association.

2.3 Problem Areas

2.3.1. The problem areas raising ethical issues directly are not necessarily universal due to cultural and governmental differences. Each national association is encouraged to promote discussion and clarification of important issues and problems particularly relevant to its country. The following problem areas are, however, widely recognized:

(Continued on next page)

BOX 1.3 (Continued)

1) *when the loyalty of the social worker is in the middle of conflicting interests*
- between those of the social worker's own and the client's
- between conflicting interests of individual clients and other individuals
- between the conflicting interests of groups of clients
- between groups of clients and the rest of the population
- between systems/institutions and groups of clients
- between system/institution/employer and social workers
- between different groups of professionals

2) *the fact that the social worker functions both as a helper and controller*

The relation between these two opposite aspects of social work demands a clarification based on an explicit choice of values in order to avoid a mixing-up of motives or the lack of clarity in motives, actions and consequences of actions. When social workers are expected to play a role in the state control of citizens they are obliged to clarify the ethical implications of this role and to what extent this role is acceptable in relation to the basic ethical principles of social work.

3) *the duty of the social worker to protect the interests of the client will easily come into conflict with demands for efficiency and utility*

This problem is becoming important with the introduction and use of information technology within the fields of social work.

2.3.3. The principles declared in section 2.2 should always be at the base of any consideration given or choice made by social workers in dealing with issues/problems within these areas.

2.4. Methods for the Solution of Issues/ Problems

2.4.1. The various national associations of social workers are obliged to treat matters in such a way that ethical issues/problems may be considered and tried to be solved in collective forums within the organization. Such forums should enable the individual social worker to discuss, analyse and consider ethical issues/problems in collaboration with colleagues, other expert groups and parties affected by the matter under discussion. In addition such forums should give the social worker opportunity to receive advice from colleagues and others.

(Continued on next page)

BOX 1.3 (Continued)

Ethical analysis and discussion should always seek to create possibilities and options.

2.4.2. The member associations are required to produce and/or adapt ethical standards for the different fields of work, especially for those fields where there are complicated ethical issues/problems as well as areas where the ethical principles of social work may come into conflict with the respective country's legal system or the policy of the authorities.

2.4.3. When ethical foundations are laid down as guidelines for actions within the practice of social work, it is the duty of the associations to aid the individual social worker in analysing and considering ethical issues/problems on the basis of:

1) The basic *principles* of the Declaration (section 2.2)

2) The ethical/moral and political *context* of the actions, i.e. an analysis of the values and forces constituting the framing conditions of the action.

3) The *motives* of the action, i.e. to advocate a higher level of consciousness of the aims and intentions the individual social worker might have regarding a course of action.

4) The *nature* of the action, i.e. help in providing an analysis of the moral content of

the action, e.g. the use of compulsion as opposed to voluntary co-operation, guardianship vs participation, etc.

5) The *consequences* the action might have for different groups, i.e. an analysis of the consequences of different ways of action for all involved parties in both the short and long term.

2.4.4. The member associations are responsible for promoting debate, education and research regarding ethical questions.

3. International Ethical Standards for Social Workers

(This section is based on the *"International Code of Ethics for the Professional Social Worker"* adopted by the IFSW in 1976, but does not include ethical principles since these are now contained in the new separate *International Declaration of Ethical Principles of Social Work* in section 2.2 of the present document.)

3.1 Preamble

Social work originates variously from humanitarian, religious and democratic ideals and philosophies and has universal application to meet human needs arising from personal-societal interactions and to develop human potential. Professional social

(Continued on next page)

BOX 1.3 (Continued)

workers are dedicated to service for the welfare and self-fulfillment of human beings; to the development and disciplined use of validated knowledge regarding human and social behaviour; to the development of resources to meet individual, group, national and international needs and aspirations; and to the achievement of social justice. On the basis of the *International Declaration of Ethical Principles of Social Work,* the social worker is obliged to recognize these standards of ethical conduct.

3.2. General Standards of Ethical Conduct

3.2.1. Seek to understand each individual client and the client system, and the elements which affect behaviour and the service required.

3.2.2. Uphold and advance the values, knowledge and methodology of the profession, refraining from any behaviour which damages the functioning of the profession.

3.2.3. Recognise professional and personal limitations.

3.2.4. Encourage the utilization of all relevant knowledge and skills.

3.2.5. Apply relevant methods in the development and validation of knowledge.

3.2.6. Contribute professional expertise to the development of policies and programs which improve the quality of life in society.

3.2.7. Identify and interpret social needs.

3.2.8. Identify and interpret the basis and nature of individual, group, community, national, and international social problems.

3.2.9. Identify and interpret the work of the social work profession.

3.2.10. Clarify whether public statements are made or actions performed on an individual basis or as representative of a professional association, agency or organization, or other group.

3.3. Social Work Standards Relative to Clients

3.3.1. Accept primary responsibility to identified clients, but within limitations set by the ethical claims of others.

3.3.2. Maintain the client's right to a relationship of trust, to privacy and confidentiality, and to responsible use of information. The collection and sharing of information or data is related to the professional service function with the client informed as to its necessity and use. No information is released without prior knowledge and informed consent of the client, except where the client cannot be responsible or others may be seriously jeopardized. A client

(Continued on next page)

BOX 1.3 (Continued)

has access to social work records concerning them.

3.3.3. Recognize and respect the individual goals, responsibilities, and differences of clients. Within the scope of the agency and the client's social milieu, the professional service shall assist clients to take responsibility for personal actions and help all clients with equal willingness. Where the professional service cannot be provided under such conditions the clients shall be so informed in such a way as to leave the clients free to act.

3.3.4. Help the client — individual, group, community, or society — to achieve self-fulfillment and maximum potential within the limits of the respective rights of others. The service shall be based upon helping the client to understand and use the professional relationship, in furtherance of the client's legitimate desires and interests.

3.4 Social Work Standards Relative to Agencies and Organizations

3.4.1. Work and/or cooperate with those agencies and organizations whose policies, procedures, and operations are directed toward adequate service delivery and encouragement of professional practice consistent with the ethical principles of the IFSW.

3.4.2. Responsibly execute the stated aims and functions of the agency or organizations, contributing to the development of sound policies, procedures, and practice in order to obtain the best possible standards or practice.

3.4.3. Sustain ultimate responsibility to the client, initiating desirable alterations of policies, procedures, and practice, through appropriate agency and organization channels. If necessary remedies are not achieved after channels have been exhausted, initiate appropriate appeals to higher authorities or the wider community of interest.

3.4.4. Ensure professional accountability to client and community for efficiency and effectiveness through periodic review of the process of service provision.

3.4.5. Use all possible ethical means to bring unethical practice to an end when policies, procedures and practices are in direct conflict with the ethical principles of social work.

3.5. Social Work Standards Relative to Colleagues

3.5.1. Acknowledge the education, training, and performance of social work colleagues and professionals from other

(Continued on next page)

CHAPTER 1: SOCIAL VALUES: THE THEORETICAL CONTEXT

BOX 1.3 (Continued)

disciplines, extending all necessary cooperation that will enhance effective services.

3.5.2. Recognize differences of opinion and practice of social work colleagues and other professionals, expressing criticism through channels in a responsible manner.

3.5.3. Promote and share opportunities for knowledge, experience, and ideas with all social work colleagues, professionals from other disciplines and volunteers for the purpose of mutual improvement.

3.5.4. Bring any violations of professional ethics and standards to the attention of the appropriate bodies inside and outside the profession, and ensure that relevant clients are properly involved.

3.5.5. Defend colleagues against unjust actions.

3.6. Standards Relative to the Profession

3.6.1. Maintain the values, ethical principles, knowledge and methodology of the profession and contribute to their clarification and improvement.

3.6.2. Uphold the professional standards of practice and work for their advancement.

3.6.3. Defend the profession against unjust criticism and work to increase confidence in the necessity for professional practice.

3.6.4. Present constructive criticism of the profession, its theories, methods and practices.

3.6.5. Encourage new approaches and methodologies needed to meet new and existing needs.

Source: Adopted by the IFSW General Meeting, Colombo, Sri Lanka, July 6–8, 1994.

---

responsibility (Marmor et al., 1990). Meanwhile, social workers, with their commitment to helping the most vulnerable members of society and their person-in-the-environment focus, provide what Federico (1990) calls a combination of caring, curing, and changing activities that help promote the general social welfare. The holistic perspective of social work readily extends from the person to the global environment.

This was a chapter, then, of theory, definitions, and frameworks to introduce the reader to the idea of the welfare state that welfare programs both create and define. We will return again and again to the fundamental concepts of the social sciences presented in this chapter. Later chapters will attempt to amplify the social welfare programs throughout the world that are enormously complex amalgams of values and economics. Our concern here, however, has been to depict the unifying themes pertinent to social welfare policy in the United States. A secondary concern has been to differentiate social work from the more purely academic disciplines—social work is a discipline with a mission. The mission is not only to study but to alleviate social problems and affect social change, though perhaps working against overwhelming and inexorable odds.

REVIEW QUESTIONS

1. Define social welfare and trace linguistic origins of this concept.
2. Differentiate among social workers, psychiatrists, and psychologists.
3. Discuss two major drawbacks to use of the term, *developing country*. Is the term, *Third World* country an improvement? How or how not?
4. Discuss the news story about the elderly couple caught shoplifting. How is this a study in cultural contradiction?
5. Discuss Maslow's concept of human needs.
6. How do sociologists utilize the concept social values?
7. Using functional analysis, discuss manifest and latent functions of various social institutions.
8. What is Piven and Cloward's conceptualization of the social welfare system? How does this differ from the traditional view?
9. Define power and relate this concept to the achievement of needs. How do the power elites manage the flow of information concerning matters of relevance to social welfare?
10. What do social psychology and social work have in common?
11. Briefly define the following concepts from social psychology—blaming the victim, displaced aggression.
12. From anthropology, discuss the connection between language and culture.
13. According to box 1.2, how do economic/work pressures affect family life in Japan? How can one account for women's delay in marriage?
14. Discuss the notion of ethnocentrism and ways to broaden one's perspective.
15. How does the metaphor of finding four-leaf clovers relate to understanding a culture?
16. Choose three of the seven U.S. value dimensions relevant to social welfare and describe the relationship of each to welfare.
17. Referring back to the reading in box 1.1, how does the news story indicate the contradiction in American values?

REFERENCES

Abercrombie, N., S. Hill, and B. Turner. (1988). *The Penguin Dictionary of Sociology.* London: Penguin.

Allport, G. (1981/1954). *The Nature of Prejudice.* Reading, MA: Addison-Wesley.

Barker, R., ed. (1995). *The Social Work Dictionary*, 3d ed. Washington, DC: NASW Press.

Baron, R. and W. Graziano. (1991). *Social Psychology.* Fort Worth, TX: Holt, Rinehart and Winston.

Bateson, M. (1984). *With a Daughter's Eye: A Memoir of Margaret Mead and Gregory Bateson.* New York: Pocket Books.

Berger, R., R. Federico, and J. McBreen. (1991). *Human Behavior: A Perspective for the Helping Professions.* New York: Longman.

Bibus, A. (1995). Reflections on Social Work from Cuernavaca, Mexico. *International Social Work* 38(3): 243–252.

Bogardus, E. (1928). *Immigration and Race Attitudes.* Boston: D. C. Heath.

Bryson, L. (1992). *Welfare and the State: Who Benefits?* New York: St. Martin's Press.

Cooley, C. (1983/1909). *Social Organization: A Study of the Larger Mind.* New Brunswick, NJ: Transaction.

Cox, D. (1994, July 10–15). *Social Work Education: State of the Art.* Paper presented at the International Association of Schools of Social Work Conference, Amsterdam.

de Roche, C. (1989). Empathy and the Anthropological Imagination. *Practicing Anthropology* 11(3): 6–7.

de Tocqueville, A. (1966/1835). *Democracy in America.* New York: Harper and Row.

Dolgoff, R., D. Feldstein, and L. Skolnik. (1993). *Understanding Social Welfare*, 3d ed. New York: Longman.

Encyclopaedia Britannica. (1993). Cultural Anthropology. *The New Encyclopaedia Britannica* 27: 375. Chicago: University of Chicago Press.

Esber, G. (1989). Anthropological Contributions for Social Work Education. *Practicing Anthropology* 11(3): 4,11.

Estes, R. (1992). Models, Social Modeling, and Models of International Social Work Education. In R. Estes, ed. *Internationalizing Social Work Education: A Guide to Resources for a New Century* (20–37). Feasterville, PA: Americor.

Faulkner, W. (1936). *Absalom, Absalom!* New York: Random House.

Federico, R. (1990). *Social Welfare in Today's World.* New York: McGraw-Hill.

George, V. and P. Wilding. (1976). *Identity and Social Welfare.* London: Routledge & Kegan Paul.

Goffman, E. (1961). *Asylums: Essays on the Social Situation of Mental Patients and Other Inmates.* Garden City, NY: Anchor Books.

Gould, A. (1993). *Capitalist Welfare Systems: A Comparison of Japan, Britain, and Sweden.* New York: Longman.

Healy, L. (1992). *Introducing International Development Content in the Social Work Curriculum.* Washington, DC: NASW Press.

Herrnstein, R. and C. Murray. (1994). *The Bell Curve.* New York: The Free Press.

Hoff, M. (1994). Environmental Foundations of Social Welfare: Theoretical Resources. In M. Hoff and J. McNutt, eds. *The Global Environmental Crisis: Implications for Social Welfare and Social Work.* Aldershot, England: Avebury, pp 12–35.

Horton, P. and C. Hunt. (1976). *Sociology,* 4th ed. New York: McGraw-Hill.

Kaplan, C. and L. Kaplan. (1993). Public Opinion and the "Economic Bill of Rights." *Journal of Progressive Human Services* 4(1): 43–58.

Karger, H. and D. Stoesz. (1990). *American Social Welfare Policy: A Structural Approach.* New York: Longman.

Katz, J. (1985). The Sociopolitical Nature of Counseling. *The Counseling Psychologist* 13: 615–624.

Lerner, M. (1971). All the World Loathes a Loser. *Psychology Today* 5(1): 54–56, 66.

Locke, D. (1992). *Increasing Muticultural Understanding: A Comprehensive Model.* Newbury Park, CA: SAGE.

Macionis, J. (1994). *Society: The Basics.* Englewood Cliffs, NJ: Prentice Hall.

Marmor, T., J. Matow, and P. Harvey. (1990). *America's Misunderstood Welfare State: Persistent Myths, Enduring Realities.* New York: Basic Books.

Maslow, A. (1970). *Motivation and Personality.* New York: Harper & Row.

McMahon, M. (1994). *Advanced Generalist Practice: With An International Perspective.* Englewood Cliffs, NJ: Prentice Hall.

Mead, M. (1972). *Blackberry Winter: My Earlier Years.* New York: William Morrow.

Merton, R. (1949). *Social Theory and Social Structure.* Glencoe, IL: The Free Press.

Morales, A. and B. Sheafor. (1995). *Social Work: A Profession of Many Faces.* Boston: Allyn & Bacon.

Nakanishi, M. and B. Rittner. (1992). The Inclusionary Cultural Model. *Journal of Social Work Education* 28(1): 27–35.

Piven, F. and R. Cloward. (1993). *Regulating the Poor: The Functions of Public Welfare.* New York: Vintage Books.

Podolefsky, A. and P. Brown., eds. (1994). *Applied Cultural Anthropology,* 2d ed. Mountain View, CA: Mayfield, Introduction.

Reamer, F. (1994). Ethics and Values. *Encyclopedia of Social Work,* 19th ed. (893–902.) Washington, DC: NASW Press.

Ryan, W. (1976). *Blaming the Victim.* New York: Random House.

Sherif, M., et al. (1961). Intergroup Conflict and Cooperation: The Robber Care Experiment. Norman Institute of Group Relations: University of Oklahoma.

Steward, E. (1972). *American Cultural Patterns.* La Grange Park, IL: Intercultural Network.

Sumner, W. (1940/1906). *Folkways*. Boston, MA: Ginn and Co.

Tester, F. (1994). In an Age of Ecology: Limits to Voluntarism and Traditional Theory in Social Work Practice. In M. Hoff and J. McNutt, eds., *The Global Environmental Crisis: Implications for Social Welfare and Social Work*. Aldershot, England: Avebury, 75–99.

Theodorson, G. and A. Theodorson. (1969). *Modern Dictionary of Sociology*. New York: Thomas Crowell Co.

Tropman, J. (1989). *American Values and Social Welfare: Cultural Contradictions in the Welfare State*. Englewood Cliffs, NJ: Prentice Hall.

Webster's New World Dictionary of the English Language, 3d ed. (1993). New York: Simon and Schuster.

Wilensky, H. and C. Lebeaux. (1958). *Industrial Society and Social Welfare*. New York: The Free Press.

Williams, R. (1979). Change and Stability in Values and Value Systems: A Sociological Perspective. In M. Rokeach, ed. *Understanding Human Values: Individual and Societal*. New York: The Free Press.

Zastrow, C. (1996). *Introduction to Social Work and Social Welfare*, 6th ed. Pacific Grove, CA: Brooks/Cole.

2

PURPOSE AND STRUCTURE

OF SOCIAL WELFARE POLICY

Taxes are what we pay for civilized society.— Oliver Wendell Holmes, Jr., 1927

S ocial welfare policies are not created in a vacuum, but are embedded in the social fabric of the society of which they are a part. The very social and personal values which give them life and meaning at one point in history may be their undoing later on. In hard times when public hysteria is voiced against welfare mothers, criminals, and illegal immigrants, the political pendulum shifts. Social welfare policy makers are under pressure to "reform welfare as we know it." New legislation is introduced, and if there is no mass counterattack by concerned parties, the legislation passes.

The previous chapter examined American social policy as an outgrowth of American cultural values. Merely to list the concerns of social policy: poverty, distribution of wealth, crime, mental illness, health care, and so on is to underscore the value/policy interconnection. Here, in chapter 2, the concern is with how these values are played out in the world of social welfare. The focus of this chapter is on the organization or structure of social welfare, while chapter 3, which is closely related, will delve into the historical foundations of the present policies. Specifically, this chapter will examine the purpose and organization of U.S. social welfare, key governmental services such as social security and Medicare, and federal attempts at cutting costs through privatization. In addition, this chapter will analyze social welfare services — "social security" — in other

51

countries, mainly Canada, Japan, Mexico, Sweden, and Great Britain. Underlying assumptions of the present discussion are that political interest groups
and economic principles enter into the formulation of social policy, and that
the perception of the working of the economy is often more influential in shaping
policy than the state of the economy itself.

RESIDUAL VERSUS INSTITUTIONAL APPROACH

The design of social programs reflects differing philosophies about who should
be served and when services should be given. The residual-institutional dichotomy
is an ideal-typical construct best conceptualized by Wilensky and Lebeaux (1958).
The *residual* (also known as the safety-net) approach holds that social welfare
services should be provided only when an individual's needs are not properly
met through other societal institutions such as the family or market economy.
Aid is strictly on a short-term basis. The values that underpin residual thinking
are capitalism, independence, and belief in opportunity.

In social welfare, residual thinking leads to the kind of programs in which
eligibility is based on proving a need — proving the breakdown of the other systems that should be working (Dolgoff et al., 1993). In order to investigate eligibility, officials must be thoroughly familiar with the circumstances of their clients'
lives, thereby ensuring that only the deserving poor receive assistance. Programs
are deemed successful in terms of reducing rather than expanding the numbers
who receive help: Getting the able-bodied off welfare and on the work rolls
is the rallying cry. In the United States and Japan, and to a lesser extent in Canada
and Australia, the residualist view prevails.

In the residually-oriented society, a stigma is attached to receiving welfare
aid. As Zastrow (1993) notes, the causes of welfare clients' difficulties are often
seen as rooted in their own malfunctioning — the persons themselves are blamed
for problems perceived as stemming from their own inadequacies. Only when
unemployment becomes extremely high overall (such as in the Great Depression) do we begin to reduce the stigma and move from a residual position to
an institutional one. Under conditions of mass economic crisis, then, the system rather than the individual receives the blame.

An *institutional* or social insurance concept of service, on the other hand,
is preventive rather than curative, and universal rather than particularist. Social

welfare, according to the institutional view, is a necessary and desirable part of the social structure. To provide economic security as an alternative to the historic patterns of inadequate, piecemeal relief is the basic purpose of the welfare state. Why allow people to fall into destitution at all when you can offset poverty at its source? An individual's difficulties are attributed to causes beyond his or her control.

Flexible eligibility requirements, lack of stigma in asking for or getting help, the absence of a sense that the family or anybody else has failed—these are among the precepts of the institutional or universal view. Blame, if there is any, is placed on structural factors in the workplace or society, not on the people themselves. Universal or institutional programs include redistribution of wealth, guaranteed income, negative income tax, children's allowance schemes, and socialized health care services (Kohlert, 1989). When benefits are universally available, poverty is prevented. When there are no poor peoples' programs that can be abolished in the next political campaign but just peoples' programs, then there will be no war on welfare. Such services belong to "us" not to "them," and therein lies their strength. In order to maintain user satisfaction and financial support, universal services are of singularly high quality. Public education is the archetype of the universal program in countries in which education is regarded as a right for the many rather than a privilege for the few.

The metaphor of the safety net, associated with the residual approach is, in fact, a better descriptive term for the institutional mode of social welfare. To grasp the meaning of the metaphor, first, imagine the trapeze artist losing his or her balance and falling down hundreds of feet to be saved by the safety net below. This metaphor is relevant to U.S. welfare, in the sense that the individual was allowed to fall. Yet, in contrast to the trapeze artist who can recover to perform again, the American worker who contracts a disease may never by able to start afresh, even following a full recovery. The job may be gone; the house may be sold; and the health insurance may expire. There is the element of shame, besides. Although there is some distress in a failed acrobatic feat, perhaps, there is no deep humiliation at such a mishap. As the artist rebounds, the audience claps in admiration or at the least, support. In the case of an individual requiring society's safety net, however, help may not be forthcoming; the criteria for receiving aid may not be met. If there is help, the recipient does not receive a hand of applause from the onlooker. The universalist social welfare state, in contrast, does provide a real safety net to the troubled citizen. See box 2.1 for a comparative view of health care treatment in Sweden and the

---

BOX 2.1

THE WORKER STUMBLES:
A COMPARISON OF SWEDEN
AND THE UNITED STATES

The difference between benefits that are work-related and those that are not is illustrated in the following realistic account of the resources provided to two workers and their respective families confronting similar situations in Sweden and the United States.

The situation is the following: A forty-five-year-old researcher with two teenage children and a spouse who is employed by a consulting company becomes permanently disabled because of alcoholism and related medical problems. The spouse, like the worker, is also employed outside the home in a full-time professional-level position. The strains on the family result in a nervous breakdown for one of the two teenage children. Both the worker and the teenager have to be hospitalized, the worker several times for serious medical complications related to alcoholism. In such a situation, what resources are available to this family?

As we shall see, the resources available in Sweden and the United States are quite different. In Sweden, government disability, pension, and health programs provide nearly comprehensive protection for workers and their families. Benefits in the United States are much less comprehensive and tied to employment, leaving workers much more vulnerable.

Sweden

In Sweden, the researcher, once diagnosed as suffering from chronic alcoholism, is declared disabled and begins receiving a monthly government disability payment. This money, along with the spouse's income, ensures the family's continued economic security. Hospital care for both the researcher and the teenage child is free, while the cost of longer-term medical and psychiatric care and prescriptions is minimal. The family's only medically related expenses are a very small set fee for each of the first ten visits to the doctor and the first ten prescriptions. Thereafter, all medical care and prescriptions are free. The researcher's spouse makes use of the five-week annual vacation to which all Swedes are entitled by law to help care for the researcher and the teenage child. In addition, the spouse is able to use paid sick leave as needed to deal with any additional family crises.

(Continued on next page)

BOX 2.1 (Continued)

As a result of the benefits available to Swedish workers, the family's lifestyle is preserved while its disabled members struggle to reestablish themselves.

Should the researcher's disability become permanent, both spouses, upon reaching retirement age, will still receive their individual government pension based on their own work history. Thus the researcher's interrupted earnings will not reduce the spouse's pension.

United States

As in Sweden, the researcher is diagnosed as suffering from chronic alcoholism and determined to be eligible for disability benefits from the government. This, along with the spouse's income, protects the family's economic security to some degree. The disabled worker qualifies for health insurance through the employer's private plan. Under this plan, the family is reimbursed for 80 percent of the cost of all medical and hospital care, but receives no reimbursement for prescription costs. Fifty percent of the cost of the teenager's psychiatric care is covered by the spouse's health insurance plan provided by the spouse's employer. This plan, however,

limits hospitalization coverage to thirty days and outpatient treatment to one year. The spouse's employer also provides two weeks' paid vacation and twelve days of sick leave that the spouse is able to use during the course of dealing with the family's medical crises.

As a result of its circumstances, the family amasses large medical and drug bills that force severe economies in its lifestyle. A second mortgage is used to help pay the medical bills, and the second child has postponed graduate school to work and help support the family. Throughout the crisis, the amount of time the spouse is able to spend with ill family members is limited by the amount of the available vacation time and sick leave.

Should the researcher's disability become permanent, the family's retirement income will be reduced because the working spouse's pension will be tied to the worker's now-interrupted work history.

_____

Source: Federico, R., *Social Welfare in Today's World* (New York: McGraw Hill, 1990), p. 228. Reprinted with permission of McGraw Hill.

United States offered by Federico (1990). This entry includes a hypothetical situation involving alcoholism and its impact under two very different circumstances. The reader may want to compare Sweden and the United States in terms of the degree of safety and security provided to workers and their families.

Throughout the remainder of this book, and especially in part II which covers care across the life span, various patterns of providing social welfare throughout the world will be compared. Family and children's policies, workers' welfare treatment of the ill and injured, and provisions for the elderly will be compared and contrasted along residual/institutional lines. By studying alternative programs such as the welfare capitalism of Japan or the advanced welfare state of Sweden, we can gain a perspective on our own programs.

Before examining the wealth of social services and institutions which comprise the social welfare structure in the United States, let us ponder the following philosophical question: What is the aim of social welfare? Or, in other words, what functions does it serve for the society? Why have such a system at all?

SOCIAL CONTROL FUNCTION

The manifest function of social welfare is to provide for the common good through a distribution of resources. Ideally, it would mean that those who have more than they need share with those who have too little. Social welfare, however, is not only an institution for dispensing wealth — it contributes to the maintenance, and indeed, the survival of society (Karger and Stoesz, 1990). This aspect can be considered the latent function of social welfare. In systems terminology, one can say that social welfare policies exist primarily to keep the society in a state of balance or homeostasis. When people perceive themselves as having nothing to lose, a revolt or revolution becomes an omnipresent reality. So, either the class of have-nots must be eliminated through generous sharing of resources, or they must be mollified or otherwise subdued in some way. This is the social control aspect of social welfare. *Social control* is defined in the *Social Work Dictionary* (Barker, 1995) as:

1. The organized effort of a society or some of its members to maintain a stable social order and to manage the process of social change.
2. Efforts to constrain people, requiring them to adhere to established norms and laws.

Often the aim of social control is to prevent social change entirely so that the ruling classes may maintain their present favorable political, economic, and social positions. Social control, according to Johnson et al. (1995), is inherent in subtle ways in what social work is and does. Compassion for the poor has always been tinged with an element of punishment, a way of penalizing them for their presumed lack of work ethic or frugality, according to Tropman, (1989). For social workers in the corrections, substance abuse, and child welfare fields, because of the involvement of the courts or the state, the control mechanisms are, of course, obvious.

According to Piven and Cloward (1993), the poor are carefully and deliberately regulated. Poor relief, as we will see in the following chapter, was invented and periodically expanded to cope with the widespread strife of dispossessed people wandering about the countryside. Relief given to the poor was just enough to prevent revolt, yet too insubstantial to be a threat to employers who paid low wages. In the United States, the peculiar combination of racism and the lack of a political-working class solidarity combined to prevent the emergence of a viable welfare state. One explanation for the distinctive pattern in the United States—the narrow reach of the social security programs, and persistence of restrictive, means-tested programs—may be the weakness of working class organizations in electoral politics (Piven and Cloward, 1993). In Europe, the rise of strong labor parties offered an ever-present check on punitive social legislation of the kind intermittently advanced in the United States.

The use of social welfare as a controlling function within nations finds its parallel between and among nations as well. Elliot (1990a) perceives social control as a recurring theme internationally: Control is exercised by means of fiscal policies, free trade agreements favorable to the dominant nation, and through corporate and professional imperialism which perpetuates the disadvantaged position of the poorer countries. Often, according to Elliot, international rebels portrayed in the Western media as "bad guys" are the "good guys" in terms of support for the poor in their countries. For example, the Sandinistas in Nicaragua who were fought as the enemies of capitalism were considered the heroes in some circles, and in Cuba the revolution was quite popular after American businesses were seized. Engaged in an unhealthy dependency on the industrialized nations whose first interest is their own economic hegemony, debtor nations often find their agricultural and manufacturing arrangements tightly monitored by external forces. The concern of the free market economy, in short, is in cornering markets for company products and technology. Human rights violations and basic needs deprivations in dependent nations may cause embarrassment for international corporations; however, they are not a primary consideration in conducting trade.

Writing from a radical feminist point of view, sociologist Bryson (1992) argues that the provision of social welfare services maintains the legitimacy of the capitalist system. Welfare, according to Bryson, represents the human face of capitalism without which workers might be unprepared to contract their labor. Fear of succumbing to the care of the state, in other words, helps maintain a tractable work force. Further, according to Bryson, welfare provisions reinforce the sexual status quo. In the absence of extensive social service benefits, women often feel compelled to assume caretaking functions for ailing relatives. In Japan, particularly, this use of women's unpaid labor provides tremendous savings to the state.

The fact that cash assistance for the poor has never been a part of the U.S. state welfare is indicative of the impetus of control. Use of vouchers and food stamps, for example, ensures that money is not spent on inessential items. Stipulations that require job training, substance abuse treatment, or children's school attendance are attached to the receipt of welfare payments as additional efforts to control clients' behavior in a fashion desired by the state. The fact that the outcomes may be favorable in no way diminishes the social control nature of the program. One of the most coercive policies in the world is China's "one child, one family" policy—a drastic attempt to control population growth. Strong social and financial sanctions are enforced upon parents who have more than one child; coercive abortion is probably the most unpalatable aspect of this "one child, one family" program. China's policy, unlike the United States', is more or less universal. It is not just a program for the poor. The fact that social control functions are a part of the social welfare even in the most advanced welfare state is revealed in the following example from Sweden: A man who was to be scheduled for a triple by-pass operation was denied surgery. Why? He refused to quit smoking.

SOCIALIST MODEL

The present welfare system, according to socialists, responds to human needs in a way designed to further the growth of capitalism. The costs of capitalism in the form of social problems are met by the state. The unjust economic system, in turn, continues to generate problems requiring social programs to ameliorate the damage incurred by the system in the first place (Karger and Stoesz, 1990).

The ideas of Karl Marx—with his radical economic determinism—have had considerable impact on social welfare. Following the Second World War, labor-dominated governments in Europe implemented sweeping social reforms. Today, strong unionization and socialist party political affiliations are characteristic of many European members of the social work profession. U.S. social welfare and social work, in contrast, were stymied at crucial historic periods by a strict capitalist political economy. The McCarthyism of the fifties had a decidedly inhibiting effect on radical thinking and organization.

Seeking revolutionary social change such as social criticism and intervention at a collective level, the socialist tradition advocates work with communities and large groups of disadvantaged and oppressed people (Payne, 1991). Instead of remedial treatment for the disadvantaged, eradication of the oppressive economic and political structures is advocated. Class advantages and disadvantages are opposed (Day, 1997). Former colonies on various continents rejected the rudiments of Western thought, stressing instead, community development based on indigenous ideas. Keefe (1980) cites the radical work of Freire (see chapter 4) as a particularly important Latin American perspective for consciousness raising of workers (including social workers) throughout the world. Freire (1973) is concerned with the education of people whose communities are oppressed by poverty and gross inequalities. The problems pertaining to social welfare are seen as arising in a structural, not an individual context.

Reacting against the social control aspect of social work, radical views on social welfare rose to prominence in the United States in the 1970s (Payne, 1991). The community organization tradition which stresses systematic collective action, and the emphasis on client advocacy and empowerment both have their roots in formulations from Europe and countries undergoing rapid socioeconomic change.

In its history of advocacy for the poor and in its public service, the U.S. social work profession today is influenced not only by the Judeo-Christian tradition (discussed in the following chapter) but also by the radical views of Marxism. Extending a neo-Marxist perspective, for instance, Fabricant and Burghardt (1992) highlight several key trends in the social services field—bureaucratization, high caseloads, and loss of control over decisions—that are alienating welfare workers from their craft. Likening human service personnel—powerless and alienated from their labor—to factory workers, Fabricant and Burghardt urge collective resistance against the increasing bureaucratization. In a similar vein, *The Journal of Progressive Human Services* publishes critiques of leading social issues from a radical, socialist perspective. Articles on struggles by workers and clients on the job and in the community address the need for building caring societies based on equality and justice.

The Canadian radical tradition is more pronounced. Mullaly (1993) recounts the rise of structural social work which now is assuming an increasing importance as a major perspective and theory in Canada. Unlike the liberal approach which accepts the social system, the structural school seeks to transform it. This view, according to Mullaly, has much more in common with socialist than with capitalist paradigms. In the contemporary United States, the liberal but not radical social work tradition is strong; mainstream journals of the National Association of Social Workers persistently call for a massive government anti-poverty effort. A parallel, more conservative trend with a marked influence in U.S. social work circles today is the influence of the private sector.

CAPITALISM

The most powerful global force today is not world communism but free enterprise capitalism. National borders are dissolving at a rapid rate as is job security as the international corporations seek cheap labor in economically depressed regions and nations. Efficiency and profit, not for nations but for companies, are the single-minded goal. Cost-benefit analysis measures human and health safety against corporate profits. Workers may be maimed, crippled, and poisoned in the process. In the advanced industrialized countries, political leaders assume that the combination of more police, more prisons, a well-disciplined media, and increasing political apathy will enable the economy to function with lower wages and smaller welfare benefits (Bishop, 1994). Any effective political and social organization by the poor in economically developing nations is opposed by force. Such grass-roots organizations, according to Bishop, are incompatible with a market-driven society.

During the 1980s, Europe, Canada, and the United States went through a period of political transformation in conjunction with the conservative "minimum state" ideology—a response to the prevailing fiscal currents (Kramer et al., 1993). What are these fiscal currents? In an analysis of what he calls the global, info-technological revolution, Toffler (1990), in *Power Shift*, perceives an emerging pattern through all the refinancing, reorganizations, and mergers. It all adds up, claims Toffler, to the biggest shake-up the business world has known since the industrial revolution. The increasing centralization of economic power through mergers and buy outs, according to Federico (1990), has made workers more vulnerable to the policies and decisions of the political corporate economy. Under conditions of the market economy, state welfare grows increasingly fragile: It is challenged both by ideological and practical pressures. According to the capitalist model (epitomized in Japan and Korea), those in middle class occupations depend more on the private than the public sector for employment and equally on employers as much as the state for welfare benefits. By ameliorating the excesses of capitalism while doing little to advance the power base of the working class, capitalist social policies reinforce the strengths of capitalism. In the conservative view, economic and social problems are blamed on creeping socialism and vested interests of those such as social workers employed in the public sector (Gould, 1993).

Corporations influence social welfare policy, reflecting the preference of business leaders for the transfer of activities from government to business. Privatization, or the shift from public to private responsibility for social welfare, is emphasized. Major policy issues such as the control and distribution of society's wealth and the citizens' rights to health, education, and shelter are bound up in the privatization issue. We will consider the impact on social welfare services later in the discussion. Corporations influence social welfare policy though the transmission of ideas (through well-financed think tanks) and through political influence in the form of contributions to political action committees (PACs).

Karger and Stoesz (1990) utilize a structural approach to the forging of new directions for public policy which reflects the preferences of corporate donors. During the 1970s, the corporate sector funded specialized research institutes for the purpose of introducing policy initiatives, as these authors indicate. The Heritage Foundation today has assumed the leadership in defining a pro-business and anti-government outlook on social policy. Established by the Coors family, this intellectual foundation with a budget of millions, finances studies that espouse a militant conservative ideology. Heritage social policy initiatives emphasize private alternatives to public programs compatible with the philosophy of the religious right. The Heritage Foundation took an aggressive stance in urban development, income security, and social welfare policies. Its proposals and concepts have shaped conservative government proposals since the 1980s. Charles Murray, whose influential works *Losing Ground* (1984) and *The Bell Curve* (co-authored with Herrnstein, 1994) have caused a storm of controversy, is associated with this conservative think tank. Both of his books propose that the welfare system itself is the cause of poverty among the so-called black American underclass. What is the solution? The elimination of social support for working-aged persons. The rationale for the assault on federal welfare programs today has been provided in writings such as these.

A second means of transforming the climate of opinion is through direct contributions to political campaigns. The influence of the corporate PACs is out of proportion to their representation in the population. In contrast, labor organizations represent far greater numbers and have less wealth at their disposal for political influence.

The 1994 health care reform battle has been the biggest, costliest, and most heavily lobbied battle to come before Congress. Tens of millions of dollars were spent on congressional campaigns, especially on the campaigns of members of House and Senate committees concerned with health care. Tens of millions more were poured into television, radio, and newspaper advertising. According to a *USA Today* article by Welch (1994), the health care industry has sponsored 181 trips for 85 members of Congress in the past two years.

Other examples of intensive lobbying efforts are the National Rifle Association's battle against gun control regulations and the defense industry's support for the production of billion dollar weapons systems.

PRIVATIZATION

Corporate growth and privatization go hand in hand. Privatizing human services for increasing efficiency is a trend that questions the fundamental nature of social welfare itself (Bell-Lowther, 1988). The increasing reliance on private health, educational, and social institutions to provide services is not merely national, but international in scope. Widely accepted in the Anglo-American countries since the early 1960s, privatization is currently gaining ground in more advanced welfare states such as Denmark, Norway, and Sweden.

Privatization is controversial. Views differ according to the political orientation of the writer. Proponents of privatization focus on cost pressures and efficiency. There is a sense of a kind of survival-of-the-fittest mentality coupled with the belief that a free and private market place will ensure the well-being of citizens through unhindered competition.

A strong critic of privatization, Abramovitz (1986) traces its history in a resurgence of interest stimulated in part by the growth of public programs during the Great Society epoch of the sixties. The growth itself led to a counter-reaction as the threatened private markets sought to retrench. Privatization, argues Abramovitz, strengthens the two-class welfare state and reproduces the inequalities that the free market inevitably creates. When people begin to seek private rather than public programs, support for the public programs eventually dwindles. These programs become associated with the poor, and sometimes the consequences of inadequate services are fatal. Karger and Stoesz (1990) cite instances in which private hospitals have transferred indigent patients with traumatic injuries to distant public facilities with dire results. Many patients have died, in fact, during transportation. There are press reports of women in labor delivering their babies in transit after being turned away at private facilities or due to the closings of regional hospitals.

Organizations whose primary goal is to gain profit have subordinated and will subordinate the social good to sustain private gain (Reisch, 1992). Reisch goes so far as to suggest that social workers should not work in for-profit organizations. These settings are noted for screening out the most needy clients and the least able to pay; cost-efficiency is paramount (Karger and Stoesz, 1990). Nevertheless, 22.1 percent of National Association of Social Workers members currently obtain their primary income from such settings (Ginsberg, 1995).

The United States' health and mental health systems, in short, have seen private initiatives in each of its components. Managed care services, alcoholism units of hospitals, inpatient mental health care, adolescent psychiatric treatment, correctional facilities — these are all examples of areas in which private sector initiatives have been the most pronounced. Savings in private settings include marketing practices to attract paying clients, more efficient use of personnel, use of part-time labor and volunteer labor, and fewer employee benefits paid out (Simons, 1989). An example of this is the extensive use of volunteer staff to conduct group sessions as a near fiat in alcoholism treatments today.

PUBLIC AND PRIVATE AGENCIES

Although U.S. public welfare expenditures relative to the gross national product are far below that of most other industrialized nations and English-speaking countries, the American public social welfare system looms large. It includes social insurance for old age, disability, unemployment, assistance for poor families, government health provisions, veterans' programs, housing and social welfare services, and so on. Public agencies are established by law, operate on local, state, or federal levels, and are administered by public officials according to legal mandates.

Federico (1990) differentiates public and private agencies in terms of accountability, responsibility, resources, and participation. Accountability refers to the body of persons to whom an agency answers. With public agencies the power resides in the legislation, not in a board of individuals. Whereas public agencies are accountable to the public and records are open to inspection, private agencies are accountable only to their governing body, usually a board of directors. Private agencies are nongovernmental and are sometimes called voluntary agencies because they were established by voluntary, often religious groups. Many now receive part of their funding from a local United Way. In relation to Maslow's hierarchy of needs, voluntary social programs are focused on lower-level, survival-based priority needs (Morales and Sheafor, 1995). In order for higher level needs, such as self-esteem and self-actualization, to be met, well-funded public human service programs are required. Wilensky and Lebeaux (1958) relate the prominence of private social welfare activity in America to individualism and religious freedom combined with the market economy.

In terms of responsibility, public agencies have been created with the aim of meeting the basic needs of all citizens. Private agencies, however, may specialize, meeting the needs of only a few. For example, some forms of cosmetic surgery may be offered on a private fee basis only. Because the most desirable patients are those who can afford such "extras," a creaming of the top or paying clients may occur.

Resources for social benefits for the public come from three tiers of government—federal, state, and local (city and county) levels. Increasingly federal subsidies to the states have been cut and responsibility is being passed down the line, often to the county level. In Iowa, for example, the county pays for mental health and alcoholism services for the indigent. The building of county jails is a major expenditure across the country. Many of the southern counties have built up huge deficits due to the expense of the appeals process associated with the death penalty. Meanwhile, at the federal level, the relative claims of social welfare and defense on federal monies is a continuing source of controversy. The size of the budget deficit and the unwillingness of the American people to raise levels of taxation in order to reduce it, exacerbate the controversy. In any case, public programs do have access to government funding. Their resource base is considerably larger than that of private programs. Table 2.1 reveals the priorities in U.S. government outlays.

Private agencies depend on contributions, fees, and contracts, such as a contract to operate a jail. Often the contracts, however, are from federal, state, and local sources, an arrangement which generally emanates from cost-effectiveness measures. The Department of Human Services (DHS), the local child welfare agency, typically subcontracts out family preservation services. The situation may thus arise that the front-line workers with the family are less well paid and less qualified than the DHS social workers employed by the state.

Participation, in Federico's usage, refers to the relationships between public and private agencies in providing services. In Mexico for some time, the system has encouraged the use of private funds to build agencies which are then publicly operated. Many of the formerly communist countries of eastern Europe are beginning to build voluntary associations to meet people's needs no longer being met by the government. In the United States, similarly, the boundaries between public and private gradually are becoming obscured. The belief that capitalist profit-making strategies can be used by the welfare state is gaining in currency. The majority of nursing homes are operated for profit with public funds (through Medicare and Medicaid programs) accounting for two-thirds of their revenues. For-profit hospital chains are a major American industry. CEOs (Chief Executive Officers) of the top health corporations, in fact, are among the highest paid CEOs in the United States, if not in the world. For-profit prisons and juvenile correctional facilities are springing up and virtually every state prison system contracts out for services such as health care and food service.

The distinction between nonprofit private agencies — those that use all their resources to provide services, and for-profit agencies — those from the business sector that seek to maximize income and reduce expenditures in order to make a profit, is increasingly blurred. Nonprofit agencies reap tremendous tax funding as well as public relations advantages.

Morales and Sheafor (1995) chronicle the transformation in the funding of human service programs. From the 1930s through the 1970s, government agencies provided services directly to clients. A relatively large public sector developed, therefore, and social workers generally were employed by the state or county. Then, in the interest of budget cuts, the pattern shifted to purchase-of-service agreements with private, nonprofit agencies providing the services. Today,

TABLE 2.1
Federal Government Finances and Employment
Federal outlays by detailed function: 1980 to 1993

(In millions of dollars. For fiscal years ending in year shown; outlays stated in terms of checks issued or cash payments.)

Function	1980	1985	1990	1991	1992	1993, est.	Percent Distribution 1980	1993, est.
Total outlays	590,947	946,391	1,252,691	1,323,785	1,381,791	1,474,935	100.00	100.00
Legislative branch	1,224	1,610	2,241	2,296	2,677	2,847	0.21	0.19
The Judiciary	567	966	1,641	1,989	2,299	2,531	0.10	0.17
Funds appropriate to President	8,542	11,858	10,087	11,724	11,109	11,855	1.45	0.80
Departments:								
Agriculture	34,785	55,523	46,012	54,119	56,465	67,169	5.89	4.55
Commerce	3,129	2,140	3,734	2,585	2,567	3,061	0.53	0.21
Defense-Military	130,912	245,154	289,755	261,925	286,632	276,037	22.15	18.72
Defense-Civil	15,161	18,770	24,975	26,543	28,267	29,471	2.57	2.00
Education	14,770	16,682	23,109	25,339	26,047	30,880	2.50	2.09
Energy	6,467	10,587	12,084	12,479	15,523	16,859	1.09	1.14
Health and Human Services	76,374	132,104	193,678	217,969	257,961	292,695	12.92	19.84
Housing and Urban Development	12,735	28,720	20,167	22,751	24,470	25,573	2.16	1.73
Interior	4,477	4,825	5,796	6,097	6,555	7,155	0.76	0.49
Justice	2,641	3,586	6,507	8,244	9,826	10,519	0.45	0.71
Labor	29,731	23,893	25,316	34,040	47,163	43,343	5.03	2.94
State	1,940	2,645	3,979	4,252	5,007	5,238	0.33	0.36
Transportation	19,802	25,020	28,637	30,503	32,477	35,913	3.35	2.43
Treasury	76,568	164,967	255,172	276,339	293,428	303,023	12.96	20.54
Veterans Affairs	21,137	26,333	28,998	31,214	33,894	35,361	3.58	2.40
Independent agencies:								
Environmental Protection Agency	5,603	4,490	5,108	5,769	5,950	6,444	0.95	0.44
General Services Administration	249	2	123	487	469	1,327	0.04	0.09
NASA	4,959	7,251	12,429	13,878	13,961	14,092	0.84	0.96
Office of Personnel Management	15,056	23,727	31,949	34,808	35,596	37,229	2.55	2.52
Small Business Administration	2,026	680	692	613	394	975	0.34	0.07
Other independent agencies	16,112	9,974	74,523	81,240	18,556	35,608	2.73	2.41
Undistributed offsetting receipts	31,988	58,656	98,930	110,005	117,111	119,242	−5.41	−8.08
Outlays by function	590,947	946,391	1,252,691	1,323,785	1,381,791	1,474,935	100.00	100.00

Source: U.S. Department of Commerce, *Statistical Abstract of the United States* (1993), p. 332.

for-profit organizations, often owned by large corporations, are providing the services on a subcontracted-out basis. A conflict between the service orientation of the professions and the profit motive of big business is apparent. Emphasis invariably appears to be on the quantity, not quality, of services provided: "How much for how little," has become a tacit theme.

To reiterate, public and private enterprises are closely intertwined. When government agencies under the influence of neoconservative ideologies initiated a pattern of contracting with private for-profit sources to provide services, the federal and state role in human services became more subsidiary. Whereas liberals would generally favor strong government programs and perceive the causes of many human problems to be structural/economic, the conservative viewpoint argues for the benefits of relying on the competition of private enterprise to offer direct services. Predictions are that in light of current economic trends the expansion of public-private partnerships only will continue (Dolgoff et al., 1993). The unprecedented level of the federal debt, the secular drift toward private enterprise as a way of life, and the growing recognition of the role of the private sector in social service delivery, enhance the attractiveness of this option. However, government intervention is as necessary as ever, perhaps even more necessary to protect individuals from uncertainties inherent in a market-based economy.

INCOME MAINTENANCE: SOCIAL INSURANCE

Income maintenance programs are social welfare programs designed to prevent or combat poverty through contributions to the income of individuals or families. Included in this category are the seeming opposites: social insurance programs and public assistance. The former is a universal-style program in which people receive benefits as legal entitlement based on their own contributions. The latter, the public welfare dimension, is financed out of general tax revenues. Public assistance is not universally available but rather, means tested.

Aptly described by Karger and Stoesz (1990) as a complex labyrinth of programs, policies, and services with little or no coordination among them, the American social welfare state sometimes comes across as a helter-skelter mix of programs that defy a systematic understanding. Because the United States has been historically ambivalent about providing public relief, most welfare legislation, suggest Karger and Stoesz, has resulted from compromises and adroit maneuvering rather than from a systematic plan. The separate state and local governments in a vast, heterogenous country further complicate welfare arrangements. Small European countries, in contrast, operate under a comprehensive and integrated welfare plan.

Included under the auspices of social insurance programs are social security, Medicare, unemployment insurance, and workers' compensation. Social insurance operates much like any other type of insurance; people pay against future risk. Social insurance programs are government programs to protect citizens from the full consequences of the risks and situations (such as unemployment) to which they are vulnerable (Barker, 1995).

Although politicians and the media complain about the costs of public assistance programs, social insurance schemes are financed at a level about four times higher than public welfare. The principal beneficiaries of U.S. social insurance programs are the elderly.

Social Security—OASDI

OASDI (Old Age, Survivors, and Disability Insurance), popularly referred to as social security, was created by the 1935 Social Security Act and later amendments. This, the largest income maintenance program in the United States, accounts for 40 percent of all social insurance payments. Nine out of ten workers are covered. Under this program, people are compelled to pay—through payroll taxes—to insure themselves against their own loss of earnings through retirement or physical disability or death of the family breadwinner. Cash benefits are paid as a matter of earned right to survivors of insured workers. Participation is compulsory for most employees; employer and employee pay equal amounts. The current Federal Insurance Act (FICA) tax rate applicable to each employee and employer is 6.2 percent for OASDI. HI (Health Insurance and Medicare) is an additional 1.45 percent (Social Security Bulletin, 1993). The self–employed pay double these rates.

Retirement benefits from this program are provided to fully insured workers age sixty-five or older. Dependent spouses over sixty-two and dependent children under age sixteen are also covered. The minimum retirement age for full old-age social security benefits has been raised beginning in the year 2027 from sixty-five to sixty-seven.

A major concern in recent years has been the financial soundness of the social insurance programs (Zastrow, 1993). A putative crisis was fueled by demographic changes (a dropping birth rate plus an increase in life expectancy), more liberal benefits paid to retiring workers, high unemployment, and the cost-of-living adjustments passed by Congress (Karger and Stoesz, 1990). However, Marmor et al. argue that social security, the most popular and successful social welfare program ever launched in America, has become a scapegoat for the anxieties engendered by a distressingly volatile economic environment. The fact that this self-paying insurance program, according to Marmor et al., is regarded within the context of crisis is scapegoating at its worst.

Walz (1994) argues compellingly that in this age of global capitalism when modern technology has replaced workers, a social security system based on a payroll tax is obsolete. Workers today are forced to retire earlier and earlier, and with perpetual downsizing of industry, payment into any insurance scheme will be predictably unstable. The reality that the poor pay a greater share of their income to social security than do the rich is an inequity built into this system and made worse by the fact that the wealth of the rich comes not from salary but from capital gains.

Tracy (1994) counters Walz's argument with a simple question, "Do we really want to abandon social security in favor of income-test programs and private initiatives?" Voluntary social security is an oxymoron, according to this author. Just as the social security systems of other nations have responded to new work patterns, so can ours also. Innovative provisions include partial retirement, pensions for the long-term unemployed, and pensions for partially disabled persons and for the prematurely aged.

Medicare

Federal health insurance for the aged, Medicare was incorporated in law in 1965 and OASDI became OASDHI (Old Age, Survivors, Disability, and Health Insurance). Medicare consists of two separate but coordinated programs: part A is hospital insurance and part B is supplementary medical insurance of which beneficiaries are charged a monthly premium. Hospital insurance helps pay for inpatient hospital care, inpatient care in a skilled nursing facility, home health care, and hospice care (Zastrow, 1993). Coverage is limited to ninety days in a hospital and to one-hundred days in a nursing home. A fairly substantial payment of a deductible is required before any benefits can be paid. Moreover, only a portion of the medical bill, usually 80 percent of reasonable charges, is paid by this program. The supplementary plan helps pay for physicians' services and a variety of other procedures and treatments.

In 1983, a system of diagnostic-related groups (DRGs) was established by the federal government. Under this cost saving measure, Medicare's reimbursement rates to hospitals were set according to illness category. This reimbursement plan has resulted in intensified discharge planning to remove patients from the hospitals as soon as their allotted time is up.

Unemployment Insurance

Created by the 1935 Social Security Act, unemployment insurance provides benefits to workers who have lost their jobs due to no fault of their own. This program is available through federal and state cooperation. The weekly benefit amount for which the unemployed are eligible, along with the number of weeks of eligibility for payment (usually for up to twenty-six weeks), varies from state to state. In most states, the formula is designed to compensate for a fraction of the usual weekly wage, normally about 50 percent, subject to specified dollar maximums (*Social Security Bulletin*, 1993). Extensions are granted during periods of economic recession. Eligibility requirements in most states are that the worker must have worked a certain number of weeks in covered employment, must be able to work, available for work, and be free from disqualifications.

The unemployment benefit program is fraught with difficulties, according to Karger and Stoesz (1990). For one thing, many of the states have steadily tightened eligibility requirements. For another, older workers separated from their jobs, may have little chance of finding new, gainful employment when competing with younger applicants. Additionally, restrictions against students receiving benefits hinders recipients in long-term preparation for career change. Due to the very temporary nature of the coverage, when the unemployment rate is high, as it is today, only a fraction of unemployed workers are receiving benefits.

Workers' Compensation

Designed to provide cash benefits and medical care when workers are injured on the job, workers' compensation was the first form of social insurance to develop widely in the United States. The first workers' compensation program was the Federal Employees Compensation Act of 1908. Individual states eventually followed suit and enacted their own laws. When state programs failed to take any responsibility for the health hazards of coal mining, however, notably "black lung" disease, a federal program was set up to provide for compensation and medical care.

As Karger and Stoesz (1990) indicate, workers' compensation programs are problematic in several ways. Out of court settlements may seem attractive on the surface, yet fail to match the loss in actual wages. Benefits are limited to one-third of the worker's salary. Finally, long delays exist between the injury and the time of the payment.

INCOME MAINTENANCE: PUBLIC ASSISTANCE

Sometimes called "welfare" by the general public, programs restricted to the poor in which applicants must undergo a "means test" are highly stigmatized. Instead of being financed by the employee through his or her job, support for public assistance comes out of general tax revenues.

Zastrow (1993) succinctly lists five aspects of public aid characteristic of adherents of the residual view of social welfare:

1. Assistance should be made as unpleasant as possible as a deterrent to use. Tedious paperwork, continual reevaluation of need, avoidance of cash benefits for greater control, and impersonal treatment by bureaucrats—these are all qualities of these types of programs.
2. Recipients should be made to work regardless of the conditions of the work or the level of the pay.
3. Payments must be lower than wages as an incentive to work.
4. Aid should be only temporary.
5. Assistance should be denied to those who voluntarily quit their jobs.

Examples of means-tested programs are Aid to Families with Dependent Children (AFDC), food stamps, supplemental security income (SSI), Medicaid, and housing assistance. These programs, in contrast to social insurance programs, are all based on need rather than entitlement.

Aid to Families with Dependent Children (AFDC)

AFDC, the nation's largest public assistance program, is the most stigmatized public assistance program (Zastrow, 1993). Society, according to Dolgoff et al. (1993), is often depicted as needing to protect itself against a horde of unwed mothers, deadbeat fathers, and other "cheats" striving to live off the public dole. Mass media exposés of welfare fraud are increasingly common. Considered somehow expendable, there is talk in the mid-nineties of turning over the responsibility for the care of children in poor families to the states. Already, there are drastic differences in state rates of allocation. In 1991, a family in Mississippi received $121 per month, while a family in Iowa received $379. This compares to Minnesota's allotment of $523 and Alaska's $690.

Significantly, the family aid program started in 1935 as a method of keeping mothers at home. Mothers were being paid, in effect, for their child care activities. Today, with middle class mothers working and a fiercely renewed work ethic, a major objective of the program is to compel single mothers to work or to train for work.

In the past, AFDC was widely criticized because of its provision of aid only to families without an able-bodied male present. This created conditions favorable to a break up of the family. Meanwhile, intellectual rationales for reductions in welfare spending came with the publication of Murray's *Losing Ground* (1984). Since the anti-poverty programs of the 1960s, according to Murray's argument, failed to reduce poverty, promoted dependency, and did not support the work ethic, they were actually harmful. This ideology was reified in the Family Support Act of 1988.

Work expense and child care may be provided for up to twelve months after a family leaves the AFDC rolls because of employment. States have adopted a variety of approaches from workfare to job training and education programs. Supporters point to the desire to end the dependency and stigma of the program. Detractors argue that welfare is punitive and reduces the number of well-

BOX 2.2

REALITY BITES

Suzanne McDevitt

Sometimes reality bites.

It's as true in policy development as in life. Theories, however carefully worked out, are never quite the same in real life as they are on the floor of a legislative house. Sometimes the idea works well. Sometimes it doesn't. For example, Headstart, after 30 years, appears to have sustained its initial vision. It's a keeper. Supply-side economics, on the other hand, after 10 years, is generally agreed not to be.

Academicians, politicians, and other policy mavens are always brimming with ideas. These ideas often get taken up by interest groups. Sometimes based on research, sometimes based on "instinct," often as a response to changing societal conditions, policy debate is frequently fueled by emotion and closely held opinion irrespective of research studies. After all, as Lincoln said, the occasion is piled high with difficulties, and we must rise with the occasion. New problems demand new remedies. And today's potential Lincolns stand in line with them. Yet approaches are often inconsistent and poorly tested before implementation.

While the FDA submits any new drug or treatment to a rigorous safety evaluation, we often implement domestic social policies as a result of discussions and debates that can only be described as political, if not ideological. Lacking prior evaluation, welfare reform—for example—could turn out to be penicillin, *but* it could also turn out to be thalidomide.

In terms of consistency, take—for example—the system of Aid to Families with Dependent Children, which is being extensively scrutinized in the new welfare-reform initiatives. AFDC is under fire for allowing women to stay home with children rather than working. However, the Social Security System—through survivor's benefits—creates the same incentive for a parent to stay home with dependent children if the deceased parent was covered under the program, i.e., had enough credits. But no one is calling for a reform of Social Security based on the incentives it creates.

Welfare reform presents a series of interesting questions. A great deal of scientific literature exists on some aspects of it; very little on others. For example, many of the current federal initiatives derive from research on welfare mothers done by David Elwood and Mary Jo Bane, formerly of Harvard, now serving at the Department of Health and Human Services, using a large

(Continued on next page)

BOX 2.2 (Continued)

database called the Panel Study of Income Dynamics. Their studies have charted trends exclusively, including how long mothers stay on welfare and what tends to take them off. One study found that one third of AFDC mothers go off the rolls due to wage income; one third, due to marriage (or reconciliation); and the final third, for a variety of other reasons.

This sounds pretty plain, but look at it another way. How many of these mothers finished in the top half of their high school class? If they did, had they had any prior work experience before receiving AFDC? How did that affect their time on welfare? While one study did find that prior work experience predicted a shorter time on AFDC, what about those mothers who are on, say, for over two years? While some studies can demonstrate that over time some mothers will receive benefits for a much longer time period than others, nothing really points to why.

What is keeping these mothers out of the work force? Are these mothers incapacitated by learning disabilities? By social circumstances? What kinds of social circumstances are so incapacitating anyway? Are there labor market reasons? Interpersonal reasons? Do they have trouble getting and keeping jobs because they have trouble getting along with other people? Are they handicapped by lack of education and training or lack of world view? No one really knows; and lacking the cause, solutions are hard to develop.

During the past eight years, spurred by the enactment of the Family Support Act in 1988, a number of experimental welfare programs (the now infamous 'waivers') have been implemented in states ranging from Iowa to California. Some concepts can be generalized from these experiments. First, it is hard to enroll participants. Second, while earnings may increase, clients often — because of the low-wage jobs they tend to be qualified for — remain eligible for benefits. It has also become apparent that, even with extended transitional benefits, many recipients run into trouble when medical and daycare benefits lapse. This provides an incentive to return to AFDC. In fact, it's been estimated that the introduction of national health insurance would spontaneously shrink the welfare roles.

Some of this information has contributed to the short-term debate. For example, having clients complete mandatory job-search programs has increased both employment rates and average earnings. Using this information, many states now see it as possible to use welfare reform to get clients off welfare and thereby cut the rolls. Yet studies also show that the gains were influenced by the nature (urban or rural) and status (weak or strong) of the labor market.

(Continued on next page)

BOX 2.2 (Continued)

And when one part of the system cuts back (for example, when general assistance was abolished by the state of Michigan), other parts of the system, i.e., the counties and the federal government, tended to be impacted.

Of course we'll go on having these debates and making decisions without regard to data on welfare reform and many other issues, for example, the tax structure. Objective data will remain hard to find.

Feelings of the populace, the politician, and the policy analyst are important. So are the issues raised by interest groups. But what happens if, God forbid, we make a mistake?

What if welfare reform doesn't work out as well in practice as we think it will? What if all these mothers who will lose eligibility can't find jobs and end up living in tents, or start leaving children on the front steps of churches or even the county courthouse? Shouldn't we think about these things (or try to) a little more objectively than we sometimes do? Anybody remember thalidomide?

Reality can bite.

Source: Institute of Politics *Reprint,* Fall, 1995, #12. Reprinted with permission of Suzanne McDevitt.

---

paying jobs. In fact, claims DiNitto (1994), recipients are now not only responsible for their own behavior, but they can be held hostage for the behavior of others. Young children may be denied part of their family's AFDC benefits if their teenage parents do not attend school. In Wisconsin, parents can be denied aid if a teenage child misses three days or more from school without a valid excuse.

The myths about AFDC are persistent (see Karger and Stoesz, 1990). The facts to refute such myths are as follows:

- Some of the lowest benefit states have the highest out-of-wedlock birthrates.
- Nearly three-fourths of all recipients have just one or two children.
- Two-thirds of the poor receive no money from AFDC.
- Ninety-three percent of AFDC families are headed by one parent.
- Less than one percent of recipients are able-bodied males.
- The majority receive help for a short time only.
- Benefit levels have not kept pace with inflation so AFDC families are worse off than previously.

- The number of black families receiving AFDC is approximately the same as the number of white families. However, since African Americans make up only 12 percent of the U.S. population and over 45 percent of the recipients, the stigma attached to AFDC may be partly due to racial prejudice (Zastrow, 1993).

Food Stamps

Initiated on a pilot basis in 1961, the food stamp program providing a monthly amount of coupons to be exchanged for food was formally established by the Food Stamp Act of 1964 with twenty-two states participating (*Social Security Bulletin,* 1993). For years, food stamp coupons were purchased by participants, the amount varying according to household income. Poor families, however, had problems accumulating the cash to exchange for stamps, and in 1977 the method of procuring stamps was changed.

As of 1992, a four-person household with no income received $370 monthly in food stamps. Households with income receive the difference between the amount of a nutritionally adequate diet and 30 percent of their income after allowable deductions. Medical expenses, for instance, may be deducted for aged and disabled persons. One- and two-person households that meet the applicable standard receive at least $10 a month in food stamps. Unlike AFDC, the food stamp program is not a cash supplement but rather an in-kind benefit. The receipt of food stamps boosts a poor family's standard of living substantially. Benefits are entirely federally funded. Who is eligible? Eligibility of a household is determined by its assets, income, and size. Persons who receive AFDC and/or disability payments automatically qualify to receive food stamps. Also eligible are drug addicts in a half-way house, victims of domestic violence, and the homeless. Boarders (or persons who do not prepare their own meals) and persons on strike are prohibited from participating in the program and illegal aliens are not eligible for the program.

Objections to the program include the humiliating fact that the recipients must publicly display the food stamps when purchasing items and the controlling aspect of being able to purchase only certain items with the coupons. Nevertheless, as Dolgoff et al. (1993) suggest, the food stamp program has notable strengths: It helps the poor meet basic nutritional needs and is uniform in its allocation across the states. Additionally, this arrangement helps guarantee that children, even children of addicted or spendthrift parents, receive food.

Supplemental Security Income

The Supplemental Security Income (SSI) program is a federal public assistance program which provides income support to persons age sixty-five or older, blind or disabled adults, and blind or disabled children (*Social Security Bulletin*, 1993). The 1995 federal SSI benefit rate for an individual living in his or her own household and with no other countable income is $458 monthly. Often several members in one family are eligible. Individuals who are eligible include the mentally retarded and mentally impaired, the aged with little or no income, the legally blind, the physically disabled, and drug addicts and alcoholics who enter treatment.

A recent liberal criticism of SSI is the fact that men are more likely to be SSI recipients rather than AFDC recipients, and are therefore receiving more money than the women who predominate the AFDC rolls. Another liberal argument against SSI states that SSI is a very insecure source of income since people may be knocked off the rolls in response to public outcry.

From the conservative perspective, there has been resentment towards SSI concerning the scandal involving drug addicts using their income for drugs rather than treatment. Since benefits are sometimes given retroactively in a lump sum, there have been cases of addicts squandering their money to purchase drugs. Sometimes bartenders have been named as their monitors, or people who officially supervise their spending of compensation. Additionally, according to mass media accounts, parents have obtained SSI benefits on behalf of their children who are encouraged to "act crazy" when evaluated. Under the influence of a Republican-controlled Congress, plans are currently underway to curb such abuses in this system. Recently, in 1996, legislation was passed to deny eligibility for alcoholism or other drug addiction in the absence of another disabling condition.

Medicaid (Title 19)

Title XIX of the Social Security Act is a jointly funded cooperative venture between the federal and state governments to assist states in the provision of adequate medical care to the poor (*Social Security Bulletin*, 1993). Known as Medicaid, this program became law in 1965. Because each of the states administers its own program, specific policies vary from state to state.

To be eligible for federal funds, states are required to provide coverage for individuals who receive federally assisted income-maintenance payments such as AFDC or SSI. Pregnant women without resources are generally required to be provided with services also.

The *Social Security Bulletin* (1993: 89) describes the scope of service as follows:

> Title XIX of the Social Security Act requires that, in order to receive federal matching funds, certain basic services must be offered in any state program:
>
> 1. inpatient hospital services
> 2. outpatient hospital services
> 3. prenatal services
> 4. nursing facility services for individuals age twenty-one or older
> 5. home health care for persons eligible for skilled nursing services
> 6. family planning services and supplies
> 7. rural health clinic services
> 8. laboratory and X-ray services
> 9. pediatric and family nurse practitioners services
> 10. certain federally qualified ambulatory and health-center services
> 11. nurse-midwife services
> 12. early and periodic screening, diagnosis, and treatment services for individuals under the age of twenty-one

According to the *Social Security Bulletin* (1993: 92), increases in expenditures have exceeded the rate of inflation. The continued growth can be attributed to:

1. the increase in rates of payments to providers of medical and health care services, when compared to general inflation
2. the results of technological advances to keep more low birth-weight babies and other critically ill or severely injured persons alive, and in need of very expensive care
3. the increase in the numbers of very old and disabled persons requiring extensive acute and/or long-term health care and related services
4. the increase in size of the Medicaid-covered populations (a result of the economic recession and federal mandates)

Problems reported with the Medicaid system are as follows: the low eligibility limits which mean many poorly paid workers are not covered; the fact that nursing home residents, though few in number, account for over 40 percent of the cost; and the reality that in many communities doctors refuse to treat Medicaid patients. Under a program of nationalized health care, the above difficulties would all be alleviated.

Housing Assistance

Enacted in 1937, the U.S. Housing Act was passed to help the poor get adequate housing. Similar to food stamps and Medicaid, housing assistance is an in-kind program to ensure the purchase of services. Several public programs assist in the purchase or rental of housing for low-income families. The Section 8 rental assistance program is currently the best known housing support for low-income families. Often assistance is provided in the form of public housing, usually government-owned projects. It is evident that such programs are inadequate to meet the needs of the increasing number of homeless people crowding the streets and under bridges everywhere.

PRIVATE PROGRAMS IN THE UNITED STATES

All social welfare programs are not directed toward the poor. Although most writers on the welfare state do not comment on what Bryson (1992) terms occupational welfare, work related benefits account for a large proportion of the nation's total social welfare expenditures. Dolgoff et al. (1993) estimate that expenditures by the private social welfare sector account for forty percent of the total social welfare expenditures, both public and private. Major expenses include health care, private pension plans, disability payments, and life and death insurance. Persons employed full-time and their families may receive benefits that cover medical treatment, mental health and substance abuse treatment, disability, retirement, and dental care. Blue Cross and Blue Shield, according to Dolgoff et al., are the giants among private health care systems. Such occupational or employee benefits are paid for by employers and sometimes, in part, by employees.

Pensions

Only one-third of all workers in the United States are covered under private-sector retirement schemes. Retired workers who receive a pension get monthly payments according to accumulated earnings. Social security payments are generally received also. Unlike social security, only a fraction of the private plans are indexed for inflation. Critics of reliance on private pension plans point to their general unreliability (Karger and Stoesz, 1990). Employees who switch jobs may lose pension rights. Some companies may become insolvent and others may raid pension funds in a financial crisis.

Whereas the U.S. pension scheme is entirely work related, many other countries have a flat rate pension with no income test. This approach is found mainly in Scandinavia and the Commonwealth countries. New Zealand, for instance, pays a flat rate pension financed from general taxes to all who meet residence requirements at age sixty. The Netherlands, likewise, provides all residents with a substantial pension at age sixty-five.

Voluntary Human Service Organizations

Nonprofit, private agencies offer numerous welfare services often defined as pioneering solutions to major social problems in the local community. Private agencies such as emergency shelters and outreach substance abuse treatment centers have the advantages of being small and located in the community. Religious organizations such as the Salvation Army, Catholic Charities, and Lutheran Social Services play an active and vital role in offering emergency and long-term aid to the needy. As a result of the work of paid and unpaid workers at private agencies, many people are saved from hunger and homelessness. A major work-related, fundraising drive, the United Way, disburses contributions received to a wide range of community agencies. Because private agencies receive a substantial share of their funding from government sources, they, like public agencies, sometimes experience constraints in program innovation (Morales and Sheafor, 1995).

LOOKING TOWARD THE NEXT CENTURY

The liberal rhetoric of an earlier day has begun to seem curiously passé. A national opinion poll of 4,809 people taken by the Times Micro Center for the

People and the Press (*Waterloo Courier*, 1994) confirms a shift in public attitude. Angry at their government and anxious about job security, Americans are becoming less altruistic, according to this report. Throughout the seven years of the survey, significant changes have been noted. Whereas in 1987, for example 71 percent said the government should take care of people who can't take care of themselves. By 1994, this number had fallen to 57 percent.

In 1994 only 41 percent said the government should help the needy "even if it means going deeper in debt." This marked a significant decline from previous polls. Other changes found that a majority of whites believe that equal rights have been pushed too far, and most want much stricter immigration laws.

Not only is there a neoconservative trend in the United States, but these sentiments expressed in the survey have been echoed recently in such disparate places as Alberta, Canada where severe cutbacks are straining hospitals, universities, and child care providers; New Brunswick, Canada, where the stress on individual responsibility overrides the notion of provincial welfare; Australia and New Zealand where cost-cutting efforts are presently underway; and the United Kingdom where retrenchment of the welfare state has been reflected in vast reductions in the area of subsidized housing and unemployment benefits. Throughout the Anglo-Saxon world, in fact, the tendency has been for universal services to escape unscathed whereas reductions in means-tested programs are exceedingly popular. Means-tested programs invariably are stigmatized as programs for the poor. British social scientist Mishra (1990) credits the market economy and the alter ego, the right-wing think tanks, for the present-day draconian welfare reduction proposals. The difference between the United States and the United Kingdom, according to Mishra, is that universal services are a good deal less developed in the United States than they are in the United Kingdom. Because it is often a revelation to see how the United States looks and how its policies appear from a foreign land, Mishra's (1990: 25) description is quoted in full:

> There is no general health insurance for the population, only an insurance program for those over sixty-five (Medicare). Income-maintenance programs such as sickness and maternity benefits (temporary disability) and family allowances, which are commonplace in most industrialized nations, have not been instituted in the United States. Not surprisingly, means-tested services account for a sizeable proportion of social expenditure. In the early 1980s for instance, more than 20 percent of social expenditure in the United States was on means-tested benefits, compared with less than 1 percent in Sweden . . . Ideological and political support for the welfare state has been a good deal weaker in the United States than in the United Kingdom.

The proliferation of low-wage jobs is another trend which is pronounced in the United States, according to Mishra. Kohlert (1989) profiled the "no help" position—no help for the needy—that was beginning to be articulated at the time of her writing. She was remarkably optimistic, however, in her anticipation of a labor shortage which would ultimately raise the clout of workers. On a grimmer note, Cox (1994), in his keynote speech at the International Association of Schools of Social Work Conference in Amsterdam, cited the serious limitations of corporate economic growth in improving overall human well-being. The three major avenues of change, according to Cox, are economic, social, and political. New attitudes that were once old attitudes are resurfacing; concomitant with them are new and harsher realities. According to a Canadian, Mullaly (1993: 22), "the great irony of the welfare state crisis is that we seem to be returning to the very conditions that gave rise to the welfare state in the first place."

A long time ago, Sir Thomas More wrote *Utopia* (1949, originally 1551: 81). Lambasting the English social structure of his day, this great religious and political leader (ultimately beheaded under the orders of Henry VIII), claimed that hard labor, like the laborer, was demeaned. More's words are vitriolic and on the brink of overkill yet eerily timeless in the sentiment conveyed:

> So when I weigh in my mind all the other states which flourish today, so help me God, I can discover nothing but a conspiracy of the rich, who pursue their own aggrandizement under the name and title of the Commonwealth. They devise ways and means to keep safely what they have unjustly acquired, and to buy up the toil and labor of the poor as cheaply as possible and oppress them. When these schemes of the rich become established by the government, which is meant to protect the poor as well as the rich, then they are law. With insatiable greed these wicked men divide among themselves the goods which would have been enough for all.

In some ways the social welfare programs of today and attitudes toward the poor are not so different from those Elizabethan times. DiNitto (1991: 31) echoes More's views. The tone, however, is markedly different:

> The rich get most of their help directly from the tax system through various loopholes, first and second homes and for property taxes and charitable contributions. These deductions, and credits (called tax expenditures) favor the more affluent over the less affluent. Some of these deductions are for

the mortgage interest paid on first and second homes. These deductions are also taken by middle-class families although the amount of their deductions is generally smaller.

Considered in this perspective, all groups benefit from government assistance and it has been argued that redistribution of income that results from public policy favors the rich rather than the less affluent.

As the twenty-first century approaches, the theme is social change—not the kind of social change that is a transformation of the social order, but change that is reactionary and punitive. Liberals and conservatives alike are reconsidering the philosophical basis of the social welfare state. The locus of the attack is not the undeserving rich and super-rich, but the undeserving poor. Welfare reform and entitlement cutting have been proposed as the solutions to the national deficit. Expected to be hard hit are single mothers, the elderly, and disabled. To date, a comprehensive program for containing health care costs has not been forthcoming. Key decisions about the shape of welfare for the next century will depend on how these issues are resolved. This will depend, in turn, on the future of welfare state ideology (Karger and Stoesz, 1990).

Demographic trends with implications for the future are the aging of the population at one level, and the influx of illegal immigrants at the other. The entry of the baby boom cohorts into the over sixty-five category will create a population bulge disproportionate to the number of workers in the young and middle-aged sector. The pressures of the aging population on the social and economic structure, particularly on the family and social services, are already being anticipated. From the social welfare standpoint, we can predict increasing health care costs and Social Security expenditures. We can expect the retirement age to rise; in the United Kingdom and Sweden it has done so already. In the United States, business firms encumbered with employee expenses increasingly are reducing retirement benefits including health care for newly retired employees. Such cut backs would have been unthinkable previously. Implicit in this demographic transition in age structure is a stepped-up demand for care providers of services to meet the needs of the expanding elderly population.

Shifting immigration patterns, a less predictable demographic change, have created grave concerns in border states on the local level. In California, Florida, Arizona, and Texas, for instance, an indiscriminate backlash against immigrants has arisen as state and local budgets have been stretched to the maximum in providing welfare services. A major task for the nation's future will be the determination of what kind of immigration policy will be feasible, enforceable, consistent with American values including human rights and family values, and serve the interests of the U.S. economy. Public sentiment about the need to control immigration is strong and growing. Politicians both reflect and inflame this sentiment. A safe prediction is that, at least in those regions of the United States where the influx of migrants is most pronounced, internal and external controls on newcomers will be tightened.

The consequences of the perceived economic crises for social welfare professionals are far-reaching. Major cut backs in health, housing, and mental health services are taking a toll on social welfare clients and, indirectly, on their service providers. Details of these and related issues are provided in the following chapters.

In the United States, both the climate of opinion and harsh economic realities play into the social welfare configuration. With the climate of opinion focusing on crime, the national debt, and "welfare cheats," and the business sector promoting residual, privately owned (yet publicly financed) services, serious welfare reform is inevitable. At the heart of every effort across the country are two simple principles: make people work, and give the states free reign to enforce it. Trends underway in the United States have their counterparts in Canada, Japan, Mexico, Sweden, and Great Britain as we will see shortly. Global economic interdependency is reflected in parallel crises and concerns throughout the world.

SOCIAL WELFARE STRUCTURE IN OTHER COUNTRIES

Often overwhelmed by the domestic scene and uninformed by mass media "world-in-a-minute" news coverage, Americans who have not lived abroad tend to be unaware of social welfare institutions in other parts of the world. The following section will explore the structural components of social welfare in five countries with close linkage to the United States.

Canada

The largest country in the western hemisphere and one of the the most sparsely populated areas, Canada, like the United States, is a land of immigrants. The cultural heterogeneity is pronounced; although close ties with Britain prevail, only 40 percent of the citizens of Canada are Anglo-Saxon. The two official languages are French and English.

Millar (1990) discussed five themes which permeate the historical development of social welfare in Canada. Each one will be considered separately. The first theme is the shift from a residual to an institutional concept of social welfare. Particularly, since World War II, there is less expectation that an individual can rely on savings or help from relatives in getting through a crisis of major proportions. Post-war Canadian social welfare has been built on a recognition that risks to an individual's well-being arise from the uncertainties in a modern, urban, industrialized society. However, the extensive network of universal social programs including child benefits, parental leave, day care, education, and medical care is currently being trimmed. Monthly child care payments—family allowance given to all parents of young children—have been canceled.

Related to this theme of universalism, Millar designates as a second theme, the attempt to establish a social minimum standard of living for all Canadians or a point below which no one is allowed to fall. Third, the process of defining and redefining the causes of poverty and dependency is a pervasive element in the history and structure of Canadian social welfare. As in the United States, an unmitigated belief in opportunity and classlessness hindered a recognition that intransigent poverty was a reality. Pioneer values of independence and individualism hung on, even following industrialization after the 1860s (*Canadian Encyclopedia*, 1988). Nevertheless, today the rate of poverty in Canada is one half that of the United States. An observer from the United States cannot help but be struck by Canada's much broader coverage and higher benefit levels.

The fourth theme singled out by Millar is the increasing amount of public interest in the form and operation of social welfare programs. When the wrath of influential groups such as senior citizens is aroused, the government is inclined to listen. Significantly, today much of the wrath is coming from the right wing directed against the poor. The Canadian mass media are replete with passionate commentary on both sides of the welfare spending issue.

A final theme with strong bearing on Canadian welfare history is the federal political system—the division of powers, responsibilities, and duties between the federal and provincial governments. While the federal government is responsible for native people, clients, war veterans, and criminal law, the provinces assume responsibility for health, education, and social services. Among the provinces, Quebec with its French heritage, has sought increasing autonomy. Not unlike the United States, there are grave disparities nationwide in the level of social services provided; the "have-not" provinces provide only the more basic services such as financial assistance and child protection, and rarely provide preventive social services.

McQuaig (1993) provides an analysis of current trends regarding Canadian workers, women, children, and the elderly. How are they faring, asks McQuaig, in comparison with those in other countries such as the United States and Europe? With conservatives steadily chipping away at the welfare state model, Canada has become increasingly imitative of its neighbor to the south. The tendency has become to rely on the private market place to take care of the citizenry and to leave the poor pretty much on their own. McQuaig's recommendation for Canada's future is to turn toward a model such as the Europeans' where everything from raising children to retaining redundant workers is the responsibility not just of individuals, but of the whole community.

A study of comparative international tables in the *Statistical Abstract of the United States* (U.S. Bureau of the Census, 1994) indicates: an average life expectancy of 78.1 (compared to 75.9 in the United States), a divorce rate for women that is half that of the United States, a comparable suicide rate, and an unemployment rate that is considerably higher than that of the United States. Health care expenditures constitute 10 percent of the gross domestic product compared to 13.4 percent for the United States. Canada, nevertheless, has a universal health care system that is largely publicly funded. This system will be described in detail in chapter 8. Read the interview in box 2.3 for a full appreciation of Canadian welfare benefits, at least as they existed in Ontario prior to more recent politically inspired cut backs.

Finn (1994) describes current issues of significance to the Canadian welfare state. Since 1991, average incomes have dropped as has the purchasing power of the Canadian dollar. Unemployment has reached 11 percent, one of the highest among industrialized countries. Canada ranks below European countries in the amount and duration of maternity leave (but far above Australia and the United States which have no government-funded paid maternity leave). The homicide rate of 2.7 per 100,000, is relatively high. (However, the United States' rate is 12.4 per 100,000). To reduce the homicide rate, proposals are presently underway to further restrict firearms (Wilson-Smith, 1994).

Canadian social work educator Mullaly (1993: 21) does not equivocate:

Government retrenchment has led to the formation of depression-type soup kitchens, food banks, and clothing depots, while the number of homeless

BOX 2.3

A STUDENT RESEARCHES BENEFITS IN CANADA

Jamie Paige

In September, 1993, I decided I was not getting anywhere with the fifteen books I had checked out on Canadian social welfare. There was only one way I was going to get the information I wanted to share with my classmates, and that was to talk to the people themselves . . . the people in Canada. I have found through my own personal experiences that everything always looks great on paper, but if you really want to know if a program is working within the system of social welfare just ask somebody who is actually in the system.

I decided to start with Mary, an old acquaintance of mine who had lived in Florida until she married and moved to Canada. "What is it like living in Canada?" I asked. "What is the social welfare system like?"

"Do you know," Mary replied, "that people in Canada get paid for having children?" Well, when her first child was born, they received $24 a month and that money was taxable. At first, she thought, "Well, what good can I do with $24?" But they soon changed the system and she is currently getting $100 tax free a month. With this money she can do what she wants: buy food, clothing, etc. for the kids, or simply start a college fund. Remember, Mary and her husband

are happily married and her husband has a very good job. This is just an extra benefit from her government. This money is based on income, so a very poor family would receive even more money a month.

Mary loves the free health care provided for her family. When children are born in Canada they receive a health care number. She borrowed her husband Ron's number for two years after which she received her own number. She is not quite sure what would have happened to her had she and her husband divorced before that two year period. She thinks she may not have been covered.

Mary was very excited about the birth of her babies. It is definitely cheaper than any birth in the United States. She had all her children by cesarean section. With the last child she received a bill from the hospital but only to show what the hospital had charged the government. It cost $3500 for the care of her infant son for seven days and $2500 for her surgery and aftercare. She firmly believes this would have been much higher in the United States.

At this point she said she would look in the blue pages (what we in the United

(Continued on next page)

BOX 2.3 (Continued)

States call the yellow pages) and find government numbers I could call for more information. This was no simple task since we really didn't know what we were looking for. Listed were such things as community and social services, family benefits. Under federal government was the health and welfare program. I gave the department of social and family services a call. The receptionist suggested that I talk with Tracey Hertel. Immediately, a whole new world opened up to me. All the following information came from this interview

First, I learned that every province has its own unique policies. In Ontario, each city has its own funding for certain social problems. Services at this level include aid to families in which the breadwinner has been laid off, and to students who can no longer live at home but can't make it on their own. Tracey and I discussed a hypothetical situation in which a mother recently had been divorced. This woman had two children, ages eight and thirteen. She had no education, no job prospects, and needed help immediately. I wanted to know what would happen to such a person in Canada. In this situation, although this woman's aid would be funded by provincial money, it is understood she would go to the municipal office to fill out all paper work. By starting with the municipal level, she can work through the system a little quicker. Her money will come from the provincial level.

Once this mother has been accepted into the system, she would receive the following benefits:

1. $707 a month . . . for Rent-Hydro (which means utilities) and rent.
2. $730 a month . . . Living expenses (laundry soap, food, clothing, etc.)
3. A drug card and a dental card so that emergency dental care could be given to her and basic care for her children.

I asked Tracey if there is a way to work off the system. In the United States it is very difficult as most benefits decrease if any extra income is earned. Tracey responded that a program titled Support to Employment Program (STEP) encourages people to seek employment opportunities. The way this program runs is quite simple. The formula is shown below.

Net income
− $120
Keep 25% of this sum for herself
− Daycare
Sum that is deducted off monthly benefits

(Continued on next page)

BOX 2.3 (Continued)

Actual example using hypothetical family situation:

$1,000 woman's take home money
− $120

$880
− 25%

$660
− $250 daycare expense
$410.00 taken off woman's benefits

Woman's benefits were:

$1,437.00 welfare
+ $1000.00 income
$2,437.00
− $ 410.00
$2,027.00 monthly

In my interview, I asked Tracey if a formal education was necessary for her position as an income maintenance officer. She said although it is good to have some background in the social services area, it wasn't always necessary. There are workers within the office who have advanced from different levels to these positions. She, however, does have her degree in social and family relations from the University of Guelph.

I took the opportunity to discuss homelessness with Tracey. In Owensound, according to Tracey, many of the homeless were mentally ill patients that did not want to be helped. She felt there were many opportunities that could have helped them change their lifestyles, but instead many chose to stay homeless. These people would quit taking their medication and since it was against their rights to be forced to take medication, they could not be helped.

Lastly, I asked Tracey how she liked her job and if people in her position suffered from burn-out. Tracey stated that personally, she liked her job but could relate to the high level of burn-out that case workers are subject to in the United States. It is hard not to be able to help all the people that need it, and it is hard helping the people who don't want help. There are people in Tracey's office who have worked for eighteen years at the same job, and the job has worn on them. She shared that their case load is four to five hundred cases per worker. This makes it impossible to know all your clients on a first name basis. We also spoke of the governments everywhere constantly cutting funds. Tracey said Canada has the same problem. In fact, the $120 exemption given in the STEP program example used to be $175 before August 1, 1993. So, Canada's programs are being cut too.

I ended our conversation by offering to send information on our food stamp program as Tracey expressed interest in this approach. In conclusion, I believe the United States has a lot to learn from Canada and from the support system they offer. This information I have gathered has given me some insight into the international social welfare system.

Reprinted by permission of Jamie Paige.

people continues to increase. Churches and voluntary organizations have had to pick up the slack . . . The absurdity of soup kitchens and food banks should make us question an economic and political system that takes an enormous endowment of natural resources . . . and converts them . . . into misery, want, and scarcity.

Ethnic diversity issues with serious importance for Canadian social welfare are Native Canadians' poor living conditions (reflected in a staggeringly high tuberculosis rate) and Quebec's perennial thrust for independence (an issue with drastic implications for Canada's status as a nation-state).

Millar (1990) perceives the U.S.–Canada Free Trade Agreement, an opening of the market for trade and investment in goods and services between the world's two largest trading partners, as an issue with potentially serious implications for the social welfare system. The reduction in trade barriers could ultimately entail a relocation of Canadian industry south of the border, where a less-unionized work force means lower labor costs. Clayton (1994) perceives the Canadian debt crisis—measured in terms of the percentage of the gross domestic product—as totally out of hand and well beyond that of other industrial-advanced nations (except for Italy). If the debt crisis is not relieved, massive budget cutting in Canada is inevitable.

Japan

Phenomenal rates of economic growth in the 1960s followed by a rapid recovery from the 1970s recession, have transformed Japan into a world superpower (Gould, 1993). Economically, Japan has moved from the imitator of western technologies to the model of economic success and efficiency. The Japanese state, according to Gould, was not hampered by enormous public responsibilities: Japanese parents had to save for their children's higher education; the family (i.e., female family members) had to take care of children and elderly relatives. The Japanese business firm had a core work force which saw its interests as inextricably tied with a career in the company. Moreover, Japanese socialization emphasizes the development of a "we-self" and a "familial-self," the suppression of one's personal needs (especially by women) for the needs of the group, and favors compliance and avoidance of conflict (Tomita, 1994).

Whereas past studies in comparative social policy have been preoccupied with Europe, the United States, and the links between the two, the inclusion of Japan in comparative work is essential today for an understanding of global economic interdependency. Chapter 7 discusses the notion of the "Japanization" of the American and European work forces. Japanization refers to the developments in western economies with parallel developments in western welfare systems. Universal welfare benefits are being devalued while the state is exercising more control of the discipline of the work force (and getting people to work) instead. As social problems mount in Japan, however, and as the traditional network for providing care for vulnerable people breaks down, a reshaping and a modernization of social welfare is imminent.

Several interrelated issues complicate the future of social welfare in Japan: an aging society, the rapidly changing roles for women, and the need for more adequate social services for disadvantaged groups. After a review of the unique history of Japan's social welfare structure and relevant statistical data, we will discuss each of the major social welfare issues for Japan.

Charity or philanthropic work was carried out from the olden days under the influence of Buddhism (Japanese National Committee, 1990). Much later, a social welfare system started from organized activities to help the poor. The Poor Relief Law was enacted in 1932. This law established that aid be provided in the categories of livelihood, occupation, medical care, and maternal care. After World War II, Japan instituted its new constitution which stipulated that it was the state's responsibility to promote and develop social welfare, social security, and public health. Based on the constitution, the national and local government assumed responsibility for voluntary and social welfare agencies to function complementarily (Japanese National Committee, 1990). Because the foundations of the social welfare system were established during the Allied occupation of Japan, Japan virtually imported and applied the U.S. model of social services and social work to meet the needs of its society (Matsubara, 1992). Social welfare laws were enacted in the 1950s and 1960s which set up welfare offices and provided care for the mentally retarded and pensions for the elderly. The provision of services was entrusted by the national government to the local authorities.

Comparative international statistics (U.S. Bureau of the Census, 1994) provide indicators of a society with few, but mounting, social problems. Educational attainment and literacy are exceptionally high; the fertility rate is low (1.55 children per family); life expectancy is 79.3 years (compared to 75.9 for the United

States); the divorce rate is just under one-third of the U.S. rate; the suicide rate is roughly the same for males as the U.S. rate but twice as high for females; health care is largely publicly funded (expenditures occupy half of the percentage of the gross domestic product in Japan that they do in the United States, and yet comprehensive coverage is provided); infant mortality is very low.

For the sake of international comparison of alcoholism rates, cirrhosis of the liver rates are considered the optimum measure (Royce, 1989; van Wormer, 1995). Strikingly, the Japanese cirrhosis rate is actually somewhat higher than that of the United States. Alcohol addiction in Japan is most likely related to the fact that male employees customarily congregate after work for extended social (drinking) rituals (Helzer and Canino, 1992). Many husbands arrive home from the after-work gatherings at midnight.

The homicide rate in Japan is very low. According to one newspaper account (Smillie, 1994), there are more gun deaths in a single afternoon in the United States than Japan records all year. In 1994 there were thirty-eight fatal shootings in Japan, a marked increase, however, from the previous year. Although antigun laws are very strict, illegal firearms made in the United States are increasingly available.

The extent of social problems in Japan is surprisingly low when one considers the population density. One-third of the very large population of Japan inhabits 1 percent of the land area. Parks and recreational facilities are sparse; housing, by American standards, is incredibly overcrowded. The cost of living is probably the highest in the world.

Japan's aging society is taxing the ability of the system to provide adequate services as it is complicated by a low fertility rate and the longest lifespan in the world, and by a tradition of family care for the elderly which may be breaking down as women seek work outside the home. The percentage of people over age sixty-five—4.7 percent of the population in 1940—rose to 12 percent in 1990. It is estimated to peak at 23.6 percent by 2021 (Matsubara, 1992). The increase in the elderly population has created an acute need for expanded health care services and financial assistance. Although most elderly parents still live with their grown children, this number is declining.

As in other countries, rising economic prosperity and materialism in Japan is associated with the breakup of the traditional family and reliance on the nuclear family for its flexibility and mobility. The tendency for women to marry at later ages and to have a career and fewer children is likely to lead to social changes affecting all levels of society. The more women participate in the labor market, the greater will be the demand for services for the care of children and the elderly. More job opportunities should be created in the field of social work to meet the country's changing needs. The professionalization of social work, however, is only in the beginning stages; reservations about using social services in Japan are strong (Gould, 1993; Matsubara, 1992). With the failure of the Japanese public sector to meet the needs of an economy in transition, the question of how to utilize the power of private social welfare activities becomes crucial for the future (Japanese National Committee, 1990). Another major challenge for the future is the creation of equal opportunities for women in a society in which they have played a predominantly nurturant, caretaking role, and in which discrimination against women is deep-rooted (Gould, 1993).

The recession in Japan in the mid-nineties and the unparalleled rise of service industries have caused part-time employment to expand rapidly. Women form a large proportion of the part-time work force in which wages compare unfavorably with those provided to full-time corporate employees. The absence of enforced minimum wage standards and of adequate social assistance puts the Japanese worker in a poor bargaining position. Because working opportunities for women are limited (their earnings per hour are 50 percent of males' earnings) and few reach leadership positions, educational opportunities at prestigious universities are limited also (Gould, 1993). Paralleling the discrimination against women in this society built on finely graded hierarchical differences and traditional loyalty, is intense discrimination against ethnic outgroups such as the Koreans who comprise a large portion of the 4 percent of Japan's residents who are degraded minorities—a truly outcast group.

The need for more adequate social services for disadvantaged groups is the third major issue to be resolved by Japanese social welfare. In his discussion of medical and social services, Gould singles out the overuse of prescription drugs, and the intense reliance on institutionalized care for the old, sick, and mentally ill as a waste of economic and human resources. Many of the institutionalized patients, according to Gould, are simply deviant or beyond familial control. The stigma of mental illness for one family member will be generalized to the whole family who may, in turn, be discriminated against. Therefore, the temptation is to shut the mentally ill away.

Another curious phenomenon connected with Japanese health care is the widespread use of abortion by women as a form of birth control. On average, according to Gould's calculations, abortions outnumber live births; Japanese women on average undergo two abortions. The reasons: economic pressures, male reluctance to use contraceptives, and difficulties in dealing with physical and mental impairment. As Matsubara (1992) indicates, the role of the social worker in the field of medical care in Japan is practically nonexistent.

Community-based services are expanding rapidly to offer counseling and rehabilitative and recreational services in rural as well as urban areas. The need, however, is far greater than what these very limited programs can provide. Japan, in the next ten years, will be forced to make choices as how to accommodate the needs of vulnerable persons in a society in transition, both internally and on the international stage.

In early 1995, the worst earthquake in a half-century struck Japan; over five thousand were killed and one hundred thousand immediately left homeless. The once-modern port city of Kobe stood in ruins. International headlines told the story and much more besides: "A Disaster Nobody Could Even Imagine"; "Even Those Who Cry Do So Quietly"; "Stealing Won't Happen in Kobe"; "Rebuilding May Lift Economy"; "A Tokyo Quake Could Rock World Economy"; and "Mob Steps in Where Japan Fails." To social scientists natural disasters offer a rare glimpse not only into a nation's cultural values and traditions, but also into the workings of a nation's social welfare system. What the world learned about Japan in a near-overwhelming crisis was that: the government was immediately ready to spend one billion dollars out of a reserve fund to help finance reconstruction; relatively few citizens had insurance money to help them rebuild; and the Red Cross moved in rapidly with aid supplies and medical teams. Concurrently, even as the death toll was mounting, harsh criticism was vented by the people over the slow start at helping the disaster's victims. In fact, in the vacuum created by the government's laggard response in food distribution, the *yakuza*, Japan's largest organized crime group, ran a huge operation to provide food and supplies to earthquake victims. A safe prediction is that out of the rubble of the devastating earthquake of 1995 governmental relief efforts will be revamped. The overall social welfare apparatus might become regenerated as well.

Mexico

Located in North America, Mexico previously included California, Nevada, Texas, Utah, most of Arizona and New Mexico, and parts of Wyoming and Colorado, ceded to the United States in the 1800s (*Information Please Almanac,* 1994). The current population is primarily Indian, with significant groups of mestizos (descendants of both native and Spanish people). Roman Catholicism is the predominant religion, although evangelical Protestants are a viable minority. The total population is over ninety-two million. In terms of population per square mile, Mexico has only one-eighth the population density that Japan has (U.S. Bureau of the Census, 1994). Compared to Japan and the United States, the Mexican population is far younger and the infant mortality rate is substantial. Life expectancy, however, is 72.9 years, quite high by world standards and a significant gain over the past years.

Robinson (1994) analyzes data for the Mexican government which reveal that nearly 30 percent of Mexico's work force are either unemployed or underemployed. The top 20 percent of the country's families earn 54.2 percent of its national income (compared to 44.4 percent for the United States); the inflation rate has decreased significantly to 6 percent; and the federal government debt has decreased but is still 24.7 percent of the gross domestic product.

A recent economic crisis caused by mounting national debt and reflected in a dramatic decline in the value of the peso may have far-reaching consequences in both Mexico and the United States. Mexico is the United States' second largest export market, second only to Canada. America's stake in Mexico's prosperity is therefore very high. Any turmoil south of the border has consequences in the form of an upsurge in unregulated emigration across the two thousand mile border with the United States. Economic crises, furthermore, have consequences for the social welfare of people worldwide. In the event that the value of the peso was allowed to shrink drastically, investors in the Mexican stock market stood to lose millions. Middle-class pension and mutual-fund investors were also vulnerable. So were the seven hundred thousand American jobs that, according to the Treasury Department, relied directly on exports to Mexico. Accordingly, President Clinton, even in the absence of Congressional support, took swift action to arrange for emergency loans to bolster the peso. Capitalists breathed a sigh of relief. As widely reported in the mass media, the reality of economic interdependence was brought home in the 1995 currency crisis in one nation linked by a free market to other nations.

The North American Free Trade Agreement (NAFTA) allowing a free flow of goods and services among Mexico, Canada, and the United States would predictably bring more low-wage employment to Mexico, threaten the indigenous small businesses and farms (20 percent of the population are farmers and 80 percent of the farms are under twenty-five acres), and make cheap products available from the United States. Mexico is a key supplier of U.S. imported oil, and outside the bounds of the law, Mexico is the number one U.S. source, either as grower or transporter, of illegal drugs such as marijuana, heroin, and cocaine (Oster, 1989). Cross-border pollution problems, often from U.S. owned industry in Mexico, affect populations in both countries. Birth defects in conjunction with contaminated water and soil are reported. Hopefully, tightened NAFTA regulations will have a salutary effect.

Oster (1989) describes Mexican living conditions in detail—the squatter slums, wages too low to live on, unaffordable medical care, impure water, few telephones, unreliable mail system, lack of indoor water and indoor plumbing, and absence of resources for children to complete an education. Directly related to the social welfare system are the limited social security and pension systems, lack of unemployment benefits, extremely high crime rates, and ubiquitous corruption. As Oster (1989: 75) indicates:

> Though Mexico has the thirteenth largest economy and can boast world-class beach resorts, steel-and-glass high-rises, training grounds for Olympic equestrian teams, satellite communication systems, and lavish neighborhoods for the rich, it has a medical profile of a dirt-poor Third World country. People die of intestinal ailments and lung disease.

Balderrabano et al. (1990) perceive a tremendous gap between Mexico's availability of social welfare services and the reality. The economic imperative, according to these writers, is that the government must designate a high portion of its budget to service the external and internal debt. However, an impressive range of social welfare services does exist; innovative devices such as eligibility for services in exchange for labor, self-help, and reciprocity with neighboring countries, are used.

In their discussion of social assistance and social welfare in Mexico, Balderrabano et al. (1990) present a largely positive portrait. The historical origins are related to the revolution of 1910 when workers demanded more protection against work-related risks as well as benefits for other circumstances such as disability, retirement, and death. The Constitution of 1917, accordingly, provided for such worker protection (not implemented until much later) as well as health care for all citizens. In 1941 the Social Security law was drafted. The term *social security* was used in the international sense to denote general social welfare benefits. The mandatory portion of this law covers: work-related accidents, illness and paid maternity leave of three months, disability and old age, and day-care centers for children of insured workers. An especially appealing aspect of this coverage is that parents of the worker or spouse are also provided with health care if they live with their adult children and are economically dependent on them. Only approximately 45 percent of the population, however, are covered under one of the social security systems. Pensions are based on income, and income at the minimum wage in Mexico is less than four American dollars per day as of 1990. On the whole, conclude Balderrabano et al. (1990), the general well-being of the Mexican population has been more influenced by poor economic conditions than by the social welfare programs themselves. Whether the newly strengthened international trade options will lead to local enrichment or to the outflow of international (and national) capital will have drastic implications on the ability of the social welfare system to meet the needs of its people.

Sweden

Sweden is chosen for special emphasis in this book not because of economic or cultural interdependency with the United States but because of the possibilities that Sweden, like Norway, represents. As a welfare state, Sweden is generally recognized as the prototype. Both Sweden and Norway, together in fact, have been idealized as the most successful examples of postwar social democracy and equality. The social welfare structure in both countries is, like the language, remarkably similar. Economic prosperity is evidenced everywhere. In the future, however, as Sweden joins the European Union (E.U.) and Norway (which has voted against union) maintains its fiscal independence, the two countries will go their separate ways. Norway can be expected to maintain greater government support for services; Sweden, as Denmark did earlier, will have to bring policies in line with those of fellow member countries.

A homogeneous nation of approximately eight million, Sweden has a history of mutual aid and universalism characteristic of an agrarian society, yet has also had an absence of feudalism. For instance, health, according to Olsson (1990), has been a public concern since the seventeenth century. With industrialization, which came late and was associated with the social problems related to rapid urbanization, emerged two significant forces: the temperance movement and the labor movement. Efforts were made to control the production and consumption of alcohol. Trade unions emerged slowly to attain a scope and breadth without parallel in democratic countries (Chakrabarti, 1987). The fact that Sweden is a nation which has not been at war for over 165 years probably both reflects and augments its peaceful character. Sweden is overwhelmingly Lutheran; the major minority groups are the Sami (Laplanders of the North) who are a Mongolian people with their own language, Finns, and political refugees from Chile, Vietnam, and eastern Europe. Sweden, like Norway, is a constitutional monarchy and a capitalist state. Politically, socialism, with its philosophy of sharing the wealth and cradle-to-grave social protection, is a major governmental force. Universal health policies provide an exceptionally high standard of care for all members of society. Norms of equality pervade the political, health, and educational systems. High taxation and extensive benefits are characteristic. There is only a small differentiation among employee wages at the various occupational levels.

A study of comparative international statistics (U.S. Bureau of the Census, 1994) provides an interesting array of facts about Sweden. Suicide rates are higher than both Japan and the United States; almost half of all births are to unmarried women; the divorce rate is midway between that of Japan and the United States; health expenditures as a percentage of the gross domestic product are relatively low; the population growth is minimal; the cirrhosis of the liver rate is low reflecting a low alcohol rate; the infant mortality rate is slightly above Japan's, but below that of the United States; the literacy rate is near 100 percent; crime rates are low but rising; and the unemployment rate has shot up suddenly to more than 13 percent. Not only are income taxes high in Sweden; the value added tax or sales tax is approximately 25 percent for residents. Major issues relevant to the Swedish system of social welfare are the national debt, the high unemployment rate, the privatization trend related to E.U. membership, and the aging of the population.

A growing concern over the government's insecure economic position (Norway as it is rich in North Sea oil is doing much better) has produced a crisis mentality with even the Social Democratic Party which is the architect of the welfare state working toward serious structural reform. Changes in sick pay have been introduced with reportedly good results according to Carnegy (1994). In the past three years absenteeism in Sweden, once a chronic problem, has fallen sharply from the levels at which three out of ten workers were off "sick" at any time to fewer than one in ten today. The high unemployment rate, additionally, has prompted workers to work harder and value their jobs more. At the same time, changes in the generous state-pension system have been introduced to generate work incentives and to stimulate job creation.

Traditionally, the emphasis in Sweden has been on cooperation and sharing of resources between the "haves" and the "have-nots." Increasingly, today the emphasis is on competition and preparation for the international market. Even in one of the least privatized countries in the world, privatization has become a key theme. Membership in E.U. requires it; regulation in E.U. comes from economic market forces instead of from the public sector. The tax system itself will become internationized (see van Wormer, 1994). High tax revenues from alcohol and tobacco will no longer be allowed; the subsidies for medicine will be removed; farmers in Nordic latitudes will now have to compete with farmers of the South; and cheap goods from other lands will be readily available. Eventually, welfare benefits will be tied more to one's work than provided universally as in Germany.

Despite the sense of doom in some quarters (social workers, socialist, farmers, feminists, and residents of northern Sweden have fought against joining E.U.), Sweden shows no intention of surrendering its basic welfare provisions. Cuts in unemployment benefits still leave the level at 80 percent of salary; child day care is universally available and affordable; excellent health care is provided for all; family allowances are paid to all families with children; and generous maternity and paternity leave is firmly in place (Carnegy, 1994).

The following forces are still operating today to protect the Swedish model of social democracy from internal and external economic forces:

- A tradition of egalitarianism that has survived centuries of political and economic turbulence; an achievement of near equality for men and women.
- The existence of a strong highly respected Social Democratic Party and the continuing strength of an opposition left-wing Socialist Party.
- The viability of a powerful union system with strong Social Democratic Party ties.
- The enjoyment of universal types of social programs in which all citizens benefit.
- A strong work ethic and resourcefulness of the people despite the economic security provided.
- High investment by the state in job training for the unemployed.
- National pride in an advanced standard of living for all.
- Strong vociferous resistance to the development of profit-making health care services.

- Health and other social benefits that are tied to the government rather than to the job; this fact gives privatization no particular economic advantage (such as in cutting company benefits).
- Wage levels that are standardized at high levels for all types of work.

A final issue complicating social welfare for Sweden is the nearly universal problem of the aging of the population at one level matched by a serious decline in the numbers of youth at the other. Unlike Japan, services for the elderly are provided not by families, but by the state. Extensive government-funded homemaker help employs large numbers of workers and enables the elderly to maintain their independence. How to finance the final years of the "cradle to grave" care offered the society is a major issue for countries such as Sweden. A major criticism of Swedish society is that despite the vast resources available, one is left with the feeling that the relationship between the client and welfare bureaucrat is formal and goal-oriented (Gould, 1993). Immigrants, according to Gould, feel totally isolated from what seems an unfriendly and cold culture. And the elderly seem lonely and isolated.

Throughout the rest of this book, Sweden, an advanced welfare society, will be presented for comparative purposes. Similarly, information on Norway, the country directly to the west of Sweden with an even stronger tradition of social equality and cooperation, will be provided. From 1988 to 1990, I was a social worker and program director at a treatment center in eastern Norway. My experience of the social welfare system was sometimes baffling, sometimes heartening. The reading in chapter 5, box 5.5 records my impressions of a land where poverty was not so much offset as prevented, and where the social values and social welfare are intertwined.

Great Britain

As in Norway, the British welfare state is financed from North Sea oil (Segalman, 1986). But this is where the similarity ends. Great Britain, unlike Norway, is a society divided against itself—the power elite and business classes against the working class. Angry attacks by one group against the other are characteristic; the antagonism sometimes erupts into crippling strikes which paralyze the nation for long periods. In contrast, in Scandinavia labor interests are represented within the government and not peripheral to it.

The literature on the British welfare system reflects the spirit of doom and gloom. Thus Mishra (1990: 43) points to:

> Monetarism and unemployment, the retrenchment of programs serving the working class and the poor,...the emasculation of trade unions, as well as massive tax reductions for the wealthy. . . .

Segalman (1986: 22), from a more conservative view, comments:

> [The] United Kingdom has a growing number of people who are losing their ability to support themselves, and the burden is fast becoming intolerable for the nation to carry.

Gould (1993: 91) surveys the historical context:

> Many of Britain's problems are rooted in its imperial past and its antiquated class structure. It struggles to be modern but seems to be held back by the accumulated deadweight of the past, its decaying infrastructure, its archaic political institutions, and entrenched social attitudes.

Jones (1992: 55) extends her commentary to the social work profession itself:

> Despite a few hopeful signs, the outlook is gloomy. . . . It seems that until the political climate changes and there is a polar rejection of the precepts of the New Right, social work will survive as an occupation but may perish as a caring and liberal profession.

What is the basic social welfare structure in Great Britain, and what are the political/economic currents of change? Despite these negative reports (all written by British commentators), the comparative international statistics (U.S. Bureau of the Census, 1994) paint a mostly positive portrait of this densely populated island nation. The population of England, Scotland, and Wales is over fifty-seven million. Suicide, cirrhosis of the liver, divorce, and infant mortality rates are significantly below the levels of the United States. As in most of the countries studied in this section of the book, homicide rates are extremely far below the rates for the United States. (Even Belfast, Northern Ireland compares favorably to American cities in terms of crime reports.)

The modern welfare state emerged in Britain out of the severe depression and mass unemployment of the 1930s, the threat of the spread of communism, and the death and destruction of World War II. The former director of the London School of Economics, Sir William Beveridge, was the architect of the revolutionary welfare scheme which included the National Health Service, a comprehensive program of free medical care for all. Much of the Beveridge Report was enacted into laws providing for social security for all citizens. This was not the first time that academically inspired theory would inform governmental policy; nor would it be the last. Elliot (1990b) credits the sense of solidarity and commitment following the war with shaping the recognition that social and economic changes in the country were necessary, and that a more egalitarian society would lead to greater social justice. The social welfare state has grown steadily over the years. However, with the advent of radical conservatism in the late 1970s under the Thatcher (Conservative) government, the idea of restructuring the welfare state has become accepted ideology (Elliott, 1990b; Jones, 1992).

Back in 1945, however, when the Labor Party swept to power on a platform to implement the popular Beveridge proposals, the government subsequently enacted legislation that still forms the basis for the British system of poor relief. A compulsory insurance scheme for all in the work force became the mainstay of the system; workers and employers paid a specified sum as did the government (Ford, 1987). As a necessary base to this scheme, there is a free National Health Service and a safety net of national assistance for those without work.

The social security system (a term used here in the European sense, roughly equivalent to social welfare) was modified in the 1970s to include a family allowance and child tax allowance combined into a child benefit. Supplementary rental assistance was provided to help with housing. Many benefits were index-linked annually to price or wage increases to reflect changes in the value of the pound. In these ways, the Labor government succeeded in its aim of providing a universal program of aid to ensure a minimum standard of living for all citizens (Gould, 1993).

Perhaps too many people were taking advantage of the system and living off the state. And perhaps competition from international markets was putting pressure on Britain to "measure up." Whatever the reason, the end of the decade witnessed a fundamental shift in thinking about the nature of participation in public services. Neoconservative doctrine promoted individualistic consumerism in Britain as in the United States. What distinguished the New Right, argues Mishra (1990), from other more pragmatic responses was its rejection of the welfare state in principle. Rolling back the frontier of social welfare was deemed necessary to enable the market economy and free society to survive. The goal of full employment was abandoned; the new ideology stressed that full employment created adverse effects such as inflation and declining productivity. Unemployment is the price to be paid for freedom of enterprise and growth. In a more efficient economy, according to the New Right agenda, everybody would benefit. Meanwhile, charitable funds would trickle down to victims of a society that was deliberately being made more unequal, according to Keegan (1994).

With one in three births now taking place outside of marriage, and the divorce rate among those who do marry having increased dramatically, blame has been placed squarely on women, and on "the feminist ideology" of female independence. However, as Roberts (1993) indicates, the family wage earned by the man is no longer sufficient. The woman who is the sole breadwinner works, not so much as an expression of her emancipation, but because she must.

Contemporarily facing Britain are the concerns of unemployment, homelessness, the weakening of union power, increased poverty, and a proliferation of low-wage jobs. Due to heavy immigration from countries of the British Commonwealth over the past few decades, Great Britain is today a multi-racial and multi-ethnic society, especially in the urban areas. Increasing numbers of people living in the inner cities are living in overcrowded conditions, unemployed, and very poor. Moreover, in Britain 37 percent of all elderly people are in poverty as compared to 15 percent in Germany and 2 percent in Sweden (Elliott, 1990). However, as Mishra (1990) indicates, general poverty is still far more prominent in the United States than in Britain. And, in Britain, thanks to their popularity, universal social programs remain largely intact. British medical care, contrary to continuous negative mass media accounts in the United States, consumes a modest share of the gross domestic product and is even considered by the government and general public to be comparatively cheap, efficient, and effective (Gould, 1993).

CONCLUSION AND SUMMARY

The purpose of this chapter has been to present the design or structure of social welfare in the United States and in five other nations economically and politically linked with the United States. The examination of comparative social welfare systems raises important questions for American social welfare: What is society's responsibility for providing care for all its members? What is the distribution of wealth and distribution of benefits? What is the level of protection offered to citizens against the ravages of personal and family illness, financial ruin, and unemployment? What kinds of controls should be placed on persons who receive aid? And should the aid come from public or private sources? How a society answers these basic needs questions determines the standard of living shared by a people. Whether a society takes an institutional (or preventive) or residual (or after-the-fact) approach is a reflection of values and traditions guiding the conceptualization of social services.

Social welfare, accordingly, is not just a collection of unrelated programs. Instead, it represents a system that seeks both to address the needs of deserving members of the society and to keep potentially rebellious elements in check. The ultimate purpose of social welfare as we have seen is to provide progams for the smooth functioning of the society, to reduce social problems, and to maintain the status quo. Socialist and capitalist models perceive the motives behind social policy through very different lenses; where one sees exploitation of workers, the other sees exploitation of the system. Where one seeks social change, the other favors stability. Social welfare policy in the United States and in the other countries studied in this chapter is actually a combination of both socialist and capitalist ideologies. Social work, as the profession most closely associated with social welfare, has been shaped by both opposing viewpoints. Today in the United States, considerable economic influences are at work, especially through the irrepressible political action committees which shape legislation by financing campaigns of politicians. Most PACs are established by the corporate sector and reflect the policy preferences of big business. The structural arrangement which has emerged over time has become a major component of getting congressional bills passed or stymied. The periodic attempts to pass strict gun control laws and to broaden health care coverage are two recent instances where special interest groups have had a major impact on public policy.

Throughout the world the trend toward privatization is pronounced. The underlying rationale of the thrust to privatize is the belief that reliance on the marketplace is the best way to ensure economic growth and stimulation of the economy so as to create job opportunities, both locally and globally. Critics of privatization contend that the rich are only getting richer, and that wealth accumulated by the international corporations does not necessarily trickle down to the lower echelons.

This chapter has looked not only at the U.S. social welfare system and how it operates but at the specific programs which constitute it. We have analyzed two means of social welfare provision: social insurance and public assistance programs. While social insurance helps workers protect themselves and their dependents against poverty, public assistance programs benefit the poor from general tax revenues. The latter programs are means-tested and lack enthusiastic support from taxpayers.

Modern trends include a lessening of government regulations on business and a tightening of controls on the recipients of public welfare. The stress on enforced work requirements and a reduction in the numbers of government employees (combined with the contracting out of services) are popular themes of the neoconservative era of today. The ideology for the period has been formulated in part from well-financed think tanks which provide the intellectual rhetoric behind much of the political legislation being proposed in Congress.

We have seen how various countries are coping with the same issues, sometimes with the same, sometimes with diverse solutions. We have also seen how, given the global interconnectedness associated with open communications and trade, the key issues are international in scope. How to pay workers a decent wage, provide company benefits, and produce cheap products to compete on the world market: this is the universal dilemma. Cost effectiveness, efficiency, and accountability are buzzwords on the international stage. Concerns of social welfare, seemingly, are taking a backseat everywhere. Advocates for the poor and vulnerable must, accordingly, understand the economic and political processes and be adept at working within the system in order to make their voices heard.

Now that the function and structure of the social welfare system have been presented, let us take a digression back in time to learn how the present set of circumstances evolved, how events and values and technologies somehow coalesced into the present complicated configuration. The roots of social welfare and of all its contradictions go back to antiquity. We now will turn in chapter 3 to the American experience from colonial times to today, but not before we have reviewed Biblical and European antecedents of what we now know as the U.S. social welfare system. Before we know where we are going, we must find out where we have been.

REVIEW QUESTIONS

1. Differentiate the residual versus institutional approach to social welfare in terms of values, eligibility, and ultimate goals. How does stigma enter the picture?
2. Discuss the metaphor of the safety net and its applicability and inapplicability to the residual approach with which it is generally associated.
3. What is the lesson of box 2.1 for the alcoholic worker and his family in two very different societies?
4. Discuss organized social welfare systems in terms of manifest and latent functions of institutions.
5. What is the connection, according to Piven and Cloward, between poor relief and social control? What did they say about the absence of viable working class organizations in the United States?
6. How does social control operate between one nation and another?
7. How do punitive social welfare policies operate in the United States, China, and even Sweden?
8. How have the ideas of Karl Marx had an impact on social welfare in Europe and the United States in the seventies?
9. Discuss radical U.S. and Canadian social work traditions. How do liberal and structural schools differ?
10. What are some of the trends today relevant to capitalism and its impact on social welfare?
11. What is the influence of think tanks. For example, the Heritage Foundation?
12. How have PACs influenced social legislation?
13. How has privatization affected health care in this country?
14. Discuss how public and private agencies differ in terms of accountability, responsibility, resources, and participation.
15. What are social insurance programs? Compare them to public assistance programs in terms of cost. Give some examples of these kinds of programs.
16. Discuss several key aspects of public aid. What are some examples of means-tested programs.
17. How has AFDC changed over the years? What is the basic thesis of Murray's *Losing Ground?*
18. Differentiate Medicare from Medicaid. What are the problems with the Medicaid system?
19. Compare U.S. and Scandinavian pension schemes.
20. Discuss the opinion poll on altruism from 1994 in terms of its implications for welfare.
21. What is the nature of the attack on social welfare at the present time?

22. Discuss demographic changes today in terms of implications for social welfare.
23. Compare Canada and the United States in terms of similarities and differences in providing aid for their citizens.
24. Discuss the extent of social problems in Japan. Refer to international statistics. How are the abortion rates socially significant?
25. Discuss the major challenges to Mexico for the future.
26. Describe the major trends in Swedish society, including membership in the European Union.
27. How do British writers criticize their own system? What are some of the positive aspects of their social security offerings?

REFERENCES

Abramovitz, M. (1986). The Privatization of the Welfare State: A Review. *Social Work* 3(4): 257–264.

Balderrabano, A., et al. (1990). Social Assistance and Social Security in Mexico. In D. Elliot, N. Mayadas, and T. Watts, eds. *The World of Social Welfare*. Springfield, IL: Charles C. Thomas.

Barker, R., ed. (1995). *The Social Work Dictionary,* 3d ed. Washington, DC: NASW Press.

Bell-Lowther, E. (1988). Privatization: Increasing Government Efficiency or Dismantling the Welfare State? *The Social Worker* 56(3), 101–104.

Bishop, J. (1994, June 17). Who Pays the Price for Free Trade? *Commonwealth:* 15–17.

Bryson, L. (1992). *Welfare and the State: Who Benefits?* New York: St. Martin's Press.

Canadian Encyclopedia. (1988). Social Security. *Canadian Encyclopedia:* 2032–2035. Edmonton: Hurtig Publications.

Carnegy, H. (1994). The "Swedish Model" Gropes for Reform. *World Press Review* 41(1): 12–13.

Chakrabarti, M. (1987). Social Welfare Provision in Sweden. In R. Ford and M. Chakrabarti, eds. *Welfare Abroad: An Introduction to Social Welfare in Seven Countries*. Edinburgh: Scottish Academic Press.

Clayton, M. (1994, December 27). Will Canada's Rising Debt Hit the Proverbial "Well"? *The Christian Science Monitor* 9.

Cox, D. (1994, July 10-15). Social Work Education: State of the Art. Paper presented at the International Association of Schools of Social Work Conference, Amsterdam. *The World of Social Welfare*. Springfield, IL: Charles C. Thomas.

Day, P. (1997). *A New History of Social Welfare*. Boston: Allyn and Bacon.

DiNitto, D. (1991). *Social Welfare: Politics and Public Policy,* 3d ed. Englewood Cliffs, NJ: Prentice Hall.

———. (1994). Should We Expect to Change Client's Behavior in Exchange for Aid? No. In H. Karger and J. Midgley, eds. *Controversial Issues in Social Policy.* Boston: Allyn and Bacon.

Dolgoff, R., D. Feldstein, and L. Skolnic. (1993). *Understanding Social Welfare.* New York: Longman.

Elliot, D. (1990a). Epilogue. In D. Elliot, N. Mayadas, and T. Watts, eds. *The World of Social Welfare.* Springfield, IL: Charles C. Thomas.

———. (1990b). Social Welfare in Britain. In D. Elliot, N. Mayadas, and T. Watts, eds. *The World of Social Welfare.* Springfield, IL: Charles C. Thomas.

Fabricant, M. and S. Burghardt. (1992). *The Welfare State Crisis and the Transformation of Social Service Work.* New York: M.E. Sharpe.

Federico, R. (1990). *Social Welfare in Today's World.* New York: McGraw-Hill.

Finn, E. (1994). First Among Equals: Why We're Not Number One. *Canadian Forum* 73: 833.

Ford, J. (1987). Social Welfare Provision in the United Kingdom. In R. Ford and M. Chakrabarti, eds. *Welfare Abroad: An Introduction to Social Welfare in Seven Countries.* Edinburgh: Scottish Academic Press.

Freire, P. (1973). *Education for Critical Consciousness.* New York: Seaburg Press.

Ginsberg, L. (1995). *Social Work Almanac,* 2d ed. Washington, DC: NASW Press.

Gould, A. (1993). *Capitalist Welfare Systems: A Comparison of Japan, Britain and Sweden.* New York: Longman.

Healy, L. (1992). *Introducing International Development Content in the Social Work Curriculum.* Washington, DC: NASW Press.

Helzer, J. and G. Canino. (1992). Comparative Analysis of Alcoholism in Ten Cultural Regions. In J. Helzer and G. Canino, eds. *Alcoholism in North America, Europe and Asia.* New York: Oxford University Press.

Herrnstein, R. and C. Murray. (1994). *The Bell Curve.* New York: The Free Press.

Information Please Almanac, 47th ed. (1994). Boston: Houghton Mifflin.

Japanese National Committee of the International Council on Welfare. (1990). Social Welfare Systems in Japan. In D. Elliot, N. Mayadas, and T. Watts, eds. *The World of Social Welfare.* Springfield, IL: Charles C. Thomas.

Johnson, H., et al. (1995). *The Social Services: An Introduction,* 4th ed. Itasca, IL: F.E. Peacock.

Jones, C. (1992). Social Work in Great Britain: Surviving the Challenge of Conservative Ideology. In M. Hokenstad, S. Khinduka, and J. Midgley, eds. *Profiles in International Social Work.* (43–56). Washington, DC: NASW Press.

Kaplan, C. and L. Kaplan. (1993). Public Opinion and the "Economic Bill of Rights." *Journal of Progressive Human Services* 4(1): 43–60.

Karger, H. and D. Stoesz. (1990). *American Social Welfare Policy: A Structural Approach.* New York: Longman.

Keefe, T. (1980). Empathy Skill and Critical Consciousness. *Social Casework* 61: 387–393.

Keegan, W. (1994, October 2). The Myth of the "Trickle Down" Society. *The Observer*: 8–9.

Kohlert, N. (1989). Welfare Reform: A Historic Consensus. *Social Work* 34: 303–306.

Kramer, R., et al. (1993). *Privatization in Four European Countries: Comparative Studies in Government—Third Sector Relationships.* Armonk, NY: M.E. Sharpe.

Marmor, T., J. Mastow, and P. Harvey. (1990). *America's Misunderstood Welfare State: Persistent Myths, Enduring Realities.* New York: Basic Books.

Matsubara, Y. (1992). Social Work in Japan: Responding to Demographic Dilemmas. In M. Hockenstad, S. Khinduka, and J. Midgley, eds. *Profiles in International Social Work.* (85–47). Washington, DC: NASW Press.

McQuaig, L. (1993). *The Wealthy Banker's Wife: The Assault on Equality in Canada.* London: Penguin.

Millar, K. (1990). Social Welfare in Canada. In D. Elliot, N. Mayadas, and T. Watts, eds. *The World of Social Welfare.* (35–50). Springfield, IL: Charles C. Thomas.

Mishra, R. (1990). *The Welfare State in Capitalist Society.* London: Harvester/Wheatheaf.

Morales, A. and B. Sheafor. (1995). *Social Work: A Profession of Many Faces.* Boston: Allyn and Bacon.

More, T. (1994/1951). *Utopia.* New York: Appleton-Century-Crofts.

Mullaly, R. (1993). *Structural Social Work: Ideology, Theory, and Practice.* Toronto: McClelland and Stewart.

Murray, C. (1984). *Losing Ground.* New York: Basic Books.

Olsson, S. (1990). Swedish Social Policy: Toward the Year 2000. In D. Elliot, N. Mayadas, and T. Watt, eds. *The World of Social Welfare.* Springfield, IL: Charles C. Thomas.

Oster, P. (1989). *The Mexicans: A Personal Portrait of a People.* New York: Harper and Row.

Payne, M. (1991). *Modern Social Work Theory: A Critical Introduction.* Chicago: Lyceum Books.

Piven, F. and R. Cloward. (1993). *Regulating the Poor: The Functions of Public Welfare.* New York: Vintage.

Reisch, M. (1992). Should Social Workers Work for For-Profit Firms? In E. Gambrill and R. Pruger, eds. *Controversial Issues in Social Work.* Boston: Allyn and Bacon.

Roberts, Y. (1993, September 24). We are Becoming Divorced from Reality. *New Statesman and Society* 24: 16–19.

Robinson, L. (1994). Mexico's New Revolution. *U.S. News and World Report* 117(7), 40–44.

Rocha, G. (1994). Redefining the Role of the Bourgeoisie in Dependent Capitalist Development: Privatization and Liberalization in Brazil. *Latin American Perspectives* 80(1): 72–98.

Royce, J. (1989). *Alcohol Problems and Alcoholism: A Comprehensive Survey.* New York: The Free Press.

Segalman, R. (1986). *The Swiss Way of Welfare.* New York: Praeger Special Studies.

Simons, L. (1989). Privatization and Mental Health System: A Private Sector View. *American Psychologist* 44(8): 1138–1141.

Smillie, B. (1994, December 24–25). Japan, Long Known for Safety Sees a "Gun Society" Developing. *Daily News*: 7A.

Social Security Administration (1993). *Social Security Bulletin.* Baltimore, MD: Social Security Administration.

Toffler, A. (1990). *Power Shift.* New York: Bantam Books.

Tomita, S. (1994). The Consideration of Cultural Factors in the Research of Elder Mistreatment with an In-depth Look at the Japanese. *Journal of Cross-Cultural Gerontology* 9: 39–52.

Tracy, M. (1994). Should Social Security Be Made Voluntary? No. In H. Karger and J. Midgley, eds. *Controversial Issues in Social Policy.* Boston: Allyn and Bacon.

Tropman, J. (1989). *American Values and Social Welfare: Cultural Contradictions in the Welfare State.* Englewood Cliffs, NJ: Prentice Hall.

U.S. Bureau of the Census. (1994). *Statistical Abstract of the United States.* Washington, DC: U.S. Department of Commerce.

van Wormer, K. (1994). Privatization in the Social Welfare State: The Case of Norway. *Scandinavian Journal of Social Welfare* 3: 39–44.

————. (1995). *Alcoholism Treatment: A Social Work Perspective.* Chicago: Nelson-Hall.

Walz, T. (1994). Should Social Security be Made Voluntary? Yes. In H. Karger and J. Midlgley, eds. *Controversial Issues in Social Policy.* Boston: Allyn and Bacon.

Waterloo Courier. (1994). Poll Finds U.S. Angry, Anxious, Less Altruistic. *Waterloo Courier.* September 21: A2.

Welch, W. (1994, July 22). Battle of the Big Bucks: Historically Unprecedented. *USA Today*: 5A.

Wilensky, H. and C. Lebeaux. (1958). *Industrial Society and Social Welfare.* New York: The Free Press.

Wilson-Smith, A. (1994). Allan Rock's War on Guns. *MacLeans* 107(50): 22–23.

Zastrow, C. (1993). *Introduction to Social Work and Social Welfare,* 5th ed. Pacific Grove, CA: Brooks/Cole.

3

HISTORICAL FOUNDATIONS OF SOCIAL WELFARE

History, despite its wrenching pain,
Cannot be unlived, and faced
With courage, need not be lived again.
—Maya Angelou, On the Pulse of Morning

The history of social welfare beginning in Europe and continuing in America over the last several hundred years is a tale of neglect and cruelty; of paternalism (or maternalism) and compassion; of integrity and deceit; of arrogant social control punctuated by racism, sexism, and classism; of new ideas superimposed on old ideas; and finally, of old ideas superimposed on the new. One thing is for certain: the need to balance the care for the weak and deprived against strong work incentives is an age old dilemma of society. A society too soft may breed laziness and malingering; one too harsh may breed death and isolation. Over the centuries, nation-states have leaned one way or another and espoused varying doctrines based on ideas such as survival of the fittest, requiring people to work in order to eat, and taxing the rich to provide for the poor.

RELIGIOUS TEACHINGS

Because the philosophical basis for social welfare is found for the most part in our religious heritage (even organized social work grew out of organized

111

religion), this chapter begins with an examination of the religious roots of social welfare. As a powerful incentive for helping to relieve the personal sufferings of the poor, religious devotion is universal in its altruism. Cited in Moses (1989), the Dalai Lama observed:

> Every major religion of the world has similar ideals of love, the same goal of benefiting humanity through spiritual practice, and the same effect of making their followers into better human beings.

Hinduism

Indian civilization is very old. Based on a belief in the spiritual oneness, Hinduism has a four thousand year history that began with Aryan invaders. As Day (1997) indicates, the Hindu caste tradition became reified following the great patriarchal invasions. Under the caste system, poverty was not a condition for the personal blame in the present life. Rather, persons were placed in poverty to atone for past lives or to prepare for future ones. Nonviolence and giving charity to beggars are basic principles for living under Hinduism (Moses, 1989). As early as 300 B.C., in fact, hospitals and shelters for both people and animals were endowed by Prince Asoka of India.

Ethics are an important part of life in India; according to Fellows (1979). They permeate the whole culture. Rather than following a doctrine about the divine or a system of ritual, Hinduism is a way of life. The notions of care for others, responsibility, and duty are embodied in the concept of *dharma*. Dharma is the good way of life for every person according to his or her station. A certain fatalism applies as caste and poverty—fortune in life—are viewed as inevitable (Day, 1997).

Buddhism

Like Hinduism, Buddhism originated in India; yet this religion has consistently denied the religious status of caste. One of the great Asian religions, Buddhism was founded in the sixth and fifth centuries B.C. by Siddhartha Gautama, later known as the Buddha. Among the teachings of the Buddha relevant to social welfare is the "eightfold noble path" of right views, right action, right livelihood, etc. Altruism is primary to Buddhist belief. The altruistic response to human welfare is provided through the ethical virtues of loving-kindness and compassion (Fellows, 1979). In understanding the interdependence of all things, the Buddhist recognizes that everything we do has consequences. Hence, the emphasis on compassion.

In the first century A.D. Buddhism entered China, and through its priests, exhorted China's rulers to care for the poor, and poverty was redefined as a holy state (Day, 1997). A meager system of welfare developed, providing only food and shelter. In times of natural disaster, according to Day, the Chinese government's relief policy enabled the poor to buy food from its granaries or, if they could not pay, to receive free grain. Additionally, the poor were taken from ravaged areas and resettled on new lands.

Judaism

A most significant cultural source for the values of the Western world has been the Judeo-Christian heritage. Emerging out of a desert existence, the sense of Judaic community was strong; hospitality was provided to the stranger. As stated in the Bible:

> You shall give to him (your poor brother) freely, and your heart shall not be grudging when you give to him because for this the Lord your God will bless you in all your work and in all that you undertake.—*Deuteronomy* 15:7–10.

And:

> Love ye therefore the strangers for ye were strangers in the land of Egypt.— *Exodus* 23:9.

The Talmud is the second great collection of Jewish scripture after the Torah, the first five books of the Bible. The Talmud consists of interpretations of the Torah for its application to new circumstances (Fellows, 1979). Charity, justice, and loving kindness—these are the basic precepts of Judaism. To honor the poor was to honor God. These concepts, which form the basis for altruism were codified in the Talmud after the Babylonian captivity around 600 B.C. (Day, 1997). Social welfare, according to Dolgoff et al. (1993), became institutionalized in two important aspects: expected behavior and providing for the poor without demeaning them. In Talmudic times, for example, there was a community charity box devised in such a way that when people put their hands into it others would not know whether they were giving or taking money.

Among the social welfare practices developed by the Jews were hospitable reception of strangers; education of orphans; redemption of lawbreakers; endowment of marriages; visitation of the ill and infirm; burial of the dead; consolation of the bereaved; and care of widows, slaves, divorcees, and the aged (Popple and Leighninger, 1993).

Christianity

The ideals of Christianity were a blending of all that had gone before—Jewish teachings and later Greek and Roman influences. Christianity is a religion based on Jesus Christ. Facts known to us about the life of Jesus are contained in the four gospels of the New Testament and in the writings of Flavius Josephus, a Jewish-Roman historian who lived to about 100 A.D. Because of Jesus' remarkably zealous followers, chief among them, Paul, the teachings of Jesus were spread across the ancient world, and immortalized in scripture.

Jesus taught that every person would someday be judged by God. And what was the basis for this judgment? The standard was not to be the individual's belief in certain creeds, but rather his or her compassion (Landon, 1986). In words which may be highly familiar to the reader, Jesus is quoted as saying:

> When saw we thee a stranger, and took thee in? Or naked and clothed thee? Or when saw we thee sick, or in prison, and came unto thee? And the King shall answer and say unto them, Verily I say unto you, Inasmuch as ye have done it unto one of the least of these my brethren, ye have done it unto me.—*Matthew* 25:38-40

The development of Christianity held profound implications for social welfare (Dolgoff et al., 1993). Charity, near sanctification of the poor, and the denigration of conspicuous consumption or materialism were the central themes. Until the Protestant reformation, in fact, these themes were fundamental to Western social welfare practice.

After the death of Jesus, Paul, in his writings, stressed the importance of individual responsibility, "If any would not work, neither should he eat" (2 Thessalonians 3:10). The early Christian church and the generations which followed took seriously the command of Jesus, a revolutionary, to carry out the expression of love and compassion. The poor, slaves, widows, orphans, and those persecuted for their Christian beliefs were aided. Women were actively engaged in charitable works from the very start (Day, 1997). By the fourth century, Christianity was legalized by the Roman emperor, Constantine. Christians donated funds openly; they built hospitals for the sick and established a network of charitable activities. Monasteries often served as all-purpose but primitive social service agencies for the needy. Later, saints renounced material goods and family ties, and led lives of poverty.

Islam

Founded by the prophet Muhammad who died in 632 A.D., Islam is the youngest and, according to Fellows (1979), in some ways, the most simple and direct of the world's great religions. The focus of this religion is on the worshiping of the one true God—Allah. The meaning of Islam is submission to God. Islam is the dominant religion today in larger parts of Asia and North Africa, the Middle East, Pakistan, Malaysia, and Indonesia, and an adherent of Islam is called a Muslim or Moslem. Islam's salient feature is its devotion to the Koran. Based on revelations given to Mohammed over a period of time, the Koran expresses the need for intelligence in deciphering messages from God, and the wrongness of stockpiling wealth.

In 650 A.D., the followers of the prophet Mohammed were told they had an obligation to help poor people and that paying a *zakat,* or "purification" tax, to care for the poor was one of their obligatory duties of Islam (Barker, 1995). This duty to give alms to the poorer class alternated from being voluntary to mandatory, to voluntary once again. Benevolence toward the needy is the prime social responsibility of a Muslim (Fellows, 1989). By the twelfth century, Islamic hospitals were magnificently built and equipped, and Islamic universities were the centers of scholarship and culture (Day, 1997).

The second-largest faith worldwide next to Christianity, Islam is the third largest religious group in the United States with a billion adherents. Its phenomenal growth within the U.S. prison system will be recounted in chapter 11.

FROM FEUDALISM TO THE GROWTH OF CAPITALISM: BRITISH HERITAGE

Just as religion was one force changing Western society through church power and the institutionalization of religious practices, the scientific revolution and its growing agricultural technology reaped a revolution in its own right. Ultimately, the world of feudalism, with its rigid statuses, roles, and obligations, was turned upside down. The barter and subsistence economy of medieval society was gradually replaced by a capitalist economy, a development that has had profound social and political consequences (Jansson, 1993). To follow the chronology refer to table 3.1.

Feudal Society Unraveled

William the Conqueror brought the Frankish form of feudalism to England when he invaded in 1066. A Norman (meaning descendent from the Norsemen or Vikings), William built castles and redistributed land titles on a feudal basis to his followers from Normandy. Under the tradition of serfdom, peasants were bonded to a lord in return for protection and rights to land use. For all the virtues of knowing one's place in a communal society, the lack of mobility, freedom, and low standard of living along with the inability to store grain caused widespread discontentment (Dolgoff et al., 1993). As population increased and agricultural technology changed—the invention of the oxen-drawn plow, for instance, put more land into production faster, and the soil began to lack fertility—serfdom became less and less economically feasible for lords. Nobles began to convert their fields from crops to livestock, thus reducing the number of peasants who were needed to cultivate their land. Peasants were further displaced from their land as owners enclosed their fields with hedges. During the land enclosure movement, common lands for gardens, domestic animals, and

CHAPTER 3: HISTORICAL FOUNDATIONS OF SOCIAL WELFARE

TABLE 3.1
Milestones in the Development of British Social Welfare

1066: Norman conquest.

1348: The bubonic plague kills one third of the population of Europe.

1349: The Statute of Laborers forbids mobility of workers.

1517: Martin Luther posts ninety-five theses on door of Catholic church.

1533: Henry VIII breaks away from Rome.

1536: John Calvin systematizes Protestant thought.

1750–1850: Industrial Revolution.

1769: Steam engine invented.

1776: Adam Smith publishes *The Wealth of Nations.*

1789: Malthus publishes *Essay on the Principles of Population.*

1800: London's population reaches one million.

1834: The New Poor Law.

1838: Dickens's *Oliver Twist* is published.

1845–1855: Irish potato famine kills nearly one million while more emigrate.

1848: Marx and Engel's *Communist Manifesto* published.

1859: Darwin's *Origins of Species* published.

1869: Charity Organization Society established.

1881: Germ theory of disease generally accepted.

1884: Toynbee Hall the first settlement house established in London.

1942: Beveridge Report recommends an integrated social security system for Britain.

1946: National Health Service established.

community water supply were taken over by landowners for pasturing sheep for wool export on the international market. For the poor, this loss of access to the land was yet another in a series of catastrophes for them. Sir Thomas More (1949/1516: 10) writes poignantly of the human misery, which arose during the late Middle Ages from the new economic system and was repeated in successive periods of modernization:

> These miserable people . . . leave their familiar hearths and can find no place where they may settle down. They sell their household goods, which would not bring much even if they could wait for a buyer, for little or nothing. . . . And if they beg, they are thrown into prison as idle vagabonds. . . . One herdsman can look after a flock of sheep large enough to

stock an area that would require many hands if it were ploughed or reaped. This enclosure has likewise raised the price of grain in many places.

Jansson (1993) pinpoints the historic development of the use of paper money, coins, and precious metals as mediums of exchange. In a money economy, the dictates of the market began to determine the price of goods. The buying and selling for profit and hoarding of wealth which ensued, in turn, created new and powerful classes of merchants and bankers. The buying and selling of land for capital reinforced the removal of peasants from their homes. Destitute, peasants increasingly had to seek whatever work was available.

The Black Death

The greatest mass killer in history arrived in Europe from Asia in 1348 without fanfare. Transmitted to humans by fleas from infected rats carried on ships, the Black Death or bubonic plague was to wipe out nearly one third of the population of Europe. Along with numerous victims, something else was to perish as well—the world of classic feudalism, and the predictability surrounding it. Day (1997) records in detail the turmoil of the age, how a frantic populace began to attack scapegoats with a vengeance—slaughtering Jews, Moslems, lepers, the disabled, homosexuals, and women on a mass basis. Because women in the 1300s exceeded the population of men, their status was very low. Over the next three hundred years, according to Day, hundreds of thousands of women were accused of witchcraft and killed. In most cases, the women were older beggars who had asked for charity and been denied. In a strange psychological twist, persons who felt guilty for turning away a beggar now could place blame on the charity seeker instead.

In any case, the phenomenal loss of life during this period created a severe labor shortage. As the workers' bargaining power increased so did the clamor for laws to regulate labor. The Statute of Laborers became law in England in 1349. Peasants were now required to remain on their home manors when their labor was needed and to work for whatever the lords wanted to pay. Begging and almsgiving were outlawed except for the old and the disabled. For the first time, according to Barker (1995), a distinction was made between the "worthy poor" (the aged, disabled, widows, and dependent children) and the "unworthy poor." The primary role of the church in caring for the disadvantaged fell to the wayside as the poor came to be viewed negatively and as a threat.

An impetus for new technology was concomitant with the shortage of labor. It was necessary to reduce the need for human power. Although the Industrial Revolution was not to get under way until much later, the climate that produced the scientific discoveries was presaged in the devastation of the Black Death. The massive depopulation caused by the great contagion and lesser recurrences of the plague over the next century undercut the manorial system that had held peasants in serfdom for so long (Parshall, 1991). The decline in the number of workers spurred labor-saving inventions and paved the way for a more scientific outlook yet to come.

The Protestant Reformation

By far the most important event for the growth of mercantilism, capitalism, and ultimately social welfare itself, was Martin Luther's break from the Catholic Church in 1517 (Day, 1989). After he was excommunicated for posting his ninety-five theses on the door of a Catholic church in Wittenberg (opposing the use of indulgences and other corrupt church practices), Luther founded what later would turn out to be Protestantism. By challenging the notion of papal authority, encouraging church members to read and study the scriptures in their own language, and replacing rituals with sermons, the Protestant church increased the involvement of parishioners in their own religious lives.

While Luther's memorable act of defiance weakened the Holy Roman Empire politically and fostered the development of the nation-state, socio-culturally the impact was equally profound. The course of social welfare history, in fact, was forever changed. At the heart of the change was Luther's introduction of the notion of vocation as a calling to do God's work in all things—whether as a member of the clergy or as a teacher, farmer, or laborer. This notion of a calling ultimately revolutionized the social system; it gave a meaning to work which went beyond the work itself. As Dolgoff et al. (1993) indicate, Luther's teachings improved the morale of laborers giving them a sense of duty in an honest day's toil. All of this, however, would not have been of such ultimate significance for American society had Henry VIII of England borne a son. Desperate to have a male heir through remarriage and forbidden by the Pope from divorce, the monarch wrested control of the English branch of the Catholic Church. England accordingly and very promptly, became Protestant. We will discuss the ideology of the Protestant ethic and the growth of capitalism under the section on colonial America.

ELIZABETHAN POOR LAW

In the wake of enclosures, population growth, and urbanization in addition to the end of the Catholic Church charities, government authorities appointed overseers of the poor to administer laws providing for public relief. The series of measures that were passed throughout the 1500s culminated in the famous Elizabethan Poor Law of 1601. The fact that some people could not find work on their own was formally recognized. Local parishes were now required to provide work for the poor and houses of correction for rogues and idlers (*Encyclopaedia Britannica*, 1993). When parishes could not provide proper relief, counties were required to assume responsibility for welfare. In effect, then, the government had become the chief enforcer of poor relief. For the first time care for the poor was a secular, not a church, function.

The Elizabethan Poor Law was to remain the major codification of laws for dealing with poor and disadvantaged people for over two hundred years (Barker, 1995). It also was destined to become the basis for dealing with the poor people in colonial America. What did the Poor Law entail? The principal provisions of this law are listed by Johnson (1995) as follows:

1. Administration of poor relief at the local level.
2. Relative responsibility which was the doctrine that parents were responsible for the support of their children and grandchildren, and grown children for their dependent parents and grandparents.
3. The taxing of people in each parish to pay for their own poor.
4. The classification of the destitute into three categories: the able-bodied or "sturdy beggars," the impotent poor who could be cared for at the poorhouse ("indoor relief") or be given "outdoor relief" or aid in their homes such as food or fuel, and dependent children who could be given apprenticeships or trained for domestic service.

Considerable regional variation in the administration of this law ensued. Compassion and punitiveness were skillfully linked in one composite piece of legislation. Separating the poor into "deserving" and "undeserving" made poverty for some a blameworthy condition. This significant development still has an impact on us centuries later throughout the Anglo-Saxon world (Johnson, 1995).

Consistent with their structuralist approach to regulating the poor, Piven and Cloward (1993) argue that western relief systems arise not out of benevolence by the advantaged but in the mass disturbances that erupt, especially during periods of mass unemployment. Unemployment diminishes the capacity of other institutions to bind and constrain people and threatens the entire structure of social control. Therefore, according to this argument, when the emergence of the wool industry began to transform the economic and social arrangements governing agriculture, and when the impact on the dispossessed farmers was devastating and caused political unrest, a new expansion of relief resulted.

THE INDUSTRIAL REVOLUTION

While across the Atlantic, America was being settled by religious dissenters and later by indentured servants and slaves, the mother country was experiencing dynamic social changes of her own. Once again, improved technology was creating new working conditions and an alteration in the distribution of wealth. The ideology shifted with the technology. From the seventeenth through the nineteenth centuries, Protestantism, the Industrial Revolution, and capitalism all became intermeshed to promote the work ethic and laissez-faire economic ideas (Johnson, 1995).

The British *Industrial Revolution* is the term applied to the social and economic changes that took place from around 1750 to 1850 when the transition from a stable agricultural and commercial society to a society based on factory production materialized. To begin to grasp the impact of these changes, a systems framework is immensely helpful. Through viewing the society in its intricate interconnectedness we can come to conceptualize how social change induced by technology affects the society as a whole, the various parts of the social structure, and individuals within the society. Change in one part of the system—the introduction of the steam engine for example in 1769—brings about a ricocheting effect that impinges upon other parts of the system. Thus, the invention of power machinery that could be driven by the wind or water transferred production from villages and small towns to larger cities where water transportation was available, and from the home of the craftsperson to larger workshops and mills (Friedlander and Apte, 1974). With the change in the place and nature of work, family life changed commensurately. The days of large, extended families sharing work and the fruits of labor from the land were over. No longer, in hard times, could families survive on the food they grew and the animals they raised. Now smaller families migrated to urban areas, care for children and the elderly was more difficult in the nuclear family, and urban overcrowding was associated with polluted water and spread of disease. Each wage earner — man, woman, and child — went out of the home to hard work in distant factories (Day, 1997). In the early days, most people thought of the application of mechanical power to industry as a major advance. The poets, however, questioned the price of progress. To Burns and Blake, both born in the mid-eighteenth century, the mills were the work of Satan. In the poem *The New Jerusalem* Blake (1960) asked: "And was Jerusalem builded here, Among these dark Satanic mills?"

The employer, rather than the worker, became the beneficiary of the products of labor. The worker, as Max Weber (1911) pointed out, was reduced to being a mere cog in the machine. In the new wage-based industrial society, the livelihoods of larger segments of the population were placed at the mercy of the whims of economic markets. One severe economic depression could wipe out everything a family had acquired and force relocation of members into the nefarious workplace.

Conditions in the workhouse were intended to ensure that no one with any conceivable alternatives would seek public aid (Piven and Cloward, 1993). According to the philosophy of the day, if people were poor and out of work it was because they were lazy and idle. The coldhearted inhumanity that treated pauperism as a crime while at the same time creating its own appalling harvest of criminality and squalor, was immortalized for all time in the voluminous works of nineteenth century novelist Charles Dickens. In this seething passage from *Oliver Twist,* Dickens (1941/1838: 14–15) imagines the kind of conniving that may have gone on at higher levels:

> The members of this board were very sage, deep, philosophical men; and when they came to turn their attention to the workhouse, they found out at once, what ordinary folks would never have discovered — the poor people liked it! It was a regular place of public entertainment for the poorer classes; a tavern where there was nothing to pay; a public breakfast, dinner, tea, and supper all the year round; a brick and mortar Elysium, where it was

all play and no work. "Oh!" said the board, looking very knowing; "we are fellows to set this to rights; we'll stop it all, in no time." So, they established the rule, that all poor people should have the alternative (for they would compel nobody, not they), of being starved by gradual process in the house, or by a quick one out of it. With this view, they contracted with the water-works to lay on an unlimited supply of water; and with a corn-factor to supply periodically small quantities of oatmeal; and issued three meals of thin gruel a day, with an onion twice a week, and half a roll on Sundays. They made a great many otherwise and humane regulations, having reference to the ladies, which it is not necessary to repeat; kindly undertook to divorce poor married people, in consequence of the great expense of a suit in Doctors' Commons; and, instead of compelling a man to support his family, as they had theretofore done, took his family away from him, and made him a bachelor! There is no saying how many applicants for relief, under these last two heads, might have started up in all classes of society, if it had not been coupled with the workhouse; but the board were long-headed men, and had provided for this difficulty. The relief was inseparable from the workhouse and the gruel; and that frightened people.

For the first six months after *Oliver Twist* was removed, the system was in full operation. It was rather expensive at first, in consequence of the increase in the undertaker's bill, and the necessity of taking in the clothes of all the paupers, which fluttered loosely on their wasted, shrunken forms, after a week or two's gruel. But the number of workhouse inmates got thin as well as the paupers; and the board were in ecstasy.

"A Christmas Carol" (Dickens, 1843: 10–11), written much later, personifies the businessman's haughty attitude toward the poor in the memorable character of Ebenezer Scrooge:

"At this festive season of the year, Mr. Scrooge," said the gentleman, taking up a pen, "it is more than usually desirable that we should make some slight provision for the Poor and destitute, who suffer greatly at the present time. Many thousand are in want of common necessaries; hundreds of thousands are in want of common comforts, sir."

"Are there no prisons?" asked Scrooge.

"Plenty of prisons," said the gentleman, laying down the pen again.

"And the Union workhouses?" demanded Scrooge. "Are they still in operation?"

"They are. Still," returned the gentleman, "I wish I could say they were not."

"The Treadmill and the Poor Law are in full vigor, then?" said Scrooge.

"Both very busy, sir."

"Oh! I was afraid, from what you said at first, that something had occurred to stop them in their useful course," said Scrooge. "I'm glad to hear it. . . ."

"I don't make merry myself at Christmas and I can't afford to make idle people merry. I help to support the establishments I have mentioned — they cost enough; and those who are badly off must go there."

"Many can't go there; and many would rather die."

"If they would rather die," said Scrooge, "they had better do it, and decrease the surplus population."

Scrooge's words continue to resonate.

The children of the parish were an ideal labor force for new manufacturers; they were suitably docile and had a light touch at the loom (Piven and Cloward, 1993). The death rate among child laborers, who could be made to work for their own room and board, was exceedingly high. Even more staggering was the death rate in workhouses where infants were dumped — abandoned by their impoverished parents.

In all, hundreds of new factories were built through the use of new labor-saving technologies: Real wages decreased, and vast numbers of workers were displaced (Day, 1997). In 1832, during a time of much economic and social distress, a royal commission was established to review the poor laws. According to Dolgoff et al. (1993), however, the commission was biased from the start. Several ideological strands, such as the laissez-faire capitalism of Adam Smith and the economic pessimism of Malthus carried the day. Before turning to the specifics of the new Poor Law of 1834, let us examine the theories of these two influential economists.

In 1776 while a major rebellion was under way in the colonies, Scottish social philosopher Adam Smith published his landmark work, *The Wealth of*

Nations. Arguing that the most efficient and productive system was one based on the principles of laissez faire (from French, literally, "let do"), Smith advocated the least possible intervention of the government into economic activities. Sometimes, he conceded, restrictions on free trade might be necessary. Public welfare, according to Smith, would arise naturally out of economic self interest of the "powers that be." A formal system of social welfare, therefore, was not necessary.

Robert Malthus (1789), an English clergyman and economist, similarly called the usefulness of social welfare into question in his renowned *Essay on Population*. Using mathematical models, Malthus argued that human capacity to reproduce would exceed the food supply, and that to raise the living standards would only increase the population further. Malthus' "contribution" was to provide scientific theories supporting the neglecting of the poor. The poor law system could now be viewed as downright harmful in its interference with the smooth functioning of the market economy.

Such theories both shaped and were consistent with the new conceptions of the social order which had developed in an age of a money economy and rapid industrial expansion. Intellectual currents promoting individualism and governmental noninterference were reified when the Royal Commission on Poor Relief completed their formal document in 1834.

THE POOR LAW OF 1834

The New Poor Law of 1834 was an attempt to reform the prior Elizabethan Poor Law. The underlying emphasis of the new law was on self-reliance. Poor relief itself was seen as responsible for "permanent paupery" (Frielander and Apte, 1974). The new, harsh moral view of poverty reflected in this law allowed the destitute to be admitted to the workhouse for the in-kind form of relief only. In short, no cash allotments. Public assistance was not considered a right, and government was not seen as responsible for the unemployed (Barker, 1995). The principle of *less eligibility* was established. According to this principle, people who were given aid had to get less than the lowest-paid worker. The aim of this Poor Law, in short, was not to end poverty but to force relief applicants to accept any type of labor available. The reader will not be hard put to see how many of the attitudes of the mid-nineteenth century, incorporated into the New Poor Law, remain with us today.

Harsh ideologies notwithstanding, in Britain and on the continent, modifying elements were at work to counter, in a way, some of the harshness of the New Poor Law. As Day (1997) observes, serious reform got under way in England only when studies revealed the malnutrition and unsanitary living conditions among the poor. In his comprehensive survey of Western culture, *Civilization,* Kenneth Clark (1969) credits Dickens' popular works as having produced reforms in the law, in prisons, and in another dozen directions, though sadly, without eradicating poverty itself. Meanwhile, Quaker activist Elizabeth Fry's valiant prison reform work stirred the public conscience. The early reformers' struggle with industrialized society illustrates what Clark suspects is the greatest civilizing achievement of the nineteenth century—humanitarianism. The laborers of Victorian England— the flogging on naval ships, the chained woman being transported, and so on— seemed to have unleashed an awakening of sorts, according to Clark.

The writings of Karl Marx (1818–1883), who was preeminently a theorist of capitalist society, set the stage for much revolution and bloodshed when he and Engels collaborated to write the *Communist Manifesto* (1848). Exiled from Europe after the Revolutions of 1848, Marx and Engels moved to London. The economic and political philosophy introduced by these writers and known as Marxism, views the history of society as the history of class struggle. In capitalist societies the relationship between capitalists and workers is based on the control the capitalist has over both forces of production and the product (Abercrombie et al., 1988).

Political organizations such as the Fabian Society, an English Socialist group, were influential in instituting practical reforms such as working hours legislation, housing projects, and mass education. Charity organizations and settlement houses sprang up. In the United States, less influenced by a socialist and labor party voice, however, the welfare system was modeled on the English poor laws and the ideologies which undergirded them. The enforcement of such laws was unmitigated by equally potent counter impulses (see Jansson, 1993; Landon, 1986; Piven and Cloward, 1993; and Trattner, 1994).

COLONIAL AMERICA

Just after the passage of the Elizabethan Poor Law in 1601, settlements began to be established by colonists in North America. As dissenters from the Church

TABLE 3.2

Milestones in the Development of American Social Welfare

1776: Declaration of Independence.

1788: Constitution ratified by the states.

1791: Bill of Rights ratified.

1838–1839: Forced march of the Cherokees.

1854: President Pierce vetoes bill inspired by Dorothea Dix to provide federal aid for the mentally ill.

1860: Over twenty-seven thousand miles of railroad track built.

1861–1865: Civil War.

1865: Thirteenth Amendment to the Constitution abolishing slavery.

1865–1872: Freedmen's Bureau provides relief for newly freed slaves.

1865–1900: Rapid industrialization.

1877: America's first Charity Organization Society.

1880–1914: Twenty-one million immigrants arrive.

1881: Practice of medicine revolutionized through germ theory of disease.

1889: Hull House opened.

1898: First school for social workers established, later becomes Columbia University School of Social Work.

1899: First juvenile court in Chicago.

1919–1933: Prohibition.

1920: Nineteenth Amendment grants suffrage to women.

1929: Great Depression begins with crash of stock market.

1933: New Deal proclaimed by Franklin Roosevelt.

1935: U.S. Social Security Act.

Alcoholics Anonymous founded.

1955: The National Association of Social Workers (NASW) is created through a merger of existing organizations.

1964: Great Society programs, food stamp program, Civil Rights Act.

1965: Medicare and Medicaid are added to the Social Security Act.

1969: Stonewall Inn riot initiates gay rights movement.

1972: Supplemental Security Income Program enacted

of England, Puritans were inspired by Calvinist theology and favored a religious service Spartan in ritual, yet strict in rigor. As one would expect, the settlers, being English, carried much of the British culture and traditions over on the boat with them and a sense of cultural superiority prevailed. Except for the Quakers, the early American settlers replicated the brutal policies of the European explorers in their dealings with the native inhabitants. At first the members of trading companies and colonists relied on friendly natives to help them through severe winters. Soon, however, colonists took the land they wanted, killing or enslaving its inhabitants (Day, 1989). In addition to the genocide, diseases introduced by Europeans eventually resulted in the deaths of most of this hemisphere's indigenous population.

Following the Puritan migrations of the 1630s, approximately half of all white immigrants to the colonies were indentured servants or convicts. With much land to be cultivated, there was a serious labor shortage. In the latter part of the seventeenth century, the settlers modeled the Europeans in Brazil and the Caribbean by establishing slavery in many of their colonies.

A market economy emerged rapidly in the New World; this growth was precipitated by the tremendous demand abroad for agricultural products and other raw material (Jansson, 1993). The belief in capitalism was reinforced by prosperity and the widespread ownership of land. For white people, opportunities must have seemed inexhaustible. Imbued with the works of John Locke, Adam Smith, and Robert Malthus, all of which set the stage for the growth of capitalism, colonists in positions of leadership championed limited government, an embryonic individualism that looks almost modern, and the growth of a free market economy. A peculiar system arose in the American colonies, however, due to the geographical realities. Local governments grew strong at the expense of the federal system which would be forever relatively weak.

In an analysis of early town records in seventeenth century Massachusetts and Connecticut, Dolgoff et al. (1993) reveal how the deserving poor were maintained and supported by the townships. Vagrant and idle persons, on the other hand, were warned to leave town. Vagrants and those who harbored them were subject to prosecution. The Poor Law mentality was alive and well in the so-called New World; provisions were followed scrupulously because they were widely familiar to England's emigrants, and because they helped maintain order in the new land. Concepts of the worthy and unworthy poor, the favoring of indoor (such as in a workhouse) over outdoor relief, and the principle of less eligibility (the poor must be supported below the level of the lowest paid worker) were implanted early in the Atlantic coast colonies. Because of the absence of unemployment, the work ethic made even more sense here than in the home country. And then, there was the religious factor: the ethos of the Protestant ethic was suffused throughout the whole social system. The strength of this religioeconomic ideology is shown in its ability to outlast its religious roots and to influence welfare policy to this very day.

The Protestant Ethic

The German scholar, Max Weber in *The Protestant Ethic and the Spirit of Capitalism* (1958/1905) compared work productivity levels in Protestant and Catholic regions of Germany, and elsewhere, as evidence for his theory correlating Protestantism and capitalism. Protestantism emphasized the autonomy of the individual and repudiated dependence on the Church, priesthood, and ritual, according to Weber. The qualities of self-discipline, hard work, and communal service were viewed as a likely sign of salvation. Martin Luther's belief in work as a "calling" gave Protestantism a singularly practical bent. John Calvin, who was Luther's counterpart in France and later Switzerland, provided the first great systematic formulation of the Reformation faith. Taking Luther's argument one step further, Calvin introduced the notion of predestination into the Protestant vocabulary. Predestination is the doctrine of God's election or choice of souls to salvation or damnation. The interpretation of predestination carried by way of England and Scotland (through the preaching of John Knox) to America, was that those predestined to salvation could be identified in this life through the evidence of their wealth. Although one's fate was sealed, in a sense, Calvinist philosophy posited that indications of this fate could be detected on earth. Using this line of reasoning, suggests Day (1997), the wealthy could justify not only their wealth but also their exploitation of workers to accumulate it. The belief system also legitimated forcing people to work for their own good. Max Weber described Calvinism as that which was not leisure and enjoyment but activity which served to increase the glory of god. Waste of time thus was perceived as a deadly sin. And condemnation of the sinner was justified. With its emphasis on individual achievement, frugality, and opportunity, the creed of Calvinism has very much affected the American character, even long after the direct religious connection was lost. For instance, the eighteenth century inventor and atheist, Benjamin Franklin, espoused the principles of the Protestant work ethic in his often cited sayings: e.g., "early to bed, early to rise makes a man healthy, wealthy, and wise;" "the early bird catches the worm;" "time is money;" "a penny saved is a penny earned."

One technological development that turned society upside down and became a major threat to social stability was the distillation of alcohol. See box 3.1 for a historical account of the extent of the devastation that accompanied one much-heralded invention.

Slavery

The counterpart of the North American belief in salvation for the elect few is the sense of superiority over persons of other religions and cultures who did not worship the Christian God. In this, the Protestant religioeconomic creed fed a darker, less salutary force—the institution of slavery. In contrast to Latin American practices and even to customs in New Orleans which took on a somewhat more benevolent cast under Catholicism, North American slavery operated in the absence of legal or cultural restraints. After the middle of the seventeenth century until the slave trade ended, *all* Africans came to America as enslaved persons. The paradox of slavery, with regard to the Protestant ethic, is that the hard work in the service of wealth was performed by slaves while their carefree masters reaped all the benefits, presumably in the afterlife too. A second related paradox, noted by Clark (1969), is that slavery was, in every sense of its being, contrary to Christian teaching.

SOCIAL WELFARE IN THE CIVIL WAR ERA

Fought to preserve the union (in the North) and for independence (in the South) and winding up as a war about slavery, approximately six hundred thousand soldiers died either in battle, or from deadly, infectious diseases during the Civil War. Much of the South was laid waste; an entire generation of young men was decimated. Following the war, the opposing southern states elected a solid block of Democrats to Congress. For generations up to the present day, these

BOX 3.1

ALCOHOL TECHNOLOGY

Before liquor reached Norway in earnest in the seventeenth century, beer brewed from oats and barley was the predominant alcoholic beverage. Peasants were required to brew this substance for harvest festivals. With grains somewhat scarce at these northern latitudes, beer must have been in short supply (Brun-Gulbrandsen, 1988). As time went by, distilling to make stronger, alcoholic beverages was done on most of the farms.

The early to mid-eighteenth century in England offers a prime example of the impact of technology on society. Founded in 1575, the oldest distillery in the world still in operation is in Amsterdam. From a concoction of grains, herbs, and juniper berries, *jenever* or gin was produced. (The word *booze* is thought to be a corruption of the middle Dutch *busen* — "drink much alcohol.") The availability of cheap gin, combined with the population displacement caused by industrialization and associated with the growth of an urban proletariat, contributed to an epidemic of drunkenness (Levin, 1990). The devastation was so great, in fact, that a staggering infant mortality rate and child starvation rate combined to prevent a growth in population from 1700 to 1750. Crimes of violence and immorality among all social classes, but most evident among the poor, gave the age a debaucher-

ous character, preserved in political commentary and the early novel.

On North American Shores

Drinking had been a part of the European cultural scene. Transplanted to what used to be considered the "new world," the drinking culture took on some peculiarities of the new land. The pilgrims chose to land at Plymouth, in fact, in order to dispense the dwindling supplies of beer with all due speed. A fight between the settlers, who faced a long cold winter, and the sailors, who faced a long dry return home, was averted when supplies were divided up. In these early days, beer was considered indispensable to health and life. The early settlers did not plan to rely on water for subsistence. It is not surprising, therefore, that more beer than water was carried on the *Mayflower* (Lender and Martin, 1982). The colonists did learn to drink water, but they also learned to make a brew from Indian corn which satisfied their needs for a time. Improvements in the technology of the manufacture of distilled beverages, however, was to change all this.

With the passage of time, liquor came to be valued for both its high alcohol content and its shipping advantages. The Puritans

(Continued on next page)

BOX 3.1 (Continued)

regarded rum as "God's good creature." Although an occasional drunk was placed in the stocks, the tavern was the center of social, economic, and political activity (Levin, 1990). As time passed, Jamaican rum seemed to have become the solution to the new nation's thirst. For rum's sake, New Englanders became the bankers of the slave trade that supplied the sugar cane and molasses needed to produce rum (Kinney and Leaton, 1991).

As the colonists turned to distilling hard liquor, they proved as adaptable as they had earlier in producing passable beer. Honey, corn, rye, berries, and apples were used in domestic production. A general lack of concern about alcoholism and its problems was one of the most significant features of the colonial era (Lender and Martin, 1982). Strong drink was thought to protect against disease and to be conducive to good health. Since good drinking water was not always available, there was some substance to this argument. And as long as the social norms were followed, drinking excesses could be tolerated. Unlike beer, however, the stronger stuff soon acquired a dubious reputation.

The relationship of alcohol abuse, the availability of cheap spirits, and the weakening of social controls in a given society or culture can be easily documented (Levin,

1990). In both England and her colonies, moral depravity, especially among the poor, was seen to be both the cause and effect of habitual intoxication. Distilled spirits in early America appeared side-by-side with easy money, the image of manliness, and all-around good cheer (Moynihan, 1993). Drinking whiskey at breakfast became routine; laborers digging the Erie Canal were allotted a quart of whiskey a day.

Severe restrictions, on the other hand, were placed on drinking by slaves. Although masters might reward slaves with alcoholic beverages, especially at holiday times, drinking was seen as a hindrance to work. Besides, there was a deep-seated fear among whites that blacks, like Indians, were especially prone to violence when intoxicated (Lender and Martin, 1982). Slave codes mandated harsh measures against slaves who drank without permission. The typical drinking pattern taught to the slaves by their masters was a long period of abstinence punctuated by a binge. Abolitionist Frederick Douglass declared that one might just as well be a slave to man as to rum.

Source: K. van Wormer, *Alcoholism Treatment: A Social Work Perspective* (Chicago: Nelson-Hall, 1993). Reprinted with permission of Nelson-Hall, Inc.

influential politicians romanticized the past and fought for states' rights against federal interference.

Although the nation had abolished slavery forever, little thought was given for the welfare of the former slaves or of the society in which they would live. Thousands of ex-slaves took to the roads, wandering aimlessly from county to county. It is safe to say that more families were broken up by the first year of freedom than by any year of slavery (Nevins and Commager, 1981). Thousands of newly freed men and women died of disease and starvation or were the victims of violence. The vast majority became share-croppers who worked on white people's farms. Meanwhile, in the North, sweeping industrial activity resumed. The American Industrial Revolution which got under way later than its British counterpart, was based on coal, iron, and eventually, electricity. We will discuss the social welfare implications shortly.

Informal and Semi-formal Helping

Most of the help for the poor has come from its own—the poor helping the poor with limited resources. Mutual aid among African Americans was based on their cultural heritage which stressed strong extended family ties and the tradition of adopting nonrelatives into the family network. Individual interests were not placed above the group; cooperation and sense of community prevailed. Before the Civil War, there were half a million free persons of African descent in the United States (and four million slaves); half of the freed slaves were in the South (Day, 1989). A great deal of charity work was done by these free blacks; they had churches, relief associations, and societies for mutual aid. Among the slaves obligations to kin and a general altruistic behavior promoted the collective survival of a people in a cruel and racist society.

Farmers of all races and ethnicity historically have maintained their common welfare through offering collective aid in times of need—crop failures, barn burnings, illness. Men have generally been responsible for the heavy labor while women have bonded together for childbirth, childcare, cooking, and other nurturant activities. Such a sense of communalism is preserved to some extent in rural areas and maintains its pure form among the Amish today.

Since the early colonial period, much help has been provided by the churches. Good works were viewed as an obligation owed to God and as more rewarding to the giver than to the receiver. In the North, as private fortunes accumulated, individuals and private groups supplemented public relief activities or assisted families whom they knew. In the South private efforts, especially large-scale giving, were even more sustained (Trattner, 1994). There, according to Trattner, Calvinist principles of hard work were less pressing, while the spirit of *noblesse oblige* was engendered in a class of people who were trying to maintain a social system not unlike that of feudalism. The tradition of chivalry in the South in fact, is thought to have originated and been sustained through the writings of Sir Walter Scott whose works formed an essential part of virtually every southern planter's library. Paternalistic treatment of African American women (and of white women defined as ladies), demeaning as it was, was consistent with the bestowing of charity upon the poor and care upon the weak.

In the United States, in contrast to many European nations, the separation of church and state had a significant bearing on the manner in which aid to the indigent was distributed. The flourishing of numerous sects in America led to a near-competitive atmosphere for helping the poor and hopefully of winning converts. Nearly all forms of relief emanated from church groups, and all major denominations had some mechanism for providing help for the indigent. Protestants established orphanages, reform schools, mental hospitals, new kinds of prisons (an area of recognized Quaker activity) and institutions for the handicapped. The Quakers, in particular, spent an enormous amount of time, effort, and money aiding the needy (Trattner, 1994). Their work in rescuing slaves and abetting their escape is well known. Generally, however, in comparison to Protestant churches, the Catholic church gave more attention to the needs of African and Native Americans, and especially to needy children (Day, 1989). Formed in the eighteenth century in New Orleans, the Ursuline Sisters ran a private home for mothers and children left homeless, initially from wars with the Indians. This home became America's first residential institution for orphaned children (Barker, 1995).

Formal Helping

Whereas outdoor relief was more common in the South, poorhouses in the North existed as a carryover from poor laws modeled on the original English laws.

By 1832, practically all of New York's counties had poorhouses run by political appointees whose pay was drawn from the inmates' work. The deserving and undeserving poor alike were confined in places where the rates for malnutrition and disease were quite high. The death rate for children was astronomical. After 1875, laws removed children from these work "dungeons of death" and placed them elsewhere.

When Sunday school teacher Dorothea Dix volunteered to teach at an insane asylum in 1841, she was set to embark on one of the most memorable crusades of the century—an effort to end the barbaric treatment of the indigent mentally ill. To Dix, the only way to rectify the problem lay in federal intervention. Building a network of support from the clergy, press, and politicians, Dix ultimately got a bill to allocate funds and land for the construction of mental hospitals passed by both houses of Congress. President Pierce's veto of the bill was based on the argument that the states, not the federal government, should provide charity. This single act set a precedent for the next seventy-five years that the federal government refrain from providing social welfare services. However, as Dolgoff et al. indicate, federal aid and land were given readily for the building of railroads and to reward soldiers.

Like other major catastrophes, the Civil War created conditions which desperately needed direct public aid of an urgent nature. Singularly, affirming federal responsibility over states' rights, this war laid the groundwork for the United States to ultimately become a welfare state (Day, 1997). First, even before the war was over, the social welfare needs of soldiers and their families demanded attention. Whether in regard to medical care, housing, or financial support, the needs of the veterans were considered apart from the needs of the civilian population. The veterans' needs were addressed without stigma or vacillation. In fact, from the time of the Revolutionary War veterans were recipients of aid, universally, in recognition of their personal service and sacrifice. Generous grants to federal lands, pensions, and other types of aid were bestowed upon them.

Noteworthy in regard to the formation of women's voluntary organizations that later became institutionalized, was the federation of organizations that served the needs of Union troops during the Civil War, supplying bandages, clothing, and food. Out of this campaign evolved the U.S. Sanitation Commission, the first important national public health organization.

Though reluctant to assume a welfare role, the federal government in 1865, during Reconstruction, established the Freedmen's Bureau as part of the War Department. The purpose of this first federal welfare agency was to provide temporary relief, education, employment, and health care for the newly freed slaves. One of the interesting functions of the Bureau was the work it did in reuniting families separated by slavery and the war, solemnizing prior slave unions, and arranging for the adoption of orphans. By 1870, according to Dolgoff et al., a large majority of African Americans lived in two-parent households. Despite the fact that it was seriously underfunded and ended its work abruptly, the Freedmen's Bureau established an important precedent in its offering of emergency, comprehensive relief during a serious social upheaval. Foreshadowing the New Deal of the 1930s, and the War on Poverty of the 1960s, the history surrounding the Freedmen's Bureau provides backing for Piven and Cloward's (1993: XV) basic premise that, "relief arrangements are initiated or expanded during outbreaks of civil disorder produced by mass unemployment, and are then abolished or contracted when political stability is restored."

EUROPE: A CONTRAST

While the Protestant ethic still prevailed in "the land of pilgrims' pride" and the British reform movement got under way in earnest, over in Europe, the birthplace of Protestantism, the first general social insurance scheme was introduced. Chancellor Otto von Bismarck's sickness insurance law provided to employees, in defined types of industry, medical care and cash benefits during a period of sickness. These benefits were to be financed through contributions by both employers and employees. In 1884 accident insurance was made compulsory. Several years later, workers' pensions were introduced. Austria followed suit, as did Sweden and the Netherlands in 1901. In contrast, in Britain and the United States, where the threat of revolution was less, self-help through friendly societies and savings banks was seen as the solution (*Encyclopaedia Britannica*, 1993).

Bryson (1992) offers an interesting contrast between England and Sweden in terms of treatment of the landless poor. Whereas England engaged in a brutal process of forcing the rural poor off the land, Sweden, where industrialization arrived later, transferred land to peasant ownership. These historical differences between the two countries, notes Bryson, remain fundamental to understanding the more positive attitudes of Swedish people to government and the welfare state to the present day.

Industrial Growth in the United States

Within the span of one person's lifetime, industrialization, which came later than in Britain and was first apparent in the North, literally transformed the American landscape (Ehrenreich, 1985). Energy production soared to such an extent that the nation went from being primarily agricultural in 1859 to primarily producing manufactured goods fifty years later. The vast increases in both the population and the physical size of the cities presented the country with a set of problems reminiscent of England in earlier days. The streets of American cities were overcrowded, filthy, and rampant with disease (tuberculosis was common) and crime. Factory conditions were abominable—eighteen hour days were not unheard of; women worked night shifts; and industrial accidents were frequent.

Two countertrends responded to the dehumanizing social conditions of the day: social Darwinism and Christian charity. *The Origin of Species,* written by Charles Darwin in 1859, discussed the evolution of plants and animals. Social theorists such as Herbert Spencer of England took Darwin's theories one step further. Spencer coined the term "survival of the fittest," still widely used today, and applied the concept to human beings. Essentially, Social Darwinists argued that competition benefits the species; therefore, subsidizing the poor would only weaken the gene pool. A happy union of laissez-faire economics and the doctrine of survival of the fittest, social Darwinism became the prevailing philosophy of the era (Trattner, 1994). As the wounds of the Civil War were healed and wealth became almost an end in itself, the poor were once again blamed for their condition.

When a severe economic depression of the 1870s threw large numbers of people out of work, rioting and disorder ensued. Unions, which were just beginning to organize, were blamed by many for the economic crisis of the nation. Churches and private citizens set up soup kitchens and distributed fuel and clothing to the poor. Regarding the emergency aid that was provided, however, fraud, inefficiency, and duplicity were characteristic (Trattner, 1994). Accordingly, even among the reformers, a national outcry sounded. The search was for a more scientific approach to social welfare.

The two seemingly disparate forces, then—social Darwinism and Christian charity—ultimately merged toward the common goal of organizing relief giving efforts. Charity organization societies and settlement houses were established to provide formal but voluntary services to the poor.

Charity Organization Societies

Patterned after the London Charity Organization Society (COS), the development of the COS in the United States in 1877 was implemented by an Episcopal clergyman, who was an Englishman by birth. The purpose of the COS, soon to become the COS movement, was to institute a rational, objective system of poor relief, emphasizing the investigation of individual cases and the coordination of services with other agencies. The success of the movement was evidenced in the fact that within twenty years virtually every large city in the country had a Charity Organization Society. Why, though, were the charity societies so successful?

Trattner (1994) attributes the success of the COS movement to the organization's compatibility with the values of the day—emphasis on trust in science, belief in progress, and the belief that the poor needed moral supervision to help them combat such vices as intemperance, indolence, and improvidence. In carrying out their work, these privately funded societies relied on corps of "friendly visitors." These visitors or agents were entrusted to investigate appeals for assistance, distinguish between the worthy and unworthy poor, and above all, provide the needy with the proper amount of moral exhortation (Trattner, 1994). COS workers (volunteers in the early days) were to become the forerunners of today's social workers, and their methods (record-keeping and counseling) anticipated social casework. To summarize, the COS emphasis was on outdoor (noninstitutional) relief; the principles of Calvin, the work ethic, and social Darwinism guided their work. Not surprisingly, COS workers believed the source of poverty was located in the individual. Over time, however, as they gained experience with human suffering, the COS workers came to identify, to some extent, with their charges and then joined social action efforts to produce much needed change.

Settlement Houses

Also an outgrowth of the deplorable urban conditions of the time and also modeled on English innovations, the settlement house movement began in the 1880s. After visiting Toynbee Hall, a house for the poor in the worst part of

London in 1889, Jane Addams returned to Chicago to found with her associate, Ellen Gates Starr, the American equivalent of Toynbee Hall at Hull House. Eventually, Hull House was to become the most famous settlement in the world. Secular from the beginning, settlement houses in the United States had social change as their focus rather than spiritual goals. The individual religious motivation of the founders and volunteers, however, is not to be underestimated.

Settlements sprang up in most large cities over the next fifteen years, their number reaching three hundred at their peak in 1915. Set up in immigrant neighborhoods, upper and middle class people themselves—unmarried women, college students, teachers, and doctors—moved into the slums as residents. Rather than engaging in friendly visiting, the upper-middle class settlement leaders tried to bridge class differences and to develop a less patronizing form of charity than had existed previously (Karger and Stoesz, 1990). Settlement leaders taught the immigrants English, American customs, crafts, and recreation, and advocated for their rights in the area of housing codes, child protection, and work conditions. An important role of the settlement house was to prevent the spread of disease. Following the revolutionary germ theory of disease pioneered by the work of Louis Pasteur in France, the cause of disease was demystified and one bacteriological discovery occurred after another. Fortified with the exciting new knowledge concerning the spread of infection, settlement house workers fought for sanitation and public health programs. These developments included efforts to sanitize drinking water, sewage disposal, housing, and work conditions in the crowded urban areas. For further discussion of this remarkable period of history including the racial dimension, dynamic social welfare activism, and community organization, see the following chapter on the growth of social work.

Some Modern Examples of Industrialization

So far we have been talking about the social costs of the Industrial Revolution and of the social unrest accompanying it during certain defining points in British and American history. Yet today, many nations are undergoing technological change at a pace that is quite dramatic. In these rapidly industrializing nations, new technologies are superimposed upon the culture from without. Accordingly, the progress of centuries in countries of the North is being condensed into one brief decade or less in parts of Africa and Central and South America. See box 3.2 for a global view of economic development in historical and geographical context.

BOX 3.2

ON DEVELOPMENT

*Develop, v. To expand or realize the
potentialities of; bring gradually
to a fuller, greater, or better state.*
—The American Heritage Dictionary

Until the 1700s, the human condition was
much the same around the world. People
lived in poverty, suffered from a number of
diseases and were largely illiterate. With the
coming of the industrial revolution, and
changes brought by scientific and technological breakthroughs, quality of living began
to gradually improve for most people in
North America and Europe as their countries industrialized. Yet as the world entered
the twentieth century, the majority of people in Africa, Latin America and Asia (continents in the Southern Hemisphere, often
referred to as the South,) continued to live
in squalor. Many of these countries did not
reap the benefits of industrialization. They
were the colonies of the North (North
America and Europe) and their minerals,
agricultural products and other natural
resources supported growth and industrialization there.

• After World War II, *development* efforts
began in earnest in the less industrialized
countries of the South. (Usually, but not
always, the term *development* is used to refer
to *economic* development, the process by

which a country improves the well-being of
its people through economic means.) Industrialization efforts in the South gained
momentum as many of the colonies became
independent. There was also an interest
among the industrialized countries of the
North in assisting the South in creating markets where the North could sell their goods
and services. Still others wanted to help the
South alleviate poverty through economic
development projects.

• The *dominant paradigm* or *mainstream
model* for development has been characterized by a push for capital intensive industrialization and economic growth. In these
models, modernization is valued over tradition. It is posited that benefits brought by
economic modernization undertaken by
elites within a country will eventually trickle
down to the poorest within that country, thus
improving the economic and social situation
of the population as a whole. In undertaking development initiatives, the Northern,
industrialized countries have long advocated
the *mainstream model,* citing their own economic growth as proof that the model works.

• According to mainstream theorists, a
country is developed once a certain level of

(Continued on next page)

BOX 3.2 (Continued)

economic growth is attained, as indicated by such figures as a high gross national product (GNP). The relatively rich countries of the North, with a high GNP, are called *developed countries,* while traditional societies which have only begun to modernize in the middle of the twentieth century and are still at an early stage of economic growth, are called *developing countries.* Countries that started to modernize at the turn of the century, but have made significant economic progress are known as *newly industrialized countries* or NICs. Mexico, Brazil and South Korea are examples of NICs.

• Developing countries are also known as Third World countries. The term originates from the French and was used to describe nations shaking off colonial rule. It is not meant to be pejorative, as if to imply that these countries are third rate, yet many people do not like to use the term. Developed countries make up the First World, while Second World refers to the traditionally communist countries.

• Many in the South, as well as the North, refute mainstream theories of development, criticizing them for being ethnocentric, ahistorical, and culturally insensitive. Too much emphasis is placed on a country's economic growth, with little regard for the social, spiritual and cultural well-being of people.

• In fact, the mainstream notion of "trickle down" has been proven false by development scholars. Case studies done in developing countries as economically diverse as Brazil, Costa Rica, Ecuador, Hong Kong, Kenya, Korea, Namibia, Singapore, Sri Lanka and Taiwan "suggest that balanced social and economic development will only take place if governments combine economic growth strategies with egalitarian redistributive measures . . ." (Midgley, 1988) It is not surprising that market forces alone have not increased the well-being of all people in the South, since similar issues are relevant in the North.

• Alternative views on development, often rooted in an ethical/humanistic framework, see development as having to do more with people and less with economic growth. The concern is for justice, peace, self-determination and self-reliance. In the South, development is often thought of as a revolutionary process; what is needed is to change existing social, political and economic relationships that keep people from reaching their full potential. Furthermore, development is more than a national issue, it is a global process of liberation from the kind of wealth and greed in society which are ultimately destructive to *human development.* (Carr, 1987)

(Continued on next page)

BOX 3.2 (Continued)

• Broader views about development are also beginning to be heard within the development assistance community. A 1989 report put out by the Administrator of the Agency for International Development stresses that real development must come from the bottom up, not the top down. Individuals need to be the focus of development efforts. (Woods, 1989)

• There is also a growing concern about our environment. That concern stems in part from a fear that we have over-developed and over-industrialized to the point of harming the earth, thus putting it and humankind at risk. Calls for development have been replaced with a move toward sustainable development, which "meets the needs of the present without compromising the ability of future generations to meet their own needs." (IIED-Earthscan) Lessons from failed development efforts, stronger voices from the South, increased interdependence and heightened awareness about the future of planet Earth, are all contributing to a new paradigm of development for the twenty-first century.

Fact Sheet prepared by Michelle Reynolds for the National Association of Social Workers, February 1990.
Source: Child and Family Well-Being Development Education Program (Washington, DC: NASW, 1990). Reprinted with permission of NASW.

Federico (1990) offers a positive view of the industrial revolution in Mexico. Prior to the 1910 Revolution, writes Federico, Mexico was an agricultural society in which the church, through its landholdings and spiritual teachings, wielded a great deal of power. Following the Revolution, which was in part a response to industrialization, the government assumed ownership of the land and later, responsibility for many social welfare functions including the regulation of work conditions. Thus we can see how the rise of industrialization ultimately can have a positive impact on the social structure by breaking down feudal arrangements.

On the other hand, a recent Associated Press news story (1994) recorded some of the social costs to ordinary Mexican citizens and their families in the wake of changes brought by the North American Free Trade Agreement (NAFTA). After NAFTA took effect, according to the article, production of goods such as television sets and tractors is rising rapidly; yet as companies increase their economic assets, they invest in more machinery rather than workers. "It's cheaper to bring in machines," a personnel manager declares. "Machines don't need training, don't quit, and don't get paid vacations." Smaller businesses, meanwhile, are folding against the competition. And thousands of unemployed men gather at Mexico City's main bus station each morning in a desperate attempt to be picked up for work.

According to anthropologist Bodley (1994), the benefits of economic development are not equally distributed within a developing society. Tribal peoples throughout the world may discover their resources are depleted and through this that their self-sufficiency is lost. Under the impact of major economic change, family life and traditional culture are disrupted while rates of malnutrition, alcoholism, crime, and suicide may increase. Industrial civilization may therefore be a mixed blessing, simultaneously benefiting one portion of a modernizing society at the expense of another. The international marketing of harmful yet appealing products such as alcohol and tobacco exacerbates the situation for the masses in newly industrialized countries.

THE PROGRESSIVE ERA IN THE UNITED STATES

It was during the Progressive Era—between 1900 and World War I—that social work became almost synonymous with social welfare itself. As a reaction to the heartlessness that had characterized the preceding period, Progressives campaigned against the ruthless practices of big business and advocated strong government regulation for the public good. The Progressive Party was supported by the nation's most respected social workers, women reformers, and many intellectuals. Under pressure from this political party and the burgeoning socialists, impressive government reforms were enacted. Laws increased workers' rights; many states established minimum wage and maximum hour legislation. The most impressive social welfare reform of this era, as Day (1997) indicates, was the granting of mothers' pensions to poverty-stricken widows. Then World War I broke out, and the liberal fervor diminished. Following the war, proponents of liberal ideas were accused of being Bolsheviks (Karger and Stoesz, 1990). The settlement house fell out of favor. Women, however, did win the right to vote in 1920.

THE GREAT DEPRESSION AND THE NEW DEAL

A second American industrial revolution occurred in the 1920s. Consumer products were the focus of economic activity. Advertisers helped induce demand for cars, radios, and so on. A trickle-down economic philosophy dominated (Jansson, 1993) claiming that benefits to the rich will eventually trickle down to the poorer classes. When the Great Depression hit following the stock market crash of 1929, the unemployment rate reached a high of 24 percent. President Herbert Hoover's response was to rely on the voluntary social welfare sector. Demonstrations, strikes, and riots occurred nationwide as the financial panic worsened. Images recalled by Olsen (1994) represent the decade: apple sellers, the bread line, the migrant-worker, and the man with his sign stating, "I will work for food." When Franklin Roosevelt assumed the presidency in 1933, the banking system was threatened with collapse; millions of transients roamed the nation and one of every four farms was foreclosed. Roosevelt stated, "I see one-third of a nation, ill-housed, ill-clad, ill-nourished." The magnitude of mass suffering, in short, was intense; everyone was affected one way or another by the crisis. In the climate of social upheaval which was fast approaching, the time was right for a startling departure from prior welfare traditions. As Roosevelt promised in his campaign speeches, he worked to regularize production, provide federal public works and unemployment insurance, and to get the federal government to assume responsibility for relief. Much of what he accomplished was done in a dazzling one hundred days.

As a part of a wave of New Deal legislation, the Civilian Conservation Corps provided jobs immediately in the national forests. The Public Works Administration, in contrast, was slower to get started but had more impact when it did so. Social worker Harry Hopkins was appointed to head the Emergency Relief Act program. To all needy, unemployed persons and their dependents, massive relief grants were provided under the auspices of the Federal Emergency Relief Administration. In order to preserve people's self-respect, the president called for a public works program to provide a job for every able-bodied unemployed person; wages were to be below those paid by private employers but higher than relief payments. Piven and Cloward (1993: 97) assess the overall significance:

> Work relief is remembered mainly for these accomplishments—for the dams and roads and schools and hospitals and other public facilities built by so

many men in so short of time. . . . By once more enmeshing people in the work role, the cornerstone of social control in any society, it went far toward moderating civil disorder.

Roosevelt's reform of the economic system established safeguards to curb exploitation of workers while obtaining the benefits of regulation of prices, wages, and production for businesses and the nation. Business leaders had to agree to refrain from using child labor, to allow workers to join unions, and to honor specified minimum working conditions (Jansson, 1993).

The greatest legacy, by far, from the wave of measures known collectively as the New Deal was the Social Security Act of 1935. Designed to alleviate financial dependency through two lines of defense—contributory social assurance and public assistance—the Social Security Act included: a national old-age insurance system; federal grants to states for maternal and child welfare services, aid to dependent children (ADC known today as AFDC), medical care and rehabilitation for the handicapped; and a federal-state unemployment system. Opposition from the American Medical Association prevented the adoption of a national health plan (Day, 1989; Karger and Stoesz, 1990). Health insurance for the elderly (Medicare) and for the very poor (Medicaid) were added to the Social Security Act in 1965.

The lack of provision for the unemployed, able-bodied worker was a significant deficiency in the Social Security Act. Yet, despite its shortcomings, the legislation contained in the Social Security Act in 1935 provided the framework for the United States' social welfare system and was a demonstration of the federal responsibility for meeting the urgent needs of the nation's citizens. Above all, the solution for social problems was sought at this historic time, in the system or in the social and economic conditions of the day, not in the individuals themselves. What transformed the thirties, recalls Olsen (1994: 27), was when the president of the United States became part of our struggle, "How simply and directly he spoke to us from the beginning: Relief, recovery, reform." See box 3.3 for a cogent personal account shared by an African American professor of social work who started life as a "mother's aid child."

While the United States moved swiftly to offset social unrest under the leadership of a determined President Roosevelt, north of the border in Canada men were herded, military style, into boot camps reminiscent of poorhouses (Guest, 1988). By the end of the decade, however, Canadians also realized that it was the economy at fault, not the individuals. World War II solved the

BOX 3.3

WELFARE ENTERS OUR LIVES—1933

Ruth B. Anderson

Two days later, in the early afternoon, the white lady came. Mama was still at work in the Hotel Martin. Mama was sure right. The lady did ask a lot of questions, such as, "Who gets you off to school in the morning? Who fixes your breakfast, your lunch? Do you like school? Do you like living with your Mom? Would you like to live with your Dad? Does your Dad come to see you often? How long does your Dad stay when he comes," and so on and so on. R. J. and I answered all the questions as best we could. We told her about Mama's friend, an older lady, named Ms. Cotton who looked in on us all the time when Mama was gone.

I asked the lady what her name was and who she was. She said, "My name is Ms. Hobbs, and I'm your mother's friend." I thought that for a friend she sure asked lots of questions.

After this visit, this lady, my mother's friend, came to see us often. Later, Mama told us that Ms. Hobbs was a welfare lady, and I came to know her both as the welfare lady and Mama's friend.

Ms. Hobbs must have decided that we were being adequately cared for by Mama and that we were not without parental care or proper guardianship. She must have also decided that we were in need of some kind

of public support. Our family became a welfare case, eligible for poor relief.

I don't remember much about cash money, but I know that we began to get a lot of foodstuffs such as rice, beans, and canned beef with white wrappers printed "Not to be sold." There was also many pounds of what at first seemed to be lard, but a little purple looking pill came with the lard. When you mixed the little purple pill with the lard, the lard turned yellow. We learned that it was not butter. Instead, it was called "oleo." Lard came in tin containers, also marked "Not to be sold." We were on relief and we were eligible for commodities.

Woodbury County Board of Supervisors provided part of our clothing through W.P.A. sewing project. The local overseer of the poor had determined that we could receive this clothing. In accordance with his duty, he also determined what amount of clothing we could receive. Sometime after our eligibility was established, Mama was also certified as eligible for work in the sewing room. I hated this room located in the basement of the Court House. I hated having to get my clothes from there. It seemed as if there were hundreds of dresses all cut

(Continued on next page)

BOX 3.3 (Continued)

from the same batch of cloth and the same pattern. Mama would get remnants of cloth and add some trimming to our dresses to try to make them different. She used to change the collars and sleeves, sometimes adding a fancy ruffle to the bottom of the dresses. My sister and I were really pleased with these slight changes, but on the whole we could tell that our clothes came from the sewing room—and we knew that others could too.

I made up my mind right then that I would never buy a dress if I saw lots of them on a rack in a store. Over the years, this decision was a very costly one. When I realized that this was one of the very painful and unpleasant memories from my welfare days, I became more able to deal with this feeling. I also realized that clothes do not make a person. I remembered Mama. "Pretty is as pretty does," she always said.

Christmas of 1933 was one of the biggest and best Christmas's that we ever had. Three welfare ladies came on Christmas eve. At least I thought they were all welfare ladies since they came with Ms. Hobbs. They had lots of boxes—all sealed up so I couldn't see inside—and several bags and sacks. Mama was full of smiles and gracious "Thank you's." My sister and three brothers had been sent to bed early to wait for Santa. We had a custom in our house that as soon thereafter as midnight came we could see what Santa brought. I remember that I rarely went to sleep, that is real sleep. I suspected that my little sister and brothers were not sleeping very soundly.

I helped Mama open boxes and put out the toys. There were books, games and puzzles, two dolls, trucks, trains, and toy guns. Mama always said I told her, "Mattie can have *both* dolls. I'll take the books." The toys weren't all. There was a piece of clothing for each of us, pants and dresses. There were dozens of oranges, apples, lots of candy and nuts. It looked as if we had enough to fill the whole "front room."

Midnight came and went. Mama and I heard a voice from the bedroom say, "Is it time yet?" Mama said, "Santa's been here." My sister and brothers bounded out of bed and into the front room with almost two leaps. The "oh's" and "ah's" seemed to go on forever as they moved from one toy to the next, holding their new clothes up as if to determine the fit. All presents opened and quieting down at last, we sat around the tree and stuffed ourselves with candy, nuts, apples, and oranges until Mama said, "That's enuf, now get back to bed."

Years later, whenever we recalled Christmas of 1933, Mama would recount how happy she was and how good she felt to see all of us so happy. She told us a little story about that Christmas Eve that I have never forgotten. She said she had worked so hard and worried so much about that

(Continued on next page)

BOX 3.3 (Continued)

Christmas. Yet, it looked as if it was all over in just a few minutes, particularly when my brother, R.J., with his mouth poked full, looked up at her and said, "I sho' be glad when *next* Christmas come." Over the years, even with Mama gone, we have told this story many times and laughed just as heartily each time.

I grew up rather fast. I helped out a lot with fixing supper, washing clothes, getting my brothers and sister ready for school. I particularly liked washing clothes on the rub board, which was fun, although quite tiring. I'd get soaked and sometimes it seemed as if there was more water on me than there was on the clothes. I liked it when Mama used to say I was "a regular little ole' woman."

Mama kept her job as a maid at Hotel Martin. In fact, she had two jobs. She also worked as a cleaning lady doing "day work" for a very light colored lady who really was colored but looked white. Ms. Crimp really liked Mama, and like so many people, she

was always giving Mama things. She also let us kids come out to her house often, and she'd give us lots of good things to eat, too. Ms. Crimp was very strict. We couldn't go out of her yard and had to be very mannerly and "lady-like." Ms. Crimp had a beautiful big house on the West side, and we used to say, "She's rich."

Daddy didn't pay child support. Mama stopped holding his checks. Our life became settled, quite peaceful and centered around home, school, the Community House, and church which provided many activities for us. In the summer, there was day camp and a week-long overnight camp for myself and for R. J. and Mattie as they grew older. These were fun years.

Source: Ruth B. Anderson, *From Mother's Aid Child to University Professor* (Iowa City: University of Iowa School of Social Work). Reprinted with permission of Ruth Anderson and the University of Iowa School of Social Work.

unemployment problem (as in the United States), but Canadians demanded full economic and social security and therefore a comprehensive welfare program was launched. A universal system of family allowances and old age benefits was included in the program. Universal health care, however, had to wait until later.

THE WAR ON POVERTY

Wills (1994: 40) poignantly captures the mood of the sixties:

> The sixties split the skies. Only the Civil and two world wars so neatly clove our history into a Before and After. And the sixties were more division than World War II, which drew people together for the war effort. The sixties drove people apart — husbands from wives, children from parents, students from teachers, citizens from their government. Authority was strengthened by World War II. It was challenged by the sixties.

Central to an understanding of the ethos of the age (an ethos which was not even apparent until the decade was over) is a recognition of the transformation of young people that occurred through the hope and optimism generated by the Civil Rights movement. As a result of mass mobilization, public martyrdom, and a sympathetic press, justice prevailed. People said, "We shall overcome," and in truth, they did overcome. This brilliantly successful movement set the pattern for others to demand their and others' rights — women, gays and lesbians, Native Americans, and the elderly. Catholics in Northern Ireland, similarly, sang Civil Rights songs and held sit-ins and mass rallies to protest discrimination against Roman Catholics. In the United States and Europe, mobilized protests against the war in Vietnam helped bring that conflict to a close even in the absence of military victory.

Concurrently with politics and even more tangibly, perhaps, the hair length for men — from the military crew cut to the long and shaggy — underwent a drastic alteration though the effects again were not apparent until the sixties were almost over. "The intensity of the reaction to long hair is hard to recapture now. Children were kicked out of school, or kicked out of their homes, for the length of their hair," recalls Wills (1994: 40). Into this climate of fashion change and social change emerged President Lyndon Johnson. After he helped push the Civil Rights Act through Congress, perhaps sensing the mood of the nation, Johnson declared a War on Poverty and a major expansion of social welfare programs followed.

The optimism of the era is captured in the use of the term, the Great Society, to refer to the War on Poverty and what it represented. The phrase sounds grandiose today; then it did not. Under the umbrella of the Office of Economic Opportunity, many programs were tried incuding: Volunteers in Service to America (VISTA); Upward Bound, a program to help poor and ghetto children enter college; Operation Head Start to prepare lower-income children for school; Legal Services; and Job Corps. Part of the impetus for these programs sprang out of massive urban riots in poor black communities of the mid-sixties.

When the war in Vietnam began to absorb the nation's resources, President Johnson announced that the nation could have both guns and butter. However, the war on poverty and the war in Vietnam could not be conducted at once, and the American people ultimately lost patience with both of them. Today, one often hears the comment that all the effort of the sixties was in vain. Karger and Stoesz (1990: 49) offer this response:

> Despite the grim post-mortem offered by subsequent scholars, however, during the Great Society period the number of people below the poverty line was cut almost in half, from about 25 percent in the early 1960s to around 12 percent by 1969.

THE WAR ON WELFARE

During the 1940s, according to Kaplan and Kaplan (1993) who utilized extensive documentation from public opinion polls of the day, the general public strongly supported Roosevelt's plan for sweeping social policy reforms to produce the programs of the New Deal. The American population, during that moment in history, argue the Kaplans, did think in collectivist terms except for the South during the mid-sixties. Unfortunately, this spirit was diverted by vested interests acting to oppose it. During the Cold War and the era of McCarthyism, new ideologies favoring absolute conformity and unswerving patriotism prevailed. The fact that American values vary over time is indicated by the historical evidence.

In the final analysis, who can say why the pendulum swings the way it does throughout history? Some historians have looked to social psychology for explanations as to why concern for the lower class is characteristic of one epoch and punishment of the lower class is characteristic of another. According to social psychologists, mass insecurity generated by external forces (such as the threat of business downsizing and reduction in benefits) and fueled by mass media exposés of welfare fraud and/or illegal immigrants, may cause the public to lash out against an already dispossessed group of people. It is a strange phenomenon that persons oppressed from above will often strike downward—the man hits the child; the child hits the dog. The displaced aggression argument will be addressed more thoroughly in the following pages.

Piven and Cloward (1993) offer an alternate but not necessarily contradictory explanation for decisive shifts in national policy. We should never underestimate, according to these authors, the power of the mass, lower-class social action or the threat of such action in compelling the administration to embark on a change of course. Fear of a major challenge to the established order, indeed, may be a key motivating factor in gaining concessions for workers and others. Conversely, mass apathy and lack of organization by the working and lower classes can be their undoing. Whatever the reasons, for the first time since the 1920s, under the leadership of newly elected President Ronald Reagan, the radical right boldly attempted to reform American society. In the absence of viable opposition, laissez-faire capitalism resumed its hold on the nation. This ideology cast high taxes, regulation, and welfare assistance to the poor as the major impediments to economic growth and prosperity (West, 1994). The decade brought us a tax cut, particularly for the highest income group, large cuts in domestic spending, and the largest peacetime military buildup in American history. This paradigm shift which edged up slowly on the nation, was reinforced in externally funded academic writings and in the corporate controlled mass media. The idea that government programs (such as Aid to Families with Dependent Children and food stamps) represent a giant drain on tax dollars went virtually unchallenged by political leaders. In the political rhetoric of the time, only those governmental programs and services that were intended to help the poor and the powerless were seen as a problem.

In 1988, drawing on negative stereotypes of poor women, advocates of welfare reform justified the need for a mandatory work program designed to channel welfare recipients into the low-wage labor market (Rose, 1990). The Family Support Act transformed AFDC from an income-maintenance program to what Rose calls a punitive government work program. Various invasive and expensive programs have been conceived to monitor the morality of welfare clients with the underlying premise that aid is for the deserving poor only, and that aid can be used to control behavior. How different the workfare programs are from the job creation programs of the thirties!

The mood of the mid-nineties is captured by Piven's (1995, 22–23) apt description:

> For the poor, it's back to the workhouse and the orphanage. The press tends to credit Newt Gingrich (Speaker of the House) with this Nineteenth Century scenario, embodied in the House Republicans' Contract with America.

But Gingrich certainly didn't invent the assault on welfare. He only had to modify a script written and rehearsed by the Clinton Administration, and then by Congress, where some twenty welfare "reform" bills were introduced over the past year . . . Democrats and Republicans alike have hit upon welfare-bashing as a way to appease an anxious and increasingly angry electorate.

CONCLUSION AND SUMMARY

The history of social welfare is as old as humankind. To understand the universality of social welfare, we have ventured in this chapter across time, geography, and religion. Throughout the ages, as we have seen, the scriptures of all religions have proclaimed that humanity is one great family. The Golden Rule (Do unto others as you would have them do unto you); love thy neighbor; honor thy father and mother; speak the truth; it is more blessed to give than to receive—these principles are common to all major religions, and they are the principles on which social welfare systems are based.

Contemporary social welfare can trace its roots back, in part at least, to the mutual aid of an agrarian community, the medieval church, and the paternalism associated with feudalism. We have seen, in every era, the inherent connections among religions, social values, economics, and technology. In understanding how the social welfare system grew and changed, it is important to note not only the milestones (such as the codification of laws), but also the upheavals—the kinds of unpredictable, cataclysmic events that throw the whole social system out of balance. The impact on one part of the system—the mass desolation wrought by war or plague—evokes compensatory change in other parts of the system as well. The path from migration to urbanization and then to stratification has perhaps been more circular than linear. The one thing we can say with certainty is that when massive and threatening social movements of the poor have arisen, social institutions have quashed them. One such major social institution is, of course, social welfare.

In summary, paralleling the growth of a complex class and gender stratification associated with wage labor, we have seen social welfare emerge from communal mutual aid into a formalized system of social control. The poor (beggars, transients, and disabled) were provided with help according to a standardized set of criteria.

Generally considered the first great landmark in modern social welfare history, the English Poor Law of 1601 became the basis for ensuring welfare throughout the Anglo-Saxon world. The workhouse became a major center of activity. Conditions were deplorable, and the death rate was staggering. The old Poor Law was not designed to abolish poverty, in essence, but to subdue the potentially dangerous classes. In the southern United States, a new kind of feudalism developed; the society was built on slave labor. Unlike serfs who belonged to the land, the slaves were property and belonged to their owners. But like serfs, slaves worked on the land. As the Industrial Revolution was getting under way in England, the North American continent was a land of opportunity. The vast personal space, absence of aristocracy, and openness to immigration provided a climate of hope and perpetual optimism. The American breed of Protestantism espoused a link between success in this world and success in the next world. Later, when the factory replaced the farm as the center of livelihood, however, the Protestant work ethic, laissez-faire economic ideas, and capitalism culminated in a pattern of worker exploitation not unlike that found on the European continent.

An outgrowth of the turmoil engendered by the Industrial Revolution in England, the Poor Law of 1834 was a set-back for humanitarianism. Still, because of its significance, the nineteenth century Poor Law can be regarded as the second landmark in social welfare history. The system of providing aid now was centralized for the first time and was made increasingly harsh. Fortunately, an active reform movement helped expose and temper the worst abuses. Several decades later, in the United States, out of the human and environmental wreckage of the Civil War, newly freed slaves struggled to live on broken promises. As economic growth, associated with the accumulation of capital, made it possible to meet pressing current needs, social values changed and required solutions to widespread problems. Forerunners of professionalized social workers, the Charity Organization Societies' friendly visitors and settlement house workers helped poor women in an attempt to motivate them toward better ways of living. Two new forms of social protection — social insurance and employer liability programs — emerged to offer public relief.

Often regarded as the third great landmark in U.S. social welfare history, the Social Security Act of 1935, was an outgrowth of the Great Depression in the 1930s. The question that needs to be addressed is this: given the popularity of the laissez-faire philosophy, how did significant governmental intervention succeed? The magnitude of the economic crisis, the precedent set by relief to

Civil War veterans, and the influence of non-Anglo Saxon immigrants united to undercut the individualistic motif. In any case, through decisive political action, the formation of an angry, unified working class which might have presented a real challenge to the capitalist order, was aborted. The New Deal, of which the Social Security Act was a part, was an attempt to meet head on the challenges of massive unemployment, poverty, and an immobilized economy. In the process, the role of the government in social welfare essentially was transformed: relief giving became a function of the public rather than the private sector.

The year 1935 marks the emergence of the American welfare state. The Social Security Act was not the beginning of a process of welfare state growth, however. It was for a long time the high point, as Piven and Cloward (1993) suggest. While in western Europe, welfare programs expanded after World War II, on this side of the Atlantic many of the most progressive programs were allowed to languish. An expanding economy, resistance of southern democrats advocating states' rights, and organized labor that looked to employers rather than the government for protective measures, shaped the course of what is often termed "the reluctant welfare state."

A second war on poverty was launched in the 1960s during a period of ideological shift spurred by the Civil Rights movement. Successful programs such as Head Start, Medicare, and Medicaid sprang out to the fervor of the 1965–1975 decade. Curiously absent were guaranteed income payments and universal health care. The rhetoric of political mobilization was uplifting, however. Today, the optimism is gone. The rhetoric is, in a word, angry: The trend has gone from getting the government to end poverty to "getting government off the backs of people," and from a war on poverty to a war on welfare. Global economic development is associated with alienation and the accumulation of wealth at one level of society, and much human misery at the other. A significant growth in the so-called underclass has put immense pressure on the welfare state. This issue will be developed further in the following chapter on poverty.

REVIEW QUESTIONS

1. Discuss similarities among the major religions of the world consistent with caring for the disadvantaged.
2. Review the history of the founding of Hinduism, Buddhism, Judaism, Christianity, and Islam.

3. Trace the basic forces which were responsible for unraveling feudalism in England.
4. What was the impact of a money economy on the social structure of the society?
5. Describe the origins of the Black Death and its impact on the labor situation. Relate the concept, displaced aggression, introduced in chapter 1 to people's behavior following the bubonic plague in the 1300s.
6. How did Martin Luther's split with his church's practices come to have such impact in England?
7. Relate Luther's teaching to the work ethic.
8. List the principal provisions of the Elizabethan Poor Law. How did it come about? What is the historical significance?
9. Discuss the British Industrial Revolution using concepts from systems theory.
10. Discuss poet Blake's concept of the "dark Satanic mills."
11. How does Charles Dickens satirize the capitalists of the day?
12. Summarize the thesis of Malthus' *Essay on Population*.
13. Compare the New Poor Law with its predecessor. What is the principle of less eligibility? Is that principle still with us today?
14. Discuss how British humanitarianism had a modifying effect on the harshness of the nineteenth century laws. How did the United States' social climate differ?
15. Describe the culture brought by the early European settlers to the so-called New World.
16. How were the "deserving" and the "non-deserving poor" treated in colonial America?
17. Briefly summarize Max Weber's thesis in *The Protestant Ethic and the Spirit of Capitalism*.
18. Discuss factors in the perpetuation of slavery and of its demise. Describe the form that mutual aid took among African Americans in the South.
19. What was the role of the churches in providing informal care?
20. Explain the meaning of this statement: the Civil War laid the groundwork for the United States ultimately to become a welfare state. Include the Freedmen's Bureau in your discussion.
21. Describe European welfare programs at the turn of the century.
22. Recount how industrialization transformed the American landscape.
23. Compare and contrast social Darwinism and Christian charity. How did these two forces ultimately move in the same direction.
24. Trace the history of the COS. Compare the philosophy and work of the COS and settlement home workers.
25. In box 3.1, what are the author's reservations about the course of development? What is sustainable development?
26. Describe the economic and social situation that existed in 1933 when Franklin Roosevelt assumed the presidency.
27. What were the highlights of the New Deal legislation? What is the significance of the Social Security Act of 1935? What are the deficiencies?

156

PART 1: SOCIAL WELFARE FUNCTIONS AND STRUCTURE

28. Describe how welfare helped change the life of the African American college professor who tells her story in box 3.2.
29. Describe the climate of social change that the sixties represents. What was the Great Society and what were the results?
30. Summarize the Kaplans' arguments concerning the American values. What are some possible explanations for shifts in attributes over time?

REFERENCES

Abercrombie, N., S. Hill, and B. Turner. (1988). *The Penguin Dictionary of Sociology.* London: Penguin.

Baldwin, H. and B. R. Larson. (1986). *The Developing World.* Washington, DC: The World Bank.

Barker, R. (1995). *Social Work Dictionary*, 3d ed. Washington, DC: NASW Press.

Blake, W. (1960/1808). *The New Jerusalem.* In A. Swallow, ed. *The Rinehart Book of Verse.* New York: Holt, Rinehart and Winston: 174.

Bodley, J. (1994). The Price of Progress. In A. Podolefsky and P. Brown, eds. *Applying Anthropology*, 3d ed. (329–337). Mountain View, CA: Mayfield.

Brun-Gulbransen, S. (1986). Drinking Habits in Norway. In D. J. Skog and R. Waahlberg, eds. *Alcohol and Drugs: The Norwegian Experience.* Oslo, Norway: National Directorate for Prevention of Alcohol and Drug Problems.

Bryson, L. (1992). *Welfare and the State: Who Benefits?* New York: St. Martin's Press.

Carr, B. (1987). Developmental Education in an Ethical/Humanistic Framework. In C. Joy and W. Kniep, eds. *The International Development Crisis & American Education: Challenges, Opportunities, and Instructional Strategies.* New York: The American Forum.

Clark, K. (1969). *Civilization.* New York: Harper and Row.

Darwin, C. (1859). *The Origin of Species.* London: Murray.

Day, P. (1989). *A New History of Social Welfare.* Englewood Cliffs, NJ: Prentice Hall.

Dickens, C. (1941/1838). *Oliver Twist.* New York: Dodd, Mead and Co.

_____. (1976/1843). A Christmas Carol. In *A Charles Dickens Christmas.* New York: Oxford University Press.

Dolgoff, R., D. Feldstein, and L. Skolnik. (1993). *Understanding Social Welfare.* New York: Longman.

Ehrenreich, J. (1985). *The Altruistic Imagination: A History of Social Work and Social Policy in the U.S.* Ithaca, N.Y.: Cornell University Press.

Encyclopaedia Britannica (1993). Social Welfare. *The New Encyclpaedia Britannica* (27: 372–392). Chicago: University of Chicago Press.

Federico, R. (1990). *Social Welfare in Today's World*. New York: McGraw Hill.

Fellows, W. (1979). *Religions East and West*. New York: Holt, Rinehart and Winston.

Friedlander, W. and R. Apte. (1974). *Introduction to Social Welfare*. Englewood Cliffs, NJ: Prentice Hall.

Guest, D. (1988). Social Security. *Canadian Encyclopedia* 3: 2032–2034). Edmonton, Canada: Hurtig Publications.

IIED-Earthscan. Our Common Future: A Reader's Guide. Washington, DC: IIED-Earthscan.

Jansson, B. (1993). *The Reluctant Welfare State: A History of American Social Welfare Policies*. Pacific Grove, CA: Brooks/Cole.

Johnson, H. (1995). Historical Development. In H. Johnson, et al. *The Social Services: An Introduction* (3–10). Itasca, IL: F.E. Peacock.

Kaplan, C. and L. Kaplan. (1993). Public Opinion and the "Economic Bill of Rights." *Journal of Progressive Human Services* 4(1): 43–58.

Karger, H. and D. Stoesz. (1990). *American Social Welfare Policy: A Structural Approach*. New York: Longman.

Kinney, J. and G. Leaton. (1991). *Loosening the Grip*. St. Louis: Mosby.

Landon, J. (1986). *The Development of Social Welfare*. New York: Human Services Press.

Lender, M. and J. Martin. (1982). *Drinking in America: A History*. New York: Hemisphere.

Levin, J.D. (1990). *Alcoholism: A Bio-Psycho-Social Approach*. New York: Hemisphere.

Malthus, T. (1914/1789). *Essay on Population* II London: J.M. Dent.

McGowan, P. (1987). Key Concepts for Developmental Studies. In C. Joy and W. Kniep, eds. *The International Development Crisis & American Education: Challenges, Opportunities, and Instructional Strategies*. New York: The American Forum.

Midgley, J. (1988). Inequality, The Third World and Development. *The International Journal of Contemporary Sociology* 25: 3–4.

More, T. (1949/1516). *Utopia*. New York: Appleton-Century-Crofts.

Moses, J. (1989). *Oneness: Great Principles Shared by All Religions*. New York: Fawcett Columbine.

Moynihan, D. (1993, summer). Iatrogenic Government: Social Policy and Drug Research. *American Scholar*: 351–363.

NAFTA Fails to Deliver Jobs Boom in Mexico. (1994, December 18). *The Bellingham Herald*: D9.

Nevins, A. and S. Commager. (1981). *A Pocket History of the United States,* 7th ed. New York: Simon and Schuster.

Olsen, T. (1994, January 3). The Thirties: A Vision of Fear and Hope. *Newsweek,* 26–27.

Parshall, G. (1991). Life after the Plague. *U.S. News and World Report* 110(15): 56–58.

Piven, F. (1995). Poorhouse Politics. *The Progressive* 59(2): 22–24.

Piven, F. and R. Cloward. (1993). *Regulating the Poor: The Functions of Public Welfare,* 2d ed. New York: Vintage Books.

Popple, P. and L. Leigninger. (1993). *Social Work, Social Welfare, and American Society,* 2d ed. Boston: Allyn and Bacon.

Rose, N. (1990). From WPA to Workfare: It's Time for a Truly Progressive Government Work Program. *Journal of Progressive Human Services* (2): 17–42.

Smith, A. (1937/1776). *The Wealth of Nations.* New York: Modern Library.

Society for International Development-U.S.A. Chapters Center. (SID-U.S.A.). Washington, DC.

Trattner, W. (1994). *From Poor Law to Welfare State: A History of Social Welfare in America,* 5th ed. New York: The Free Press.

van Wormer, K. (1995). *Alcoholism Treatment: A Social Work Perspective.* Chicago: Nelson-Hall.

Weber, M. (1911). *Gesammelte Aufsaetze zur Soziologie und Sozialpolitik.* Tubinge, Germany: J.C.B. Mohr.

Weber, M. (1958/1930). *The Protestant Ethic and the Spirit of Capitalism.* New York: Charles Scibner's Sons.

West, C. (1994, January 3). The '80s: Market Culture Run Amok. *Newsweek*: 48–49.

Wills, G. (1994, January 3). The Sixties: Tornado of Wrath. *Newsweek*: 26–27.

Woods, A. (1989). *Development and the National Interest: U.S. Economic Assistance into the Twenty-first Century.* Washington, DC: U.S. Agency for International Development (AID).

4

HISTORICAL FOUNDATIONS OF SOCIAL WORK

God grant me the Serenity
To accept the things I cannot change,
Courage to change the things I can,
And the wisdom to know the difference.
    —Reinhold Niebur, 1934

The social work profession the world over is concerned with the devastating effects of poverty, hunger, illness, homelessness, inequality, injustice, and violence (Burt, 1994). The globalization of the economy and society affects social work practice in every nation. Just as the nations of the Northern Hemisphere have dominated free market economics and the diffusion of technologies, social work practice knowledge has pursued a similar course with knowledge flowing in one direction—from north to south. From the global perspective a fact that has so often been overlooked is that social workers in industrialized nations, where there increasingly are problems of poverty and homelessness, have much to learn from social workers in countries who have been facing myriad human and social ills for some time.

In recognition of the need for the mutual exchange of knowledge, the Council on Social Work Education (CSWE) has issued the following curriculum policy statement: "Effective social work education programs recognize the interdependence of nations and the need for worldwide professional cooperation" (CSWE,

159

1994). The National Association of Social Workers (NASW), similarly, has joined the alliance for a global community to launch a drive to promote greater awareness of world events and of their importance to Americans (*NASW News*, 1994). The recognition of the need to internationalize social work programs, nevertheless, has been slow in coming and in many places amounts to more talk than action.

Before presenting the case for an international focus in social work education as an imperative for the twenty-first century, this chapter will chronicle the emergence of social work in the United States. As a profession whose roots are planted in the informal and formal responses to human misery in England and North America, and as a profession which was both shaped by historical movements and helped to fashion them, social work has managed to survive by blending with the times. This remains no less true now than formerly and no less true in other parts of the world than in the West. Taking a comparative view, this chapter will provide information about social work training and practice in Iran, India, Japan, Uganda, and Norway as well as in North America and the United Kingdom. Information will also be provided on various collaborative efforts among teaching institutions internationally.

SOCIAL WORK AND PARADIGM SHIFTS

Social work in the United States began in the 1890s in response to problems caused by industrialization and its corollary, urbanization. An outgrowth of the charities and corrections movements, social work practice has been greatly influenced by the development of the social welfare system. Whereas technological advances have often outpaced our ethical and political understanding of how to cope with them, social workers and their antecedents have been key mediators between societal forces and the people they serve. Social workers, in other words, have helped those caught in the grip of rapid social change adjust to new circumstances. As society's "great humanizers," social workers alternately have been accused of overidentifying with the poor and of "being co-opted" by the system. This apparent dualism, between individual and society and between inner and outer directedness, in fact, is as old as social policy and, of course, far older than its professional link, social work. This dualism has haunted the profession since well before it even could be considered a profession.

Let us digress for a moment to differentiate between personal troubles and public issues and then examine the connection between them. Sociologist C. Wright Mills (1959) introduced a distinction between "the personal troubles of milieu" and "the public issues of social structure." A *trouble* is a private matter according to Mills. In contrast, an *issue* is a public matter or something beyond the control of the individual. The significance from the social work standpoint is that structural problems, such as poor employment conditions, are generally experienced as private troubles. By the same token, a surfeit of private troubles creates the climate for public discourse. The personal thus becomes political, and the political becomes personal. Any attempt to separate the two is relatively futile.

In their work as professional change agents, social workers have rarely pursued the relationship between individual change and social change. While some have focused their energies on changing individuals to fit the system, others have focused on changing society. To put this another way, the slogan "change yourself, change the world"—the individualistic view—can be juxtaposed with, "change the world, change yourself"—the social psychological perspective. Although there is truth in both slogans, each by itself is incomplete. Each fails to capture the whole picture.

The social/self dualism mentioned earlier is characteristic of social welfare history. Ehrenreich (1985) describes this history as one long series of pendulum swings between two opposite poles with the focus of individual diagnosis at one end and the focus of social reform at the other. Although both of these currents have run simultaneously throughout the last century, one side or the other typically has tended to dominate at any one time. One generation's certainty has become the next generation's foolishness and blindness, to use Ehrenreich's apt phraseology. Or to continue with the metaphor, we might say that gravity invariably pulls the pendulum downward toward the other direction. A community action emphasis, for instance, characterized the Progressive Era before World War I, the 1930s, and the 1960s. The foremother of social work, Jane Addams, is associated with the social reforms of the Progressive Era; social worker Harry Hopkins helped initiate the New Deal and the creation of the modern welfare state; and the idealistic war on poverty offered a bonanza in jobs for community action workers.

And then there were those in-between years when individualism triumphed. The private interest of the hedonistic 1920s, the political hysteria and anti-idealism of the 1950s, and the attack-the-underdog mentality of the Reagan era were all manifestations of ideological shifts away from the social activism of the previous age.

Franklin (1990) offers a cyclical framework to the emergence of three social work methods of practice—social casework, group work, and community organization. The origin of each method is linked, curiously, to the prevailing ideology of a specific political cycle in U.S. history, as Franklin's framework suggests. We could almost say, taking a literal meaning of the term, that each dominant practice modality was "politically correct" in its day. Whether society's focus was more on personal troubles, on public issues, or somewhere in-between, the priorities of social work and the methods of treatment have followed. In this chapter we will view the paradigm shifts as social work has oscillated between opposite ends of the political pendulum in response to the ideological and socio-economic influences of the times.

THE ORIGINS OF THE PROFESSION

Two social movements in social welfare that began at the end of the nineteenth century shaped the development of the profession of social work: the Charity Organization Societies (COS) and the settlement house establishments. Both movements were based largely on English models and tradition, as we saw in chapter 3. Patronage, piety, poor laws, and philanthropy: these are the four Ps singled out by Specht and Courtney (1994) in their incisive book, *Unfaithful Angels: How Social Work Has Abandoned Its Mission.* The four Ps are different arrangements for dealing with social problems that developed after the breakup of feudal society but which preceded the modern period. Patronage, an ancient custom still extant today, entails an independent system for boosting some members of the population (often minorities) into prominence. Political patronage for a particular ethnic group (e.g., the Irish immigrants in Boston) and social worker advocacy on behalf of the poor are two obvious examples. Piety, a term used to refer to the religious aspect of serving needy people, is another historically derived aspect of social work. Throughout history, thousands of church organizations have provided such help. The values of the Poor Laws are reflected in the middle-class morality that regulates the poor and their receipt of government aid. Programs for the poor, as Specht and Courtney cleverly put it, are both "means tested and mean spirited," and most are deliberately made unattractive. Private philanthropies frequently served as a desirable alternative to public relief. "Alms for the poor" in its present form is represented in help provided by the private/voluntary sector; this includes support ranging from United Way agencies to employee assistance programs.

Charities and Corrections Movement

Claiming that individual failure was the reason for poverty was the underlying rationale of the Charity Organization Society which was founded in London in 1869. The COS quickly moved to numerous American communities beginning with Buffalo, New York. Central to its approach was the idea of organizing and coordinating relief-giving units, developing a control register of the needy, and using friendly visitors as volunteers to visit applicants for help (Johnson, 1995).

The decades from 1877 to World War I were a time of deep economic, social, and political crisis. Consistent with the ethos of the age, a scientific solution was directed to both the protection of the poor from starvation and a validation of the work incentive. Ehrenreich (1985) refers to three organizing principles of the operation of the COS: the use of business methods in controlling the flow of allocations, the perpetual focus on the moral status of the clients (were they deserving of aid?), and the key role of the friendly visitor or caring helper and mentor. As these often upper-class charity workers grew immersed in the world of the poor, a curious but predictable thing happened to them—they began to recoil at the paternalism and victim blaming inherent in the social system and to see poverty as a cause as well as a result of certain forms of social behavior (Ehrenriech, 1985; Franklin, 1990).

Mary Richmond, later renowned for establishing the principles of social work education, began her career with the COS of Baltimore in 1888. Unlike other founders of the profession, Richmond was not a member of privileged classes; she was entirely self educated, in fact. Although she did not intend it, Richmond's individualistic, casework focus helped prepare the profession for its later embrace of psychiatry, psychoanalysis, and psychotherapy (Specht and Courtney, 1994). Nevertheless, Richmond's keen attention to the individual as a part of a social unit and her advocacy of understanding the person-in-the-situation is surprisingly consistent with modern multifocused formulations.

Richmond's ideas were set forth in *Social Diagnosis* (1917), the first major textbook to be used by practicing social workers. The psychosocial conceptualization of human behavior introduced in this work might have come to fruition in the years that followed with the usual revision and reformulation of new theoretical paradigms had it not been for the influence of something even more magnificent—the voluminous works on the unconscious by Sigmund Freud.

In the meantime, as the COS began to develop a relevant knowledge base and to formalize techniques of social service and delivery, the casework model of practice was born. With this well formulated model, the way was paved for the emergence of a new profession. Emphasizing personal attention and individual work with clients, the casework method gained preeminence in conjunction with social work's transition from a voluntary to a paid enterprise. The inevitable tendency of scientific charity, with its emphasis on the objective and factual, was to make the use of volunteer visitors, untrained and part time, increasingly difficult to justify (Trattner, 1994).

The first social worker became employed in Europe in 1895. A trained COS worker, Mary Stewart was hired to interview patients at the Royal Free Hospital in London. Her major role was to determine whether or not patients qualified for free treatment at the clinic (Amundsen, 1994). By the turn of the century, the organized charities were establishing formal training as the first step in professionalization. Volunteers now were being placed under the authority of social workers who shaped policy and covered the field. The professional charity workers, not the volunteers, began to be acknowledged authorities on the needs of disadvantaged and/or deviant people (Day, 1997). As mentioned earlier, social work derived from two movements, each with a very different ideological base. Whereas the individualistic casework method had come to prominence later when the emphasis on personality superseded the social action thrust, the community oriented focus never had been entirely absent from the profession bent on "helping others help themselves." Nor is it entirely absent today.

The Settlement House Movement

The belief that poverty perhaps could be eliminated was a theme of the liberal Progressive Era. The settlement house movement, as we have seen in chapter 3, began in England in the late 1800s with the establishment of Toynbee Hall. In contrast to their friendly visitor counterparts, settlement house workers regarded themselves as social reformers rather than charity workers. With their goal to bridge the gap between classes and their emphasis on prevention rather than treatment, these workers lived side by side their urban neighbors and worked together with them to improve social conditions. In actively participating in the life of the neighborhood and of their poor and immigrant clients (in the United States), these upper- and upper-middle-class young men and women (mainly women) sought to raise the cultural, moral, and intellectual level of the community. The settlements provided a day nursery for working mothers, health clinics, and classes in dance, drama, art, and sewing. Gradually, as a result of their intimate knowledge of their charges, the settlement workers became politicized and pursued social reform through legislation and social policy change. These reformers helped bring about changes in child labor laws, in women's labor laws, and in the institutional care of the disabled and the "feeble minded" (Johnson and Schwartz, 1994). The establishment of child welfare services and juvenile courts, likewise, had its inception here. Rather than looking down upon the poor or seeking to impose their way of life upon them, settlement workers geared their efforts toward the needs and desires of those with whom they were working (Trattner, 1994). As Jane Addams stated in her autobiography (1910: 167).

> We early found ourselves spending many hours in efforts to secure support for deserted women, insurance for bewildered widows, damages for injured operators, furniture from the clutches of the installment store. The settlement . . . constantly acts between the various institutions of the city and the people for whose benefit these institutions were erected.

A question not addressed in the autobiography is how did the settlement movement respond to the needs of blacks who were just beginning to migrate into the northern cities during the Progressive Era? Trattner contrasts attitudes of the COS workers who stressed the individual moral causes of poverty and were largely indifferent to the problems of destitute blacks, with settlement house workers who advocated the unpopular cause of equality for all Americans. Long before it was in vogue to do so, at least some settlement house workers helped foster black pride and Afro-American culture, according to Trattner. To their credit, settlement leaders actively participated in the creation of the National

Association for the Advancement of Colored People (NAACP) and the National Urban League. Yet consistent with the social climate of the day, while they opposed racism these leaders did not advocate integration (Philpott, 1978). Realists as well as idealists, these women, such as Jane Addams and Mary McDowell, knew that neighborhood prejudices militated against the mixing of blacks and whites in settlement houses.

After 1900, according to Philpott, the settlements for "colored people" never had the capacity to provide black Chicago with adequate, much less equal, service. On the other hand, the nation's settlement houses were largely segregated, with many in the South reserved for blacks only created and staffed by African American women. In Chicago, according to Trattner, the Frederick Douglass Center had workshops and clubrooms for boys, and held classes in manual training for boys and domestic service for girls to prepare black youths for the only jobs open to them in that day. Philpott (1978), in his interpretation of history, however, is less charitable. His documentation, drawn from historical records of the day, suggests that the Douglass Center's true purpose was not to help the poor blacks but to attract the black elite and to insulate them from the less educated blacks who were pouring into "the black belt" in large numbers. The Emmanuel Settlement, founded and directed by Fannie Emmanuel, a dedicated African American, operated under a different philosophy. Fostering neighborhood pride, this center was a place where a person could get relief, relief both in a monetary and emotional sense. With little or no financial support from whites, however, the settlement closed in less than five years.

Portrait of Jane Addams

By the turn of the century, as Specht and Courtney (1994) indicate, Jane Addams was the most famous woman in America. By the culmination of her career in 1931, she was awarded the Nobel Prize for her efforts for peace during World War I. But who was Jane Addams really?

Although recounting some facts from her early life, Addams' autobiography *Twenty Years at Hull House* reveals very little personal detail about the author. The qualities that do shine forth are an abiding concern for the underdog, optimism, perseverance, and feisty leadership. Her fondness for her father, a devout Quaker to whom the book is dedicated, clearly set the stage for Addams' unpopular pacifism during World War I—a position which branded her a subversive and radical for the rest of her life. Jane Addams was to be given the dubious honor of first being made a life member of the Daughters of the American Revolution and then subsequently being expelled.

Works on Quaker history include Jane Addams and others associated with the settlement movement as Quakers by upbringing. As described in *The Story of Quaker Women in America* (Bacon 1986: 147): "Jane Addams herself was the daughter of self-styled Hicksite John Addams, whom she adored. Although never a member of a Quaker meeting, she maintained close ties with Quakers throughout her life." Addams, in fact, was sent as a representative of the Society of Friends to distribute aid following the human wreckage of World War I.

Feminist and lesbian sources, too, proudly claim Addams as one of their own. Faderman (1991) includes Addams among those whose love for women was at least in part a search for allies to help wage the battle against women's social impoverishment. Changing the lives of the poor, these women themselves were changed by their confrontation with the cruel realities from which they otherwise would have been sheltered. Ellen Starr, the close friend with whom Addams cofounded the Hull House, was Addams' first serious attachment according to Faderman. Her devoted companion throughout most of her life, however, was Mary Rozet Smith. Most historians and social work scholars, nevertheless, have preferred to present Addams as one who never knew love. In 1985, the silence was broken when the editors of *Lesbian and Gay Issues: A Resource Manual for Social Workers* (Hidalgo et al., 1984) dedicated their work to Jane Addams. Their dedication said in part:

> This great woman-identified woman led social work in its obligations to counteract oppression and injustice with liberation and empowerment. For too long, the profession has acclaimed her leadership as a social change agent while denying that her lesbian identification existed as a major influence in her life, her work, and her understanding of oppression.

Barring definitive evidence, however, the extent of Addams' lesbian identification cannot be known. The pairing off of unmarried women did not raise comment in her day.

PART 1: SOCIAL WELFARE FUNCTIONS AND STRUCTURE

A Profession: Social Work

Less interesting perhaps, but of more significance to the development of the social work profession was the training furnished to the friendly visitors and resident workers of the COS and settlement houses—respectively, the two precursors of social work. At first, the training consisted mainly of apprenticeship. Then, in addition to teaching on the job, agencies began to use more formal training which consisted of lectures, reading, and discussion (Johnson and Schwartz, 1994). Participation at the annual National Conference of Charities and Corrections drew together all those concerned with social welfare issues. Although their reform efforts were major, and considered radical by the standards of the day (for example, they rallied for a forty hour work week), the charities and corrections people were ruled by a fierce Victorian morality. Perhaps facetiously or to give a flavor of the times, Specht and Courtney (1994: 73) quote from the pages of the *Proceedings of the Conference of Charities and Corrections of 1914* on the unsalutary influences of the candy store:

> During the cooler evenings of the spring, fall, and winter, both sexes, little boys and little girls, gather in these centers which sometimes keep open as late as the saloon. In the pool room we have only young men, in the saloon men, but in the candy store and other like centers, where children gather, we allow both sexes to associate without any supervision of the places which harbor them. . . .
>
> The things sold in the store which the children eat are frequently injurious to health. The study of some two hundred children, largely newsboys, showed that nearly one-third had chronic indigestion. . . .
>
> Irregular eating, and eating of harmful food and sweets, means that by the time our children have reached the age of twenty-five to thirty they will be wrecked physically. Digestive organs are injured beyond repair. Again the candy store promotes physical inactivity—sitting, which means that the muscles and organs of the body cannot be normally developed.
>
> The candy store develops habits of thriftlessness and a desire to spend money for foolish, worthless things.

These passages provide a flavor of the concerns of the times. They confirm how each generation tries to guard the morals of youth from modern sources of corruption. The passages also say more about the attendees of the Conference of Charities and Correction—their fear of idleness and sex and self-indulgence—than about the children themselves.

Earlier, toward the end of the nineteenth century, Mary Richmond presented a paper titled "The Need for Training Schools in Applied Philanthropy." The impact of this presentation was considerable because it paved the way for the founding of formal social work education. In 1898, a professional summer course was sponsored by the Charity Organization Society of New York. This led, in 1904, to a one year graduate program of what was to become the first American School of Social Work at Columbia University. In the United Kingdom, at about the same time, lectures and practical training were provided at the Women's University Settlement in London. Parallel developments took place in Germany as well. But the credit for establishing the first clearly defined school of social work goes to a group of social reformers in the Netherlands (Hokenstad and Kendall, 1995). According to Lorenz (1994) the first school of social work was founded in Amsterdam in 1896, and owed its existence to philanthropy and the international settlement movement.

A basic principle known in the sociology of professional development is that every occupation striving to gain recognition as a profession is in search of a solid, theoretical foundation. In the period before World War I, social work's knowledge base was derived largely from sociology, a social science geared toward the understanding of poverty and the need for community-based social care. Drawing on scientific surveys, sociology showed that persistent poverty in society was not primarily the result of personal failings but of systematic structural inequality. Yet social work practice still remained focused on individuals, generating a search for theories that primarily explained interpersonal processes.

The term *social work* was used for the first time, according to Lorenz (1994), in Germany (*Sozial Arbeit*) and in the American settlement movement. The use of the term attests to the social nature of the profession, and is consistent with the occupation's historical origins. In his historic address to the National Conference of Charities and Correction in 1915, Abraham Flexner, M.D., uttered a stinging rebuke to the social work occupation much to the disappointment of his audience. Social work he declared, unlike law and medicine, could not claim to be a profession. The field lacked a systematic body of knowledge and theory, and autonomy as social workers merely assisted the real professionals as auxiliary staff. Although this historic commentary could have been regarded as a male attacking a female-dominated profession using criteria of the male model of achievement, the listeners buckled under. They would acquire professional status somehow. The social workers were determined to get the recognition due them.

THE FREUDIAN INFLUENCE AND GROWTH OF CASEWORK

The lifeline thrown to a fledgling profession came in the form of psychoanalytic theory, the teachings of which began to disseminate among U.S. social work educators after Freud's historic visit to Clark University in 1912. However, according to Lorenz (1994), the wholesale adoption of these theories in the United States and in Britain still would have failed to satisfy the criteria set forth by Flexner. For one thing, the principles were borrowed from another discipline and offered little in the way of practical guidelines for everyday social work practice. Yet, as Specht and Courtney (1994) point out, the ascendancy of psychiatric and psychoanalytic theory had important treatment implications which would be recognized later when many soldiers returned severely traumatized from World War I. For treatment of the mentally ill, these theories also would hold some practical value.

Never immune to society's fickleness and trepidations and still chafing under Flexner's earlier provocative rebuke, social work was ready to move in a new direction. Logically and inexorably, the field turned inward toward the psychiatric realm. It was as if the theory of psychoanalysis could somehow simultaneously provide the promise of professionalism and respectability. So in no time the talent and creativity from the field were concentrated into what would become the prestigious specialization of psychiatric social work. Ultimately (but not before still another major paradigm shift during the Great Depression), the significance of the adoption of the Freudian paradigm was in that it paved the way for social workers to reinvent themselves in the form of psychotherapists.

The liberal political climate disappeared almost overnight when, under the presidency of Woodrow Wilson, the United States entered World War I. This was when settlement house leaders fell out of favor with the public sentiment because of their active opposition to the military buildup and ensuing aggression. Other factors also reinforced the reactionary drift of the country. The victory of bolshevism in Russia, which culminated in the Red Scare of 1919–1920, put a taint on all community-type collective activity. As public suspicion and distrust grew, the settlement houses suffered considerably (Trattner, 1994). Financial support was withdrawn, and people began to look elsewhere to solve social problems. Social reform became now equated with radicalism, and radicalism was considered dangerous.

As the war ended, women also lost much of the independence they had acquired. As Macht and Ashford (1990) indicate, women who had assumed traditional male work roles to help the war effort, now were pressed to surrender their well-paying jobs to the returning men, and to go back to work in the home or in unskilled work such as domestic service. Identifying women as the weaker sex, Freudian theory provided a rationale to justify a return to the status quo at a time when women, having had a taste of power, might otherwise have been inclined to want to keep it (women were given the right to vote but very little else.)

Then there was the matter of racism. As the middle classes and socially mobile immigrants moved out of the central city into the suburbs, new people moved in—Puerto Ricans, Mexicans, and African Americans replaced the Europeans of an earlier day. Less public sympathy was generated toward these darker-skinned residents; assimilation was less an option for them than for their predecessors, in any case.

With the settlement house philosophy demoted in the public eye, Mary Richmond was catapulted to leadership within the profession. In 1922 she "clarified" the social casework method to bring it more in line with the personality focus which was rapidly gaining currency. The psychosocial view of human behavior was replaced by a more narrow perspective, but one which was as exciting as it was revolutionary. In her autobiography, Bertha Reynolds (1963: 58–59) uniquely captures the thrill of her own education into the mysteries of the human mind and beyond:

> We learned about the working of the subconscious, and many things in everyday life became clear to us. We saw fears displaced from childhood, jealousy displaced from other persons, hostility disguised as solicitude, desire as fear, and wish as certainty. We watched each other's slips of the tongue with glee and lived in a world where nothing was quite as it seemed and was frequently the opposite. We learned that the normal could best be understood through study of the abnormal, just because, in states of disease, inhibitions are lost and the workings of the mental mechanism can be seen, as are the works of a clock when its back is removed. No wonder we felt that we had been fooled by appearances all our lives and that we now had the key to wisdom in human relations.

But alas, no sooner had the discovery of the unconscious rewritten our understanding of human behavior, a national economic calamity struck. A fascination with probing the unconscious gave way to more immediate concerns.

THE NEW DEAL ERA AND THE EMERGENCE OF GROUP WORK

The Great Depression had a radicalizing effect on the nation's conscience and on the social work profession as well. During a time of disillusionment and despair with the capitalist system, caseworkers grew critical of the narrow Freudian focus. The growing prevalence of poverty made it difficult to lay the blame on individual weakness. Nevertheless, many professionals, in the words of Specht and Courtney (1994), continued "to worship at the altar of" psychoanalysis. Later these same devotees would emerge at the forefront of social work education and train students for work in the private sector. In the 1930s, however, the government, not the profession, called the shots. Due to the massive programming introduced "to get America moving again," the demand for social workers, especially trained social workers, increased exponentially. Under social legislation enacted under the New Deal, the administrators and planners drew heavily upon the knowledge, assistance, and heritage of social workers, and the profession assumed an unprecedented importance in American life (Trattner, 1994). So, as always, the focus of social work shifted in tandem with the exigencies and ideologies of the day, and caseworkers moved away from one-on-one counseling and probing of the mind, to client advocacy and intervention geared toward resource linkage (Macht and Ashford, 1990).

As new public welfare workers faced taxing working conditions, huge caseloads, crowded workplaces, and little job security, they looked toward social work unions and other activist groups for help (Popple and Leighninger, 1993). Despite the heightened awareness of the effectiveness of collective action during a period of social change, American social workers were torn between their image of professionalism and the desire to better working conditions through collective bargaining. In the depression era, according to Popple and Leighninger, mainstream social work chose to resolve the dilemma by endorsing the roles of "expert witness" and "consultant" to policy workers, rather than assuming a more adversarial stance. This resolution of a potentially volatile issue has never been seriously challenged. European social workers, in contrast, perceived no inherent conflict between unionization and professionalism and in many countries, in fact, the professional organization is the union.

On both the North American and European continent, the pendulum, which so recently had swung toward social action and government relief efforts, now has predictably gravitated toward the other direction. A growing national backlash against New Deal reforms and union strikes, along with the escalation of war in Europe and Asia, contributed not only to hostility against the labor movement in the early 1940s, but also to social work's renewed interest in the individual treatment aspects of the field (Popple and Leighninger, 1993). So social work was back to shaping the individual to fit the system instead of adjusting the system to help the individual, back to wrestling with private troubles over public issues.

The Emergence of Group Work

For all practical purposes then, the settlement house days were over. It was not so much that the settlements disintegrated, in fact, as that they evolved into new forms. The settlement houses evolved from group living centers to community recreational and youth club activities centers. Leisure time agencies such as the YMCA and Girl Scouts grew in number. *Group work*, a term coined in 1927 by a member of the faculty at Western Reserve University (now Case Western University), grew in stature and achieved recognition as a major social work activity. True, there had been a certain resistance to acceptance of the group process as an intrinsic part of social work earlier, a resistance that as Brieland (1990) explains, was due to the fact that group activities—offered for recreation, socialization, and character development—were disparaged as they required no professional training. But then, after World War II a new development enhanced the prestige of this social work specialty. Group work, as the astute reader might guess, actually borrowed a reconceptualization of Freudian thought to relate the basic principles (transference, defense mechanisms such as regression and repression, and so on) to the dynamics of group interaction. Then as professional training was required, this form of social work practice "came of age."

An Overview of Women's Leadership in the Profession, 1910–1955

Unique among the social sciences and most of the professions, the field of social work was created and given its shape and character by women. Or, in the words of Kendall (1989: 23):

> There were men in the field—even some good men—but women ran the show. Many, if not most, of the great deans of schools of social work in that period were women. Private agencies were run by women, even when they were headed by men . . .

The field of social work, as we have seen, emerged out of the work of charity organization societies and the engagement of the settlement movement in immigrant and working class neighborhoods. Of the top best-selling and most influential books in social work, six of eight were written by women (Chambers, 1986). While men outnumbered women in executive positions, according to Chambers, women dominated in supervisory roles.

The women's influence in Europe was especially strong. Lorenz (1994) recounts the history. As women were regarded by society as the natural and traditional embodiment of charity, most schools of social work founded by churches had a clearly defined "mission" for women within the organizations. Middle-class women entered social work as a means of carving out personally rewarding and socially acceptable occupations for themselves. The energetic pioneer of German social work, Alice Salomon, who had a Ph.D. in economics and was closely linked to the American settlement movement, was convinced that only women could create a culture of caring that would raise welfare services above a preoccupation with material concerns. To preserve women's preeminence in the field, Salomon reserved the schools of social work exclusively for women. Furthermore, the schools effectively resisted being accorded university status to resist absorption by male-dominated institutions. Although by far the largest number of women's schools of social work existed in Germany, a practice which continued until after the Second World War, other European countries also had separate social work schools for women. In Austria, France, Hungary, Italy, Norway, Portugal, Romania, and Switzerland, these women's schools represented the only social work training institutions. The underlying theme of the early female social work schools, according to Lorenz, was the commonly heard motto, "the personal is political." For the pioneers of social work education, the transfer of female nurturant qualities into professional attributes was a means of transforming society to being maternalistic rather than paternalistic or bureaucratic.

Examining events which led to an eventual male "takeover" of the profession in the United States, Jan Andrews (1990) argues that women not only led the profession in its early years but also continued to shape the course of social work until as late as 1955. Seeking an explanation of the shift toward male dominance in leadership positions in the field, Andrews conducted an extensive search through the social work archives. The four basic explanations gleaned from the literature are as follows: the decline of feminism after 1920 when women had won the right to vote; the decline in the settlement house community living experience which had provided a home and sense of mission for single women; reinforcement of women's family roles (under the influence of psychoanalytical thought); and the effects of major cataclysmic events such as the Great Depression and World War II which favored male over female wage earners and elevated war veterans to positions of prominence.

Perhaps for a combination of all these reasons, the unique partnership of "strong women and gentle men," which shaped the profession of social work during the formative periods, began to fragment when men emerged largely in command of agencies, graduate school education, public policy, and welfare administration (Chambers, 1986). The rapid and vast expansion of welfare bureaucracies and the emphasis on public accountability, cost effectiveness, and the like tended to favor having men in management positions and women in hands on positions.

European Influence

Rarely in the American literature is the European influence on the U.S. social work profession mentioned. The reader of American textbooks, therefore, is apt to be unfamiliar with the international sweep of knowledge or with the historical precedence of ideas. A kind of historical and cultural amnesia prevails. Sorokin (1956) deplored this amnesia by the "the new Columbuses" among American social scientists in his day. Yet knowledge, like the economy, reflects the global interconnectedness of human phenomena; ideas and methodologies are enriched cross-culturally. German social work educator (currently university lecturer in Cork, Ireland) Walter Lorenz (1994) presents a comprehensive evaluation of the profession today. The fact that the many divergent patterns in social work are intrinsically historical processes is a basic thesis of Lorenz's writing. Only by recognizing our historical contingency as social workers, writes Lorenz, can we begin to transcend and transform the field in the way that social movements transcend and transform national and European boundaries.

In his evaluation of the profession's unwitting service as pawns of the Nazi state, surely the grimmest episode in social work history, Lorenz reveals the repercussions on both sides of the Atlantic. Because of a climate of patriotism, tyranny, and lack of organized resistance to an immoral regime, social work ended up complying with the fascist, exclusionary policies of the Nazi period. In turn, the inevitable siege against the profession took the form of direct threats to its members and particularly to its educators. The large proportion of social workers who were Jewish or who had Jewish connections were forced to surrender their positions and flee the country. Many others were attacked and persecuted for their social democratic leanings. Through this enforced wave of emigration, American social work was considerably enriched. The work of Gisela Konopka, a political prisoner who escaped Germany and fled to the United States, provided a theoretical grounding for group work practice which enhanced its prestige and professional image. Under skilled leadership, the group could become a powerful mechanism for interpersonal growth and development; the therapeutic possibilities of the group process were unlimited. The new psychologically-oriented group approach was especially appealing to practitioners seeking to attract an expanding middle-class clientele (Franklin, 1990).

German and Scandinavian social work benefited from cross-fertilization as Konopka and many other visiting experts forged the link between European and American traditions. In Europe, as Lorenz indicates, social work had an important part to play in rebuilding societies devastated by war. Through imparting self-help skills and replacing fascist authoritarianism (and countering the communist variety) with egalitarian practices, American social work methods had high priority within foreign aid programs of the United States and the United Nations. The availability of American social work literature translated into several European languages enhanced the assimilation of American methods in social work education on the wider European horizon. The spirit of progress was infectious, and yet we must recognize as Lorenz argues, that the massive program of "re-education" provided to postwar Europe represented, in an ideological sense, a retreat from the social and worldly humanistic mission of social work.

PROFESSIONAL VULNERABILITY AND THE McCARTHY ERA

Social work, as we have seen throughout this chapter, cannot be understood apart from the dynamics of the larger society. To know the temper of the age is to know social work. As Bertha Reynolds (1963: 261) observed from personal bitter experience, "Adaptation to the climate of community opinion was, of course, as old as social work itself." Although social work values flow from the democratic principles on which Western society is based and share the beliefs of equality and independence, they are, like those of the larger society, often burdened with dilemmas and conflict (Weick and Vandiver, 1981). Between the reality and the ideal, and the politics and values, the tension at times can be overpowering. Inasmuch as social workers tend to work for the state either directly or indirectly (through funding) they have to answer to the state. Therefore, their helping roles, at times, may be circumscribed. Under Hitler, as we have seen, social work's vulnerability to political misuses was especially pronounced. Social work assessments, in fact, were used to separate out the unworthy and non-productive elements from society; this use of professionals trained in scientific methods helped justify the ultimate annihilation of large segments of the population. Social workers, in effect, were rendered accomplices to murder. First the state came for their clients; welfare workers failed to protest; and, in the end, the state came for them—the workers.

Social work's vulnerability to serving the interests of the state is evident in the extreme of Nazi Germany. In Khomeini's Iran, similarly, as we will see toward the end of the chapter, social workers and students of social work found it impossible to uphold their professional values under the severe duress of a reactionary social revolution. Under repressive regimes in Chile and South Africa, the vendetta against social workers has included political imprisonment. Although the magnitude of comparable events in the United States pales beside the horrors inflicted elsewhere, the ethical dilemma—how to maintain one's personal and professional integrity in an unfree society—is the same. We are talking here of that ultraconservative and almost paranoid period during the late 1940s and early 1950s when free speech was stymied under the banner of anticommunism, and the social work profession was effectively quashed.

The emphasis on security in a repressive and war-ready society perpetuated a climate of suspicion of all behavior outside of the mainstream. This hysterical climate was personified by Senator Joseph McCarthy who stood in the national limelight to ferret out Communists and "fellow travelers." In the melee that followed, thousands of teachers, social workers, journalists, and government workers lost their jobs for supporting unions or other liberal causes. The age—the 1950s—has since been characterized as the McCarthy era.

In the United States and Canada (where anticommunist campaigns were somewhat less public and extensive than in the United States), homosexuality became viewed as a national, social, and sexual danger. In right-wing, conservative, and even liberal discourse, gays and lesbians were associated with communism and spying for the U.S.S.R. due to their supposed targeting for blackmail (Kinsman, 1994). Homosexual vulnerability to compromise with Soviet agents was taken for granted even in the absence of evidence to back it up. Mass firings and transfers were carried out in the U.S. military and among the Canadian police, national defense units, and civil servants. The criminalization of homosexual behavior made the task in both countries that much easier than it would have been otherwise.

In the southern United States, the uncertainty and budding paranoia on the part of the power structure pertained to the issue of integration. Change was in the air and many southern whites feared that their society would be turned upside down as "separate but equal" was ruled to be unequal. Many white southerners claimed that states rights was the real issue and they suddenly became concerned with the importance of voter literacy. White and black integrationists were branded as red; since the emergent movement for civil rights was labeled as communist-inspired, an accusation that stuck well into the next decade.

Out of the political darkness and enforced silence of the McCarthy era, women were also suppressed. Freudian teachings about proper roles for women, which had been played down during the duration of the war when women were needed for industrial work, now resurfaced to send white women home and African American women back to their menial labor. Ambitious women "did not know their place" as it was said and they were not considered appropriately feminine. Female social workers, likewise, had to step aside for the sake of men who now became the majority of those who held doctorates in social work. Tracked into dead-end casework positions, women watched while men were groomed for agency administration and policy leadership (Brandwein, 1995).

Mass persecutions, witch-hunts, fallout shelters, air raids, the mandate for conformity in word, deed, and dress styles—all attributes of the 1950s—raise the difficult question of why these phenomena occurred at this time. Macht and Ashford (1990) provide a partial explanation: Despite the sense of prosperity and optimism, the 1950s also included a sense of insecurity. An ever-present possibility of war and an economic system undergoing major changes involving stepped-up specialization and routinization of work contributed to a generalized sense of uncertainty. The buildup of defense industry, labeled by President Eisenhower as "the military-industrial complex," was another probable factor in the growth of a repressive mentality. Then the propaganda machine, launched to perpetuate the war industry in the absence of a major war, helped stimulate a national hysteria. Whatever the reasons for the climate of intolerance that shook the nation in the 1950s, the important point is that everywhere critics of the government and of "the American way of life" were branded as public enemies and socially and professionally ostracized.

Even during this time of severe repression, however, there were internal challenges urging the social work profession to take a stand. These challenges, however, fell on deaf ears until the emergence of a completely new political experience of the turbulent 1960s (Franklin, 1990). In *Security Risk* (1986) Fisher, a progressive social worker, recalls how, labeled a risk to national security, he was discharged as a result of the Truman loyalty program, the purpose of which was to weed out radicals and dissenters from politically sensitive positions. In those times, in light of the political nature of their profession, social workers found themselves especially vulnerable. Refusing to stand together, they were "bumped off" one by one for signing petitions for peace, attending a radical meeting, or merely being so accused. Although most social workers suffered from the fallout of the climate of fear, the profession did little or nothing to protect them (Schreiber, 1995). The social work literature of the day does not mention the kinds of pressures people in public service were under. So while group work was evolving into group psychotherapy, social workers were playing it safe politically, and, sadly, a mood of quiescence prevailed. Many good people were sacrificed and had their high profiles suppressed never to be regained.

Bertha Reynolds

The flight from social reform and service to the poor could not proceed without uneasy words of warning from at least some quarters (Trattner, 1994). In any historic period in any country, there are always people who stray from the common mentality or, as in the words of Thomas Gray's *Elegy,* "far from the madding crowd." Bertha Reynolds (1963) was one of those people. Written from the perspective of her later years, Reynolds' autobiography recounts the closing of the prison gates around social work during the public hysteria that accompanied the Cold War period.

The impact on social work, according to Reynolds, was immediate and profound. While schooled in psychiatric social work and a major contributor to this approach, Reynolds was acutely conscious of the impact of economic and social conditions on her clients; politically, she was an acknowledged Marxist and union organizer. Her writings record in extraordinary detail events of the political scene when prominent radical figures, such as herself, found themselves jobless, shunned, and uninvited to professional meetings and conferences (Ehrenreich, 1985). Reynolds' memoir, *An Uncharted Journey,* provides an excellent resource for grasping the essence of a bygone era, a time which is often forgotten but of no small consequence. Events at the 1940 social workers' national conference are described by Reynolds (1963: 263) as follows:

> Our whole profession was jolted out of any complacency it may have had by the news from California that relief allowances had been cut to starvation levels and denied entirely unless clients would accept labor at starvation wages; that trained social workers in public assistance who protested were replaced by untrained political henchmen; that social workers even suspected of being members of the CIO union were fired. . . .

At the convention Reynolds, true to character, delivered a speech which addressed the issues of client rights and their rapid deterioration. In the years ahead, in fact, conditions were only to get that much worse. The growth of the social work profession was significantly affected by the demolition of social work unions, whose existence was a legacy of the leftist rank and file movement of the 1930s. While the discredited social work profession requested government help for their needy clients who were reduced to paupery, the mass media focused on accounts of clients who refused to work and on others who received special coddling from the welfare office. The attacks on public assistance in the press prepared the way for new stern "economic" measures against the sick, aged, and children in New York and elsewhere. Thus the intolerance in one area of life (for example of the poor) was matched by intolerance in another area (of the sick and the aged). In the impetus to restrict care of the nation's most vulnerable citizens, parallels between this period and the 1990s are as striking as the differences.

In 1950, the national government moved against persons with ties to the Communist Party or to any organization from a long list of "Communist-front organizations." The Soviet Union was seen as a serious menace to the Western world, and fear, according to Reynolds, reached into every corner of American life. So great was the fear generated, in fact, that schools of social work were under extreme pressure not even to discuss McCarthyism or its impact. Thus, as Reynolds noted, even at a university whose mission it was to educate in an atmosphere of freedom of thought, all academic freedom was stifled.

SOCIAL WORK IN THE 1960S AND BEYOND

The dualism between the social and psychological strains in social work came to a head during the 1960s. Practitioners at the time, according to Macht and Ashford (1990), tended to limit their practice to focusing on either the person without addressing the environmental forces impacting the client, or on the environment without addressing the emotional or personal behavior of the client. Thus there was a false dichotomy between individual and society which did not get resolved until ecosystems theory caught the excitement of theorists in the 1980s.

Franklin (1990), as mentioned at the beginning of the chapter, linked three distinct methods of social work practice—casework, group work, and community organization—to the socio-economic and political forces in American society. With the advent of the sixties, the neo-Freudian formulations and emphasis on human development gave way to an impetus to change the system to promote social welfare. While community organization as a social work process was hardly new, direct action as a strategy was rejuvenated and refined for the sixties. There was a great deal of criticism of social casework, some from outside the profession. Most notably Saul Alinsky (1971) urged against helping people adjust to the system as opposed to radically changing the system.

Strongly influenced by the Civil Rights movement and the Great Society program in 1964, the social work profession began to shift its focus from case-work to social policy. The new goals of the eradication of poverty and racism fired up a new generation of social workers. The shift in the profession's emphasis became apparent in the editorial content of social work's leading journals. This progressivism, in fact, is still evident today as editors of the mainstream journals continue to focus on the crises in social welfare, human rights issues, and the need for social and political action. The social work code of ethics (see box 4.1) reflects an expanded interest in social policy and in the ramifications of such policy for the poor.

SOCIAL WORK IN TODAY'S WORLD

Writing in *Social Work*, Ann Hartman (1989: 387) editorializes:

> We have not attained a just society. In fact, despite the gains in social and economic participation achieved during the reform periods of the 1930s and 1960s, the resource and power gaps continue to grow. . . . Furthermore, in the past eight years, we have witnessed a major dismantling of most social programs—a dismantling that has deprived a large segment of our population of needed economic, social, educational, and health services.

Yet the need for intensive social programs is as great today as ever before. This need is related to the severity of economic and social problems that is not unique to the United States. Links between mental health impairments and social problems were uncovered in a recent report directed by Dr. Arthur Kleinman which drew on the work of more than eighty experts in more than thirty nations in Asia, Africa, Latin America, and the Middle East. According to this comprehensive international study (Ritter, 1995), communities with politically inspired violence often have high rates of alcohol abuse and violent abuse. Violence across ethnic or religious lines often produces depression and hopelessness in youth and high rates of suicide and homicide. The growing rate of dire poverty is associated with serious social problems. Mental retardation, for instance, is two to eight times more common in poor nations than in industrialized nations due

BOX 4.1

THE NASW CODE OF ETHICS

I. The Social Worker's Conduct and Comportment as a Social Worker

A. Propriety—The social worker should maintain high standards of personal conduct in the capacity or identity as social worker.

1. The private conduct of the social worker is a personal matter to the same degree as is any other person's, except when such conduct compromises the fulfillment of professional responsibilities.
2. The social worker should not participate in, condone, or be associated with dishonesty, fraud, deceit, or misrepresentation.
3. The social worker should distinguish clearly between statements and actions made as a private individual and as a representative of the social work profession or an organization or group.

B. Competence and Professional Development—The social worker should strive to become and remain proficient in professional practice and the performance of professional functions.

1. The social worker should accept responsibility or employment only on the basis of existing competence or the intention to acquire the necessary competence.
2. The social worker should not misrepresent professional qualifications, education, experience, or affiliations.

C. Service—The social worker should regard as primary the service obligation of the social work profession.

1. The social worker should retain ultimate responsibility for the quality and extent of the service that individual assumes, assigns, or performs.
2. The social worker should act to prevent practices that are inhumane or discriminatory against any person or group of persons.

D. Integrity—The social worker should act in accordance with the highest standards of professional integrity and impartiality.

1. The social worker should be alert to and resist the influences and pressures that interfere with the exercise of professional discretion and impartial judgment required for the performance of professional functions.
2. The social worker should not exploit professional relationships for personal gain.

E. Scholarship and Research—The social worker engaged in study and research should be guided by the conventions of scholarly inquiry.

1. The social worker engaged in research should consider carefully its possible consequences for human beings.

(Continued on next page)

BOX 4.1 (Continued)

2. The social worker engaged in research should ascertain that the consent of participants in the research is voluntary and informed, without any implied deprivation or penalty for refusal to participate, and with due regard for participants' privacy and dignity.
3. The social worker engaged in research should protect participants from unwarranted physical or mental discomfort, distress, harm, danger, or deprivation.
4. The social worker who engages in the evaluation of services or cases should discuss them only for professional purposes and only with persons directly and professionally concerned with them.
5. Information obtained about participants in research should be treated as confidential.
6. The social worker should take credit only for work actually done in connection with scholarly and research endeavors and credit contributions made by others.

II. The Social Worker's Ethical Responsibility to Clients

F. Primacy of Clients' Interests—The social worker's primary responsibility is to clients.
1. The social worker should serve clients with devotion, loyalty, determination, and the maximum application of professional skill and competence.

2. The social worker should not exploit relationships with clients for personal advantage.
3. The social worker should not practice, condone, facilitate or collaborate with any form of discrimination on the basis of race, color, sex, sexual orientation, age, religion, national origin, marital status, political belief, mental or physical handicap, or any other preference or personal characteristic, condition or status.
4. The social worker should avoid relationships or commitments that conflict with the interests of clients.
5. The social worker should under no circumstances engage in sexual activities with clients.
6. The social worker should provide clients with accurate and complete information regarding the extent and nature of the services available to them.
7. The social worker should apprise clients of their risks, rights, opportunities, and obligations associated with social service to them.
8. The social worker should seek advice and counsel of colleagues and supervisors whenever such consultation is in the best interest of clients.
9. The social worker should terminate service to clients, and professional relationships with them, when such service and

(Continued on next page)

BOX 4.1 (Continued)

relationships are no longer required or no longer serve the clients' needs or interests.

10. The social worker should withdraw services precipitously only under unusual circumstances, giving careful consideration to all factors in the situation and taking care to minimize possible adverse effects.

11. The social worker who anticipates the termination or interruption of service to clients should notify clients promptly and seek the transfer, referral, or continuation of service in relation to the clients' needs and preferences.

G. Rights and Prerogatives of Clients— The social worker should make every effort to foster maximum self-determination on the part of clients.

1. When the social worker must act on behalf of a client who has been adjudged legally incompetent, the social worker should safeguard the interests and rights of that client.

2. When another individual has been legally authorized to act in behalf of a client, the social worker should deal with that person always with the client's best interest in mind.

3. The social worker should not engage in any action that violates or diminishes the civil or legal rights of clients.

H. Confidentiality and Privacy—The social worker should respect the privacy

of clients and hold in confidence all information obtained in the course of professional service.

1. The social worker should share with others confidences revealed by clients, without their consent, only for compelling professional reasons.

2. The social worker should inform clients fully about the limits of confidentiality in a given situation, the purposes for which information is obtained, and how it may be used.

3. The social worker should afford clients reasonable access to any official social work records concerning them.

4. When providing clients with access to records, the social worker should take due care to protect the confidences of others contained in those records.

5. The social worker should obtain informed consent of clients before taping, recording, or permitting third party observation of their activities.

I. Fees—When setting fees, the social worker should ensure that they are fair, reasonable, considerate, and commensurate with the service performed and with due regard for the clients' ability to pay.

1. The social worker should not accept anything of value for making a referral.

(Continued on next page)

BOX 4.1 (Continued)

III. The Social Worker's Ethical Responsibility to Colleagues

J. Respect, Fairness, and Courtesy—The social worker should treat colleagues with respect, courtesy, fairness, and good faith.

1. The social worker should cooperate with colleagues to promote professional interests and concerns.
2. The social worker should respect confidences shared by colleagues in the course of their professional relationships and transactions.
3. The social worker should create and maintain conditions of practice that facilitate ethical and competent professional performance by colleagues.
4. The social worker should treat with respect, and represent accurately and fairly, the qualifications, views, and findings of colleagues and use appropriate channels to express judgments on these matters.
5. The social worker who replaces or is replaced by a colleague in professional practice should act with consideration for the interest, character, and reputation of that colleague.
6. The social worker should not exploit a dispute between a colleague and employers to obtain a position or otherwise advance the social worker's interest.
7. The social worker should seek arbitration or mediation when conflicts with col-

leagues require resolution for compelling professional reasons.

8. The social worker should extend to colleagues of other professions the same respect and cooperation that is extended to social work colleagues.
9. The social worker who serves as an employer, supervisor, or mentor to colleagues should make orderly and explicit arrangements regarding the conditions of their continuing professional relationship.
10. The social worker who has the responsibility for employing and evaluating the performance of other staff members, should fulfill such responsibility in a fair, considerate, and equitable manner, on the basis of clearly enunciated criteria.
11. The social worker who has the responsibility for evaluating the performance of employees, supervisees, or students should share evaluations with them.

K. Dealing with Colleagues' Clients—The social worker has the responsibility to relate to the clients of colleagues with full professional consideration.

1. The social worker should not assume professional responsibility for the clients of another agency or a colleague without appropriate communication with that agency or colleague.

(Continued on next page)

BOX 4.1 (Continued)

2. The social worker who serves the clients of colleagues, during a temporary absence or emergency, should serve those clients with the same consideration as that afforded any client.

IV. The Social Worker's Ethical Responsibility to Employers and Employing Organizations

L. Commitments to Employing Organization—The social worker should adhere to commitments made to the employing organization.
1. The social worker should work to improve the employing agency's policies and procedures, and the efficiency and effectiveness of its services.
2. The social worker should not accept employment or arrange student field placements in an organization which is currently under public sanction by NASW for violating personnel standards, or imposing limitations on or penalties for professional actions on behalf of clients.
3. The social worker should act to prevent and eliminate discrimination in the employing organization's work assignments and in its employment policies and practices.
4. The social worker should use with scrupulous regard, and only for the purpose for which they are intended, the resources of the employing organization.

V. The Social Worker's Ethical Responsibility to the Social Work Profession

M. Maintaining the Integrity of the Profession—The social worker should uphold and advance the values, ethics, knowledge, and mission of the profession.
1. The social worker should protect and enhance the dignity and integrity of the profession and should be responsible and vigorous in discussion and criticism of the profession.
2. The social worker should take action through appropriate channels against unethical conduct by any member of the profession.
3. The social worker should act to prevent the unauthorized and unqualified practice of social work.
4. The social worker should make no misrepresentation in advertising as to qualifications, competence, service, or results to be achieved.

N. Community Service—The social worker should assist the profession in making social services available to the general public.
1. The social worker should contribute time and professional expertise to activities that promote respect for the utility, the integrity, and the competence of the social work profession.

(Continued on next page)

BOX 4.1 (Continued)

2. The social worker should support the formulation, development, enactment and implementation of social policies of concern to the profession.

O. Development of Knowledge—The social worker should take responsibility for identifying, developing, and fully utilizing knowledge for professional practice.

1. The social worker should base practice upon recognized knowledge relevant to social work.
2. The social worker should critically examine, and keep current with emerging knowledge relevant to social work.
3. The social worker should contribute to the knowledge base of social work and share research knowledge and practice wisdom with colleagues.

VI. The Social Worker's Ethical Responsibility to Society

P. Promoting the General Welfare—The social worker should promote the general welfare of society.

1. The social worker should act to prevent and eliminate discrimination against any person or group on the basis of race, color, sex, sexual orientation, age, religion, national origin, marital status, political belief, mental or physical handicap, or any other preference or personal characteristic, condition, or status.
2. The social worker should act to ensure that all persons have access to the resources, services, and opportunities which they require.
3. The social worker should act to expand choice and opportunity for all persons, with special regard for disadvantaged or oppressed groups and persons.
4. The social worker should promote conditions that encourage respect for the diversity of cultures which constitute American society.
5. The social worker should provide appropriate professional services in public emergencies.
6. The social worker should advocate changes in policy and legislation to improve social conditions and to promote social justice.
7. The social worker should encourage informed participation by the public in shaping social policies and institutions.

Source: NASW Code of Ethics (1990). Reprinted with permission of NASW, Washington, DC.

to nutritional deficiencies and lack of prenatal care. Another threat to health that is poverty related is the exchange of sex for food in African shanty towns, a practice leading to infection of the AIDS virus. Kleinman's report which has been presented to the United Nations, calls for an international emphasis on mental health services and changes in government policies to prevent violence against women.

Mental health problems are rampant in the United States also. Problems at the macro-level filter down to the micro-level. Generally, social work responds through its clinical interventions. Thus, when psychological depression strikes or child abuse or wife battering occurs, social workers trained in therapy can aid in the decision-making process toward change and in providing appropriate referrals. Yet personal problems may be linked to the larger picture. The same factors affecting the wider society—the relocation of industry to poorer nations, the technology revolution and the associated dislocations of labor, the huge national debt, the incentive for major corporations to privatize and hire temporary workers—affect the provision of social services as well. Personal crises mount and just when services are most needed, in times of economic hardship for example, economic funding is cut back. Public policy often is guided by a commitment to remain competitive in the high-tech race for control of the global marketplace rather than by humanitarian goals (Walz 1995).

What happens to social workers, asks Hartman, who cherish Reynolds' ideals as they attempt to serve clients in conservative America? The means available to help clients increasingly are limited. The near obsessive emphasis on accountability for every dollar spent and cost-effectiveness translates into mounds of paperwork and fund-raising efforts by progressively harried staff. Most social workers, observes Hartman, remain in stressful positions and make the most of it. Some others move into areas of greater political influences; still others leave the profession altogether. Many social workers, perhaps reluctantly, flee to private practice. As they explore the issue in *Unfaithful Angels: How Social Work Has Abandoned its Mission*, Specht and Courtney (1994: 8) are far less empathetic toward members of the profession who establish careers in psychotherapy:

> In increasing numbers, social workers are flocking to psychotherapeutic pastures, hanging out their shingles to advertise themselves as psychotherapists just as quickly as licensing laws will permit. For the most part, professional associations of social workers and schools of social work are active participants in the great transformation of social work from a professional

corps concerned with helping people deal with their social problems to a major platoon in the psychotherapeutic armies.

Well-written and refreshingly iconoclastic, *Unfaithful Angels* is a highly useful resource for viewing today's variety of social work practitioners in a historical context. Specht and Courtney correctly take the psychotherapeutic field to task for having fallen captive in many instances to popular therapies such as "codependency work," excessive individualism, and the like. They also take the social work field to task for bestowing professionalism, prestige, and respect singularly to clinicians. Still, as one who has engaged in clinical work in private treatment settings and yet has opposed privatization in the United States and abroad, I wish to make the opposite point. No, social work has not abandoned its mission. The next section will articulate this position.

HAS SOCIAL WORK ABANDONED ITS MISSION?

Unlike related fields in the social and behavioral sciences and counseling education, social work is highly self-critical, culturally-aware, and therefore, introspective. Every accredited social work program stresses policy as well as counseling issues. The fact that academics of the caliber of the late Harry Specht and his associate Mark Courtney have chastised the field for its parochialism, paradoxically, may actually be one of many encouraging developments in social work today. Specht and Courtney's book offers a kind of soul-searching that is the attribute of a truly altruistic profession. Other positives in this enduring field are: the outpouring of politically relevant articles, editorials, and policy statements in *Social Work* and *NASW News,* the leading professional journals in the field; the continuing idealism of social work students; the strident, multicultural, and policy emphasis including progressive mandates by the Council on Social Work Education; the strong feminist influence in social work and social work education; the new impetus for global and environmental awareness; and the dominant ecosystems framework which informs practice on both the micro and macro level.

Editorials and Policy Statements

The National Association of Social Workers is a politically viable and dynamic organization with a membership of over 140,000 (keep in mind that only approximately one-fourth of social workers are official members). With membership, subscription to *Social Work, NASW News,* and a regional newsletter is automatic. Anxious for endorsement and funding by the generous Political Action Committees, politicians at the local and national levels court NASW support. Social workers can thus be said to belong to an organization with professional clout. NASW lobbies extensively for improved social welfare programs as well as for its own professional representations in health care, mental health treatment, etc. As an academic discipline, the political involvement sets social work apart from other related areas of specialization. Graduates of nationally accredited programs are able to benefit from having a credential that is regarded as professional (applied) rather than as strictly academic, or a degree which qualifies the recipient for a specific job.

Headlines from 1995 *NASW News* reports and editorials reveal social work's continuing social action on behalf of the poor and oppressed: "Court Briefs (by NASW) Back Gay, Lesbian Rights," "NASW Urges Hill to Fund '96 Programs," "1995 Agenda Urges Nonpunitive Policies," "Welfare Bill is Wrong Vehicle, Congress Told."

Among journals in the field devoted specifically to human rights and poverty issues are: *Affilia: Journal of Women and Social Work, Journal of Gay/Lesbian Social Services, Multicultural Social Work,* and *Journal of Progressive Social Work.* A serious omission is one or more social work journals dealing with specific racial and ethnic minorities. As the editor-in-chief of *Social Work,* Hartman (1989: 388) proudly acknowledged her faith in the vitality and relevance of the profession:

> Possibly, when we help people to improve their lives we are working against major regulatory processes in our society. This inconsistency is the fundamental dilemma. This dilemma is the vulnerability of our position between client and community.

> However, it is just this position, our attention to person and situation and our refusal to retreat from mounting social problems by redefining them as personal defects, that creates the special character of social work. Such a position creates both dilemma and opportunities.

The Idealism of Social Work Students

What brings students to major in social work? Has their motivation shifted in the last ten years? In a nonrandom sample survey of over seven hundred

Midwestern undergraduate social work majors, Hanson and McCullagh (1995) addressed these questions. The purpose of the study, conducted over a ten year period, was to determine if monetary rewards and prestige surpass altruistic motivations as reasons for pursuing social work as a career. Although men scored slightly higher than women on the self-interest factor, for both genders service to others emerged as an overriding reason for choosing the social work major. This was a motivation, moreover, that did not change significantly over the course of the study. The predominant reason for entry into social work was to make a contribution to society.

Compared to undergraduate students, as one would expect, graduate social work (MSW) students are more inclined to seek career opportunities and autonomy in the relatively lucrative area of private practice. Recent studies indicate that between one-fifth and one-third of incoming MSW students plan to have full-time private practice careers (Specht and Courtney, 1994). A survey of NASW members (97 percent of whom have MSW degrees or above) indicates that only 18.6 percent of the members are engaged in private solo or group based full-time practice (Ginsberg, 1995), a 5 percent increase from 1988. Many other social workers engage in private practice part-time in addition perhaps to an agency job. Social workers, as shown in the 1995 membership survey, are primarily employed in mental health, family, and child practice areas, with most working in agencies, hospitals, or clinics. These data do not offer much support for Specht and Courtney's (1994: 149) statement that, "As social work has drifted into the field of psychotherapy, most schools of social work have drifted along with it." As these authors concede, recent surveys of MSW students do indicate that students express a desire to work with at least one of the disadvantaged groups traditionally associated with social work practice. In fact, the social work constituency is diverse. According to the latest statistics available, of students who received BSW degrees in 1992, 23.1 percent were members of minority groups, the majority being African American (Ginsberg, 1995). Of those awarded master's degrees, 17.17 percent were minorities. This figure is up slightly at the doctoral level. Of social work faculty, approximately 25 percent were minorities in 1992. These figures are strikingly high compared to the figures for other occupational groups. Women are even more disproportionately represented in the social work profession. Of those receiving MSW degrees, 80 percent are women as are two-thirds of those receiving doctorate degrees. The majority of social work faculty are women; however, men constitute a much higher percentage of the faculty than of the profession as a whole and are highly represented at the upper echelons of the academic world.

In light of the cultural and gender diversity of the profession, the keen attention to social issues of the literature, and the continued idealism of students, one can only conclude that social work has not abandoned the mission of its foremothers. Yet, given the forces of the radical right, the market economy, managed care, and the media campaign launched against the recipients of aid, the challenges to social work are formidable. To what extent the budding social workers of today can maintain their idealism and enthusiasm under the circumstances remains to be seen.

Multicultural Social Work Education

Due to the importance of accreditation to university social work programs—graduates must have degrees from accredited programs to be considered professional social workers—the Council on Social Work Education fulfills a vital, and as some critics would say, a dictatorial function. A positive aspect of the CSWE is its ability to enforce a strong antidiscrimination policy. On the other hand a negative aspect is the often rigid standardization of the social work curriculum.

People of color and other diverse groups constitute a large proportion of the clients social workers serve. In recognition of the need for multicultural competence, the CSWE mandate is for the social work course curriculum to include content on ethnic minorities, women, and sexual orientation, ideally infused throughout the entire curriculum. Integrated accrediting teams monitor the programs to ensure that course syllabi and textbooks are geared toward human diversity. The importance of the recruitment and retention of minority and female faculty and students is emphasized. In a systematic analysis of leading social work journals and practice textbooks, however, Lum (1992) challenges the notion that attention to minority aspects of practice has been adequate. Since much of the material that Lum studied was written in the 1970s, it is possible that an up-to-date literature analysis would more accurately reflect social work's multicultural emphasis. In any case, social work is far more minority-oriented than other comparable academic fields.

Although the United States may not lead the world in its social welfare policies, in the area of antidiscrimination legislation, it has paved the way. Paralleling national legislation, U.S. social work has moved from a reactive to a pro-active stance. In social work education in most of Europe, a multicultural, pluralistic approach is espoused. The aim, however, is to be gender blind and color blind rather than pro-active. According to Lorenz (1994), this tolerance perspective does not address racism and discrimination as realities. Belatedly, the United Kingdom took a decisive lead when the accrediting body directed social work educators to teach not only the skills for ethnically sensitive practice but the skills for challenging institutional and personal racism as well. Since the publication of Lorenz's text, however, this process of infusion of multicultural content has suffered a set-back stemming from reactionary government legislation, as we will see shortly.

America's Council on Social Work Education requires that five areas be covered in all social work training institutions: human behavior and the social environment, social work practice skills, research, social policy, and the field practicum. The combination of macro- and micro-level offerings reinforces the person-in-the-environment conceptualization of the profession. Thus, while social workers may engage in community organization work, they may draw upon the basic counseling and interviewing skills in community activism and negotiation. Similarly, social work clinicians ideally will be aware of the external policy issues impinging on their clients' lives and of the importance of political advocacy on behalf of the disadvantaged and vulnerable.

Ethnic-sensitive practice raises social workers' awareness of racism in wider society, and of how social conditions related to powerlessness are integral to the experiences of persons of color. To be effective, social workers must be aware of their own prejudices and fears before they can help their clients achieve self-awareness. By identifying and building upon existing strengths, the worker empowers the client to get involved in mutual aid groups for social support as a first step in the change process (Gutiérrez, 1991). In Canada the British Columbia Association of Social Workers is pursuing initiatives to promulgate muticulturalism through cross-cultural immersion activities (Seebaran and George, 1990). In British Columbia, where over 22 percent of the population is now foreign-born, the establishment of a specific committee for the development of training programs and policy initiatives was essential.

The Feminist Influence

Just as the African American and gay/lesbian lobbies within social work have been well-organized and effective in shaping CSWE and NASW policies, feminism has also been a major influence in the field. Feminist social work, the aim of which is to remove oppression due to sexism, has its roots in the women's movement of the 1970s. Yet as we know from the history of social work, strong women have shaped the profession from the start. The antifemale bias of psychodynamic theory which has been widely noted (Payne, 1991) can be viewed as a bit of an anomaly within social work history. In any case, when the psychoanalytical therapies were dominant in the 1920s and again in 1950s, the special needs of women clients and therapists took a backseat to protect men from women who might otherwise undermine them. Regarded as highly vulnerable to female wiles, men were viewed as having egos that could shatter easily. Women's egos were considered only in conjunction with the male. Freudianism carried the authority of the male medical establishment: its influence spread from medicine to the behavioral and social sciences. Rape victims were regarded as having "wished for it" or even having "imagined it;" rape and wife battering were studied in popular criminology textbooks as "victim-precipitated" crime. Labeled as "castrating," assertive (then called aggressive) women were widely regarded as maladjusted, and as having "a complex" about men stemming from early childhood experiences. Typically viewed as denying their feminine role and as "frustrated," women in leadership positions became fewer and fewer in the 1950s and 1960s. This trend was true for the social work profession as for society as a whole. The dramatic decrease in female authorship of policy and planning publications was a tangible indicator of women's declining role in policy leadership during this period (Brandwein, 1995).

Thanks to the grass-roots feminist movement that reemerged in the 1970s, awareness of women's needs and issues became paramount. Women's problems were depathologized and then politicized. Founded as a field of strong women (most of whom remained unmarried by choice) and gentle men who stood alongside them, social work stands uniquely among the professions as woman-centered, as Chambers (1986) notes. The fact that writers of the feminist school today decry the underrepresentation of females in top administrative positions shows that the feminist voice in social work is alive and well (see Andrews, 1990; Chambers, 1986; Dominelli and McCleod, 1989; and Payne, 1991).

In both its history and approach, then, social work is fundamentally feminist in nature (Collins, 1986; Andrews and Parnell, 1994; Stere, 1986). Parallels between feminist thought and social work are found in their mutual belief that: the personal is political and vice versa; problems lie in the structures of society rather than in the fault of the disadvantaged; the perpetration of poverty in women is systemic; and violence inflicted against women and children is an instrument of power (Andrews and Parnell, 1994). Both perspectives—feminism and social work—seek to bridge the gap between the personal and the political through the process of empowerment. Both perspectives challenge all forms of institutionalized oppression. The generalist model in social work, the predominant approach which incorporates ecosystems concepts and directs interventions at all levels of the system—the individual, the family, the community, and society—also guides feminist practice. Or perhaps it is the feminist perspective which shapes the form that the generalist approach has acquired. Or perhaps it is a combination of both. In any case, Stere (1986: 49) effectively encapsulates the sweep of feminist practice:

> I consider my practice to be feminist in that my interventions, which are intended to serve better the needs of women, include the regular offering of women's groups and workshops for networking and skill building, organizing all-women self-help groups and therapy groups, charging fees on a sliding scale, doing therapy with lesbian couples with a woman cotherapist, providing information and referral services for women, and using models for social and personal intervention that are based on the developing theories about women.

Stere's multidimensional formulation belies the presumed dichotomy between psychotherapy and community organization and neatly bridges the gap between them.

Although the majority of social workers may not have the kind of ideological commitment to call themselves feminist therapists and to employ a systematic feminist methodology in their work, many therapists have come to question the highly normative views of the family that earlier had been *de rigueur* in family therapy. A proliferation of workshops, papers, and conference sessions focused on women's issues and gender sensitivity has given credence to the female voice and experience (Hartman, 1995). Canadian social work educator Don Collins recommends the feminist approach (with reservations) for therapists in child and youth counseling. Gutiérrez (1991) and Turner (1991) find feminist practice especially amenable to work with women of color.

Social work practice with women has developed in the last two decades from a concern about sexism and women's issues to an emerging model of practice grounded in feminist theory, scholarship, and action (Bricker-Jenkins and Lockett, 1995). So, far from arguing that social work today has abandoned its mission, one could much more accurately conclude that social work, on the contrary, has expanded its horizons, moving into new directions without losing sight of the old. One cautionary note: a right-wing backlash against victims of society in conjunction with the economic dictates of managed care has created a barrage of criticism against the entire therapy field and against feminist therapists, in particular. This development with important consequences for all members of the helping professions will be discussed more fully later.

The New Impetus for Global Awareness

A very encouraging development is the awareness of how "Americentric" social work education has become over the years. "But," declares Hartman (1990: 291), "it is a new world, a different world, a world that demands new responses and major changes on the international, national, professional, and personal levels." The profession's growing international commitment is evident in current initiatives such as the NASW Child and Family Well-Being Development Education Project; the link between regional NASW chapters with social workers in other countries (twinning partnerships); federal funding of a three-year NASW Development Education Project on Violence to examine the causes, impact, and solutions to violence internationally; and the existence of the International Federation of Social Workers (IFSW) of which NASW is a member, and of the International Association of Schools of Social Workers (IASSW) in which the United States is actively involved. In 1992, in a cooperative effort between NASW and CSWE, a curriculum manual *Introducing International Development Content in the Social Work Curriculum* was developed (Healy, 1992). Contained in the manual are teaching modules for use by social work programs.

In recent years the perspective of social work had broadened to challenge widely-held assumptions of industrial society, assumptions equating non-sustainable economic growth with progress. The sustainable development model, a central theme of such books as *Social Development* by Midgley (1995b) and *The Global Environmental Crisis: Implications for Social Welfare and Social Work* edited by Hoff and McNutt (1994) integrate environmental concerns and ecological principles. What is needed now, argue Hoff and McNutt, is nothing less than a complete re-thinking of our relationship to the natural world. An understanding of the interplay between poverty and environmental degradation is central to the social development model. The imminent threat of global environmental collapse compels the social work profession to adopt a truly comprehensive ecological framework and to take a pro-active stance toward the depletion of resources and the promotion of policies toward sustainable social development.

Yet American social workers are just at the crossroads of assuming a worldwide and environmental focus, and of grasping the fact that social problems are becoming more interconnected and nations more interdependent in a global economy. Mary and Morris (1994) urge social workers to get involved in some of the many international exchange opportunities available through their professional membership.

Excellent resources are now available for social workers and researchers to learn of challenges, problems, and solutions in other lands. The *British Journal of Social Work* and the *Scandinavian Journal of Social Welfare* often publish articles with an international focus. *International Social Work* is the official journal of IFSW and IASSW. The *Journal of Multicultural Social Work* is an exciting addition to the literature. *Social Development Issues*, like the *Journal of International and Comparative Social Welfare*, focuses on nations of the south from an international social work perspective.

The Ecosystems Framework

The final source of knowledge for the argument that social work has not abandoned its mission is drawn from the nature of the dominant perspective in the field, the breadth of the ecosystems conceptualization. A holistic, systemic-ecologically oriented, and singularly rich perspective, ecosystems theory is as relevant to individual therapy as it is to policy issues, and as meaningful to the treatment of the mentally ill as to intervening in the environment (perhaps advocating the need for a halfway house). In its understanding, in the words of social psychologist Cooley (1909) of "the society and self as twin born," the ecosystems framework does not dichotomize social phenomena but rather perceives reality in terms of reciprocity or interactionism. Ecosystems theorists do not separate the person from the environment or the environment from the people who comprise it. The nature—some would say the uniqueness—of social work is in its intervention at both individual and environmental levels, often at the point of their intersection. Logically, therapists and community organizers are not regarded as on opposite ends of the (personal/political) continuum. Just as the therapist works in the community, the community worker relies on therapy skills. In our clients, we see the personal dimension of political legislation; in the political enterprise we view the human aspect.

To review the concepts of the ecosystems construct described in chapter 1, this approach encompasses awareness of the impact of internal forces (such as disease) on the individual in the context of the larger social and economic considerations. According to this nonlinear perspective, one looks not for a single cause and effect but at the person and society in dynamic interaction. It is not either A or B but both A and B; and not either/or then, but both/and. For example, it may not be alcohol abuse that causes homelessness but abuse of alcohol and transient living which mutually reinforce each other. Similar connections can be found between depression and relationship problems and between poverty and lack of motivation to get job training.

Translated into practice, the ecosystems model is sometimes known as *generalist practice*, a repertoire as we have seen earlier that contains strategies appropriate for work with a variety of systems—individuals, families, small groups, agencies, and communities (Johnson, 1995). Johnson (1995) and Germain and Gitterman (1995) emphasize the social worker's role in maximizing the client's social functioning. The core of the social work endeavor is the worker and client interacting in relation to present or future problems in social functioning. A major omission from the classic formulation—and this is so throughout the ecosystems literature—has been the inattention to the interaction between past and present which affect future phenomena. Elsewhere, the concept of interactionism has been expanded to include the past, the essence of which is stored in memory and meaning, for example, the meaning of sex to one who has been sexually traumatized, or the meaning of trust to the survivors of bloodshed in Cambodia, Bosnia, or the Persian Gulf (see van Wormer, 1995).

Present behaviors may appear incomprehensible unless understood in the context not only of culture but of time and past experience. Recently, however, Germain and Gitterman (1995) have included attention to the client's presentation of his or her life story as an integral part of self-discovery, guided by attentive prompting from the therapist. Another way the ecosystems model can be expanded conceptually is by incorporating the explicit recognition of the centrality of the economic dimension to virtually all human development. To fully see the person-in-the-environment, the social worker needs a grasp of the importance of worldwide systems for individual, family, and community functioning.

As an evolving theory and practice modality, the ecosystems approach is continuously open to newly developing ideas and knowledge. The same conceptual framework is adaptable to practice with individuals as well as to work with communities and political advocacy (Germain and Gitterman, 1995). The potential of this theoretical bounty is immense; the notion of interactionism or reciprocity (which has its wellsprings in symbolic interactionism of social psychology) does not view reality statically but in terms of continual motion and feedback. This interactionist premise provides for an exciting framework for viewing global interdependence.

In summary, social work has not abandoned its mission merely because members of the profession are practicing clinical social work. A truly "Renaissance woman," Bertha Reynolds was a psychiatric social worker, union organizer, and writer/commentator on the McCarthy era. In all her endeavors, her major contribution was to the mission of social work. And what was/is this mission? As Hartman (1991: 195) defines it, "The profession's mission is to improve the quality of life of its clients, enhance social functioning, and intervene to make the environment on all levels more supportive and enabling." This perspective is consistent with understanding the individual needs of clients and in addressing much broader issues impinging upon their happiness. Yet a critical issue for the profession as singled out by Hopps and Pinderhughes (1992) is its need to come to grips with its dual obligation to social justice and the amelioration of individual problems. To build on an ethos of justice, schools of social work must help students integrate political-economic dynamics into their chosen fields of practice. Policy and practice, and community and individual work, must be seen in mutual interdependence.

Therapist, group worker, and community organizer—all are caught up in a backlash of international proportions. Whether one works in the confines of an office, in the wider community, or as a professional lobbyist, the social worker qua social worker has a vital function to perform in the dialectic of public policy. An appreciation of the common bond among all members of the profession will help insulate the field from the kind of helplessness against the cyclical nature of concerns—the either/or formulation that has characterized much of social work history. Following her historical analysis of the profession's vacillation between addressing personal troubles and public issues, Franklin (1990: 75) concludes, "The profession needs to develop a way of addressing the imbalance of the previous cycle, preparing for the opportunities of the next cycle, and developing 'shorter run' integrative methods." A major challenge, according to Franklin, is how to integrate the social treatment technologies with social work's knowledge of social change into one coherent strategy. Thus only if united can social work prepare for the besiegement from the radical right.

THE IMPACT OF THE RADICAL RIGHT

The single most important trend in social welfare during the past decade has been the conservative onslaught on the welfare state (Glennerster and Midgley, 1991). The onslaught is the ideological counterpart of the mass market economy, and its impact is international. The welfare state (in rich countries) or the state of the welfare (in poor nations) is experiencing a crisis rooted in the need for industrial countries to compete in a new global economy. Competition is inversely related to working conditions and the provision of benefits. According to conservative philosophy, national survival can only be assured if government, like business, cuts costs and becomes more efficient (Karger, 1993). The emphasis on efficiency and profitability often leads, according to Karger, to industrial reorganization which in turn leads to rapidly changing production technologies that can displace workers with machines.

What does all this have to do with social work? Increased demand for services generated by economic changes are met by government cuts in services. Government cuts entail employee layoffs and a decline in worker morale and bargaining power. In the United States, argues Hartman (1991), the work with the poor that social workers do is not valued by society. The destruction of programs, the transfer of resources away from the poor to the rich and to military causes, and the fact that the society has grown leaner and meaner, profoundly affect the systems within which social workers work.

By combining notions of economic individualism with cultural and religious traditionalism and with what Midgley and Jones (1994) call "authoritarian populism," the radical right has managed to solidify its political position. Immigrants, criminals, the chemically dependent, welfare mothers, disabled children, the elderly: these are among the groups targeted by those who represent the "taxpayers" and "moral America." The populations targeted represent the primary users of social services and indirectly, the social workers who serve them.

The free market system advocates that social services be delivered through the provision of private commercial practitioners/entrepreneurs (Mullaly, 1993). Social welfare assistance would not be preventive, but would come into play in emergency situations where the family and economic structures were unable to help. According to Mullaly, emphasis in the market economy is on getting people to accept their personal, family, and social obligations and not on social or environmental reform. The context of economic and work related realities is apt to be overlooked. The social work role, under this scenario, is one of control and coercion of people. The values represented by neoconservatism are the antithesis of progressive and feminist social work.

The Radical Right and Social Work

The effect of the media cannot be separated from the public reaction since the media both reflect and mold public opinion. In the United States, as Specht and Courtney (1994) maintain, social workers have been society's unwelcome messengers who have borne the brunt of much of the public's scorn. Ambivalence toward this centuries-old profession has been the result. At once applauded for their altruistic spirit, professional social workers are simultaneously derided in the belief that the welfare benefits and programs provided by them place a great and unnecessary burden on the taxpayers. People worried about their own jobs in a rapidly shifting economy are not likely to support government services for the poor.

Related to the right-wing backlash is the barrage of media attacks on psychotherapists, mostly women, concerning the issue of recovered memories (this involves the revival of previously repressed material usually repressed due to trauma). Cases have been reported in which therapists, through suggestion, apparently encouraged false memories which clients actively believed. Some of the "retrieved" memories led to court prosecutions of crimes ranging from child molestation to murder. The unfortunate result of several widely reported prosecutions of innocent people probably says more about our limited knowledge of the unconscious mind than it does about the motives of therapists. For an in-depth study of this explosive issue involving over one hundred lawsuits against therapists, see Butler (1996) and Neimarke (1995). In any case, the trauma of victimization is currently being disparaged as is much of the work of feminist

therapists who help clients confront their past as treatment for present afflic-
tions (for example, eating disorders, alcoholism, sexual dysfunction). In all the
furor against "therapists who plant memories," many other therapists today are
reluctant to engage in family-of-origin work at all. The risk of any systematic
media attack (as has happened to the priesthood with a spate of molestation
scandals) is a decline in public esteem.

In the United Kingdom, against a backdrop of declining governmental
resources and a growing minority population, social work has been much more
seriously affected by virulent right-wing ideology than in the United States and
Canada (Midgley and Jones, 1994). Political animosity has taken the form of
attacks on social workers' court testimony in child sexual abuse cases. Defense
attorneys try to brand social workers as influenced by feminism. As reported
by Jones (1992), courtroom questioning concerning social workers' personal
lifestyles and beliefs is indicative of the manner in which conservative critics
have sought to undermine the authority of social work. Social work education,
additionally, has been the source of a vendetta by politicians and journalists.
Philip Guy (1994) correctly puts much of the blame for the hostility directed
against social work and its academic training ground on the media. "Almost
without exception" argues Guy (266), "media coverage of social work has been
highly critical: at times derisory does not seem too strong a term." Events are
sensationalized, especially in the tabloid press and the focus is invariably on
one area of social work—child protection. In Norway cases involving removal
of children receive a great deal of negative tabloid press attention as well. Factors that play into the intensity of the hostility against social workers in Britain
are the statutory character of contemporary social work (the occupation is almost
entirely located within the state sector); social work's virtual preoccupation with
the marginalized and poor; and the fact that social work is bound up in the
public mind with social welfare at a time of the rise of the radical right (Guy,
1994; Midgley and Jones, 1994).

Throughout Latin America, similarly, the welfare state is highly criticized
and the professional profile of social work is in danger of becoming blurred
or less distinct (Quiroz, 1992). Pressures from the International Monetary Fund
translate the conservative ideology into action in Latin America, according to
Quiroz, the coordinator of the Rural Women's Program of the Chilean Center
for Adult Education. The monetary plan involves forcing countries to reduce
their national debt as a condition for receiving international aid. This has resulted
in severe retrenchments in expenditures in the areas of health, social housing,

and education. In a situation where only the rich are prospering, Quiroz's recommendation is for intervention to occur at the community level rather than through institutional channels or through privatization, both of which have failed earlier.

Throughout the world *privatization*—the transfer of government services and functions to private agencies—is transforming the means of social welfare provision. To cope with the lingering fiscal crises at state and local levels, agencies are turned over to private services. Lower wages and benefits reduce labor costs while worker autonomy has been sharply curtailed by the increasing control by funding sources in defining the nature of practice (Hartman, 1991). The pressure is often on workers to do more with less; the process of social work is routinized due to the evermore demanding bureaucratic constraints.

Tambor (1995) points to an often overlooked aspect (and latent function) of privatization—the breaking of unions. Although in the United States the social work professional organization does not operate as a union, an estimated 25 percent of the social work labor force (especially those employed in the public sector) are members of unions. NASW confirms the right of social work and other employees to engage in collective bargaining and negotiate provisions such as caseload size, ethical practice, and working conditions. Their Canadian counterparts are far more highly unionized.

To defend their membership base and protect the equity in these jobs, as Tambor indicates, unions have strongly opposed the contracting out of human services. Social workers surrender their control of the profession as agencies such as the Department of Human Services contracts services out such as family preservation teams to assume responsibility for intensive therapy work with high-risk families. These private companies bid for contracts; they hire recent graduates often without social work experience. A related phenomenon which also saves money for the state is the declassification of jobs.

Declassification, sometimes called deprofessionalization, is the trend initiated during the Reagan years which downgrades requirements for specific social work positions so people with lesser degrees and professional training can fill them and be paid lower salaries (Hopps and Pinderhughes, 1992). The modification has resulted in a situation in which the majority of those who deliver social services are not members of the profession. Work in child protection services has been especially affected. This trend is related to the push for governmental deregulation. An advantage of declassification is the flexibility allowed for hiring indigenous or bilingual workers who have attributes more directly relevant to working with the community. The disadvantages are the lowering of standards, pay levels, professional standing of engaging in a certain line of work, and a disregard of the social work profession. Social work has sought to stop such attempts to open traditional social work to the general public through extensive lobbying of state legislatures for strict licensing laws and negotiations with third party payers (such as insurance companies) to require professionally trained staff for services provided. All the states have enacted legislation legally regulating social work. This development protects the profession in regard to restricting the use of the title of social worker, in assuring base levels of competence and ethics, and in enabling practitioners to receive third party payments (W. Johnson, 1995).

In Australia a major challenge to the social work profession comes from a combination of forces in government, labor, and business advocating *multi-skilling* or moving of the work force freely from one arena to another. Deprofessionalization is a major trend endorsed by unions. Social worker salaries are set by the government in Australia, an indication of a lack of autonomy of the profession. Exacerbating the situation is the absence of licensing or registration of social workers. Only the Northern Territory currently requires it.

THE SOCIAL WORK IMAGINATION AND CRITICAL THINKING

To perceive the congruities in the incongruities, to discern the false dualism between the private and the public, to experience the beauty of social work against the bureaucratic assaults, and to see the past in the present and know this too shall pass—this is resilience. And what is the opposite of resilience? Burnout. There are also qualities pertaining to resilience that are intuitive and perhaps innate such as a faith in the good you are doing, a cardinal faith that it matters. (See box 4.2).

In this age of predictability, accountability, and manageability in education, sometimes there is little room for the kind of growth that comes from nurturance and the give and take of often unplanned dialogue. Bradley and Harris (1993: 63) describe the creative process accordingly: "To the extent that social work involves forms of creativity as well as technology, experience as well as knowledge, there is as a necessary dimension of the activity a form of creative chaos which surfaces, as it were, 'naturally,' given the right environment."

But then there is the more tangible, learned aspect—the critical thinking. If you can somehow come to possess or develop these qualities then you have what I will label the *social work imagination*.

A mark of greatness, writes Kendall (1989), is breadth of vision. In her portrait of three extraordinary social work leaders of the 1930s—Alice Salomon of Germany, Eileen Younghusband of the United Kingdom, and Edith Abbott of the United States—Kendall stresses their deep commitment to international concerns. Every social work graduate at the University of Chicago in

BOX 4.2

BECAUSE IT MATTERS

Paul A. Lacey

Because it matters
  to read books
  jagged as boulders,
  serene as a Mozart concerto;

to correct our lives
by the plumb-line
of Jeremiah or Plato;

and to comfort our hearts
with Isaiah and Bach;

to know the world anew
in the witness
of Galileo, Darwin,
Teilhard de Chardin;

and to savor a new creation
with Woolman and Blake
and Thomas More;

Because it matters
  that we can be companions
  in a learning fellowship
  which begins here and now
  and may reach to our
  final darkness;

Because it matters so much,
  I am where I am
  and do what I do.

Source: The Earlhamite, Annual Report Issue, Autumn 1979. Reprinted with permission of *The Earlhamite,* Earlham College.

Abbott's day, for example, was exposed to a view of the field and the profession that encompassed history and comparative study. Salomon and Younghusband worked with the League of Nations and the United Nations. In their international vision and flexibility, these female pioneers personify what I mean by social work imagination. As Kendall (30) concludes, "In embracing the necessity to join social reform with individual help, they long ago settled the question of whether social work should be equally concerned with therapeutic action and social action."

Critical thinking can be defined as the ability to put phenomena (problematic and triumphant) in perspective. We need to be able to see parts of the whole—practitioners urge clients to partialize problems or to break them down into manageable parts—and the whole in parts, or the context.

Two aspects of critical thinking delineated by Keefe (1980) are empathy and critical consciousness. Each social work skill complements the other along a continuum of individual to social change. We will discuss these attributes of critical thinking along with a third and closely related concept—cultural competence.

Empathy, the ability to put oneself in place of another, requires both cognitive and emotional responses to the client on the part of the worker. Awareness of the client's emotional state and of the impact of the social and cultural environment are essential. Only through empathy can a therapist work with a wife batterer or sexual offender and help such persons move away from such destructive behavior. Often understanding for the sorriest client may accrue from knowing his or her childhood histories.

Critical consciousness involves an understanding of the encompassing social-structural context of human problems. According to Keefe (389): "That there are serious problems with the economic structure of this society and that the status quo is not static are part of the professional's collective wisdom." Larochelle and Campfens (1992) discuss the importance of inculcating student social workers with the ability to link the personal with the political in the tradition of C. Wright Mills' (1959) "sociological imagination." Several Canadian undergraduate university social work programs have developed an integrated approach gearing change efforts at both the personal and collective levels, according to Larochelle and Campfens. However, many other Canadian students and seasoned social workers fail to respond appropriately to the socioeconomic realities of their clientele. Larochelle and Campfens attribute this failing to the Canadians' exaggerated emphasis on individual responsibility and technocratic solutions when dealing with social problems. In a simulated attribution-of-cause experiment, Bell (1979) documented a similar tendency in American social workers to attribute another person's actions solely to innate personality characteristics rather than to a combination of factors.

Another shortcoming in social work education which few have recognized is that while the training of social workers seems to prepare them too well regarding their limits in dealing with the clients, and their problems, there is little done to help social workers recognize the consequences of their silence much less the possibilities of instituting change (Larochelle and Campfens, 1992). In this vein, Keefe locates the kind of resourcefulness that exemplifies the social work imagination in the form of collective field activities developed in Latin America. Having lost confidence in the capacity of their official leaders to bring development to their countries, grass-roots organizations have formed to work among the poorest and most needy groups of society. Chilean social work education was revolutionized as a result of the pedagogical instruction of Paulo Freire, an exiled Brazilian educator living in Chile. From 1965 to 1973 when a military dictatorship intervened to suppress the program and persecute the social workers who were organizing the countryside, a real participatory democracy characterized social work education. Today, while human rights are being restored in Chile, there and throughout Latin America schools of social work are training their students in this collectivist form of organization. Keefe cites Freire (1973: 17) who describes his emancipatory pedagogy as follows:

> The critically transitive consciousness is characterized by depth in the interpenetration of problems; by the substitution of causal principles for magical explanations; by the testing of one's findings and by openness to revision; by the attempt to avoid distortion when perceiving problems and to avoid preconceived notions when analyzing them; by refusing to transfer responsibility; by rejecting passive positions; by soundness of argumentation; by the practice of dialogue rather than polemics; by receptivity to the new for reasons beyond mere novelty and by the good sense not to reject the old just because it is old—by accepting what is valid in both the old and new.

The Women's Community for Feminist Social Work or Fem-School organizes a summer training session to develop and teach methods of practice that advance feminist world views. This annual gathering (not conference) of women-oriented women engages in mutual consciousness-raising activities as a process of enhancing both awareness and commitment. The process is cerebral as well as emotional. As Bricker-Jenkins (1991: 294) succinctly describes it, "It is a search for meanings, and how those meanings were derived." Freire's theory of critical pedagogy and approach to knowledge where the students are active participants is the chosen paradigm for the Fem-School. The goal is individual and collective growth; the means is feminist education designed to engage all participants in the process of personal and political transformation.

Feminist educator bell hooks (1994: 202) similarly articulates Freierian premises in terms of "teaching/learning to transgress," and critical thinking as "the primary element allowing the possibility of change." This summarizes critical thinking. A related aspect is, of course, cultural competence, an indispensable ingredient for working in a multiculturally diverse and complex environment.

Cultural competence entails a recognition of society's prejudices — ethnocentrism, sexism, classism, heterosexism, and racism — and of our own possession of many of these traits. As Ronnau (1994) enunciates, to fully appreciate cultural differences, self-awareness is a must. Social workers must recognize the influence of their own culture, family, and peers on how they think and act. Cultural competence requires continuous efforts to gain more knowledge about the client's culture — the norms, vocabulary, symbols, and strengths. Ronnau argues against the color blind and gender blind notions of many European-American social workers. Through accepting that significant differences do exist between people of different ethnic backgrounds, professionals are recognizing a person's wholeness and individuality. To tell a lesbian or gay person, "Just stay in the closet and you'll be all right," is to deny that person an important part of him- or herself. To tell an African American "we're all the same under the skin," is to deny the importance of race in the society. Multicultural social welfare education exposes students to divergent thinking as they are forced to examine formerly taken for granted assumptions.

Cultural competence becomes more and more critical to effective social work practice as global interdependency increases. Professional developments in other countries are becoming especially relevant to those in the United States as social problems become universal. Much as nations of the south have looked to nations of the north for models of social work education, truly reciprocal exchanges would be more beneficial for all concerned. Today, recognition exists of the need to internationalize the programs of professional education to prepare graduates for the increasingly global nature of social work practice — e.g., with clients of diverse national, ethnic, religious, social, and cultural backgrounds and with persons from other countries (Estes, 1992).

PART 1: SOCIAL WELFARE FUNCTIONS AND STRUCTURE

INTERNATIONAL KNOWLEDGE

Healy (1992) asks us to consider the following:

- A social worker in a family and children's agency meets with a prospective adoptive couple to discuss whether they should consider adopting a Latin American child.
- A social worker at a women's shelter ponders whether the practice principles she has learned are appropriate for counseling a Cambodian refugee woman.
- A community-based social worker advocates for special services from a school system, unaware of his Haitian client's undocumented status.
- A woman asks a legal aid social worker to assist in a custody dispute. The client's husband has fled with their child to his native Sri Lanka where the Sri Lankan court will consider the case.

To these I would add:

- A retired couple living on social security payments seeks advice on relocating to a retirement settlement in Mexico where they can afford the medicine they need.
- A social worker helps document the case of the trauma that would be caused to girls if returned to Nigeria where they would risk genital mutilation.
- A military social worker relocates to a base in Germany to counsel American military families in which there is reported wife abuse.
- A Chinese-American social worker working in a veterans administration unit finds that her presence triggers flashbacks in some Vietnam veterans.
- A lesbian couple meets with a social worker in hopes of adopting a child from a foreign country.
- A Mexican migrant worker who does not speak English requires inpatient treatment for alcoholism.

The common denominator in every case is the link between the United States and another country; often the link is via the client. International and intercultural knowledge is necessary for social work practice in an ever-shrinking world. Child and family problems in the United States, too, increasingly resemble those on distant shores. Healy (1992) provides the following examples:

- Children toil long hours on the streets of Bombay, and a recent investigation uncovers thousands of labor law violations in New England.

211

- Babies with AIDS languish in New Haven, Connecticut; in Kampala, Uganda; and in Bucharest, Romania.
- Street children in Bogota, Colombia, and homeless children in U.S. cities miss out on the education that could provide a chance for their future.
- Refugee children around the world and children in the United States are frequent victims and witnesses of violence.

For the kinds of real situations described in the vignettes above, human service workers require a vast knowledge of the resources relevant to the resolution of social problems rooted in worldwide political economic realities. Connections must be made between the private violence of child abuse and the public violence of war, and between the individual's futile denial of drug addiction and the international denial of nuclear and military addiction and destruction of the environment (Mary and Morris, 1994). Recent efforts such as Estes' guide to internationalizing social work education (1992), the curriculum manual for introducing international development content (Healy, 1992), and the kinds of collaborative educational efforts between countries are described in the following section. Estes (1994: 77) articulates a New World Order Model (NWOM) of social development practice that is at once visionary and integrative:

> The New World Order asserts that the most serious problems confronting humanity are rooted in the fundamental inequalities that exist in the present world *order*; that is, in the system of international social, political, and economic institutions that govern relationships between nations and, within nations, between groups of people. In promoting its social change objectives, the NWOM calls for the creation of a *new world order* based on (a) recognition of and respect for the unity of life on earth, (b) the minimization of violence, (c) the satisfaction of basic human needs, (d) the primacy of human dignity, (e) the retention of diversity and pluralism, and (f) the need for universal participation in the process of attaining worldwide social transformation.

SOCIAL WORK EDUCATION FOR INTERNATIONAL LIVING

The best way to learn of diverse approaches to caring for one another is to live among the people but not before learning to speak their language. The next best way is to have representatives from different countries come to us. In their reactions to the strangeness of our customs, we come to see ourselves as others see us and are made aware of other ways of doing things. We also have to explain ourselves: Why do Americans think they need to carry guns? Don't we get any vacations? Who takes care of us if we can't find work? Why do small families need such big houses?

Most of the academic efforts in the United States and Canada to foster an international orientation have focused on the MSW education, and yet the majority of training programs for social workers worldwide are at the undergraduate level (Johnson, 1994). Some of the means by which programs can be internationalized, according to Johnson, include introducing special courses on international social welfare, integrating this content throughout the curriculum, offering field placements in cross national or overseas settings, and offering reciprocal faculty and student exchanges among various countries. Box 4.3 describes the very intensive and carefully engineered collaborative undertaking between Augsburg College's undergraduate and graduate programs and social workers in Cuernavaca, Mexico. There is also a close connection between Augsburg and the University of Bristol in England. This multifaceted undertaking is a prime example, in Midgley's (1995a) words, of mutual collaboration among professionals in different parts of the world, exchanges that require a discerning attitude, the selective adaptation of practice approaches, and the careful testing and evaluation of innovations. An underlying assumption of the Augsburg program is that practice and policy are interlocked; social work is defined as social policy in action.

Outside the continental United States, at the Brigham Young University-Hawaii Campus, a Pacific/Asian Rim social welfare course is offered to undergraduates (Furuto, 1992). Since a majority of the students in the course and at the university are Asians, often from Japan, and Pacific Islanders, many of whom plan to return to their home countries to practice social work, the classroom atmosphere is uniquely international. The welfare systems of Japan and selected Pacific Island countries are studied in depth.

Undergraduate students at the University of Northern Iowa were astonished to learn of the *harm reduction model* of substance abuse, a model in which substance users work with social workers (in cooperation with doctors and the police) to reduce the harmful effects of drug use on their lives. (Americans are much more apt to subscribe to an abstinence model.) This education was introduced as a part of an official exchange between the departments of social

BOX 4.3

EXPANDING IDEAS ABOUT SOCIAL WORK THROUGH EXPERIENCE IN MEXICO

Rosemary Link and Vincent Peters, Augsburg College

Since 1989 a collaborative course has been developed between the Global Center for Education and Augsburg College's Social Work Department, as part of a full semester program in Cuernavaca, Mexico. Open to students nationally, the program includes Spanish language immersion, social policy, social work internships, family living and comparative models of social work. Much has been learned with students, faculty, and Mexican colleagues as we have shared common ground and met very new realities. The following paragraphs outline some of the questions raised when exploring social work internationally.

The key for us in experiencing social work across national boundaries is the recognition that focusing only on our familiar domestic environment puts false limits on our sense of what can be. To widen our perspective and learn from others gives us more choices and opens us to alternative approaches to human needs. It challenges our ethnocentrism and alerts us to the denigration of difference in our own communities. For example, recently the *Star Tribune* ran a story about Mexican people in Wilmar entitled "Migrant families changing the face of rural Minnesota." (Doyle, 1988). The article concentrated on "problems" and negative stereotypes in a way which demeaned and lacked respect for people making major changes in their lives for survival's sake.

For many of us, to study the questioning among social workers in Mexico is to learn about our own attitudes and possibly, professional complacency. Mexican social work is in the midst of transformation. There are two main arenas for social work activity there, which are distinct and obvious. Social workers have been trained in the past in the traditional "Western" tripartite model (of casework-group-community work) but in recent years there has been a breaking away—a conscientization or new consciousness of the roots of poverty and the need for social workers to become politically aware, creative and risk-taking community organizers. The new mode of social work or "reconceptualization" involves empowering people in their communities, focusing on their felt needs and contributing to local resources and natural helping networks. One

(Continued on next page)

BOX 4.3 (Continued)

example of this is the Women Domestic Workers' Center where our students intern on literacy, employee rights and family projects. However, there are still many social workers employed by the state, especially in the Department of Health and schools. They work with individual needs, often in the casework style and are part of a system which identifies problems as individually created. Often their jobs come with guaranteed state benefits, such as health care and training. Clearly, for some social workers with families to support, it would be hard to critique a system offering these benefits. Nevertheless, for many the traditional styles of social work have not fitted their communities well.

Josefina Perez, our Mexican field liaison speaks of her social work education, including studying Mary Richmond. This produced, as she puts it, "a shock on graduation. I came out of the University as a social worker and felt I hit a brick wall. My training did not fit me for the needs of the people around me." (Perez, Cuernavaca Seminar, 1990) Increasingly numbers of people live the idea of "conscientization" which was defined by Brazilian educator Paulo Freire, "as the process by which an individual learns to perceive the contradictions of reality in the political, social and economic spheres." This conscientization is then "mediated" by practical, social action—such as literacy projects, children's centers, and clean water action. Instead of focusing on individual and family

dysfunction, these social workers are seeking a change, moving away from blaming individual families for their situation, to asking the system to hear their concerns.

Perhaps the acute living problems of health, sanitation, literacy, and housing in Mexico make these issues seem far away from the Midwest. However, we must pause. This week in the press we hear that measles outbreaks are becoming common in the United States, that 10 percent of the children in Minnesota are going hungry and often without shelter (as the 410 Agency can clearly confirm), and teen pregnancies, especially between thirteen and fifteen are on the increase while parents protest a bill introduced to strengthen sex and relationship education in schools. (*Star Tribune,* March 26, 1991) The term "dysfunctional" family is frequently heard in our environment: perhaps it is time for us too, to rethink our negative terminology and focus on social work opportunity which does not blame but focuses on the strengths of individuals and communities. In Mexico we meet with women who have been battered. Sometimes they want individualized help over a crisis and ask for it. There will always be a place for individual pain to be attended to in social work. Most of the time, however, they are working together with social workers to increase women's knowledge of community

(Continued on next page)

BOX 4.3 (Continued)

support and resources combatting violence. The emphasis is collective voice, empowerment, and social change, rather than private assessment of personal deficit.

As social workers we widen our choices by sharing knowledge of different ways of doing things in other countries—not to lay judgment on better or worse, but to equip ourselves to challenge a future which perceives the lack of fit between violent crime and gun control, teen pregnancy and sex education, marital violence and military violence, welfare "dependency" and family income, family crisis and structural unemployment. Both the United States and Mexico have enormous challenges for social workers. The response we have seen, is to be more consciously aware of why things are as they are, and what needs to be done.

———————

Source: Minnesota NASW Chapter Newsletter, Winter, 1991–1992, p. 6. Reprinted by permission of Minnesota NASW.

work at the University of Northern Iowa and at the University of Hull in England. A common bond between the two programs is that they both offer an addictions emphasis.

The University of Iowa, where the journal *Social Development Issues* is published, is heading a faculty and practitioner exchange with Russia. Graduate students from Iowa and Canada also do field work in gerontology in Mexico. Links with India and Australia offer further diversity to an already internationalized program. At the University of Denver, a rare tripartite venture is underway involving this graduate school of social work (offering evaluative research) and professionals in Hong Kong and China. This collaboration was created so that China could learn from Hong Kong expertise on offering services for persons who are handicapped. The undertaking came at the initiative of the Chinese government. The emphasis which China places on community development, and the dedication and expertise in the provision sources in Hong Kong are both a boon to the Denver school of social work (see Jones, 1993).

Following years of careful planning, the International Association of Schools of Social Work (IASSW) conferences were held in Hong Kong in July 1996. The International Federation of Social Workers and International Council on Social Welfare also held their biennial conferences at the same time and place, making for a diversified social work gathering. Previously, the IASSW played an active role in preparing for the Fourth World Conference on Women in Beijing, China, in 1995. Such global interchange of concerns and ideas enriches the field of social work in every participating country. It also prepares the case for humanitarian representation by the world's social workers at the next United Nations world summit.

Faculty at the Columbia University School of Social Work are engaged in a twenty-four-country cooperative effort to study family change in Western and Eastern Europe. Washington University at St. Louis and the University of Pennsylvania have established graduate-level concentrations in social and economic development. The specializations are intended for students who wish to pursue macro-level practice careers in international social work. The University of Connecticut School of Social Work has opened the Center for International Social Work Studies to encourage international education and linkages with social work programs in other parts of the world, especially with Canada and the Caribbean region. Extensive collaboration is currently getting underway among the members of the newly formed North American and Caribbean Regional Association. A linkage with the school of social work in Esbjerg, Denmark, provides field internships for students from Denmark.

A growing collaboration between Canadian schools of social work and schools in industrializing nations reflects the active role that Canadian social workers have played in international development for some time (Gilchrist and Splane, 1995). In 1984 three international welfare conferences were held in Montreal. This kind of activity has spurred the effort to offer international social welfare course material throughout the schools of social work in Canada.

The University of Calgary offers an international concentration as one option in the community organization, management, and social policy specialization at the masters-level. International field placement opportunities are available on five continents and in over thirty countries. In the summer of 1995 the University of Calgary hosted an international conference on social change which was attended by hundreds of participants from over the world.

One of the most ambitious, flexible, well-financed exchange efforts in the world is the European Mobility Program (ERASMUS) which provides funding for faculty exchanges to explore collaboration among teaching institutions in countries that are members of the European Union (Bradley and Harris, 1993). Students are actively involved in exchanges, especially from non-English speaking countries to English speaking ones. The key issue seems to be language facility.

Located at the seaport town of Hull in northeastern England, the University of Hull is in close contact with German universities, and both faculty and students are actively involved. Visitors to Germany benefit from observing a social welfare system that is more generous in many ways, while Germans can enjoy some of the British innovations in community-based care. At the University of Bristol, French visitors, meanwhile, are mystified upon exposure to the anti-oppression and anti-racism workshops based on North American models. The advantage of such exchanges is in the cultural enrichment and opportunity to examine new ways of addressing old problems. The fact that practicing social workers are not excluded from the opening of borders among countries further enhances the exchange of models and approaches. To facilitate the geographical mobility of social workers, the move is underway to standardize occupational training and qualifications (Hokenstad and Kendall, 1995).

Wagner (1992) contrasts the creative exchange among equal partners which underpins "the integration through sharing" taking place in Europe today with the gift-giving or unilateral approach used when knowledge is exchanged from teacher to student. In the latter instances, after World War II for example, when United States experts transported concepts and methods to a war-weary Europe, and in the early phase of contact with Eastern Europe, transactions were one-way and noninteractive. Gradually, the American "import" came under critical scrutiny and the Europeanization of social work got under way, paralleling closely the developments toward European community. Following upheavals in Eastern Europe, interprofessional contacts were intensified with Hungary and Poland.

The development of social work in much of Eastern and East Central Europe, except for Poland and former Yugoslavia, is in embryonic stage. Today Poland reaches back seven decades to its beginnings in social work to redevelop its social welfare legislation and promote social work in over thirty-four professional schools of social work; the school of social work in Zagreb, Yugoslovia, is over forty years old (Mechta and Constable, 1994). In an international social work event in 1991 in Vienna (sponsored by the IASSW), initiatives were undertaken to formalize social work training in Hungary, the Czech Republic, Slovakia, Albania, Estonia, Lithuania, Latvia, Romania, and Russia, among others. The disappearance of central control following the revolutions of 1989 through 1991 in Eastern Europe demanded reconstruction of every social institution. In most Communist states prior to the revolutionary changes, social work and social work training were not permitted or were eliminated where they existed (Garber, 1994). How could one need social assistance when everyone was employed and housing and health care were universally available? This was the Marxist point of view concerning social work; the ideology was consistent with the denial of social problems in societies ruled by the people. The concept of an independent social work profession was alien also. Under the new democratic and capitalist regimes of today, the political and social disorganization compounded by severe economic problems has created a setting where the need for active social work (community centered practice) is apparent. Exchanges with countries having strong traditions of social work are offering exciting educational and cultural opportunities for East and West alike.

COMPARATIVE SOCIAL WORK

Social Work Education and Status

In most parts of the world—in rich and poor countries, in rural areas and large cities, under capitalism and socialism—in one form or another, there is social work. Internationally, there is no uniform set of standards for educational training. Within Europe, three conditions must be met in order for social workers to be recognized as professionals throughout the E.U.: the profession must be regulated by an official body; education must be beyond high school; and training must be of three years duration (Wagner, 1992). Yet, even within Europe there are varied educational traditions. Whereas in Italy and Spain, social workers are educated solely at universities, there are mixed postsecondary programs in Denmark, France, Germany, and the United Kingdom. In Belgium, Greece, the Netherlands, Norway, and Portugal, social work education is at specialized postsecondary, technical schools. In Eastern Europe, Poland and Hungary offer university-based education. Social work education is at a very early stage of development in Russia, according to Hokenstad and Kendall (1995).

The university pattern of education is strong throughout Latin America with the exception that in Mexico most social workers are educated in nonuniversity training programs. Many of the African nations provide three to four year undergraduate university programs. Most Asian countries have organized social work education along American lines, as have Australia and New Zealand.

Although there are differences in how the social work profession presents itself throughout the world, there are interesting similarities in the status of social workers which unfortunately is quite low. The conflict between capitalist and humanitarian values and the materialism of the modern world shape the context of social work practice. Then there is the stigma, an almost universal stigma or a kind of "guilt by association" of working with the poor and downtrodden of society.

The resentment of the high cost of the social welfare system is a further factor adversely affecting human service workers in Western nations especially since the resentment seems to translate into ever declining prestige and income (Federico, 1990). Outside of Africa, women are represented in disproportionately high numbers in the professional membership, no doubt a fact accounting for the relatively modest salaries, political powerlessness, and lack of public prestige accorded to persons in this line of work. Where the social welfare traditions are more ingrained, however, and where social workers are able to shape laws affecting their practice and constituents, such as in Scandinavia, the power that social workers wield increases commensurately. However, this very power, such as in the always controversial area of child protection, is likely to be greatly resented at the same time. Moreover, the social workers' close alliance with left-wing politics (stronger in Europe than in the United States) may leave the profession in disrepute in times of conservative insurgency. Today's conservative and economic onslaught against the vestiges of the welfare state does not bode well for the poor or for social workers employed in the public sector.

SOCIAL WORK ROLES AND MODELS

Although the education may vary in all countries, social work values transcend the national boundaries. In emerging nations, the social work role is cast in terms of the challenge of nation building; in communities divided ethnically or racially, social workers are expected to be agents of reconciliation (Hokenstad, Khinduka, and Midgley, 1992). Due to war and conquest, colonialism, immigration, and the scarcity of resources, ethnic rivalries and disturbances are facts of life everywhere. The challenge for social workers is a difficult one: to look beyond the divisions between people and toward the common human connectedness while recognizing the strengths in diversity. In actively working for world peace and justice, through what Wagner (1992) calls "global acting/thinking," social workers are respecting the individual worth of every person.

There is an emergent recognition today that traditional social work practice models grooming professionals for office work with individual clients is of limited practical value against the timeless plagues of disease, war, homelessness, and overpopulation. Whereas many in the countries of the North deal with poverty indirectly in a social control capacity or in working toward individual change, social workers internationally are taking note of what is happening in the South, particularly in Latin America, where the poor have mobilized themselves into empowering social movements to improve living conditions and where indigenous social workers have joined the struggle. To combat the horrendous social problems facing the twenty-first century, Mary and Morris (1994) call for a major paradigm shift; this would include a shift in social work focus from treatment to prevention, and from residual problem solving to more transformational, preventive formulations. Such proponents of radical community action, interestingly, put little faith in the government's willingness or ability to promote social welfare for the masses. Although sometimes the state joins the struggle of the poor, according to this model for change, the leadership flows from the bottom up (at the grass-roots level) rather than in being dictated from the top down. In many countries, expenditures for government initiated programs end up in the hands of government workers and politicians rather than with the poor. Social work theorists from the industrialized countries are asking why such models can work in Peru and Honduras then why not in New York City and London? This evolving grass-roots community action approach has come to be labeled the *social development perspective* (Midgley, 1995). This perspective should be distinguished from an economic development approach which assumes that as a country develops economically, the prosperity will benefit the whole population. Social development focuses on social welfare development in health, education, and living conditions for all people. The journal, *Social Development Issues*, explores the dynamics of social development from an international social work perspective. Typical articles chronicle successful grass-roots activities such as setting up programs to promote literacy, nutrition, and organized day care in rural areas in countries where government organizations are weak. An underlying theme throughout all the developmental literature is the centrality of world economic variables in human affairs. For a closer view of the challenges facing social work in various parts of the world, we will look briefly at the profession in various nations—in India, Iran, Uganda, and Norway.

India

The disjunction between the needs of the people to be helped and the training of the helpers is the defining characteristic of Indian social work. Organized mainly at the master's degree level, social work education draws students (most are female) largely from middle-class backgrounds. Despite the dire need for social welfare activities in rural communities, textbooks and theoretical frameworks are borrowed overwhelmingly from the United States and are often desperately out-of-date besides (Nagpaul, 1993). These deficiencies are further exacerbated by the fact that university talent and training are largely wasted in a nation which does not recognize social work education as necessary to the performing of tasks related to social welfare (Bose, 1992). Today, according to Bose, there is virtually no possibility of professionally trained social workers being employed in decision-making positions that require social work expertise. The absence of effective professional associations is largely responsible for this state of affairs.

Ejaz (1991) describes the dilemma confronting caseworkers who are torn between social worker goals of self-determination and clients' dependency and fatalism. Because of these traditions, client-centered therapy, so popular in the West, is largely culturally alien to India. What is in tune with Indian culture is to seek advice of elders and of educated persons. Caseworkers, therefore, tend to become directive and even authoritarian in their approach. In this way, despite their Western-based education, Indian workers are conditioned by their clients to respond to them in the way they expect.

On the positive side, at one of the oldest schools of social work in Asia, established in Bombay in 1936, the Tata Institute of Social Sciences offers a diversified curriculum leading up to the doctorate level. In India, professional social work education is well-developed, and is provided at a higher level than in many European countries (Midgley, 1981). There are over thirty professional schools of social work, the great majority of which offer a master's degree. Two social work specialties where social work training is valued by employers are labor welfare (which resembles personnel management) and medical-psychiatric social work. The former specialization is entirely indigenous, according to Nagpaul, and is derived from the Indian Factories Act of 1948 and its various amendments. Although there has been a trend to downgrade all such terms of prestige and job opportunities, labor welfare continues to be the dominant field of study in India. With regard to the medical/psychiatric specialty, Nagpaul (1993: 210) argues: "In a society where the problems of physical health are massive as reflected through higher rates of infant mortality, maternal mortality, malnutrition, and many other forms of morbidity, the establishment and promotion of medical and psychiatric social work seem rather questionable."

Published by the Tata Institute of Social Sciences in Bombay, *The Indian Journal of Social Work* grapples heroically with such issues as mass poverty, and maternal and child health. The authors, generally professors of social work in India, are concerned with social welfare issues from a preventive, not a curative perspective.

Iran

There is a wealth of recent literature concerning the disaster of implanting Western models of social work to non-Western countries, models which are often irrelevant to the magnitude of the task at hand. It is true that when colonial powers set up European social work programs in non-European countries, a kind of elitism prevailed. In many places, social work (before the 1970s) became a caricature of its worst instincts. And yet Sattareh Farman-Farmaian (1992), a native Iranian, found the weapon she was looking for "to fight Iran's human miseries" at the University of Southern California (USC) in the "profession called social work." Her fascinating autobiography, *Daughter of Persia: A Woman's Journey from Her Father's Harem through the Islamic Revolution*, offers invaluable insight into the intricacies of adapting the principles of American social work into one's native land. The detailed description of the rise and fall of the establishment of a school of social work in Tehran, Iran, is a revelation not only in terms of the political obstacles that had to be overcome in a country where at that time "women couldn't vote, much less run for office," but also a vital documentation of social work education history. Here, Farman-Farmaian reveals her sense of inspiration in what was imparted to her at USC in 1946 (1992: 167):

> Whereas in my country help came to the needy only through alms, for the first time I saw how social workers developed ways to address the problems that made people needy: well-regulated orphanages, licensed homes for the

aged, the disabled, and the mentally ill. There were thousands of family service agencies, hospital clinics, and training programs in which social workers not only assisted human beings in emergencies but tried to give them ways of dealing themselves with broken families, sickness, physical disability, mental illness, old age, relocation, unemployment, alcoholism, and other problems—always with the goal of helping them to rely not on benefactors and protectors, but on themselves.

Inspired by her dedicated mentors at USC School of Social Work, teachers who engaged in a constant fight for social reform and "who had the gift of making us feel we had been chosen, like physicians, to heal all the ills of society," Farman-Farmaian returned to her home country to pursue her mission. Blessed by high family connections that extended to the royal palace, Farman-Farmaian was authorized (with a limited stipend) in 1953 to start a graduate training school—the Tehran School of Social Work. The social work literature which had been written with an American audience in mind was entirely unsuitable for use in a non-industrialized nation. Since there was not even a Persian word for social worker, the term *madadkar* was invented, meaning "one who helps." According to Farman-Farmaian (1992: 212), the education for a madadkar was comprehensive:

> I was requiring them to study numerous subjects: planning a family's diet, hygiene, first aid, human physical development and reproduction, family finances, and social and individual psychology. (There were no courses in psychotherapy, a subject of exceedingly limited use to social workers in the developing nations of the world, whose inhabitants are mainly concerned with surviving from one day to the next.)

In their field placements, the students, women from middle-class backgrounds and men from working-class backgrounds, encountered a wretchedness they had never dreamed existed. Visiting insane asylums and orphanages, they found the inhabitants literally groveling in filth. Together, with a host of volunteers, the social work students physically cleaned (shoveling out excrement) the premises as a first step in providing care. Family planning was another area of intensive organizing activity. Soon over time, the students' integrity and unselfish devotion to social work enhanced the reputation of the school and a BSW program was established. The number of applications soared and the school was accorded university status in 1961.

Although Iran under the Shah or king (Reza Pahlavi), was a country in which free speech was unknown and the extreme social problems could not be publicly documented, when governmental pressures became too much, the school was protected by the active support and influence of the Shah's westernized wife, Queen Farah.

Prigmore (1990) was impressed with the modernization and efficient bureaucratization of Iran that he observed in 1977. An elaborate health and welfare network delivered a variety of needed services to the people. There were over 2,500 family planning clinics. A trip to the welfare office in one of the large cities indicated that thirty-four social workers served the city, and a shortage of trained social workers continued to be a primary problem. In events which culminated in the revolution of 1979, however, religious fundamentalists destroyed everything that smacked of secular culture. Ordered to return to covering themselves from head to toe with a black garment called the chador, women were driven from their jobs as factories and offices were segregated by sex. Farman-Farmaian found herself arrested for establishing birth control clinics. With the forced closing of the school of social work, the "daughter of Persia" fled at great personal risk to the United States. All that had been was no more.

Due to the heavy censorship concerning social welfare in Iran, Prigmore notes the enormous difficulty in discovering the true state of affairs today. Most significant is the suppression of women who had earlier been a decisive force in social welfare thought and action. We do know from international reports that while the country struggles with a shattered economy and high unemployment, its leaders spend billions on a massive arms build up (Sivard, 1993). The birthrate is now one of the highest in the world and polygamy, or the practice of marriage between one (usually wealthy) man and several wives, has been restored (Prigmore, 1990).

The short history of social work in Iran illustrates the universalism of the spirit of social work ("together we can") if not always of the specific content. The integration of social work with community development was possible due to a complex but favorable government response as well as to the political pull, personal charisma, and dedication of a remarkable woman. This same history also underscores the political vulnerability of schools of social work to political and social repression forces, especially when they are directed against women and ethnic minorities (against "Zionists" or Jews in this case).

Both Farman-Farmaian and Prigmore agree that the hope of the future lies in the women of Iran. While the laws are against them, the legacy of strength, strong family roles, and the experience of a period of liberation unite them.

Uganda

Although most professional schools of social work in Africa were not established until the 1960s, in Egypt, South Africa, and Uganda, social work training began in the 1930s (Midgley, 1981). British colonialists introduced social work into Ugandan society, and, as in other parts of Africa under British influence, the professional schools of social work eventually were located within universities. The residual, individualized approach dominated social work for the first thirty years, with the focus ranging from various marginal groups such as orphans and juvenile offenders to the neglect of the vast needs of the general population (Ankrah, 1992). Then, with the independence of East African countries in the early 1960s, the social work focus changed to challenge the poverty, malnutrition, and poor sanitation affecting the country as a whole. Community organization, empowerment, and social development are themes of the Afrocentric social work programs offered today. According to Ankrah, a member of the Department of Social Work and Social Administration at Makerere University in Kampala, Uganda, who conducted an extensive survey of qualified practitioners, a new generation of social workers is emerging. These social workers, mostly male, are not caseworkers but are employed as public and social administrators, policymakers, researchers, community mobilizers, and educators. Public health is opening up as a major new arena for professional social workers in Africa; one reason being that Uganda is being ravaged by AIDS.

An alarming one out of every six people in the African nation is HIV-positive. An article in the British medical journal, *The Lancet* (Mulder et al., 1994), provides the facts: for HIV-positive women in Uganda, the highest number of deaths occur among those between thirteen and thirty-four years old; for men the comparable ages are twenty-five to thirty-four years old. The age difference is explained by the fact that African men, according to Anderson and May (1992), tend to form sexual partnerships with women who are five to ten years younger than themselves. Because somewhat more women than men are dying of AIDS, and because these women are of childbearing age, the result is the birth of large numbers of AIDS-infected children. Many other children are orphaned. AIDS is already causing serious demographic changes; the social consequences are staggering.

Because of the AIDS epidemic, urban and rural families are being impoverished by the expense of caring for the ill and by the loss of breadwinners. The largest influx of professionals engaged in working to control the epidemic has been in the nongovernmental, indigenous, and international humanitarian organizations (Ankrah, 1992). Supportive counseling and building extended family networks and community-based support systems are two of the major social worker roles. Under the auspices of the World Health Organization, the social work department of Makerere University is spearheading research to be used in policy-making and program development.

Government resources to pay for AIDS prevention or any other social services are depleted due to the International Monetary Fund's (IMF) requirements for "structural adjustment" as a condition of economic aid. IMF's terms require reduction in government support for such social services as health and education as well as retrenchment in the civil service (Ankrah, 1992). Nevertheless, an active role for professionally trained social workers is assured in rural and social development. Private agencies, international organizations, and home-grown, health care operations will be the recruiting grounds of the future.

Norway

Sometimes a crop or breed of animal when transported to a different land does better than in the native country. Perhaps the soil is richer or the climate is more hospitable or maybe the process of challenge and adaptation creates a new vitality. So it also is with social institutions. Introduced relatively late from England and the United States, social work seems to have "taken root" in the fertile Scandinavian soil where traditions of helping and cooperation are legendary.

The social work profession began outside of Norway. The casework approach, with its Freudian, psychodynamic focus, was borrowed from the United States and England. But in Norway, social casework took on an altruistic character from the start. In 1920, the first Norwegian women's social work course was instituted; this grew into a full social work college by 1950. Not long afterwards, the first professional association—the hospital consultant's organization—evolved into the militant organization, NOSO (Norsk Sosionomforbud), now the FO (Fellesorganisjonen). Men, despite being in the minority, assumed the leadership roles. The 1960s were characterized by political radicalism coupled with the fight for acknowledgement of social work as a profession. Although American and British textbooks were widely used, a strong flavor of anti-Americanism characterized the new generation of students (Editorial, 1989).

A profession requires a distinct, exclusive title. Swedish social workers coined the name *Sosionom* in 1966. *Sosio* is from Latin and *nomos* from Greek meaning one who knows the community. The word *social worker* is used in a general way and the word *sosionom* is used to denote a specific professional membership and training. This precise designation of an exclusive title prevents the kind of confusion engendered over the generic term, social worker, as applied on the North American continent and in the United Kingdom.

Since the 1970s, when NOSO joined the predominant and powerful master trade union in Norway, the question of pay has assumed a central importance. Furthermore, NOSO has consistently fought for a four year higher education. Pay raises have been granted and educational opportunities have improved. Social workers in Norway are highly unionized; the professional organization which publishes the social work journal *Sosionomen* is itself the union, providing extensive labor protection where required.

According to an extensive survey (Avgedal and Thyness, 1990), the typical social work student is a thirty-year-old female with children. Today, 86 percent of the new students are female who mostly plan to do therapy work while a disproportionately high number of males choose administration. Eight percent of social work students plan to specialize in addictions work and 30 percent plan to work with children. For those students private practice is not an option. Entrance into a school of social work is competitive: in 1990 there were 4310 applications for 525 places.

U.S. social workers may smile enviously at typical job announcements such as the following: "An opening for family therapist. Five weeks vacation and one year paid leave after five year's service. We have our own kindergarten." Such benefits are given, in light of the scarcity of social workers, to attract applicants. Since there are too few kindergartens in the country, this final enticement should produce the desired results. Norwegian social workers are lobbying for a six-hour work day for themselves and for workers in other professions. A major argument for this is that childcare responsibilities will be more easily met with a shorter work day. Plans are underway to equalize social work pay in order to lessen pay differentials between administrators and frontline workers.

Social work education is offered, generally, in specialized schools with undergraduate status. The social work program lasts three years and leads to a certificate or degree. Only one university at Trondheim offers a program in social work. Until 1975, Norwegian social work educators were largely trained in the United States since there were no advanced social work courses in Norway prior to that time. The traditions of psychologically-oriented individual case-work were predominant until the late 1960s when social workers were made responsible for carrying out new social policies of the state. Training in law, political, or administrative theory was provided; the influence of sociology was strongly felt.

The social work curriculum is standardized across the country, as it is in the United States. Standardization in Norway, however, is imposed by government rather than academic bodies. The course curriculum prospectus from the University of Trondheim reveals an intensive two and a half year curriculum designed for the training of administrators, social planners, and social work educators. Approximately one-third of the program consists of field experience. Research methods are stressed as in the fields of administration and law, and lawyers teach on the faculty. Interestingly, the *rektor* or director of one of the social work colleges is a distinguished judge. Sociologists and psychologists are also on the faculty of all these colleges.

Norwegian social workers are well-represented in government and have a close association with the socialist political parties, especially at regional levels. The position of *sosialsjef* (social chief) is held by a social worker. The post, which comes below that of the mayor, involves overseeing budgetary and child welfare matters. A governmental link between social work and community institutions is thus "closer in the Norwegian welfare state than in the United States and England" (Lingas, 1991: 7). At the national level, members of the profession operate in an advisory capacity to the government, especially with regard to shaping child welfare law (van Wormer, 1990).

Since Norway recently voted in a national referendum not to join the European Union, but to retain their high standards of social welfare and subsidization of farmers, Norwegian social workers are in a position preferable to that of their Danish and now Swedish and Finish counterparts. Vast deposits of oil in the North Sea, largely government owned, bolster the Norwegian economy making independence possible.

A survey of editorials in the professional social work journal, *Sosiono-men*, reveals that Norwegian social worker concerns, the political and ethical issues of interest, are strikingly similar to concerns of their North American counterparts. Child welfare, care for the elderly, and day care are highlighted as areas requiring institutional attention. Common to Norwegian and North American social work journals is advocacy on behalf of clients in the face of deteriorating or nonexistent social services. To the extent that there is a difference between social work in a welfare state or in a society of high militarism, the difference is more one of degree than of substance. While the Norwegian journals fight to maintain the high standards of living, journals in the United States must reckon with abject poverty, homelessness, poor health care, and high incarceration rates, on top of a public backlash against those who receive help from the state.

CONCLUSION AND SUMMARY

Social workers share a global mission. The social ills confronting the profession—inflation, national indebtedness, the influx of political and economic refugees, underemployment, homelessness, the AIDS pandemic—differ in degree but not in kind. Every country's economy today is affected by a global market and intense competition to market products. In the past, models of practice have been superimposed into various educational structures by representatives from the Euro-American world: visiting instructors were British and American; the textbooks were in English and emphasized individualized models; and therefore the transfer of knowledge was largely unilateral.

But as British social work educator Robert Harris (1990) reminds us, the development of an understanding for local customs and policy is something which is absorbed as much as learned; it is a part of a context of learning and living which is simply unique in different places. Knowledge imparted from the outside, in this context, develops a life of its own. Frameworks employed that do not fit are discarded and modified or exchanged for those that do. In Africa, Latin America, Asia, the forms of social work have been molded to the contours of the landscape. Meanwhile, social work educators in the West are seeking new forms of intervention. The days of unilateral exchange of knowledge from West to East or North to South may be over.

One of the delights of talking to overseas colleagues lies in the differences we perceive, and the capacity of those differences to make us look with fresh eyes on that which we thought we knew and understood.

Grass-roots activity, or organizing from the ground level up, is a hallmark of the new generation of social workers in countries of the South. Other countries can learn a lesson from this. In the bewildering new order of the global economy and the resurgent conservatism, the impetus of the international exchange of ideas and solutions is formidable. There is a mounting awareness that social workers in places like North America, Europe, and Japan can study the innovations developed in Latin America and Africa that can be adapted to address mutual social problems.

To summarize the themes of this chapter, the history of social work is a proud history, the story of strong women and gentle men in many ways ahead of their time who worked for social reform or to help individuals in distress. There were, of course, some low moments—conformity under Hitler's Germany and under McCarthyism in the United States, and the dominance of psychoanalytical theory in the 1920s and 1950s.

The history of the development of the social work profession and of its educational institutions reveals that evolution is circular rather than linear and occurs in rotating shifts. These shifts tend to reflect the ideological rhythms of the wider society. Historically, the movement has altered between two seemingly opposing forces: personal troubles and public issues. Franklin (1990) has revealed how social work responded to the ideological influence of the times by offering interventions—community action, social casework, group therapy— that were compatible with the popular currents. We have to remember there was much overlap between the interventions, until one or the other won out, and that countervailing forces were always present simultaneously.

Whereas the Charity Organization Societies founded prior to the 1890s generally are regarded as individualistic in focus with the emphasis mainly on determining individual eligibility to receive charity, the settlement house movement tends to be presented as the prototype of community organization in motion, as an organization for social reform but also for cultural education. World War I changed things as did Flexner's stunning and somewhat insensitive rebuke of social work for failure to qualify as a genuine profession. These dual influences, in conjunction with growing anti-immigrant and racist sentiment in the United States, created a situation ripe for a wholehearted endorsement of the very intriguing psychoanalytical concepts. With its relatively coherent theory of personality, psychoanalysis provided a rationale for diagnosis and treatment that had previously been lacking.

When the Great Depression hit, social workers thrived under the New Deal as society set out to rebuild itself. Canada experienced a comparable shift from attention to personal attributes (or lack thereof) to putting the "social" back in social work.

Going from action to counteraction or counterreaction, a new war fever built up and a conservative mood followed. Group-work, psychodynamically oriented, was introduced as a new trend, the teaching of which rapidly spread to Europe. Minimal attention was paid to social concerns until the sixties, another period of rejuvenation for the community approach. The radical right once again is a major force to reckon with, an international ideology associated with competition in the global economy. Privatization is a related worldwide trend affecting social work conditions of employment, the strength of the unions, and the means of payment reimbursement for clients. Conditions ripe for mass unemployment related to technological advances are countered by a media-generated public outcry to force public welfare recipients to go to work. Meanwhile, in countries around the world the increasing chasm between rich and poor and the conservative onslaught on the social welfare state have created difficulties for the social work profession universally. A deliberate, targeted attack on Britain's social workers has been especially forthright. While some nations, such as those in Scandinavia, continue to look to the government for solutions to the social ills, other nations, such as those to the South have been drawn to community intervention starting at the grass-roots level and working upwards. International social work is taking note of such populist innovations.

This chapter has introduced the term *social work imagination* to represent the wealth of creative and innovative activity taking place across the globe. A prime example was the introduction of social work as a home grown and culturally indigenous enterprise in Iran. As Europe opens its borders — France and England are now physically joined for the first time — the exchange of faculty and students is bringing a cross-fertilization of ideas and approaches in its wake. The social work profession in the United States, Canada, and Britain has established leadership in feminist therapy with Britain making inroads in feminist activism and the United States and Britain making progress in antidiscrimination policies, which are now being adopted internationally.

The quest for creative responses to near universal problems has led the social work profession to look for sources of inspiration in other parts of the world. In recognition of the fact that the exchange of knowledge — previously from the North to the South — is a contradiction in terms, attention is being directed toward the social developmental, community-centered focus as a model for advocacy and empowerment. Such an approach has been successfully used in Chile, Honduras, and South Africa. Although in the United States and Canada growing numbers of social workers, frustrated with narrow agency constraints, are seizing opportunities to practice privately, many working from an individualist perspective, there are promising counterforces at work. Among them is the constant, sometimes scolding reminder in the literature of the social work mission and traditions which emerged out of the cruelties of the industrial age. Another is in the feminist, multicultural perspective adopted by many contemporary practitioners. Nevertheless, the major threat to social work today, and this is true worldwide, does not come from *within,* it comes from *without.* It is the thrust toward privatization associated with subcontracting out of services, declassification of job requirements, the threat of agency layoffs, and a reduction in pay, benefits, and job security. The political war on welfare combined with a decline in skilled employment is also an assault on the profession most closely associated with social welfare. The overall situation was summed up well in a cartoon published about ten years ago in which one worker said to the other, "These are the good old days."

So how to resolve the age-old questions in social work: Does one aim the interventions at the individual or at society? Which is the cause and which is the effect? Consistent with the ecosystems model prevalent in social work today and with contemporary historical analysis, this chapter has argued against the either/or construct and looked toward a both/and conceptualization to encompass both the person and his or her environment. Multicultural practice and feminist therapy, which highlight oppression and empowerment, are encouraging new approaches. Social work education's efforts to internationalize the curriculum is another laudatory development. Whether social workers are employed by governmental agencies or engage in independent practice, whether their method is via therapy or community action, and whether they work in Singapore, Ireland, Canada, or the United States, they are united by common social work values that emphasize altruism and goodwill and transcend the professional nuances of national borders.

REVIEW QUESTIONS

1. Discuss the evolution of social work in light of political shifts of the pendulum. Can the personal and political be truly separated?

2. Discuss C. Wright Mills' distinction between personal troubles and public issues and how they come together.
3. What is the significance of the slogan, "Change the world, change yourself?"
4. During which periods was a community action emphasis apparent? When did individualism triumph?
5. What are Specht and Courtney's four Ps? Relate each one to social welfare today.
6. What are Mary Richmond's contributions to social work? How was interpretation of her theoretical formulation reshaped by psychoanalytical thought?
7. Trace the history of the settlement house movement. Compare this development with the COS movement.
8. How did the settlement house leaders respond to the needs of African Americans? What was the contribution of the Emanuel Settlement?
9. Give the personal history of Jane Addams. How did she fall out of public favor?
10. Discuss the growth of formal training for social workers. How did the new profession get a name?
11. What was the impact of Flexner's stinging rebuke to social work in 1915? How did the profession strive to subscribe to the role model?
12. How did the effects of World War I and racism catapult Mary Richmond to leadership within the profession? How did she "clarify" her method for public consumption?
13. Describe the excitement generated by the new Freudian view of human behavior.
14. How did the Great Depression change things? How did the New Deal impact social workers?
15. Discuss the backlash against the New Deal reforms that followed World War II.
16. Discuss women's leadership in the social work profession. What was Alice Salomon's role? What were factors leading to a male "takeover"?
17. Recall the pioneering work of Gisela Konopka. How did she combine theory with method in a unique way?
18. How did social workers in Germany end up, unwittingly, as "accomplices to murder"? What are some later parallels?
19. Discuss the role of the anticommunist hysteria. How did homosexuality enter the picture? What happened to social work?
20. What were some factors in the rise of McCarthyism? What was the view of persons receiving social welfare benefits? Discuss parallels between the 1950s and 1990s.
21. Discuss the impact of the Civil Rights movement on social work.
22. What is the basic thesis of *Unfaithful Angels: How Social Work Has Abandoned Its Mission?* Argue in favor or against the position taken by Specht and Courtney.
23. Describe NASW and its political viability. Describe the make-up of the profession and students' attitudes.

24. Differentiate the European tolerance position from the North American antidiscrimination stand.
25. What is ethnic sensitive practice?
26. Discuss the parallels between feminist thought and social work.
27. How is the profession's growing international commitment evidenced?
28. How is the barrage of attacks against psychotherapists related to the right-wing backlash?
29. How have pressures from the International Monetary Fund affected social welfare in Latin America?
30. Relate *declassification* to professionalization.
31. What is the *social work imagination*? Relate this to international vision.
32. Define empathy, critical consciousness, and cultural competence as components of critical thinking.
33. What is Freire's theory of critical pedagogy? How does feminist theory relate to this model?
34. Give some examples of international situations the social worker might encounter.
35. Describe the ERASMUS program in Europe and its purpose.
36. Discuss the status of social work in various parts of the world.
37. Discuss the social development perspective with regard to grass-roots activities.
38. Describe how the importation into India of Western social work models has not always been effective.
39. Recount the remarkable and remarkably short history of social work education in Iran.
40. What are some of the social problems facing Uganda today?
41. Compare and contrast the social work profession in Norway with its counterpart in the United States.

REFERENCES

Addams, J. (1910). *Twenty Years at Hull-House*. Norwood, MA: Norwood Press.

Alinsky, S. (1971). *Rules for Radicals: A Practical Primer for Realistic Radicals*. New York: Random House.

Amundsen, R. (1994). Da Sosionomyrket Ble Til. (When Social Work Began). *Sosionomen* 9: 26–30.

Anderson, R. and R. May. (1992, May). Understanding the AIDS Pandemic. *Scientific American*: 58–66.

Andrews, J. (1990). Female Social Workers in the Second Generation. *Affilia* 5(2): 46–59.

Andrews, J. and Parnell, S. (1994, April 29). *A Training Model to Integrate Feminist Principles into Education.* Paper presented at the Biennial Midwest Social Work Education Conference, St. Paul, MN.

Ankrah, E. (1992). Social Work in Uganda: Survival in the Midst of Turbulence. In M. Hokenstad, S. Khinduka, and J. Midgley, eds. *Profiles in International Social Work* (145–162). Washington, DC: NASW Press.

Avgedal, E. and P. Thyness. (1990). 86% Kvinner. *Sosionomen* 5: 32–5.

Bacon, M. (1986). *The Story of Quaker Women in America.* San Francisco, CA: Harper and Row.

Bell, W. (1979). *The Attribution of Cause in the Assessment Process.* Doctoral dissertation: Tulane University, New Orleans, LA.

Bose, A. (1992). Social Work in India: Developmental Roles for a Helping Profession. In M. Hokenstad, S. Khinduka, and J. Midgley, *Profiles in International Social Work.* Washington, DC: NASW Press, 71–83.

Bradley, G. and R. Harris. (1993). Social Work in Europe: An ERASMUS Initiative. *Social Work Education* 12: 51–66.

Brandwein, R. (1995). Women in Social Policy. In *Encyclopedia of Social Work*, 19th ed., 2552–2560. Washington, DC: NASW Press.

Bricker-Jenkins, M. (1991). The Propositions and Assumptions of Feminist Social Work Practice. In M. Bricker-Jenkins, N. Hooyman, and N. Gottlieb, eds. *Feminist Social Work Practice in Clinical Settings.* Newbury Park, CA: SAGE.

Bricker-Jenkins, M. and P. Lockett. (1995). Women: Direct Practice. In *Encyclopedia of Social Work,* 19th ed., 2529–2539. Washington, DC: NASW Press.

Brieland, D. (1990). The Hull-House Tradition and the Contemporary Social Worker: Was Jane Addams Really a Social Worker? *Social Work* 35(2): 134–138.

Burt, W. (1994, July 11–15). *The Social Components of Foreign Policy: Implications for Social Work Involvement.* Paper presented at the 27th Congress of the International Association of Schools of Social Work, Amsterdam.

Butler, K. (1995). Therapy under the Glass: Caught in the Cross Fire. *The Family Therapy Networker* 19(2): 24–34, 68–79.

Chambers, C. (1986). Women in the Creation of the Profession of Social Work. *Social Service Review* 60(1): 1–26.

Collins, B. (1986). Defining Feminist Social Work. *Social Work* 31(3): 214–219.

Collins, D. (1992). Thoughts of a Male Counsellor Attempting a Feminist Approach. *Journal of Child and Youth Care* 7(2): 69–74.

Cooley, C. (1983/1909). Social Organization: A Study of the Larger Mind. New Brunswick, N.J.: Transaction.

CSWE. (1994). *Social Work Education Reporter* 42(3): 5–6.

Day, P. (1997). *A New History of Social Welfare.* Boston: Allyn and Bacon.

Dominelli, L. and E. McCleod. (1989). *Feminist Social Work.* London: Macmillan.

Editorial. (1989). "Trekk fra Forbundets Historie." *Sosionomen* 21: 6–13.

Ehrenreich, J. (1985). *The Altruistic Imagination: A History of Social Work and Social Policy in the U.S.* Ithaca, NY: Cornell University Press.

Ejaz, F. (1991). Self-Determination: Lessons to be Learned for Social Work Practice in India. *British Journal of Social Work* 21: 127–142.

Estes, R. (1994). Education for Social Development: Curricular Issues and Models. *Social Development Issues* 16(3): 68–90.

———., ed. (1992). Internationalizing Social Work. *Internationalizing Social Work Education.* Philadelphia: University of Pennsylvania: 10–19.

Ewalt, P. (1994). Welfare—How Much Reform? *Social Work* 39(5): 485–586.

Faderman, L. (1991). *Odd Girls and Twilight Lovers: A History of Lesbian Life in Twentieth-Century America.* New York: Columbia University Press.

Farman-Farmaian, S. (1992). *Daughter of Persia: A Woman's Journey from her Father's Harem through the Islamic Revolution.* New York: Crown.

Federico, R. (1990). *Social Welfare in Today's World.* New York: McGraw Hill.

Fisher, J. (1986). *Security Risk.* Sarasota, FL: Piney Branch Press.

Franklin, D. (1990). The Cycles of Social Work Practice: Social Action vs. Individual Interest. *Journal of Progressive Human Services* 1(2): 59–80.

Freire, P. (1973). *Education for Critical Consciousness.* New York: The Seabury Press.

Furuto, S. (1992, March 3). *The International Community at the BSW Level: Outline of a Pacific Basin/Asian Rim SocialWelfare Course.* Paper presented at the annual meeting of the Council on Social Work Education: St. Louis, MO.

Garber, R. (1994). Introduction. In R. Constable and V. Mehta, eds. *Education for Social Work in Eastern Europe.* Chicago: Lyceum, 1–4.

Germain, C. and A. Gitterman. (1995). Ecological Perspective. In *Encyclopedia of Social Work*, 19th ed., 816–823, 824. Washington, DC: NASW Press.

Gilchrist, G. and J. Splane. (1995). Canada's Role in International Social Welfare. In J. Turner and F. Turner, eds. *Canadian Social Welfare,* 3d ed. Scarborough, Canada: Allyn and Bacon, 574–596.

Ginsberg, L. (1995). *Social Work Almanac,* 2d ed. Washington DC: NASW Press.

Glennerster, H. and J. Midgley, eds. (1991). *The Radical Right and the Welfare State: An International Assessment.* London: Harvester Wheat Sheaf.

Gutiérrez, L. (1991). Empowering Women of Color: A Feminist Model. In M. Bricker-Jenkins, N. Hooyman, and N. Gottlieb, eds. *Feminist Social Work Practice in Clinical Settings.* Newbury Park: SAGE, 119–211.

Guy, P. (1994). A General Social Work Council—A Critical Look at the Issues. *British Journal of Social Work* 24: 261–271.

Hanson, J. and J. McCullagh. (1995). Career Choice Factors for BSW Students: A 10-Year Perspective. *Journal of Social Work Education* 31(1): 28–37.

Harris, R. (1990). Beyond Rhetoric: A Challenge for International Social Work. *International Social Work* 33: 203–212.

Hartman, A. (1995). Family Therapy. In *Encyclopedia of Social Work,* 19th ed., 983–990. Washington, DC: NASW Press.

_____. (1991). Social Worker-in-Situation: Editorial. *Social Work* 36(3): 195–196.

_____. (1990). Our Global Village: Editorial. *Social Work* 35(4): 291–292.

_____. (1989). Still Between Client and Community. *Social Work* 34(5): 387–388.

Healy, L. (1992). *Introducing International Development Content in Social Work Curriculum.* Washington, DC: NASW Press.

Hidalgo, H., T. Peterson, and N. Woodman, eds. *Lesbian and Gay Issues: A Resource Manual for Social Workers.* Annapolis, MD: NASW.

Hokenstad, M. and K. Kendall. (1995). International Social Work Education. In *Encyclopedia of Social Work,* 19th ed., 1511–1520. Washington, DC: NASW Press.

Hokenstad, M., S. Khinduka, and J. Midgley. (1992). Social Work Today and Tomorrow: An International Perspective. In M. Hokenstad, S. Khinduka, and J. Midgley, eds., *Profiles in International Social Work.* Washington, DC: NASW Press, 184–193.

hooks, b. (1994). *Teaching to Transgress: Education as the Practice of Freedom.* New York: Routledge.

Hopps, J. and E. Pinderhughes. (1992). Social Work in the United States: History, Context, and Issues. In M. Hokenstad, S. Khinduka, and J. Midgley, eds. *Profiles in International Social Work* (163–179). Washington, DC: NASW Press.

Johnson, L. (1995). *Social Work Practice: A Generalist Approach.* Boston: Allyn and Bacon.

Johnson, L. and C. Schwartz. (1994). *Social Welfare: A Response to Human Need.* Boston: Allyn and Bacon.

Johnson, W. (1995). Historical Development. In W. Johnson, et al., eds. *The Social Services: An Introduction* (3–10). Itasca, IL: F.E. Peacock Publishers.

_____. (1994, April 29). *Do Tomorrow's BSW Practitioners Have an International Perspective?* Paper presented at the Biennial Midwest Social Work Education Conference: St. Paul, MN.

Jones, C. (1992). Social Work in Great Britain: Surviving the Challenge of Conservative Ideology. In M. Hokenstad, S. Khinduka, and J. Midgley, eds. *Profiles in International Social Work* (43–56). Washington, DC: NASW Press.

Jones, J. (1993). Training Across the Borders: A Study in Collaboration. *Social Development Issues* 15(3): 71–81.

Karger, J. (1993). The Future of Social Work in a Changing Economy: Preparing for the year 2000. *Journal of International and Comparative Social Welfare* 9(1 & 2): 21–32.

Keefe, T. (1980). Empathy Skill and Critical Consciousness. *Social Casework* 61: 387–393.

Kendall, K. (1989). Women at the Helm: Three Extraordinary Leaders. *Affilia* 4(1): 23–32.

Kinsman, G. (1994). Heterosexual Hegemony. *Canadian Dimension* 26(3): 21–23.

Larochelle, C. and H. Camfens (1992). The Structure of Poverty: A Challenge for the Training of Social Workers in the North and South. *International Social Work* 35: 105–119.

Lingas, L. G. (1991). "For Mye Tro-For Lite Viten." *Sosionomen* 16: 2–13.

Lorenz, W. (1994). Social Work in a Changing Europe. London: Routledge.

Lum, D. (1992). *Social Work Practice and People of Color: A Process—Stage Approach,* 2d ed. Pacific Grove, CA: Brooks/Cole.

Macht, M. and J. Ashford. (1990). *Introduction to Social Work and Social Welfare,* 2d ed. New York: Macmillan.

Mary, N. and T. Morris. (1994). The Future and Social Work: A Global Perspective. *Journal of Multicultural Social Work* 3(4): 89–101.

Mehta, V. and R. Constable. (1994). Preface. In R. Constable and V. Mehta, *Education for Social Work in Eastern Europe.* Chicago: Lyceum: vi–x.

Midgley, J. (1995a). International and Comparative Social Welfare. In *Encyclopedia of Social Work,* 19th ed., 1490–1499. Washington, DC: NASW Press.

———. (1995b). *Social Development: The Development Perspective in Social Work.* London: SAGE.

———. (1981). *Professional Imperialism: Social Work in the Third World.* London: Heinemann.

Midgley, J. and C. Jones. (1994). Social Work and the Radical Right: Impact of Developments in Britain and the United States. *International Social Work* 37: 115–126.

Mills, C. (1959). *The Sociological Imagination.* New York: Oxford University Press.

Mulder, D., et al. (1994, April 23). Two-Year HIV-1-Associated Mortality in a Ugandan Rural Population. *The Lancet*: 1021.

Mullaly, R. (1993). *Structural Social Work: Ideology, Theory and Practice.* Toronto, Canada: McClelland and Stewart.

Nagpaul, H. (1993). Analysis of Social Work Teaching Material in India and the Need for Indigenous Foundations. *International Social Work* 36: 207–220.

NASW News. (1995). Court Briefs (by NASW) Back Gay, Lesbian Rights. *NASW News* 40(3): 15.

———. (1995). NASW Urges Hill to Fund '96 Programs. *NASW News* 40(5): 1.

———. (1995). 1995 Agenda Urges Nonpunitive Policies. *NASW News* 40(3): 6.

———. (1995). Welfare Bill is Wrong Vehicle, Congress Told. *NASW News* 40(3): 1.

———. (1994, October 8). See Third World's Strengths, Group Urges. *NASW News* 8.

Neimark, J. (1996). The Diva of Disclosure. *Psychology Today* 29(1): 48–52, 78–80.

Niebuhr, R. (1934). *Prayer.* Delivered in a sermon in Heath, MA.

Payne, M. (1991). *Modern Social Work Theory: A Critical Introduction.* Chicago: Lyceum Books.

Philpott, T. (1978). *The Slum and the Ghetto: Neighborhood Deterioration and the Middle-Class Reform.* New York: Oxford University Press.

Popple, P. and L. Leighninger. (1993). *Social Work, Social Welfare, and American Society,* 2d ed. Boston: Allyn and Bacon.

Prigmore, C. (1990). Social Welfare in Iran. In D. Elliott, N. Mayadas, and T. Watts, eds. *The World of Social Welfare* (171–182). Springfield, IL: Charles C. Thomas.

Quiroz, T. (1992). Social Policies and the Role of Social Work for the New Times. *International Social Work* 35:121–133.

Reynolds, B. (1963). *An Uncharted Journey.* New York: The Citadel Press.

Ritter, M. (1995, May 23). Mental Health Crisis Contributing to Violent Society: Study. New York: Associated Press.

Ronnau, J. (1994). Teaching Cultural Competence: Practical Ideas for Social Work Educators. *Journal of Multicultural Social Work* 3(1): 29–42.

Schreiber, M. (1995). Labeling a Social Worker a National Security Risk: A Memoir. *Social Work* 40(5): 656–660.

Seebaran, R. and C. George. (1990). Multiculturalism: Initiatives by the British Columbia Association of Social Workers. *The Social Worker* 58(4): 157–160.

Sivard, R. (1993). *World Military and Social Expenditures.* Washington, DC: World Priorities.

Sorokin, P. (1956). *Fads and Foibles in Modern Sociology.* Chicago: Henry Regency Company.

Specht, H. and M. Courtney. (1994). *Unfaithful Angels: How Social Work Has Abandoned Its Mission.* New York: The Free Press.

Stere, L. (1986). A Reformist Perspective on Feminist Practice. In M. Bricker-Jenkins and N. Hooyman, eds. *Not for Women Only.* Washington, DC: NASW Press.

Tambor, M. (1995). Unions. In *Encyclopedia of Social Work Education*, 19th ed., 2418–2429. Washington, DC: NASW Press.

Trattner, W. (1994). *From Poor Law to Welfare State: A History of Social Welfare in America*, 5th ed. New York: The Free Press.

Turner, C. (1991). Feminist Practice with Women of Color. In M. Bricker-Jenkins, N. Hooyman, and N. Gottlieb, eds. *Feminist Social Work Practice in Clinical Settings.* Newbury Park: SAGE.

van Wormer, K. (1995). *Alcoholism Treatment: A Social Work Perspective.* Chicago: Nelson-Hall.

———. (1990). The Hidden Juvenile Justice System in Norway: A Journey Back in Time. *Federal Probation* 54(1): 57–61.

Wagner, A. (1992). Social Work Education in an Integrated Europe: Plea for a Global Perspective. *Journal of Teaching Social Work* 6(2): 115–130.

Walz, T. (1995). Social Work: A Futures Perspective. In Johnson, H., et al., eds. *The Social Services: An Introduction*, 4th ed. Itasca, IL: Peacock Publishers.

Weick, A. and S. Vandiver, eds. (1981). *Women, Power and Change.* Washington, DC: NASW Press.

5

POVERTY AND SOCIAL

INSTITUTIONS

Before I had a chance to take these courses (from the church),
I never really understood how the world worked. I was so
caught up in surviving from day to day that I never had
a chance to figure out where my problems came from.
—Elvia Alvarado, Don't Be Afraid Gringo

One in seven Americans is poor, while one in four U.S. children lives in poverty. Yet the nature and extent of poverty in this country pales beside the nature and extent of poverty in the world. Among the tasks for this chapter are to:

1. View the problem of poverty on a world scale.
2. Define what is meant by poverty and examine the distribution of wealth in the United States.
3. Explore the notion of welfare for the rich.
4. Consider the functions and dysfunctions of poverty.
5. Describe the psychological effects of living in poverty.
6. Look at the social psychology of blaming the poor.
7. Identify the connections between poverty and gender, and poverty and race/ethnicity.
8. Describe and refute some of the myths about public welfare.
9. View poverty in a comparative, cross-cultural context.
10. Present strategies for the prevention of poverty.

POVERTY ON A WORLD SCALE

The outstanding economic and social problem in the world is poverty. An estimated one billion people—one fifth of humankind—are unable to afford a minimum adequate diet and other bare necessities of life (*UN Chronicle*, 1993). An unnecessary scourge in this modern age, poverty stunts people's growth physically, psychologically, and socially (Cox, 1994). World hunger must be considered one of the most serious problems facing humanity today. Although most of the poorest of the poor come from rural areas of Asia and Africa, there are also pockets of poverty in the industrialized world. The weight of poverty falls most heavily on vulnerable groups in every society—women, the elderly, minority groups, and children. In poor households on the Indian subcontinent, for example, men and boys usually get more sustenance than do women and girls, while the elderly get less to eat than the young (Dasgupta, 1995). So intense is the suffering rendered by absolute, wretched poverty, in fact, that the grievances of people who have satisfied their basic needs seem trivial in contrast.

Definition

In rich societies, most discussions of poverty focus on relative poverty or deprivation in relation to the greater resources of others (Macionis, 1994). Relative poverty is defined by the general standard of living in various societies and by what is culturally defined as living poorly. Thus by the standards of most inhabitants of India, the Mexican villager would be "well off." The Mexican, in turn, would perceive migrant work in the United States as an opportunity to "get ahead" (Macionis, 1994). In the United States, the official government poverty level is based on the cash income for individuals to satisfy minimum living needs according to comparative expectations.

In contrast, absolute poverty which readily can be identified in a global context, is a deprivation of resources that is life-threatening. Arguably, there is a degree of absolute poverty even in a rich nation such as the United States where inadequate nutrition, health care, and heating are unfortunate realities. Yet, as Macionis reminds us, such immediately life-threatening poverty in a modernized nation strikes only a small proportion of the population. By contrast, at least one person in four of the population in the non-industrialized world is not able to satisfy such basic needs as adequate nutrition, access to safe and sufficient water, clean air to breathe, proper sanitation, and health care including vaccines and family planning (Sivard, 1993).

In *The Vast Majority: A Journey to the World's Poor,* Harrington (1977: 86) describes how he slowly becomes inured to poverty, even in the course of weeks:

> During the last two weeks in India, I have seen more poverty than in a life-time in the United States . . . Soon one became incredibly relativistic. If a battered, dilapidated hut by the side of the road had a bike in front, if a miserable little shop whose total inventory of cigarettes or soda was not worth what a tourist would spend on a good meal, also had a harsh, naked light bulb, one thought, this is not so bad. Had I seen those things the day after I arrived, I would have wanted to throw myself on the ground and beg for-giveness of these people. Not now. This is not to say that I have become indifferent to them. Quite the contrary. I am more determined than ever before that I will work however best I can to alleviate—to eradicate—this intolerable agony.

Global Hunger

Close to 75 percent of the world's population live in poor nations of the world, most of the poor in the Southern hemisphere. Overdependence on the exporta-tion of cash crops to other nations in exchange for hard currencies has added considerably to the food shortage problems of some developing nations such as Ethiopia, India, and China (Estes, 1992b). The extent of world hunger is staggering. The number of people who die every few days of hunger and star-vation, according to Estes, is equivalent to the number who were killed ins-tantly in the bombing of Hiroshima. Simply put, poverty has a global face; people are dying every minute of the day from lack of basic nutrition.

In a frightening passage from her book, *Don't Be Afraid Gringo*—a power-ful diatribe against the United States—Alvarado (1987: 24) of Honduras speaks from the heart:

> Look at my granddaughter. She's a year old and has diarrhea right now.
> My daughter took her to the doctor, but the medicine they gave her only

made the child sicker. Now they say she has second-degree malnutrition, and that we have to feed her healthier food—eggs and milk and things like that. But where are we supposed to get the money for these foods?

Drawing on international data from the United Nations, North Atlantic Trade Organization, and the U.S. government, Sivard (1993) documents the ravages of warfare and the international trade in weapons. Where massive supplies of arms have been shipped into countries in desperate need of economic aid, both the death toll and the flood of refugees have increased. Prolonged fighting across the globe has destroyed crops and devastated agricultural areas, turning countries into ecological wastelands. In Somalia, for example, torn by tribal warfare in the early 1990s, famine claimed as many as one thousand victims a day.

Warfare is predominantly a male activity. The economic costs of war and the preparation of war often fall more heavily on girls and women as they become less valued than boys and men. This inequity is reflected in infanticide, and in reduced health care and nutrition for females. In some regions, and especially in South Asia, men and boys eat first. Girls in impoverished nations are more than four times as likely to be malnourished as boys (United Nations, 1995).

Macionis (1994) provides a graphic portrait of the face of poverty in Madras, India, one of the largest cities in a country which contains one of three of the total number of the world's hungry. In his powerful description, Macionis juxtaposes the western visitor's response of horror with the traditional coping strategies of the survivors: Arriving in Madras, the visitor immediately recoils from the smell of human sewage and contaminated water which is unsafe to drink. Madras, like other cities of India, teems with millions of homeless people; people work, talk, bathe, and sleep in the streets. Macionis suggests that the deadly cruelty of poverty in India is eased, however, by the strength of families, the religious tradition of *dharma*—the Hindu concept of duty and destiny—and a sense of purpose to life. The absence of danger, illegal drug activity, and anger are striking to the outsider. Compared to North Americans, Indians have an altogether different experience of poverty, as of life itself.

Causes of Poverty

Central to an understanding of the persistence of poverty throughout the world is a recognition of the barriers to its alleviation. As accurately stated in Harrington's searching investigation of poverty (1962: 22): "There are mighty historical and economic forces that keep the poor down; and there are human beings who help out in this grim business, many of them unwittingly" (Harrington, 1962). Cox (1994) has filtered out from the vast international literature five levels of activity relevant to poverty perpetuation: international competition in a global market, state structures, service delivery systems, social welfare arrangements, and community organization. The interrelationship of these factors is readily apparent.

International forces shape the economic structures of all nations. Trade imbalances stemming from a combination of declining exports and increasing imports have had an especially devastating impact on nations with already high levels of foreign indebtedness. Overdependence on food imports has threatened local agricultural efforts and reduced the level of self-sufficiency still further (for appreciation of the complex realities of global interdependence see box 5.1). The poorest countries whose inhabitants are on the brink of starvation end up exporting their own scarce food grains as cash crops to generate the foreign exchange required to pay their foreign debts (Estes, 1992a). Multinationals appear to have added to, not allayed, the world's hunger problems, argues Bell (1987). As agribusiness has gained control of considerable arable land, both meaningful work and economic self-sufficiency have been destroyed. Multinationals, moreover, push the sale of nonessential, even harmful items such as soft drinks, tobacco, white bread, and infant formula. The latter product has become downright lethal for infants in the absence of pure water and sanitary cooking equipment.

Survival in a highly competitive global economy affects the modern social welfare state of the industrialized world. To compete, corporations and government are compelled to become more efficient (Karger, 1994). To aid corporations, as Karger explains, government often frees up investment capital through curbing corporate tax rates. The loss of tax revenue encouraged by corporate growth exacerbates the staggering levels of governmental debt and leads to an eventual deterioration in public services (Karger, 1994). These policies practically ensure a host of social problems and a downsizing in social welfare programs to rectify them. For the corporations themselves, the pressures of international competition can lead to economic restructuring, which in turn, promotes rapidly changing technology and a reduced need for workers. The greater the accumulated capital by industry, the greater the investment in technology to manufacture the products. Meanwhile, the lack of stable employment in a community is associated with mounting social problems.

BOX 5.1

ON INTERDEPENDENCE

Interdependence is a term that is used frequently these days by individuals in fields as diverse as trade, agriculture, the environment, communications and health. Interdependence is a reality because events and forces outside national borders can and *do* profoundly affect events and forces in other countries. As we begin to understand our interconnections to the developing world, we can reach a deeper understanding of development issues there without ever leaving our own communities.

• Global economics and trade issues have dominated discussions of interdependence. Major international events dramatically illustrate economic interdependence. For example, during the rapid decline in the stock market in October, 1987, investors around the globe closely followed foreign stocks in order to predict what might happen in their own countries.

• An event which vividly illustrates interdependence between the United States and the developing world was the oil crisis of the 1970s. The oil-producing countries ushered in a rapid rise in oil prices, putting profound financial pressures on the rest of the world. While the United States was able to survive the recession, it was forced to spend fewer U.S. dollars to buy goods from developing countries. Fragile economies in the developing world, losing U.S. and other overseas markets, had to borrow from commercial banks, mostly in the United States. By 1980, the developing world was facing an external debt crisis of $500 billion. In 1982, 25 percent of U.S. commercial banks' international activity was with developing countries. (*Hamilton, 1988; Sommer, 1987*)

• Economic adjustment policies, enacted to assist developing countries to pay back their debts, have forced developing countries to cut back on their imports from the United States. This has hurt U.S. farmers, and is partly responsible for the farm crisis in the U.S. Foreign trade has been important for American farmers throughout history. Agricultural products made up 80 percent of U.S. exports in the nineteenth century and helped to pull the U.S. economy out of depressions. (*Hamilton, 1988*) Today, the soybean, sent primarily to developing countries, is the United States' largest export product. Yet more and more, developing countries are not able to afford our exports. Lessons from the oil crisis and the debt crisis demonstrate that if the economies of the developing world are unhealthy, then the U.S. economy is negatively affected, and visa versa.

(Continued on next page)

BOX 5.1 (Continued)

• The global economy provides only a partial illustration of interdependence. Environmental problems in one part of the world are often problems for everyone. Ocean pollution on the other side of the globe can make itself apparent on our shores. Deforestation in India and Nepal has led to catastrophic flooding in Bangladesh. Emissions of industrial chemicals have been shown to cause acid rain and deplete the ozone layer; while the use of fossil fuels can harm distant forests and contribute to global warming.

• Infections and diseases know no national borders. All major flu epidemics in the United States have originated abroad, primarily in the developing world. In fact, the Russian flu of 1977 actually started in China. (*Hamilton, 1988*) Whether or not AIDS originated in Africa, as some experts maintain, it has now spread throughout the world. Agricultural pests, inadvertently brought to the United States, have been known to wipe out entire crop yields. Poverty and scarce resources in the developing world make it difficult for people to identify, study and treat diseases and eradicate pests. Ironically, their poverty affects us all.

• The drug problem in the United States is also connected to poverty in the developing world. Primary illegal drug producing countries are developing countries. Coca used to make cocaine, a drug of great concern to our society and administration, is grown by poor Latin American farmers who can make several times the profit selling coca than they could get from other crops. Moreover, income generated from drug-related crops helps the debt-ridden developing countries repay their foreign loans. Tackling the drug problem is not a local or national concern, but an international one that will demand an examination of international development issues.

• The United States is further connected to the developing world because a growing number of people from Asia, Africa and Latin America live within our borders, as students and citizens. The large refugee and immigrant populations in the United States have brought important changes in education, as well as in the social and health service fields, with an eye towards increased understanding and appreciation of cross-cultural differences.

• The realities of interdependence are inescapable. Countries may be politically independent, but in today's world they are also interdependent in so many ways. The effects of interdependence reach beyond the level of the national government and into our

(Continued on next page)

BOX 5.1 (Continued)

communities, impacting on the lives of each and every one of us. Because of this, knowledge of international development is not only important in an academic or humanitarian sense. Understanding our connections to the developing world is important also to our own well-being.

Fact Sheet prepared by Michelle Reynolds for the National Association of Social Workers, February 1990.
Source: Child and Family Well-Being Development Education Program (Washington, DC: NASW, 1990). Reprinted with permission of NASW.

In addition to the transnational corporations' reliance on cheap labor, Cox lists the following as being associated with the impoverishment of nations striving toward development: the history of colonial exploitation, the low proportion of official development assistance that is targeted at priority human needs, and the now acknowledged biases in the International Monetary Fund's structural adjustment requirements. Nations depend on the International Monetary Fund, an organization that promotes the stabilization of the world's currencies and which exerts tremendous pressure on debt-ridden nations to correct any deficit in their balance of payments.

Some people point to population growth as a major cause of poverty; others reverse the proposition and argue poverty to be the determinant of population growth. In fact, as economist Dasgupta (1995) concludes from his analysis of collected research, each element (in the system of global commerce) simultaneously influences the other. Focusing on the vast numbers of small, rural communities in the poorest regions of the world, investigators have identified circumstances in which population growth, poverty, and degradation of local resources often fuel one another. Dasgupta (1995: 41) explains world poverty in terms of a self-perpetuating cycle as follows:

Fetching water in Rajasthan, in the west of India, takes up several hours a day for each household. As resources become increasingly sparse and distant, additional hands become more valuable for such daily tasks, creating a demand for families to have more children. The burgeoning population puts more pressure on the environment spurring a need for even more offspring in a cycle of increasing poverty, population, and environment damage.

CHAPTER 5: POVERTY AND SOCIAL INSTITUTIONS

In the age of the global economy, the gap between rich and poor nations has widened considerably. Over 80 percent of the world's income is concentrated in the richest 20 percent of the world's nations (Sivard, 1993). Only in South and East Asia have the nations expanded their economies over the last decade (UN Chronicle, 1993). The largest increase in people suffering from hunger has been in Africa, where a combination of natural and human-created disasters has created mass starvation and environmental deterioration. Modern technologies introduced from abroad increase the national debt and benefit the top echelons at the expense of the others.

Within nations, likewise, the gap between rich and poor has been getting larger. In Mexico, the poorest 40 percent receive less than 10 percent of the gross national product and in Brazil the poor receive only 7 percent. In South Africa, 5 percent of the population, mostly whites, own 88 percent of all private property. Within the poor counties, existing wealth is diverted to the rich, leaving the majority of the population in absolute poverty (Healy and Whitaker, 1992)

Now we turn from the international realm in shaping policy to the role of the nation itself. As the number two barrier to poverty alleviation, the state is responsible for negotiating international relations and managing the redistribution of available resources, according to Cox. Global economics, population growth, and local politics may interact in such a way as to create a vicious circle of despair. Consider box 5.2 as a case in point.

Social service systems can help offset social problems by enhancing the quality of life through the provision of a set of health (including family planning), educational, housing and other services. According to Cox, reduction in the funding of such universal services is the third barrier to preventing poverty. As a nation's indebtedness to foreign powers increases, and as a small group of elite capitalists comes to control the wealth in a country, cut backs in social delivery systems are inevitable. Some thirty-seven of the world's poorest countries, in fact, cut their health budgets by half in the 1980s, according to a comprehensive United Nations (1991) report. These cuts were accompanied by increased military expenditures during the same period, especially in African nations. Maternal and infant mortality rates increased accordingly (Sivard, 1993).

Social welfare arrangements, the fourth of Cox's levels of activity related to poverty, refer to provisions (nonuniversal) for disabled and vulnerable people in a society. Whether care is formal or informal, the availability of help in times of severe crisis is essential to ensure survival of a population. The lack of such aid compounds the social problems related to poverty.

BOX 5.2

HAITI: POLITICAL AND ECOLOGICAL CATASTROPHE

Wallace E. Akin

There is something peculiarly Roman in the air of Haiti: Roman in cruelty, in its corruption and in its heroism . . . We are nearer to the Europe of Nero and Tiberius than to the Africa of Nkrumah — thus did the late author Graham Greene characterize the country.

Haiti is surrounded by other poor island nations in the Caribbean struggling to raise their standard of living. The others are, for the most part, slowly succeeding. Why is Haiti the tragic exception? The reasons are complex, stemming from historical, political and environmental roots.

The second-oldest republic in the Western Hemisphere, and once the richest colony in the Caribbean, "The Pearl of the Antilles" today is more a poorhouse than a pearl, and more oligarchy than republic.

Haiti occupies the western third of the island of Hispaniola; the Dominican Republic has the rest of the island. Spain claimed the island in 1492, but soon lost interest in the western side.

During 200 years of Spanish neglect, French pirates and adventurers gradually moved in, and in 1697 France claimed sovereignty over what now is Haiti. There they developed a thriving plantation econ-omy based on sugar, rum and coffee, but African slaves created this wealth, and harsh treatment by their masters led to continual revolts.

Haitians became independent in 1804 following a bloody rebellion in which the slaves defeated the French and expelled them. Free at last, shunning further labor in the sugarcane fields, the former slaves fled to the mountains, becoming subsistence farmers in the West African tradition. Flames of revolt destroyed plantations and mills, in essence both symbols and realities of the old colonial order — bountiful for the French, brutal for the slaves.

With neither slave labor nor skilled management, the plantation economy collapsed and never fully recovered. The mulatto elite, only 5 to 10 percent of the population, fell heir to political power and what wealth remained. These descendants of French planters and slaves, often educated in France, preserved the French language and culture and, unfortunately, they also retained the racial attitudes of the former masters, distrusted each other and feared the black

(Continued on next page)

BOX 5.2 (Continued)

majority. This minority has ruled directly, and through black surrogates, for almost two centuries with perpetual political turmoil.

The United States invaded Haiti in 1915 during World War I to protect American business interests from German competition and to secure routes to the Panama Canal. The occupation lasted until 1934.

The United States brought material benefits, American investments and improved public health, but it wasted a golden opportunity to help initiate a political system beneficial for all Haitians. Rather, it left behind a well-organized Haitian military that today is a source of present political problems, and it also left a reservoir of widespread anti-Americanism, emanating from racist attitudes. The mulatto elite never forgave the Americans' refusal to accept them as social equals.

During the dictatorship of Francois "Papa Doc" Duvalier (1957–71), the misery of the Haitian people deepened. Traditionally isolated, peasants became participants and victims of the political horrors of Papa Doc's private police, the dreaded *Tonton Macoutes,* who extended their bloody tentacles from the cities deep into the countryside and retained their grip after the death of Papa Doc. Although his long reign of terror ended, life for the poor has never improved. Escape is their only hope.

The Haitian dilemma lies not only in politics but in the unbalanced relationship between land and people—too many people, not enough land. Haiti's 10,500 square miles must support almost seven million people. With less than one-third of its land even marginally suited to crops, and more than half of its labor force engaged in agriculture, rural population densities are among the highest in the world. There are some two thousand Haitians for each square mile of cultivated land.

Only 5 percent of the original forest remains, and rapid soil erosion has destroyed 20 percent of arable land. With the loss of an estimated 1 percent of its potential cropland annually, Haiti could face mass starvation. Ecological damage may be reversible but only if competent and responsible leaders emerge soon.

Against this backdrop of limited and deteriorating resources and the longest record of political failure among the world's nations, sadly, one cannot be optimistic about Haiti's future. The focus keeps returning to the leadership—to the elite. Somehow they must find a political solution for bringing the poor majority into effective political and economic participation. Only through genuine efforts in this direction can Haiti awaken from this social, political, and ecological nightmare.

———

Source: The Des Moines Register, September 17, 1994, p. 7A. Reprinted with permission of the *Des Moines Register.*

Community organization at the local level helps shape the political, economic, and social realities and can be instrumental in obtaining benefits for otherwise overlooked groups such as the mentally ill. The role of social work in alleviating poverty is especially pronounced at this community level; services, however, are of course closely dependent on funding. There is a need today for community-based, grass-roots based programs that improve conditions such as health, schooling, and sanitation for inhabitants in rural areas. In light of the increasingly global economy which boosts the corporations' fortunes while investing in new technologies to cut factory jobs and wages, poor nations may find themselves locked in an endless cycle of misery. The lack of hope and morale in a country characterized by elitism and an "us" and "them" mentality are a barrier to the kind of community action that is so desperately needed. Such demoralization is the final factor identified by Cox precluding the alleviation of poverty.

Whether modernization increases the economic dependency of poor nations on the more technologically advanced nations of the world as Cox and others suggest, or whether such development helps the non-industrialized surge forward, constitutes the debate of global inequality. Macionis (1994) thoughtfully reconciles opposing arguments in this debate by producing evidence to support each view. In some regions of the world, especially in the "Pacific Rim" of eastern Asia, market forces are raising living standards rapidly and substantially. In central Africa and parts of Latin America, on the other hand, economic turmoil frustrates hopes for market-based development. To survive economically, and compete on the world stage, agricultural and industrial productivity are a must, as is equity in the distribution of educational opportunity and economic resources across all layers of the society.

DISTRIBUTION OF WEALTH IN THE UNITED STATES

Paralleling the gap between rich and poor countries is the gap between rich and poor people within rich countries such as the United States which now ranks sixth after Japan, Canada, Norway, Switzerland, and Sweden for its standard of living on the United Nations' Human Development Index. Disparities among ethnic, gender, and economic groups are stark. When separated by ethnic groups, U.S. whites rank first in the world, while African Americans are ranked thirty-first (reported in the *Des Moines Register*, 1993).

Among the advanced, industrialized nations, this country leads in the proportion of income going to the wealthiest fifth (who receive almost half of

U.S. income according to Bernstein, 1994). Yet the average spread between the richest and poorest fifths of the population is still less than half that found in Brazil (Sivard, 1993). *Class polarization* is the term used by Phyllis Day (1989) for the widening of the economic gap between the poor and the wealthy which, according to Day, is one of the most crucial problems facing the American institution of social welfare at the present time. While more of the middle classes are moving into a lower standard of living through unemployment, lower wages, and a rise in the number of single-parent families, people with wealth are consolidating their holdings. Because of the indirect but very significant impact of the global economy on all of us, including social work clients, Day suggests that an internationalist perspective is vital. For many of the same reasons, the poor are growing poorer the world over. Let us now explore in more detail the economic inequality in the United States.

According to the Census Bureau's annual report, 39.3 million people (15.1 percent of all Americans) fell below the poverty level in 1993, the most since 1961 when 22 percent of the population fell below this level (U.S. Bureau of the Census, 1995). Refer to table 4.1 for the statistical breakdown. Labor Secretary Robert Reich termed the figures "deeply disturbing" and commented that we have the most unequal distribution of income of any industrialized nation (Associated Press, 1994). Poverty in the United States is determined in terms of *poverty line* which is treated as an absolute measure of deprivation. It is absolute in the sense of being based on established, fixed standards of living. Defined in the *Dictionary of Social Work* (Barker, 1995) as follows, the *poverty line* is:

> a measure of the amount of money a government or a society believes is necessary for a person to live at a minimum level of subsistence or standard of living. The first measure of this type was issued by the United States in 1964. The original poverty line was calculated by a formula that multiplied the cost of a subsistence food budget by a factor of three. Since 1989 the poverty line has meant the previous year's poverty line adjusted for the change in the *Consumer Price Index.*

Who Are the Poor?

Of poor people in the United States, the vast majority are women and children. Products of divorce, abandonment, de-institutionalization, demolition of low-rent housing, punitive immigration laws, technological advances and global competition, plant closings, medical expenses, welfare benefit restrictions, and the agricultural depression, the poor, in short, represent the downside of competition and opportunity. In 1996, in a land of vast resources and wealth millions of Americans continue to struggle to meet their most basic needs. Poverty cuts occur across a wide spectrum of the population and exist in all regions of the United States. More whites than blacks or Hispanics are poor. In proportion to their numbers, however, African Americans and Hispanics are much more likely to live in poverty. Of whites, 12.2 percent are below the poverty level, compared to 30.6 percent of Hispanics, and 33.1 percent of blacks (U.S. Bureau of the Census, 1995).

According to the Census Bureau, 15.1 percent of all Americans (or one out of every seven persons) was below the poverty threshold in 1993. When in-kind benefits such as food stamps and housing are added into the formula, however, the poverty rate is reduced to 12 percent. Regardless of the measures used, we can see in table 5.1 the sizeable disparities by race and ethnicity for the various forms of family composition. The poorest of the poor are households headed by females. More than half of African-American children are growing up in single-parent homes, which is almost three times the rate of white Americans.

Who are the poor? An encouraging trend, historically, is that over the last one hundred years the poverty rate has been reduced considerably. Prior to the twentieth century a majority of the people lived in poverty (Zastrow, 1996). At the time of the New Deal, over one-third of the nation was wretchedly poor. In 1978, however, following great efforts of the second war on poverty (the New Deal being the first), a low of 11.4 percent of the population was below the poverty line. A significant decrease in poverty among the elderly was also a positive outcome of new social policies. War on poverty programs initiated in the sixties, in fact, have done more to help those over age sixty-five than any other group. From over 25 percent in 1964, the poverty rate of the elderly has been reduced to approximately 12 percent in 1993 (U.S. Bureau of Census, 1995).

Today, alas, the numbers of the poor are shooting up drastically. Unlike the poor of previous periods in history, the contemporary poor have no political voice. The poor do not fill the rosters of labor organizations. Politically, the poor are both powerless and invisible.

Nationwide, one in four children lived in poverty in 1995. Most of the affected children had parents who worked at least part time, and fewer than

CHAPTER 5: POVERTY AND SOCIAL INSTITUTIONS

a third of the families relied entirely on cash public assistance (Associated Press, 1995). A parent working full time for the federal minimum wage would find his or her family far below the poverty line, even with a family of only two.

Unemployment accounts for the poorest families; over 80 percent of children living with unemployed parents are poor. The unemployment rate for African Americans consistently has been about twice that of white people. In 1994, 5.2 percent of whites were officially unemployed compared to 10.6 percent of

TABLE 5.1

Statistical Breakdown of the Poor in the United States, 1993

Total
39.3 million poor persons
15.1 percent of the population

Poverty threshold, family of four	$14,763

	Median Family Income
United States	$36,959
White	39,300
African American	21,542
Hispanic	23,654
Married couples	43,005
White	43,675
African American	35,218
Hispanic	28,454
Female householder family, no husband present	17,443
White	20,000
African American	11,909
Hispanic	12,047

	Percent Below Poverty Level
White	12.2
African American	33.1
Hispanic	30.6
Children	22.7

Source: U.S. Bureau of the Census, *Statistical Abstract of the United States,* 115th edition (1995). Washington, D.C., pp. 479–483.

blacks and 9.7 percent of Hispanics (U.S. Bureau of Census, 1995) We need to recognize, moreover, that the official unemployment rates seriously underestimate actual levels of persons out of work. Those no longer looking for work are not included in unemployment statistics.

The Feminization of Poverty

The fact that of families in the United States headed by single women, 38.5 percent are below the poverty line has led some scholars to coin the term, *feminization of poverty*. The combined effects of the dual labor market, occupational segregation, and sex and race discrimination have resulted in a 1993 median income for full-time, working, single women of $18,545 compared to a comparable figure for males of $29,849 (U.S. Bureau of the Census, 1995). When the ratio of women's full-time income reached 72 percent in 1990, it was an all-time high. This is a reflection, however, not of a rise in women's income as much as a decline in men's income during this period. Nevertheless, men still earn substantially higher wages than woman, even when they are working in traditionally "female" occupations such as nursing and social work.

The causes of female poverty are complex. The high divorce rate coupled with the infrequency of mothers receiving child support from the fathers forces many women to find jobs immediately or go on welfare. Low-paying service jobs—such as waiting tables in fast-food restaurants and motel housekeeping work—drive many women to welfare dependency as a means of escape from such daily drudgery, lack of essential work benefits, and childcare concerns. Programs designed to compensate for the absence of a male breadwinner in the family are means-tested and highly punitive. When men are absent, women's prescribed role as family caretaker is ignored and devalued by the system—a fact which reinforces women's marginality in society and ensures women and their children's high representation among the destitute. Until the importance of nurturing and shaping young lives through domestic caretaking is regarded as primary work, the feminization of poverty will continue. The federal and state program reductions in job training, education, and childcare implemented by the Reagan, Bush, and Clinton administrations have had a major impact on already poor women and children. Ruth Sidel's (1992: 21) commentary on an earlier assault on persons receiving benefits is highly applicable today:

"Perhaps the most serious result of the Reagan administration's economic policies, particularly the cut backs in human services, has been the legitimization of the negative attitudes held by many Americans toward the poor." For a poetic presentation of a strong welfare woman read Maya Angelou's "Mamma Welfare Roll" in box 5.3.

More and more women are working; this is true for married and single women both. Three out of every five women with children work. Only one type of family saw its average income rise in the 1980s—married couples with working wives. While average wages have fallen at an annual rate of .7 percent per year over the past twenty years, women are taking up difficult and poorly paid jobs to help feed their families (Mead, 1994). A major barrier to permanent, full-time female employment centers around the absence of adequate and affordable childcare and subsidized childcare leaves.

BOX 5.3

MOMMA WELFARE ROLL

Maya Angelou

Her arms semaphore fat triangles,
Pudgy hands bunched on layered hips
Where bones idle under years of fatback
And lima beans.
Her jowls shiver in accusation
Of crimes clichéd by
Repetition. Her children, strangers
To childhood's toys, play
Best the games of darkened doorways,
Rooftop tag, and know the slick feel of
Other people's property.

Too fat to whore,
Too mad to work,

Searches her dreams for the
Lucky sign and walks bare-handed
Into a den of bureaucrats for
Her portion.
"They don't give me welfare.
I take it."

Source: Maya Angelou, *The Poetry of Maya Angelou* (New York: Quality Paperback Book Club, 1993), p. 148. Reprinted with permission from Random House, Inc.

At the end of the life span, women pay again for their abbreviated, low-paid work careers. Qualifying far less frequently than men for adequate pension plans, most elderly women must rely on Social Security as their sole source of income. Accordingly, 15 percent of elderly females compared to 9 percent of elderly males are in poverty.

How are women doing worldwide? A United Nations report summarized in *Facts on File* (1995) reveals that although female literacy and life expectancy have increased in the past two decades, women around the world still lag behind men in many areas:

- Of the 1.3 billion people in poverty, 70 percent are women.
- In illiteracy, women outnumber men 2 to 1.
- Worldwide, women make up half of electorates but hold just 10 percent of legislative seats and 6 percent of cabinet posts.
- In all regions, women outnumber men among the unemployed.
- The average wage paid to females was three-fourths males' average wage in nonagricultural jobs.

For more details on the plight of the world's women see the section women and work in chapter 7, the war against women in chapter 10, and women and health care in chapter 8.

WELFARE FOR THE RICH

The male-dominant welfare system for the rich provides benefits that demand honor and respect. The bulk of government assistance is meted out not to the economically disadvantaged—the women and children and elderly, and not to the middle classes whose real wage earnings have declined steadily over the past decade—but to the richest 10 percent of the U.S. population. There is a kind of welfare for the wealthy and for large corporations (such as tax relief for mismanaged savings and loans institutions) not available to the poor (Dolgoff et al., 1993). In fact, the share of the national wealth going to the richest segment of the population continues to rise. But how can this be? How can so much be spent on the affluent while massive budget cuts threaten the already low-living standards of the poor?

CHAPTER 5: POVERTY AND SOCIAL INSTITUTIONS

Economist John Galbraith (1992) provides the rationale given by those who are "contented" and wish to perpetuate their contentment. To serve contentment, there are three basic requirements, according to Galbraith: commitment to laissez-faire government policies, demonstration to the class immediately below that the case for the rich is a benefit to society, and dismissal of the underclass as architects of their own unhappy fate. The argument is bolstered in a disturbing interview (Greider, 1981) with David Stockman who was an economist in the Reagan administration. The newly espoused doctrines and the recycled trickle down theory were, according to Stockman, simply a serviceable cover story. The actual and deeper purpose of the rhetoric was to lower taxes on the affluent. The interview caused a furor in conservative quarters.

Cynically and angrily, Huff (1992) writes of what he calls "the upside down welfare state." The national agenda, according to this argument, is to redistribute wealth to American businesses. Through a variety of programs the non-poor are provided with such benefits as low-cost government insurance for their oceanside vacation houses, tax breaks for their investments, subsidized medical care, and supplemental retirement benefits. But this is child's play, according to Huff, compared to the redistribution system that annually transfers billions of dollars from ordinary taxpayers to the major corporations. Subsidies to massive agribusiness operations and the defense industry are examples of gigantic public relief programs. Income tax law provides breaks for individuals who are self-employed and derive their income from investments rather than salary. Tax breaks to corporations are considerable also. In Puerto Rico, not only do individuals pay no federal taxes, for instance, but the hundreds of factories located there pay no U.S. taxes either. The pharmaceutical companies have benefited tremendously from this arrangement.

The course we are pursuing today is not entirely new. In his classic work on poverty, *The Other America*, Harrington (1962: 172) observed:

> As long as the illusion persists that the poor are merrily freeloading on the
> public dole, so long will the other America continue unthreatened. The truth,
> it must be understood, is the exact opposite. The poor get less out of the
> welfare state than any group in America.

History and ideology, in short, have caused us to take one attitude toward public or private welfare services for the affluent, another attitude toward subsidy for the upper-middle classes, and still another attitude toward public welfare services for the poor.

THE FUNCTIONS OF POVERTY

Functional analysis allows us to look at things from a unique perspective and consider the negatives from a positive point of view. In a frequently cited article, Gans (1976) explains the persistence of poverty in terms of fifteen functions which poverty and the poor perform for the rest of U.S. society. Gans' economic, social, cultural, and political functions of poverty and the poor are as follows:

1. assuring that society's "dirty work" is done;
2. subsidizing through low wages many activities of the affluent;
3. the creation of jobs for a number of occupations and professions (e.g., correctional officers, the police, and Pentecostal ministers) which serve the poor;
4. providing buyers for goods—such as day-old bread—that no one else wants;
5. maintaining the legitimacy of dominant norms by identifying the poor as deviants;
6. allowing helpers to feel noble and altruistic;
7. providing vicarious pleasure for the affluent in the supposed wild sexual doings of the lower classes;
8. guaranteeing the status of those in higher classes;
9. furthering the upward mobility of the nonpoor through restricting channels of mobility to the poor;
10. helping to keep the aristocracy busy in caring for and teaching the poor;
11. making high culture possible by providing labor to create monuments of civilization;
12. providing "low" culture which is frequently enjoyed by the rich;
13. acting as a source for arousing conservative opposition such as against "welfare chiselers;"
14. providing foot soldiers for wars and land for urban renewal;
15. by not voting, keeping their interests from "cramping the style" of others.

Gans concludes his article with a clarification; what is functional for affluent groups in the society is not necessarily functional for the society as a whole.

Taking the argument to a global level, what are the functions of poverty for rich countries when dealing with poor countries? The rich countries' access to money spells power through the ability to offer loans and markets for dependent nations' goods. Sometimes the mere threat of economic sanctions can be quite effective in controlling the internal affairs of foreign governments. International corporations are in a position to exploit poor nations in terms of cheap labor, natural resources such as oil and forests, and as markets for weapons, cigarettes, alcohol, and herbicides which are banned in industrialized countries.

THE DYSFUNCTIONS OF POVERTY

Poverty does not just mean the absence of wealth in a society of plenty; it means people having to live on diets consisting of beans, macaroni and cheese, stale bread, and even dog and cat food. It means lack of security against criminals — high susceptibility to victimization by shooting, robbery, rape, and/or assault. Privation is associated with the urgent social ills of homelessness, substance abuse, and infectious diseases such as tuberculosis and AIDS.

In short, being poor is not just one aspect of a person's or family's life; it is a whole way of living. Each deprivation and disability becomes all the more intense because it exists within a web of deprivations and disabilities (Harrington, 1962). Perhaps the harshest and most unmitigated poverty in the United States is to be found in the agricultural fields. In a news article entitled "Harvest of Shame," Sallah (1994) equates life in the squalor of run-down migrant camps in Belle Glade, Florida, with life in Third World countries. The downtown area of this community is a jungle of dilapidated rooming houses, most of them with communal toilets, exposed wiring, and broken windows. Crack cocaine and "hustling" (prostitution) are a way of life. The death rate from AIDS is four and a half times the national average.

Mechanization of farms, especially of sugar cane farms, has reduced the need for farm labor in this part of Florida. Meanwhile, an influx of immigrants from Haiti and Jamaica has created a labor surplus. Most of the farms are corporately owned; the growers are some of the wealthiest in the country. Their political influence in Florida and Washington is considerable. Accordingly, there is little hope of alleviation of present conditions described in Sallah's article.

Although people in the United States are not facing the dire starvation situation experienced by people in other parts of the world, rural America is where the greatest pockets of hunger are found. The paradox is that in the food growing regions of the United States, the infrastructure is designed to get food out, not to distribute it from within. Moreover, rural food banks are scarce, and social services agencies are often distant. The elderly rural are especially susceptible to hunger. The hungry can be found among the nation's homeless and illegal immigrants as well. For many children, even when their parents are scraping by on public aid, dietary needs are not met at the end of the month when the family's allotment of food stamps runs out. According to a new study from Second Harvest, a nationwide network of food banks, one out of ten Americans—many from working families—makes use of food banks to get enough to eat (Shapiro, 1994). What Harrington observed in 1962 (p. 20) is eerily true today:

> The other Americans are the victims of the very inventions and machines that have provided a higher living standard for the rest of the society. They are upside down in the economy, and for them greater productivity often means worse jobs; agricultural advance becomes hunger.

Children

The impact of poverty falls most heavily on the nation's children. Hunger and malnutrition rob children of their health, making them susceptible to frequent colds, ear infections, and irritability. An article by Bower (1994) in *Science News* summarizes recent research findings from longitudinal studies of the children of the poor. By age five, children in impoverished families have markedly lower IQs and display more fearfulness, anxiety, and unhappiness than never-poor youngsters. Behavioral problems in the children proliferated. Interviews with unemployed women revealed a high rate of depression, with the most depressed mothers citing the greatest reliance on harsh violent forms of discipline. Conflict between parents escalates as well when financial difficulties keep stress perpetually high; if the father smokes, family resources may be used to get cigarettes instead of food for the children. The old saying, "When poverty comes in the door, love goes out the window," is very possibly true.

A problem that has become a symbol of the United States' failure to cope with appalling poverty is the disgracefully high infant mortality rate. Twenty-three other nations have lower infant mortality rates than the United States. Twice as many black as white infants die within their first year. Money not spent on prenatal care is hardly a savings when the cost for medical care during the child's first year is at least three times the cost of preventive care.

For every year that fifteen million children are brought up in poverty, the nation loses thirty-six billion dollars in future productivity, according to a 1994 report from the Children's Defense Fund. Additionally, poverty:

- Decreases babies' chances of being born healthy.
- Makes children twice as likely to suffer from a host of health problems.
- Slows educational development.
- Strains families, increasing odds of abuse and neglect.
- Increases adolescents' risk of pregnancy, delinquency, and crime.

Economy

Business Week (Bernstein, 1994) adopts a strictly pragmatic perspective to the dysfunctions of inequality. Due to import competition and the decline of unions, according to the article, families in the bottom fifth of the economic structure are stranded in low-wage limbo. While in every industry, the new technologies demand progressively more advanced skills, workers unable to afford higher education will be a drain on the national economy. U.S. companies, in turn, will suffer from a great skill shortage which will hinder their competitiveness on the world market. Besides, according to Bernstein, a society divided between the "haves" and the "have-nots" will fail to be prosperous and stable. Widening inequality furthermore hurts education in poor communities deprived of school tax dollars and the role models of professional parents.

Unemployment

Whatever the circumstances of unemployment, whether the experience is personal or shared with hundreds of workers (as in mass layoffs), the psychological impact of job loss is enormous. The sense of personal failure, a concomitant of the North American work ethic, creates further difficulties for the worker and his or her family that go far beyond even the loss of income itself. The human cost of unemployment can be measured in the number of admissions to psychiatric hospitals, suicide rates, rates of violence in the family, and alcohol abuse and alcoholism. Bell (1987) defines the mass tragedy of the geographical flight of corporations forever in search of lower taxes and cheaper labor. After an extensive review of the literature, Bell concludes that American families pay an extremely high price for our boom-and-bust economy and for the tradition of corporations moving at will. Disrupted lives, disturbed children, and broken marriages are the result. This is true whether families follow the corporate trek, or more likely, are left behind to frantically find another means of income before the unemployment benefits run out.

Typically, the unemployment rate for African Americans is double the white rate. The limited educational opportunities in the inner city where African Americans are concentrated helps create conditions for family instability and a host of related social problems. Studies have shown a clear correlation between unemployment and family violence, desertion, separation, and divorce (Sidel, 1992). As people suddenly feel themselves to be rejects and outcasts, becoming a part of the affluent society which surrounds them ceases to be a reality or even a hope; it becomes a taunt (Harrington, 1962). Psychological deprivation thereby becomes one of the chief components of poverty.

The traumatic effects of the loss and absence of work over generations are analyzed in considerable depth by Cattell-Gordon (1990). Introducing the concept of culturally transmitted traumatic stress syndrome to describe the character of a people—the Southern Appalachian people—Cattell-Gordon records the history of those who have been alternately exploited and abandoned throughout the twentieth century. The distinct but not unique history of Appalachia reveals how external exploitation can leave a land and its people broken and bruised, and how the normative adaptations to the crises of unemployment and grinding poverty of yesterday have become ingrained in the culture today. According to Cattell-Gordon (1990: 43):

> These particular cultural traits then—an enduring sense of resignation, deep depression, disrupted relationships and hurtful forms of dependency—appear, again and again, in the culture as each new generation faces unemployment.

Although oppressed populations, such as inner-city African Americans and Native Americans, manifest a similar pattern of cultural transmission that are at odds, we might say, with the work ethic of the wider society, Cattell-Gordon argues vehemently against a culture of poverty premise. Whereas the culture of poverty theorists perceive a virtually autonomous subculture extant among the poor, they overlook the fact that the individual or group cannot easily break out of this vicious circle of social isolation and lack of faith in a system which appears to have very little to offer. Ultimately, the causes of a culture's poverty are structural, and the solutions will have to stem from the help and resources of external society. Otherwise, the sources of dysfunctions of poverty will be seen not only with the unemployed and alienated but in the descendants of the unemployed as well. The social cost of demoralizing generation after generation, which seek to outsmart the system but lack the will or the way to make a contribution to the system, is immeasurable. Gradually, the norm of working the system comes to replace the norm of working; rage, crime, and fatalism prevail. Commentators blame these attitudes (and the welfare) for poverty. The interactive nature of external realities and belief systems may not be recognized; cause is confused with effect.

Dysfunctions of World Poverty

The shackles of poverty prevent a fifth of humanity from attaining the most basic of human needs—adequate food, safe and sufficient water, sanitation, and access to health and education. According to painstakingly documented reports from United Nations agencies, there is a clear consensus that development means far more than per capita gross national product. Development also means action to protect the vulnerable and to provide adequate nutrition, safe water, primary health care, basic education, and family planning (Adamson, 1994).

In the poorest parts of the world such as Sub-Saharan Africa, lack of physical resources is paired with rapid population increase. The pressures of poverty and overcrowding also ravage the environment, as land-poor farmers seek short-term solutions to eke out their meager living (Sivard, 1993). They clear woodlands and bushes, soon exhausting the earth. In this way, poverty begets poverty.

An especially tragic example of how dysfunctional poverty can be is seen in the link between poverty and the mistreatment of women. Where survival is at stake, daughters will be sacrificed for sons. Girls may be sold to brothels for the highest bidder. In Thailand, for example, whole villages are being depleted by the deaths of daughters sold into slave-prostitution who then return home to die along with their HIV-infected babies. In sub-Saharan Africa, one adult in forty is HIV-infected. In India, poverty breeds dowry burnings of brides whose families are unable to meet dowry obligations. All these issues are explored in more depth in chapter 10.

Poverty anywhere affects the standard of living everywhere. Infectious diseases, such as AIDS and tuberculosis, are carried across the world. Disparities in wealth, whether within nations or between nations, are associated with greed, resentment, and war. Wars in one part of the world invariably involve nations from another part. War refugees migrate from the poor countries into the wealthier ones, joining the already large number of immigrants who cross borders for economic reasons. A major loss to the poor countries is the brain drain of doctors and scientists who were educated at their governments' expense but whose talents will be utilized elsewhere.

The work of the United Nations has been instrumental in documenting the causes and extent of poverty worldwide and in seeking to alleviate the causes of poverty through gaining the cooperation of the international community. A major effort to move social development to center stage in every country, and to translate economic resources into real human progress was seen, for example, in the World Summit for Social Development in Copenhagen in 1995, the fiftieth anniversary of the United Nations. At such world summits, heads of state come to consensus on issues of global import such as the need to ensure child nutrition and promote public health. Often commitments to agreed-upon goals are made through the signing of documents such as the Convention on the Elimination of all Forms of Discrimination against Women.

The dysfunctions of poverty at home and abroad clearly are paramount, despite academic exercises in locating social functions. A major dysfunction in regard to mass poverty is engendered in the system of rationalization which arises to justify it. Just as we dehumanize the enemy during wartime in order to reduce any qualms in battle, so we dehumanize the poor and homeless in order to justify our handling of them. In dehumanizing the poor, we are dehumanizing ourselves. We are blaming the victims for even being victims in the first place.

BLAMING THE VICTIM

Sorting out the multiple misfortunes that have befallen the poor in recent years is not easy. Cut backs in every conceivable type of welfare program, from nutrition to heating assistance to aid for dependent children, have been imposed. Even though, as Macht and Ashford (1991) indicate, many cultures value achievement, the United States is unusual in its victimization of "underachievers." Today, underachievers are regarded with disdain by their working neighbors; the poor welfare mother has become a national pariah. Unfavorable portraits of welfare mothers cheating the system have surfaced on virtually all the major television news programs.

What are some of the reasons that we blame the victim? As indicated in chapter 1, blaming the victim is a tendency that serves several social psychological functions: it makes us feel superior and distances us from the pain and suffering of other people's poverty; and it allows us to express hostility toward a class of people but without making us appear to be racist or sexist. The use of terms such as underclass and unwed mothers is sometimes a way of referring to the black poor without explicitly doing so. From the mid-eighties, according to Katz (1989), a new image dominated poverty discourse—the image of menacing blacks increasingly clustered and isolated in postindustrial cities. What bothered observers most was not their suffering; rather, it was their sexuality and welfare dependence. In any case, blaming the poor is easier than fixing what is really wrong in our society. Externally, blame allows prospering individuals to reap economic benefits in the short term if not also in the long run. In focusing on the moral shortcomings of society's victims, we cleverly can avoid dealing with the more complicated structural problems including technologically-based unemployment, inadequate health care, segregated schools, and low wages.

Most people who are poor, according to Dolgoff et al. (1993), do not choose their victimization nor do they gain satisfaction from it. The status is thrust upon them, often by cruel circumstances. Yet, and this is the sad part, those who are deemed to be receiving money for nothing come to internalize the blaming as they see others working hard and having to pick up the tab for their aid. As one welfare mother cited in Sidel (1992: 9), "Now when I feed my children I feel I am taking money out of the pockets of my working neighbors." To be poor in America, concludes Sidel, is to let America down. The self-fulfilling prophecy falls into place as conditions defined as true, come to actually be true in their consequences. When the poor are treated as biologically and morally inferior, when they are allowed to fail, they almost certainly will do so. Bitter and angry at a system that fails to provide hope, some members of society retreat. When given opportunities, however, such as college educations for AFDC recipients in Iowa, and philanthropic programs in Kansas City and New York City where inner-city children are closely monitored and groomed for vocational training or college, success stories abound. The film *Stand and Deliver* recounts the true story of a Hispanic math teacher who led his inner-city students against insurmountable odds to score high achievements on advanced placement calculus tests. While administrators derided the students as educationally and culturally backward, one inspiring teacher showed the nation what his students could do when given the needed encouragement.

In the 1960s, the well-publicized "Moynihan Report" identified the disintegration of black family life as the cause rather than the effect of urban poverty. Today we have the "Charles Murray Report." Ignoring many of the root causes of poverty suggested in this chapter—technology, politics, and the free market economy—Murray, in *Losing Ground* (1984), blamed welfare itself and the progressive programs of previous decades for a host of social problems associated with persistent poverty. He continued that argument in a much-talked-about essay in the *Wall Street Journal* (Murray, 1993). In this article, Murray states (1993: A14):

> Illegitimacy is the single most important social problem of our time—more important than crime, drugs, poverty, illiteracy, welfare, or homelessness because it drives everything else.

His solution? "End all economic support for single mothers. . . . The government should spend lavishly on orphanages." Regarding the article, in a controversial interview in the British radical press (Bunting, 1993), Murray was cited as saying:

> The things I was savaged for in 1984 are now conventional wisdom . . . I wrote a piece in the *Wall Street Journal* last October in which I came out and said we really had to get rid of the welfare system. Period. The response was phenomenal.

Apparently, according to the British commentator, Murray has not only been able to lay claim to responsibility and to being a major influence on U.S. government policy, but his ideas have been snapped up by British Toryism as well.

Murray's work, financed by the conservative think tank the American Enterprise Institute, provides a strange twist on victim-blaming. In *The Bell Curve,*

Herrnstein and Murray (1994) present the case that low IQ scores of the poor white and poor black Americans are the reason for their poverty, that low-functioning individuals cannot achieve success in a highly technological society. Basic assumptions of these authors are that the IQ test is an important measure of intelligence; that little or nothing can be done educationally to raise the ability of the IQ-impaired; and that one's ability to make a contribution to society is reflected in such scores. Studies cited indicate that Asians have top scores, then Caucasians, then Africans Americans, and lastly, Africans in Africa. *The Bell Curve* has been branded as racist in its implications and in its reliance on culturally biased, nonscholarly sources.

A unique phenomenon of the blaming-the-poor rhetoric of the 1990s is the success in enlisting the lower-middle classes in the service of the upper class establishment in targeting the poor as society's scapegoats. During the Great Depression, in contrast, those who had amassed great fortunes were the ones put on the defensive and attacked by politicians and the press. Although each state spends only about 3.4 percent of taxes on welfare (i.e., aid for the poor), the reason for the national budget deficit is pinned on the poor and their purported lack of morality. The new crop of social programs seems intent on controlling the behavior of the so-called underclass. The problem with such approaches is that they are based on myths. Despite conventional wisdom to the contrary, the real value of welfare benefits has been declining as the rate of infants born to single mothers has been rising.

WELFARE MYTHS

Not all American commentators, of course, share the outlook of Murray and his political allies. Noted social welfare historian Trattner (1994) takes Murray to task for ignoring the fact that during the years between 1960 and 1972, precisely the years when welfare programs really proliferated, poverty in the United States was cut in half. The significant growth in poverty that occurred later paralleled the subsequent curtailment, not expansion, of such programs. If welfare programs did fail, it was perhaps because they did too little, not too much.

Trattner, furthermore, challenges the dubious assumptions of recent state statutes—assumptions proved incorrect by a variety of scholarly studies—that claim that most recipients have been on welfare for long periods of time by choice, that they are able to get and to hold decently paying jobs, and that they will enter the labor force only when threatened with starvation. The tacit assumption that benefits have been too generous is belied by an actual 40 percent decline in welfare recipients' "real" dollar purchasing power since the early 1970s.

Marmor et al. (1990) in their book *America's Misunderstood Welfare State* deplore the harm that is done by mistaken ideas when they get translated into public policies. On the subject of misconceptions, these authors (1990: 213) state:

> A quite remarkable proportion of what is written and spoken about social welfare policy in the United States is, to put it charitably, mistaken. These mistakes are repeated by popular media addicted to the current and the quotable. Misconceptions thus insinuate themselves into the national consciousness; they can easily become the conventional wisdom.

Are welfare mothers promiscuous teenagers who have babies to get on the dole? Or are they down-on-their-luck women who need a temporary helping hand? *Business Week* (Valle and McNamee, 1995) analyzes Census Bureau data which reveal that only a fraction of AFDC mothers are seventeen or under and unmarried; and that 15 percent of AFDC mothers, moreover, are still pursuing an education. Some states with the highest benefits, such as California, have the lowest birth rates for unwed teens while some low-paying states, such as Georgia, have high pregnancy rates for such youths. On the other hand, AFDC recipients do have more children than nonwelfare mothers—2.6 versus 2.1—though far fewer than is commonly believed.

Much of the negativism vented against immigrants concerns their putative role as parasites who live on welfare. In a *U.S. News and World Report* review of census data (Friedman, 1994), immigrants were shown to constitute only 5 percent of all families getting federal welfare checks or food stamps. Exceptions were political refugees, typically from communist countries, who have quick access to welfare programs, and older immigrants who qualify for Supplemental Security Income (SSI) due to ailing health. A backlash is forming, however, against this latter provision of assistance.

What are the facts concerning social welfare recipients? In the political mouthpiece of the National Association of Social Workers (*NASW News*), Landers (1995) draws on congressional and other sources to get the record straight. The information presented in box 5.4 helps refute much of the reform debate's rhetoric.

BOX 5.4

UNTANGLING WELFARE DEBATE'S WEB OF MYTH

Susan Landers

As welfare reform moves to the top of the Republican agenda and both parties prepare to promote their "get tough" approaches in the 104th Congress, NASW is intent upon smashing myths that have surrounded welfare recipients.

According to the "myth busters" compiled by NASW's government-relations staff from congressional and other sources:

• More than two-thirds of the fourteen million Aid to Families and Dependent Children (AFDC) recipients are, in fact, children.
• According to 1992 statistics, 80 percent of the children lived in families headed by mothers in their twenties and thirties while only 8 percent lived in families headed by teenage parents.
• Out-of-wedlock births are increasing much faster among women in their twenties than among teenagers. These births increased among teens by 150 percent between 1970 and 1990, while among unmarried women twenty to twenty-four years old the number tripled, and among those twenty-five to twenty-nine years old, it increased almost six times.

• Only 30 percent of teenage mothers go on welfare within three years of the birth of their children, compared to 20 percent of all women who become single mothers through divorce of death of a spouse. Among unmarried teens, 50 percent go on welfare within three years, and the average teenage mother stays on welfare only one year longer than mothers in their twenties. Because the majority of teen parents have been sexually or physically abused as children, living at home should not be presumed to be the best option for them, NASW believes.
• Families receiving AFDC typically have the same number of children as families that do not receive welfare benefits. In 1991, more than 70 percent of all AFDC families had two or fewer children, more than 40 percent had only one child, and just 10 percent had four or more. The AFDC benefit structure in most states effectively penalizes families with more children, failing to increase benefits by an amount sufficient to cover the costs of providing for additional children. Payment is limited to an average of $65 per month for each additional child.

(Continued on next page)

BOX 5.4 (Continued)

- A change in marital status—whether through divorce or death of a spouse—that results in a female-headed family is the most powerful predictor of welfare receipt. Seventy-five percent of AFDC cases begin this way, while only 15 percent begin with a drop in family earnings.
- The vast majority (70 percent) of all people entering the welfare system leave within two years, and 50 percent leave within one year. Only 15 percent of all AFDC clients receive benefits for more than five years over the course of their lives, and only 25 percent receive benefits for ten years or longer. It is estimated that at least half of AFDC families who leave the system are forced to return—often after jobs or child care fall through—but welfare as a way of life is not the reality for most recipients.
- A significant number of adults who receive AFDC are single parents who are employed at some point during the year. In 1989, nearly 15 percent of adult female recipients and more than 22 percent of adult male recipients were either employed or in school while receiving aid, and another 65 percent of the men and nearly 40 percent of the women were enrolled in work or training programs.
- Less than 1 percent of the total federal budget funded AFDC in fiscal year 1991. That percentage has remained basically unchanged for the past ten years. In 1991,

the average state spent 2 percent of its revenue on AFDC.
- AFDC benefits have fallen in value during the past twenty years. Unlike Social Security, AFDC is not adjusted each year to keep pace with the rising cost of living. When adjusted for the inflation between 1970 and 1992, AFDC benefits show a 45 percent decrease in value.
- The average benefit per AFDC family in fiscal year 1992 was $388 monthly, $4,656 annually. In January 1992, state payments for families of three ranged from $120 per month in Mississippi to $924 in Alaska. Even when payments are combined with food stamps, the benefit is below the poverty level ($11,521 per year for a family of three) in every state and below 75 percent of the poverty level in almost four-fifths of the states.
- Not all AFDC families receive benefits under other poverty programs. About 15 percent of AFDC families do not receive food stamps and 63 percent live in private rental housing for which they receive no housing assistance. In two-thirds of the states (thirty-eight), the cost of the lowest-priced rental housing unit exceeds a family's entire monthly AFDC payment, leaving most families in substandard housing or without housing at all.
- Families receiving AFDC are about as likely to be white as black. In 1991, 38

(Continued on next page)

BOX 5.4 (Continued)

percent of families receiving welfare benefits were non-Hispanic white, 39 percent were black and 17 percent were Hispanic.

- A multi-year evaluation of Wisconsin's Learnfare program—which ties a family's AFDC grant to a child's attendance at school—found that the program failed to improve school attendance or graduation

rates. After one year, about one-third of Learnfare students had improved their attendance, while more than half showed poorer attendance. Graduation rates were the same for teens subject to Learnfare as for those who were not.

Source: NASW NEWS, 40(1) (January 1995): 5. Reprinted with permission of NASW.

For comparison purposes, poverty and the impact of poverty on present and future generations will be viewed from the perspective of Mexico, Russia, Canada, Great Britain, and Norway.

POVERTY IN MEXICO

Of all the countries in the world, only the United States, Germany, and Japan have more billionaires than Mexico which has twenty-four. Yet the combined worth of the twenty-four billionaires in Mexico has been shown to equal the total wealth of the twenty-five million least affluent Mexicans. In light of the general poverty of the country, many consider the huge Mexican fortunes now being amassed as downright obscene. According to a commentary in *The Christian Science Monitor* (Seid, 1994), the imposition of estate and inheritance taxes is essential to help redistribute the wealth and ensure social stability.

Carrington (1994) of *The Wall Street Journal* concurs that the region's extreme social inequities are in need of immediate attention. The rebellion of impoverished Indians from Mexico's Chiapan highlands serves as a warning to the nation that people at the margins see themselves disadvantaged by economic reforms in conjunction with the North American Free Trade Agreement (NAFTA); 70 percent of Mexico's extreme poor live in the Chiapas state.

Not only the impoverished are threatened by competition with free trade from the United States and Canada; home-grown businesses, large and small, are experiencing tremendous losses. From national airlines and local banks to the corner bakeries, grocery stores, and other small businesses, manufacturers and shop owners cannot compete with the offerings of stores like Wal-Mart and other warehouse-style chains. For every business opened in 1993, in fact, two were closed.

The general well-being of the population has been influenced by the extremely large national debt and the recent devaluation of the peso. With regard to shaping up the economy, Mexico faces serious obstacles, among them being an infrastructure that is in appalling shape. Telephone lines constantly get crossed, and phone rates to the United States are very expensive. The ports are badly managed, and the railroads are a disaster. Due to killer highways and reckless driving, the accident rate is incalculably high. The bribery rate to traffic police is staggering. Oster (1989), an award-winning journalist on location in Mexico, refers to one police officer informant as a clear exception to the rule as "a Mexican oxymoron, an honest cop."

In terms of pollution and crime, poverty takes its toll on Mexicans at all levels. All those who visit Mexico's cities are affected also. Noise and air pollution from unmuffled cars and buses is, according to Oster's description, beyond belief. Acid rain is killing what few trees are left. Crime, in its own way a response to the economic crisis, is reflected in extensive gang activity. Mexico City has a homicide rate which is about twice that of New York City. The burglary rate is extraordinary and affects all citizens. The poor, however, are affected in unique and terrible ways by the dual health standards—private care for the rich and very little preventive or other care for the poor. Malnutrition is endemic; respiratory ailments from pollution, and diarrhea from lack of water sanitation are common. The poor's children must drop out of school at around age twelve to hustle on the streets for money. With inflation skyrocketing, nearly 30 percent of Mexico's work force is unemployed.

POVERTY IN RUSSIA

As the teachings of Karl Marx get swapped for the teachings of Adam Smith, and vast economic changes are underway, the Russian people have collectively experienced a serious decline in living standards. Thirty percent of the population are below the poverty line. The deputy minister of Social Protection in Moscow, Andrey Panov (1995), contrasts the situation in 1993 when a single mother could support two children on federal allowances and compensation payments with the situation now when a great deal more help would be required to meet the family's basic needs. In fact, due to economic uncertainty and chaos, the system of social welfare is breaking down and social problems are mounting. Drawing on research which shows that alcoholism and drug addiction rates have soared, Panov shows that the rate of birth defects, inborn or otherwise, has soared also. With standards of medical treatment in a state of rapid decline and the cost of adequate medical treatment prohibitive, virtually all families with children with disabilities are on the verge of poverty. A greatly diminished life expectancy has resulted.

Other desperate problems related to economic instability are homelessness; an influx of refugees from areas of civil unrest; widespread prostitution; the warehousing of orphans in institutions; a significant rise in the number of child abuse cases and other forms of violence; and high unemployment, inflation, and infant and maternal mortality rates.

In short, some individuals are getting rich in capitalist Russia, many through illegal enterprises; the conspicuous consumption of the *nouveau riche* has been widely reported in the world press. At the other end of the social spectrum, workers are in a state of increasing insecurity in a country engaged in a constant struggle against the forces of political and economic turbulence.

POVERTY IN CANADA

Canada, which has long taken pride in providing European-style social programs, has assumed an abrupt about-face in light of forces from the global economy. As angry, middle-class taxpayers stage rallies across the country demanding "no new taxes," and as the national budget debt continues to mount, drastic cuts in federal spending are inevitable, according to an article in *Maclean's* the Canadian weekly news-magazine (Janigan, 1995). Average family income is declining, meanwhile, and rising taxes (including provincial and federal income taxes and sales taxes) have steadily eroded Canadians' purchasing power. In contrast to the United States, corporate income taxes have steadily crept upward and individuals in the upper income brackets are taxed up to 54 percent on a progressive basis. With the middle and upper classes already bearing the brunt of the tax burden, the most likely direction of the Canadian government, especially at the provincial level, will be to reduce spending on programs for the already impoverished and vulnerable. Already, the universal, much lauded family allowance program has been eliminated.

A study from Statistics Canada (reported by Mitchell, 1994) provides compelling evidence that restrictive social policy is preventing single mothers from taking their place in the work force. Married mothers with children under three years of age were found to be almost twice as likely to work outside the home as single mothers with children of the same age. Yet, once the children are of school age, single and married mothers work at the same rate. The key variable, according to the study, is the lack of available, affordable, around-the-clock child care. As in the United States, single mother families tend to be poor. The poverty rate for single mother families of which a family member did work was found to be 40.4 percent. The report also said that in 1992, women who worked at full-time year-round jobs earned (as in the United States) only 72 percent of what men did.

As recently as 1992, the article "Why Canada Has Less Poverty" (Hanratty, 1992) recounted in glowing terms the success story of Canada in eradicating, really preventing, poverty in comparison with the United States. Canada's programs were recognized for their generosity to unemployed workers and families in need of assistance, and the universality of the coverage—whether for health care or old age security pension. Total social welfare payments exceeded the poverty line in seven out of ten provinces. Hanratty explained the differences between the neighboring countries in terms of Canada's lower military spending, much higher unionization rate, and fairly homogenous racial composition which means the poor are perceived as more similar to the rest of Canadians. How far Canada will be able to adhere to its tradition of caring for the disadvantaged in light of free market forces, including tremendous competition from commerce south of the border, remains to be seen.

POVERTY IN GREAT BRITAIN

Over four hundred people, largely a white, male, and middle-aged population, sleep outdoors in central London. For London's homeless, glue-sniffing is common among the young and drinking among the old. Some live in tents and make-shift shacks. Charities bring blankets, clothes, and sleeping bags, and soup is delivered by church vans. Any homeless who want to shower or wash clothes has access to these facilities in day centers. Although a government program provides beds in hostels, many of those on the streets refuse to move (facts from *The Economist*, 1993)

The past super power of the nineteenth century ("The sun never sets on the British empire"), Britain has suffered a significant economic and political decline on the stage of world affairs. Competitors in Europe, Japan, and the United States have obtained dominance in international markets and global politics (Gould, 1993). Due to global forces and the influence of technology in the 1980s, the unemployment rate grew considerably. Trade unions, in turn, have lost much of their political clout. In combination with a surge in conservatism, class elitism, and racism (against immigrants from the Commonwealth and their descendants), social problems including poverty and crime have mounted. Minorities have suffered unemployment at twice the rate of other British residents. Welfare provisions, according to Gould, have been seen increasingly as something "blacks" (a term used to refer to those of Asian as well as African descent) were only too eager to take advantage of. The call has gone out in sizeable sections of the middle and upper classes to "roll back the frontiers of the state" and return to "Victorian values." The failure of the British welfare state to resolve the problems of poverty and the rising demands and pressures it faces has created, especially for poor people, a monolithic structure that is inadequate, unresponsive, and often impenetrable (Jones, 1992).

Instead of being a proud industrial giant, Britain has become the sweatshop of Europe, according to Knightley (1994). Both minimum wages and maximum working hours have been abolished. The rich, meanwhile, are getting richer; the top rate of income tax has been valued at 40 percent. Billions of dollars worth of state industries have been sold to the private sector. The top 20 percent of the population takes 40 percent of the nation's income, while real incomes for the bottom 10 percent of the population are down nearly 15 percent since 1979. Knightley's (1994: 18) commentary in the article "End of the Great in Britain" is harsh:

> As it slips back to the 19th century standards, Britain is regarded with ridicule in the rest of Europe. It has more children living in poverty today than does any other Western European country except Ireland or Portugal. More than

a third of the British work force now earns less than the minimum the Council of Europe considers necessary to exist decently. The welfare state is collapsing. . . . Everywhere there is a clearly discernible atmosphere of decay, a palpable feeling that something is rotten. . . .

POVERTY IN NORWAY

All countries are affected by competition from the global corporations, and Norway is no exception. The Norwegian social work journal *Sosionomen* (quite radical by North American standards) decries recent trends of privatization and efforts to reduce what must be the world's most generous social welfare benefits. The social workers' union is calling for a maximum work week of thirty hours. Norway's recent decision against joining the European Union was influenced largely by the women's vote (women stood to lose benefits) and opposition from farmers and inhabitants of north Norway. In contrast to Sweden, which in a referendum voted narrowly in favor of membership and is now forced to bring its extensive social welfare programs in line with the rest of Europe, Norway and Iceland have preserved much of their fiscal and social welfare independence. In box 5.5 I argue that Norway remains, for the most part, a society without poverty.

CONCLUSION AND SUMMARY

The prospects for substantially lessening poverty are dimmed by the relentless expansion of population, poverty's companion (Sivard, 1993). Overpopulation, discussed in chapter 10, is one of the major obstacles to economic and social progress. In the future, as population growth continues unchecked, rural areas will be depleted of resources and giant cities will be tinderboxes of seething slums with devastating health and political consequences. When fertility is controlled through centralized family planning, the health of mothers and children will be greatly improved. Although fertility rates are declining significantly, even in parts of sub-Saharan Africa, the need for birth control information and accessibility is urgent.

BOX 5.5

A SOCIETY WITHOUT POVERTY— THE NORWEGIAN EXPERIENCE

Yes, there is another way.

I went to Norway to teach American methods of alcoholism treatment and to learn of life in a welfare state. My stay of almost two years informed me in the way that firsthand experience informs—rudely, indelibly. My family and I have experienced the Norwegian community—the schools, social services, the health care system. And I have come to see how each dimension is connected to every other dimension of the cultural whole. In the high quality of life in Norway is the key to the larger pattern.

To the American visitor, the lack of poverty is striking, even puzzling. The outsider is inclined to see what *is* in terms of what is not: the southerner noting, for instance, the complete absence of palm trees. The Norwegian, meanwhile, is aware neither of the lack of poverty nor the absence of palm trees.

To understand the lack of poverty, you have to first understand poverty. And I am speaking of poverty in a rich society, there being no need to explain poverty in the absence of resources. The sociologists of the 1960s conceived of the existence of poverty in a prosperous society as functional for the total community. What were the social functions of poverty? (For a literature review, see Blau, 1988). Poverty or the threat of poverty provided a steady pool of compliant workers; poverty provided jobs for bureaucrats who were to ameliorate the poverty; the poverty of some provided for a natural division of classes. The existence of poverty in America is consistent with teachings of the Protestant ethic and the survival-of-the-fittest mentality.

Whereas Americans think individually, Norwegians tend to think collectively. Whereas Americans value competition, Norwegians value cooperation. The thesis of this article is that poverty persists in the United States because our values say it will persist. It does not persist in Norway because the society chooses not to tolerate it. This article examines the general economic conditions in Norway and views them against the Norwegian cultural context—values of egalitarianism and the collective will, trust in the social system, and above all a tradition of kindness to the weaker members of society. Implications for the United States and for American social workers are drawn.

Norwegian Economy

Norway is a socialist country in terms of social policy but a capitalist nation in terms of the ownership of business. Because of

(Continued on next page)

BOX 5.5 (Continued)

Norwegian control of North Sea oil industries, a great deal of wealth is available to the nation. This fact helps compensate for the poor agricultural conditions — rocky, mountainous land and a short growing season.

Personal income taxes in Norway are among the highest in the world. The higher the income, the higher the percentage of taxes paid. The value-added tax is a sales tax of 20 percent on virtually all items sold. Consequently, food and services are extremely expensive in Norway.

Income differences across occupational groups are relatively slight. Virtually no group of employees earns more than twice the average earnings of all employees (Selbyg, 1987). The equalization of income is a reality in Norway.

Poverty

Official estimates put the percentage of people living in poverty at 16.0 percent in the United States and 4.8 percent in Norway (Zimbalist, 1988). In fact, these figures were based on relative income in each country. My personal impression is that the gap between poverty in the United States and Norway is much higher than the numbers indicate. Even in my work with alcoholics, I did not come across one truly impoverished person. When an individual gets into economic trouble, the state provides help. Statistics on poverty thus do not portray the reality in a cradle-to-grave, highly protective society.

Kohlert's (1989) description of the universalism philosophy in welfare is pertinent to Norway. Universalism views those in need as no different from other people. Benefits-for-all programs can effectively prevent the occurrence of poverty in the first place. Such programs as redistribution of wealth, guaranteed income, and children's allowance schemes are examples. Theoretically, benefits from the state are rights, not privileges, and schools teach children that they have earned them. No one will go homeless, hungry, or sick (Henriksen, 1988).

Norway's family policy provides a universal tax-free child allowance for all children younger than sixteen. Single mothers or fathers receive double the allowance for each child. Older children are eligible for educational stipends. Actually, the amount of the family allowance, about $100 per child per month, is far below the cost of caring for a child and needs to be increased considerably to keep up with inflation. Elderly people are guaranteed a basic pension. In short, considerable sums are filtered through the tax and social systems to those who need assistance. The result is a society in which there are few truly rich or poor individuals.

Homelessness and Housing

Homelessness is simply not a problem in Norway as it is in some other countries. The

(Continued on next page)

BOX 5.5 (Continued)

government subsidizes low-cost housing so that adequate housing is available to everyone. If a person loses a home through inability to pay the rent, for instance, the social office will assist that person in finding other suitable housing. Housing and income are provided for refugees when they arrive. Like Sweden (Zimbalist, 1988), Norway has no deteriorated housing anywhere. Buildings are well-maintained and warmly heated. In many homes, flowers, visible through well-lighted windows, give a cheerful impression in all the neighborhoods.

Health Care

A recent feature article in the leading Oslo paper carried the headline "Norway Teaches USA on Health Services for Children" (1990). The medical professor interviewed in the article described an international conference attended in Washington, DC. According to Professor Lie, "America totally lacks official health care for children. . . . In infant mortality and death of children due to violence and accidents, the USA is far ahead of Europe and Canada. Twenty-five percent of American children live in poverty" [author's translation] (p. 11).

The public health service and the hospitals are the responsibility of the government. A hospital stay is free, and medicine and primary health care cost minor sums. Mothers or fathers of newborn infants receive extended paid leaves of absence.

Present health policies give Norwegians one of the longest life expectancy rates in the world. Access to excellent health care is not available only to a certain class of citizens but to all members of society. In contrast to the United States, which has the best technology in health care in the world but lags behind other developed countries in coverage, care in Norway is readily available to all.

Norwegian Culture

Two countries of great natural resources and highly industrious people move in different directions. Why? The persistence of poverty in the United States and the elimination of poverty in the Nordic countries reflect the cultural values of the two respective countries. In the United States there are many opportunities, but the cost of failure is high; in Norway there is great security, but the cost of security is high.

Three dominant cultural orientations of Norwegians may provide clues to the economic structure: (1) egalitarianism and the collective ideal, (2) trust in the social system, and (3) kindness toward the weak and vulnerable. These cultural orientations are consistent with those observed by Stevens (1989).

Egalitarianism and the Collective Ideal
The link between these dual concepts is in the tendency toward unity that is evidenced

(Continued on next page)

BOX 5.5 (Continued)

in all areas of Norwegian life. The stress on egalitarianism is exemplified in the organization of schools. Competition is largely absent. Children do not receive grades until they are thirteen, and then only rarely. Homework is minimal, and there are no special classes according to achievement level. Sports are noncompetitive as well; there are no school teams. There are no class officers. Teachers are addressed by their first names until the gymnasium, or high school. Norms favor belonging to the group and not rising above the group (Stevens, 1989).

Group conformity experiments by Milgram (1977) objectify the phenomenon of the collective ideal. A cultural comparative study of conformity to group norms in Norway and France indicated that the pull toward conformity, even to obvious judgmental fallacies, was significantly stronger among the Norwegians than among the French. In addition, although Norwegians accepted criticism impassively, the French subjects made pointed retaliatory responses.

"Do not stand out from the crowd" is the unwritten cultural norm. In my work in alcoholism treatment, the group was used to positive and compelling effect. Clients who were full of denial and minimization of their problems on day one seemed to have undergone some sort of strange transformation by day twenty-eight. Never have I observed such consistent turnover of arguments and beliefs in treatment groups in the United States.

Trust in the group is exceedingly strong in Norway (Ekstrom, 1988). The group in America is powerful, but in Norway it is more powerful still.

Woe to the group member in Norway who even mentioned connections with wealth or power! Indeed, the only insults uttered in the treatment groups were related either to lying or to bragging. "You are not one of us. You feel superior to the rest of the group" is a hard-hitting complaint.

This verbal enforcement of egalitarianism is reified in the tax system, which demands a heavy toll from those with high incomes, as well as in wage distribution. The disparity in wages among occupational groups is slight (Selby, 1987). As they do in the United States, however, capitalists earning money from investments have available to them the usual loopholes that effectively preserve their control of the nation's wealth. The elimination of poverty does not always carry with it the elimination of great wealth. Every system is full of contradictions.

Trust in the Social System
Security is provided by the social system. Economic security is available to all, even to malingerers. Extended sick leave provides 100 percent of their pay to people suffering from such intangible conditions as back pain and nervousness from stress. Money is provided

(Continued on next page)

BOX 5.5 (Continued)

by the employer for the first two weeks, then by the government thereafter.

Social workers have a great deal of authority within the social system, especially in regard to child welfare and public welfare. (For a critical analysis, see van Wormer, 1990.) Professionally trained practitioners work with families in need; they arrange for people in economic difficulty to receive allotments from the state. Because the stigma attached to receiving aid is absent or very slight, no stigma attaches to working at the "social office."

Trust in the system that is for the most part not corrupt and that provides help when needed is logical. A latent effect of the tendency to turn to the state for help is reflected in the small minority of elderly people who live with their families or in nursing homes. Most often they live in easily accessible apartment buildings, where they receive extensive home help and health care. The emphasis on independence, however, is often at the price of loneliness. The very system that takes care of sick and elderly people appears to reduce the responsibility of the family proportionately.

Kindness toward the Weak and Vulernable
Even the dogs do not bite in Norway; they rarely even bark. Owners of disobedient dogs speak quietly to them. These remarkable animals ride the trains with their owners and often accompany them to work. This illustrates one aspect of Norwegian life that is consistent with other aspects — kindness and nonaggression.

The kindness toward children in Norway is evidenced in law and social custom. Laws forbid corporal punishment against children by teachers and by parents. These laws are widely accepted and vigorously enforced. Norwegian visitors to the Anglo-American countries often remark on the shocking display of violence against children they encountered there. Americans, in contrast, often remark that children in Norway are babied and pampered. Indeed they are! Very large babies are pushed around in baby carriages and continue to take the bottle as long as they wish. They do not start school before age seven and are not taught to read before then.

Norway is not a punitive society. By international standards, criminals receive remarkably light sentences. The treatment of children, poor people, and even criminals is all of a pattern, and this pattern is characterized by individual and systematic kindness to people of all sorts.

Implications for U.S. Social Policy

To grasp the meaning of poverty or its absence is to grasp the sense of cultural style. The poverty that exists so ubiquitously in America, North or South, and the poverty that is prevented in a country like Norway mirrors the larger system. To understand a

(Continued on next page)

BOX 5.5 (Continued)

living system, it is necessary to look at a constellation of factors, not in and of themselves, but in their relationships and in their contexts (Bateson, 1984). To know one living system in its uniqueness is to learn of another in terms of the contrast.

Change will come in the United States when the values begin to change and emulate those in Norway. Generally, the laws in a society are consistent with traditional or current values. Hoefer (1988) used the example of Sweden's shift in politics and social welfare policies to illustrate the theory of changes in personal values (postmaterialism) as related to structural change.

To change the social system with reference to poverty in the United States, the country will need to change its values. For instance, both the collective good and individual protections will have to be emphasized above individual growth. Leaders in both the public and private sectors will have to articulate this consciousness. Coverage in the mass media will help. Once a collective sense of urgency is established (such as a demand for national health care), the mobilization of forces to carry out the prerequisite tasks will follow. I emphasize the word "urgency" because a passive belief system will not suffice. The equivalent of wartime fervor, however, would breed rapid mobilization and concomitant change.

Recently, U.S. national leaders talked of a "kinder, gentler society." Also, some action

has been taken to shift from counterproductive defense spending to a reform of public welfare spending. Social workers, individually and as a profession, are speaking out for a reprioritizing of interests (Day, 1989). The consensus of social workers seems to be that they must work toward policy change (Hartman, 1989). They must also work toward achieving value change. But whether these diverse "voices in the wilderness" will lead to institutionalization of the efforts will depend on the national sense of urgency and the belief that something can be done.

Meanwhile, Norway is an example of the possible. The solution is simple and described by Selbyg (1987) as follows: "Norway is a welfare state, a country where extensive systems of social care and social insurance make most residents who find themselves in a difficult economic situation legally entitled to aid from the government" (p. 72). Instead of the work ethic, a helping ethic prevails. This ethic is not an individualistic, Band-Aid approach but rather a universal, preventive one, a policy consistent with a value system based on care and absolute security. Norway has found another way, and, in my opinion, a far better way.

References

Bateson, M. C. (1984). *With a daughter's eye: A memoir of Margaret Mead and Gregory Bateson.* New York: William Morrow.

(Continued on next page)

BOX 5.5 (Continued)

Blau, J. (1988). On the uses of homelessness: A literature review. *Catalyst, 6*(2), 5–27.

Day, P. (1989). The new poor in America: Isolationism in an international political community. *Social Work, 34,* 227–232.

Ekstrom, J. (1988, July–August). *Cross cultural adaptation of drug and alcohol educational program.* Paper presented to the 35th International Congress on Alcoholism and Drug Dependency, Oslo, Norway.

Hartman, A. (1989). Homelessness: Public issue and private trouble [Editorial]. *Social Work, 34,* 483–484.

Henriksen, J. F. (1988). On being retired in Norway: Is the welfare state living up to expectations? *Norseman, 6,* 8–10.

Hoefer, R. (1988). Postmaterialism at work in social welfare policy: The Swedish case. *Social Service Review, 62,* 383–395.

Kohlert, N. (1989). Welfare reform: A historic consensus. *Social Work, 34,* 303–306.

Milgram, S. (1977). Nationality and conformity. In S. Milgram et al. (Eds.), *The individual in a social world: Essays and experiments* (pp. 159–173). Reading, MA: Addison-Wesley Press.

Norge laerer USA on helsetjeneste for barn. [Norway teaches USA about health services for children.] (1990, March 28). *Aftenposten,* p. 11.

Selbyg, A. (1987). *Norway today.* Oslo: Norwegian University Press.

Stevens, R. (1989). Cultural values and Norwegian health services: Dominant themes and recurring dilemmas. *Scandinavian Studies, 61*(2–3), 199–212.

van Wormer, K. (1990). The hidden juvenile justice system in Norway: A journey back in time. *Federal Probation, 54*(1), 57–61.

Zimbalist, S. (1988). Winning the war on poverty: The Swedish strategy. *Social Work, 33,* 46–49.

Source: K. van Wormer, *Social Work* 39 (1994) (3): 324–327. Reprinted with permission of NASW.

Poverty, population growth, environmental degradation, education of women, illness, and malnutrition all interact in a cyclical pattern. Generally, the poorer the country is, the higher the level of fertility. In the poorest regions of the world, the most potent solution is to deploy a number of policies simultaneously (Dasgupta, 1995). Family planning services allied with health services and measures that empower women are essential.

In the United States and other countries in the industrialized world, the social costs of poverty are tremendous. The costs can be measured in the billions spent on treatment after the fact—for infectious diseases, low-weight births, imprisonment, and widespread unemployment—as opposed to prevention in the form of preventive health care, adequate income for food and housing, work programs, and family planning. As a modest movement toward a more equitable distribution of the nation's economic resources, Sidel (1992) calls for a comprehensive U.S. family policy. Such a policy would entail universal support for children, and appropriate maternity leave and childcare provisions; this would enable women to participate equally in the work force. In a commentary contained in the United Nations report, *The Progress of Nations,* Edelman (1994) similarly refutes the argument that the U.S. government cannot afford investments to meet peoples' human needs. What we cannot afford is to spend $274 billion a year on external defense when the real enemy is within.

Recent rhetoric from the U.S. Congress has portrayed government itself as the enemy of social progress. Marmor et al.'s (1990) extensive review of the research supports the perspective that social welfare programs can and do make a significant dent in the sources of poverty. Demonstrating the effectiveness of much maligned programs as Head Start, food stamps, Medicare, and Social Security, the authors advocate the continuation and expansion of such efforts. From a strictly pragmatic perspective, Farrell (1990) writes in *Business Week* that we should invest in human capital and thereby protect our citizens from economic hardship. The key to healthy corporate profits, economic growth, and higher living standards, states Farrell, is through productivity which depends on investing in a people's social welfare.

Harrington's (1962: 9) remarks made before the War on Poverty are sadly as timely today as they were originally:

> To be sure, the other America is not impoverished in the same sense as those poor nations where millions cling to hunger as a defense against starvation. This country has escaped such extremes. That does not change the fact that tens of millions of Americans are, at this very moment, maimed in body and spirit, existing at levels beneath those necessary for human decency.

See box 5.6 for a commentary by a sociologist and former social worker concerning proposed welfare cuts.

To summarize, three facts that emerge from this chapter on poverty are poverty is global; the statistics shock; and solutions are fairly obvious. The causes of poverty are external and political; nations are striving toward the accumulation of vast sums of capital for investment in industries including military production. In the age of the global economy, the gap between rich and poor nations has widened, while within nations, the gap between rich and poor likewise has grown wider.

BOX 5.6

SHE WANTS MORE FOR POOR

Betsy Rubiner

If there is anything Ruth Sidel and Newt Gingrich agree on, it is that welfare doesn't work. But Sidel, a nationally known expert on poverty, argues that welfare programs have failed because too little—not too much—has been spent on them.

"It has left (people) in abject poverty and has not given them opportunities to move out," said Sidel, a sociology professor at Hunter College in New York.

The author of several books about women and children, Sidel is "disheartened and dismayed" by the House Republican welfare reform bill that was approved Friday in Washington D.C.

While public opinion polls show Americans support cuts in welfare programs and think poorly of adults on welfare, this support drops when they're asked if they approve of cutting programs that help poor children, Sidel said.

She hopes public support for the Republican initiatives will diminish when the focus is shifted away from the adults on welfare and onto the plight of their children.

"When people realize what's going to be cut, they won't be nearly so willing to let it happen," she said. "We're hurting children. It's foolhardy. It's going to cost us much more in the long run—in prisons, drug addiction, medical bills, violence."

She argues that many people on welfare need a lot of help—and prodding—to become independent. "We haven't invested enough, and we have not invested wisely," she said. "If we're really serious about helping people back into the mainstream, we have to give them enough to pay rent, to have decent clothes and heat. Anything else ostracizes them."

What is needed, she said, are higher welfare payments that really help people get out of poverty, training programs for real jobs, quality child care, financial support for poor people who get a low-paying job or try to attend a four-year college.

"To have people feel they're part of society, with jobs and homes, is certainly much more cost-effective than having people out there without any resources who are going hungry."

Right now, people on welfare don't get enough in payments and food stamps to rise above poverty, Sidel said. If they receive any training, it's for low-paying or non-existent jobs, she added. Plus there is little incentive

(Continued on next page)

BOX 5.6 (Continued)

for them to leave welfare, when the alternative is a low-paying job and no assurance of quality child care.

"They are exchanging welfare with Medicaid for a job that still leaves them in poverty without benefits," she said.

Sidel also points to what she calls "a great double standard."

"We don't want (Los Angeles prosecutor) Marcia Clark to be away from her children too much. Why is it OK for poor women to be away from their children earning poverty wages?" she said.

She views the attack on programs for the poor as a thinly veiled attack on women and minorities by a middle class frustrated by its own lack of economic progress. "People are losing ground and want someone to blame," she said.

Sidel says they're asking, "Why are my neighborhoods so dangerous? Why are my schools deteriorating? Why am I being laid off my job at age fifty? Why has my income deteriorated? Why will my children not do better than I am?

"The quintessential American dream is that their children will do better. This generation doesn't believe that. They need someone to blame."

Shifting the responsibility for welfare programs to the states, Sidel said, means the poor will no longer be guaranteed help.

"We know there are states out there that are racist and sexist and will treat people differently depending on their race and marital status. If there isn't federal . . . oversight, guidelines and standards, states will be free to do anything they want to the poor."

She said state politicians can "very easily" use this new power to discriminate against the poor in favor of powerful business interests. "State governments are much more susceptible to the political and economic clout of the owners of companies in their state. That's who put them there, contributed to their campaigns," said Sidel. "The poor don't have that clout."

Sidel notes that proponents of the Republican measures justify the cuts by arguing that without them, the next generation will be burdened with an even larger national debt.

But she warns that if the welfare programs are cut, the next generation will inherit a world in which "millions are put on the margins of society without enough education or decent health care or a feeling that they can participate. We don't even know what we may be in for."

Source: Des Moines Register, March 25, 1995, pp. 1T–2T. Reprinted with permission of *The Des Moines Register.*

Using the official government poverty level as our measure of deprivation, we see that over 15 percent of the population live below the poverty level. The poverty level had declined substantially in the 1970s, but it is rapidly rising today. Poverty is most frequently found among African and Hispanic Americans and in households headed by single women. The poverty rate appears less bleak for the elderly, once the poorest group in the United States. For children, however, living standards have declined considerably; over one in four children now lives below the poverty level. Poverty is strongly associated with a national decline in well-paying jobs, unemployment, and health care provisions.

In light of the historical intransigence of poverty, sociologists such as Gans have pondered the functions of poverty for those in society who shape the social policies. The functions listed are economic, social, cultural, and political. In short, poverty keeps one segment of society humble and grateful for work from the other segment. This theory relates to Piven and Cloward's thesis reviewed in the previous chapter that states that a minimum degree of social welfare must be provided to keep the poor believing in the system, or in other words, to prevent social unrest.

Even in industrially advanced nations, the dysfunctions of poverty are considerable; as a family's income declines, every aspect of life is ineradicably altered accordingly. The struggle to make ends meet becomes all consuming. Family members suffer—psychologically, physically, and socially. Communities suffer also. The social costs can be measured in terms of disease, infant mortality and retardation, substance abuse, crime, and inferior education. In impoverished parts of the world, one's standard of living can very well make the difference between life and death. Being born female is especially hazardous throughout much of the Southern Hemisphere. Regional poverty is not confined to just this one area; its effects are echoed globally. Diseases spread; warfare reverberates; and refugees flock into nations where conditions are better. We live in a highly complex global society in which we are ineluctably interdependent.

To the roots of reluctance in the creation of a viable American welfare state discussed in the opening chapters of this book, we must add the persistence of racial, ethnic, gender, and class divisions and, above all, the tendency for members of the mainstream to attach blame to the victims of the socioeconomic system. Victim blaming of those mired in poverty becomes an additional factor in perpetuating the poverty. The poor make easy scapegoats in a society facing economic and vocational stress. Charles Murray's contribution to blaming the poor was described in this chapter. His solution to "end welfare as we know it" was challenged by facts drawn from government and business news sources. A related aspect of impoverishment is the perpetration of myths about persons "on welfare." Facts refuting the popular rhetoric can be found in the U.S. Census data published annually.

The way poverty is perceived in a given country has important implications for strategies to alleviate the problem. Following an overview of possible solutions to the seemingly intractable poverty in this United States, this chapter considered the nature of poverty in Mexico, Russia, Canada, Great Britain, and Norway.

REVIEW QUESTIONS

1. Differentiate absolute from relative poverty. Use these concepts with regard to Mexico and India.
2. Discuss the relationship between warfare and poverty. How have women been affected?
3. How, according to Macionis (1994), does the quality of poverty in India take on a unique character?
4. How has agribusiness affected regional economies in poor countries?
5. Referring to box 5.1, discuss aspects of global interdependence connecting the United States with Asia, Africa, and Latin America.
6. Discuss the relationship between economic restructuring and unemployment.
7. Explain the connection between poverty and overpopulation. How is a vicious cycle produced?
8. Referring to box 5.2, recount the ecological history of Haiti.
9. Discuss the concept of class polarization and the impact of the global economy.
10. Discuss the statistics from the U.S. Bureau of the Census provided in table 5.1.
11. Cite the statistics to indicate a relationship between race and poverty. Discuss the concept of the feminization of poverty.
12. What are three basic requirements, according to Galbraith, serving contentment of the upper classes? How does the "upside down welfare state" work?
13. What do longitudinal studies of children in poverty show? Discuss the cost factor in child poverty.
14. How does *Business Week* approach the pragmatic side of inequality?
15. Discuss the mass tragedy that unemployment entails. Relate culturally transmitted traumatic stress syndrome to the Appalachian people. How does this argument differ from the culture of poverty premise?

16. Discuss the following statement: "Poverty anywhere affects the standard of living everywhere."
17. Relate victim-blaming to poverty.
18. Argue in favor of or against Charles Murray's basic contentions.
19. List the most commonly accepted welfare myths, and counter the myths with facts.
20. Discuss poverty in Mexico with regard to economic developments of the 1990s.
21. What are the major challenges facing capitalist Russia?
22. How have events in Canada changed under the impact of world economic forces?
23. Is Britain a proud industrial giant according to this chapter? Why or why not?
24. Discuss the cultural values in Norway in terms of the alleviation of poverty.

REFERENCES

Adamson, P. (1994). One Small Step for a Summit. In UNICEF *The Progress of Nations.* New York: United Nations Children's Fund.

Alvarado, E. (1987). *Don't Be Afraid Gringo.* New York: Harper and Row.

Assessing Social Welfare: A Mixed Success. (1993, June). *UN Chronicle:* 62–64.

Associated Press. (1995). One in Four U.S. Children Live in Poverty. *Waterloo Courier.* January 30: A1.

———. (1994). Poverty at Highest Level Since '61. *The Des Moines Register.* October 7: 1A, 4A.

Barker, R, ed. (1995). *The Social Work Dictionary,* 3d ed. Washington, DC: NASW Press.

Bell, W. (1987). *Contemporary Social Welfare,* 2d ed. Washington, DC: Macmillan.

Bernstein, A. (1994, August 15). Inequality: How the Gap between Rich and Poor Hurts the Economy. *Business Week* 3385: 78–83.

Bower, B. (1994, July 9). Growing up Poor. *Science News* 46: 24–25.

Carrington, T. (1994, October 28). The Unfinished Agenda. *Wall Street Journal:* R10.

Cattell-Gordon, D. (1990). The Appalachian Inheritance: A Culturally Transmitted Traumatic Stress Syndrome. *Journal of Progressive Human Services* 1(1): 41–57.

Cox, D. (1994, July 10–15). *Adapting Social Work Education to Training for Poverty Alleviation in the Third World.* Paper presented at the International Association of Schools of Social Work Conference, Amsterdam. *The World of Social Welfare.* Springfield, IL: Charles C. Thomas.

Dasgupta, P. (1995, February). Population, Poverty, and the Local Environment. *Scientific American* 272: 40–45.

Day, P. (1989). The New Poor in America: Isolationism in an International Political Economy. *Social Work* 34, 227–233.

Dolgoff, R., D. Feldstein, and L. Skolnik. (1993). *Understanding Social Welfare*, 3d ed. New York: Longman.

Economist. (1993). Homelessness: Move Along. *The Economist*. February 6; 65.

Edelman, M. (1994). This Is Not Who We Are. *The Progress of Nations*. New York: UNICEF.

Estes, R. (1992a). The Debt Crisis and Development. In R. Estes, ed. *Internalizing Social Work Education: A Guide to Resources for a New Century* 272: 181–188. Philadelphia: School of Social Work.

———. (1992b). World Hunger and Malnutrition. In R. Estes, ed. *Internalizing Social Education: A Guide to Resources for a New Century* (168–175). Philadelphia: School of Social Work.

Facts on File (1995, September 21). Statistics on Women. *Facts on File*, 688.

Farrell, C. (1990). Why We Should Invest in Human Capital. *Business Week* 3192: 88–90.

Friedman, D. (1994). Immigrants and Welfare: The Myth of the Parasites. *U.S. News and World Report* 117(13): 38.

Galbraith, J. (1992). *The Culture of Contentment*. Boston: Houghton Mifflin.

Gans, H. (1976). The Positive Functions of Poverty. *American Journal of Sociology* 78(2): 275–289.

Global Tomorrow Coalition. (1989). *Citizen's Guide to Sustainable Development*. Washington, DC: GTC.

Gould, A. (1993). *Capitalist Welfare System: A Comparison of Japan, Britain and Sweden*. London: Longman.

Greider, W. (1981, December). Education of David Stockman. *The Atlantic*.

Hamilton, J. M. (1988). *Main Street America and the Third World*. Cabin John, MD: Seven Locks Press.

Hanratty, M. (1992, summer). Why Canada Has Less Poverty. *Social Policy*: 32–37.

Harrington, M. (1962). *The Other America: Poverty in the United States*. Baltimore, MD: Penguin.

———. (1972). *The Vast Majority: A Journey to the World's People*. New York: Simon and Schuster.

Healy, L. and W. Whitaker. (1992). Global Poverty, Hunger, and Development: Basic Issues and Impact on Family and Child Well-Being. In L. Healy, ed. *Introducing International Development Content in the Social Work Curriculum*. Washington, DC: NASW Press.

Herrnstein, R. and C. Murray. (1994). *The Bell Curve: Intelligence and Class Structure in American Life*. New York: The Free Press.

Homelessness: Move Along. (1993, February 6). *The Economist* 65.

Huff, F. (1992, winter). Upside-Down Welfare. *Public Welfare*:36–40.

Janigan, M. (1995, March 6). The Middle Class: Blown Away. *Maclean's* 108(10): 48–51.

Jones, C. (1992). Social Work in Great Britain: Surviving the Challenge of Conservative Ideology. In M. Hokenstad, S. Khinduka, and J. Midgley, eds. *Profiles in International Social Work.* Washington, DC: NASW Press.

Karger, H. (1991). The Global Economy and the American Welfare State. *Journal of Sociology and Social Welfare* 18: 3–20.

———. (1994). Toward Redefining Social Development in the Global Economy: Free Markets, Privatization, and the Development of a Welfare State in Eastern Europe. *Social Development Issues* 16(3): 32–44.

Katz, M. (1989). *The Undeserving Poor: From the War on Poverty to the War on Welfare.* New York: Pantheon Books.

Knightley, P. (1994, August). The End of Great Britain. *World Press Review*: 18–20.

Landers, S. (1995). Untangling Welfare Debate's Web of Myth. *NASW News* 40(1): 5.

Macht, M. and J. Ashford. (1991). *Introduction to Social Work and Social Welfare,* 2d ed. New York: Macmillan.

Macionis, J. (1994). *Society: The Basics,* 2d ed. Englewood Cliffs, NJ: Prentice Hall.

Marmor, T., J. Mashaw, and P. Harvey. (1990). *America's Misunderstood Welfare State: Persistent Myths, Enduring Realities.* New York: Basic Books.

Mead, W. (1994, September 11). When the Economy Heads Uphill it Usually Takes the President with It—But not this Time. *Waterloo/Cedar Falls Courier*: F1–F2.

Mitchell, A. (1994, October 26). Social Policy Hurts Single Mothers, Study Says. *Toronto Globe*: A7.

Murray, C. (1984). *Losing Ground: American Social Policy, 1950–1980.* New York: Basic Books.

———. (1993, October 29). The Coming White Underclass. *The Wall Street Journal*: A14.

Oster, P. (1989). *The Mexicans: A Personal Portrait of a People.* New York: Harper and Row.

Panov, A. (1995, March 2). Social Work in Russia: Problems and Perspective. *International News*: 3.

Sallah, M. (1994, April 17). In Fertile Land, A Harvest of Shame. *Waterloo/Cedar Falls Courier*: 1. (Reprinted from the *Toledo Blade.*)

Seid, R. (1994, October 31). Why Billions of Mexican Pesos Should Be Redistributed. *The Christian Science Monitor*: 2.

Shapiro, L. (1994, March 14). How Hungry is America? *Newsweek*: 58–59.

Sidel, R. (1992). *Women and Children Last: The Plight of Poor Women in Affluent America.* New York: Penguin Books.

Sivard, R. (1993). *World Military and Social Expenditures.* Washington, DC: World Priorities.

Society for International Development-U.S.A. Chapters Center. (SID-U.S.A.). Washington, DC.

Sommer, J. G. (1987). Development: What's the Problem? In C. Joy and W. Kniep, eds. *The International Development Crisis & American Education: Challenges, Opportunities, and Instructional Strategies.* New York: The American Forum.

Trattner, W. (1994). *From Poor Law to Welfare State: A History of Social Welfare in America.* New York: The Free Press.

UN Chronicle. (1993). Assessing Social Welfare: A Mixed Success. *UN Chronicle* 30(2): 62–64.

United Nations. (1995). *The World's Women 1995: Trends and Statistics.* New York: United Nations.

U.S. Bureau of the Census. (1995). *Statistical Abstract of the United States.* Washington, DC: U.S. Department of Commerce.

Valle, C. and M. McNamee. (1995, March 13). *Business Week* 44.

Women Challenges to the Year 2000. (1991). New York: United Nations.

Woods, A. (1989). *Development and the National Interest: U.S. Economic Assistance into the Twenty-first Century.* Washington, DC: U.S. Agency for International Development (AID).

Zastrow, C. (1996). *Introduction to Social Work and Social Welfare,* 6th ed. Pacific Grove, CA: Brooks/Cole.

PART II

CARE THROUGH THE LIFE CYCLE

6

CHILD WELFARE

Barndomen kommer aldrig igen.
Childhood never comes again.—old Swedish saying

From around the world, first there are the images:

- Disabled orphans in Russia, many the victims of nuclear radiation and industrial pollution.
- Street children of Brazil shot by police officers.
- Child refugees roaming the earth, many traumatized by war.
- Children on the street of New York City shot from stray bullets.
- Child warriors forced to engage in horrible acts of slaughter in Liberia.

Then there are the statistics:

- About 10 percent of all Russian children are born with deformities or other defects, many caused by pollution.
- About 55 percent of the world's deaths under age five are caused by malnutrition.
- Over eighty thousand children have been orphaned due to genocide in Rwanda.
- There are over one million child prostitutes in Asia.
- One in five American children lives in poverty.

This chapter will go beyond the statistics to examine issues that know no geographical boundaries. The title of this chapter refers not to its social work meaning of "a specialized field of practice" but to its literal meaning of the general well-being of children. Underlying assumptions of this chapter are that children are the most powerless members of the human community, and that the primary source of help and nurturance for children is the family, which often cannot do the job alone. In societies which have formal, *residually* based child welfare services, intervention only occurs when the child's needs are believed not to be met. Under the contrasting *institutional* orientation, on the other hand, child welfare services routinely are made available to all children in the society (Kadushin and Martin, 1988).

Under the conditions of plague, economic crisis, overpopulation, and war, the standards of child welfare are worsening. In the United States, an over-burdened child welfare system is straining at the seams with the victims of paren-tal disease, addictions, and maltreatment (McFadden, 1991). Additionally, throughout the world, the health and lives of children are threatened when their society discriminates on the basis of race, ethnicity, and gender. In many places, children's human rights are endangered because their families are at risk for genocide, political persecution, or grinding poverty.

Central to the treatment of children is the societal notion of childhood itself. This chapter traces the historical development of the concept of child-hood and of child welfare services in western society. In providing this over-view we will be addressing Ann Hartman's (1990: 118) provocative though rhetorical questions, "What is happening in this country (and elsewhere)? How is it that this society, which is supposed to be so child-centered, can be guilty of such unconscionable neglect?" To this we can add our own, "What can we do to protect the world's children?"

In an imperfect world, the well-being of children requires political action at the highest levels. In 1990 such action was provided by the United Nations Convention on the Rights of the Child, a landmark agreement in international law which is widely considered to be the most progressive, detailed, and specific human rights treaty ever adopted by the member states of the United Nations (UNICEF, 1995). After examining the principles of human rights as spelled out in the document, we will consider some of the specific problems threatening children's survival. These problems include the effects of disease and war as well as the more mundane cut backs in essential government services. Throughout the world, children are deliberately and cruelly exploited as prostitutes, slave labor, and combat soldiers; these violations will be discussed as well as the plight of homeless, street children. In its final section, this chapter explores the treatment of children in trouble and those who have been victimized, violently and sexually, by their families. International standards of treatment of children and of provisions for childcare are compared. The conclusion addresses the choices and challenges facing the social work profession and other interested associations as they work on both national and international fronts to advance justice for children.

HISTORY OF CHILDHOOD AND CHILD WELFARE

No concern in the United States has been more heavily studied and documented than the condition of the nation's sixty-four million children, especially those at risk for drug use, crime, and child abuse. Yet no problem, perhaps, has been such a consistent source of misguided or inadequate effort. As a review of Euro-American history will show, the field of child welfare has focused on individuals—children and mothers—out of the context of societal forces. Often the problems (for example, child neglect) have been more economic than personal. Yet out of reluctance to risk providing support for family members who, it was feared, might lose their work ethic if they received aid, the state sometimes has resorted to the removal of children from the home. Today, in parts of the United States, disabled children in need of expensive special care may be placed with foster or adoptive families. Such homes qualify for payments for special needs children while the biological homes do not. (I know personally of a case of a child in Kentucky placed in foster care for a sufficient period so that she could get braces for her seriously malaligned teeth.) In other industrialized nations, universal health care policies provide protection for families so children can get the kind of care they need. The question we will want to consider is why the United States is unique in this regard. There are two aspects of the issue to explore—the macro (or state) level of care for children and the micro (or family) level of care.

Without a historical perspective that traces the relation of economic forces—from feudalism and postindustrial capitalism to the development of child and family welfare polices—a nation's treatment of children cannot be understood or evaluated. Without a grasping, furthermore, of the power of cultural proclivities bearing on the treatment of infants and children, Hartman's pointed query asking how can we "be guilty of such unconscionable neglect" can only lead to bewilderment. Let us start with the culture.

In his article, "Our Forebears Made Childhood a Nightmare," DeMause (1975) reviews the facts concerning the horrors that children once endured. The further back in history one goes, according to this author, the lower the level of childcare, and the more likely children were to have been killed, abandoned, whipped, sexually abused, and terrorized by their caretakers. Battering, which was recommended in all the early childrearing tracts, began in infancy. The sexual use of children, well documented in ancient Greece and Rome, was so ingrained in the male culture that slave boys were commonly kept for sexual use by older men.

Like it or not, claims Chase (1995), the killing of children is a constant and important feature of human social history. Child sacrifice was common in ancient and biblical times. Infanticide served as a means of rendering sacrifice to the gods, as a eugenic device to weed out the sickly and deformed, as a tool of population control, and as the last resort of unmarried mothers. In China, the killing of infant girls was the custom. In Japan's feudal era farmers killed their second or third sons at birth. Infanticide was a regular feature of Eskimo, Scandinavian, Polynesian, African, American Indian, Australian aborigine, and Hawaiian cultures. The taboo, concludes Chase, has not been so much to forbid the act, but to avoid mentioning it. Until the relatively recent "discovery" of child abuse and neglect, in fact, there has long been a norm of silence concerning the maltreatment of children.

Centuries of Childhood by Aries (1965) documents some of the sadistic punishments carried out against children in England during the seventeenth, and especially the eighteenth and nineteenth centuries. Deliberate pain was inflicted to teach school lessons, social norms, and even self-control. Both in England and in early America, disobedient children were flogged and executed, traditions that reflected the harshness of a society that was aggressive as well as punitively religious. Although children in North America and Britain today have some protection against life-threatening physical abuse, they are not protected, as adults are, against ordinary assault and battery. Children are apt to be physically assaulted by practically anyone including neighbors, babysitters, teachers, and most commonly, by parents. Many adults are furious that there are far more restrictions in this regard than formerly, and believe that their rights are being tampered with.

The most pervasive form of abuse against children, however, has come not directly but indirectly through the cruelty in the social order. A society in which survival-of-the-fittest rather than justice and equality has been the predominant cultural mode could not fail to be oppressive toward children. For, as we will see in the remainder of this chapter, when families suffer, children invariably suffer also.

Child welfare practice is a gauge by which we can observe the values of a society. A society's attitude toward the treatment of children is a part of a whole texture of values: This one cultural attribute is the clue to the cultural whole. Thus we see Anglo-Saxon punitiveness reflected in tough childrearing patterns of childhood, rigid sentencing of criminals, creation of conditions conducive to poverty, and vast resources invested in the military rather than in people.

The egalitarianism and kindness evidenced in Norwegian society today reach back to the Viking Age, a time when regional assemblies passed statutes which provided for relief to destitute persons (Selbyg, 1987). These statutes became incorporated into the first national civil code in the thirteenth century. Also in the thirteenth century, came recognition of the fact that society cannot react to juvenile lawbreaking with the same severity reserved for adult lawbreaking. In 1621, Norwegian law provided for public guardians to assume responsibility for youngsters not adequately cared for by their parents (Flekkoy, 1989). The evils inherent in the merciless factory system inevitably followed, but they were met by subsequent reforms.

Similarly, in Sweden, solicitude for its people did not stop with care for the aged, the physically handicapped, the mentally sick, and the criminal. Children have been well cared for also (Berfenstam, 1973). A free upbringing was advocated for children by Ellen Key, an author and journalist who wrote in 1900. Her work was exceedingly influential in the care and upbringing of children.

There are conflicting estimates of when the notion of childhood as a special developmental stage began and of precisely when and where institutionalized child welfare began. First, "The whole concept of childhood as a special, unique phase of human development," argues Richette (1969: 56), "is a twentieth century idea." Before that, children were considered the chattel of their parents (Aries, 1965). Yet Chase (1975) records the process of separating children from adults as occurring as early as the 1600s. Children, according to Chase, were separated from adults in styles of clothing and from other children of different ages. It was a process, however, that developed over time. Perhaps these seemingly contradictory estimates of when childhood began can be reconciled by realizing there was a gradual transition toward the notion of childhood and of children as individuals that we have today. The child-saving and child-rescue movements of the nineteenth century eventually crystallized into a system of services which emphasized removal of children from the home as a solution to family and cultural problems. Although many states established orphanages during the early nineteenth century, current child welfare policy did not get underway until the 1870s.

For the beginnings of institutionalized child welfare, Hegar (1989) and Moe (1990) point to Norway's Child Welfare Act of 1896 as a protectionist act and as the first in history to protect children from punishment, abuse, and exploitation by adults. However, across the Atlantic, several years before this, the seeds of the Canadian "child's movement" already were being sown. Out of this movement sprang the first Children's Aid Society in Canada in 1891 as well as the promotion of legislation in Ontario that protected children living with their own families and those who were abandoned or orphaned (Swift, 1991). As early as 1888, the province was given the right to oversee the child's environment if deemed in the child's interest. Shortly thereafter, more specific legislation was passed to prevent cruelty to children. In the United States, spawned by a response to industrialization and urbanization which often left children unprotected and homeless, the first separate juvenile court was established in 1899 in Chicago. Not a criminal court, this institution theoretically considered the needs of children in trouble and those who were neglected by their parents. In fact, children under the jurisdiction of the court were often removed from their homes and placed in institutions. Parents had no right to voice objections. The significance of these developments, and of parallel developments throughout Europe, was in the newly carved out role for the state, an undertaking which was eventually to transform philanthropic child-saving into public child welfare. This was the birth of the idea that all children were the special concern of the state. The role of the state in child education expanded simultaneously.

It should be noted, however, that care for orphans is not a strictly modern phenomenon. As early as the third century, the Roman emperor established a series of institutions for children who lacked adult protectors (Richette, 1969). Society, in fact, has expressed a concern for homeless, orphaned children since antiquity.

In the 1890s, orphanages or "orphan asylums" were very popular; most of the children confined there were not orphans, in actuality, but children with one working parent who could not provide the care needed (Smith, 1995). Since before the 1920s, impoverished children started work by age twelve or fourteen, few teens resided in the institutions. Alternatives to orphanages were proposed by progressives. Adoption, foster care, and in the United States, "widow's pensions" as aid to single mothers was then informally called, helped improve the lives of children. The most dramatic alternative to institutionalization was the "orphan train" on which some 200,000 children from Eastern cities were transported for adoption and farm labor to the rural West. This practice ended in 1930. The goal was to get as many immigrant children away from the crime-ridden cities and, reportedly, from Catholicism as possible as prejudice against Catholics was strong at this time. Protestants feared Catholics both because of their rising political solidarity and their religious beliefs and practices.

In the summer of 1995, the Glenbow Museum in Calgary, Alberta, provided a culturally sensitive exhibit, "Youth in Western Canada." Child visitors were greeted with the question, "How would you feel if you were taken from your family and sent far away?" On the wall were disturbing images from history: Japanese-Canadian children being herded away from their parents who were to be shipped to internment centers during World War II; infants and children of a militant group of Doukhobors (a religious sect who fled Russia and moved to British Columbia) who in 1953 while their parents were engaged in rebellion, were made wards of the government and kept in orphanages; and the systematic removal of aboriginal children who were forced into boarding schools far away from the native community so that they would be acculturated into Canadian society. This last policy was longstanding and affected more than one generation.

In pre-modern Africa, as in other parts of the world, there was no administrative system to organize childcare nor was there any need to do so. By virtue of the extended nature of the family system, adoption has not been necessary. Relatives have taken responsibility for children in need. The much-quoted African saying and subject of first lady Hillary Rodham Clinton's (1996) best-selling book, "It takes a village to bring up a child," comes to mind. Urbanization, as an outgrowth of market economy, however, has weakened the traditional forms of mutual aid (Kadushin and Martin, 1988). The gap between present-day needs and institutional forms to meet those needs is great.

How about child welfare developments in the early twentieth century for African Americans? Neglect or imprisonment of black children by public officials was commonplace. Meanwhile, mutual aid activities on the part of African American churches and voluntary associations were directed toward troubled children. Peebles-Wilkins (1995) chronicles the nature of these early social welfare developments, highlighting the work of Janie Porter Barrett who in 1915 founded and directed the Virginia Industrial School for Colored Girls. Barrett's background was as fascinating as her work. Reared in Athens, Georgia, as a family member in the home where her mother was employed as a maid, Barrett was given a refined education including teacher's training in Virginia. As the head of the Virginia Federation of Colored Women's Clubs, Barrett was instrumental in raising money for an industrial school for "wayward colored girls" to keep them out of jail. When she read of an eight-year-old sentenced to six months in jail, Barrett began fund-raising in earnest, then appealed to the judge against "making a baby like this serve a sentence." Against the traditions of her day, Barrett managed to organize an integrated board of directors to ensure the success of the school. The Virginia Industrial School became a model school that other states tried to emulate.

In the United States, due to the economic circumstances of poor families, child labor emerged as a primary social problem (Karger and Stoesz, 1990). The absence of public relief compelled children to work full shifts in coal mines and textile mills. Child labor was finally prohibited over the protests of capitalists. The greatest boost to child welfare in general was Aid to Dependent Children, a preventive measure enacted under the auspices of the Social Security Act. Significantly, both family relief and child welfare services were to be administered by the states through public welfare departments.

France has been very child-oriented as far back as the 1800s when a slew of bills were enacted decreeing standards of protection, suitable housing, child labor, and education, etc. (Hegar, 1989). By the 1880s in Great Britain, similarly, the groundwork was laid for an expanded state role in child welfare. The work of family service units in Great Britain started during World War I when conscientious objectors cared for disorganized, bombed-out families in English cities. Today, staff live together in community houses to demonstrate how standards can be maintained even under conditions of poor housing. Additionally, they may help troubled families in their own houses (Kadushin and Martin, 1988). A universally-operated program is the public health nurse visitation (in the United Kingdom and Ireland) to the homes of all new mothers to provide instruction in childcare. Many European countries also have such preventive programs.

Even more significant for children's welfare is the European tradition of providing automatic family allowances to all families with children. Canada had across-the-board family allowances until recently when the government instituted a means-tested alternative. Generous childcare provisions help compensate Canadian families for day care arrangements. Maternity leave benefits allow mothers and sometimes fathers to take up to a year off from work to stay home with an infant. Japan's Child Welfare Law was passed after the war in 1949. Expenditures in the area of child welfare and education are high. The Children's Allowance Law provides allowances for parents. Japan has an extensive network of child guidance centers with shelter facilities for children who have run away or whose families have abandoned them.

Today, in most countries, the trend toward reduced funding for social services has serious implications for child welfare. The parallel trends toward international free trade agreements and the reduction of labor, likewise, have serious ramifications for the well-being of a nation's children. A related issue, directly and indirectly related to economic factors (as well as to cultural tradition), is children's rights.

CHILDREN'S LEGAL RIGHTS

In an extraordinary gathering in September, 1990, more than seventy heads of state came together for the largest global summit meeting in history and pledged their commitment to the protection of the children of the world. The United Nations Convention on the Rights of the Child (*New York Times,* 1990: 1A) states in its introduction:

> Each day, countless children around the world are exposed to dangers that hamper their growth and development. They suffer immensely as casualties of war and violence; as victims of racial discrimination, apartheid, aggression, foreign occupation and annexation; as refugees and displaced children, forced to abandon their homes and their roots; as disabled; or as victims of neglect, cruelty and exploitation.

> Each day, millions of children suffer from the scourges of poverty and economic crisis—from hunger and homelessnes, from epidemics and illiteracy, from degradation of the environment. They suffer from the grave effects of the problems of external indebtedness and also from the lack of sustained and sustainable growth in many developing countries, particularly the least developed ones.

> Each day, forty thousand children die from malnutrition and disease, including acquired immunodeficiency syndrome (AIDS), from the lack of

clean water and inadequate sanitation and from the effects of the drug problem.

These are challenges that we, as political leaders, must meet.

The Opportunity

Together, our nations have the means and the knowledge to protect the lives and to diminish enormously the suffering of children, to promote the full development of their human potential and to make them aware of their needs, rights and opportunities. The Convention of the Rights of the Child provides a new opportunity to make respect for children's rights and welfare truly universal.

Leaving no stone unturned, the convention, and this is its triumph, is all-encompassing. Its clauses provide uncompromising protection not only in the usual areas—health, education, and nutrition—but also in the less tangible areas of economic and sexual exploitation, torture and war, and homelessness. Stephen Lewis (1994) of the United Nations Children's Fund (UNICEF) expresses his excitement over the significance of this document, now signed by 177 nations. What does the convention do? The convention, writes Lewis, provides a standard or a benchmark against which the behavior of nations can be measured. Even though there is no international court enforcing the clauses, there is the judgment of the world community, and today, this is powerful. Because of this document, continues Lewis (1994: 37), governments are rewriting their laws and policies of enforcement:

> *Look at Vietnam:* it's reforming its juvenile justice system because of the Convention. Look at Barbados: it passed legislation prohibiting the execution of minors because of the Convention. . . . Look at Bangladesh: it made schooling compulsory for girls, in part because of the Convention.

Norway has also made some changes since the convention. In Norway, the welfare of children has been a primary concern for some time. Symbolically, the national independence day celebration is a parade not of the military but of all the children in Norway who march in national dress with their teachers. Yet the tradition of the child welfare boards was so ingrained that children in trouble and others were removed from home with very little fanfare (van Wormer,

1993). In fact, by international standards children's rights and those of their parents were clearly violated. Today, however, to meet the standards of the U.N. Convention, a new legalistic board has been instituted. Attorneys play a key role in the proceedings to ensure that children are represented.

In Sweden a new office with a toll-free help line was set up by the Children's Ombudsman. In response to the U.N. Convention, Swedish children have been offered an official channel to voice their needs (Sloane, 1995). The office has a full-time staff of twelve which deals with issues including abuse, teenage motherhood, and refugees about to be departed to unsafe countries. Only a handful of countries—Norway, New Zealand, Costa Rica, and Iceland—have children's ombudsmen.

In the United States, although the convention has been signed by President Clinton it has not yet been ratified by the U.S. Senate. Endorsement of this document is problematic in that the United States is in violation of the convention's principle forbidding the use of the death penalty for crimes committed by persons under the age of eighteen. This nation also falls short of meeting the treaty's requirements to provide "within its means" an adequate standard of living and health for children. For poor and minority children, the level of health care is abysmally low. Whether or not the laws will be changed to bring this country up to the international standards of social welfare remains to be seen.

The convention's requirement that children in child custody hearings be accorded their legal rights and that in decisions "the best interest of the child" becomes primary, has not been heeded in recent American court decisions favoring the biological parents over adoptive parents in contested cases. The conservative "family values" focus is, in part, a throwback to the earlier "children as property" conceptualization (see Mason, 1994). Child advocacy groups deplore the apparent "biological bias" of court decisions. In a major setback to children's rights advocates, the U.S. Supreme Court in 1989 ruled that the state could not be held liable for the return of a four-year-old boy to an abusive home situation (Jost, 1993). The boy suffered permanent brain injuries in the beating that resulted from this placement. Following this precedent, the 1993 custody battle over Baby Jessica and the 1995 Baby Richard case both involved riveting transitions of children from adoptive to biological homes. Because the public reaction to these cases was overwhelming, many states including Iowa and Illinois have rewritten their laws to prevent such tragedies in the future.

Writing in the *Encyclopedia of Social Work*, Wineman (1995: 474) questions to what extent child protection laws are honored in practice:

Yet it is children who, without access to the courts, may be legally beaten by a parent short of medically significant physical harm, when similar spousal maltreatment would constitute a criminal assault. It is children who, in twenty-four states, can be assaulted by a teacher, having been denied by the Supreme Court the protection accorded a convicted felon in prison.

The Convention on the Rights of the Child may have, as Lewis claims, transformed the struggle around human rights of children. Nevertheless, under the effects of overpopulation, war, and famine, there is no indication that the world's children are better off today than formerly. The stories, as Lewis (1994: 37) observes, "pour forth an avalanche of horror." For example:

> From Bosnia, young girls raped, raped again, mutilated, murdered. From Angola, Cambodia, Afghanistan, Mozambique, children literally torn to shreds by landmines or, at best, dismembered, consigned to live entire lives as amputees. . . . From Thailand, young girls, very young girls, girls who are still pre-pubescent, stolen from their Myanmar (Burma) villages to be locked in brothels, servicing ten, fifteen, twenty, thirty male sexual predators every twenty-four hours. From Somalia, Sudan, Rwanda, child refugees on the run. . . .

For such children it is not their legal rights or even quality of life, but their right to life itself that is at stake. Now we come to a closer look at children experiencing this sort of risk.

CHILDREN AT RISK

From the global perspective, children at risk must hope for survival. They are at level one of Maslow's hierarchy of needs (1954) — meeting basic physiological needs such as nutrition, clothing, health, and housing. The meeting of such needs is clearly delineated in the United Nations Convention on the Rights of the Child as a right, not a privilege (United Nations, 1989). Parents are considered the primary providers with the state assuring the provision of material assistance and support as necessary. In many parts of the world, especially in Asia and sub-Sahara Africa, a high proportion of children suffer from chronic and brutal deprivation. Infant mortality rates are high, prenatal and natal care

are inadequate, malnutrition is rampant, and preventable illnesses take an enormous toll. High child death rates and low levels of education for women mean that the demand for family planning remains low (UNICEF, 1994b). Three areas of special concern that put children at risk are poverty, poor health, and war.

Poverty

In total, about 220 million Africans—about half of the population south of the Sahara—now live in absolute poverty, unable to meet their most basic needs. The percentage of children who are malnourished has risen to 25 percent in the last decade. According to *The State of the World's Children* (UNICEF, 1995), a vast proportion of Africa's resources and external aid has been diverted to military purposes. At the same time, the continent of Africa has been devastated by debt and annual repayments that are enormously draining on the meager resources. Rural poverty in many parts of Africa has been a cause of much of the current strife. A record number of war-related deaths, fanned by a heavy flow of weapons from industrialized nations, has left millions of orphans to die from starvation and preventable illnesses. In the words of the former Secretary General of the United Nations, Jarvier Perez de Cuellar (1990):

> Poverty, I repeat, is the main enemy of children. Hunger, disease, illiteracy, despair—these constitute the enemy's fearful train. There is no way in which issues relating to children can be segregated from the issues of the overall social and economic environment.

Environmental deterioration is both a cause and an effect of dire poverty; it is exacerbated by war and closely related to overpopulation. Fortunately, fertility rates have been falling rapidly in most regions of the world since 1970. At the same time, however, international support for family planning services appears to be on the decline. When births are spaced, the child survival rate goes up; and as more children survive, there is more demand by women for family planning (UNICEF, 1994b).

Although the level of suffering and hardship does not come close to that of the poorest nations, poverty among American children is high relative to that of children in other industrialized countries. In the United States, in fact, child poverty has hit a thirty-year high. Over one in five of all U.S. children lives in poverty compared to the all-time low point of 14 percent in 1969. Approximately half of African American children and over 40 percent of Hispanic children are below the poverty level. In Canada, West Germany, Norway, Switzerland, and the United Kingdom, the child poverty rate is 37 to 70 percent lower than in the United States (Plotnick, 1989). Australia's rate is higher than Europe's but still half that of the United States (UNICEF, 1994). Compared to these other nations, the United States has a substantially higher rate of children in single-parent families. However, New Zealand and the United Kingdom seem to be doing their best to catch up. What really makes the United States unique, however, is the incredibly high rate of early teenage pregnancy. In 1990 there were 1,000 pregnancies for teens under age fifteen, and 95.9 per 1,000 among girls ages fifteen to nineteen. These rates are the highest ratio in the industrialized world.

In the United States, even under progressive regimes, policies to ameliorate the impact of harsh economic and social realities have not been forthcoming. In a political climate where the current political impetus is upon behavior control and eliminating dependency programs, policies directed toward eliminating poverty for children have fallen out of favor (Keefe and McCullagh, 1995). As welfare programs benefiting poor families and providing a safety net for children have been cut back, families with children have come to comprise 31 percent of the homeless, up from 21 percent in the early 1980s. In inner-city areas, child immunization rates have fallen drastically, and infant mortality is on a par with that of much poorer nations.

To counteract the vicissitudes of the economy, Jones (1995) recommends that a child benefit be paid to all families with children. Often known as a family allowance, this is an effective way of providing a minimum income guarantee to ensure a provision of the basic necessities without reducing the work incentive. A family allowance constitutes a compact between the federal government and its citizens so that all children will be afforded an opportunity to prosper regardless of the contingencies of birth (Keefe and McCullagh, 1995). Most industrialized nations provide such support.

For every year that fifteen million U.S. children remain poor, they are robbed of health, education, and dreams — and the nation loses thirty-six billion dollars in worker productivity, according to a study released by the Children's Defense Fund (summarized by Edmonds, 1994). Child poverty, according to the report, decreases babies' chances of being born healthy, increases the prevalence of children's health problems, slows educational development, strains families increasing odds of abuse and neglect, and increases adolescents' risk of pregnancy, delinquency, and crime. Therefore, reducing child poverty would be tremendously cost effective in reducing the waste of government resources. A national program of a direct cash transfer to low-income families similar to the programs of other industrial countries or an income tax credit or refundable children's credit — all such arrangements are viable as military expenditures are reduced (Keefe and McCullagh, 1995).

As the president of the Children's Defense Fund, Marian Wright Edelman (1994: 41) comments:

> Many millions of our young people feel they have no economic and social place in our society, that they have little to respect in themselves or to be respected for by others. And from this point of alienation and frustration, the path to drugs, alcohol abuse, crime, violence, and prison is ever open. . . . We need to acknowledge that what we are now seeing is the result of years of neglect and lack of investment in our children. . . . To reverse the decline, we must first of all create jobs.

In Canada, similarly, there has been a call by child advocates to end child poverty and build for the future. The activities and contributions of Campaign 2000, a pan-Canadian movement intended to secure full implementation of the 1989 Canadian House of Commons resolution to eliminate child poverty, have been impressive (Hughes, 1995). Although public opinion polls indicate overwhelming public approval to end child poverty, the recent replacement of the family allowance as universal program with a child benefit scheme, has put the fate of poor children on the line. The Canadian record may be far superior to that of the United States, yet as Wharf (1995) observes, subsidy programs to meet the needs of low-income families are entirely inadequate to alleviate poverty.

Health

Viewed globally, malnutrition and illness are inextricably linked. All illnesses are a threat to physical development as they depress the appetite and drain nutrients from the body (Jonsson, 1994). Nutrition is not, as Jonsson emphasizes, a simple matter of providing food. It is a matter of using knowledge to prevent nutritional deficiencies, such as of vitamin A, protein, and iodine. Through government educational programs—encouraging breast feeding, for instance—several nations have reduced malnutrition even in the midst of poverty. Tanzania and Zimbabwe are among the success stories. Large scale preventive action is underway in seventeen nations, mostly in Central America and Asia, to ensure that all children have adequate vitamin A (UNICEF, 1994a). In some countries, such as India, Bangladesh, and the Philippines, the levels of child nutrition are far above what they would be expected to be based on gross national product levels alone. Bangladesh, for instance, is making considerable progress through massive government efforts directed at immunization and water sanitation. With government health services reaching into almost every village, the total birth rate has fallen drastically.

Every year, two million children die from vaccine-preventable disease and another three million die from diarrhea (Rohde, 1994). Deaths from pneumonia take an equally high toll. Yet low-cost methods of preventing such diseases have been long available. There is some cause for optimism in that immunization rates in the disease-ridden parts of the world have gone from 15 percent of the population to almost 80 percent immunized. The reduction in polio rates is particularly striking.

In several countries, however, AIDS is overtaking measles and malaria as a leading killer of children, and hard-won gains in reducing child mortality are being reversed (UNICEF, 1995). In sub-Saharan Africa about one adult in forty is infected with HIV, in some cities the rate is one in three, and in Thailand the rate is one in fifty. The AIDS epidemic is hitting women and children the hardest. In the southern regions of the world, teenage girls are twice as likely to develop AIDS as teenage boys due to their earlier sexual contact. There is some hope, however, as programs for AIDS prevention are increasingly widespread. In Thailand, the use of condoms has risen wherever the public has been informed. Everywhere sex educational mass media and school programs are being introduced. Before significant progress can occur, according to the Children Fund's annual report (UNICEF, 1994a: 20), nations must educate their girls, "In the long term, almost every other aspect of progress, from nutrition to family planning, from child health to women's rights, is profoundly affected by whether or not a nation educates its girls." Unfortunately, far more boys are educated than girls, and therefore many girls are illiterate.

In the United States, similarly, women are especially vulnerable to infection, either through sexual contact or through personal injecting of needles. In some cases these women pass the virus on to their unborn children. Ninety-four percent of HIV-infected children are Latino or African American (Taylor-Brown and Garcia, 1995). Many of these children and others are made orphans as their parents die of this disease.

In this country, an estimated eight million children are without health care. Paralleling the rise in the number of families in poverty, child immunization rates have fallen to as low as 10 percent in certain inner-city areas. In the Western Hemisphere, only Bolivia and Haiti had lower overall rates (UNICEF, 1994b). The rate of preventable disease has begun to rise as a result.

The immunization rate in Russia, similarly, has fallen drastically. In fact, a serious deterioration in the quality of health care there and in countries of the former eastern bloc has resulted from the economic changes in the region. Average life expectancy has declined somewhat in all these countries and most significantly in Russia. Mysterious birth defects are cropping up all over Russia, a result of heavy industrial pollution. About 10 percent of all Russian children are born with serious deformities or other birth defects, according to a recent report (York, 1995). The overall infant mortality rate in Russia is twice as high as in North America. More than half of pregnant women are suffering from some kind of disease and many die in childbirth. The growing level of poverty in the newly capitalist country is associated with a shortage of the basic necessities of food and medical care. About half the Russian children are lacking these essentials.

Widely circulated press accounts reveal that hundreds of thousands of unwanted children in China—females or handicapped children—are kept in grisly orphanages (Schmetzer, 1995). Toddlers are leashed to nursery stools equipped with chamber pots, and babies sleep in crowded conditions, often on bare floors. Secret documentary footage shot by a British Broadcasting Company (BBC) film crew exposed orphans allegedly dying of starvation and neglect, awash in their own urine.

Juvenile violence including the act of suicide puts many children, especially children of color, in the United States and Canada at risk. The terrors of growing up in the Chicago housing projects are captured in graphic detail by Kotlowitz (1991) in the book, *There Are No Children Here*. This text follows the lives of two brothers and their family in a Chicago housing project. While other children wonder what they will do when they grow up, these boys wonder if they'll grow up. Children in the inner city must often huddle up against the walls of their apartment as gangs exchange gunfire outside. Violence and death are all around them. Juvenile violence is a major concern in the United States with homicide ranking as the second highest cause of death among those fifteen to twenty-five years old and with deaths from gun wounds as the leading killer of teenage males (Hopps and Collins, 1995).

The number of suicides among youths has risen steadily. Canada's rate of teen suicide is the third highest among major countries, just below that of New Zealand and Finland (Nemeth, 1994). Canadian Indian youths have a suicide rate five or six times that of other Canadian youths. Some of the factors involved are the high numbers of divorced parents, increased competition for available jobs, and the impact of street drugs. In the United States, the accessibility to guns increases the rate of impulsive suicides during a personal crisis.

Suicide prevention workers in Calgary, Alberta, are working within the school system with high-risk young people (Mitchell, 1995). The gay factor in suicide attempts is being openly addressed in light of recent findings that gay and lesbian youth are more at risk of suicide than others. Extreme peer harassment, lack of respected role models, and family and church condemnation, are all factors in causing a young gay or lesbian person to become completely overwhelmed. There is a great deal that schools can do, however, to provide much needed counseling and educational programs for those for whom sexual orientation is a concern. For all students, work in the cognitive area—learning stress management techniques, positive self talk, and seeing things in perspective—can be helpful in times of crisis.

Children in War

Inner-city children terrified of getting shot is the small scale version of children caught in the cross fire of war. In Shakespeare's *Julius Caesar*, Mark Antony refers to the horrors of war which become so dreadful "that mothers shall but smile when they behold their infants quartered. . . . All pity chok'd with custom of fell deeds." From the battlefields of Bosnia to the killing fields of Cambodia and Rwanda, more than 1.5 million children have been killed by wars over the past decade (Associated Press, 1994). Millions more around the globe are homeless, orphaned, or maimed. For those children who survive, war traumas significantly damage their psychosocial development. Some children, as we will see later, become instruments of war themselves as they are recruited as militia fighters and deliberately brutalized. The rape of girls has been used as a systematic weapon of war in former Yugoslavia and Rwanda. Hundreds of thousands of children have been crippled by land mines (UNICEF, 1994b). Others become extremely passive, insecure, and adopt a catastrophic view of the future (Macksoud, 1994).

In all of these situations of threatened survival—threats from dire poverty, disabling illness, and the scourge of war—the future of the world's children has been placed at risk of perpetuating the cycle of suffering, hating, and killing. A new framework has emerged specifically directed toward the protection of children in armed conflicts through the provisions of the Convention on the Rights of the Child. Thanks to the convention, the notion of "days of tranquility" has been gaining ground. During El Salvador's civil war, for instance, all parties agreed to a time out on several days each year for children to be immunized. Similar events took place in Lebanon and the Sudan (UNICEF, 1994b).

Child Labor

Impoverished children find many creative and desperate ways to survive. Viewed outside the context of despair and misery, the survival strategies make little or no sense. The exploitation of children, likewise, takes shape within the context of human misery, and against a background of what Erik Erikson (1963: 422) calls the "prolonged inequality of child and adult, as one of the facts of existence which makes for exploitability." This section will first examine child labor and the way in which children are sometimes used to perform the dirty work of society despite the injuries inflicted upon them in the process. Writing in the *Encyclopedia of Social Work,* Otis (1995) has written the definitive work on the subject. In fact, as Otis indicates, the profession of social work through its child welfare specialty has been remarkably inattentive to the abuse and neglect inherent in the practice of child labor. Child welfare practice in the United States today is concerned with neglect and abuse in the home, but not with neglect and abuse at the macro level. Historically, however, our social work foremothers advocated for children in regard to housing, sanitation, and more specifically, child labor laws. Due to well-organized opposition, however, child labor standards were not established until 1938 in the Fair Labor Standards Act (Barker, 1995).

Before discussing the matter further, it is important to distinguish between *child work* and *child labor.* Child work, as defined by the International Labor Organization (ILO), refers to adult-guided activities whose focus is the child's learning of vocational or cultural skills. Child labor, in contrast, as it is used here, does not refer to after-school work such as at a car wash, but rather to "paid or forced employment of children who are younger than a legally defined age" (Barker, 1995: 55). A pejorative term, *child labor,* includes activities that are potentially hazardous, interfere with education, and represent clear exploitation of the child. As a truly comprehensive document, the Convention on the Rights of the Child recognizes the right of the child to be protected from economic exploitation and from performing work harmful to his or her health.

Otis cites a number of sources to indicate that child labor, such as the labor of migrant children in the United States, and of factory workers in India, is perhaps the single most common form of child abuse and neglect in much of the world today. Consider the following examples assembled by Otis from various news sources:

- In Bangladesh, children as young as seven work long hours in the booming export garment industry.
- The discovery in the gold-mining region of Peru of over seventy common graves of child laborers.
- In the Philippines, children work 90 to 110 hours a week in tiny factories.
- In Brazil, many of seven million abandoned children survive through street crime.
- Children throughout southeast Asia pressed into prostitution in light of their apparent AIDS-free status.

Why would parents allow their children to be victimized as child-slaves? Why would the state turn the other way? The answer on both accounts is money. Families living in extreme poverty may feel compelled to exploit their children's labor for the family's survival. Many other parents who hardly can feed themselves find it nearly impossible to refuse a man's cash payment in exchange for sexual acts with one of their daughters (Sachs, 1994). As environmental stress associated with global trade pushes rural families toward ruination, children become economic liabilities. In desperation, such children may be sold to a sweatshop or brothel. The recent boom in these forms of child labor is endemic in countries with a rapidly widening gap between rich and poor and an export-oriented economy. Children are in demand as sex objects—both boys and girls—and also as factory workers where their nimble fingers, docility, and inexpensive upkeep make them valuable commodities.

Resistance to such activities is curbed, often with the cooperation of authorities. According to a recent report in *Maclean's* (1995), India's chief opponent of child labor, Kailash Satyarthi, has been subjected to extensive police harassment, including his arrest for "defrauding" a New Delhi carpet manufacturer. Satyarthi's "crime" was to appear in a German TV documentary depicting child slavery in India. In Pakistan, where poor families sell their children to factory owners because they need the money for food, child bondage is common. Activists in Pakistan, similarly, have been arrested for opposing child labor practices in that country. Iqbal Masih, a twelve-year-old child who actively spoke out against child labor and became an international sensation, was mysteriously shot and killed. His murder has brought a worldwide outcry and more demands for tougher action against child bondage (Bokhari, 1995). The Pakistani government has condemned this killing and plans are now underway to make primary education compulsory for children. In fact, strict enforcement of universal compulsory education is a major remedy against child labor, as Otis (1995) effectively illustrates in his review of the history of child labor in the United States. Successful campaigns have been launched in Japan, North and South Korea, and China, as well as in the United States.

To protect children from such vile forms of exploitation, Otis recommends the following: the conducting of public information campaigns into working conditions; the establishment of intragovernment agencies to expose conditions and coordinate activities to rectify them; that a more active and less equivocal role be played by the U.N. Children's Fund (UNICEF) and the World Health Organization—organizations sometimes inhibited by sensitivities of the United Nations member states; and, finally, international boycotts of products produced by child labor.

Child Prostitution

Sex has become a multibillion dollar industry, and today children are being bought, sold, and traded like any other mass-produced good (Sachs, 1994). In places as geographically diverse as Brazil, Columbia, and Russia, the trade in children's bodies is booming. But the center of the child sex industry is in Asia.

According to a report from the World Watch Institute (Sachs, 1994), international tour agencies, affluent travelers, and even governments turn a blind eye. An article in *The Humanist* (Leuchtag, 1995) entitled "Merchants of Flesh: International Prostitution and the War on Women's Rights" describes the horror facing girls in Brazil, some as young as nine years of age, forced into prostitution in remote Amazon gold-mining regions. As many as twenty-five thousand girls are "recruited" with the promise of well-paying jobs, then delivered in airplanes to brothels. Those caught trying to escape are tortured and killed.

In India, because of their low worth, more girls than boys are forced into child labor. Sometimes tied to looms, girls weave up to fourteen hours a day to "earn" their dowries. With the help of new technologies to determine the sex of unborn children, girls can now be gotten rid of before they are born. Accordingly, one state in India now has a ratio of 874 women per 1,000 men (*The Economist*, 1995). As an experiment to combat sex bias, the Indian government is setting up a savings scheme that will give money to girls from poor families at age eighteen if they are still unmarried. To what extent this scheme will improve life for girls remains to be seen.

Increasingly, the plight of child prostitutes is gaining international attention. Following a successful conference in Bangkok on the urgent situation for both girls and boys who are being sexually exploited in Thailand, the Swedish government sponsored a "First World Congress on the Commercial Sexual Exploitation of Children" in 1996. Meanwhile more and more women in all parts of the world are discussing the global politics of prostitution: the links between policies pushed by the World Bank and the International Monetary Fund to boost the tourist industry and the bitter sexual exploitation of fourteen and fifteen-year-old village girls in such countries as Kenya, India, Nepal, the Philippines, Brazil, and Honduras (Leuchtag, 1995). In some places, activists are organizing to demand an end to policies and practices conducive to the promotion of prostitution.

Boy Soldiers

Throughout the world and against international law, children are being turned into willing, ruthless warriors. The front ranks, hospital beds, and battlefield graves of the armies of poor nations around the world are increasingly filled with mere kids—boys well below age fifteen, the minimum age established for combat by international conventions (Frankel, 1995).

The recruitment of children for war has some key advantages. Boys will do things like torturing whole families and burning houses that men would shy away from, and the children's belief in magic renders them remarkably fearless. The kind of sadistic brutality immortalized in the novel, *Lord of the Flies* (Golding, 1954) which tells of the antics of schoolboys marooned on a remote island, is practiced every day on the modern battlefield. The violence done to small boy recruits defies description; this abuse helps train them for savagery. In Mozambique, children have been terrorized by being hanged upside down. Many have been forced to kill their parents (Frankel, 1995). Later these boys will willingly terrorize others. Tens of thousands of children are brandishing arms in places such as Sudan, Somalia, Liberia, and Thailand, frequently terrorizing adults by rape and death. Liberia's civil war has taken the concept of child soldiering to alarming new proportions (Sly, 1995). In many places, boys are pressed into service, but in Liberia, the existence of small boy units in itself encourages other children to join up. War orphans in Rwanda, similarly, find "family" in the army; they want to fight in order to avenge the death of their families.

A sad fact in the brutalization of children is that the brutalized learn to enjoy the killing. Belief in magic and use of drugs seem to subdue fears or inhibitions. Children brag about raping and killing members of whole families and about the sense of exhilaration they felt as they looted their things (Sly, 1995). Except for Palestinian youth growing up under occupation, political ideology usually does not enter the picture. In many places, according to a story in *Newsweek* (Frankel, 1995), picking up a gun is simply the best survival option available. A child soldier gets a bright-colored uniform, shoes, and a weapon — symbols of power and status. In addition, the children get three meals a day and medical care.

Limited programs, under the auspices of the U.N. Children's Fund, prepare the ex-soldiers to resume school and ordinary life. When the children arrived in these programs' camps, according to reports, they were aggressive, refused to listen to adults, and tried to rape female staff members. The children blamed their nightmares on the staff for "taking away their powers."

Street Children

Street children are victims and victimizers both; they are pushed out of their homes by family poverty and neglect, while pulled into a life on the streets by the availability of work and income. At once attracted and repelled by their lifestyle, these children tend to be boys, and their numbers are increasing dramatically worldwide. Known in the United States as runaways or homeless children, as *street sparrow* in Zaire, *pelone* in Mexico, *gamine* in Columbia, such children are identified by the United Nations as street children. *Street children* are defined as minors who earn their living by working on the streets or as children who reside on the streets full-time (Peralta, 1995). It is estimated that over forty million children live on the streets worldwide; twenty-five million of them are in Latin America. Street children are differentiated from abandoned or runaway children by the permanency of their condition and their exploitation in connection with illegal activities.

In a comparative study of children who inhabit the streets in the United States, India, and Columbia, Viswanathar and Arje (1995) perceive the economic conditions as paramount: The plight of the street children, according to these authors, is shaped by poverty, gender, and child labor conditions. In the United States, children of all social classes gravitate to the streets often to escape situations of abuse and neglect in their homes, and are drawn into deviant subcultures. In Columbia, on the other hand, children are on the street more to ease family economic burdens where they are active participants in the underground economy, especially drug traffic. The large majority of street children in Columbia and in other parts of Latin America maintain some continuing relationship with their families. In India, on the other hand, girls whose parents could not afford to keep them are often entrapped in brothels and prostitution as a way of life.

In a 1995 study conducted in Mexico City, Peralta found that of the 195 street children interviewed, 66 percent were male, and the majority were on the streets for economic reasons. Compared to his previous study, however, 14 percent (compared to the 5 percent in 1989) lived on the streets on a full-time basis and had severed contact with their families. This supports the theory, as Peralta concludes, that the recent financial crisis has contributed to the numbers of throwaway children in Mexico.

Except at the macro level, remedies for children living on the streets are few and far between. Peralta suggests the establishment of multi-service centers for high-risk youth. In a realistic essay in *Social Work Today* describing a professional team operation with the street children of Mexico City, Webb (1992) reaches a similar conclusion. Although the goal of their practice is prevention, the usual procedure is for social workers to get involved only after juveniles have been picked up by the police. Housed together in a "clearing house" center, some of the street children are returned to their families while others are sent to specialized institutions. In either case, many are destined to be caught up in the criminal justice system all their lives.

In Brazil, with over twenty-five million street children the situation is even more grave (de Oliveira, Baizerman, and Pellet, 1992). Heavy drug use at an early age is characteristic; child drug users live in the slums of Brazil and are frequent targets of violent police action. In Sao Paulo, Brazil, 80 percent of the prison population is comprised of former street children (Reynolds, 1992). International organizations such as UNICEF advocate for programs that see street children not as delinquents but as victims of societal underdevelopment and neglect.

Child labor, prostitution, boy soldiers, and street children are all examples of the abuse and neglect of children on a mass scale, often committed by the social system itself. Now, abuse and neglect at the familial level and the role of social service agencies in protecting children will be discussed.

FAMILIAL LEVEL OFFENSES AGAINST CHILDREN

Child Abuse

As stated in the United Nations Convention on the Rights of the Child (1989):

> Children have a right to protection from all forms of physical or mental violence, injury or abuse, negligent treatment, maltreatment, or exploitation, including sexual abuse, while in the care of parents, legal guardians, or any other person who has the care of the child.

The hitting of children by parents (euphemistically called spanking) is clearly contrary to this declaration, as the U.N. Committee on the Rights of the Child has indicated (UNICEF, 1994a). Austria, Denmark, Finland, Norway, and Sweden have already passed laws forbidding all forms of physical punishment of children — in the home, at school, or in juvenile facilities.

Physical punishment of children is an appropriate place to begin a discussion of child abuse because as research generally shows, child abuse often stems from harsh disciplinary practices over which the parent loses control (Brissett-Chapman, 1995). Yet, as one of America's top researchers on family violence, Murray Straus (1994) argues that despite the evidence that corporal punishment of children increases the risk of abuse substantially, this fact is largely ignored in the literature. Moreover, while several organizations to combat child abuse have fought to end corporal punishment by teachers, they have failed to mention that parents should not hit children. Straus attributes these omissions to the fact that we live in a society where assault of a child is defined as discipline rather than assault and where 84 percent of the population believes that "a good hard spanking is sometimes necessary." (Similar approval rates are found in England and New Zealand). Over 90 percent of American parents acknowledge that they punish their toddlers physically. Yet a correlation between parents' use of corporal punishment and children's later rates of hitting others is a consistent finding in the research-on-aggression literature (see the summary in Kandel, 1991). Drawing on data from two National Violence Surveys, Straus shows the close association between corporal punishment in childhood and increased risk of juvenile delinquency, spouse abuse, and criminal behavior later in life.

Physical punishment of children, in fact, is practically universal; the only exception might be in some hunting and gathering societies where cooperation is stressed over obedience. The Scandinavian countries, similarly, are nonpunitive societies with a strong tradition of cooperation and sharing, facts reflected in their laws against striking children. The British, on the other hand, with a tradition stressing "getting children under control" have recently ruled through their government that parents have the right to permit caretakers to "smack" their children (Willow, 1995).

Physical abuse is defined as hitting a child to the point at which the child sustains some physical damage (Kadushin and Martin, 1988). In their textbook titled *Child Welfare Services*, Kadushin and Martin make a lame attempt to distinguish discipline as "legitimate violence" from abuse which is viewed as excessive. However, they acknowledge that there is a fine line between them. "Discipline is more clearly related to the child's behavior; it has a clearly corrective purpose," these writers (1988: 229) further contend. Interestingly, up until the late nineteenth century, the hitting of servants, apprentices, wives, prisoners, and soldiers was permitted for the same correctional purpose, and there were often legal limits to the degree of violence allowed. To the extent that the past can be our guide, we might concur with Wells (1995) who says that many practices and conditions currently tolerated will seem barbaric in another time and place and will undoubtedly be frowned on, as infanticide and wife beating are now frowned on.

Chase's (1975: 1) definition of child abuse as "the deliberate and willful injury of a child by a caretaker" is more inclusive but no less ambiguous than Kadushin and Martin's. For the purposes of this book, and since corporal punishment, although legal is in actuality merely a culturally acceptable form of child abuse, we will define *child abuse* as behavior that is so labeled by the authorities. Now we can look at the facts:

- Reported child abuse cases in the United States tripled during the 1980s; about three children die each day from maltreatment (UNICEF, 1994b).
- Out of a ranking of twenty-three industrialized countries on deaths of infants by presumed abuse, Czechoslovakia, the United States, and former Soviet Union had the highest rates; Spain, Italy, and Sweden, the lowest rates (UNICEF, 1994a).
- Economic stress due to poverty, unemployment, and related work concerns are factors behind the increase in child abuse reports in recent years. Substance abuse was another contributing factor (NASW News, 1994).
- Ninety-five percent of physical abuse cases do not involve severe injuries and are typically rooted in punishment rather than psychopathology (Straus, 1994).
- Physically abused children have high rates of violence and crime later in life (Widom, 1989).

The National Association of Social Workers has adopted a position statement opposing all forms of corporal punishment. In order to limit violence in the family, social workers are teaching parents nonviolent forms of child discipline. At women's shelters, similarly, counselors and childcare workers forbid violence and model acceptable parenting skills. Otherwise the cycle of violence will merely perpetuate itself, generation after generation.

A similar philosophy prevails among social workers in the United Kingdom. For the National Children's Bureau, there is a concept of "not for sale." Link (1993) describes this as referring to elements of the worker role that cannot be negotiated, including their commitment to nonviolent discipline and children's physical, sexual, and emotional well-being. The family centers which provide crises intervention counseling all over Britain teach parents what can be negotiated and what is "not for sale."

Childhood pain can become adult abuse of power. Sometimes, explains Bishop (1994), the victims themselves will abuse a less powerful person if their survival reaction has been triggered because they think their victim has power over them. For example, parents who abuse their children and men who abuse their partners are apt to see their actions as controlling a person who might hurt them otherwise. Abuse is sometimes deliberately used, as we have seen with the child soldiers, to help mold children into the norms of a tough social system. Schools for the British upper classes and military academies offer ritualized Spartan treatment for their students. This entails such elements as cold showers, hard beds, tasteless meals, early rising, and harsh discipline; hazing compounds the psychological pressure. "First you have to learn to take orders before you can learn to give orders" is the theme of this form of socialization. The novel *The Lords of Discipline* (Conroy, 1982), loosely based on practices at the Citadel, magnificently captures the rigors of military socialization.

Child Neglect

In the United States, reports of neglect far outnumber reports of physical abuse. As with abuse, there is little agreement on the definition of neglect. Unlike physical abuse which refers to the commission of acts of aggression against the child, neglect refers to acts of omission by caregivers that are potentially life threatening. Kadushin and Martin (1988) discuss various types of neglect, such as the deprivation of necessities, inadequate supervision, medical neglect, and failure to protect the child from injury. Neglect is usually characterized by the social worker descriptively, for example, "the child is found living in a house that is rat-infested and full of fleas; the child was dirty, her hair matted, and clothes reeking of urine." The ultimate form of neglect, as Kadushin and Martin point out, is child abandonment.

Although there seems to be a fairly clear cross-cultural agreement on the minimal level of care a parent should provide (Polansky et al., 1983), there is some controversy concerning where the responsibility for the child's care rests. Should it be with the family or society? The family itself, rather than external conditions such as poverty and lack of childcare, continues to be targeted for correction. Since more mothers than fathers are apt to take responsibility for their children, mothers are often the subject of formal complaints. In anticipation of future court action, child welfare workers in the United States and Canada gather evidence against mothers. When drugs are involved, the legal consequences may be severe.

Kasinsky (1994) sees major continuities between the state's reaction to pregnant mothers who use drugs and the Progressive Era's response to mothers accused of child neglect. Mothers have been disempowered by the state in both eras, argues Kasinsky. A major impetus for state intervention in the lives of the "underclass" today is the climate of opinion associated with the "war on drugs," which in turn, has created new responses to infants exposed to drugs. According to a carefully documented study in the *New England Journal of Medicine* (Chasnoff et al., 1990), African American pregnant drug users were ten times as likely as other users to be reported to state authorities. This racial discrepancy held in both public and private hospitals. The reporting of a positive drug test, in fact, has become a standard event in child neglect proceedings. The need for an alternative emphasis on good prenatal care and substance abuse treatment is self-evident. How much better to help produce a healthy mother and child than to remove a drug-affected child after birth! The earlier the help is provided, the more economical and effective it is in the long run. Schorr (1988) favors intensive junior high school programs to prevent unplanned teen pregnancy and adequate financial support for families so that their children's needs might be met.

The climate of child protection in the United States, Britain, and in Norway (after recent changes) is highly legalistic. In France, the continental system of justice prevails (Pitts, 1994). The judge and social worker work together to come up with a solution; the child is not an actor in court. Proceedings are inquisitional, not adversarial and focus on the suffering of the child, not the evidence. The child protection system in France, unlike elsewhere, attracts no media attention at all. Social workers there, according to Pitts, are accorded high status and are trusted by the people.

The fact that there is a close correlation between poverty and neglect is confirmed by numerous studies: according to a recent comprehensive review of the literature, many families that are involved with child protective service agencies are also recipients of AFDC (McDevitt et al., 1995). An important question to consider, however, is why so many poor mothers manage to provide adequate care for their children. Traditionally, this has been explained by psychological inadequacies in those mothers who do not provide physical care for their children (Polansky et al., 1974). Swift (1991), however, takes a more comprehensive approach to examine the interaction of a number of factors. Such high risk factors as poverty, single-parent status, heavy drinking or other drug use, multiple children, and social isolation are significant in combination with each other. For two parent households, wife abuse may be a key factor in preventing the mother from providing consistent quality care for her children. Poverty alone, however, may not cause neglect in the absence of other negative variables.

Child Sexual Abuse

A general definition of child sexual abuse is forced, tricked, or manipulated contact with a child by an older person (usually five or more years older) for the purpose of the sexual gratification of the older person (Conte, 1995). Child sexual abuse includes incest, sexual molestation, sexual assault, and exposing the child for purposes of pornography or prostitution. Although there has been concern with sexual abuse of children previously in history—in nineteenth century France and at the turn of the century when the French brought the issue out in the open—for the most part, there has been a conspiracy of silence concerning its very existence. For personal, societal, and political reasons, it has always been more expedient for society to deny this problem than to face it head on. This unhappy synergy is well-illustrated by Canadian journalist Judy Steed (1995), in her bone-chilling description of a system that shields the abusers while children are condemned to excruciating psychological pain by adults who cannot bring themselves to face the truth. In *Our Little Secret* Steed recounts in suspense-filled detail the crimes, the concealment, and the shock to the victims' families as the horrible truth gradually unfolds. For sixteen years, the choirmaster at the renowned St. George's Cathedral in Kingston, Ontario, had been sexually abusing many of his charges. Two of the boys had committed suicide. Although some children tried to tell adults, and one went to the police, no one listened. Only when thirteen former students came forward did the choirmaster plead guilty. Incredibly, the church leadership and many in the congregation still maintain their loyalty to the choirmaster. The story of the ultimate betrayal of children, first by the church's representative, then by the church itself, more than justify Steed's bold conclusion that we tend to let our children conceal their shame and suffer in silence while we adults indulge our ignorance and get on with our lives.

In 1969, in her memorable *I Know Why the Caged Bird Sings,* Maya Angelou broke through the wall of silence with her powerful autobiographical account of childhood violation (1969: 76):

Then there was the pain. A breaking and entering when even the senses are torn apart. The act of rape on an eight-year-old body is a matter of the needle giving because the camel can't. The child gives, because the body can, and the mind of the violator cannot.

I thought I had died—I woke up in a white-walled world, and it had to be heaven. But Mr. Freeman was there and he was washing me. His hands shook, but he held me upright in the tub and washed my legs. "I didn't mean to hurt you, Ritie. I didn't mean it. But don't you tell. . . . Remember, don't tell a soul."

Sexual child abuse was rediscovered in the late 1970s and early 1980s when a deluge of newspaper articles, books, and TV movies appeared in North America and western Europe. Historically, political progress in child welfare has been linked to the success of feminism, and the fact that women are disporportionately victims of sexual abuse has cemented the linkage in the modern period (Finkelhor, 1994). When feminists joined forces with child welfare professionals, who tend for the most part to be trained in social work, child protection advocacy got off the ground. Despite a formidable backlash in recent years, there is a public and professional awareness of the exploitation of children that did not exist in previous decades.

The percentage of women in the general population who report having been sexually abused as children varies according to the study conducted. Reports range from a low of 6 percent of all females to a high of 62 percent (Kadushin and Martin, 1988) and 3 to 31 percent of males (Conte, 1995). Since the overwhelming majority of cases are not known to authorities, and national crime statistics do not include crimes against children, the only measures available are small sample, retrospective surveys.

Comparative international research about sexual abuse is relatively hard to find. In all countries studied, however, the presence of widespread incest and child molestation has been confirmed. Everywhere when researchers have asked, a sizable percentage of the adult population acknowledges a history of sexual abuse (Finkelhor, 1994). The available data, mostly from industrialized nations, reveals sexual abuse histories in at least 7 percent of the females and 3 percent of the males, ranging up to 36 percent of women (Austria) and 29 percent of men (South Africa) according to Finkelhor's comprehensive review of the literature.

In both clinical and nonclinical American samples, perpetrators are predominantly male. In general population samples which reflect reality more accurately than do samples of persons in treatment, sexual abuse by parent figures constitutes 6 to 16 percent of the cases, abuse by other relatives constitutes 25 percent, abuse by strangers equals 5 to 15 percent, and the rest of the cases by acquaintances (Berliner, 1995). Boys unlike girls are more likely to be abused by nonfamily members. All types of sexual acts occur with attempted or completed intercourse reported in 20 to 40 percent of the cases.

A great deal of media attention in North America has been given to false reports. The fact that there have actually been innocent persons sentenced to prison based on flimsy evidence is undeniable. Some false reports have been inspired by parents in custody battles or visitation disputes; others have been promoted through suggestion by therapists who possibly had a fixed agenda. In carefully controlled laboratory experiments children have been shown to be highly suggestible and to actually "build memories" in response to repeated questions. Emotionally disturbed clients are also highly suggestible as they try to make sense of their psychological distress. The risk is that because some children were too readily believed in the past, too few will be believed in the future.

Myers (1994), a professor of law, attributes the backlash against reports of sexual abuse partly to society's tendency toward denial of sexual abuse and partly to the shortcomings of the child protection system itself—the overload of cases, the inadequate funding, the crises in foster care, and the absence of a focus on the needs of children. But a large part of the backlash Myers perceives as self-inflicted by the professionals themselves. For instance, the exaggerated cliché, "children never lie about sexual abuse" is without scientific proof. To say that fabrication of sexual abuse is uncommon would more accurately reflect reality. When professionals exceed the bounds of current knowledge, and when contradictory expert testimony is offered (much of it being oversimplistic and biased) the professional community can anticipate criticism and even ridicule.

Whatever the reasons, whether stemming from anger over believing reports that were later shown to be false, or from the right-wing rhetoric promoting family inviolability, the backlash is evident in extensive news reports of retracted allegations which were generated by overzealous therapists. The sense from the barrage of stories—many on TV news-magazine programs—is that many falsely accused people are going to prison. The numerous cases in which the system works efficiently to protect children from would-be predators are ignored.

In any case, two facts are clear: sexual abuse of children is relatively common, and such abuse is associated with a host of emotional, often long-term problems. In an extensive review of international studies that looked at long-term effects, Finkelhor (1994) found an association between early sexual abuse and adult mental health impairments. Symptoms of anxiety and fear that are consistent with posttraumatic stress disorder (PTSD) are found in approximately one-third to one-half of sexually abused children (Berliner, 1995). PTSD includes intrusive, unpleasant recollections of the event and avoidance and numbing symptoms. Guilt feelings and a generalized sense of feeling dirty and damaged are common. Long-term sexual dysfunction is a corollary of childhood abuse. Repressed memories may be associated with phobias of a disabling sort. In short, the destruction of childhoods and wreckage of adult lives, in the wake of child abuse, is monumental (Steed, 1995).

In chemical dependency treatment centers and eating disorders clinics, early childhood sexual abuse has emerged as an unresolved issue in up to 50 percent of the female clients and in a significant percentage of male clients (see Miller, Downs, and Testa, 1993; and van Wormer, 1995). Use of alcohol and other drugs is a common way of dealing with the pain of buried memories and damaged self-image. The risk of rape, sexual harassment, or battering is doubled for survivors of childhood sexual abuse (Herman, 1992). Some of the survivors driven by adult pain pursue a course in the helping professions to help alleviate the suffering of others. Although most victims do not become abusers, without early intervention a small but significant minority of abused children will grow up to repeat the cycle of sexual violation.

A growing body of research, including a recent study by the Alan Guttmacher Institute, indicates that childhood sexual abuse is a potent factor in teenage childbearing (reported in *NASW News*, 1995). Up to two-thirds of teen mothers say they had had sex forced on them earlier by older men; an earlier study of almost 200,000 births by teenage mothers revealed that 70 percent were fathered by adults. These findings put a different angle on the early teenage pregnancy phenomenon that is so persistent in the United States. The accumulating evidence reveals that young teen girls who get pregnant are often suffering from earlier trauma which has led to self destructive links with older men. Sometimes the pregnancy itself is the result of rape. In any case, the provision of psychological counseling would seem to be more effective in altering undesirable behavior patterns than cut backs in welfare benefits.

In her in-depth Canadian investigation into pedophilia, the sexual perversion in which children are the preferred sexual object, Steed was deeply disturbed by the forces stacked against child victims and by the depth of the pain experienced by the survivors, even many years following the abuse. Some of what she learned includes (214):

I had not understood that abusers often romance and seduce their victims before closing the trap. The adults can basically do anything they want to a child. That children hardly ever disclose right away, and when they do, non-offending adults usually instantly deny the allegations and align themselves with abusers. I had not understood that the sexual touching of a child by an adult is psychologically destructive because it's an invasion of personal boundaries that can lead to the obliteration of the child's ego, the erasure of identity, the end of autonomy.

Mental health professionals have important roles to play in child protection: in deciding treatment of both the survivors and the perpetrators, in preparing a child for court, and in working with a shocked and bereaved family.

Child Protective Services

The needs of children and youth have been a central concern to the social welfare systems in the United States and Canada since their very beginnings. Social work has been the most prominent profession in the development of child welfare services.

The social upheaval and family disruption resulting from large-scale immigration and rapid industrial and urban growth were especially hard on children (Trattner, 1994). As a result, a broad child welfare movement swept through America. The movement, according to Trattner, took many forms including the removal of dependent, neglected, and delinquent children from their families and the creation of juvenile courts and probation systems, the provision of mothers' or widows' pensions, and crusades against child labor. The "childsavers" were bent on safeguarding youths as the key to social control for future generations.

In 1874, the Society for the Prevention of Cruelty to Children was formed to protect children in the way animals (yes, protection of animals came first) had been protected from maltreatment. Many states at this time passed laws against endangerment of the health of a child and child cruelty. In 1893 Ontario, Canada, passed the Children's Protection Act which provided the administrative machinery to care for neglected children and for those found in bad company. Children could be removed from deficient homes.

CHAPTER 6: CHILD WELFARE

In the passage of Norwegian Child Welfare Act of 1896 various motives—some benevolent, some paternalistic or maternalistic—came together to allow for the removal of children from the harmful and criminal influence of the streets. A child welfare board of lay persons with education as the superior goal was set up to encourage, admonish, judge, and punish both parents and children who had been remiss in their parental duties (Dahl, 1985). In the United States and other countries in contrast, the usual procedure was to refer children to the courts.

The history of child welfare reform reveals the extent to which women were at the forefront in setting up today's institutions for child protection. See box 6.1 for the role of men and women in child welfare history.

The creation of the Children's Bureau in 1912 represented the U.S. federal government's first foray into the realm of child welfare. Emphasis was placed on the quality of care rather than poverty alone as a reason to separate children from their parents. A broad range of child welfare issues from health and child labor to delinquency and abandonment were among the concerns of the bureau (DiNitto, 1995). Under the Social Security Act, the bureau was directed to cooperate with the states to develop child welfare services. In 1962, with the identification of the "battered child syndrome," a medically defined condition that could be determined by the use of X-rays to reveal long bone fractures, the public's interest in child abuse was intensified. Services thereafter expanded rapidly. In 1974, Congress passed the Child Abuse Prevention and Treatment Act to ensure the effective coordination of policies and the development of model programs and services. But because federal policy had stressed placement of the child, usually in a foster home resulting in children being moved from home to home, the Adoption Assistance and Child Welfare Act of 1980 was passed and "permanency planning" became the buzzword of the decade. Funding now was to be provided for in-home services instead of for out-of-home placement. Adoption was to be encouraged if family reunification was not possible. This family preservation approach was strengthened further by the Omnibus Budget Reconciliation Act of 1993, an act directed toward offering sufficient services to keep families together.

In Canada, parallel developments have taken place, with Canadian law having incorporated the "least intrusive" principles of family preservation. Because of public wariness of the intrusiveness of past child welfare efforts, this law designed to strengthen the family has enjoyed wide support (Swift, 1995). Native Canadians, like their U.S. and Australian counterparts, have borne the

BOX 6.1

WOMEN'S WORK IN THE HISTORY OF CHILD WELFARE AND HOW TO CHANGE HISTORY

At the turn of the century, women like Jane Addams, Grace Abbott, Mary Richmond, and Charlotte Whitten became leaders and respected professionals in the emerging social work field. Because of the nature of the field, they were able to exert leadership without abandoning the traditional feminine emphasis on caring and connectedness. Their strategies included individual superperformance and the development of innovative and even separate services for women. Most of the strength of women in those early years, however, came from the collective consciousness and the active networks they created.

Women's dominance began to diminish after the 1920s, as men, a minority population in the social welfare field, assumed the highly visible leadership positions and the pay and privilege that went with them. Women made child welfare a profession, but history had already made male perspective and experience implicit in the very definition of the term.

Women's Work

From the male-dominated heights of objectivity and science, child welfare is often seen as subjective, ambiguous, and therefore, less than respectable. Even feminists ignored the field until recently because of its image as a refuge for "do-gooders." No doubt this generally low valuing increased the vulnerability of child welfare workers to attacks on their "amateurish" methods and "judgmental" decision making during the 1970s and '80s. Some saw subjectivity in the work practices of (mostly) female service providers as *the* reason for injustices and failures within the child welfare system. Serious errors by workers were brought forward as evidence of the need to legalize and objectify practice methods.

When the male model of professionalism was imposed on child welfare, it brought a new emphasis on training, testing, objective recording, and ever more factual evidence gathering and court testimony. These measures, generally viewed as demonstrating greater professionalism, have also increased the regimentation of social workers and stripped them of much of their professional autonomy. Meanwhile, the women's work has continued to earn low status and poor pay within the social work profession.

Women who do child welfare work are among the superwomen of the 1990s, and

(Continued on next page)

BOX 6.1 (Continued)

they pay a high emotional price for this "honor." Often they must surmount a wearying array of tasks, barriers, and problems before they even arrive at the workplace—largely because they are women, for whom connectedness and maintenance of the family are supreme values. Then these same women become instrumental in removing children from other families.

Some workers have tried to apply feminist thinking to the dilemmas they and their clients face, for example, by helping women understand and resist violence. The organization and values of the agency setting, however, resist this approach. Feminist ideas and language have not been incorporated into legislation, policy, or professional literature. In the absence of such legitimizing processes, women who introduce *patriarchy* or *sexism* into a team meeting or supervisory session are open to charges of subjectivity or defensiveness—serious female crimes, as we know.

So although women remain a large share of all direct service providers, our visibility is restricted largely to catastrophic mistakes, our influence has diminished with increasing professionalization of the field, and our concerns have yet to find a voice. Meanwhile, as a quick survey will demonstrate, men are the field's executive directors, funded researchers, and chief spokespersons.

The labor of a host of low-paid and unpaid women, primarily clerical staff and direct service workers, keeps the child welfare system afloat. Untold numbers of women provide child care and in-home supports, serve as parent aides, and volunteer with agencies. Homemakers, who are absolutely key to the current Canadian child welfare service structure, are certainly the most disadvantaged members of the female labor force—immigrants and visible minorities—and their pay is abysmally low. These women are organized, credited, and paid in accordance with a hierarchy of class and race.

A second group of women upon whom child welfare services depend are foster mothers. Some foster mothers are held up as icons of womanhood, representing the heights of selfless caregiving to which all women should aspire. The everyday reality, of course, is one of ongoing and usually invisible caregiving labor provided at extremely low cost. In fact, family foster care represents the epitome of class relations in child welfare, in which the impoverished mother is replaced by a working class woman who is supervised by a middle class woman.

Lowest of all in the power hierarchy, while often highest in notorious visibility, are child welfare clients, the vast majority of them women. These women, overwhelmingly poor, single, and members of ethnic minorities, cannot be written off simply as inadequate caregivers or as victims of the system.

(Continued on next page)

BOX 6.1 (Continued)

As workers know, many of these women demonstrate superior strength, resiliency, and resourcefulness in their efforts to survive and raise their children in a hostile world. Neither our literature nor our practice reflects this reality—very serious omissions given the viciousness of the current public attack on these mothers.

Future Directions

Clearly, women bring not only numbers but considerable strengths to child welfare: obvious competence in managing diverse roles and responsibilities, provision of care in the most difficult of circumstances, the valuing of relationships, our common consciousness, and our potential for network building. What can be done to move these strengths to the very center of child welfare work?

This late in the twentieth century, the main work of women continues to be consciousness raising. We have considerable work to do in renaming, revaluing, and relegitimizing women's experience in a way that reveals our strengths and considerable achievements. Historically, women's strength comes not from the triumphs of individual superwomen but from the formation of active networks and alliances through which we can challenge our common exclusion from power. We must begin to create alliances by actively increasing communication among women in child welfare. There cannot be enough meet-

ings, conferences, and workshops that involve women in all aspects of the field, including clients. And let us not forget the "information highway" for sharing knowledge and experience. We must cite, honor, and promote the achievements of women at all levels within the system on every possible occasion. We must monitor our spokespeople in the public sphere and protest loudly when they fail to represent the viewpoints and needs of women.

Child welfare can and should be infused with feminist thought, forms, practices, and principles. Reclaimed and reinvented by women, child welfare would be less hierarchical, less divisive, less competitive, more participatory, and vastly more preventive in its directions. To achieve this, women must take on systems and find ways to incorporate both the labor and the emotional attachments involved in caregiving into all our programs and services. Finally, it is essential that we overcome the race and class divisions that now permeate the organization of child welfare. Women working together can develop the influence and power to reshape child welfare and truly honor "women's work."

Source: K. Swift, *Children's Voice,* 4 (1995) (3), 28–29. Child Welfare League of America: Washington, DC. Reprinted by permission of Child Welfare League.

brunt of the most destructive of the "child saving efforts." Sent away to culturally alien boarding schools, children were abused emotionally, physically, and
in some of the Canadian schools, sexually (pedophile priests and teachers took
advantage of their Indian charges to an extent only recently coming to light).
Today, the loss of language, spirituality, and an economic base, abuse from
residential church schools, and forced relocation, are cited by native Canadians
as root causes of the high rate of child sexual abuse, physical abuse, and wife
beating that take place (Timpson, 1995).

In the United States, the Indian Child Welfare Act of 1978 was passed to
reverse the pattern of placing American Indian children in non-Indian foster
and adoptive homes and to tighten the legal protection given biological parents and families in child custody matters. Tribal courts, under this law, were
recognized as the authority in child welfare matters. In Canada, decentralized,
community-based child and family services have been provided by First Nations
agencies since the mid-eighties. Reports in the literature highlight the successes
of the fully mandated, indigenously administered child welfare services as, for
example, those offered in Manitoba (see McKenzie et al., 1995). In Australia,
to correct past abuses, a legalistic, juvenile justice model has replaced the more
informal child welfare bureaucracies. Today, however, as O'Connor (1994: 210)
charges, continuing removals of Aboriginal children are simply "masked behind
the facade of the impartial criminal justice system."

FAMILY PRESERVATION

Child welfare agencies have dual roles—the investigative, policing, and child-
removing role, and the helping, teaching role (Pelton, 1993). In order to cut
costs, much of the counseling work is subcontracted out to private agencies.
Child welfare workers do a lot of documentation and follow-up of cases, increasingly through use of computer programs. The key roles of preserving and
strengthening families are thus "farmed out" to private agencies lacking the social
work traditions of the state and county welfare departments. Although decisions for child removal are in the hands of the juvenile court judge and his
or her hands may be tied by fiscal constraints, social workers get the blame
for too-hasty or too-reluctant placement of children. Today's tendency in North
America and Britain is to err on the side of "saving the home" rather than "saving

the child." In a refreshingly honest critique of efforts to transplant America's Families First program to Australia, Scott (1993) fears for the program's success unless a number of conditions are satisfied. The situation of "too little expertise, spread too thinly" must end and programs must be extensive as well as intensive, declares Scott. Some very, very troubled families should be excluded based on established criteria; otherwise for vulnerable children, the attempt at family preservation is dangerous.

In the United States a disturbing statistic from a profile of forty-five states for the year 1991 was released by the National Center on Child Abuse and Neglect (1993): 1081 children "who were known to child protective services" died from abuse and neglect in a single year. This figure is an underestimate, moreover, because many child deaths that appear to be from natural causes may not be so. There is much confusion, for instance, over the label *sudden infant death syndrome* (SIDS) which may be used when the true cause of death is unknown.

In theory, keeping families together and focusing on their strengths rather than deficiencies are laudable goals. Intensive Families First programs in Iowa, Michigan, and Washington state have been successful in many cases in teaching parents how to parent; this often includes the setting of realistic expectations for small children. Lack of sufficient funding, however, has rendered most programs extremely ephemeral and has jeopardized the results and placed some children in danger. Recent assessment of intensive family preservation services indicates that although they improve family functioning initially, out-of-home placement is often necessary in the end (DiNitto, 1995).

Gelles (1992), a nationally recognized authority on domestic violence and earlier advocate of family reunification, reversed his position when the data on child homicide came to light. According to national crime reports, 30 to 50 percent of children killed by parents or caretakers are killed *after* they have been identified by agencies and have been involved in interventions. Gelles' recommendations are emphatic:

> "Child protection" and "child advocacy" need to replace family reunification as the guiding policy of child welfare agencies. Child welfare workers need to "listen" to the actions of maltreating parents. Parents who fracture the skulls or bones of six-month-old children, who have sexual intercourse with 12-month-old daughters, and whose drug abuse patterns compromise their ability to care for their children are simply not entitled to "three strikes" before they lose their rights as parents. With severe child maltreatment, "one strike" is sufficient to warrant terminating parental rights.

In a hard-hitting editorial, the then editor of *Social Work* (1990) Ann Hartman bemoaned the traditional American individualism which has helped create a society extremely reluctant to interfere with the family until a child is in serious danger and it is really too late. In the United States, according to Hartman, a person's destiny is determined by the "accident of birth"—by the parents to whom the child is born. There is no conviction that the children belong to themselves, to the community, or to the future. Thus children do not enjoy full legal rights.

The mass media both reflect and shape social change. In recent times, as reported cases of abuse rise, many states are reconsidering their reluctance to remove children from troubled families. A *Christian Science Monitor* headline is typical, "Tide Shifts on How to Protect Abused Children" (Gardner, 1996). Social workers can be expected to be given more latitude to remove children from high-risk homes in the future.

In the United States and Germany, the issue of children's rights versus parents' rights is resolved on the side of the parents, whereas in Norway, the child's interest takes precedence. Sometimes where the risk of mistreatment is seemingly high, children are removed at birth and freed for adoption. Foster parents are generously reimbursed, and these homes appear to be fairly stable. The Norwegian equivalent of "permanency planning" is that once removed from their biological families, the children are not returned. They have a new home for the duration. Even if the biological parents "turn their lives around" as through alcoholism recovery, or even if the original decision was mistaken, the "social office" does not as a practice return the child. Moe (1990) describes a progressive, alternative supervisory program for borderline cases where child welfare authorities are concerned about the quality of care being offered. Visits, often unscheduled, may continue for years until the child is eighteen. Similar prevention work is done in Denmark, Sweden, and Finland. At Arhus, Denmark, the Family Workplace provides a kind of recreational therapy for family members who come several hours a week to learn how to communicate. Families work at tasks such as cooking, painting, or gardening under social worker guidance (see Pecora, 1992).

The universal paradox is whether to risk erring on the side of the child or on the side of the family. Perhaps the issue is not either/or but both/and as Wharf (1995) helpfully suggests. Maybe it is not an issue of whether you should protect the child or support the family but rather how to provide a means of empowerment for clients. This can be achieved, according to Wharf, through the building of mutual aid associations and group and community approaches to provide the maximum benefit for all family members. This has been successfully tried in New Zealand and Canada. The Family Group Conference in New Zealand, for example, utilizes the technique of support network development to map out a plan for stopping the violence. Instead of the social workers playing a directive role, the family is respected for the expertise it can offer. Similarly, in the Canadian middle-range approach, clients are viewed as colleagues in the helping process. Consistent with this approach, as Wharf explains, demeaning and dehumanizing language such as "target populations," "multiproblem families," and "case management" are avoided.

In the United Kingdom, the Children Act, passed by the government in 1989, transformed children's services as they had previously existed. The transition was from not listening to children to respecting their wishes, from policing parents to supporting them, and from labeling families to providing de-stigmatized care (Rickford, 1992). Practical help, such as procuring good child care, is provided. Family centers are now widespread—here families live in self-contained flats for a program of intensive relationship work. The center employs eleven staff members and families can stay as long as six months. Another alternative project to help families is the residential respite center for teenagers which allows young people to stay away from home for several days at a time. This gives the parents a break and keeps the kids off the street.

CONCLUSION AND SUMMARY

In the shattering Depression documentary, *Let Us Now Praise Famous Men,* James Agee (1939: 263) grasps the essence of life accordingly, "In every child who is born, under no matter what circumstances, and of no matter what parents, the potentiality of the human race is born again." Under conditions of dire poverty, however, children's growth is stunted (literally and figuratively) so that they never can achieve their potentiality.

With regard to children, the United States is a study in contrasts. While this nation prides itself on youth-orientation, and the amount of money spent on expensive toys in some quarters borders on the obscene, U.S. children actively suffer poverty, homelessness, and violence. Today, here, as in many other countries, the pressures on families and therefore on the child welfare system have become relentless. Despite the intention to preserve the family unit, the number of children in foster homes and before the courts has skyrocketed in recent years. Under the burden of drug addiction, AIDS, poverty, unemployment, and teenage pregnancy, the number of children at risk has exploded. Contradictory philosophies that alter with the political winds contribute to the chaos. Over the past decade, the government has promoted family preservation and permanency placement. Often the children end up in transit—going back and forth between biological family and rotating foster families.

While social agencies cope with ever mounting paper work (now done on computers) and struggle to hold together extremely unhealthy families, the families themselves are demoralized through lack of resources for housing, childcare, and alcoholism treatment. Money spent on prevention is far more cost-effective in the long run than money poured out after the harm of neglect—societal neglect—has taken its toll. As so clearly enunciated by Ruth Sidel (1992) in her book, *Women and Children Last,* it is far cheaper to make sure people are well fed than to treat malnutrition; it is far cheaper to immunize children against infectious disease than to treat them once they are sick. And, we might add, all nations can learn the importance of reducing teenage pregnancy. The key, as we have seen from a perusal of United Nations' comparative data, lies in offering flexible and available family planning services but also, and the point should be underscored, in providing a climate for women in which educational and employment opportunities offer attractive alternatives to early childbearing. Over the long term, almost every other aspect of progress, from nutrition and child health to family planning and women's rights, is profoundly affected by whether or not a nation educates its girls, according to *The Progress of Nations* (UNICEF, 1994a). For situations of child abuse and neglect some of the best preventatives may be a reduction in stress on families, especially on single parent families. All families require bolstering through provision of health care, day care, and jobs that pay an adequate wage. A program of parent education for all parents-to-be and a program of periodic public health nurse home visits to monitor the progress of children is invaluable in ensuring children's health. For all its talk of "family values," the United States is not a family-friendly society. In contrast, in Sweden and Norway, a year of maternity leave at near-full salary is provided to ensure that one of the parents will stay home with the child. Childcare fees are set on a sliding scale and the standards of public day care are extraordinarily high. At the heart of such policies is the premise that the whole community thrives when families and children thrive. The United

States would do well to look toward policies that strengthen rather than weaken the ability of vulnerable families to raise healthy children. By not catching problems early, we pay the price later in escalating crime, drug use, and spread of disease. What we must keep in mind, as Sidel observes, is that these problems are not insoluble. There are models from other countries where the rates of poverty, infant mortality and morbidity, crime and drug abuse, and child neglect and abuse are quite low and, in short, where protection of families and children is intertwined. While countries of the world today are investing in advanced systems of weaponry and reducing investment in social services for people, the povertization of the world's women has advanced also. Against the throes of an uncaring social welfare state, the caring offered by child welfare services is so limited as to appear inconsequential. These things will not change in the immediate future, but perhaps one day nations will see the light. Perhaps as the *Progress of Nations* (foreword) eloquently predicts:

> The day will come when the progress of nations will be judged not by their military or economic strength, nor by the splendor of their capital cities and public buildings, but by the well-being of their peoples: by their levels of health, nutrition, and education; by their opportunities to earn a fair reward for their labors; by their ability to participate in the decisions that affect their lives; by the respect that is shown for their civil and political liberties; by the provision that is made for those who are vulnerable and disadvantaged; and by the protection that is afforded to the growing minds and bodies of their children.

In summary, from a world perspective, many very poor nations of the world face nearly insurmountable challenges in child welfare policy and practice. And when survival is a key issue, child welfare services may not exist, or if so, they may cater only to the needs of a fraction of the populace. Against the backdrop of poverty and starvation, attention to parents' maltreatment of children might seem more like a luxury than a necessity. Moreover, the meaning to the family of one form of behavior, such as child labor, may be different in Pakistan and Latin America than in Australia or the United States.

International social welfare considers the universal questions and dilemmas and, in the cultural context, their solutions. It examines the role of this one profession in shaping and enforcing these solutions. For the purposes of this chapter, the universal question concerns society's monitoring of the care and well-being of its children. For a starting point, we considered the nature of childhood, past, present, and evolving. Some notions die hard: the notion of the child as property of the parents is still with us in many ways. In the United States, often children who don't want to return to a home in which they were neglected and beaten are forced to return home. Adopted children may be reunited with a family they never knew due to an irregularity in the adoption procedures. Children of a different race from their foster parents may be removed from their foster homes, similarly, against the interests of the child but in the interest of the state or of a race or tribe. Active and flexible recruitment of suitable substitute homes, however, could avoid unnecessary tragedy later (Hairston and Williams, 1989).

Other countries, meanwhile, such as those in Scandinavia, may lean in the opposite direction where the child's interest is paramount. Children placed in foster care remain in foster care. Even if a mistake has been made and the biological parents falsely accused, once the child has adjusted to new surroundings chances are that he or she will stay in placement. The tension between family rights and public interest in the child, therefore, may be resolved one way in one society and a different way in another. The means of resolution has to do with the society's values and traditions of an earlier day. All nations share an interest in the welfare of their children; the children represent the future, the link between today and tomorrow. Sometimes, however, the public's interest in the child has been a nationalist and colonialist one as when aboriginal children were taken from their families in the United States, Canada, and Australia to be socialized into mainstream culture. This brings us to the issue of children's rights.

The passage by the United Nations General Assembly in 1989 of the Convention on the Rights of the Child was a breakthrough in international law. Many nations have already revised their policies regarding children to be in compliance with international standards. According to the declaration, children have a right to due process in court, a right not to be hit, abused, or exploited, and a right to health and nutrition. In times of war and famine and other national crises, however, children's rights fall to the wayside. Orphaned children must scrounge out a living roaming the countryside. Even in some rich countries such as the United States, and in less prosperous ones such as Russia, the health standards are below what they should be, and the rate of preventable diseases is on the rise.

In this chapter, child work was differentiated from child labor, the former referring to a didactic process, the latter to an exploitative one. Child labor was presented in this chapter as a form of societal abuse and neglect. Images were presented of small children laboring long days under appalling and sometimes life-threatening conditions. Boys and girls may be forced into prostitution, with young children being in great demand in Asia under the mistaken belief that they are likely to be AIDS free. The lot of boy soldiers, hardened to be fighters through torture, is equally severe. The final topic under child labor concerned children who survive on the streets, children who either may be helping their families get by and who may be completely on their own. Despised by their compatriots, these children are sometimes killed through institutionalized murder as in Brazil, or by isolated crime as in places further north.

Turning to maltreatment by the family as regulated by the state, this chapter discussed child abuse, neglect, and sexual abuse. Use of violence by parents is so ingrained in the system that most societies (a throwback to the child-as-property premise) allow children to be hit by their parents and many others allow teachers to hit children at school (in British private schools children can be caned). Sometimes the physical punishment gets out of hand and children are noticeably injured or killed. In countries with well-developed child welfare systems, the authorities intervene, perhaps removing the children from the home and placing them in foster care. In the United States, Canada, and Great Britain, the emphasis is on family preservation. Many child homicides, as we have seen, take place each year *following* family intervention. Nevertheless, some excellent programs of family intervention have been instituted in various parts of Europe, Canada, and New Zealand. Serious underfunding, of which understaffing is a reflection, jeopardizes American programs such as the family reunification program in Iowa, however. Foster care in many parts of the world is buckling under increased pressure from the combination of drug addiction, poverty, lack of low-income housing, teenage pregnancy, and the AIDS epidemic. To what extent the United States and other countries in similar positions will devote their resources and creative energy to real family protection by bolstering families to enable them to provide good care, and to what extent the money will be diverted into furthering the military-industrial-complex, remains to be seen. The key point of this chapter, generally speaking, is that a society that is good to its members will have members who are good to their children. Treat the parents well, and they will treat their children well. Kindness transcends the system, as does leanness and meanness.

REVIEW QUESTIONS

1. What is the lesson of DeMause's article discussed in this chapter, "Our Forebears Made Childhood a Nightmare?"
2. Discuss some of the horrors children faced in the past.
3. Discuss the statement, "Child welfare is a gauge by which we can observe the values of a society." Give some examples from various times and places.
4. Discuss the differences of opinion over when the notion of childhood began. When did child welfare as a system begin?
5. Describe the early orphanages and the "orphan train." What is the significance of the display housed at the Glenbow Museum in Calgary, Canada?
6. Discuss the meaning of the African quote, "It takes a village to bring up a child."
7. Describe the Virginia Industrial School for Colored Girls in light of its significance.
8. What is the system of family allowances? How does it relate to child welfare?
9. What is the significance of the U.N. Convention on the Rights of the Child? How does it influence policy? Give examples.
10. Name three ways the United States is in violation of the principles of the convention.
11. Compare poverty in the United States with the situation in some African countries. Explain how reducing child poverty in the United States would be cost effective.
12. From a global perspective, discuss nutritional neglect and its ramifications. What is the impact of AIDS?
13. Describe some of the health problems in Russia.
14. What is the message of the book, *There Are No Children Here?*
15. Discuss suicide prevention work in Canada. How does the "gay factor" enter in?
16. Describe the difference between *child work* and *child labor*. Give some examples from around the world of child labor. What are Otis' recommendations for reform?
17. Describe child prostitution in Thailand.
18. How can children be programmed for war? Discuss the life of boy soldiers.
19. Discuss the findings on studies of street children. What draws them to the streets? Are there any remedies?
20. What does the U.N. Convention on the Rights of the Child say about violence against children? What are the implications for parents?
21. Discuss different ways of viewing physical punishment of children throughout the world.
22. What is the connection between economic stress and child abuse? What is NASW's position on violence against children? How is this controversial?
23. Define child neglect and describe different types. How do various factors interact in situations of abuse?

24. What facts were uncovered in the book, *Our Little Secret*? What do we know of instances of sexual abuse in different parts of the world?
25. Discuss the recent backlash relevant to reports of child sexual abuse.
26. What is PTSD and how does it relate to sexual abuse? What do we learn from substance abuse treatment centers? How about early pregnancy?
27. Discuss the role of child protective services yesterday and today. What is "permanency planning?"
28. What were the reasons for the Indian Child Welfare Act of 1978?
29. Discuss the advantages and disadvantages of the family preservation movement. How might it be improved?
30. What striking facts brought about Gelles' reversal in his stand on family reunification?
31. How does Norway "lean the other way" on the child protection issue?
32. Agree or disagree with the following statement and back up your arguments, "For all its talk of 'family values,' the United States is not a family-friendly society."

REFERENCES

Agee, J. (1939). *Let Us Now Praise Famous Men.* New York: Ballantine Books.

Angelou, M. (1969). *I Know Why the Caged Bird Sings.* New York: Random House.

Aries, P. (1965). *Centuries of Childhood: A Social History of Family Life.* New York: Vintage Books.

Associated Press. (1994, December 11). Children of War "Feel Nothing." *Bellingham Herald*: A3.

Barker, R. (1995). References. *The Social Work Dictionary*, 3d ed. Washington, DC: NASW Press.

Berfenstam, R. (1973). *Early Child Care in Sweden.* London: Gordon and Breach.

Berliner, L. (1995). Child Sexual Abuse: Direct Practice. *Encyclopedia of Social Work,* 19th ed. Washington, DC: NASW Press, 408–417.

Bishop, A. (1994). Becoming an Ally: Breaking the Cycle of Oppression. Halifax, Canada: Fernwood.

Bokhari, F. (1995, May 1). Death Spotlights Plight of Child Laborers. *The Christian Science Monitor*: 15.

Bricker-Jenkins, M. and L. Sindos. (1986). Making Capital on Kids: The Economic Context of Day Care Policy Debates. *Catalyst* 20: 36–51.

Brissett-Chapman, S. (1995). Child Abuse and Neglect: Direct Practice. In *Encyclopedia of Social Work,* 19th ed.: 355–365. Washington, DC: NASW Press.

Chase, N. (1975). *A Child is Being Beaten.* New York: McGraw-Hill.

Chasnoff, I., H. Landress, and M. Barrett. (1990). The Prevalence of Illicit Drug or Alcohol Use during Pregnancy and Discrepancies in Mandatory Reporting in Pinellas County, Florida. *New England Journal of Medicine* 322: 1202–1205.

Children of War "Feeling Nothing." (1994, December 11). *The Bellingham Herald*: A3.

Clinton, H. (1996). *It Takes a Village and Other Lessons Children Teach Us*. New York: Simon and Schuster.

Conroy, P. (1982). *The Lords of Discipline*. New York: Bantam Books.

Conte, J. (1995). Child Sexual Abuse Overview. In *Encyclopedia of Social Work,* 19th ed.: 402–408). Washington, DC: NASW Press.

Dahl, T. (1985). *Child Welfare and Social Defence*. Oslo: Norwegian University Press.

de Cuellar, J. (1990, October 2.) Excerpts from Remarks by Leaders at U.N. Work Summit for Children. *The New York Times*: A1.

DeMuse, L. (1995, April). Our Forebears Made Childhood a Nightmare. *Psychology Today*: 85–88.

de Oliveira, W., M. Baizerman, and L. Pellet. (1992). Street Children in Brazil and their Helpers: Comparative Views on Aspirations and the Future. *International Social Work* 35: 163–176.

DiNitto, D. (1993). *Social Welfare: Politics and Public Policy,* 4th ed. Boston: Allyn and Bacon.

Economist. (1995, March 11). India's Rich Little Poor Girls. *The Economist*: 40.

Edmonds, P. (1994, November 16). The Bottom Line of Poverty: New Study Says It Costs Billions. *USA Today*: 3A.

Edelman, M. (1994). This Is Not Who We Are. In UNICEF, *The Progress of Nations*. New York: UNICEF, 40–41.

Erikson, E. (1963). *Childhood and Society,* 2d ed. New York: W. Norton and Company.

Excerpts from the United Nations Declaration on Children. (1995, October 2). *New York Times*: A1 and following.

Finkelhor, D. (1994). The International Epidemiology of Child Sexual Abuse. *Child Abuse and Neglect* 18: 409–417.

Flekkoy, M. (1989). Child Advocacy in Norway: The Ombudsman. *Child Welfare* 68(2): 113–122.

Frankel, M. (1995, August 14). Boy Soldiers. *Newsweek*: 44–46.

Gardner, M. (1996, March 2). Tide Shifts on How to Protect Abused Children. *The Christian Science Monitor*: 12.

Gelles, R. (1992). Abandon Reunification Goal for Abusive Families and Replace with Child Protection. *Child and Adolescent Behavior Letter* 8(6): 1, 6.

Golding, W. (1954). *Lord of the Flies*. New York: Coward-McCann.

Hairston, C. and V. Williams. (1989). Black Adoptive Parents: How They View Agency Adoption Practices. *Social Casework* 70(9): 534–539.

Hartman, A. (1990). Children in a Careless Society. *Social Work* 35(6): 483–484.

Hegar, R. (1989). The Rights and Status of Children: International Concerns for Social Work. *International Social Work* 32: 107–116.

Herman, J. (1992). *Trauma and Recovery.* New York: Basic Books.

Hopps, J. and P. Collins. (1995). Social Work Profession Overview. In *Encyclopedia of Social Work,* 19th ed.: 2266–2282. Washington, DC: NASW Press.

Hughes, C. (1995). Child Poverty, Campaign 2000, and Child Welfare Practice: Working to End Child Poverty in Canada. *Child Welfare* 74(3): 779–794.

Jones, R. (1995). The Price of Welfare Dependency: Children Pay. *Social Work* 40(4): 496–505.

Jonsson, U. (1994). Nutrition. In UNICEF, *The Progress of Nations.* New York: UNICEF, 6–11.

Jost, K. (1993). Children's Legal Rights. *CQ Researcher* 3(15): 339–354.

Kadushin, A. and J. Martin. (1988). *Child Welfare Services,* 4th ed. New York: Macmillan Publishing Company.

Kandel, E. (1991). *Physical Punishment and the Development of Aggressive and Violent Behavior: A Review.* Unpublished manuscript. University of New Hampshire, Durham, NH: Family Research Laboratory.

Karger, H. and D. Stoesz. (1990). American Social Welfare Policy: A Structural Approach. New York: Longman.

Kasinsky, R. (1994). Child Neglect and "Unfit" Mothers: Child Savers in the Progressive Era and Today. *Women and Criminal Justice* 6(1): 97–129.

Keefe, T. and J. McCullagh. (1995). Child Poverty: A "Fair Deal" for Children. *Social Development Issues* 17(1): 87–98.

Kotlowitz, A. (1991). *There Are No Children Here: The Story of Two Boys Growing Up in the Other America.* New York: Doubleday.

Leuchtag, A. (1995, March/April). Merchants of Flesh: International Prostitution and the War on Women's Rights. *The Humanist*: 11–16.

Lewis, S. (1994). They Will Not Get Away With It Forever. In UNICEF, *The Progress of Nations.* New York: UNICEF.

Link, R. (1993, March). *Parent Participation in British Family Centres.* Paper presented at the CSWE Annual Program Meeting, New York.

Macksoud, M. (1994). Children in War. *World Health* 47(2): 21–23.

Maclean's (1995). Child Labor. *Maclean's* 108(25): 43.

Maslow, A. (1954). *Motivation and Personality.* New York: Harper and Row.

Mason, M. (1994). *From Father's Property to Children's Rights: The History of Child Custody in the United States.* New York: Columbia University Press.

McDevitt, S., A. Henkin, W. Downs, and C. Henkin (1995, September 19). *Social and Political Trends of the Nineties in the U.S.A.: Implications of Welfare Reform Agendas for the Family.* Paper presented at the ERASMUS Conference, Vienna.

McFadden, E. (1991). Preface. *Child Welfare* 70(20): 99–105.

McKenzie, B., E. Seidl, and N. Bone. (1995). Child and Family Service Standards in First Nations: An Action Research Project. *Child Welfare* 74: 633–653.

Miller, B., W. Downs, and M. Testa. (1993). Interrelationships between Victimization Experience and Women's Alcohol Use. *Journal of Studies on Alcohol* 1 (Suppl. 11): 115–123.

Mitchell, A. (1995, June 23). Tackling the Issue of Homosexuality at School. *The Globe and Mail*: A2.

Moe, A. (1990). *Tilsyn i Forebyggende Barnevern*. Trondheim, Norway: University of Trondheim.

Myers, J. (1994). Definition and Origins of the Backlash against Child Protection. In J. Myers, ed. *The Backlash: Child Protection Under Fire*: 17–30). Thousand Oaks, CA: SAGE.

NASW News. (1994, October). Economic Abuse. *NASW News*: 9.

———. (1995, October). Teens and Age Difference. *NASW News*: 13.

National Center on Child Abuse and Neglect. (1993). *National Child Abuse and Data System: Working Paper 2—1991 Summary Data Component*. Washington, DC: U.S. Government Printing Office.

Nemeth, M. (1994). An Alarming Trend. *Maclean's* 107(44): 15.

New York Times. (1990, October 2). Excerpts from the United Nations Declaration on Children. *New York Times*: 1A.

O'Connor, I. (1994). The New Removals: Aboriginal Youth in the Queensland Juvenile Justice System. *International Social Work* 37: 197–212.

Otis, J. (1995). Child Labor. In *Encyclopedia of Social Work,* 19th ed.: 390–402). Washington, DC: NASW Press.

Pecora, P. (1992). A Guide to the Family Workshop Program in Denmark. Washington, DC: NASW.

Peebles-Wilkins, W. (1995). Janie Parker Barrett and the Virginia Industrial School for Colored Girls: Community Response to the Needs of African American Children. *Child Welfare* 74(1): 143–161.

Pelton, L. (1993). Enabling Public Child Welfare Agencies to Promote Family Preservation. *Social Work* 38(4): 491–493.

Peralta, F. (1995, July 29-August 1). *Street Children of Mexico City*. Paper presented at the International Social Welfare in a Changing World Conference: Calgary, Alberta.

Phillips, L. (1995, August 31). Sex Abuse: Silent Factor in Teen Welfare Equation. *USA Today*: 6A.

Pitts, J. (1994). What Can We Learn from Europe? *Social Work in Europe* 70(1): 48–53.

Plotnick, R. (1989). Directions for Reducing Child Poverty. *Social Work* 34(6): 523–530.

Polansky, N., P. Ammons, and B. Weatherby. (1983). Is There an American Standard of Child Care? *Social Work* 28: 341–346.

Polansky, N. and C. Hally. (1974). *Profile of Neglect Survey of the State of Knowledge of Child Neglect.* Washington, DC: U.S. Department of Education and Welfare, Community Services Administration.

Reynolds, M. (1992). On Street Children. Fact sheet in L. Healy, *Introducing International Development Content in Social Work Curriculum.* Washington, DC: NASW, 141–142.

Richette, L. (1969). *The Throwaway Children.* New York: Delta.

Rickford, F. (1992). Happy Families. *Social Work Today,* 23(38): 20–21.

Rohde, J. (1994). Health. In UNICEF, *The Progress of Nations.* New York: UNICEF, 12–17.

Sachs, A. (1994). The Last Commodity: Child Prostitution in the Developing World. *World Watch* 7(4): 24–30.

Schmetzer, U. (1995, August 23). Grisly Orphanages Haunting China on Eve of UN Meeting. *Chicago Tribune*: 1, 8.

Schorr, E. (1988). *Within Our Reach: Breaking the Life Cycle of Disadvantage.* New York: Doubleday.

Scott, D. (1993). International Technology Transfer in Family Preservation: Differences Between the Australian and U.S. Context. The *Prevention Report:* Publication of the University of Iowa School of Social Work: 1–7.

Selbyg, A. (1987). *Norway Today.* Oslo: Norwegian University Press.

Sidel, R. (1992). *Women and Children Last,* 2d ed. New York: Penguin Books.

Sloane, W. (1995, October 12). Swedish Gadfly for Kids Keeps Officials Honest. *Christian Science Monitor*: 1, 3.

Sly, L. (1995, August 9). Child Soldiers. *Chicago Tribune*: 1, 5.

Smith, E. (1995). Bring Back the Orphanages? What Policymakers of Today Can Learn from the Past. *Child Welfare* 74(1): 115–142.

Steed, J. (1995). *Our Little Secret: Confronting Child Sexual Abuse in Canada.* Toronto: Vintage Canada.

Straus, M. (1994). *Beating the Devil Out of Them. Corporal Punishment in American Families.* New York: Lexington Books.

Swift, K. (1995). An Outrage to Common Decency: Historical Perspectives on Child Neglect. *Child Welfare* 74(1): 71–91.

———. (1991). Contradictions in Child Welfare: Neglect and Responsibility. In C. Baines, P. Evans, and S. Neysmith, eds. *Women's Caring: Feminist Perspectives on Social Welfare*: 234–271. Toronto: McClelland and Stewart.

Taylor-Brown, S. and A. Garcia. (1995). Social Workers and HIV-Affected Families: Is the Profession Prepared? *Social Work* 40(1): 14–15.

Timpson, J. (1995). Four Decades of Literature on Native Canadian Child Welfare: Changing Themes. *Child Welfare* 74: 537–546.

Trattner, W. (1994). *From Poor Law to Welfare State: A History of Social Welfare in America.* New York: The Free Press.

UNICEF. (1995). *The State of the World's Children 1995.* New York: United Nation's Children's Defense Fund.

_____. (1994a). *The Progress of Nations.* New York: United Nations Children's Defense Fund.

_____. (1994b). *The State of the World's Children 1994.* New York: United Nations Children's Defense Fund.

United Nations. (1989). *Convention on the Rights of the Child.* New York: U.N. Document.

van Wormer, K. (1995). *Alcoholism Treatment: A Social Work Perspective.* Chicago: Nelson-Hall.

_____. (1993). Child Welfare Practice in Cultural Context: Norway and the U.S.A. *International Social Work* 36: 301–314.

Viswanathan, N. and M. Arie. (1995). Street Children: An International Perspective. Paper presented at the International Social Welfare in a Changing World Conference. Alberta, Canada: University of Calgary.

Webb, S. (1992). Rough Justice. *Social Work Today* 23(39): 11–19.

Wells, S. (1995). Child Abuse and Neglect Overview. In *Encyclopedia of Social Work,* 19th ed.: 346–353. Washington, DC: NASW Press.

Wharf, B. (1995). Toward a New Vision for Child Welfare in Canada. *Child Welfare* 74(3): 820–839.

Widom, C. (1989). The Cycle of Violence. *Science* 244: 160–166.

Willow, C. (1995). The Double Standards in Smacking Children. *Community Care* 1075: 13.

Wineman, D. (1995). Children's Rights. In *Encyclopedia of Social Work,* 19th ed.: 465–475. Washington, DC: NASW Press.

York, G. (1995, July 24). Sickness on the Rise for Russian Children. *Globe and Mail*: A1, 6.

7

WORK AND FAMILY WELFARE

What happens to a dream deferred?
Does it dry up
like a raisin in the sun?
Or fester like a sore—
And then run?
Does it stink like rotten meat?
Or crust and sugar over—
like a syrupy sweet?

Maybe it just sags
like a heavy load.

Or does it explode?
      —Langston Hughes, 1902–1967

Economic restructuring, downsizing, accountability, cost-effectiveness, global market, productivity: these are a few of the buzzwords causing workers in various parts of the world to cringe. Job security, even in Japan, will soon be replaced as harsh competitive "realities" of intense global competition dictate the treatment that workers receive.

At a glance, the inclusion in this book of a chapter on work may seem unorthodox, an extravagance, even. Only one other of the texts in the field of social welfare provides a section or chapter on trends in the workplace (see Zastrow, 1996). Yet did not Freud say the two key ingredients for happiness were work and love? Did not the United Nations Universal Declaration on Human Rights of 1948 include the right to work, among the basic rights of citizenship? (See chapter 11 for the text of the declaration.) Today, as this chapter will make clear, there are compelling reasons to study work multidimensionally. For in the matter of work, these three dimensions—the social, psychological, and economic—all coalesce.

The study of the economic and social well-being of today's worker in nations of varying degrees of economic development reveals a commonality of pressures at the crossroads of rapidly advancing technology. "The information revolution is here at last," declared an article in *Newsweek* (Levy, 1995). *The Chicago Tribune* (McCarron, 1995: 11) warned:

> If you're the kind of worker, say, who can oversee the conversion of your company's computer systems to Windows '95, you're sitting pretty. If you're the kind of worker who performs repetitive tasks that can be done more cheaply by automation, or by somebody overseas, you are in trouble.

One worker's opportunity (the worker in a low-wage country, for example) is another's worst nightmare. And the nightmares are becoming more frequent than the opportunities. The story of labor over the past decades is a study in transition from regional bidding over cheap labor (this was bad enough) to international competition of a much more peremptory sort. Today workers in the industrialized world, who once considered themselves to be removed from workers in other places (such as Mexico or Indochina, for example), are being made painfully aware of to what extent their lives are interconnected with the lives (or livelihoods) of workers throughout the world. Now the corporations to which workers may have felt they belonged or which belonged to them or at least to their country, are no longer clearly identifiable as American or Japanese or Swedish. These are *transnational* enterprises, the operations of which flow with increasing ease back and forth across borders, gyrating in response to worldwide economic forces. Simply put: what Texas took from Michigan— factories in search of cheap labor—Mexico is now taking from Texas. And next year it will be Thailand. Wages go lower; profits go higher. But the story will not end here because if businesses can manage it, most workers will be as the British say, "redundant." In short, the models of labor which the world has grown used to are now becoming obsolete. How obsolete will be discussed in the following pages.

Every major period of technological development affects the structure and organization of society. In a book entitled *The End of Work,* but which perhaps more aptly should be called *The End of the Worker,* economist Rifkin (1995) captures the new, economic ethos. Wave after wave of technological innovation affects not only manufacturing sectors (where robots are replacing people) but the service sector as well (where computers, automated teller machines, and voice-recognition technologies are eliminating the need for human contact). But just as important as technology is the *control* of technology and the *use* of the technology. In short, the degree of regulation of industry or the government's role in ameliorating or not ameliorating the consequences of the structural changes for the benefit of people must be considered.

The social welfare of a people is intricately linked to the way they earn their living, the availability and conditions of their employment, and the sexual division or non-division of labor. In most modern or modernizing societies, an individual's sense of self worth is affected by the work that he or she does and the significance attributed to this line of work. Work is essential to human dignity, a fact set out so meaningfully in the 1948 U.N. Declaration on Human Rights. If unchecked, structural shifts in the economy can have devastating consequences for workers and their families. As self-sufficient national economies risk being overtaken by fierce competition driven by cheap and temporary labor, many workers have now grown expendable and work security and incentives are gone. It used to be "the carrot and the stick." Now it is simply, "the stick." A headline from *The Wall Street Journal*—"These Six Growth Jobs Are Dull, Dead End, Sometimes Dangerous" (Horwitz, 1994)— says it all. The United States, according to the news story, is monitoring workers' every move to assure the maximum level of productivity. Poultry processors and nursing home aides epitomize the harshness of much of the new low-wage work where workers suffer soaring injury rates and yet frequently lack health benefits. In many high-growth industries, work is faster than ever before and, therefore, the personal stress is greater also. Moreover, the once solid foundation for millions of middle-class families—the corporate career—is sinking rapidly. As workers become increasingly expendable, their sense of security vanishes. The by-products of pressure on the job—family violence, employee violence, substance abuse, divorce, and stress-related illness—are on the rise in the United States and elsewhere.

Hovering over the whole issue of work are these questions: What is the meaning of work in our lives and our family lives? How can society adapt to a rapidly changing work milieu? And what happens to "a dream deferred?" This chapter will address these questions, first from a historical perspective, viewing the role and functions of work. Then we will view the human toll, psychologically and culturally, as the worker is marginalized by the forces of what one writer calls "the McDonaldization of society" and another calls "the Third Industrial Revolution." A separate section on women and work looks at the division of labor and subordination of the female work force in a world context and in the context of competition within a global market. This chapter concludes with a discussion of solutions designed to bolster the family against the forces of fierce, global competition. The classical notion of *cultural lag* is revitalized to refer to the disjunction between changes in the economic constitution of society and cultural adaptation to the changes.

THE SOCIAL FUNCTIONS OF WORK

In industrialized and westernized societies, work fulfills economic, social, psychological, and moral functions. Economically, work provides a source of income that makes survival possible. Whether a person barely gets by or lives a life of relative ease is determined, in large part, by his or her earnings (or the earnings of family members). Profits from work, wisely invested, can multiply and themselves produce earnings.

"What do you do?" This is the question commonly asked of strangers in an effort to gauge the social standing of another. The social aspect of work relates to the status in society accruing from one's position of importance. Some occupations, usually those requiring specialized training, carry high status. Generally the well-paid, highly-skilled professions provide esteem for an individual and immediate family members. In addition to providing social acceptability which makes friendship in certain circles possible, the job itself provides a network of friends and acquaintances for oneself and one's family. Often when people lose their jobs, their friendships vanish as well. An unemployed person consequently may see his or her place in the social structure seriously altered.

Control of important aspects of life—especially work life—is viewed as central to the development of both adult potential and individual identity (Keefe,

1984). Psychologically, the value of work is paramount. Challenging, fulfilling work provides a sense of self-respect and the kind of satisfaction that comes from making a contribution to society. Working at a boring, degrading, monotonous job often leads workers to view themselves as personally insignificant (Zastrow, 1996) or in the words of Studs Terkel (1974) "a Monday through Friday sort of dying." Still, generally speaking, people get more credit for "slaving away" to support their families than for opting out of the work force. For parents, those who can't take pride in the work they do can find solace vicariously in their plans and dreams for their children; we judge ourselves not only by the work we do, but by the work our children do or will do ("my son, the doctor"). Thus even parents who have not had opportunities themselves may find hope in the potential of the next generation.

This fact is brought stunningly to life in the 1950s award-winning portrait of black Chicago family life, *A Raisin in the Sun* (Hansberry, 1994: 45–46), as Mama remembers: "Big Walter used to say . . . 'Seem like God didn't see fit to give the black man nothing but dreams—but he did give us children to make them dreams seem worthwhile.'" Mama is a maid, her son a chauffeur, but her daughter plans to be a doctor and as the son says to a white racist in the play's dramatic climax, "We are proud of her."

The social functions of a phenomenon often can be understood more in its absence than in its presence. So it is with fulfilling employment. Jobs that do not provide opportunities to learn and grow, that are mere drudgery in other words, can lead to a sense of alienation. *Alienation* is defined as the condition in industrial society in which the individual's sense of self and significant aspects of a person's physical and social environments are experienced as estranged and out of personal control (Keefe, 1984). Later in this chapter, the psychological toll that the lack of satisfying employment takes on workers and their families will be discussed. For the present, suffice it to say that joblessness, poverty, and family breakup are all highly intercorrelated (Hernandez, 1993). Substance abuse and job loss are reciprocally related. Zastrow (1996) lists suicide, emotional problems, insomnia, psychosomatic illness, social isolation, and marital unhappiness among the consequences of long-term unemployment.

Widespread unemployment can be devastating not only for the individual, but for the society. The consequences are reflected in early teenage pregnancy, homelessness, crime statistics, and even mass civil disorder, inasmuch as persons outside of the work economy are divorced from the ordinary social structure. On the financial side, widespread unemployment also leads to diminished tax revenues. This, in turn, is associated with reduced government services. Those in the work force who pay taxes are resentful of others who do not; they are apt to support punitive policies to force non-taxpayers to take low wage jobs.

From the societal point of view, then, full employment serves to provide stability of the citizenry, a healthy tax base, and a sense of community among those who have a stake in its survival. Even in a poor, working class neighborhood, law abiding role models are available to help socialize the young. Close family ties can be sustained when the adult members can find gratifying work.

HISTORICAL PERSPECTIVE

An idealized work ethic, which often stigmatizes very poor people as lazy or pathological when they are not engaged in wage labor, has dominated modern Western history (Wagner, 1994). Founded by religious dissenters, the United States, far more than any other country, attaches a moral value to work. Canada may not be that far behind. One joke broadcast on the Canadian public radio has it that in one town in Manitoba, the people are so puritanical that they can be heard to say, "Thank God it's Monday." The Anglo American emphasis on work and productivity marks quite a contrast with the beliefs of an earlier day.

The ancient Greeks, for example, viewed work as a curse imposed on humanity by the gods (Zastrow, 1996). Slaves did the heavy work to free up citizens' time for philosophic contemplation. To the ancient Hebrews, work was a penance for original sin, not a source of personal fulfillment. There were strict laws covering pay for labor. Pay had to be provided at the end of the day's toil. One of Jesus' parables tells of an employer who paid all his workers the same amount at the end of the day regardless of whether they had worked one hour or eleven hours (*Matthew* 20:1–16). According to Hebrew law, all workers had to be paid at the end of the day on which they worked. Those who worked the longest complained bitterly about the burden they had borne. This passage bridges the gap between the Hebrews and the first Christians. Although the early Christians were somewhat more positive in their attitude, not until the time of the Protestant Reformation did work, along with frugality and asceticism, become a primary virtue.

In her attack on the modern work obsession, Juliet Schor (1991) in *The Overworked American* reveals that leisure time has been plentiful throughout

357

history, with the exception of the eighteenth and nineteenth centuries. Steady employment for fifty-two weeks a year, as Schor indicates, is a modern invention. In the past, labor was seasonal, intermittent, and irregular. Capitalism which depended on making profits by getting the maximum work out of the workers, and the peasants' gradual loss of their land combined to create a factory system that was unbelievably arduous. Working hours were pushed to the brink of human endurance.

Jeremy Rifkin (1995) traces the history of technological advance, or the transition from renewable to nonrenewable sources of energy and from biological to mechanical sources of power. In the First Industrial Revolution, steam was harnessed for energy and used in the manufacture of a wide range of goods. The Second Industrial Revolution occurred between 1860 and World War I when electricity created a new source of energy to light up cities and create instant communication. Then, according to Rifkin, a Third Industrial Revolution emerged immediately after World War II and its impact is being felt today as technological breakthroughs offer the promise of a great social transformation based on a change in the need for most work, or at least for the way it is performed. We will discuss the implications of these developments later in the chapter.

Lest we become too nostalgic for the factory life that preceded automation, Jane Addams, (1910: 199-299) in her autobiography, provides this harrowing account of the Chicago industrial scene:

A south Italian peasant who has picked olives and packed oranges from his toddling babyhood, cannot see at once the difference between the outdoor healthy work which he has performed in the varying seasons, and the long hours of monotonous factory life which his child encounters when he goes to work in Chicago. An Italian father came to us in great grief over the death of his eldest child, a little girl of twelve, who had brought the largest wages into the family fund. In the midst of his genuine sorrow he said: "She was the oldest kid I had. Now I shall have to go back to work again until the next one is able to take care of me." The man was only thirty-three and had hoped to retire from work at least during the winters. No foreman cared to have him in a factory, untrained and unintelligent as he was. It was much easier for his bright, English-speaking little girl to get a chance to paste labels on a box than for him to secure an opportunity to carry pig iron.

Around the turn of the century a scientific form of management was invented. This is not only of historical interest but as Ritzer (1993) informs us, it is also the precursor of the extreme form of standardization epitomized in what he calls the "McDonaldization of society." Max Weber (1921), whose work is cited by Ritzer, captured the essence of modernized work in his classic tract on bureaucratization and rationalization. As the paradigm of formal rationality, the bureaucracy develops rules and regulations toward the ends of efficiency, predictability, quantification, and control. Ritzer regards the process of fast-food restaurant management as a logical extension of the Weberian theory of rationalization. This will be discussed later in the chapter.

Despite the advances in factory production in the early twentieth century, capitalism, according to Schor (1991), still had not consolidated its control within the workplace in either the United States or Britain until the innovations of what is now known as *Fordism*. In 1914, Henry Ford devised a sophisticated approach to labor discipline which would stifle worker resistance for years to come. The conveyor belt process, as we know, functioned in such a way that each worker did the same task over and over again. The resulting efficiency in producing cars, appliances, radios, etc., and the speedy production of identical products, reduced the prices considerably for mass consumption. Workers, engaging in highly specialized tasks, readily became interchangeable and ultimately replaceable, in fact, with machines.

Today, the greatest source of investment by industry is in the super-sophisticated high tech equipment capable of doing not only physical labor but mental tasks as well. Where does all this money come from to make the shift from humans to machines possible? For over forty years, according to Rifkin (1995), banks and insurance companies have been investing billions of dollars of workers' funds in new labor saving technologies, only to eliminate the very workers whose pension fund money is being used. In the end, they might not be around long enough to get the pension.

Throughout much of the twentieth century, a strong recognition existed that the interests of capitalism and of the worker did not always coincide. Labor legislation, passed through the activism of unions, settlement workers, and politicians, curbed the worst abuses in the industrialized nations. As unions grew in power, they were able to demand for their workers pay increases, reduced hours, and fringe benefits. Since 1980, however, in the face of fierce international competition and advanced technologies, the bargaining power of labor has been seriously eroded, especially in the United States where labor interests were not represented within a political party and have had little leverage accordingly.

Link Between Work and the Family

Social change in one central area of life often has important ramifications in other areas. So it is with economic change and the family. As new technologies revolutionized the way work was conducted, the functioning of families was altered. This, in turn, altered the capacity of families to meet the needs of their members through mutual aid. When the Industrial Revolution swept across Europe, and later in other countries, there was a steady migration to factories located along rivers as sources of power. The separation of home and workplace marked a pivotal change in the structure and composition of the family. A vastly increased mobility of the population accompanied industrialization. We witness the impact in currently industrializing nations—movement from the countryside to the booming city; the daily commute between home and work; movement within an occupation to different specializations; periodic transfers from one place of work to another; socially upward mobility in reference to family of origin. With industrialization, families are uprooted and pushed into a situation of worker dependence on the employer company and labor market for a livelihood. With cumulatively changing technology, skills become obsolete and the stress of worker competition mounts. The impact on the family has been so consequential (some would say devastating) that, as Wilensky and Lebeaux (1965) suggest, much of social welfare service may relate indirectly to the demands made on the family by the forces of modernization.

In her historical overview of the family, Kamerman (1995) attributes the "stripping the family of its traditional functions" to the multifaceted social change associated with the Industrial Revolution. Broadly, the history of modernization can be described as a story of the loss to the family of its educational, religious, social control, and vocational functions as formal and bureaucratic structures arise to meet the needs. Schools, churches, prisons, and workshops come into play. Kamerman stresses the impact of such changes on young people: In addition to the physical separation of parents and children, new technologies and labor recruitment have made it possible for youths to work and obtain independence. Compulsory public education emerged out of society's desire to socialize youth and to prepare them to be a disciplined work force. In her provocative book, *The Overworked American*, Schor (1991) takes this argument one step further: As the first generation of workers were, on the whole, a motley crew with poor work habits, the school was now looked to to break the laboring classes into docility. Putting small children to work at school for very long hours at dull subjects habituated them to labor and monotony.

The breakup of the economically self-sufficient extended family is a concomitant of the factory system and commercial agriculture everywhere (Wilensky and Lebeaux, 1965). As the nuclear family relocates near the source of labor, the emphasis is on youth and the elderly get left behind, no longer an active part of the family unit. In the industrial society, parenthood no longer provides old-age insurance. In this type of society, similarly, marriage fails to provide life-time security either. With extended kinship systems thus loosened through geographical and social mobility, the pressures put on the small nuclear family are enormous. Simultaneously, pressures forcing unhappy couples to stay together are weakened as community ties are weakened. As women in non-agricultural societies have fewer children and as their work tends to be independent of their spouses, they are able, if need be, to make it on their own. The breakup of the extended family and close-knit community, therefore, is often accompanied by a disintegration of the nuclear family as well.

Philip Slater (1976), in *The Pursuit of Loneliness,* a popular but grim sociological treatise of the 1970s, dealt with the chronic sources of stress in American society stemming from the extreme competitiveness and depersonalization of everyday life. Slater also probed the connection between households and the market economy. He viewed the history of industrial capitalism as one long, sad story of economic functions being "sucked out of the home" and put into the industrial market where they came to be performed by larger and larger organizations. Becoming less rooted to each other at the local community level, individuals found themselves increasingly at the mercy of uncaring and distant bureaucracies. The process of which Slater wrote has been going on for over a hundred years.

Every now and then in the course of human history along comes an innovation, a breakthrough perhaps, that opens the door to another and another. We live during such a time, as we might say, of invention spawning invention, and of rapid social change the historical essence of which it is still too early to digest. This much we know or will know soon: Because of new technologies, a revolution is underway in the workplace. According to Green (1995: 322), what we are experiencing is "the decomposition of the national working classes upon whose struggles the social welfare states were based." Cahill (1994: 17), similarly, bemoans the "decline in the traditional core of the industrial working class," while Hutton (1995: 2) refers simply to the "revolution in men's employment patterns." The latter two writers are viewing events from the eastern side of the Atlantic, but in America, too, we can observe the entire occupational structure shifting throughout this post-industrial world. In short, this nation's and much of the world's economy is undergoing a transformation of depth and scope which we can compare to other historic movements—for example, the industrial revolution and the shift to mass production techniques or Fordism. As in earlier times, the victims of progress are hardworking, respected people, who find themselves no longer needed by society. Against the clamor of "welfare reformers" for workfare and job training, U.S. Secretary of Labor Robert Reich (1994: 36), acknowledges that "the comfortable landscape of steady, sturdy mass production and rock-solid corporations has been altered irrevocably." In many countries today, in essence, much of the population is becoming simply surplus: unemployed or underemployed, impoverished, and discarded (Rifkin, 1995).

The social consequences of having a surplus population are severe: When there is an absence of attractive, remunerative employment for men, the marriage rate of pregnant females goes down. Yet families headed by single parents are particularly vulnerable to high levels of stress caused by role overload and continuing economic struggle. Unable to maintain a home, pay for higher education for their children, save for retirement, or maintain their purchasing power, the stress on poor families is palpable. In all families, when there is a shortage of money, tensions mount and conflict often develops among individual members. Members may blame themselves or each other for problems that are external to themselves and to their community. Such family crisis is occurring not only in North America but universally. In Mexico City, small children are sometimes literally tied to their beds while the parents work. This lack of childcare is a worldwide phenomenon, as a report on world trends released by the Population Council in New York states (Knight-Ridder, 1995). Increasingly, according to this report, mothers are raising children alone and also working outside the home; fathers are absent because they have migrated for work and/or formed new families; and children are at high risk of being poor and left to fend for themselves. In terms of workload, women everywhere are found to work many more hours than men when nonpaid work is counted.

A second aspect of what can be viewed as a backlash against labor and the laborer is somewhat unique to the United States. This backlash, for workers who are not laid off, is the rise of the number of hours in their average workweek. During the 1980s, as Schor (1991) documents, companies reduced the length of vacations, rest periods, and other paid time off. Under conditions of cutthroat competition for work, legal protection for employees was eroded. Furthermore, with a majority of U.S. workers experiencing a steady decline in the value of their wages, workers were finding it necessary to work more hours to make ends meet. While even in Japan vacations have grown longer (now up to three weeks), in the United States, they have grown shorter. Parents spend less time with their children who are often left at home due to inadequate or unaffordable childcare. The human toll of those who overwork and of those who underwork will be considered in a later section of this chapter.

According to Johnson and Schwartz (1994), one of the reasons we need a strong social welfare system as a safety valve is to help individuals and their families make the adjustment to a world in which they suddenly may have become alien because of rapid social change. While the effect of the global marketplace is transforming the conditions of work and the bargaining power of workers, family welfare is being threatened from another front as well. Theisen and Waltz (1995) provide the historical context for welfare developments in the United States. Whereas welfare reform proposals from the Kennedy through the Reagan administrations stressed the responsibility of the state for meeting the needs of the vulnerable, a major welfare policy shift occurred in the nineties. Three dimensions of this policy shift set it apart from previous models. As delineated by Theisen and Waltz, the first dimension is the reconceptualization of welfare recipients as *victims* of the welfare program which encourages nonwork, teen pregnancy, and "illegitimacy." The second dimension extolls *work* as an end in itself, quite apart from whether or not money earned is sufficient to meet the family's basic needs. Third, the *responsibilities* of the recipients of aid to the state to train for work or find work are stressed in the form of a written contract. Above all else, the idea that aid is strictly temporary is a guiding principle.

Under what Theisen and Waltz correctly call "the new model of public welfare," a reformulation of welfare has quietly taken place. Society's sense of obligation to the poor and to their children, a notion that has been with us for the better part of a century, is no more. Perhaps, as Theisen and Waltz dramatically suggest, this reformulation is the most important change since the Social Security Act replaced the poor laws.

A similar change forcing the poor to work low-paying jobs is underway in the United Kingdom as well. The British Conservative agenda is a crusade for intensified individualism and self-reliance, argues journalist Hutton (1995), and for welfare "claimants," the agenda calls for more rigid eligibility requirements. Despite all the moral panic about single mothers depending on the state for support, the problem is in the declining wages paid to the "underclass." The attack on workers is no accident. As Hutton (2) puts it:

> The willingness to run the economy with a reserve army of unemployed to lower inflation, the weakening of trade unions and the build-up of pressure on companies to achieve impossibly high financial returns, has interacted with the powerful forces of new technology and international trade to transform the prospects for men's work. At the bottom of society this has produced near desperation in a brutish fight for survival.

From the family standpoint, the quality of life will be less than what it has been in decades past as societal forces combine to encourage more members of the family to work especially in the low-paying, service industries. As Hutton (1995: 3) realistically predicts, "Conditions for the millions at the bottom of our society, already tough, will get tougher still."

WORK AND THE GLOBAL ECONOMY

The attack on workers' rights is virtually worldwide. In one advanced country after another, the revolution in computer and information technology has contributed to rising profits and productivity, while eliminating blue collar jobs or sending them elsewhere. Middle management is being eliminated as well. Business profits are up and not *in spite of* but *because of* continually falling wages. What is happening here?

For an understanding of globalization and its impact on work, it is necessary to grasp the nature of some of the technologies linking (but also locking) the world in tight interdependency. The impact of information technology has been momentous. Micro electronics, the routine and widespread application of computer technology, has revolutionized the manufacture and distribution of goods and services (Cahill, 1994). With the enhanced access to information which computers provide, many workers have seen their efficiency and horizons expand.

For the first time in history, large numbers of people can be freed from tedious, mindless tasks with no overall threat to the nation's levels of productivity. For students, the process of doing a research paper is greatly expedited as, within minutes, a computer program available at most libraries, provides an extensive bibliography complete with article abstracts. In much the same way, the fax machine and electronic mail can bring messages from around the world into our living rooms instantaneously. The possibilities are exciting and far-reaching. The information highway, according to computer magnate Bill Gates (1995), is better understood as "the ultimate market." This market, he says, will enable capabilities that seem magical when they are described, but represent technology at work to make our lives easier and better. In diminishing the salience of national borders, the new information technology means that a government (for example, Iraq) can no longer control the flow of information in or out of the country. For people oppressed by their governments, this access to world news can be a godsend. In short, although the pace of change is fast enough to be scary, few who experience the wonders of such things as cyberspace will be willing to turn the clock back.

The new information technology has heralded an age in which industrial production is being organized on a global basis: one important ramification is that a product now can be manufactured in one country and assembled in another. The transfer of semi-skilled jobs overseas is hardly new. The shift is taking place, however, at an accelerating rate and involves ever-higher paying jobs (Bradsher, 1995). Computer programmers in India, for instance, are fluent in English, highly trained in computer science, and willing to work for a fraction of their American counterparts. The pressure on corporations, as we have seen, to cut costs and raise profits in order to survive in a competitive global market encourages management to downsize their operations and look to foreign labor to meet their production needs. The lion's share of the growth in the United States (in Canada and Britain also) is being captured by the top 20 percent of the labor force (McCarron, 1995). The political and economic consequences of this trend have yet to be acknowledged.

One point that should be clarified is the implication that an industrialized country's loss is the low-wage country's gain. The cheap-labor-abroad phenomenon is more a legacy of earlier industrial technologies of mass production than the way of the future. The new labor-saving technology has simply not reached many places yet.

"To begin with," explains Rifkin (1995: 5), an economist who takes an international perspective, "more than 75 percent of the labor force in most industrial nations engage in work that is little more than simple repetitive tasks." With current surveys showing less than 5 percent of companies around the world having even begun to make the transition from human workers to machine surrogates, the implications are profound and far-reaching. Today, claims Rifkin, we are at the dawn of the Third Industrial Revolution. As supranational companies build high-tech production facilities throughout the world, the ranks of the unemployed and underemployed are growing. The fact that the labor cuts are deliberate and facilitated in the new machine culture is confirmed by our corporate leaders who do not reveal their business decisions and are quoted in business news sources such as the *Wall Street Journal* and *Forbes.* In order to stay "competitive" they are restructuring the workplace to end labor as we know it, or increasingly *knew* it. For the chief executives, meanwhile, pay is skyrocketing. Whereas in the 1970s, the typical chief executive officer of a large American company earned about 40 times as much as a typical worker, now he or she earns 190 times as much! (Cassidy, 1995). Their yearly earnings, typically, are in the millions.

When the Mobil Corporation, as reported on page one of the *Wall Street Journal* (Murray, 1995), posted soaring first quarter earnings one week and then the plan to eliminate 4,700 jobs the next week, employees were baffled. Generally workers assumed that following the necessary period of leanness and sacrifice the layoffs would stop when profits increased. But, according to the article, they were wrong. While corporate profits were surging to record levels last year, the number of job cuts approached those seen at the height of the recession. Corporate restructuring is not a sign of trouble but of progress, as a Procter and Gamble chief executive explained when his company began slashing jobs. As the article further points out, when there are layoffs the stock market prices go up. In more and more countries, observes Rifkin (5), "the news is filled with talk about lean production, re-engineering, total quality management, post-Fordism, decruiting, and downsizing." In the future, it will not be a competition between one country's labor against another country's labor; it will be a competition between labor and machines which machines will win. The workerless factory and workerless office will have become realities.

AGRICULTURE

The nature of modern agriculture has been experiencing a high-technology revolution for years. Widespread use of chemical pesticides and herbicides associated with this type of land usage promotes high productivity with little land and few farm laborers. In their study of capital-intensive agricultural development, anthropologists Barlett and Brown (1994) examine the impact on the quality of life and the ability of people to meet their needs. As the forces of an increasing population, land shortage, and the desire for consumer goods combine, the temptation is to plant high-yield monoculture crops, often for international export. A typical country succumbing to these forces is Costa Rica where the process of agricultural intensification has occurred rapidly in one generation. In Costa Rica, the cultivation of tobacco, a highly profitable crop, makes possible the purchase of modern consumer goods. Through the use of dangerous chemicals, several other crops can be produced on one plot of land. In light of damage to the ecosystem and the demands for expensive equipment to maximize production, risky indebtedness results. As Barlett and Brown thoughtfully conclude, as cultures change things become different, not necessarily better.

The massive displacement and dislocation of farm labor over the past century has deprived millions of people of their chosen livelihood. Through mechanical, biological, and chemical innovations, productivity has risen considerably. Fewer and bigger farms have been the end result. Today in Iowa, work is well underway on a robot-tractor that will plow the fields by remote control.

On a global basis, unsustainable land use has led to desertification, deforestation, and environmental contamination. China, the rice capital of the world, is facing an agricultural upheaval according to a report in *The Wall Street Journal* (Kahn, 1995). Eclipsing a five thousand year history of peasant agriculture, modernization is claiming the land. Grain output, consequently, can't keep pace with the soaring demand as arable land is sacrificed for industry and meat production. Heavy importation of wheat will be necessary to feed a nation that contains one-fifth of the world population on only one-fifteenth of its arable land.

While all of the Central American countries have been devoting substantial effort to industrialization, agriculture has been an important part of their attempts to finance this process (DeWalt, 1994). Export agriculture in combination with cheap food policies is an essential part of the Southern Hemisphere's linkage with the world market. The goal of the export is to earn scarce foreign exchange. The change in land use patterns has been dramatic. Poor and indigenous people have been displaced. In Mexico, the increased concentration of land ownership in the hands of a few has led to violent uprising and much political unrest. (Read of the Chiapas rebellion in chapter 10). Throughout Latin

America, much of the land is now devoted to pasture for cattle, an export commodity that employs relatively little labor. And peasant agriculturalists have become an underemployed urban poor struggling to survive as shoeshine boys, servants, and street vendors, as DeWalt indicates. This is the key point of relevance for our discussion of work and the global economy: the destruction of the small farms in a market economy makes for decreasing employment possibilities for the populace.

FREE TRADE AGREEMENTS AND COMPETITION

Unique among economists of his day, Karl Marx saw capitalism as inherently expansionist. Marx further conceived of a state of affairs in which this expansionist drive would lead to the fashioning of an international division of labor in which one part of the globe is transformed into primarily agricultural production for the other part's primarily industrial production (Harrington, 1977). The north/south gap, notes Harrington, was based on slavery and conquest and then, in the nineteenth century, it was deepened and institutionalized by means of the world market. Marx and Engels' brilliant insights from the *The Communist Manifesto* (1848: 30) address this in the following passage which perhaps has more relevance today than when it was written:

> By exploitation of the world market, the bourgeoisie has given a cosmopolitan character to production and consumption in every land. To the despair of the reactionaries, it has deprived industry of its national foundation. Of the old-established national industries, some have already been destroyed and others are day by day undergoing destruction. They are dislodged by new industries, whose introduction is becoming a matter of life and death for all civilized nations: by industries which no longer depend upon the homeland for their raw materials, but draw these from the remotest spots; and by industries whose products are consumed, not only in the country of manufacture, but the wideworld over. Instead of the old wants, satisfied by the products of native industry, new wants appear, wants which can only be satisfied by the products of distant lands and unfamiliar climes. . . . It forces all the nations, under pain of extinction, to adopt the capitalist method of production; it constrains them to accept what is called civilization, to become bourgeois themselves. In short, it creates a world after its own image.

A fact that is striking to the reader of world press reports is of the commonality of trends the world over. At international conferences the question on every attender's lips is, "Oh, is that happening in your country too?" International trade alliances between nations standardizes an item's production and costs; free trade agreements hasten the relocation of plants, not so much for the cheap labor available any more as to be near a potential new market (Rifkin, 1995). Highly automated plants are now going up in droves along the border towns of northern Mexico. Any new jobs are offered to a work force of highly skilled technicians. There is one hitch to the capitalists' plan, however, and we may see this worldwide. When the worker suffers, the economy will eventually suffer too. For when people have no money, who then will be able to afford the products? Take Mexico as an example. Despite, a recent economic upturn leading to a rise in the stock market and general improvements in the beleaguered Mexican economy, small businesses are closing down, losing out to the international market. As in North America, whole sectors such as textiles and electronics have, with Mexico's entry into the North American Free Trade Agreement (NAFTA), collapsed under the pressure of Asian imports. With one-third of Mexico's work force now unemployed or underemployed, the buying power has decreased also. Car sales, for instance, have plummeted 56 percent (LaFranchi, 1995). As Canadian professor Hellman (1994) makes clear in her book, *Mexican Lives*, free trade has in fact turned into a personal catastrophe for many of the Mexican people.

The deleterious effects of globalization on social welfare in Canada are spelled out by Broad (1995). These effects mainly stem from the heavy job loss, now estimated to be over half a million, due to open trade between the United States and Canada. Underemployment and economic insecurity accompany the job layoffs. The increase in part-time, temporary labor is leading to impoverishment. In Canada, the issue is highly volatile. At the International Social Welfare in a Changing World Conference held at the University of Calgary in 1995, a heated panel discussion on NAFTA was very revealing, perhaps more for the depth of the sentiments expressed than for the facts presented. But the points made were compelling as well: the gap between rich and poor in Mexico, Canada, and the United States continues to increase under the NAFTA agreement; the rhetoric of free trade is only rhetoric — Canada is not moving toward free trade but toward global economics; the restrictions in favor of business are great. A politician who has supported NAFTA pointed to the many jobs created as a result; the largely Canadian audience angrily pointed to the loss of well-paying jobs, weakening of labor unions, loss in support for the arts and culture, and of social benefits.

No place in the world, in short, is exempt from the pressure to cut corners. In Japan, where unemployment previously had been barely known, fears are mounting that companies will have to slash as much as 20 percent of their white collar work force to match the low overhead of U.S.-based companies. So far women workers, many in part-time jobs, are bearing the brunt of the downsizing. In a country with the tradition of benevolent paternalism and keeping a job for life, the realities are devastating. In the European Union (E.U.), worker protection has been provided through improved labor standards legislation (Broad, 1995). Workers can move freely among the countries; agreements are currently being reached to recognize professional credentials cross-nationally. Students can attend universities throughout the E.U. as well. Perhaps the most promising dimension of the E.U. is its attention to social problems, especially those that transcend national boundaries. For instance, the Commission of the European Union, in anticipation of workers' displacement, has taken a stand in favor of shortening the work week for everyone. (NAFTA would do well to emulate this position).

On the negative side, the leveling of standards mandated in the agreement is resulting in serious "adjustments" in welfare programs in Denmark, Finland, and Sweden. Farmers cannot be subsidized as they have been — their produce will have to compete with food grown much more cheaply in southern Europe, and women stand to lose many of their special benefits. Accordingly, much political controversy has ensued throughout Scandinavia over some of the consequences of Europeanization to these welfare states and is referred to within the E.U. as the "north/south divide."

In September, 1995, I attended a social work conference of agency practice teachers for field placement at the University of Warwich, England. The impact of the E.U. in terms of stepped-up competition and stress on productivity and cost-effectiveness was strongly evidenced in the presentations and small group discussions following. "What are some of the paradoxes in your social work practice?" asked one speaker. The audience provided the following responses (most speakers were quite emotional):

- Training people for jobs that are disappearing.
- Quality standards are raised, yet there is not time to do all the work.
- The lack of resources and lack of time to meet the new demands and increased workloads.

- Being forced to be highly competitive and to document everything as opposed to valuing working together.
- The diminishing role of social work under the shift to care management.
- The feeling of being encouraged to "sell out" for the sake of bureaucracy.
- The valuing of the need to provide evidence for outcomes over the quality of the work itself—quality assurance has become quantity assurance.
- Using a model that comes from industry, viewing the clients as products.

The above quotes from the English social workers are presented in full because they demonstrate that not only in industry and agriculture, but even in the helping professions (the medical world will be looked at in the next chapter) the accelerated pace of work and pressure to produce are strongly felt and actively resented. Although the terminology is distinctively British and unique to social work, the themes are universal of the workplace in the high-tech era. Social work faculty at many universities in Britain and the United States are suffering under new forms of coercion and subtle intimidation to produce tangible results (i.e., publications) while teaching demands are accelerated. Accountability to supervisors who must verify the office's output to external agencies is indicative of the kinds of sweeping "reforms" that are redefining every aspect of white collar and service work. Many in computer software industry compare the paperless office (with most clerical work eliminated) to the cashless society and expect to see much more of this sort of thing in the short run (Rifkin, 1995). Many social workers and social work faculty work directly in front of the computer, processing an unending stream of information. Clerical help has been replaced, for the most part, by machines.

In *The Welfare State Crisis and the Transformation of Social Service Work*, social work professors Fabricant and Burghardt (1992) helpfully provide a neo-Marxist framework to analyze contemporary trends which are alienating human service workers from their craft. A major complaint involves the bureaucratization associated with increased emphasis on worker productivity and quantifiable outcomes. Increasing administrative demands reduce the scope for creative problem-solving. Comparing an agency to a factory, the authors decry the new constraints on human service workers robbing them of initiative and control over the goals, values, and meaning of work. Human service workers are further alienated and "proletarianized," as Fabricant and Bughardt suggest, by the deprofessionalization or deskilling of jobs. By this process, newly mechanized tasks are passed on to lower-paid occupational groups, thus effectively depriving workers of their bargaining leverage. Finally, new accountability and structural demands that have been imposed upon agencies by the state have also brought about a reduction in professional autonomy and control. As one worker states (163), "I feel so much of the time we are cold, distant. . . . Just moving people through as we fill out their forms."

In short, the emergence of a common global market and labor pool associated with free trade agreements has had an effect on all levels of work in all parts of the world. The pressures to produce have grown so overwhelming that much of the fun and creativity, even from the most rewarding of work, is rapidly vanishing and job security is departing along with it. Shortly, the human toll will be discussed. But first, to carry the metaphor of the factory assembly line further, we will turn to a provocative book on the process of McDonaldization.

THE McDONALDIZATION OF WORK

Interchangeable workers, homogenization of the product, standardized work routines, and rigid technologies — these are among the characteristics of the fast-food restaurant singled out by sociologist George Ritzer (1993) in his popular book (especially in Britain) *The McDonaldization of Society*. The process by which the principles of the fast-food restaurant "are coming to dominate more and more sections of American society as well as of the rest of the world" (1) is epitomized in the global McDonald's chain, according to Ritzer. Not only characteristic of the restaurant business, the process is also affecting education, travel, organized leisure-time activities, politics, the family, and of course, work itself. Significantly, the term *Mc* has come to symbolize mass-produced services as in *Mc*Dentists, *Mc*Papers, *Mc*Day Care. The McDonald's model has succeeded because where time is a premium in a work-crazed society, it offers the consumer efficiency, predictability, and food for little money. For the worker, however, the setting is often dehumanizing; the average fast-food worker lasts only three months. Workers take no pride in their work or creations, they only pride themselves on the speed with which it is performed. The new technologies take care of most of the "brain" work, even down to filling cups with Coca-Cola and determining when the french fries are done. Pseudo-interactions with customers are as predictable as the food. Parting messages such as "Have a nice day," or at the department store, "Thank you for shopping at K-Mart," seemingly provide a personal touch. Despite the pseudo-personal atmosphere at the fast-food restaurant, business is the first priority. To prevent customers from lingering too long when the restaurant needs tables to be vacated quickly, seats are designed to make a customer feel uncomfortable after twenty minutes, as Ritzer carefully documents.

Speed and efficiency come to a head in a singularly bizarre way—the installing of high-tech, computerized hiring systems to screen job applications. Rifkin (*The End of Work*, 1995) describes the process in detail: An optical scanner stores images of a résumé in a computer database. In less than three seconds the résumé can be scanned to generate the appropriate acknowledgment letter. Applications are then processed by the computers and relegated to the appropriate job category. Personal sounding replies are sent to each hopeful applicant.

Most of the gains in efficiency, as Ritzer observes in *The McDonaldization of Society,* are on the side of those who are pushing rationalization upon us. Is it more efficient, for instance, to pump your own gas or use exact change on a bus? Are prerecorded voices on the telephone responsive to our needs? Borrowing from Max Weber, Ritzer shows how, with greater and greater bureaucratization, the rational has become *irrational*. In agreement with Rifkin's major thesis in *The End of Work*, Ritzer predicts that the most likely response to complaints about dehumanization of the worker will be simply to eliminate more and more of the humans. Since McDonaldization is here to stay and the advantages are numerous, the author provides these suggestions to combat it:

- Reading *The New York Times* rather than *USA Today* once a week.
- Watching PBS instead of the commercial station.
- Avoiding large college classes or courses where tests are computer-graded.
- Dining at a local "greasy spoon" instead of McDonald's.

The implications of the McDonaldization trend are worldwide. Fast-food restaurants are taking off in Russia and China along with trends toward uniformity in work, while the thrust toward "irrational rationality" is well underway in Europe. So far, some countries such as Sweden (which has experimented with breaking the assembly-line monotony in the automobile industry) and Japan (with its tradition of company-worker loyalty) have managed to resist the most noxious aspects of the rationalized workplace. Yet, in Sweden and Japan, both having some of the world's most highly advanced technology, automated vehicles and robots are replacing humans at a rapid rate.

WOMEN AND WORK

There are a lot of things I'd like to change. But what I'd like to see most is mutual respect. Now it's like a dictatorship. You can't get sick. You get a mark against you if you stay home sick — even if the plant doctor sends you home. You don't get paid. After eight marks, you're fired. And you can't stay home to take care of a sick child. I have kids and the majority of the people I work with on the line have kids. — Poultry Worker in Woodland, N.C. (Monagle, 1995): 33.

Because work of the paid variety is somehow deemed more important to men than to women, and men rather than women are considered more important to work, most of the studies in this area are of males. The American workplace, like that in other countries, is still very much of a frontier for women. The statistics represent this. Information from the Human Development Report on women in the United States (United Nations, 1995a) reveals:

- In the assessment of women's access to professional, economic, and political opportunities, the United States ranks eighth (following Sweden, Norway, Finland, Denmark, Canada, New Zealand and the Netherlands).
- Women in the United States have 35 percent of the nation's earned income; their wages for nonagricultural jobs average 74 percent of men's.
- On the human development index, a U.N. index ranking countries according to standard of living variables, racial and ethnic disparities are so great that, regardless of gender, whites would rank 1st in the world, blacks 27th, and Hispanics 32nd.
- Women occupy 40 percent of the United States' managerial and administrative jobs (compared to 14 percent for the world), and 10 percent of seats in state and federal legislatures (compared to 10 percent for the world).

The U.N. Human Development Report also concluded that in virtually every country women work longer hours (much of them unpaid) than men, yet women share less in economic rewards. The idea that men are the primary workers of the world is therefore a myth. Globally, women earn 75 percent of men's average nonfarm wages. Among the 1.3 million people in the world living in poverty, 70 percent are women. The average number of working hours a day for work of all kinds done by married women who are employed and have children in industrial countries is eleven. In its summary, the Human Development Report indicates that since 1970, women have progressed considerably in education and health, but are lagging far behind men in earnings and political power.

Other sources indicate that women's work force participation rates in the United States rose to 58.8 percent in 1994 (*Wall Street Journal*, 1995) and to 45 percent in Canada where women's earnings total 72 percent of men's earnings (Steele, 1995). The percentage of working mothers with children has increased steadily; it is now 73.6 percent (Gottlieb, 1995). African American women, out of necessity, traditionally have had higher work force participation rates than have white women and from 1970 to 1991 African American women's proportion in the work force went to 62.6 percent (Gottlieb, 1995). In Japan, women upon marriage in their late twenties leave the work force in vast numbers; Japanese women earn 59 percent what their male counterparts earn (Barr, 1995). These women's work statistics may be misleading, however, as Nichols-Casebolt et al. (1994) indicate, because wages in the informal sector (not to mention unpaid work) are not counted in these figures. Informal work includes home-based assembly work, sewing at home, growing and harvesting food for the family, and housecleaning.

The economic devaluation of women exacts a huge toll worldwide in a manner rarely understood in the West, according to Dentzer (1995). Because their daughters earn less than their sons, parents in poor countries often invest less in their daughters, especially with regard to education and health care. In consideration of the fact that well over one hundred million women are in effect "missing" from the planet, the presumed victims of premature and preventable deaths, the opening of educational and occupational opportunities for women is crucial.

Because of the growing realization of the desperate need to invest in women's future, as Dentzer indicates, more than one-third of the World Bank's $180 billion in loans to developing countries is now geared to addressing gender issues. Still, imperatives in the global economy associated with the phasing out of state-controlled industries, cut backs in social welfare programs, and the loss of available farm land, have worsened women's socio-economic condition significantly. Perhaps, as Johnson and Kramer (1995) suggest, under the present system of global economics and finance, it is a near impossibility to achieve global sustainability and successful social development. Women — the victims of the economic crisis and structural adjustment strategies imposed by international financial institutions — have been negatively affected in virtually every type of economic activity as employment, income, and conditions of work have deteriorated (United Nations, 1995b).

Working Conditions

The disadvantaged position of women in many societies and communities today is a major manifestation of what Midgley (1995) calls *distorted development*. Distorted development exists in societies where economic development has not been matched by a concomitant level of social development, and where prosperity has been achieved through exploiting natural resources, according to Midgley. With the advent of the global economy, there is a great potential for the exploitation of women and girls (Nichols-Casebolt et al., 1994). As a result of the development of cash crops, women are spending more hours engaged in tasks such as the collection of fuel, fodder, and water. In severely deforested areas of India, for example, the typical rural woman and her children now spend four to five hours per day gathering enough fuel for their evening meal.

In subsistence economies, as people are moved off the land, they gravitate to cities. Many get jobs in the formal sector in shoddily constructed factories. Because women lack labor organizing experience, can be paid low wages, and will tolerate frequent job turnover with no security, they are hired by the thousands (Wetzel, 1993). As the Communist nations such as Vietnam begin to participate in the global market and privatize, the new opportunities are not always beneficial to women (Gillotte, 1994). In newly booming economies, girls may be removed from school and higher education to help their families by working in the new factories. Harsh economic reality also takes its toll in Thailand and Russia where girls are forced or enticed into prostitution, a matter that will be discussed in chapter 10. One source of revenue in many poor countries are sex tours patronized by Western men. Most of the big prostitution operations in Asian countries were developed to service foreign troops. The disadvantaged, abuse-prone situations of women in countries in which North American factories are relocating are replicated when women become immigrants in countries like the United States. Horror stories of illegal exploitation abound. A shocking case involves seamstresses from Thailand who were lured into debt bondage in Los Angeles to be locked (literally) in a sweatshop. Those trying to escape were beaten, after which their photograph might be thrown onto the laps of others to warn them of their fate if they tried to get away (Scheer, 1995). Although this situation is an extreme example of brutal mistreatment of undocumented workers—poor, rural, single, and female—this kind of exploitation of desperate immigrant workers is widespread in many of the industrialized countries.

Single Mothers

In the United States in 1994, 65 percent of black children lived in single parent families compared to 36 percent of Hispanics and 25 percent of whites. The large majority of these families are headed by females. The Hispanic child is the most likely to live in a three-generational household (U.S. Census Bureau, 1994).

Single mothers are a marginalized population worldwide. The active stigmatization of this group gives national permission to keep these women out of the economy (Wijnberg and Weinger, 1995). Societal barriers, both religious and legal, can subordinate single women on an international scale. In order to assess the meaning of work for single mothers, Wijnberg and Weinger surveyed English and American mothers. What they found, not unexpectedly, is that mothers who achieve full-time worker or student status develop supportive network arrangements and have high life and work aspirations. Many others, however, have their dreams shattered by the harshness of the economic and social scene.

Baker (1995) pursues a similar theme in her study of work and employability of mothers in eight industrialized countries. At opposite ends of the social welfare spectrum, Sweden and the United States encourage mothers to enter the labor force. While Sweden bolsters the mother with support to help her combine work and family life, the United States leaves her to wrestle with the market forces without statutory leave, benefits, or childcare services. Accordingly, the economic status of lone mothers in the United States is low relative to that of countries like Sweden with universal benefits for families. Britain and the Netherlands, in contrast to both the United States and Sweden, accept lower working rates for mothers with small children in the belief that they provide important childcare services at home.

Taking a somewhat different tack, Eveline (1994) compares Australian and Swedish affirmative action programs geared to address labor inequality. The idea that the concept of work in modern society conforms to the male model of the worker is the underlying thesis of Eveline's study. In Australia the male model, for instance, is evident in the dearth of childcare facilities, in the lack of paid parental leave, and in the differential between time spent by women and men in unpaid caring and household work. Affirmative action schemes often produce an exaggerated level of visibility combined with social isolation and tokenism. Relative to Australia, Sweden is struggling with innovative legislation to accord men an equal place in child — and household — care. Sweden's "Free Men" parental leave campaign of 1989 encouraging fathers of small children to take a paternity leave for childcare has been partially but not wholly successful.

An issue of concern to all working mothers, but especially to single mothers, is how to care for small children and work at the same time. A world perspective on childcare woes is offered by Shellenbarger et al. (1995) in the *Wall Street Journal*. Worldwide, according to this report, the availability of childcare shapes women's economic roles in subtle but profound ways. In many countries with extended families breaking down, and women facing mounting pressure to support their families, they are limited to jobs that allow them to keep their children nearby, such as farm work or street vending. Alternatively, older sisters are expected to drop out of school to care for younger children. With exceptions in France and Scandinavia, most women face a trio of day care obstacles: poor availability, high costs, and low quality. In Nigeria, for example, one caretaker may oversee fifty children and basic health and safety practices are ignored. In rural China, it is common for farm workers to leave their four-year-olds unattended at home. Polish women are losing the convenience of state-run preschools under the former regime and now must fend for themselves.

In many parts of Europe, children between three and six years of age attend all day preschool programs associated with the educational system. This is true whether mothers work or not since the experience is widely regarded as beneficial in itself (Bell, 1987). In England, however, good childcare can consume over 35 percent of an individual's typical take-home pay. Once children start school, finding suitable afterschool care is another serious hassle. In the 1980s, the British introduced the word *carer* for home helper into their everyday vocabulary, signifying, according to Cahill (1994), that this form of home care work is now generally accepted as an occupation for which some pay is available. However, the financial support from the central government has been less than adequate and certain restrictions apply. Worldwide, as economist Gary Becker (1995) reports, women contribute about 70 percent of the total time spent at such activities as rearing children, cooking, and nursing the sick — even in egalitarian nations such as Sweden. In poorer nations such as India, women do virtually all the housework.

Importance of Work

Whether a woman chooses to spend time with her children doing unpaid household work — the significance of which tends to be underestimated in our materialistic society—or whether she can find suitable care for her children and work in the paid labor sector has profound implications for a woman's self-esteem. Work, paid or unpaid, can be liberating, oppressive, or somewhere in between depending on the working circumstances and conditions. Governmental policies to boost women (and men) in their caretaking roles are crucial to their personal and economic growth and to children's social well-being.

There are fifty-three million women in the United States earning a paycheck. Women today often are placed in a no-win situation as a result of society's ambivalence concerning mothers' employment. Dependence is a socially devalued concept that, as Miller (1991) rightly suggests, is closely related to caretaking and to women's role in the family ethic. Denounced for their dependence on society if they stay home and receive public assistance and condemned as "bad mothers" if they leave their children to find work, single mothers of small children are placed in a peculiar bind. Mothers in two parent households, similarly, are caught between norms of caregiving and norms of personal achievement. The current political impetus to force welfare mothers into the low-wage, low-skill sectors of the economy (which is about all that is open to them) is being accomplished against a backdrop of political commentary citing women's insistence on working as a factor in the breakdown of the family and, more specifically, in child neglect. In several celebrated child custody cases, preference has been given to the provider who can offer round-the-clock childcare (most often where there is a housewife in the home).

Despite some of its drawbacks, work can be highly meaningful. For a woman, the right job can be instrumental in: providing a source for creative energy of the kind that society rewards; boosting her self-confidence so that she can authoritatively speak on any number of topics; opening the door to a social network for personal empowerment; providing access to activities furthering personal and professional development; broadening her horizons educationally and culturally; raising her status at the familial level; supplying a source of income to meet her and the family's needs; and protecting her from abuse or threats of abuse by offering an avenue to independence and the confidence to take that option if needed. Work, in other words, can do for a woman much of what it does for men plus raise her consciousness as a member of an oppressed minority group. Contrary to myth—that women work only because they have to or that their incomes are only supplemental—work is an integral part of a woman's life, often a source of self-identity (for example, police officer, nurse, teacher) and personal satisfaction (editors, *MS,* 1995). Unfortunately, recent trends favoring management over workers, and neither management nor workers against market forces, are threatening to remove much of the satisfaction from many lines of work.

Trends Affecting Women

A legal secretary states, in an interview on women's work with Monagle (1995: 37), "My job and every other secretary's job is threatened. If firms are able to get computer systems to do the lion's share of secretaries' work, those computers won't require lunch breaks, days off, or benefits. . . . Longevity on the job is more of a handicap than a help now, because they don't want you to have benefits that accrue." Is this not also true of most occupations generally associated with females—telephone operator, bank teller, court reporter, general clerical work, and even nursing? Women's problems, explains Wetzel (1993) are deeply rooted in patriarchal sex discrimination and racism that segregates women in undervalued and underpaid jobs. Because of the connection of domesticity, which tends to be poorly regarded, and women, who are in a disadvantaged position by virtue of gender, anyway, the traditionally female occupations are doubly marginalized. Thus caretaking and home maintenance, work traditionally considered to be women's work, as Wetzel suggests, are viewed as something to undervalue in the first place.

Women's lack of bargaining power and employment alternatives combined with a certain culturally conditioned passive response, has rendered them especially vulnerable to corporations' money-saving schemes such as job reclassification and benefit cut backs. Turning full-time work into contingent work is a favorite ploy. As Judd and Pope (1994) report, women are taking temporary agency jobs, not to have more time at home as is a common claim but rather because employers are creating more temporary positions in the fields in which women typically work. Now one-fourth to one-third of all employees are of the temporary—here today, gone tomorrow—variety. Advantages to the companies who employ temporary workers are many: no health care and pension benefits to worry about, no need to follow protective legislation covering everything from age, sex, and racial discrimination to occupational health and safety (contingent workers are not considered employees although this is being challenged in the courts), and no need to keep workers on when their services are not needed. Particularly hard hit by this trend toward contingent work are women, and especially women of color. Office work, as Judd and Pope indicate, is a gold mine for temporary agencies. As existing jobs disappear, especially in the public sector where jobs are now subcontracted out, women find themselves affected by this second trend and settling for jobs with private companies. Job security and a living wage have become a thing of the past for many workers.

The home health care industry is a case in point. As Wetzel (1993) describes it, in its efforts to contain nursing home costs, the government is saving millions of dollars by creating a sub-employment system characterized by low wages and severely restricted benefits. A ghetto of women of poverty is created, many of whom are African American and Hispanic immigrants. For its workers home health care promotes job insecurity along with lack of opportunity for advancement.

Whether stemming from a trend or a national mood, the growing resentment against women and single mothers, in particular, is affecting the quality of support allocated to them. Even the 1988 Family Support Act intended to ease mothers' transitions from welfare to work exempts women with children under age three and requires only part-time work thereafter—with guaranteed childcare. Congress, along with the religious right now, however, is responding to—or even "manipulating," as Betty Friedan (1995) contends—the white male, economic, insecure rage against women and minorities by pushing mothers of small children into dead-end and low-wage jobs. Growing unemployment and the resultant backlash against women can also be seen in Muslim countries where women have been pushed back under the veil, and in former Soviet countries where women are being told to go back into the home, as Friedan further suggests.

A program that is popular with voters but punitive in many aspects is workfare for recipients of welfare. Many experimental programs in the United States and Canada typically have ended because they cost more to deliver than they save. Since the programs are not cost-saving, they must be designed for more sinister purposes, according to Toupin (1995) who has studied the Canadian proposals. Workfare has become a fully legal policy option for Canadian provinces since April 1996. In Canada, workfare is compulsory work as a condition of receiving benefits. Such workers are not covered by standard labor codes, and are without the right to join unions, or to be paid minimum wage, or take vacations. As a sad outcome of employment programs in Alberta and

Quebec, persons on welfare were hired instead of workers at full wages. One hospital, in fact, laid off permanent workers and replaced them with poorly qualified welfare recipients.

This trend toward using low-paid female labor is worldwide. Throughout Africa, Asia, and Latin America, in countries of high unemployment, the very conditions that make women employable—a willingness to work for dirt-cheap wages—often keep them poor. Some work in unregulated sweatshops, but even more are working in the home, according to a hard-hitting report by the World Watch Institute (Misch, 1992). "Off the books" and invisible to labor statisticians, the so-called *informal* sector or hidden labor force toils at arduous tasks— often in health-threatening conditions—for industries that pay them exploitative "piece rates" or payment according to output. Predominantly female homeworkers, usually illegal immigrants, are working under equally intolerable conditions in Europe and the United States as well, as we learned in the scandal of enslaved Thai immigrant seamstresses described earlier. A very different variety of homeworker involves the use of a computer at home. Women teleworkers, as Cahill (1994) calls them, mostly do clerical tasks taking instructions from employers. Wages are low and room for advancement is nil.

Writing in the (London) *Observer,* Whitehorn (1995: 6) tells of "a future that has to be perpetually renegotiated" in "the great drive to keep employees on their toes by constantly reassessing performance and giving short contracts." Workers, accordingly, may find themselves "on the scrapheap in their thirties." The blows to men in manufacturing, meanwhile, create havoc in the family and intensify pressures on their wives to be successful providers. The end of "jobs for life" is leading, not surprisingly, to an epidemic of stress-related illnesses, the details of which will become evident following the discussion on solutions.

Solutions

Lack of economic resources is a major obstacle to single mothers and women whose husbands face "redundancy." A further obstacle affecting primarily women is the caregiving responsibility for ailing family members. Strategies are desperately needed to act as a buffer against the contingencies of childcare crises (illness, school closings, and lack of affordable day care services) and caregiving of elderly or disabled relatives. Both of these create serious gaps in women's employment histories affecting their careers adversely as well as their contributions to private pension plans. Women's expanded participation in the labor force is associated with increased nursing home placement of family members in need of care. Strand (1995) points to an obvious solution: a universal system of benefits for families with children so that women can move between the work and home without losing income supports for day care and medical care. Gustafsson (1994) describes the mother-friendly Swedish arrangement in which the mothers work twenty to thirty-four hours per week or "long part-time" rather than working long hours or not at all. This pattern is facilitated by public policies including fifteen months paid parental leave, subsidized high quality childcare, and the right to work a six-hour day until the child is eight. Under required adjustment to E.U. standards, however, such family benefits may be reduced. Hooyman and Gonyea (1995) recommend adequate public support for home-based family care and other extensive community-based services to families. The availability of such services would lessen the economic burden on women caretakers considerably, reduce the institutionalization of the disabled and frail elderly, and create new jobs in the community at the same time.

Rifkin's focus is on women's tendency to work excessive hours—eighty hours a week sum-total on the job and in the home is the U.S. average. For workers in the United States, it is basically an all-or-nothing proposition—carry extended work schedules or be laid off. Several unions representing women are negotiating for shorter hours and/or work weeks.

From a global perspective, Midgley (1995) emphasizes the need to involve women, a population whose needs have been almost entirely overlooked by international development agencies in development efforts. He advocates the empowerment approach for social change. This approach, notes Midgley, attributes women's subjugation not only to patriarchy but to imperialism and neocolonialism. To achieve control over their lives, women must mobilize through a grass-roots strategy of campaigning and organizing. Successful examples of such empowerment efforts are campaigns for legal rights in the Philippines and for improved housing conditions in Bombay. As Stein (1992) reveals, female income generating groups, organized as a collective in Costa Rica, offer many positive benefits for the women involved. The income earned raised members' status within their families which was measured in terms of economic and sexual control, bargaining, and independence. However, argues Stein, measures need to be taken to provide workers in the informal sector with the benefits that workers in the formal sector receive—for example, a retirement plan and the complete range of health services.

To have women well represented at the policy making level is crucial. Only in this way will domestic and international policies be shaped to protect the welfare of women and children. Through a shared consciousness, women can begin to understand and communicate what is and isn't in their own interests — and they can do this from a global perspective (Nichols-Casebolt et al., 1994).

THE HUMAN TOLL

In virtually every major manufacturing activity and many clerical ones, as we have seen, the human element is steadily being replaced by machines. Millions of working men and women around the world, accordingly, find themselves trapped between economic eras, casualties of the Third Industrial Revolution and the relentless march toward ever greater technological efficiency (Rifkin, 1995). As work becomes scarce, the older and least productive workers are eliminated. Many of these reluctantly will accept jobs for paltry wages in the service sector. For the remaining workers, meanwhile, the speed of work and the technical demands increase commensurably. The essence of the strain is thus double: it falls upon those who lose their means of livelihood as well as upon those who retain it.

The American economy's response to the globalization of markets has been to turn into a nation of temporary workers. More than 60 percent of new jobs created are in three industries: health care (paraprofessional), restaurants and bars, and temporary help (Beatty, 1994). Central themes running through the new international economy are these: boom for the economy is bust for the worker; with one person's income falling, another family member may go to work as well; and everywhere among workers, insecurity mounts. There is nothing new historically in worker displacement and company downsizing. But always before where one door was closed, another had opened. Decline in one area of employment was more than offset by opportunities elsewhere. If there is something unique about the latter-day technological revolution, it is the absence of hope and the absence of belief in the future. For generations, Americans have considered a brighter future as their birthright, and upward mobility for their children a must. In light of the changing realities in the workplace, no longer will parents be able to pin their hopes on the next generation to accomplish what they could not. Workers can't count on the generosity of government assistance to help them out with innovative programs. Nor can they look to worker retraining for an economy in which the most logical question would be, retraining for what?

The computer age is already changing every aspect of human lives. Enthusiasm at the highest levels of government is generating a huge investment in further developing the new technologies to improve the United States' competitive trade advantage (Rifkin, 1994). Robotics, artificial intelligence, data storage—this is where the investment will be. What is not known is where the electronic superhighway will take us. Only when the information revolution starts spinning out of control and the concept of work is transformed in ways never before imaginable, will we see where the superhighway is leading. Maybe only then will a realistic map be worked out. Otherwise many will be lost along the way.

There are two types of stress relative to the workplace during a time of cataclysmic change. First, there is the stress of the work itself; second there is the stress caused by the loss of work. These are the topics at hand.

Employment Stress

The stress placed on the average British family today is generalizable to much of the industrialized world. As Yvonne Roberts (1993: 17) reports:

> Both sexes are now part of a "feminized" labor force, a euphemism for low pay, casualized part-time work and too few rights. A household with two full-time wage-earners, but only one who doubles as domestic servant is under strain. . . . A family in which the woman works, acts as a housewife and attempts to shore up a demoralized, unemployed "head of household" is under strain.

Depressed wages, a frenetic pace set at the workplace, the rapid rise in temporary work, decreased long-term employment, the growing disparity between the haves and have-nots, and the dramatic shrinking of the middle class are placing unprecedented stress on the American work force (Rifkin, 1995). As jobs have been eliminated, survivors are now doing the tasks of two or three people. The Japanese, similarly, dedicate themselves to their work. The human toll is so great there that they even have a name for it, *karoshi,* which literally means dropping dead at your desk.

In Iowa, an interview with therapists in a newspaper article entitled, "Money Problems Plus Extra Work Equals Stress" (Rubiner, 1994) chronicles the same phenomenon. The widespread belief that children will never have it as good as their parents fosters depression, marital discord, and emotional strain, according to this article. Farmers, suffering from the gap between expectations and reality, are especially hard hit. To support the farm they are forced to find work off the farm and as economic pressures mount, health insurance may be sacrificed as is money put away for retirement. Leisure time is reduced to a minimum. Family tensions are reportedly high and the rate of spousal abuse—physical and verbal—is up.

In a newspaper interview, Labor Secretary Robert Reich (Manegold, 1994) points to the widening gaps in wages of educated and uneducated workers. Ominous forces, claims Reich, in the way American labor issues are handled have divided the country between an overclass in the safety of elite suburbs and an underclass quarantined in surroundings that are unspeakably bleak and often violent. In the middle is a new anxious class trapped in the frenzy of effort it takes to preserve their standing. In Reich's opinion, the middle class, as historically defined, is disintegrating. There are more rich, more poor, and fewer in the middle. The pattern is clear.

If the white middle class is faring poorly, the African American middle class faces even greater obstacles. Middle class African Americans' educational backgrounds may be weak due to the low quality of many public schools in predominantly black neighborhoods. This makes it harder to compete for jobs. Fewer high-paying, blue-collar jobs will decrease the opportunities through which African Americans have been able to earn enough to help their children go to college. Blacks are over-represented in the service industries and under-represented in the professions. The clamping-down on affirmative action programs leaves blacks and Hispanics especially vulnerable to shifts in the economic winds.

Newman (1995), in a thought-provoking essay, recounts what a scholarly research team discovered about the working poor in inner-city Harlem. In contrast to the literature on the underclass which emphasizes criminality and social isolation, this researcher found that even in a depressed inner city, working for a living remains a key norm. The competition even for fast-food jobs in the area was fierce; immigrants had an advantage in getting hired over African Americans. Still there are many African Americans who work in the service industry and who must continue to live in the city's most depressed neighborhoods. Instead of dismantling the social welfare system, policy-makers would do well to help make job opportunities available, as this study implies.

After successive waves of downsizing have reshaped offices and factories, Americans have grown increasingly anxious and disillusioned, according to a series of public opinion surveys reported in *USA Today* (Magazine, 1995). The bottom line is that Americans resent that they are working longer hours, and lack job security and respect by their superiors.

A portrait of meat packer David Betts (highlighted by Voss in the *Des Moines Register*, 1994) reveals the human dimension of work stress. At age forty-two, Betts has spent most of the last twenty years packing meat. His present job entails pulling up to one hundred pounds of guts out of pig carcasses at the rate of three hundred an hour. Because of the physical stamina and speed required, Betts figures he will not be able to last beyond a few more years. In the past, the future looked more promising. Wages were good; the refrigerator was always full; bills could be paid on time. Plus there was extra money for family outings, all the basic benefits, and the reward of a pension down the road. Betts' work schedule was under his control. How different things are now!

An aspect of work in the United States that most workers take for granted is the lack of time off. Many workers are putting in sixty hour weeks. Two weeks of vacation a year is the norm. In Europe, in contrast, there are all kinds of holidays throughout the year, climaxed by five to six weeks vacation at a stretch. In Norway, workers are given a substantial sum of vacation money and expected to spend it. The greater the stress at work, the greater the need for rest. Studies on work stress indicate that at sixty hours a week, performance declines by 25 percent. The drug abuse, drinking problems, and mental illness that result from overwork cost American industry billions of dollars each year (Lawday, 1991).

Concepts from alienation theory offer insights into the link between economic forces and emotional and interpersonal problems. Keefe (1984) summarizes the alienation perspective. Lack of control in the workplace, estrangement from the products of one's work, powerlessness, and alienation from one's fellow workers, one's body, and one's creations generate an inevitable alienation from oneself. Human relationships become stressed by economic necessity. At the same time, needs that are frustrated in the workplace can be sublimated with commodity consumption in nonworking hours. Overspending and overwork reinforce each other in a self-perpetuating cycle of despair. But if work stress is bad, the stress of loss of work is infinitely worse.

Unemployment Stress

Instead of producing an employment strategy, Canada like other countries, puts its faith in market forces to create jobs. The issue then becomes welfare dependence and the advocacy of drastic cuts in social programs, as Kitchen (1995) indicates, when the jobs that would provide working age Canadians with the necessary material security and stability are not there. In Canada, the unemployment rate generally runs over 10 percent. The impact is evidenced in the large number of former Canadian workers from all walks of life reduced to dependence on food banks when they run out of money for food. As Cox (1995: 20), the assistant director of the Daily Bread Food Bank, reports:

> A food bank in Alberta reports that one-third of the people who use it now have no income at all. A Quebec food bank talks about soaring welfare rolls, about unusually high numbers of the elderly who live in poverty, about rising youth unemployment. . . . Over the last three years, more than 10,000 food bank recipients in the Metro Toronto area have lost their cars, and 4,400 have lost their homes. . . . Unemployment has become the single biggest cause of impoverishment here in Toronto. . . . The largest group are clerks, followed by construction workers and—surprisingly—professionals. You are more likely to find computer operators and teachers among their ranks than labourers, waiters or taxi drivers.

The official U.S. unemployment rate is around 6 percent, but if you include the involuntary part-timers along with workers too discouraged to look for work, then the rate more than doubles (Beatty, 1994). Over 50 percent of black teenagers look for work in vain. In Britain the unemployment rate hovers around 11 percent. Often referred to as mass unemployment, this falls unevenly on minorities, youths, and workers over the age of fifty. Recent outbreaks of rioting and looting instigated by young people are undoubtedly reflections of their demoralization related to unemployment (Cahill, 1994).

The profound psychological impact of the radical changes in the conditions and nature of work on the worker is being viewed with alarm by industry observers (Rifkin, 1995). So internalized in the American psyche is the work ethic (we are what we do; our worth is what we earn) that the trauma of job loss cannot be underestimated. Sometimes suicide results, and increasingly workplace murder is followed by suicide. Homicide is now the third major cause of death at the workplace. In a society where one's self image is built around work roles, job loss may be equated with death.

Researchers find a strong association between unemployment and emotional problems. During a recession, mental hospital admissions increase, as do suicides, divorce rates, and incidences of child abuse (Zastrow, 1993). Even children of the unemployed suffer from mental health problems as well as rejection by peers, developmental delays, and increased depression (Allen-Meares, 1995). See box 7.1 for a disturbing portrait of people in England and elsewhere who have "become unpersons, by means of the most genteel and delicate of violent suppressions, by being deprived of livelihood."

A classic description of the impoverishment — social and literal — that comes with unemployment is provided by Harrington's *The Other America* (1962: 34):

> What happens to the man who goes eighteen months without a steady job? The men told me. First, the "luxuries" go: the car, the house, everything that has been purchased on installment but not yet paid for. Then comes doubling up with relatives (and one of the persistent problems in becoming poor is that marriages are often wrecked in the process). Finally — and this is particularly true of the "older" worker — there is relief, formal admission into the other America.

Arthur Miller's (1949) Pulitzer Prize-winning drama, *Death of a Salesman,* captures the despair of a tragic hero whose failure to make it as a salesman becomes his downfall as a man. As his wife defends him to his sons:

> No, a lot of people think he's lost his — balance. But you don't have to be very smart to know what his trouble is. The man is exhausted. . . . He works for a company thirty-six years this March, opens up unheard-of territories to their trademark, and now in his old age they take his salary away.

In its entirety, *Death of a Salesman* is often interpreted as an epitaph for the American dream.

The lack of secure full-time work contributes not only to an individual's undoing but to the family's demise as well. In an analysis of U.S. Census Bureau data, Hernandez (1993) reveals that poor two parent families are twice as likely to break up as those with income above the poverty line. The breakup rate for black families experiencing job loss is higher than for white families, suggesting

BOX 7.1

THE UNPEOPLE

Jeremy Seabrook

For the second time in a decade, we are seeing a significant "shake-out" of labour. Many people now without work are those who dutifully "priced themselves into" the very service jobs promised as the salvation of those compelled to bow before the necessities of "structural adjustment" in the early 1980s. This time, however, a new group is being evicted from the labour market; and many of them are the children of the victims of the earlier wave of redundancies.

In the early 1980s, a generation of workers in heavy industry lost their function and purpose. It was a destructive, corrosive experience. Some people became depressed, prematurely old, waking up in the early morning, knowing there was no longer any mill to go to, and the factory had become a site of mangled metal and crushed brick. Some people killed themselves. I remember the family of one man in Lancashire who showed me the note he had left; a few lines apologising for his own superfluousness to the system that had discarded him. Others saw marriages fail and the bonds of affection and kinship dissolve. Some gratefully took to the poisonous consolations of alcohol, illness and psychic disintegration. It was an ugly, cruel time, which displaced and ousted people from settled ways of life that

had seemed the supreme guarantors of our continuity as an industrial power.

Many of those now being made redundant were recruited in the 1960s to the "caring society" — itself a pledge that the old brutalities of mass poverty and unemployment would never recur. Their role was, they had imagined, to heal and soothe the casualties of industrial society. Those now finding themselves deprived of function are people in social work, charity, education, the health service, public services, planning, architecture and administration. Many had implicitly believed in the creation of a better world, to which their skills were indispensable.

Already during the 1980s, the professional workers now being marginalised had become increasingly disaffected from the excesses of Conservative government. Scorn at Thatcher's politics turned to incredulity; later to outrage, anger, and, finally, numb reconciliation to the inevitable. They were constantly appalled by policy statements, cuts in public expenditure and the latest emanations from free-market think-tanks.

They clung to an archaic scheme of public morality that was being jettisoned; and they could not adapt to the rigours of

(Continued on next page)

BOX 7.1 (Continued)

the free market. But, however horrified they were, most kept their jobs during the first recession of the 1980s. Many have found it unbearably painful now to return to their elderly parents and confess that they too have been made redundant.

Perhaps they should be better armed against the experience? During the eighties, so many of them — I mean us, of course — had believed we had opted out, settled for the consolations of a well-rewarded job, even if it did seem curiously disarticulated from the high purposes with which we had entered it.

We retreated, uneasily, into private life, professing a disgust with politics, a revulsion against ideas of social progress; and unable to understand why the caring society in which we believed should be attended by so much violence, cruelty, so many addictions, the ruin of structures of kinship and neighbourhood. Although it was distasteful to us, there seemed little point in holding to notions of improvement in any area other than the economic. In a way, we had already privately conceded the case of those we still thought of as our opponents.

But now, even that tenuous and unstable job security has been swept away. Many of those now unemployed are in their forties and fifties, and are as defeated and depressed as the old industrial workers were in the early 1980s. Few calamities are worse than loss of function, especially when you have believed in the value of what you were

doing. And the old industrial workers knew their lives were bound up with the making of material necessities; just as today's redundant knew that their concern was with human values, with healing, caring, and helping.

That such areas of manifest utility and goodness should prove redundant to the majestic sweep of wealth-creation is a deeply scarring experience. In the early 1980s, I met many people bereaved of their purpose; they closed the front doors of their modest little houses in shame and sat beside gas-fires turned to a flicker in their draughty rooms, incapable of grasping why people like themselves, who had been schooled to labour, deferred pleasures and scant joys, people who had had so little, should nevertheless still be capable of being deprived of something so vital in this late season of their lives.

It still comes as a shock that we have been taken up, used and then rejected by our society. For some of us, it is not an entirely new experience; indeed, it has a certain familiarity. When we were in university, for instance, in the late 1950s and early 1960s, to be working class was itself to be highly fashionable; was to be courted and urged to amuse our peers with vignettes of northern or Midland life; was to exude a patina of glamour that those from more exalted social

(Continued on next page)

BOX 7.1 (Continued)

strata found — inexplicably to us then — exotic and desirable. This feeling of being valued was intensified during the 1960s, when we became teachers and social workers.

Since then, both the working class and caring society have been disgraced, and those tainted by contact with them have become deeply unfashionable. The miners' strike, perhaps more than any other event, dispelled any lingering glamour; the working class — or, rather, what was left of it — had proved itself once more the violent, perverse, and disruptive rabble it had always been perceived as in the early industrial era. And what could be more unambiguous than the fall of social workers, blamed now for all the social ills that they, in a more innocent era, thought they could cure?

There was one other experience that called for our energies to be employed. That was in the early 1980s, during the first flush of Thatcherism: mass daily redundancies and inner-city riots. There was a clear possibility it might all end in disaster and violence. We were useful once more, not only to absorb intensified workloads for those in the health and social services; our betters were also quite keen to learn anything we might have to say about the formation of a permanent underclass, from which they were anxious to separate the mainstream. We had what they wanted — information.

But now the transition is complete, the awkward moment safely negotiated. The existing order is no longer threatened. The only alternative has itself been vanquished, exorcised. Socialism is off the global agenda. The market reigns supreme. The West has won. There is no longer any need for dissent. Hence the time has come for silencing, for marginalising, side-lining. We have become unpersons, by means of the most genteel and delicate of violent suppressions; by being deprived of a livelihood.

These multiple expulsions have their cumulative effect; repeated blows to a sense of worth and value, a denial of skills, a repudiation of insights and energies. I have been, perhaps, more fortunate than many, for I have been able to find great strength in the struggles of many people in the third world; not as a form of escapism from the more opaque and intractable problems of my own society, but precisely because of the parallels and similarities with what I and my peers have experienced here. If there is now only one global system of which we are all part, we should expect echoes of the same experience across cultures, races and regions. And this is what is happening.

Everywhere, people are being evicted from livelihoods, displaced from their habitats by the same processes that are depriving us also of security and continuity. Indigenous peoples, tribal and forest people are being ousted for the sake of their

(Continued on next page)

BOX 7.1 (Continued)

resource-base, required by a greedy market economy to earn foreign exchange; and, in the process, sustainable traditional ways of life are violently overthrown.

The children of rice-farmers in Thailand must migrate to Bangkok and Phuket to supply the demand for sex workers, fuelled in large measure by the demands of western tourists. Subsistence farmers in India and the Philippines are being forced from their lands by the urgent need of their governments to service mountainous debts. They go to the growing cities, where they are allowed no peace either; their fragile shelters are always being demolished for the sake of "developers" and construction conglomerates who covet the land they occupy.

It has become a source of great self-congratulation to the West that there is no longer any overarching ideology to oppose the patterns of development it is now free to impose on the whole world. The market system is to be the universal means of deliverance of all the suffering peoples of the earth, whether they like it or not, no matter what violent discontinuities, what unsustainable practices it may bring.

We have already seen the effects of this dynamic process in the West. In the 1960s and 1970s, we saw that areas of human experience previously considered to be beyond the reach of the market system could readily be turned into marketed services and commodities—indeed, the caring profes-

sions themselves marked the passage into the money economy of things that human beings had traditionally offered each other freely.

The 1980s was the decade in which what was not marketable was shown to have no value. The 1990s will go further and demonstrate that what is not marketable does not exist. The power of the market, unchecked, becomes a tyranny like any other concentration of power. Indeed, precisely because it is the most dynamic and forceful feature of our lives, there is no other source of moral resistance strong enough to contest its domination. The supreme triumphal emblem of its success is, of course, the shopping mall, to which all other social institutions seek to approximate themselves. Thus, cities become halls of merchandise, adjacent to which people happen to live. Airports are shopping centres, at which aircraft call from time to time. Hospitals are franchise outlets, in which people are incidentally healed or not. Churches are bazaars in which people sometimes worship.

The ceaseless movement of peoples all over the world, the evictions and oustings, upheavals and transformations are all in the name of the market economy, whose extension and expansion is now the only serious project in the world. It represents a vast process of colonization, or recolonization,

(Continued on next page)

BOX 7.1 (Continued)

one to dwarf all previous conquests. This is why the fate of the former miner, in the bleak functionless pit village is the same as that of the tribal family, forced from its habitat, and squatting in the fetid slums of Bombay or Manila. The displaced fishing communities of Kerala and Penang are subject to the same forces as those that make families homeless in New York or Hackney; the people under the bridges of London or Paris with their fires and bottles of drink are the sisters and brothers of those under the motorways of Sao Paulo and Mexico City.

Indeed, as the logic of the global marketplace extends further, people in Bombay and Seoul will be competing for work with the people of Birmingham or Naples, or even Moscow. We must expect to see a blurring of the distinctions between first and third worlds.

This is why these times are less gloomy than they might otherwise be. So much is

becoming clearer, despite the efforts of those who would render our own experience impenetrable to us, promote incoherence and call it pluralism, preside over the spread of powerlessness and ask us to bless it as the highest freedom.

We who have been marginalised by the majestic imperatives of the market in this phase of reconstruction are no longer young. But we shall not go away. We will not fade into obscurity and silence without protest and without articulating the multiple expropriations that are imposed on the vast majority of humankind, for the sake of sustaining a system that has installed social injustice, inequality and poverty as the only motors of its aberrant definition of what constitutes wealth.

Source: New Statesman and Society, June 28, 1991, pp. 15–16. Reprint with permission of the _New Statesman and Society._

the strain is greater among blacks probably because incomes are lower. So if one parent suffers job loss, family breakup may be hastened. This look at the Census Bureau data lends strong support to the argument that well-paying jobs held by parents keep children out of poverty. A father's absence itself is not the cause of poverty, but poverty hastens family breakup.

At the community level, Donna Davis (1993) studied gender relations in Grey Rock Harbor, Newfoundland, during an ongoing decline in the fishing industry. In the face of unemployment and being forced into supposedly demeaning land bound forms of work, the men turn to a confrontational bravado to assert their threatened masculinity. Thrown into unaccustomed competition with women on the land, they react with hostility and bitterness. Many of the long daytime hours are spent in the two village bars, "literally and figuratively crying in their beer" (Davis, 1993). Thus sweeping change in the local economy, in other words, can throw family life into a state of disequilibrium and the whole social structure into a tailspin.

The Racial Factor

Contemplate these two opposing facts: (1) African Americans have made striking gains in education and in moving into the higher echelons of management and the professions; the black middle class is expanding rapidly; college educated black women earned 10 percent more than comparably educated white women. (2) Affirmative action support for minority hiring is ebbing; in many inner-city neighborhoods where industry has moved out, a majority of black adults lack gainful employment; the median income of black households is 60 percent those of whites; black households' median net worth is a mere one-tenth of whites' net worth. Based on these facts drawn from the U.S. Census Bureau, 1995, Farrell (1995) notes the gnawing fear that black economic gains will stall and that many of the powerful economic forces changing America, such as the job squeeze on the less skilled and less educated, will affect African Americans disproportionately. Given the facts, the solutions seem quite obvious. Or do they?

SOLUTIONS

The time interval between the arrival of a change and the completion of the adaptations it prompts is called *cultural lag*, a term widely used in anthropology. The lag of social institutions behind technology is the most widely cited example. W. F. Ogburn (1950), who developed the notion of cultural lag, noted that changes in culture were not always or necessarily congruent with economic changes. Cultural lag is known through hindsight when legacies of the past (for example, the belief that a woman's place is in the home, or the notion that a woman can count on finding a man to take care of her) get carried over into the modern age.

So it may be too early yet for people to see it, or even for the technological impact to be fully felt. But perhaps years from now, looking back, the tremendous discrepancy between the socioeconomic realities and current policies (pinning hopes for a job boom on high technology and for social welfare benefits through the private markets) will seem obvious. Let us review what occurred in the 1930s for its possible relevance today.

Without government intervention, the mass unemployment of the 1930s set the stage for business to break unions and cut wages. To protect labor, Franklin Roosevelt worked for the passage of the Wagner Act which guaranteed the right of collective bargaining for workers (Beatty, 1994). Minimum standards for wages were established also. These measures along with the rest of the New Deal were a victory for society over the economy, as Beatty suggests. Well-paid labor is a liability, however, in the kind of global market that exists today. The automated high-tech economy decrees the end of work as we know it and the end of the worker.

What is society's responsibility to its citizens? Shall we fight the growth of technology itself or welcome the greater efficiency as it saves people from tedious and mindless work? Should we rely on a small crew of workers doing mandatory overtime "until they drop" or should we arrange to spread the work and its rewards around more equitably?

From the literature, most of it written by economists concerned with long-term planning, sensible approaches and strategies can be gleaned. Central to these approaches are the following basic assumptions: We cannot turn the clock back; the free market is a misnomer (corporations being heavily subsidized); and an impoverishment of the working and middle classes will have serious consequences for industry and society in the long-run (who will be able to buy the manufactured goods?).

Following Midgley (1995) in his articulation of the social development approach, I look toward the mobilization of diverse social institutions including the market, community, and state to promote the general welfare. Instead of viewing the economic and social domains as in competition with each other, it would be wise to see the overall well-being of a people and the strength of the economy as intertwined. Countries which invest extensively in education, health care, child welfare, and other forms of human capital tend to have higher levels of economic development than those that do not.

A major stumbling block to industry in the United States has been the expectation that business will provide for the health care of its workers because the government does not. Skyrocketing health care costs for workers are passed on to consumers in the price of the product. Midgley describes Sweden as the prototype of a country that uses the social development model in establishing close links between social policy and economic development. Costa Rica, though with far fewer resources, similarly, promotes economic development in ways that foster social progress for the population as a whole. Emphasis in Costa Rica is on primary health care and education, not hospital construction or military spending.

Rifkin (1994), like other U.S. economists, perceives the risk in forging ahead blindly down the information highway—the risk of creating a dangerous America—one in which a small elite of corporate managers and technicians exists inside a nation of the permanently unemployed. Writing in the *Wall Street Journal*, Lowenstein (1995) envisions trends so formidable that it behooves politicians to sit up and listen. The fact is, today as never before, productivity has begun to leave wages behind. Service industries can be expected to go the way of other industries and discover the joys of laying off workers as well. What jobs will there be for the structurally unemployed, the victims either of global commerce or of automation?

There is much, in fact, that the government can do. Among helpful suggestions from the literature are these:

- Provide a tax deduction for employees facing reduced workweeks (Rifkin, 1995).
- Negotiate multilateral agreements with other nations to ensure a fair playing field; restrict trade through tariffs to foreign producers whose workers receive decent pay (Rifkin, 1995).
- Provide extensive maternity and childcare leave policies and children's allowances to help support them (Sidel, 1992).
- Labor can go global along with the corporations to keep workers from being pitted against one another (Bacon, 1995). (Stated by Marx and Engels, 1848).
- Millions of low-technology jobs can be created to build housing for the homeless and an adequate public mass transportation system both of which are desperately needed (Rifkin, 1994).
- Provide structured living in group homes for teenage mothers and their children such as has been done in New York City; mothers are taught parenting skills and given an education (Moskowitz, 1995).
- Redefine the work ethic. Learning is work. Caring for children is work. Community action is work (Terkel, 1974).

In short, efficiency and productivity have been put at the head of the agenda, and the social consequences may far exceed the immediate advantages. The concurrent reduction in social benefits on the altar of deficit reduction, the maintenance of a Cold War level military budget, the mass construction of prisons, the continuing large tax cuts for corporations and the super rich — these policies are inconsistent with the aims of social development and family values. They are not even good business.

CONCLUSION AND SUMMARY

The typical family today is stressed. A large part of this stress is due to changes in the economy and workplace over which families and their individual members have no control. As early as 1974, Studs Terkel in his book *Working* (xxii) described the present situation: "In a world of cybernetics, of an almost runaway technology, things are increasingly making things." Appropriately, in 1995 a headline in the *Chicago Tribune* (Rubin, 1995) ran, "More Find American Dream is Really a Nightmare." The perks — the promotions, raises, bonuses, and job security — are all but gone, as the article indicates.

This chapter has taken an ecosystems approach to reveal the interconnectedness of social institutions and of nations. Ecosystems theory, as presented in chapter 1, views the parts within the whole, each part of which is in constant and dynamic interaction with the others. Adapting this perspective to the sociology of work, we can come to see how a change in one area of community life impinges upon every other area, and because of international linkages, how one country's policies reverberate across the world and back again. We also can begin to grasp the spiraling impact of new technologies, an impact that cuts across the entire gamut of human experience. Let us suppose, for example, that some new automated equipment is introduced as a cost-saving measure to free up time of the workers and ultimately to replace them. First the workplace and the individuals who work there are affected. Through them their families are affected and then through their families the society is affected. Society through its general turbulence and/or remedial policies, impacts the workplace. By then the impact has come full circle. This company or factory will be highly competitive on the global market; money earned will be invested in more automated machinery. Before long, companies around the world with the resources will follow suit. Moreover, to have access to the necessary capital, many of the companies will merge into giant corporations.

One thing about history: It's invariably tough to recognize until it's over that you have lived through it. When the ramifications are not realized, however, and when yesterday's solutions are offered to the problems of today, we can claim, as has been claimed in this chapter, that a state of cultural lag exists. *Cultural lag* can be defined as the discrepancy between old concepts and new realities. Whether or not cultural lag exists today and to what extent will only become apparent over time. Only then will the unique inclusion of a chapter such as this one on work and family welfare be seen not as an anomaly but as an essential component in a study of social life and being.

While in previous times in history nations existed *sui generis* (or as one of a kind) and cooperation between labor and management was essential for the common good of the workplace and of the nation, today, on international playing fields, the rules of the game are determined by the imperatives of the market, and labor and labor movements effectively are being suppressed. While earlier industrial technologies replaced the physical side of human labor, the new computer-based equipment can handle increasingly complicated mental tasks of a sort never before imagined. Machines are already making medical diagnoses and screening job résumés. We are, no doubt, in the midst of a historic transformation, a Third Industrial Revolution. Looming large over the political landscape is the issue of how to move from a society based on an abundance of work to one in which the worker is increasingly irrelevant without crushing the human spirit.

In the three traditional work sectors—agriculture, manufacturing, and service—worker displacement has begun to take a tragic toll, locally and globally. This chapter has looked at each of the work sectors in terms of drastic changes underway. In the loss of the farm, the automation of the factory, and the replacement of service and clerical workers by computerized programs, the human toll has been considerable. The social functions of work discussed at the start of the chapter were brought to light in the later review of studies on the stress of unemployment. A question for all of us to consider is: What happens to people when there is nothing to do, no place to go, and no sense of being needed? While many former workers are demoralized (and impoverished) through job loss, those remaining on the job are overworked under conditions of heightened stress. The casualties (both from overworking and underworking) are reflected in the statistics on alcohol and drug abuse, mental disorder, home-lessness, crime, and family breakup (and a reluctance to marry in the first place). Yet societal adaptation has been slow; ideology has not yet caught up with the new realities. The belief that economic growth will benefit all levels of work; and faith that welfare cut backs will produce independence, family cohesion, and a willingness to work are instances of cultural lag characteristic in a time of rapid social change. The blaming-the-poor rhetoric overlooks the structural components in economic life.

Today many recognize, as Midgley (1995) points out, that the challenges facing society require concerted action on the part of government, communities, individuals, and that global social needs can only be addressed in a meaningful way through pragmatic policies and programs that directly address welfare issues. A full-employment, pro-worker agenda could help ease many social problems. Broadening the definition of work to include, for example, care for the young and old and domestic work, reducing the workload for each individual to spread the work among larger numbers of people, and creating jobs in the much needed arenas of public housing and transportation were among the remedies suggested.

For women torn between their household tasks and caregiving and their need to earn a living, their povertization is almost an inevitability. Already vul-nerable to discrimination in the workplace, women especially are prone to bear the consequences in times of a growing labor surplus. Because of their care-taking responsibilities, women often are not free to engage in the overtime work that is expected as the work pool is deliberately kept to a minimum. Then women who have had their jobs eliminated by computerization (such as clerical wor-kers) or by deskilling (such as nurses) have been increasingly forced into tem-porary jobs where the pay is low and the benefits nonexistent. Issues of primary concern to women workers—childcare, parental leave, and eldercare—have not been addressed. Women, many of them single mothers, are being forced off the welfare rolls into the low-wage service jobs which keep them and their chil-dren below the poverty level without any of the basic welfare protections. Mean-while, the position of women in the workplace and women on welfare are serving as scapegoats for a falling standard of living. A similar onslaught against per-sons of color is borne out in the statistics on job loss. While middle class Afri-can Americans have made striking gains educationally and professionally, the forces transforming the United States from an industrial-based economy to a high-tech one have had a devastating impact on those who are both members of a minority group and without marketable skills.

In the end, the corporations themselves and the government are being short-sighted. The relentless drive to cut labor costs, if unchecked, will produce a crisis the least of which is a reduction in the purchasing power. People who lack a connection to work also lack a stake in the social system. A second crisis that is taking a toll for opposite reasons is the propensity to overwork as revealed in Schor's penetrating study, *The Overworked American* (1991). An arrangement involving too little work for some and too much work for others is having a devastating impact on families, one way or another.

The question that opened this chapter—what happens to a dream deferred?—is the question the policy-makers would do well to ponder as the human factor in work progressively is undermined. Meanwhile, for the worker, there needs to be a balance between work and home. Crucial elements in achieving such a balance include providing sufficient time off with paid maternity and paternity leaves, sick leaves, functional childcare arrangements, adequate income and job security, and viable affirmative action programs to protect the interests of otherwise disadvantaged groups. The next chapter discusses two additional phenomena of singular relevance to families: health care and housing.

REVIEW QUESTIONS

1. Discuss the Langston Hughes poem that introduces the chapter in terms of the chapter's specific context.
2. What is the revolution in work today? How might Rifkin's book *The End of Work* be appropriately retitled? What is its basic thesis?
3. "What Texas took from Michigan, Mexico is now taking from Texas." Discuss.
4. What is the source—direct and indirect—of some of the pressures on the job?
5. How does unemployment hurt the individual? The society?
6. How was work conceptualized before and after the Protestant Reformation?
7. What do we learn of work in early twentieth century Chicago from Jane Addams?
8. Describe the connection between pension money and computerization. What will the consequences be?
9. How did the separation of home and workplace in early industrial history affect family life? How did the functions once served by the family change?
10. Discuss plans to put welfare mothers to work in light of changing employment patterns.
11. List some positive aspects of the new technologies.

12. What does the future hold for low-wage countries in terms of employment security?
13. How is modernization affecting agricultural production across the world? What were Marx and Engels' earlier insights?
14. Contrast NAFTA with the E.U. regarding conditions for the worker.
15. What is the complaint of British social workers?
16. Discuss the contribution of Ritzer's *The McDonaldization of Work*.
17. What are the working conditions for women of the world? How do single mothers tend to be marginalized?
18. What is the significance of work to women? What changes can be made to help women's work function?
19. Provide evidence of a human toll in terms of both underemployment and overemployment.
20. What does the concept *cultural lag* add to the discussion on "welfare reform" today? What are some ways society and workers can benefit both because of and in spite of the technological changes?
21. Are we at a turning point in history as the conclusion to the chapter suggests? Discuss.

REFERENCES

Addams, J. (1910). *Twenty Years at Hull House.* New York: Macmillan.
Allen-Meares, P. (1995). Children: Mental Health. In the *Encyclopedia of Social Work.* Washington, DC: NASW Press.
Bacon, D. (1995, September 18). Upsizing Labor. *The Nation*: 259–260.
Baker, M. (1995, July 29–August 1). *Poverty, Work and the Employability of Mothers: Cross-National Comparisons.* Paper presented at the International Social Welfare in a Changing World Conference, Alberta, Canada: University of Calgary.
Barlett, P. and P. Brown. (1994). Agricultural Development and the Quality of Life. In A. Podolefsky and P. Brown, eds. *Applied Cultural Anthropology,* 2d ed. Mountain View, CA: Mayfield.
Barr, C. (1995, August 16). Japanese Women Refuse to Bow to Job Discrimination. *Christian Science Monitor*: 1.
Beatty, J. (1994, May). Who Speaks for the Middle Class? *The Atlantic Monthly*: 65–77.
Becker, G. (1995, October 16). Housework: The Missing Piece of the Economic Pie. *Business Week*: 30.
Bell, W. (1987). *Contemporary Social Welfare,* 2d ed. New York: Macmillan.
Bradsher, K. (1995, September 10). High-Tech Jobs Migrating Overseas. *Des Moines Register*: 2G.

Broad, D. (1995). Globalization and Casual Labor: Marginalization of Labor in Western Countries. Paper presented at the International Social Welfare in a Changing World Conference. Alberta, Canada: University of Calgary.

Cahill, M. (1994). *The New Social Policy.* Oxford England: Blackwell.

Cassidy, J. (1995, October 16). Who Killed the Middle Class? *New Yorker:* 113–124.

Cox, S. (1995, October). Next in Line at the Food Bank. *Canadian Forum:* 20–21.

Davis, D. (1993). When Men Become "Women": Gender Antagonism and the Changing Sexual Geography of Work in Newfoundland. *Sex Roles* 29(718): 457–475.

Dentzer, S. (1995, September 11). Paying the Price of Female Neglect. *U.S. News and World Report:* 45.

DeWalt, B. (1994). The Agrarian Basis of Conflict in Central America. In A. Podolefsky and P. Brown, eds. *Applied Cultural Anthropology,* 2d ed. Mountain View, CA: Mayfield.

Editors. (1995, September/October). Introduction, How's the Job? *MS:* 32–34.

Eveline, J. (1994). "Normalization," "Leading Ladies," and "Free Men." Affirmative Actions in Sweden and Australia. *Women's Studies International Forum* 17(2/3): 157–167.

Fabricant, M. and S. Burghardt. (1992). *The Welfare State Crisis and the Transformation of Social Service Work.* Armonk, NY: M. E. Sharpe.

Farrell, C. (1995, November 6). Is Black Progress Set to Stall? *Business Week:* 71–73.

Friedan, B. (1995, September 4). Beyond Gender. *Newsweek:* 28–32.

Gates, B. (1995, November 27). The Road Ahead. *Newsweek:* 59–68.

Gillotte, T. (1994, August 17). Aiding Women in Indochina. *The Chronicle of Higher Education:* A31–32.

Gottlieb, N. (1995). Women Overview. In the *Encyclopedia of Social Work:* (2518–2528). Washington, DC: NASW Press.

Green, P. (1995, September 25). History: To Be Continued. *The Nation:* 318–322.

Gustafsson, S. (1994). Child Care and Types of Welfare Studies. In D. Sainsbury, ed. *Gendering Welfare States:* (45-61). London: SAGE.

Hansberry, L. (1994/1958). *A Raisin in the Sun.* New York: Vintage Books.

Harrington, M. (1962). *The Other America: Poverty in the United States.* Baltimore: Penguin.

———. (1977). *The Vast Majority: A Journey to the World's Poor.* New York: Simon and Schuster.

Hellman, J. (1994). *Mexican Lives.* New York: The New Press.

Hernandez, D. (1993, November). Jobs, Poverty, and Family Breakup. *USA Today:* 28–29.

Hooyman, N. and J. Gonyea. (1995). Family Caregiving. In the *Encyclopedia of Social Work:* (951–959). Washington, DC: NASW Press.

Horwitz, T. (1994, December 1). These Six Growth Jobs Are Dull, Dead-End, Sometimes Dangerous. *Wall Street Journal* A1: 8.

Hutton, W. (1995, September 18). A State of Decay. *The Guardian*: 2–3.

Johnson, C. and J. Kramer. (1995). Sustainable Development in the Climate of Global Finance, Economics and Free Trade. Paper presented at the International Social Welfare in a Changing World Conference. Alberta, Canada: University of Calgary.

Johnson, L. and C. Schwartz. (1994). *Social Welfare: A Response to Human Need,* 3d ed. Boston: Allyn and Bacon.

Judd, K. and S. Pope. (1994). The New Job Squeeze. *MS* 4(6): 86–90.

Kahn, J. (1995, March 10). China's Industrial Surge Squeezes Grain Farms. *The Wall Street Journal*: A1.

Kamerman, S. (1995). Families Overview. In the *Encyclopedia of Social Work:* (927–935). Washington DC: NASW.

Keefe, T. (1984, March). Alienation and Social Work Practice. *Social Casework*: 145–153.

Kitchen, B. (1995, May/June). Children and the Case for Distributive Justice between Generations in Canada. *Child Welfare* 74: 430–458.

Knight-Ridder. (1995, May 30). Report: Families Breaking Up, Many Women Overburdened. *Waterloo/Cedar Falls Courier*: A3.

LaFranchi, H. (1995, July 31). Despite Economic Upturn, Mexicans Say, "It's the Tortilla Prices, Stupid." *Christian Science Monitor*: 7.

Lawday, D. (1991, August 5). Letter from a Productive Lover of Leisure. *U.S. News and World Report*: 6.

Levy, S. (1995, February 27). Technomania. *Newsweek*: 25–29.

Lowenstein, R. (1995, October 12). Will Flat Wages Beget Future Trouble? *Wall Street Journal*: C1.

Manegold, C. (1994, September 25). Reich: Employee Training a Priority. *Des Moines Register*: 11A.

Marx, K. and F. Engels. (1963/1848). *The Communist Manifesto.* New York: Russell and Russell.

McCarron, J. (1995, September 4). "Days of Unrest?" *Chicago Tribune*: 11.

Midgley, J. (1995). *Social Development: The Developmental Perspective in Social Welfare.* London: SAGE.

Miller, A. (1949). *Death of a Salesman.* Harmondsworth, England: Penguin.

Miller, J. (1991). Child Welfare and the Role of Women: A Feminist Perspective. *American Journal of Orthopsychiatry* 61(4): 572–598.

Misch, A. (1992, March/April). Lost in the Shadow Economy. *World Watch*: 18–25.

Monagle, K. (1995). How's Your Job? *MS* 6(2): 32–34.

Moskowitz, E. (1995, October 2). Second-Chance Homes Clear Welfare-to-Work Path. *Christian Science Monitor*: 4.

Murray, M. (1995, May 4). Amid Record Profits, Companies Continue to Lay Off Employees. *Wall Street Journal*: 1.

Newman, K. (1995, June 23). What Scholars Can Tell Politicians about the Poor. *Chronicle of Higher Education*: B1–2.

Nichols-Casebolt, A., J. Krysik, and R. Hermann-Currie. (1994). The Povertization of Women: A Global Phenomenon. *Affilia* 9(1): 9–28.

Ogburn, W. F. (1950). *On Culture and Social Change.* Chicago: Chicago University Press.

Reich, R. (1994, March). American Workers Must Face Reality. *USA Today (The Magazine)* 122: 36–37.

Rifkin, J. (1994, May). Dangers in Pinning Our Hopes on Trickle Down Technology. *USA Today Magazine* 122: 74–76.

_____. (1995). *The End of Work: The Decline of the Global Labor Force and the Dawn of the Post-Market Era.* New York: Putnam.

Ritzer, G. (1993). *The McDonaldization of Society.* Thousand Oaks, CA: Pine Forge Press.

Roberts, Y. (1993, September 24). We are Becoming Divorced from Reality. *New Statesman and Society*: 16–19.

Rubin, B. (1995, January 30). More Find American Dream is Really a Nightmare. *Chicago Tribune.*

Rubiner, B. (1994, September 26). Money Problems Plus Extra Work Equals Stress. *Des Moines Register*: T1, 2.

Scheer, C. (1995, September 11). "Illegals" Made Slaves to Fashion. *The Nation*: 237–238.

Schor, J. (1991). *The Overworked American: The Unexpected Decline of Leisure.* New York: Basic Books.

Scott, D. (1993, Fall). International Technology Transfer in Family Preservation: Differences between the Australian and U.S. Contexts. *The Prevention Report*: 3–7.

Shellenbarger, S., M. Moffett, and K. Chen. (1995, August 25). Around the World, Women are United By Childcare Woes. *Wall Street Journal*: A1, 10.

Sidel, R. (1992). *Women and Children Last.* New York: Penguin.

Slater, P. (1976). *The Pursuit of Loneliness: American Culture at the Breaking Point.* Boston: Beacon Press.

Steele, S. (1995, August 21). Women at Work: Room to Improve. *Maclean's*: 28–29.

Stein, L. (1992). Income-Generating Strategies for Poor Women in Costa Rica: Improvement in their Social Development as Well as Economic Status? *International Social Work* 35, 177–190.

Strand, V. (1995). Single Parents. In the *Encyclopedia of Social Work* (2157–2163). Washington, DC: NASW Press.

Terkel, S. (1974). *Working.* New York: Pantheon Books.

Theisen, W. and T. Waltz. (1995, July 29–August 1). *Welfare Reform: Entitlements, Offers and Threats in the Conservative State.* Paper presented at the International Social Welfare in a Changing World. Alberta, Canada: University of Calgary.

Toupin, L. (1995, October). Index on Workfare. *Canadian Forum*: 48.

United Nations. (1995a). *Human Development Report*. New York: Oxford University Press.

_____. (1995b). *The World's Women 1995: Trends and Statistics*. New York: United Nations.

USA Today. (1995). Newsview. *USA Today* 124 (Magazine 2603): 1–2.

Voss, M. (1994, September 25). Downwardly Mobile. *Des Moines Sunday Register*: E1.

Wagner, D. (1994). Beyond the Pathologizing of Nonwork: Alternative Activities in a Street Community. Social Work 39(6): 718–727.

Wall Street Journal. (1995, March 10). Working Women Adding to Their Numbers. *Wall Street Journal*: B1.

Weber, M., ed. (1921). *Economy and Society* (vols. 1–3). Totowa, NJ: Bedminster Press.

Wetzel, J. (1993). *Women of the World*. London: Macmillan.

Whitehorn, K. (1995, October 1). Jobs for Strife and No Fortress Future. *The Observer*: 6.

Wilensky, H. and C. Lebeaux. (1965). *Industrial Society and Social Welfare*. New York: The Free Press.

Wijnberg, M. and S. Weinger. (1995, July 29–August 1). *Marginalization and the Single Mother: A Report of a Comparative Study*. Paper presented at the International Social Welfare in a Changing World Conference. Alberta, Canada: University of Calgary.

Zastrow, C. (1996). *Introduction to Social Work and Social Welfare,* 5th ed. Pacific Grove, CA: Brooks/Cole.

8

HEALTH CARE
AND HOUSING

Never clean the water until you get the pigs out of the creek.
—traditional Iowa saying, Jay Cayner, President, NASW, 1994

Even a bird has a nest.—a homeless woman

T he two aspects of social welfare encapsulated in this chapter title—health care and housing—are linked to each other in myriad ways, as both are also linked to the broader context in which government programs operate. We can see that lack of housing and physically safe shelter can be a serious health threat. Later we will read a selection from a former emergency room social worker on health problems of persons who are homeless. Less obvious is the reverse association—the health factor as a cause of loss of housing. Yet mental illness, addiction, war trauma, and other disabilities do render individuals susceptible to homelessness.

Although generally included in various international documents and initiatives, the universal rights of shelter and health care (and employment) are absent from U.S. federal and state constitutions. The tendency toward privatization in health care and housing is consistent with a renunciation of governmental responsibility in these areas.

The fact that health and well-being cannot be attained in a hazardous and deteriorating environment is a major theme of this chapter (and of the book).

This section begins with a look at health conditions in a global context. Although focusing on health care and low-income housing in the United States, this chapter assumes an international perspective on the provision of services. The problems of nutrition and preventable diseases such as AIDS, the refugee situation, natural disasters, mental illness and substance abuse, the crisis in women's health care — these issues among others will be viewed in global perspective. The section on health care in the United States will look at the privatized health care delivery system relative to universal offerings in Europe and Canada. The section on homelessness will focus on the United States, while the discussion of displaced persons will be concerned with nations at war. The chapter closes with a description of exemplary community action efforts in countries like India and Costa Rica. An argument is made that the key issues of health care, nutrition, employment, available housing, and formal community care for persons with severe disabilities be tackled at both national and international levels. Global change in key areas related to social work requires global solutions.

AN OVERVIEW OF WORLD HEALTH

On a global scale the universal system of health care is rare. Its opposite — specialized and residual care for the rich who can pay and emergency care for the poor — is the standard pattern. Much of the health care offered is curative rather than preventive and geared toward the young rather than the old; much of it is out of reach to the ordinary person.

The World Health Report 1995 provides a digest of the status of health problems throughout the world in all age groups, and of the World Health Organization's (WHO) contributions to world health. Subramanian (1995) and *Facts on File* (1995a) summarize the major findings. Much of the news is positive: the infant mortality rate has fallen considerably; a rapid decline in population growth is projected; immunization rates for children is over the target of 80 percent. Still, there are widening disparities in health status between countries and among population groups within countries. Even within families, disparities in health care exist. Poor families tend to allocate health care, like food, on the basis of gender. Rapid urbanization has further marginalized the urban poor, and the number of refugees and internally displaced persons has increased exponentially. About 2 billion of the world's 5.6 billion people are ill at any one time, and many die from preventable diseases. The report cites poverty as the primary underlying cause of disease and death worldwide. Many of the poor nations are experiencing a substantial death rate from the pandemic of AIDS, while the mortality rate from accidents and suicide for young adults is particularly high in industrialized countries.

The World Health Report 1995 outlines three priorities for international action. These are: to provide international funding and technical support for the poorest, most severely indebted countries such as in sub-Saharan Africa; to ensure that the poor, particularly families with young children and the elderly, have access to primary health care; and to improve the equity of access to health as a public health policy, especially concerning women. The World Health Report is ambitious in its aims for the future and optimistic concerning expected results.

Some writers such as Mishra (1990), Hartman (1992), Wetzel (1993), and Midgley (1995), however, have taken a less sanguine view of recent trends. Universal social provisions in the Northern Hemisphere countries, Australia, and New Zealand have been at risk of becoming means-tested income programs, and the latter have been progressively undermined as programs for the poor. The ascendancy of the Radical Right associated with serious cutbacks in social investments and mass unemployment has resulted in a significant increase in unmet social need (Midgley, 1995). In Midgley's words (p. 65), "as the twentieth century draws to a close, the human condition seems desperate."

HEALTH CARE IN THE UNITED STATES

In a sense the United States has the best medical care in the world. For complicated procedures, the world's rich people often travel to the United States' top hospitals for treatment. The United States spends substantially more per capita on health care than does any other nation. Yet, there are glaring, inexorable problems. In contrast to other industrialized nations in which health care is viewed as having a service orientation, the health care system in the United States has the dual (and often conflicting) objectives of providing a service *and* of making a profit (Zastrow, 1996). Because treatment is more profitable than prevention, preventive medicine is given low priority. Crisis-oriented medicine receives the greater share of research funding, allocation of health care personnel, and building construction. American physicians are the highest paid in the world, yet their rate of pay is declining, and it pales alongside the money that hospital CEOs get in one year, a figure that may reach into the millions. Major profits are made in private hospitals in affluent sections of large cities, nursing homes, and the drug industry. A report in the *Wall Street Journal* (Chase, 1995) puts the country's annual medical bill at a staggering one trillion dollars. Lobbying efforts are commensurate with the vested interests of the various parties who have vast sums to lose under a government-directed single-payer plan.

Federal health care policy is comprised of two major programs: Medicare and Medicaid. The structure of these programs was described in chapter 2. Medicare, the larger of the two, is a social insurance program operated by the federal government to cover all persons over age sixty-five as well as younger people with long-term disability such as kidney failure (DiNitto, 1995b). Medicaid, in contrast, is a public assistance program designed to help the very poor regardless of age. Financing is shared with the states. Two thirds of Medicaid expenditures go to the aged and disabled (much of it for nursing homes). Government medical programs have displayed a strong institutional bias; hospitals and nursing homes receive far more money than home health or community services. However, because hospitals (under constraints from third party payers) are discharging patients long before they are healed or well, home care is now the fastest growing segment of U.S. health care.

An unintended side effect of Medicaid was that it has the means to limit physician payments while reimbursing hospitals fully. As a net result, many doctors opted out of Medicaid. Preventive care was not provided and the poor resorted to expensive emergency room use in public or private hospitals. Health care rates soared as hospitals shifted costs to third-party payers and to patients who paid cash. In recent times, cost containment strategies prevent such a recoupment of costs, so private hospitals dump non-paying patients onto public hospitals, sometimes with tragic results. Each state responds differently to the public's need for health care.

Hawaii and Minnesota are generally considered to have exemplary programs. Hawaii, in fact, is the only state in the United States to provide a right to health care in its state constitution (Wronka, 1994). Hawaii requires employers to insure most of their work force and the state covers the rest. Minnesota's Health-Right extends insurance to low-income residents, charging on a sliding-fee basis (DiNitto, 1995b).

Cost Containment?

What is happening in the hospital industry is a microcosm of what is happening to the economy as a whole. The market determines the price, and the price determines who gets the business for greater profits. In a huge scramble to offer the cheapest prices, hospitals are competing to attract managed-care contracts from large insurers and Health Maintenance Organizations (HMOs) (Gordon and Baer, 1995). In order to deliver a particular treatment at a price below the competition, hospitals are engaged in a national bidding war. That's why, according to Gordon and Baer, America now has the shortest length of hospital stay of any country in the industrialized world, why managed-care plans kick patients out of hospitals twice as quickly as fee-for-service plans, and why the United States has led the way in eliminating nurses, specifically highly skilled registered nurses. Already, state nursing associations have begun to document deaths and injuries due to hospital negligence (Papazian, 1995).

The U.S. health care system is not faring well. Congress plans to cut Medicare, the federally funded health care program for the elderly, and to decimate Medicaid, the program for the poor. Other proposals tear away at standards for nursing home care and laboratory tests. The right of people injured by drugs or medical devices to collect punitive damages may be sharply curtailed. The commercialization of medicine has grown rampant; the health care providers, not the American people, are calling the shots. The question on many people's minds is, why don't elected officials do something?

When health care reform became one of the major political issues of 1994, the biggest, costliest, and most heavily lobbied battle ever to come before Congress ensued. Health care interests donated twenty-five million dollars to congressional campaigns and poured tens of millions more into mass media advertising (Welch, 1994). Members of Congress on committees working most directly on health care policies received millions in contributions and entertainment in connection with out-of-town speaking engagements. The leading sponsor of these trips was the American Medical Association. Other top health care contributors of political action committee (PAC) money were major businesses which opposed mandatory employer financing, the United Auto Workers who wanted protection, insurance companies which wanted to maintain control, and the Association of Trial Lawyers who wanted to be able to sue.

Because of the continuing role of insurance companies and managed health care organizations (MHOs) with clear vested interests in maintaining their share of the financial pie, the government is stymied from overhauling the system. Now money that could have been spent on primary health care simply will have to be used to pay for the damage caused by the lack of it—premature babies, preventable diseases, and illnesses that easily could have been arrested at an early stage. As we saw in the previous chapter on work, employers are cutting back on benefits including health care. Were the government to assume responsibility for health care, American products would be cheaper. Car-making costs in Canada are currently about a thousand dollars less per vehicle because the government foots the bill for employee benefits (*Facts on File,* 1995a). This paralysis in U.S. public policy change, according to an editorial in *Business Week* (Kuttner, 1991), reflects an underlying gridlock of diverse, profit-making constituencies. Meanwhile, the employed, like the unemployed, increasingly are without health benefits. Fifteen percent of Americans lack health insurance, and many who have it must pay for it privately (Pins, 1995). For its lack of comprehensiveness, the American health care system generally is regarded as a failure. The policy problems of today, as we have seen in the chapters on welfare history and work, become the personal problems of tomorrow.

The high cost of prescription medications is another area where the profit motive and social welfare collide. Senator Pryor of Arkansas (1994) has spoken out on behalf of the millions of senior Americans without prescription drug coverage who are exposed to potential financial catastrophe as a result of inflated prices for medication. After a special report on the lavish tax breaks bestowed upon the pharmaceutical industry while drug prices have risen astronomically, call after call came in to the Senate. As Pryor (p. 74) recalls, "We heard the heart-wrenching stories of people who described the astronomical cost of medications they must take and how they often wonder whether they will be able to afford their next refill." The drug manufacturers of the top twenty drugs have increased their profits at five times the average of the Fortune 500 companies. Older Americans at the lowest income level, who are unprotected by Medicaid, consequently spend 10 percent of their total income on prescription drugs. Where are all the profits going? To marketing, advertising, and stockholders. Americans who travel abroad are shocked to learn of the low prices charged by pharmacies for their drug prescriptions. In countries like Mexico, Canada, and Norway, the drugs are cheap in comparison with prices charged in the United States.

In short, the combination of privatization and competition has led to the development of for-profit medical facilities that can cream off well-insured high-fee paying patients. Furthermore, as Hartman (1992) notes, the distribution and character of health care have been altered by the enormously influential presence of third-party payers. The cost of health care is exorbitant, both to the individual and to the nation. The system rewards the use of drugs, unnecessary diagnostic procedures, and surgery rather than health education, sickness or crisis care, and other preventive measures. Use of life-sustaining, highly advanced technological equipment for persons who are terminally ill and in pain or who are brain-dead has raised a number of questions. This sort of treatment may appear to be prolonging death rather than prolonging life. In any case, the amount of money spent on extraordinary interventions reduces the resources available for ordinary forms of care. Because Americans do not consider health care a right but a privilege (except for emergency care) and leave it up to individuals to make their own arrangements, millions of Americans are without access.

Lack of Access

In the United States access to health care is based on one's ability to pay. There is a three tier system—the insured, including the elderly, receive care that is as good as any in the world although the urgency of hospitals to reduce costs is lowering the quality of care to some extent; the poor, most of whom work, is a steadily growing population who get only emergency care when their conditions have seriously deteriorated (as of 1995, forty-three million Americans are without health insurance); and the minority of persons below the poverty level who are eligible for Medicaid and therefore get hospital care although many doctors in private practice will not treat them.

U.S. statistics bear out the tremendous disparity in care. Among the nations of the world, the United States ranks twelfth in life expectancy, nineteenth in infant mortality, twenty-first in deaths of children under five years of age, and twenty-ninth in the percentage of low-birth weight babies. Our low immunization rates are reflected in a rise in preventable childhood diseases.

The infant mortality rate of African Americans is double the white rate. Because of its reliability, the infant mortality rate is often used as a gauge of a nation's progress in taking care of its citizens' health. The African American infant mortality rate, a consequence of the lack of prenatal and postnatal care, is at a level comparable to that of some very poor nations. Throughout their lives, African Americans have higher rates of practically every illness than whites. Membership in a lower social class is also correlated with more illness and a significantly shorter life span than that of middle and upper classes.

A highly stigmatized program because of its association with poverty, Medicaid is seen by many as a handout to the able-bodied poor; about 70 percent of its beneficiaries are women and children. Yet nearly 70 percent of the expense goes for the poor elderly and the disabled, much of it for nursing homes. In fact, argues Ornstein (1995) of the American Enterprise Institute, the program benefits middle class families. The dependence of nursing homes and their residents on Medicaid is a crucial subsidy for their middle class adult children who otherwise would have to pay out of their pockets for their parents' care. The able-bodied adult poor who are the source of so much of the public's displaced anger comprise barely 10 percent of Medicaid's outlays. Medicaid's tremendous growth reflects the graying (or "whiting") of the population; the over-eighty-five age group is growing as fast as any other age group. Also, technological advances in medical care including neonatal care and organ transplants are raising the cost of care. Treatment of AIDS patients is another factor creating heavy demands on the system.

Going beyond the statistics, Hilfiker, M.D., (1994) provides us with a painful look at the human side of inner-city medicine in his book, *Not All of Us Are Saints*. The war stories resonate: homeless people treated for frostbite and then returned to the streets; sexual abuse reports not heeded; prescriptions for home health care which can amount to a cruel joke as far as the homeless are concerned.

The human side of health care on an Indian reservation is equally disturbing. According to van Biema (1995), while the federal government spends $2600 a year for the average American's health, the average spent on Native Americans is exactly half that. Jobs on reservations nationwide are extremely scarce. For medical services and food there is only one source of income—the federal government. But, as van Biema reports, the government is about to pull the plug. In the most drastic personnel cuts of any federal agency, the Bureau of Indian Affairs is laying off one-third of its employees and the budget is being slashed by a third also. Tribal government money is being withdrawn as is money for housing and food. The cut backs are expected to have a severe impact on health, especially through cuts in policing, food distribution, child welfare, and sanitation. There is one source of encouragement: Unlike other citizens who are guaranteed no right to health care, the government is required through hundreds of treaties to maintain a reasonable level of education and health among tribal members. The resolution of this situation will determine whether Native Americans will escape from the dire poverty of their living conditions or if the next generation will be even more impoverished.

Marketing Disease and Treatment

Thanks to privatization, health care is big business throughout the world. Many forms of treatment are marketed. The first marketing step is creating a need for the service as in the grosser aspects of cosmetic surgery where there is no need. The cosmetic surgery industry in the United States takes in three hundred million dollars every year, a figure that is rapidly growing according to Naomi Wolf, author of *The Beauty Myth* (1991). "If women suddenly stopped feeling ugly," according to Wolf (p. 234), "the fastest-growing medical specialty would be the fastest dying." "The manufacture of needs" is the phrase used to describe one of the major strategies of advertisers who are manufacturing wants that otherwise would not exist. Historically, advertisers have targeted women, playing on personal insecurities and self-doubt by projecting impossible ideals of feminine beauty (Durning, 1993). Consumption is idealized as the route to happiness. Pharmaceutical companies market their products relentlessly, mostly through magazine and medical journal advertising. The equation of happiness (even euphoria) with use of the product is the basic theme of this approach, "Ask your doctor about product X." Another example of the commercialization of medicine and medical care is the reliance on television advertisements by hospitals. Substance abuse treatment programs and adolescent treatment for behavioral problems are also examples of profit-making areas which are widely marketed.

Sometimes, and this is a paradox, society creates an atmosphere conducive to harm, the harm for which treatment centers arise to try to undo. For instance, the notion of "the alcoholic society" was formulated by sociologist Denzin (1993). In providing the arena for the production of alcoholics, the mass media created demands for the product to be used heavily; the addicted drinker is the target of most of the ads. Common sense tells us that liquor companies make little profit from moderate drinkers. To study alcoholism, then, is to study the relationship between individuals and the social structure, and the relationship between the treatment center and the social forces that create and sustain it. The study of the marketing and distribution of tranquilizers (often prescribed quite freely to women) is an even clearer example of the link between business and medicine in promoting harmful outcomes. In the end, antidotal medication is often required to get a person "unhooked" from the original medication. This becomes a case of treatment to counter treatment, a truly ironic state of affairs. In one way or another the business interests, then, are behind both heavy consumption of a product and its treatment. Economics, similarly, shapes the treatment itself. The form, duration, and availability of the medical treatment are determined less by science or the convenience of the patient (such as neighborhood location) than by sharp economic realities (such as insurance company constraints).

The fact that business is allowed to push products demonstrably dangerous to human health raises an important ethical issue: To what extent should the public be protected from marketers or, for that matter, from itself? To address this issue we will look at tobacco marketing, an area, like commercials for alcohol, of great disagreement and concern throughout the Western democracies. The assault that marketers make on children has been especially worrisome. Many countries have taken steps to regulate questionable practices. Yet, tobacco marketing, despite the increasingly tough restrictions placed on it, has been highly effective in boosting tobacco sales and ultimately diseases such as lung and throat cancer. Children, who want to appear cool and grown up, and women, who want to stay slim, have been specifically targeted by marketing strategies of a highly sophisticated sort. The success of the tobacco companies in increasing sales through mass marketing campaigns has been phenomenal. The numbers of female smokers skyrocketed with the Virginia Slims brand of cigarette for women. Recent data indicate a rising market share for Camels among youths following a highly controversial cartoon campaign surreptitiously aimed at children (Pierce and Gilpin, 1995). According to a recent survey of thousands of California adolescents, the biggest turn-on to smoking comes, not from peers, but from cigarette advertising (Associated Press, 1995c). To stem the tide and create revenues for health care, the American Heart Association, American Cancer Society, and American Lung Association recommend a two dollar increase in federal tax per pack of cigarettes (Bartecchi et al., 1995).

More nefarious and of special relevance to social welfare is the marketing of harmful products to poor countries abroad. Even if tighter marketing restrictions and higher excise taxes prove successful in decreasing tobacco smoking in the United States, the industry has a means to counteract loss of revenue, according to an article in *Scientific American* by Bartecchi et al. (1995). The means is through exportation. Leading the world in tobacco exports, the United States has capitalized on markets where there are few, if any, restrictions on advertising or product labeling. This kind of exploitation—for example, the targeting of women in Hong Kong—"equates with the disgraceful export of opium by England to China in the 1830s" (Bartecchi: 50). The marketing of cigarettes (sometimes passed out for free in Asian countries to create a demand) is the marketing of addiction. With cigarette smoking as the number one preventable cause of premature death in the United States, the magnitude of tobacco-related diseases and deaths around the world cannot be overrated.

Alcohol companies are aggressively marketing their addictive products through promises of leading a sophisticated Western lifestyle. Heise (1991), who has worked with a child health project in Guatemala, offers a tragic picture of the ravages of alcohol abuse in countries where even moderate drinking competes directly with food for scarce family income. Excessive drinking constitutes a substantial drain on health care systems. In Chile, for example, over half of all patients at Santiago's three largest medical centers are there (directly or indirectly) because of drinking problems. In Mexico, liver cirrhosis, a disease closely associated with heavy drinking, is one of the country's leading causes of death. In African countries, a husband's drinking severely restricts the effort put into food production and therefore, the family's health suffers. While international advertisers maintain that their craft stimulates business growth and creates jobs, critics such as Heise (1991) and Durning (1993), question whether the skillful stimulation of wants and desires is compatible with the quest for a sustainable society, not to mention good health.

THE ECONOMY AND HEALTH CARE IN CANADA AND EUROPE

Canada

The issues in Canada are the same as in the United States—high unemployment and a global market—and the solutions are also the same—privatization and budget cuts—but the Canadian system compared to that of the United States is decidedly different. Let us consider the system which although it is widely criticized, is still highly regarded as one of the best in the world.

Founded on the basic premise that health care is a right of residency, Canada's publicly funded health system has been fully operational since 1971. Mizrahi et al. (1993) sum up its basic principles for all ten provinces as follows:

- Universal coverage not related to employment.
- Comprehensive and full coverage including medical and hospital care, mental health services, and prescription drugs for people over sixty-five and for those with catastrophic illnesses.
- Public, nonprofit administration with provincial governments as the single payers of physicians and hospitals, no draining off of resources by intermediary companies such as insurance companies and MHOs.
- A provincial responsibility under federal mandate.
- Freedom of choice of provider.

Mizrahi et al. attribute the success of this arrangement—its low cost and high quality—to its efficient structure. In the United States, 24 percent of all health care spending goes toward administration, and the red tape is excruciating. Opinion polls taken in Canada reveal a people, compared to Americans, highly satisfied with their health care system. Because Canadians value the care that is available to them, however, they fear for its future against a barrage of attacks from the political right and the medical establishment (*Economist*, 1995). In defiance of the Canada Health Act which promises all citizens free and equal care, the province of Alberta allows private specialist clinics to operate. There are hundreds of these clinics now across Canada (Dalglish, 1994).

Don Collins (1995) delivered a presentation at the International Social Welfare in a Changing World Conference at the University of Calgary. His paper entitled, "A Canadian Social Worker's Views on NAFTA," compared the Canadians' "human need" and "universal access" criteria for their health care with the United States' "ability to pay" standard. Under imposed changes associated with the free trade agreement, social programs, according to Collins, will need to become much more cost effective and efficient. The Canadian Association of Social Workers deplores these developments and has opposed the free trade agreement. As an alternative, Collins urges Mexico and the United States to adopt social programs according to the Canadian model. This is a suggestion unlikely to occur.

The concepts of cost-effectiveness, privatization, and restructuring are also creeping into the medical care vocabulary. As federal and provincial governments pressure the medical system to restrain costs, some services are being dropped. The private sector is stepping in to fill those gaps (Dalglish, 1994). Because of the urgency attached to federal deficit reduction and the growing needs of an aging population, the "Medicare wars" (the Canadian health care system is called Medicare) are expected to continue. Federal support for the system is rapidly declining and being replaced by a block transfer to the provinces. Hospitals are being closed or merging, staff are being cut, and in-patient stays shortened. The replacement of registered nurses with nursing attendants, such as in operating rooms in Alberta, has stirred an uproar in the medical community and grave fears for patient safety (Marshall, 1995). Still, Canadians continue to take great pride in their system of universal care and show no inclination to give it up (Caragata, 1995).

United Kingdom

Developed following the social upheaval after World War II, the British National Health Service (NHS) was established under government authority. The belief was adopted early on that health care was a right to be enjoyed by all. In a speech given in Iowa, Director of Nursing of Bishop Auckland Hospitals in Durham County, England, Alison Guy (1994) provided an enthusiastic defense of the British health care system, a system she said was "about looking after people." The following information is based on Guy's informative and interesting talk. The distribution of money which comes from taxation is highly centralized and flows directly from the government. Medical procedures are performed, not unnecessarily to make a profit, but only if medically appropriate. Health care was reorganized into trusts in the 1980s when community care was stressed over hospitalization. Unlike in the United States, there are age limits on certain procedures. For dialysis, for instance, sixty-two is the maximum age for which it is provided through the NHS. Care is rationed, therefore, and since 1989, there is strict accountability for how money is spent. Today, a major stress on health care is the disproportionately high number of older people in the population. Unlike the Canadian system, the salary scale for doctors is set at the same level everywhere outside of the London area. In London, the pay is approximately three thousand dollars extra to compensate for the cost of living.

In Britain people pay four dollars toward their prescription medication. Patients may choose their own physicians or change doctors except if they are diagnosed with a chronic illness such as AIDS. It is hard to get a new general practitioner because doctors are reimbursed on a per capita basis and they would be reluctant to sign on seriously ill patients who already were under a physician's care.

In contrast to the United States, social workers are not employed by the hospitals but by the social service department. Therefore, social workers advocate for patients. If in their professional belief a patient is not ready to go home, the hospital cannot release him or her.

Current nationwide surveys in Britain indicate a high level of satisfaction with the doctors and nurses of the national health system and with the system itself. Guy concluded her talk on this note, "I know I work in it, but we have a wonderful system." In light of the high unemployment rate in the United Kingdom, however, and the rising national debt, one could realistically anticipate austerity measures to be applied there as elsewhere.

Western Europe in General

In an analysis of recent European trends in health care and disability programs, Zeitzer (1994) discusses social insurance provisions in five Western European countries in comparison with the United States. Although the funding arrangements vary by country—the United Kingdom pools all the tax revenues into one fund for distribution as needed, and Germany funds each program separately—all of the European countries studied have national health insurance programs that provide virtually universal and comprehensive health care for their populations. When persons are disabled and face loss of work, they are paid cash-sickness benefits to replace income lost. Special medical equipment making their homes handicapped-accessible is provided at no charge. The problems confronting Americans in these circumstances, in short, are not encountered in Europe. The effects of economic recession and the impact of an aging society, however, are areas with major implications everywhere. In Germany, moreover, the need to absorb all of the former East German workers into its labor force is extremely difficult in what Zeiter terms "a downturned" or depressed economy. Similarly, the rapidly deteriorating public finances and declining output in Sweden is leading to program cuts and restructuring. The Netherlands has taken strict measures to reduce the numbers of new disability claimants and make the benefits of a temporary nature. The French health care system, the most expensive in Europe, has put a cap on health spending and restrictions on hospital purchases and unnecessary medical treatment. Raising the retirement age is being used in Germany and Sweden as a means of increasing the number of taxpayers, and lowering the cost of living adjustments for pensioners in Germany, Sweden, and the United Kingdom is being introduced as a cost-saving measure.

Russia

Whereas the United States devotes more than 12 percent of its federal budget to health (much of it wastefully), England devotes 6 percent, and in Russia the percentage has fallen from 4 to 1, about the same as in the poorest African nations (Specter, 1995). If a nation's health can be seen as a main indicator of its level of social welfare, Russia is in fairly sad shape. In an article aptly entitled "Failing Health," Weir (1994) deplores the degeneration of Russia's hospitals in the context of market "reform" under capitalism. "Nowhere," asserts Weir (p. 21), "is Russia's post-Soviet social disaster more visible than in the growing squalor and collapse of its once-proud hospitals." The once universal system of health care is now creating mass dissatisfaction in the large majority of Russians. While the *nouveau riche* and foreign business community are treated in expensive Western-style hospitals, the rest of Russia is denied decent health care or medicine. Many former hospitals have become little more than holding tanks for the homeless, drug addicts, and abandoned elderly people, all victims of the new social structure. The life expectancy has fallen drastically to fifty-seven years for men and seventy-one years for women (CBS News, 1995). The infant mortality rate is up significantly. Hospital administrators are helpless against the plummeting of state funds and doctors, fed up with salaries that average less than one hundred dollars a month, are leaving the medical profession or fleeing the country entirely.

According to an eye-opening CBS news report (1995), living in Russia is hazardous to your health. Not only has the health care system collapsed but following decades of Soviet environmental abuse, water is contaminated and the air fouled. Infant birth defects are four times the American rate; scientists believe the exposure to dangerous chemicals may have damaged the genetic stock.

MALNUTRITION AND PREVENTABLE DISEASES

Malnutrition and disease are inextricably linked as each causes the other. Moreover, in most situations, poverty breeds malnutrition and disease as well. A useful conceptualization proposed by Hillary Graham (1984) illustrates poverty as living on an income insufficient to purchase the material resources necessary for health. Efforts to combat poverty, according to this construct, become health work in a true sense (Bywaters, 1986). In the United States, cuts in child nutrition and food stamp programs clearly have a direct bearing on the level of malnutrition but so do cuts in other programs—housing subsidies, energy assistance, and Medicaid—which invariably mean that families have less to spend on food (Sidel, 1992). Foods high in nutritional value such as fresh fruits and vegetables are often more expensive than the high-starch, low-nutritional foods. When money runs out, according to Sidel, food is what people skimp and save on. If the choice is between rent and food, one pays the rent; if it's between medicine and food it's usually a toss-up.

Malnutrition

World hunger, which is discussed in the context of poverty in chapter 5, is a growing problem closely related to overpopulation and the shortage of arable land. Stein (1990) summarizes the roots of global hunger: population increase, the burden of debt payment, deforestation, the shortage of water for irrigation, destruction of top soil, and global warming. According to the Brundtland Report (1987) entitled *Our Common Future,* sustainable development is achievable with proper planning so that the basic needs of all can be met. A world in which poverty is endemic will always be prone to ecological and other catastrophes.

The United Nations Children's Fund (UNICEF) released its annual report, *The State of the World's Children* (1994), which recorded the progress of nations and, in agreement with the Brundtland Report, seized the opportunity to call attention to the needless malnutrition, disease, and illiteracy that still cast a shadow over the poorest quarter of the world's children. The progress reported over the last fifty years includes: the doubling of real incomes; infant and child death rates more than cut in half; average life expectancy increased by a third; school attendance rates increased; family size has fallen by half; and much greater access to safe water. At the end of the 1980s, the internationally agreed target of 80 percent immunization against the major vaccine-preventable childhood diseases was reached by almost half of those defined as developing countries, while nearly all achieved a level of 70 percent. A benefit of progress in immunization not widely recognized is its contribution to improved nutrition. Frequent illness is a threat to a child's nutritional health and long-term growth. Illness reduces appetite, inhibits the absorption of food, and drains away vital nutrients through vomiting and diarrhea.

UNICEF's 1995 report reveals a continuation of the progress in disease elimination and water sanitation, both tremendous achievements, which "must give pause to those who would take the easy step into cynicism about the value of goals established by the international community" (p. 33). Two major setbacks over the previous year indicated in this report are a decrease in family income accompanied by an increasing wealth inequality which has now reached monstrous proportions. The decrease of overall foreign aid for furthering social development is highly unfortunate and will hamper further progress toward the World Summit goals of reducing deaths, malnutrition, disease, and disability.

Through family planning, the health of women has improved considerably. By having fewer children, women's risk of dying in childbirth is less, and the nutritional health of both mother and child is much improved. Still, as UNICEF strongly recommends, an increased investment in family planning services would do much to prevent the high rate of maternal deaths. Every year an estimated 500,000 women die from causes related to pregnancy and childbirth. Reducing the number of pregnancies among girls too young to give birth safely, or who seek unsafe abortions, would save many lives. However, as it was demonstrated in chapter 6, high child death rates and low levels of education for women mean that demand for family planning remains low.

The kind of mass starvation of which the world is periodically aware in dramatic news stories is rare. Only 1 to 2 percent of the world's children exhibit visible signs of malnutrition. Yet chronic malnourishment is rampant, nevertheless. According to UNICEF's report, the risk of dying from a given disease is doubled for even mildly malnourished children. In total, malnourishment is a factor in one-third of the deaths of small children each year. Mental retardation, according to an international report funded by the MacArthur and Rockefeller foundations among others, is two to eight times more common in poor nations than in industrialized countries due to such things as nutritional deficiencies and lack of prenatal care (Ritter, 1995).

The United States does not face the severe problems of nutritional deficiency that plague some of the rest of the world, but many Americans face uncertainty about meeting basic nutritional needs (DiNitto, 1995a). The food banks and soup kitchens struggle to feed the hungry. People holding up signs declaring, "Will work for food" or eating out of garbage dumpsters near restaurants are increasingly common sights.

Nationally, some five million children younger than twelve years old go hungry each month, and millions more are at risk (Keigher, 1994). Inadequate quantity and quality in the diet of pregnant women are closely linked to low birthweight and infant mortality which is quite high in the United States. Good nutrition for children is related to intelligence. Provisions as simple as school breakfasts, notes Kriegher, improve scores on standardized tests and raise school performances. Unfortunately, this important means of providing nutrition is one of the many programs being cut back.

Other programs slated for budget cuts are school lunches, the special school milk program, food stamps, and commodity food programs. Sum total, the nation's nutrition programs will be slashed by millions. Although saving the government money immediately, in the long run such savings will be extremely costly—the toll will be expressed in wasted lives and increased poverty among the next generation. Reductions in immunization efforts by federal and state governments have led to predictable measles epidemics, especially in the inner city. Fortunately, the consequences were tangible and immediate and, after a national outcry, efforts were made to undo the damage before it was too late.

One program that is widely acclaimed is the Special Supplemental Food Program for Women, Infants, and Children (WIC). This federally funded health promotion effort is aimed at improving the nutritional status of low-income, pregnant, breast-feeding, and postpartum women and their infants and children up to age five who are considered at nutritional risk. Participants receive coupons that allow them to obtain specified nutritious food such as dairy products and fruit juice. They also receive referrals to appropriate agencies for their care and well-being. A number of statistically controlled evaluations that compared prenatal women enrolled in WIC with women of the same socio-economic background who did not receive these services reveal decreased levels of low birth weight among enrolled women's infants. Costs for overall maternal and infant hospital care were also reduced. Drawing on data from the U.S. General Accounting Office, Avruch and Cackley (1995) found that prenatal WIC enrollment reduced first-year medical costs for U.S. infants by $1.9 billion in 1992. This program, however, only reaches 55 percent of those who are eligible (DiNitto, 1995a). The U.S. General Accounting Office recommends that all low-income pregnant women be eligible regardless of their level of nutritional risk (Avruch and Cackley, 1995).

As the safety net below poor families is being shredded, serious concern is voiced across the land. Bread for the World, a Christian citizens' anti-hunger movement in conjunction with Lutheran, Presbyterian, and Catholic organizations, held a "Lunch of Stones" on Capitol Hill. This activist gathering took its symbolism from Jesus who asked, "Is there anyone among you who, if your child asks for bread, will give a stone?" McManus (1995) pursues this metaphor further in an editorial entitled, "Lawmakers are Offering Stones, not Bread, to the Hungry Children of the World." The editorial builds on the Bread of the World's landmark report on the state of world hunger. One hundred million people were at risk due to 164 armed conflicts raging in the world in 1995, according to this report. Yet the United States is getting rid of the humanitarian relief portion (for "sustainable development") of foreign aid and maintaining the military portion. Western aid is expected to decrease in the future in another area with vital implications for the world: AIDS care and prevention.

Preventable Disease: AIDS

This discussion on disease will focus on acquired immune deficiency syndrome (AIDS) as one preventable disease that dwarfs all others in terms of social and medical impact, and as an affliction with horrendous international implications. AIDS is a contagious, currently incurable disease that destroys the body's immune system (Zastrow, 1996). The human immunodeficiency virus (HIV) is a sexually transmitted and blood-borne retrovirus that ultimately destroys the immune system (Lloyd, 1995). HIV has been firmly established as the cause of AIDS. AIDS, the end-stage of HIV infection, is spread when body fluids such as blood, semen, urine, and vaginal secretions of a person infected with the virus enter the bloodstream of another.

The global toll is already staggering. According to the World Health Organization's (WHO) latest estimates, cited by Cowley (1994), four million persons have developed AIDS since the beginning of the epidemic—1.5 million in the past year alone—and seventeen million are HIV-positive. While the rate of new infections is waning in Europe and the United States, the epidemic is fierce in Africa, and Asia is bracing for an explosion of new cases. And no nation can be complacent. Given the interdependence of nations and the rate of spread of AIDS, no country can be completely safe from this disease until every country is safe.

AIDS is a calamity for humanity the spread of which is perpetuated by the other calamities, especially poverty and underdevelopment. As scientists Kalibala and Anderson (1993) of the Global Programme on AIDS of the WHO point out, the social impact of this disease is the worst among underprivileged individuals, families, and communities all over the world. By striking people during their most productive years—about two-thirds of those infected are under age 25—AIDS is robbing nations as well as families of their able-bodied workers (UNICEF, 1994).

Across the African continent, millions of children are being orphaned because of the AIDS epidemic. Another million or so of African children have died of AIDS (UNICEF, 1995). The traditional extended family is withering away in Africa just when its caring influence is most needed (Kalibala and Anderson). Partly because the pressure of so much illness is too great and partly because of the changing economic environment, urbanization and monetary considerations are taking over humanitarian and social obligations. The lure of sex, drugs, and alcohol to individuals caught up in the quest for power and money is weakening the traditional African community. The women are being overwhelmed with having to provide care for chronically ill husbands and brothers. Yet the ratio of women to men with AIDS in Africa is six to five. So who cares for the dying women? Mothers, sisters, and children are responsible. Outside help is greatly needed, as Kalibala and Anderson urge, to reinforce the role of families and to prevent the further spread of this deadly disease. Early intervention, according to UNICEF (1995), is the best hope for eradication. In Uganda, a country which has been seriously stricken—the average life expectancy has declined from age fifty-two to age forty-two since 1980—programs for AIDS prevention increasingly are mobilizing every possible resource for reaching the public. Like most countries which are taking desperate action, Uganda is using a combination of school and mass media campaigns. A unique program in Uganda targets long distance drivers and prostitutes at trading centers. These are key groups who engage in risky sexual behaviors that promote HIV transmission. For the high numbers of children orphaned in Uganda, the government has instituted a program to place children with relatives when they lose their parents to AIDS. Kenya, in contrast, has no such program so untended children roam the cities in packs (Snell, 1995).

Logan (1994) underscores the pivotal role of social work education in relation to HIV/AIDS and the contribution that the social work profession can make toward global prevention strategies. At the University of Manchester, England, HIV/AIDS-transmission awareness is integrated into the core curriculum. The dynamics of this disease, as Logan informs us, brings together a myriad of issues which occur across social work practice generally: sexuality, stigma, fear, discrimination, disability, loss and death. HIV infection can be prevented. Because the modes of transmission are well-established, it is possible to inform people about very specific behavior or activities that, if changed, reduce or eradicate their risk of infection (Lloyd, 1995). Logan (p. 45) describes how social workers will use this knowledge:

> Inevitably, the specialist knowledge required by social workers and probation officers will vary according to their particular focus of practice. Social workers in adoption and fostering will be concerned with the complexities surrounding HIV positive children or how to deal with misinformed or highly anxious foster parents. Those working with adolescents will want to know how to advise them on safer sex practices. Child protection workers are going to be increasingly faced with the implications of HIV for sexual abuse. Probation officers may need to know how to advise clients on safer drug use whilst others will want to know about treatment options. Those working directly with people living with the virus will require more specialized skills in grief counseling.

Although geared for work with British clients, this knowledge base is applicable to social workers everywhere who are wrestling with the same difficult issues.

Currently the best way to stop the spread of AIDS is through educating people to avoid known risks and to protect themselves through use of condoms. Zastrow (1996) lists the following as high-risk behaviors:

- Having anal intercourse.
- Having multiple sex partners without using condoms.
- Sharing intravenous needles.
- Having sex with prostitutes.

Drug-related transmission risk behavior is particularly difficult to curb because needles and syringes are shared. Drug injectors, furthermore, may be in double jeopardy in that drugs lower inhibitions and increase the practice of unsafe sex (Lloyd, 1995). Drug and alcohol treatment and prevention programs are therefore essential in reducing risk-taking behaviors. For confirmed drug addicts, harm reduction efforts such as extensive needle exchange programs have been effective in the United Kingdom. Such programs are being initiated on a limited basis in the United States where moralism and common sense are so often on a collision course.

Prevention in World Context

As a legacy of the Industrial Revolution, scientific and technical approaches to diseases came to dominate the medical model of health and illness, with an emphasis on illness. Although historians have provided evidence that improved nutrition and the provision of safe water and efficient disposal of sewage were responsible for the drastic reduction in mortality rates over the past century, health care policies tend to focus on cure rather than care. This emphasis is reinforced by the interests of the drug industry. In medicine, the bulk of funding is geared toward new technology to eradicate disease, while preventive policies remain relatively undeveloped (Bywaters, 1986). At the service end, likewise, there is a lack of appropriate emphasis and funding for long-term care for elderly, mentally retarded, or mentally ill persons in contrast to the provision of acute care. A related criticism of the modern health care system is its emphasis on the disease rather than the person, and on the symptoms rather than the context. Physical pain may be addressed whereas emotional pain may be neglected. Sometimes the emotional pain stems from the medical treatment itself.

A health care system built on treatment and totally neglecting prevention is found in Russia. The lack of attention to infection control, in fact, renders hospital stays extremely hazardous. Big city operating rooms resemble the clinics of rural nineteenth century America; sterile instruments are rare and blood is washed away with a garden hose (Specter, 1995). The death rates have never been higher in peacetime, and preventable infectious diseases like diphtheria and measles have reached epidemic levels. Health experts, according to Specter, say that Russia could do much to improve conditions even without spending much money. Reasonable attempts to teach disease prevention and sanitary habits would save thousands of lives a year. Even though Russians smoke and drink excessively, doctors do not try to educate them. An inexpensive vaccine could wipe out the country's diphtheria. Information on diet, cleanliness, vitamins, and exercise would cost little and help immensely.

Two-thirds of all new cases of HIV are now occurring in Africa where recent gains in child survival are accordingly being reversed. Without a vaccine available, prevention efforts geared at behavioral change are essential. Cultural change is essential also: the AIDS threat to women and children, as UNICEF (1995) indicates, will continue to increase until women have more power to say no to sex, to choose their own partners, and to influence sexual behavior. Resources are also required. Unfortunately, only 10 percent of the annual expenditure on AIDS prevention is spent in Southern Hemisphere countries of the world where 85 percent of infections are occurring (UNICEF, 1995).

COMMUNITY ACTION EFFORTS

Cuba

In its AIDS prevention efforts, Cuba, up until recently, used a system of quarantine for persons living with AIDS. The enclosure of persons who tested as HIV-positive or who had developed AIDS was reminiscent of Louisiana's leper colony, a colony established to protect the general public by isolating those with contagious diseases. The care given in these quarantines was above the standard of living for ordinary Cubans. Although the AIDS infection rate in Cuba remained quite low, this policy was discontinued in 1994, apparently due to international pressure. According to the U.S. CBS news-magazine program, *60 Minutes,* the remedy raised some questions from a human rights standpoint but as a disease-control measure, it seemed to have been effective. Some might find this remedy, in its authoritarianism, worse to contemplate than the spread of the disease itself.

Cuba's solution was consistent with its overall health care focus on prevention over cure and primary treatment over tertiary treatment. Cuba is a country, like many in Europe, where health care is considered a human right for all citizens. Iatridis (1990) draws on the example of Cuban health care which is equitable and effective in maintaining high standards despite limited resources. In terms of quantitative health indicators like the infant mortality rate, nutritional status, and life expectancy, Cuba equals or surpasses the United States, particularly in universal health coverage, preventive primary care, infant mortality, life span, and medical insurance coverage. The Cuban experience, as Iatridis asserts, demonstrates the influence of ideological commitment and policy-making on the provision of health care and challenges the assumption that high-quality care for all citizens requires massive financial investment.

Mexico

In three years, Mexico has halved the number of child deaths from diarrhea and the dehydration associated with it. Inspired by goals set for all nations at the United Nations 1990 World Summit for Children, a mass educational effort was launched to train one million women as health representatives in the simple and low-cost technique of oral rehydration therapy (UNICEF, 1995). This public health effort has paid off; approximately thirty thousand young lives have been saved as a result of the campaign. Investment in clean water and safe sanitation has aided the effort tremendously by stopping the problem before it starts. Health authorities from forty-five countries have visited Mexico to study the successful campaign to defeat the number one killer of Mexico's children. Another area of remarkable success has been in family planning. Through an extensive mass media campaign with the backing of government agencies, the family size has been reduced considerably.

Large Scale Prevention Strategies

In the Philippines, where the infant mortality rate was already quite high, an alarming decline in breast-feeding was aggravating the situation. The marketing of infant formula milk that was vitamin-deficient was threatening child survival (Mabulay and Subingsubing, 1995). A coalition of community-based groups was born in 1981 to pursue the protection of infants' health. Breast-feeding seminars were conducted for pregnant women. As community awareness was increased, community health centers also became interested, and today the alarming trend not to breast-feed has been turned around.

Costa Rica's health care has been oriented toward the poor for two decades, with the result that lower income groups now receive a considerably greater share of public health expenditures than do the middle classes. Malaysia has a similar poor-oriented policy. The Children's Fund (UNICEF, 1995) in its annual report urges "radical and far-reaching changes" to restructure government expenditures for the common good. How can this be achieved? UNICEF recommends limiting expenditures on universities (education for the elite) and hospitals and concentrating on primary school education and rural health clinics. India and Zimbabwe are two countries pursuing policies to help the masses; India by focusing on literacy for *all* instead of on university education for the few, and Zimbabwe by reducing investments in central hospitals in favor of rural health care. However, according to the United Nations report, such efforts are more the exception than the rule. The difference between what can be done and what is being done is vast.

Canada

David Smith (1995: 12) defines *health* as "the product of multiple interacting forces—physical, emotional, economic, social." Within the spirit of this holistic framework Canada's community health centers operate. Instead of the episodic care provided in a sickness-oriented system, the community health centers provide comprehensive, continuing care in a preventive mode (Smith, 1995). Staffed by a team of salaried doctors, nurses, physiotherapists, and dietitians, community health centers are springing up all over Canada (fifty-three in Ontario) to keep health care costs from being sent "through the roof." A unique aspect of the centers, originally opposed by the medical profession, is that they are consumer-run; community boards determine health policies and programs.

Suicide prevention is an area in which a large-scale effort is directed in Finland, Norway, Australia, as well as Canada (Tanney, 1995). The situation in Canada which has drawn preventive attention includes a high rate of rural suicides, with a notable increase in rates among young males, a continuing high female rate, and increased rates among native Canadians and throughout the correctional system. The province of Alberta is at the forefront in the organized implementation for preventing suicide. The main component of the program is early intervention focused on the environment and integrated with an educational component. As described in chapter 10, an effort directed in Alberta high schools focuses on students who are wrestling with sexual orientation issues, a high-risk population for suicide. Funding in Alberta for the total prevention effort is over one million Canadian dollars. Nevertheless, Tanney fears a declining interest nationwide in prevention and early intervention activities as human service activities continually shrink.

Other Industrialized Countries

Relative to the United States, other industrialized countries are advanced in the provision of preventive health care for children. Perhaps because these countries foot the bill for health care, the interest is in maintaining good health to save great expense later. Well-baby care, for instance, is provided to young mothers. European countries systematically reach newborns with home visitors, immunizations, advice, and well-baby assessments (Keigher, 1994). The truth is that in the United States public health is in crisis, especially in regard to maternal and child health. Addressing the subject of Medicaid's failure to prevent unwanted pregnancy, Keigher (1994: 146) writes, "I wonder about the usefulness of public policy in a society that, in the midst of recovery, is allowing itself to destroy its own seed corn." Keigher's agrarian imagery is reminiscent of Jay Cayner's old Iowa saying which introduced this chapter, "Never clean the water until you get the pigs out of the creek." This is prevention in a nutshell.

The community action efforts described in this section could be adapted to poor urban and rural areas in rich countries. Since the poor and women of color have higher rates of illness and shorter life expectancies than others, the availability of health care services in the inner city is vital.

HOUSING AND THE HOMELESS

Housing

Housing represents the American dream: the combination of physically safe shelter with the expectation of status, security, community resources, and independence (Mulroy, 1995). The absence of housing is the American nightmare. The importance of housing is obvious in the examples of early European immigrants having to improvise houses out of sod because there were no trees before the cold winds started to blow, and of course the Eskimos who created warmth and coziness in the midst of ice.

Housing in today's world is associated with privacy, protection from the elements and from intruders—people, wild animals, and insects—a place to take care of one's daily needs, a place to show hospitality to others, and an entertainment center. Housing serves both as a center for rest from work and as a place for work. Whereas the word *house*, in popular use refers to a "roof over one's head," the word *home* has more social emotional connotations. The difference is revealed in the expression "to find the child a home." The reference is clearly not to a building—a house—but to a place where people will take care of him or her. Home, wrote Harrington (1985: 101), "is the center of a web of human relationships."

Housing is discussed in this chapter because of its close, though often overlooked connection with health and health services. A house provides physical safety from injury—keeping small children out of the street or lamentably, in some neighborhoods, out of gunfire range. Being without shelter or in overcrowded shelter is associated, as we will see, with the spread of disease. More remotely, there is a link between housing and health care in that persons without adequate income are apt to lack both.

Federal recognition of the importance of housing was evidenced in the Housing Act of 1949 which acknowledged the need for a decent home and a suitable living environment for every American family. Thirty percent of income is generally what residents of public housing are expected to contribute to their rent. Yet nearly half of all renters have rent burdens above this level (Mulroy, 1995). In single-mother households the proportion may reach 70 to 80 percent. Only 28 percent of poor households live in public housing or receive housing subsidies such as the Section 8 program (Mulroy, 1995). Waiting lists are long since many eligible renters are unable to find qualified Section 8 housing in the private market. Cuts in federal subsidies for housing have resulted in grave limitations in the availability of low-cost housing and a staggering growth of homelessness (Johnson and Schwartz, 1994). According to Karger and Stoesz (1990), there are four major factors contributing to a severe housing crisis: escalating rents and utility rates, substantial increases in property taxes affecting both homeowners and renters, lack of moderate and low-priced housing (when buildings are substandard they are often demolished rather than repaired), and severe slashes in federal funding for rental assistance and other programs. To this list Mulroy adds the shifts in the nation's economy that have increased income gaps between the rich and the poor and produced a sharp decline in employment for men. There is a public outcry, nevertheless, over subsidies for the poor to help them obtain housing. Yet housing-related tax deductions for the middle and upper classes are valued at over three times the total cost of low-income housing assistance (Karger and Stoesz, 1990).

Today, public housing accounts for only 2 percent of the U.S. housing market compared to 46 percent of the market in England and 37 percent in France (Mulroy, 1995). Why the reluctance of the U.S. government to provide low-cost housing? From the start, such housing was perceived as potential competition with the private sector and discouraged by real estate and banking interests, according to Mulroy. Since 1980, the Department of Housing and Urban Development (HUD) has seen its funding cut drastically. The trend is to go to a voucher system where the government subsidizes rent at the fair market rate. However, the voucher system still fails to get to the heart of the problem—the absence of adequate low-income housing.

In sharp contrast to the United States where public housing is highly stigmatized, in the United Kingdom such subsidized housing is the normal pattern for the respectable working classes. Over one quarter of the people live in council (public) housing. Council housing is provided and managed by the housing departments of local authorities and varies from large estates and special housing for elderly people to large high-rise buildings in inner cities (Elliott, 1990). Local authorities take responsibility to house the homeless.

A Costa Rican grass-roots project helping slum dwellers construct decent houses has a lot in common with the United States' Habitat for Humanity program which draws on volunteer labor to remodel and construct houses for low-income families. A women's group in Costa Rica with thirty thousand members and a strong sense of community operates under the slogan, "homes, not slums" (Trejos, 1992). Its daily struggle against poverty and homelessness helped people to see all social problems as interlinked. These women fought for genuine improvements in their living conditions along with new housing. During moments of relaxation on the site where women and children are constructing blocks of a hundred living units, the volunteers give advice on such subjects as food hygiene, breast-feeding, birth control, sanitation, and social legislation. Land surrounding the houses is cultivated for the growing of vegetables and medical plants.

Japan is unique in its combination of high living standards and severely cramped housing in the large cities. Notes Waswo (1995: 25), a professor of modern Japanese history, "Here, even the well-educated and relatively well-paid tend to live in the small, cramped quarters an official of the European Union once described as 'rabbit hutches.'" Waswo holds the state responsible for not pushing apartment dwellings over single-family dwellings and for the failure to construct public housing units in the early postwar years. To escape urban overcrowding, the Japanese endure long commuting distances between home and work. The elderly and poorly paid form the majority of those who inhabit substandard public and private housing in Japan's inner cities. For a recent news report on a little known aspect of Japanese urban life—homelessness—see box 8.1.

The cities in China, similarly, are jam-packed with humanity. Beijing, for instance, faces a severe housing crisis (Associated Press, 1995b). Roughly half its ten million residents live in old one-story *hutongs* built as early as the fourteenth century. Most of the other half live in high-rise apartments in poor condition. The crumbling cities today are inundated as rural migrants, knocked off farm labor, flock in looking for jobs. The average number of urban square feet of housing space is half that of overcrowded Japan. A single outdoor water faucet may be shared by a dozen families. Two illustrations from the Associated Press story reveal the urgency of the situation: A fight erupted between a divorced man and his ex-wife who lived divided only by a curtain because neither could get new housing; a Shanghai man is now serving a life prison term for wounding his boss with a knife for failing to get him a larger home.

The case of Lithuania exemplifies the hardship of moving into capitalism without adequate large-scale planning. Housing and medical benefits have gradually eroded; inflation is rampant, and homelessness, crime, and economic exploitation by an underground market give visible evidence of the progressive movement into poverty of an entire society (Kulys and Constable, 1994). Housing expenses

BOX 8.1

HOMELESS IN TOKYO

It is a familiar scene in North America, but it has proved shocking to many Japanese. Shuffling, stooped, mostly male, a ragged group of homeless people waits patiently for a cup of hot soup, their main meal for the day. The food line, organized by Shinjuku Renraku Kai, a citizen's group aiding Japan's homeless, has grown steadily longer over the past two years. It snakes past the gleaming buildings and well-stocked shops that surround Shinjuku station, gateway to a major Tokyo office and nightlife centre. It moves in the shadow of the 48-storey, $1.9 billion Tokyo City Hall, an elegant showpiece built at the height of Japan's inflated bubble economy of the 1980s. But those times are over now, and these people are the proof.

"This is a common sight these days," says Yasue Suzuki, a volunteer for the citizens' organization. "The recession and the decay of the family as an institution are the main causes of the rise in the homeless in Japan." Ten years ago, there were virtually no street people in Japan. Today, according to government statistics, 3,300 people live rough in Tokyo, but social workers say the number is probably 10,000. Many of those in Shinjuku are older people who have lost their construction jobs and a company-provided bed space. Some have been abandoned by children, a once-unthinkable turn of events in a society that has traditionally

venerated the elderly. "In Japan, homeless people are mostly single, unemployed and elderly men and women," says sociologist Midori Komobuchi. "That is because family solidarity is breaking down and social conscience is at a low ebb. And it's going to get worse before it gets better."

The Shinjuku people live in cardboard boxes in a long passageway in the vast underground station, using the public toilets and scavenging garbage cans for food. Now, Suzuki says, even elderly couples inhabit the station. "When the husband loses his job," she says, "they have nowhere else to go."

Koichi Watanabe, 60, has lived in the passageway for the past two years. "I have been a day laborer all my life and earned quite a bit during the construction boom," he relates. "Then came the double punch. I was growing old and and economy crumbled." Watanabe manages a wash and a shave every three days in a public washroom. Once a week, he visits a charitable foundation to pick up clothes distributed to the needy. "Then I try my luck at work again," he says softly. "But the clothes don't fool anybody, apparently. The recruiter just ignores me."

When the trickle of homeless first began appearing a few years ago, authorities preferred to see them as a freak aspect

(Continued on next page)

BOX 8.1 (Continued)

of Japanese society. But as the numbers grew, they became a problem that had to be dealt with—not always deftly. At Ueno Park, a major green space in an elegant area of Tokyo, officials have launched twice-monthly eviction operations to try to get rid of homeless inhabitants. "They leave garbage lying around and their presence is unpleasant to visitors," says a park superintendent. "A park is no place to sleep."

The Shinjuku district office is enmeshed in a battle with the homeless and their supporters, who are fighting a plan to build a moving walkway where the cardboard homes now stand. In mid-December, more than one hundred aging homeless clashed with police at Tokyo City Hall after storming the building and demanding jobs. "We will not be forcibly evacuated," screamed an old man into a microphone.

The contrasting reactions the homeless provoke are familiar to North Americans. Shinjuku district officer Minoha Takeyama shakes his head in exasperation. "There are some genuinely homeless people out there, but most of them simply don't want to work and prefer to live like that," he says. "It's too much." Volunteer worker Suzuki, on the other hand, thinks the government should show more sympathy toward the homeless. "These people need to be respected and understood as victims of Japanese society, not as people to be rid of." Given Japan's painful restructuring, the country is unlikely to be rid of them soon.

Source: Suvendrini Kakuchi, "Homeless in Tokyo," *Maclean's,* January 8, 1996, p. 21. Reprinted by permission of *Maclean's.*

---

consume 50 to 75 percent of the income of most Lithuanians. Hot water is available only on weekends in large cities and heat in apartments is kept at very low levels.

A rich and highly regulated country such as Norway is a land where all new construction is aesthetically appealing. No one is allowed to live in mobile homes or manufactured houses, for instance. There is a housing shortage, however, and the government assumes responsibility for persons having problems finding a place to live. To keep the population from flocking to the cities of southern Norway, persons who live in the north are given government subsidies as are farmers. Many Norwegians have two homes—a city dwelling and a log cabin in the mountains as a place of retreat for skiing and summer holidays.

Legal refugees are provided with housing by the government often in former hotels until they are formally admitted as residents of the country.

Homelessness

One of the most powerful definitions of *home* is offered by Robert Frost in the poem, *The Death of the Hired Man* (1914), "Home is the place where, when you go there, they have to take you in." Use of the word in this sense refers to a lot more than "a roof over one's head." Here, home has an almost nurturant quality associated with warmth, openness, and acceptance. Some people find their home on the street. Others may be housed in a shelter which is not a home. The phrase "going home" may refer to a person's past or to a broad geographical area rather than to a house. All of this is to say that the term homeless is perhaps a misnomer. We are really talking about people who lack adequate shelter and are in a sense "houseless." These people, according to the dictionary, don't have "a place of residence; a place in which one's domestic affections are centered" (*Random House Dictionary*, 1980).

Nevertheless, everyone today has his or her personal image of what is meant by the homeless. Here is a snippet from conservative radio commentator Rush Limbaugh on his concept of homelessness (1992: 250–251).

> Notice that in all of them (liberal writings) the so-called homeless crisis is used by the left to drag down the American way of life. That is the common theme in all of them. The message is that the American people are at fault, and the downtrodden—whether they are drug abusers or homeless people—can't be at fault. You're never supposed to blame the downtrodden. Who, then should we blame? It's true that some of the homeless have lost their homes. But the government's disastrous policies of urban renewal are responsible for destroying many of the single-room-occupancy hotels they used to live in. And many of the homeless have only themselves to blame. They either aren't willing to assume the responsibilities that go with being a citizen or they are mentally ill or abusing drugs or alcohol. Of course, we have to find some way to help them, but is it necessary to lie to them or ourselves about their own contribution to their condition? Their actions often are responsible for their problems. . . .
>
> You don't believe me that some homeless people choose to live that way? Take the case of Richard Kreimer, a homeless man in Morristown, New Jersey,

who liked to frequent the public library there. He would stare at patrons, and many had to leave the library because of the strong stench he gave off. He refused to bathe, and would wander about the library as if it were his living room. . . .

Who Are the Homeless?

Because homeless people are elusive, and the definition of homelessness is vague, exact figures are hard to come by. According to Martha Burt of the Urban Institute (quoted in an interview by Young, 1994), the absence of recent homeless data has been a cause for lack of funding and makes interstate comparisons difficult. Advocates of the homeless estimate their numbers as three million, according to Burt, and this figure is the most widely cited.

A survey of thirty cities by the U.S. Conference of Mayors found total requests for emergency shelter up 13 percent and food requests up 12 percent (Moss and Dickson, 1994). For families the growth rate is even higher. The demographic portrait of homelessness released by the Conference of Mayors is as follows:

Single men	48%
Single women	11%
Families with children	38%
Children without families	3%
Blacks	53%
Whites	31%
Hispanics	12%
Native Americans	3%
Asians	1%
Substance abusers	43%
Mentally ill	26%
Veterans	23%
Employed full- or part-time	19%
Have AIDS or related illnesses	8%

To realize the human dimension beyond these numbers, Cheryl Hyde (1995: 192) provides an account of the death of Brenda, a homeless woman who died overnight while seeking shelter in a bus stop near the HUD office ("Homeless-ness Hitting Home: A Death on HUD's Doorstep," *New York Times*: November 30, 1993):

> As her body was removed, HUD officials and White House personnel were furiously debating funding for homeless programs. Her companions' remembrances were of a woman in her thirties with a "sharp mind" and helpful nature who was afraid of shelters. Brenda's death was not anonymous because of where she died. That we know of her death only underscores how little we know of her life, or the lives of others who are homeless, because of societal indifference and government neglect.

In Iowa, a state that is fairly representative of America's heartland, children today make up just over half of the state's homeless (Associated Press, 1995a). All the agencies involved in providing services—from schools and social services to shelters—agree that the number one need is affordable housing.

Although some people refuse to go to shelters and claim to enjoy the freedom of their life on the streets, most people are homeless not by choice but by cruel circumstance. The profile of the homeless has changed to include large numbers of women and children. One thing that can be said with certainty: the homeless are a strikingly heterogenous group. Let us look at the background factors.

Homelessness is conceptualized variously depending on the political orientation of the writer. Thus homelessness is a manifestation of class oppression (Leibow, 1993), an embodiment of the contradictions of the postindustrial city (Katz, 1989), a product of the lack of housing affordability (Mulroy and Lane, 1992) and a chosen way of life (Limbaugh, 1992). In truth, a combination of factors operating simultaneously can lead to loss of a home. The key factors, furthermore, vary by population group.

Of all the writers on homelessness, Rosenthal (1994) singularly attends to the *interaction* component in the process of becoming homeless. The chain of events, according to Rosenthal, that leads a person from residency to homelessness typically involves three stages: a predisposing *vulnerability* to homelessness (economic or physical), *precipitating incidents* (job loss, "welfare reform," or loss of affordable housing), and the *inability to find substitute housing*. How do these events work in tandem? Mental illness, say, may interact with loss of family support and structural factors (urban renewal and cuts in public assistance). Substance abuse may enter the picture also, frequently serving as a form of self-medication against a sea of troubles. More specifically, substance abuse may be associated in a reciprocal fashion with work problems or with a lack of gainful employment. Whatever the configuration of factors, the significance, consistent with ecosystems theory, is the synergism or multiplying effect of any number of elements.

The biopsychosocial model provides a framework ideally suited to an understanding of the multidimensional nature of homelessness. *Biologically,* an individual may have a health problem that precludes work, inhibits long-term relationships, and hinders his or her abilities to engage in long-term planning. *Psychological* aspects overlap with the biological—mental and drug dependency disorders both related to depression and physical abuse precipitate an individual's decline. *Social factors* include having the family as a buffer against life's cruel blows; and other socioeconomic forces such as unemployment, deinstitutionalization of mental patients, and the demolition of low income housing and alternative programs. Applied to homelessness, this biopsychosocial construct draws attention to the *biological* consequences of street-living that are often fatal as for Brenda described earlier who apparently froze to death on HUD's doorstep; the *psychological* repercussions of having no security or stability; and the loss of one's *social* support system, the building of another support network, and society's response to the homeless as a highly visible segment of the poor.

For certain groups, such as youths and women, particular factors emerge as causative. "Throwaways" are youths who have been thrown out of their home by families. Parental or child drug abuse may be a cause, or as in many cases, sexual orientation of the child can be a factor (Putnam, 1995). The number of gays and lesbians among street children has been found to be startlingly high (Athey, 1991). Many youth flee their homes to escape physical or sexual abuse. Domestic violence, similarly, is a major factor contributing to homelessness in women.

In an article entitled "Battered Welfare Syndrome," Ehrenreich (1995) views welfare benefits as not just support but as a life-saving device freeing women who may be in grave danger at home, and at work sites as well, from predatory males. Many aspects of welfare "reform," as Ehrenreich notes, threaten refugees from domestic violence. Among these reforms are the work requirement, the cuts in welfare payments and support for women's shelters, stipulations to identify the children's father, and the state residency restrictions (to qualify for benefits) preventing certain avenues of escape. Victims of abuse are especially vulnerable to poverty, and victims of poverty are especially prone to physical abuse. The backlash against mothers on welfare is pronounced; consequently survival factors may be overlooked with tragic results.

So what is it like to be homeless? How does one live from day to day? Liebow (1993) depicts the female reality of shelter life in his disturbingly dramatic book, *Tell Them Who I Am: The Lives of Homeless Women.* These women must fight for or overcome enormous obstacles to get things usually taken for granted. Shelter rules, such as having to be out on the streets by seven a.m. and not leaving any possessions behind, can create tremendous barriers to comfort. One can only imagine the inconvenience of such circumstances.

When sociologist Ron Roberts took a leave from his teaching duties to live as a homeless person, he was able to experience homelessness from the inside out. Roberts and Keefe (1986) interviewed homeless people allowing them a chance to speak for themselves. Nancy, a homeless activist and organizer, evidences a striking resilience as she speaks (p. 414):

> I'm really good friends with the rest of the street people. They've lived in my camper. We do dumpster diving, you know, garbage diving. We do some feeding. We make the best stews you can imagine.

Another homeless person, Sam, describes survival on the banks of the river in these terms (p. 406):

> You've got to have a buddy, for one thing. If you lay here on the American River, you've got to sleep with one eye open and one hand on your knife in your bag. People would just as soon kick your head in as to look at you.

From Hertzberg's (1992: 154) participation observation study comes the following view on what life is like on the streets:

> It's rough. It's not a nice place to be, unless you're drunk; then you don't care.

Having a drink and killing the pain of the rejections and frustrations of being homeless becomes an all-day routine, according to Hertzberg. Rosenthal (1994) articulates how the contingencies of time and distance (miles to walk each day) shape the survival strategies of homeless people. The stories his interviewees tell highlight an important point about homeless life: Despite their lack of a home base or other supports for creating an orderly life, most homeless people continually attempt to create one, an effort that requires some level of competency. The homeless become tremendously resourceful.

Health Care

Illness can lead to the loss of income and therefore to the loss of housing. The homeless are already at great risk for health problems due to their harsh living conditions and because of inadequate preventive health care services afforded to them. Belcher and Di Blasio (1995) summarize the health problems facing those persons we see huddled over steam vents, in doorways, on subway benches, and reaching into restaurant dumpsters. The first problem is the spread of diseases—colds, flu, acute bronchitis, tuberculosis—where people are in close confinement such as in a shelter. Secondly, there are the physical injuries— assaults, stab wounds, rape—and the health problems associated with such trauma. Finally, many unaccompanied homeless youth, both males and females, resort to prostitution as a means of survival (Putnam, 1995). Therefore, the risk of contracting AIDS is high, and is one of the most serious health problems, in fact, of homeless youth.

The inability of the homeless to find a bed and the proper coverings at night causes these people to suffer from diseases of the extremities. Foot disease is common. Malnutrition and hypertension are also major health problems (Belcher and Di Blasio, 1995). Homeless people will wait until they have serious health problems before seeking medical help, often from a hospital's emergency room. See box 8.2 for a social worker's perspective on emergency room work.

Prevention and Services

There are the temporary, band-aid solutions and preventive measures that are directed toward the long term. Current federal housing policies that fund homeless shelters and transitional housing programs do not address the long-term

BOX 8.2

EMERGENCY ROOM ENCOUNTERS
WITH THE HOMELESS

For eight years I was a social worker in the emergency room at Graduate Hospital, Philadelphia. In this inner-city setting I worked with hundreds of homeless people. Looking back on this experience now, I am impressed with the discrepancy between the image that one gets on the city sidewalks of the solitary man sleeping on a vent or the "shopping bag lady" and the wide variety of humanity that happened through our hospital doors. Patients with end-stage AIDS, drug abusers, victims of terrible violence—we saw it all.

Whatever brought the homeless to the hospital—the need for "three hots and a cot" or medical ailments associated with living on the streets—their arrival in the emergency room setting marks a rare encounter between those who live outside the social system and representatives of mainstream society, the hospital staff.

Although the basic roles of social work—broker, advocate, clinician—apply in the emergency room, the methods of carrying them out reflect the uniqueness of the atmosphere. To get a picture of what it is like, imagine a theater in the round in which the main characters are rushing to and fro in apparent chaos. The sights: blood, vomit, faces of people in shock. The sounds: shrieks

and screams, barking of orders, phones ringing off the wall. The smells: urine, feces, sweat, disinfectants. The impact jars the senses. Add to this a sense of urgency in dealing with situations of life and death.

Now upon this scene, enter the homeless, a population whose numbers are swelling for reasons external to themselves and connected to adjustments in the economy and in the provision of medical and mental health services. All areas of social work are affected, but the inner-city emergency room especially so.

To get some indications of the challenge that faced me as an emergency room social worker, let's view my work in terms of the standard social work roles. As a *broker,* I referred patients to detoxification centers, prenatal health crisis centers, homeless shelters, and battered women's shelters. Placement in these facilities was extremely hard to arrange. Detox centers refused to accept patients after five P.M. or on the weekends. As a social worker in the emergency room on the evening shift I had to convince drug and alcohol liaisons of insurance companies of the need to provide exceptions to their rigid policies and procedures. With

(Continued on next page)

BOX 8.2 (Continued)

regard to the number of battered women's shelters, there were many more shelters for animals in Philadelphia than for women. In short, due to the lack of available facilities, my job was extremely difficult.

Related to the broker's role was *advocacy.* Interceding on behalf of the patients with the doctors was a crucial aspect of this job. Sometimes this was verbal and at other times involved physical management of the patient's appearance. I found that doctors were much more responsive to patient's needs if patients were de-loused. Social workers in other fields would find this surprising, but there were times when I took patients into the shower myself to clean them before they saw the doctor. It was rewarding to be able to dress them in fresh clothes which we kept on the premises. This will sound even more strange but on occasion I found myself taking up collections from doctors and other staff members on behalf of desperate homeless people; I have seen doctors take off their socks right then to give to someone in need.

In my role as *clinician* I had to make spur of the moment decisions concerning mental illness and alcohol abuse. Relying solely on observation and listening skills, I would inform the attending physician of the need for a psychiatric consult. One problem with working with the homeless was trying to decide what was the cause and what was the effect. In other words, to what extent did

the disorientation, drinking, depression, etc. precede the homeless state, and to what extent did these traits result from the homeless experience itself?

The following cases typify the social worker's role: Frank wandered in suffering from the aftereffects of a gun shot wound to the stomach. In my role as *broker,* I rushed out to meet fire rescue and obtain the necessary information. Then as was my task, I telephoned the next-of-kin. When Frank's sister answered the phone, I told her Frank was shot. As was typical, she let out a shriek and called out to others in her house. Frank recovered. On discovering that he had a drug dependency problem, I went to great lengths to get a treatment facility to admit Frank as a patient.

Joe, who suffered from paranoid schizophrenia, was admitted with gangrene; he had not removed his shoes since 1987! "The doctor told me never to take them off," he explained. The attendants and social workers had to wear gas masks the smell was so overpowering. In the end, however, Joe recovered the use of his feet, and he got a new pair of shoes.

Bruce, appeared in the waiting room covered head to toe with excrement. He could not be bathed because of the severity of his frostbite. After staying two hours overtime to arrange a transfer for him to a shelter, I

(Continued on next page)

BOX 8.2 (Continued)

left him in the waiting room to await transportation. To my horror, I learned the next day that the security guards had thrown him out in the cold and that he froze to death on the streets.

In many ways, the emergency room, especially the inner-city emergency room, captures in microcosm society's failure to provide. The sights, sounds, and smells of this country's casualties should cause us to stand up and take note. There is only so much the doctors and nurses can do to alleviate the pain and misery often caused by the condition of homelessness—the frostbite in winter, heat exhaustion in summer, the street

victimizations, alcohol overdoses to end the pain, and flared-up psychosis caused by stress, not to mention malnutrition. There are only so many places to which the social worker can refer persons who have no place to go, and only so much that can be done at the end of the line when the problems emanate from way up ahead. When one social institution breaks down, often another one will have to pick up the pieces. So it is today with America's inner-city emergency rooms.

———

Printed with permission of Mary Boes, University of Northern Iowa.

need for permanent, habitable, affordable, and nontransient housing for all American households (Mulroy, 1995). Programs geared toward housing and income are the most directly relevant to the problems of homelessness. The solution is obvious: build more housing units and ensure that people have the income to afford them. Nevertheless, current housing programs are underfunded, fragmentary, and without clear and focused goals because the U.S. federal government is often viewed as an arbiter of the last resort (Karger and Stoesz, 1990).

One federal program of some promise is the "moving to opportunity" program now under way in Baltimore, Boston, Chicago, Los Angeles, and New York. Funding is from the Department of Housing and Urban Development (HUD) and represents a new shift in thinking by this agency (*Economist*, 1995c). The shift is away from investment in vast government-funded projects and away from local governments as opposed to communities. An earlier desegregation program in Chicago is the model. This program resettled black families from public housing into private housing in less segregated areas of the city. Over six thousand families have been moved, and the results have been reassuring.

Parents who have relocated to the suburbs have found jobs, and their children have done much better in school than those who have stayed behind. To ensure success, the program screens applicants carefully. Applicants find their own apartments. The cost of the program is about one thousand dollars per family. HUD concludes, according to the *Economist* article, that living outside an area of poverty by itself has positive effects for high-risk families.

In England, homelessness is a growing problem as well. "Rough sleepers," as the homeless are called, congregate in central London, most of them (over four hundred according to an earlier survey) sleeping in the fields. Programs to help these people are charity-based and government-funded initiatives. Charities (often church related) bring blankets, clothes, and sleeping-bags. Showers and washing machines are available nearby. The government program provides beds in hostels until permanent housing can be found. Many on the street, however, refuse to leave: they complain of rules, dirt, and bans on drink in shelters. In other parts of England, there are hostels that supply alcohol to residents during specified times during the day.

In the United States there are more proposals than programs; there is no coordinated government effort to alleviate the problem of homelessness. Suggestions made at the *micro-level* include the following:

* Provide low-cost housing (Mulroy and Lane, 1992; Zastrow, 1996).
* Increase numbers of halfway houses for the mentally ill and alcoholic (Burt, 1994; Mulroy, 1995).
* Change zoning laws so more low-income housing will be built (Burt, 1994; Liebow, 1993; Mulroy and Lane, 1992).
* Provide subsidies for doubled-up households (Rossi, 1989).
* Promote funding for temporary shelter programs to house vulnerable populations such as homeless teens and battered women (Mulroy, 1995; Hertzberg, 1992).
* Coordinate services among isolated programs such as services for people with AIDS and those for pregnant, homeless teens (Putnam, 1995).
* Increase AFDC payment (Mulroy and Lane, 1992).

Most writers on the subject, including those cited above who have proposed short-term solutions, look to the *macro-level* where the problems first originated. Liebow's (1993: 171) call for a strong initiative from the federal government "as the highest and wealthiest level of government . . . the only one that can structure compliance among lower levels" is typical. In many ways, adds Liebow, the federal government itself created homelessness through its withdrawal of commitment to public and affordable housing, a mental health system, and adequate social services. Writing the lead editorial in *Social Work,* Hartman (1989: 484) concurs:

> The problem of homelessness is a public issue and can only be resolved through public action and major changes in public policy. Poverty must be reduced and low-income housing must be made available. This effort, of course, requires a major reordering of our national agenda. It requires a major investment in the welfare of the nation's vulnerable citizens. . . . We must resist the ever-present pressure to redefine this public issue and disgrace as a private trouble.

MENTAL HEALTH CARE AND SUBSTANCE ABUSE TREATMENT

Seriously incapacitating mental illness is likely to affect 1 percent of the world's population at any given time and at least 10 percent of people in all societies at some time during their lives (Wetzel, 1994). Throughout the world, women have the highest rates of mental illness; depression and anxiety are the disorders most characteristic of women, while anti-social disorders and suicide are more likely to be diagnosed in men.

As we have seen, approximately one-third of homeless people are mentally ill and approximately one-third have substance abuse problems. There is considerable overlap between these categories because many of the homeless, about half, are dually diagnosed. There is a growing consensus that an array of basic life supports such as food, clothing, shelter, and medical care is required to respond adequately to the needs of this extremely disadvantaged population (Task Force, 1994). The homeless mentally ill and substance abusers often live in life-threatening circumstances. Their death toll is high from accidents such as being run over by cars and trains, and from exposure to frigid temperatures. Persons suffering from paranoia often will not sleep in shelters much less seek medical help. Some shelters, in any case, will not admit people who are psychotic or intoxicated. Two questions we want to consider are: How did this situation come about, and what can be done about it?

Deinstitutionalization and Care Management

The closing of large hospitals for the mentally ill and the placement of former patients in the community have been important aspects of social policy of the past four decades in the United States and Canada. A similar trend has occurred in Europe following recommendations from the World Health Organization (Holmes and Hokenstad, 1991). Some credit the Civil Rights movement of the 1960s with the recognition of the rights of disadvantaged people that led to landmark legislation in 1963 establishing community mental health centers. This movement was spearheaded by an unlikely coalition of liberals concerned with the horrors of the type of mental ward treatment portrayed in *One Flew Over the Cuckoo's Nest,* and fiscal conservatives who saw a way to save the state money by shutting down the mental hospitals. The impact of medical breakthroughs in altering mental health care services also cannot be underestimated.

The effectiveness of antipsychotic medication in controlling if not curing mental illness went a long way toward revolutionizing treatment for the mentally ill. Many of the mentally ill could now lead normal lives as long as they continued to take their medication; long-term hospitalization was no longer necessary. However, without supervision, many refused to take their medication, and for others, the side effects outweighed the benefits.

Deplorably, even short-term inpatient care was discontinued for the most part; federal support for services dwindled, and the promised community resources were not provided. The shortcoming is not in the area of outpatient treatment which is widely available, but in the lack of halfway houses to provide the daily supervision needed as well as food and shelter. The care is so inadequate, in fact, that the nation's jails have become a "dumping ground" for the mentally ill. Today more people suffering from bipolar disorders and schizophrenia are incarcerated in jails and prisons than are receiving treatment in public hospitals. A national jail survey released by the National Alliance for the Mentally Ill found that jails are still being used in some states to house mentally ill people even if they haven't been charged with a crime (Clark, 1992).

A trend of the 1990s is the shift from Medicaid funded services to managed care reimbursement programs. Managed care corporations operate as mediators between the providers of services and the state. Their goal is to keep costs down by monitoring treatment options. Stringent criteria are set up as cost-saving maneuvers, sometimes with near-fatal consequences. A Des Moines psychiatrist,

Dewdney (1995), in a newspaper editorial entitled, "Seriously Ill Iowans Are Being Forced Back into the Streets," provides the following example of the tyranny of the new criteria: A scared and depressed adolescent and his harried parents are told that he does not qualify for inpatient care because his attempt to kill himself did not occur in the last twenty-four hours. The new cost-saving measures are creating profits for the out-of-state corporation that manages care by denying care. The integrity of Iowa's mental health is being impaired by the introduction of market forces into the treatment assessment process, according to Dewdney. Mental health professionals no longer control the process, business managers do.

The idea behind deinstitutionalization is excellent: treat patients in the community, offer services in the least-restrictive environment. This — the mass release of patients from locked wards — should be seen not as the end of treatment, however, but as the beginning. The Task Force on Homelessness and Severe Mental Illness (1995) recommends outreach strategies to help those in shelters move into more stable housing situations linked to supportive services. But where is the stable housing? In recognition of the desperate need, the task force proposes that a facility known as a safe haven offer semiprivate accommodation for around twenty-five people. Such places would offer food, shelter, showers, and clothing as well as other necessities such as a telephone and safe storage space. Residents would not be required to vacate the premises during the day but instead to participate in the operation of the facility. For each resident a care manager would enhance continuity of care and link the person with programs to which he or she is entitled.

In England, considerable distress has been voiced in the media concerning the policy titled Care in the Community which "has dumped on to the streets thousands of sick people, some of whom have killed others" (Hugill, 1995). Although there is probably some truth in this kind of criticism, some positive things are happening as well. Through the department of health which stresses individualized care, effective residential programs are being set up. An array of service providers helps people who are marginalized by their illness, even to the point of hostility toward all those trying to help (Blatchford and Pidgeon, 1992). Community care can protect a person from disasters, financial and otherwise, which are likely to occur without a formal safety net. Offering such housing and care management services costs a fraction of what acute care does.

In sharp contrast to the thrust toward community care in most Northern Hemisphere countries, Japan's system is highly institutionalized. More than 60 percent of all patients are kept behind barred metal doors and windows where they are locked twenty-four hours a day. Duration is among the longest in the world with more than half of all patients having been confined in the hospital for over five years. These facts are presented by Salzberg (1994), the director of Japanese Legal Studies at the University of British Columbia. Especially bewildering to Salzberg is the payment plan which involves complete reimbursement under the national health insurance scheme to private companies who can maximize patient numbers for big profits. Patients are subdued through excessive medication, overuse of physical restraints, and isolation rooms and have no legal rights. If reform is to occur, it will have to come through sustained international pressure, according to Salzberg.

Substance Abuse Treatment

The social burden in economic costs of substance abuse is quantified by totaling the impact of substance abuse on the health care system, the general welfare and social service systems, criminal justice, and the employment market (Ware, 1995). According to a preliminary report by the National Institute of Alcohol Abuse and Alcoholism (Francis, 1995), rough estimates of the total cost of alcohol abuse alone is one hundred billion dollars a year.

However, the tragedy in human suffering and the destruction of lives, families, and futures, cannot be measured in economic terms. Although only a fraction of substance abusers ends up on skid row, and most retain their jobs, substance abuse—especially alcohol abuse and addiction—figures prominently in the lives of those on the street. Whether the addiction causes the homelessness or the homelessness causes the addiction is not easy to determine. Alcohol and other drug use is associated with stress and pain (van Wormer, 1995). Once harmful drugs are used for self-medication, to curb anxiety say, there is, of course, a lot more to be anxious about.

One very effective form of prevention may be at the societal level—the alleviation of social conditions which foster behaviors that harm physical health. Although substance abuse treatment can be very effective in helping people turn their lives around, the success rate is highly correlated with stability of home life. For the homeless, therefore, involvement in a self-help group such as Alcoholics Anonymous, or commitment to inpatient treatment center, will be effective only in combination with secure and supervised aftercare living arrangements. The nexus between health and housing, the theme of this chapter, can be discerned in this understanding of chemical dependency and how crucial acceptable housing may be to recovery. A similar claim can be made in regard to mental illness; here a cause and effect relationship can be said to exist also, inasmuch as lack of housing aggravates mental disorders (paranoia, depression, etc.), and mental illness may cause a person to lose his or her home.

DISPLACED PEOPLE AND REFUGEES

The images are heartrending and difficult for citizens of northern lands to fathom: the vast migration of genocide's survivors from Rwanda; crying children huddled over dead parents; a dump truck dropping dozens of bodies into a mass grave. Hardly a day goes by without a report of war, mass famine, or disaster, so much so, that the world spectators are getting almost inured to this kind of mass suffering.

Displaced people are those who have been uprooted within their own country; *refugees* are people who have crossed national boundaries in search of refuge (Ahearn, 1995). However, in the literature the term *displaced* is often used to refer to people who have lost their place in general, as in "globally displaced" people. To clarify the distinction, this book will use the term, *internally displaced* persons. The word *refugee* will be used to refer to persons forced to flee their homes. The United Nations, however, applies a strict standard to its definition of refugee. Refugees, in UN terms, are persons who have fled because of persecution and who are unable to return to their country. This narrow definition is, according to Kane (1995), a remnant of the Cold War and irrelevant to so many today. Those who are escaping famine or natural disasters fail to qualify as official refugees. Thus, they are ineligible for asylum in other countries; they may join internally displaced people within their country's borders or become illegal immigrants elsewhere. Whatever categories are used, the mass migrations of people which amounts to over 150 million worldwide, is unprecedented in human history (Kane, 1995). The world's official refugee population is at an all-time high of twenty-three million. The majority of refugees are in Africa, the Middle East, and South Asia. There is virtually nowhere on earth left unaffected by the huge influxes or departures of people. Overwhelmed by the magnitude of today's forever growing flow of newcomers, many countries have rolled back the welcome carpet. Anti-immigrant sentiment has risen and been exploited by politicians sometimes as a way of distracting people from their nations' internal problems.

Women constitute three-fourths of the world's refugees yet, as Fugle (1995) points out, literature on refugees tends to focus on three areas—protection within safe countries, practical concerns in resettlement, and policy reviews. Refugee women have become especially vulnerable to various forms of physical brutality and insecurity as well as to sexual intimidation and abuse. The pain that refugee women experience in transition from their home country to host country ranges from physical and psychological torture and trauma to horrendous stress associated with massive loss and acute cultural transition (Fong, 1995).

Men too suffer from the trauma of the displacement experience. They have often been injured sometimes as conscripts in war, sometimes by landmines. Witnessing violence is traumatic for the onlooker as well as for the recipient. Children who have seen their parent or relative murdered—a frequent refugee experience—invariably suffer from trauma. Unresolved psychological problems may emerge many years later (Ahearn, 1995).

Nobel Peace Prize laureate and concentration camp survivor, Elie Wiesel (1995: 5), articulates the agony of being without a country in this excerpt from his memoirs:

> The refugee's time is measured in visas, his biography in stamps on his documents. Though he has done nothing illegal, he is sure he is being followed. He begs everyone's pardon: sorry for disturbing you, for bothering you, for breathing. How well I understood Socrates, who preferred death to exile. In the twentieth century, there is nothing romantic about the life of the exile, be he stateless person or political refugee. I know whereof I speak. I was stateless, and therefore defenseless. . . .

Reasons for Mass Migrations

Writing for *State of the World: A World Watch Institute Report,* Kane (1995) has filtered out six major causes of mass migrations across the world. The *human-created form* of disaster heads the list. The Chernobyl nuclear reactor explosion is a vivid symbol of human carelessness which led to death, destruction, and relocation of over 100,000 residents. Elsewhere in the former Soviet Union, severe industrial pollution has led to massive internal migrations to cleaner, healthier regions. Environmental degradation such as soil erosion and deforestation has caused mass population shifts, often from rural to urban areas. Similarly, millions have been forced to migrate as technological feats such as dam construction and urban and highway development have claimed the land. Unlike Chernobyl, however, these disasters were planned for economic growth, not accidents.

Natural disasters are a second reason that people are uprooted in large numbers. Acute land hunger has pushed people onto uninhabitable regions such as flood plains and drought-prone areas; then when inevitable natural disaster strikes they are forced to evacuate for safety.

A *population transfer* driving people out by government decree is a third way people are uprooted. China, for example, has populated Tibet with Chinese people as a deliberate strategy for quashing Tibetan nationalism. Russia did this with its satellite countries; England did this with Northern Ireland; and the United States conquered part of Mexico in this way. Kane cites Machiavelli who advocated colonization by immigration as an effective means of conquest.

Fourth, government *eviction* may be used against minorities. Fearing Kurdish dissent, Saddam Hussein chased a million and a half Kurds out of Iraq and into neighboring Turkey. Kuwait, likewise, evicted Palestinians for similar reasons. A related strategy to encourage emigration is the government-sanctioned persecution of minority groups. The pogroms in Russia are one example. In recent years, over a million Jews have left the area to escape being the victims of prejudice.

War is a major cause for mass flight. Superpowers involvement such as in Afghanistan, Vietnam, and Cambodia exacerbates the conflict, as outside forces prop up unpopular leaders, furnishing them with massive firepower to stifle opposition (Newland, 1994). Civil war, such as has taken place in Haiti and former Yugoslavia, leaves people to feel they have no option but to escape. They often are more running away from than toward anything other than survival and peace. Sometimes to leave, however, is as treacherous as to stay. Neighboring countries when inundated with refugees can be extremely inhospitable.

Sixth, *overpopulation* and overcrowding exert extreme pressures on people that get them to branch out in search of new resources. At times, as in Vietnam, whole communities have decided to move. At other times, as in Indonesia, the government has resettled people through "transmigration" projects.

In summary, displaced people move for a variety of reasons, among them resource scarcities, ancient animosities, and pressures caused by rapid technological change. To these reasons we can add the powerful economic drives, which Kane terms "the push of poverty, the pull of wealth" which is at the root of some of the largest movements of all. The pattern of this form of migration often splits up families and communities, but at the same time it leads to the transfer of large sums of money to the home country. This movement in search of economic opportunity was discussed in the previous chapter on work and family welfare.

Interestingly, Hoff (1995) utilizes the image of an ever-widening spiral, with complex cause-and-effect interactions to represent the essence of inducements to migrate. These are the relationships Hoff perceives: as economic conditions deteriorate, rivalries break into armed conflict with modern weapons and "scorched earth" strategies; as the physical environment becomes totally decimated, waves of refugees are created along with a whole new host of problems for the countries, rich or poor, where refugees sojourn.

Health Care Needs and Services

The health care needs of the survivors of war and famine are great. Many of these needs preceded the survivors' flight itself and, in fact, precipitated the flight. The process of leaving to escape starvation, danger, and death is often fraught with additional traumatization. Treacherous sea and land voyages may compound the original misery. Insufficient food and water, the lack of medical care, inadequate housing, diseases contracted, and injuries received—the physical and mental health implications are considerable (Ahearn, 1995).

Within the United Nations system, the Office of the High Commissioner for Refugees is the primary international agency charged with responsibility for safeguarding the security and promoting the freedom of political refugees (Estes and Harding, 1992). Thousands of staff members work in eighty countries to find durable solutions for the twenty-three million persons officially classified as refugees. This agency works to ensure standards for the treatment of refugees worldwide in addition to direct social welfare work.

The Red Cross, one of the earliest relief organizations, was founded in 1863 to provide relief services and ensure the humane treatment of prisoners and civilians in time of war (Healy, 1995). The Red Cross has been joined by numerous other international private (often church related) organizations to meet the needs of refugees and victims of natural disasters.

Within the United States, as in many other industrialized nations, official services are provided to the political refugees who have been granted political asylum. This fairly generous program was set up mainly to help refugees from communism "get on their feet" and become productive citizens. Specialized services are provided through the U.S. State Department Bureau of Refugee Programs and the Department of Health and Human Services. Through special centers scattered throughout the world, refugees are evaluated, placed, and given relocation grants. Once placed in the United States, continued assistance is provided including Medicaid for health care benefits for a limited time and Supplemental Security Income (SSI) for the disabled. Today, with a political backlash sweeping the country, there is a public outcry against newcomers receiving benefits to which citizens often are not entitled. Moreover, there is a government reassessment of who is admitted as a political refugee.

A reluctance to open the borders to refugees is happening everywhere, even in Germany which, since the second World War, has had a policy of remarkable openness to foreigners. Finland's borders have been closed to immigration for years, and Norway and Sweden have accepted political refugees reluctantly. Because many people requesting political refugee status are denied asylum and returned involuntarily, an underground movement has arisen in the churches. Historically, churches have offered sanctuary, or so-called church asylum, to people. According to an *Aftenposten* article (1995), forty-one foreign nationals are still in refuge in twenty Norwegian churches; most are refugees from the war-torn Balkans. The authorities are not considering a general amnesty, according to the article.

The asylum movement in Sweden operates, similarly, to hide refugees facing deportation by the state. Churches and monasteries have been at the forefront of this movement (Nagy, 1995). The Save the Children organization has represented the human rights of refugee children. Civil disobedience has occurred on behalf of these would-be immigrants, with nuns playing a major part.

WOMEN AND HEALTH CARE

Global View

Because many of these health care issues have been given close attention elsewhere in this book, this section will simply provide an overview. Generally, across the globe, if you're poor you are more likely to be sick, less likely to receive adequate medical care, and more likely to die at an early age. In countries where women are devalued, girls may not make it to adulthood: Female infanticide takes large numbers of lives, but increasingly, because of new technology females often are eliminated before they are born. After birth, health care frequently appears to be allocated, like food, along lines of sex, age, and familial role (Santow, 1995). According to a UN Development Program survey measuring the male-female population ratio, as a result of selective abortion and infanticide, more than one hundred million women are "missing" around the world (Wright, 1995). The missing number is the estimate of males to females in a given population (which is approximately even) minus the discrepancy in the actual figures.

The leading cause of death for the world's women is given variously as AIDS (Paolisso and Leslie, 1995), domestic violence (Borrus, 1995), and maternal mortality (Dasgupta, 1995). Maternal mortality rates, indeed, are staggering — over 500,000 women die per year due to complications surrounding pregnancy (including unsafe abortions). Women suffer ill health and die because they are neglected as children, married as adolescents, poor and illiterate, underfed and overworked, subject to harmful traditional practices, and excluded from decision-making, according to a United Nations report (U.N. Chronicle, 1992).

Facts on File (1995c: 688) compiled the following data on women's health and violence against women from current U.N. and World Bank sources:

- The number of women who died from causes related to pregnancy or childbirth had dropped by half since 1970; some 500,000 women die from such causes world-wide each year.
- In developing countries, trained attendants were at hand in only 55 percent of births; only 37 percent of births took place at a hospital or clinic.
- One-fifth of all babies born worldwide each year were born to teenage women.
- More than six million women around the world were infected with HIV, the virus that causes AIDS.
- Female life expectancy has increased 20 percent faster than male life expectancy over two decades.
- Fertility rates have dropped by a third over two decades, to 3.0 live births per woman in 1990–95 from 4.7 live births in 1970–75.
- Some two million girls a year were subjected to genital mutilation.
- In India in 1994 there were about 6,300 reported cases of men (and in-laws) killing their wives because their dowries were deemed too small.

When 28,000 women from all corners of the globe convened in Beijing at the Fourth World Conference on Women to discuss how to achieve empowerment and equality, the impact on those who attended and on the women of the world was overwhelming. The biggest problem for women emerged as their treatment in their own countries which for many boils down to simple survival (Wright, 1995). Reports were made from women across the world where, in staggering numbers, women are still slaves, sold as child prostitutes, sexually mutilated, and victims of abuse in its many brutal forms. The global epidemic in violence against women was revealed in its most graphic form at the conference, not in statistics, which are too mind-boggling to absorb, but in a graphic film shown to the approximately five hundred women attending a session on genital mutilation of girls (Koch, 1995). So unexpected and so harrowing were events shown in this film, according to Koch, that women in the audience were driven to shouting and screaming in outrage in spite of themselves.

The health of women and their low status are intricately intertwined (Wetzel, 1993). Health care strategies for women should focus on prevention and encompass the whole life cycle, including family planning to prevent unwanted pregnancy, reproductive health which will benefit the unborn child as well as the mother, and nutrition. Most of the major risks to the health of the world's women are related in one way or another to the reproductive cycle.

The maternal mortality rate, as we have seen, is astoundingly high; 99 percent of the deaths occur in the poor nations of the world. Inadequate medical care (prenatal and obstetric) does nothing to stem the tide. Yet there is no need for expensive technology to increase women's survival rate. The deaths related to pregnancy and childbirth can be prevented by reliance on transfers to hospitals when an emergency arises, according to UNICEF (1995) and more medical training is needed by district-level hospital staff. Nutritional needs of women are also not being met. Anemia, or a reduced number of red blood cells due to lack of iron, is a major problem among women and poses a particular danger to those who are pregnant. Where protein foods are scarce, males receive the greater share of them. Yet women's needs are greater, at least in the childbearing years. Malnutrition combined with frequent pregnancy often results in high rates of death in pregnancy and childbirth (Wetzel, 1993).

Abortion is a related issue. Estimates of death due to illegal and unsafe abortion procedures range from 70,000 (UNICEF, 1995) to 200,000 (Jacobson, 1990) per year. In Latin America, botched abortions are the leading cause of death among young women (Baverlein, 1995). In the United States, medical students are no longer routinely trained to do abortions, and the storm of controversy concerning the procedure is driving experienced doctors away (*Journal of the American Women's Association*, 1994). The results of these practices, in conjunction with the withdrawal in most states of Medicaid funding for abortion, remains to be seen.

Women in the United States are succumbing to HIV infection at increasing rates; in New York City, AIDS is the leading cause of death among women aged twenty-five to thirty-four, most of them women of color (Wetzel, 1993). AIDS is considered a women's disease in much of the world. In places where infibulation, the most disfiguring form of genital mutilation is practiced, wives are at heightened risk of contracting AIDS from infected husbands due to the difficulty of vaginal intercourse (Santow, 1995). There is some hope, however. According to a recent report in *Newsweek* entitled "Making Men Listen" (Bogert, 1995), due to the magnitude of the AIDS situation, local feminist movements have gained momentum; many now oppose female genital mutilation and other forms of violence against women. At the World Conference in Beijing, women's voices were heard. The liberal language of the conference's final platform stressing sexual determination for women was largely attributed to the Africans' fortitude and perseverance.

In addition to the hazards to women's health related to reproduction, there are environmental health risks having a serious impact as well. Ofosu-Amaah (1994) describes the health implications of women's daily interaction with a contaminated environment. In most communities, the growing of food crops and the gathering of water and wood for fuel are women's responsibilities. They are the first to suffer, therefore, from the effects of environmental degradation such as the use of dangerous herbicides and other unsustainable agricultural practices. As environmental resources are depleted, more hands are needed to gather food and water; more children are then produced further increasing the health risks for poor women (Dasgupta, 1995). This analysis suggests that the way to reduce fertility and improve women's health is to break the spiral of destructiveness.

Women, such as those who stood up before the world at Beijing sometimes at great personal risk, need to be heard. Their voices need to be reflected in policies backed by the world's financial institutions. (Strides are, in fact, being made in this direction). Santow (1995) thoughtfully suggests that educational efforts target men rather than women. Husbands are an obvious source of influence. Bringing them into areas that are usually viewed as the natural preserve of women, such as family planning and child health, may directly and indirectly benefit every member of the family. Above all, however, improvement in women's status is key to improvements in women's health.

CONCLUSION AND SUMMARY

Midgley's (1995) contrast between *distorted development* and *social development* offers a conceptualization that is helpful in uniting the many themes of this chapter. Societies with distorted development, notes Midgley, can be contrasted with societies where a better balance between economic and social development can be found. European countries such as Austria, Sweden, and Switzerland have made systematic efforts to promote the development of *all* the people, not only of the few at the expense of the many. Extensive health and social services are provided, thereby minimizing the amount of social problems. Outside of Europe, Costa Rica, Cuba, and Taiwan have managed to foster both economic and social development. Yet, as Midgley points out, the problem of distorted development remains widespread. Concentrations of poverty that exist on an unacceptable scale are present throughout the world, and especially pronounced in the subsistence level economies and in the capitalizing regions of Eastern Europe.

The level of misery in many formerly colonial countries and nearby regions is so intense that sometimes even the poorest of the poor in a rich country like the United States have an existence that is less precarious and from which there are more avenues of escape than do most residents of the poor nations. Yet between the poorest of the poor in one nation and another there is much common ground, as we have seen in this chapter. Common ground in terms of the often crowded, unsanitary, and inadequate physical environments, the fight for survival against the elements (cold in the Northern regions, heat and drought in the South), the dearth of primary health care services, and the often terrifying stresses of everyday life.

The universal dilemma is whether the government should play a strong role, part benevolent and part coercive, in ensuring health care and housing for all, or whether nations would do better focusing on economic investment and technological advancement in the belief that the market forces will ultimately take care of the needs of the people. How this issue is played out is seen in the barter for child prostitutes in Thailand, the global epidemic in maternal mortality, the increasing overpopulation in sub-Saharan Africa, and the unconscionable level of homelessness in the United States.

This chapter has pursued health care and housing as two interlocked forms of social welfare. People without shelter are unhealthy people, and unhealthy people may end up without shelter. The issue in the United States of how to take care of people's needs has been resolved on the side of the market forces of profit-making constituencies who have a strong influence on public policy, the mass media, and maintenance of the status quo. The reduction in the federal government's involvement in housing and health care is being felt, above all, by the most vulnerable populations in society—single women and their children and people of color. The poor and racial minorities have higher rates of illnesses and shorter life expectancies than others in the population largely because of the inadequacy of preventive care such as nutritional, prenatal, and neonatal programs.

The tug-of-war between prevention and tertiary care is resolved in modern society in favor of tertiary, or after-the-fact care. This is as true of housing as it is of health care. Once people are on the street or terminally ill, all the emergency services in the world cannot undo the damage. Programs that for decades have been the bedrock of what used to be our social welfare infrastructure are being dismantled. Persons who are already disadvantaged by a myriad of factors bear the most visible cost of the transformation of American social welfare and of American cities through urban renewal and downtown revitalization. The portrait of the homeless presented in this chapter puts a human face on the misery of the daily grind to obtain food, social services, and shelter for the night. What our society fails to grasp is that applying the logic of the market place to human services is fraught with peril. The health care exchange, as Gordon and Baer (1995) convincingly argue, is not about acquisition, it's about illness, aging, vulnerability, and death.

Because our lives are influenced and controlled internationally, social change can only occur if social consciousness is global (Wetzel, 1993). Unless and until we have a global perspective on social welfare and social development, international institutions that are willing to play a meaningful role, and global funds and resources, we cannot resolve the harmful consequences of economic globalization (Gupta, 1995). In international resolutions, such as the magnificent Beijing accord, where in a most unlikely location women of all cultures came together to demand that human rights supersede national traditions, consensus must be achieved. At least for a moment, the world listened. The international impact remains to be seen.

REVIEW QUESTIONS

1. Relate the ascendancy of the Radical Right to universal health care.
2. How can the United States be considered to have the best health care in the world in spite of the deficiencies? Why is it so expensive?

3. What is the role of HMOs? Discuss the facts pertaining to various lobbying groups.
4. Drawing on illustrations provided from various sources in chapter 8, what is the human side of health care in the United States?
5. What is meant by the marketing of disease? Provide examples. What kinds of unsafe products are marketed to economically poor countries?
6. Describe the workings of the Canadian and British health care systems. What is happening in Russia today?
7. Record the progress relevant to the health of children in poor nations of the world. What are the areas in need of urgent attention?
8. How are family planning and education for women related?
9. Describe the success of the WIC program. What is the symbolism of the "Lunch of Stones" held on Capitol Hill?
10. Review the facts concerning the global toll of AIDS. What are some preventative actions that can be taken?
11. Describe various prevention strategies for health care in Cuba, Mexico, the Philippines, Costa Rica, and Canada.
12. Compare the words *house* and *home*. What is the history of public housing in the United States? What is the situation today?
13. What is the housing situation in Japan, China, and Norway?
14. Analyze with close attention to the details presented, Rush Limbaugh's reaction to homeless people.
15. Provide a demographic portrait of homeless people. Who are they?
16. What is the interaction component in the process of becoming homeless? Discuss homelessness utilizing a biopsychosocial framework.
17. Why do youths and married women sometimes end up on the streets?
18. What is life like on the streets? What is the link between homelessness and health? Discuss emergency room social work with the homeless as revealed in box 8.2.
19. Describe the "moving to opportunity" program adopted by several major cities. Contrast *micro* and *macro* solutions.
20. What is the connection between mental illness and homelessness? How did de-institutionalization contribute to the problem?
21. What are the facts pertaining to the world's refugees? What are the causes of the mass migrations of people? Discuss the impact on the host countries.
22. What are some of the leading causes of death for women in various parts of the world? Which statistic to you is the most shocking?
23. Discuss recent encouraging developments internationally.

REFERENCES

Aftenposten. (1995, May 31). Refugees Still in Church Asylum. *Aftenposten.*
Ahearn, F. (1995). Displaced People. In *Encyclopedia of Social Work,* 19th ed.: (771–780). Washington, DC: NASW Press.

Associated Press. (1995b, July 21). Chinese Squeezed into Tiny Homes. *Calgary Herald*: B11.

———. (1995a, August 24). Study Shows Homelessness Rising in Iowa. *Waterloo/Cedar Falls Courier*: C1.

———. (1995c, October 18). What's the Biggest Turn-on to Smoking? Ads, Kids Say. *The Tennessean*: 7A.

Athey, J. (1991). HIV Infection and Homeless Adolescents. *Child Welfare* 70(5): 517–528.

Avruch, S. and A. Cackley. (1995). Savings Achieved by Giving WIC Benefits to Women Prenatally. *Public Health Reports* 110(1): 27–34.

Bartecchi, C., T. Mackenzie, and R. Schrier. (1995, May). The Global Tobacco Epidemic. *Scientific American*: 44–51.

Bauerlein, M. (1995, October). Diminished Choice. *Utne Reader*: 18–22.

Belcher, J. and F. Di Blasio. (1995). Health Care: Homeless People. In *Encyclopedia of Social Work*, 19th ed.: (1175–1177). Washington, DC: NASW Press.

Blatchford, B. and J. Pidgeon. (1992, July 16). Out on a Limb. *Social Work Today*: 12–13.

Bogert, C. (1995, September 25). Making Men Listen. *Newsweek*: 52.

Borrus, A. (1995, September). What the U.N. Women's Conference Can Do for Women. *Business Week*: 42.

Brundtland Report, The. (1987). *Our Common Future*. Report of the World Commission on Environment and Development. Oxford, England: Oxford University Press.

Burt, M. (1994, November 3). *Where Are We Going?* Address given at the University of Northern Iowa, Public Policy Department.

Bywaters, P. (1986). Social Work and the Medical Profession—Arguments against Unconditional Collaboration. *British Journal of Social Work* 16: 661–677.

Caragata, W. (1995). Medicare Wars. *Maclean's* 108(14): 14.

CBS News. (1995, August 22). *CBS News*.

Chase, M. (1995, February 13). Health Care Shifts from Hospital to Home and Hearth. *Wall Street Journal*: B1.

Clark, H. (1992, November 29). Concern Voiced About Jailing of Mental Patients. *Waterloo/Cedar Falls Courier*: A1, 2.

Collins, D. (1995, July 29–August 1). *A Canadian Social Worker's Views on NAFTA*. Paper presented at the International Social Welfare in a Changing World Conference. Calgary, Alberta.

Cowley, G. (1994, August 22). The Ever-Expanding Plague. *Newsweek*: 37.

Dalglish, B. (1994). Health for Profit. *Maclean's* 107(45): 44–46.

Dasgupta, P. (1995, February). Population, Poverty and the Local Environment. *Scientific American* 272: 40–45.

Denzin, N. (1993). *The Alcoholic Society*. New Brunswick, NJ: Transaction.

Dewdney, D. (1995, September 17). Seriously Ill Iowans Are being Forced Back onto the Streets. *Des Moines Resister*: C1–2.

464

PART 2: CARE THROUGH THE LIFE CYCLE

DiNitto, D. (1995a). Hunger, Nutrition, and Food Programs. In *Encyclopedia of Social Work,* 19th ed.: (1428–1437). Washington, DC: NASW Press.

———. (1995b). *Social Welfare: Politics and Public Policy,* 4th ed. Needham Heights, MA: Allyn and Bacon.

Durning, A. (1993). Can't Live Without It. *World Watch* 6(3): 10–18.

Economist. (1995a, September 23). Canada's Medicine on the Sick-List. *Economist*: 33.

———. (1995b, February 6). Homelessness: Moving Along. *Economist*: 65.

———. (1995c, October 7). Housing Policy: From Ghetto to Suburb. *Economist*: 33.

Ehrenreich, B. (1995). Battered Welfare Syndrome. *Time* 145(14): 82.

Elliott, D. (1990). Social Welfare in Britain. In D. Elliott, N. Mayadas, and T. Wattes, eds. *The World of Social Welfare*: (91–109). Springfield, IL: Charles C. Thomas.

Estes, R. and P. Harding. (1992). Political Refugees. In R. Estes, ed. *Internationalizing Social Work Education: A Guide to Resources for a New Century*: (148–149). Philadelphia: University of Pennsylvania.

Facts on File. (1995a, May 11). WHO Issues Global Health Report. *Facts on File*: 340–341.

———. (1995b, January 12). Canada. *Facts on File*: 23.

———. (1995c, September 21). Statistics on Women. *Facts on File*: 688.

Fong, L. (1995, July 29–August 1). *The Plight of Refugee Women as Victims of Violence.* Paper presented at the International Social Welfare in a Changing World Conference. Alberta, Canada: University of Calgary.

Francis, D. (1995, September). Heavy Drinkers Hurt the Nation's Economy. *Christian Science Monitor*: 9.

Fugle, B. (1995, July 29–August 1). *The Neglect of Refugee Women.* Paper presented at the International Social Welfare in a Changing World Conference. Calgary, Alberta.

Gordon, S. and E. Baer. (1995, January 29). Market-Driven Health Care's Real Cost. *Des Moines Register*: 2C.

Graham, H. (1984). *Women, Health and the Family.* Brighton, England: Harvester.

Gupta, A. (1995, July 29–August 1). *Global Development and Global Welfare: An Indian Perspective.* Paper presented at the International Social Welfare in a Changing World Conference. Alberta, Canada: University of Calgary.

Guy, A. (1994, September). The British National Health Service. Class presentation at the University of Northern Iowa: Cedar Falls.

Harrington, M. (1985). *The New American Poverty.* New York: Viking Penguin.

Hartman, A. (1992). Health Care: Privilege or Entitlement. *Social Work* 37(3): 195–196.

———. (1989). Homelessness: Public Issue and Private Trouble. *Social Work* 34(6): 483–484.

Healy, L. (1995). International Social Welfare: Organizations and Activities. In *Encyclopedia of Social Work,* 19th ed.: (1499–1510).

Heise, L. (1991, July/August). Trouble Brewing: Alcohol in the Third World. *World Watch*: 11–18.

Hertzberg, E. (1992). The Homeless in the United States: Conditions, Typology and Interventions. *International Social Work* 35: 149–161.

Hilfiker, D. (1994). *Not All of Us Are Saints: A Doctor's Journey with the Poor.* New York: Hill and Wang.

Hoff, M. (1995). Physical Environment Decline and Violent Conflict: An Exploration of the Linkage to Economic and Social Development. Paper presented at the International Social Welfare in a Changing World Conference. Alberta, Canada: University of Calgary.

Holmes, T. and M. Hokenstad. (1991). Mental Health Services: An International Perspective. *Journal of Sociology and Social Welfare* 18(2): 5–23.

Hugill, B. (1995, September 24). Psychiatrist Goes in Fear of Schizophrenics on the Loose. *The Observer:* 7.

Hyde, C. (1995). Book Review. *Journal of Sociology and Social Welfare* 22(1): 192–195.

Iatridis, D. (1990). Cuba's Health Care Policy: Prevention and Active Community Participation. *Social Work* 35(1): 29–36.

Jacobson, J. (1990, March). Abortion in a New Light. *World Watch:* 31–38.

Johnson, L. and C. Schwartz. (1994). *Social Welfare: A Response to Human Need,* 3d ed. Boston: Allyn and Bacon.

Journal of the American Medical Women's Association. (1994, September/October). Entire issue on abortion. *Journal of the American Medical Women's Association.*

Kalibala, S. and S. Anderson. (1993). AIDS in Africa: A Family Disease. *World Health* 46(6): 8–10.

Kane, H. (1995). Leaving Home. In L. Brown et al., eds. *State of the World: A Worldwide Institute Report:* (132–149). New York: W.W. Norton and Co.

Karger, H. and D. Stoesz. (1990). *American Social Welfare Policy: A Structural Approach.* New York: Longman.

Katz, M. (1989). *The Undeserving Poor: From the War on Poverty to the War on Welfare.* New York: Pantheon Books.

Keigher, S. (1994). The Morning after Deficit Reduction: The Poverty of U.S. Maternal and Child Health Policy. *Health and Social Work* 19(2): 143–147.

Koch, S. (1995, November 5). *Reflections on Beijing.* Presentation before the National Organization for Women, Northeast Iowa Chapter. Cedar Falls, Iowa.

Kulys, R. and R. Constable. (1994). The Emergence of Social Work in Lithuania. In R. Constable and V. Mehta, eds. *Education for Social Work in Eastern Europe:* (81–90). Chicago: Lyceum Books.

Kuttner, R. (1991, April). Health Care: Why Corporate America is Paralyzed. *Business Week:* 14.

Liebow, E. (1993). *Tell Them Who I Am: The Lives of Homeless Women.* New York: Free Press.

Limbaugh, R. (1992). *The Way Things Ought to Be.* New York: Pocket Books.

Lloyd, G. (1995). HIV/AIDS Overview. In *Encyclopedia of Social Work,* 19th ed: (1257–1290). Washington, DC: NASW Press.

Logan, J. (1994, July 11–15). *The Role of Social Work Education in the Global AIDS Strategy.* Paper presented at the 27th Congress of the International Association of Schools of Social Work, Amsterdam.

Mabulay, A. and V. Subingsubing. (1995). The Key to Child Survival [Special issue]. *World Health* 48: 8–9.

Marshall, A. (1995, July 21). RNs Warn New Rules Dangerous. *Calgary Herald*: 1.

McManus, M. (1995, October 20). Lawmakers Are Offering Stones, Not Bread, to the Hungry Children of the World. *Nashville Banner*: A15.

Midgley, J. (1995). *Social Development.* London: SAGE.

Mishra, R. (1990). *The Welfare State in Capitalist Society.* Hemel, Hempstead England: Harvester Wheatsheaf.

Mizrahi, T., R. Fasano, and S. Dooha. (1993). National Health Line. *Health and Social Work* 18(1): 7–12.

Moss, D. and G. Dickson. (1994, December 23). Homeless Remembered. *USA Today*: 3A

Mulroy, E. (1995). Housing. In the *Encyclopedia of Social Work,* 19th. ed.: (1377–1384). Washington, DC: NASW Press.

Mulroy, E. and T. Lane, T. (1992). Housing Affordability, Stress and Single Mothers: Pathways to Homelessness. *Journal of Sociology and Social Welfare* 19: 51–64.

Nagy, G. (1995, July 29–August 1). *The Role of NGOs in the Welfare of the Refugees in Sweden.* Paper presented at the International Social Welfare in a Changing World. Alberta, Canada: University of Calgary.

Newland, K. (1994, May/June). Refugees: The Rising Flood. *World Watch*: 10–20.

Ofosu-Amaah, W. (1994). Remembering the Environment: Links among Health, Environment, and Women. *Family Community Health* 17(2): 22–29.

Ornstein, N. (1995, August 15). Medicaid's Middle-Class Payoff. *USA Today*: 13A.

Paolisso, M. and J. Leslie. (1995). Meeting the Changing Health Needs of Women in Developing Countries. *Social Science and Medicine* 40(1): 55–65.

Papazian, E. (1995, September/October). Are Nurses Being Phased Out? *MS*: 35.

Pierce, J. and E. Gilpin. (1995, May). Looking for a Market among Adolescents. *Scientific American*: 50–51.

Pins, K. (1995, December 18). Iowa Better Off than U.S.: 10% Here Lack Health Coverage. *Des Moines Register*: 2A.

Pryor, D. (1994, March). Prescription Drug Industry Must be Reformed. *USA Today* (Magazine): 74–75.

Putnam, K. (1995). The Developmental Impact of Homelessness on Children and Adolescents. *Social Work Perspectives* 5(1): 31–35.

Random House. (1980). *The Random House Dictionary.* New York: Random House.

Ritter, M. (1995, April). Mental Health Crisis Contributing to Violent Society Study. From the Associated Press. In *Daily News*, Bowling Green, KY.

Roberts, R. and T. Keefe. (1986). Homelessness: Residual, Institutional and Communal Solutions. *Journal of Sociology and Social Welfare* 13(2): 400–417.

Rosenthal, R. (1994). *Homeless in Paradise: A Map of the Terrain.* Philadelphia: Temple University Press.

Rossi, P. (1989). *Down and Out in America.* Chicago: University of Chicago Press.

Salzberg, S. (1994, November). In a Dark Corner: Care for the Mentally Ill in Japan. *Social Science Japan*: 12–14.

Santow, G. (1995). Social Roles and Physical Health: The Case of the Female Disadvantage in Poor Countries. *Social Science and Medicine* 40(2): 147–161.

Sidel, R. (1992). *Women and Children Last.* New York: Penguin.

Smith, D. (1995). Community Health Alternatives. *Canadian Dimension* 29: 12–13.

Snell, M. (1995, July/August). Walking in Beauty. *Utne Reader*: 73–79.

Specter, M. (1995, February 19). Russia's Declining Health: Rising Illness, Shorter Lives. *New York Times*: 1, 4.

Stein, H. (1990). International and Global Education: Implications for Social Work. In K. Kendall, ed. *The Internationalization in American Education.* Proceedings of an International Symposium. New York: Hunter College.

Subramanian, M. (1995). The World Health Report 1995: Bridging the Gaps. *World Health* 48(2): 4–5.

Tanney, B. (1995). Suicide Prevention in Canada: A National Perspective Highlighting Progress and Problems. *Suicide and Life-Threatening Behavior* 25(1): 105–121.

Task Force. (1994). Homelessness and the Mentally Ill. *USA Today* (Magazine) 122: 26–30.

Trejos, M. (1992, March). Homes not Slums. *UNESCO Courier*: 34.

UN Chronicle. (1992, September). Women's Health: Tragedy of Gender. *UN Chronicle*: 57.

UNICEF. (1994). *The State of the World's Children.* Oxford, England: Oxford University Press.

_____. (1995). *The State of the World's Children.* Oxford, England: Oxford University Press.

van Biema, D. (1995, September 18). Bury My Heart in Committee. *Time*: 48–51.

van Wormer, K. (1995). *Alcoholism Treatment: A Social Work Perspective.* Chicago: Nelson-Hall.

Ware, F. (1995). Social Services and Substance Abuse. In W. Johnson, et al. *The Social Services: An Introduction.* Itasca, Illinois: F.E. Peacock Publishers, 183–198.

Waswo, A. (1995, August). Urban Housing in Postwar Japan. *Social Science*: Japan 4: 24–25.

Weir, F. (1994, November). Failing Health. *In These Times*: 21–22.

Welch, W. (1994, July 22). Battle of the Big Bucks: "Historically Unprecedented." *USA Today*: 5A.

Wetzel, J. (1993). *The World of Women.* London: Macmillan.

_____. (1994). Women of the World: The Wonder Class—A Global Perspective on Women and Mental Health. In L. Davis, ed. *Building on Women's Strengths: A Social Work Agenda for the 21st Century*: (229–246). New York: Haworth Press.

Wiesel, E. (1995, November 5). How America and I Chose Each Other. *Parade Magazine*: 4–5. Excerpt from: Knopf, A. (1995). *All Rivers Run to the Sea.* New York: Alfred A. Knopf.

Wolf, N. (1991). *The Beauty Myth.* New York: William Morrow and Company.

Wright, R. (1995, September 10). All Over the World, Women Face Violence in Their Homes. *Waterloo/Cedar Falls Courier*: F1, 2.

Wronka, J. (1994). Human Rights and Social Policy in the United States: An Educational Agenda for the 21st Century. *Journal of Moral Education* 23(3): 261–271.

Young, J. (1994, November). Homelessness Conference Speaker Paints Bleak Picture for Future. *Waterloo Courier*: A8.

Zastrow, C. (1996). *Introduction to Social Work and Social Welfare,* 5th ed. Pacific Grove, CA: Brooks/Cole.

Zeitzer, I. (1994). Recent European Trends in Disability and Related Programs. *Social Security Bulletin* 57(2): 21–26.

9

CARE FOR THE AGED

(The) last scene of all
That ends this strange eventful history
Is second childishness, and mere oblivion
Sans teeth, sans eyes, sans taste,
  sans everything.
  —Shakespeare, As You Like It: 139

E rik Erikson (1963) sees life development as a series of tasks to be mastered at various stages. In the final stage, the challenge is to achieve integrity rather than despair. Retirement, widowhood, and the accumulation of losses can lead to loneliness and depression. Ideally, at the final stage of life, one comes to accept his or her life as having been meaningful and worthwhile. An interviewee in the book, *Understanding Older Chicanas* (Facio, 1996: 101) personalizes this acceptance: "I've done what I've had to do . . . but I don't feel useless. It's a different life now . . . I have the (retirement) center, my friends, my grandchildren, and my garden." Similarly my mother, a native Louisianan, views the final stage of her life as "lagniappe," a little something extra, a gift.

Today, one in eight Americans is age sixty-five or over. The U.S. population under six years of age is expected to decrease to 6 percent in 2010 from 11 percent in 1960, while one in seven people will be at least sixty-five in 2010 (Schenck-Yglesias, 1995). The proportion of older people in the population is rising because there are fewer births occurring. Because of the shorter lifespan of men, generally, women will continue to outnumber men in this older age group by a wide margin. The baby boom generation, as everyone else, is aging. Never before will so many people live so long as will members of this postwar cohort.

The graying of America, where one in ten Americans will be over age eighty early into the twenty-first century, is a trend found virtually everywhere. The graying of the world is bound to change the way we live and the way we view aging (Shah, 1992). This demographic revolution, depending on the viewpoint, is both a triumph and a problem.

As our nation ages, how will we respond to the population shift? How will we handle the health care demands? Social security? Who will care for the frail elderly? What lessons can we learn from other nations who have preceded us in the changing population balance? The chapter will:

- Differentiate aging as a lifetime process from old age.
- Explore the social context within which the elderly function.
- Review trends pertaining to the graying of the United States and the world and the implications of these trends.
- Describe the care of the frail elderly across the globe.
- Consider the interaction of ageism, sexism, and racism during a time of retrenchment of social programs that leave vulnerable people considerably more so.
- Discuss the economic and health care arrangements of provision for the elderly members of a society, and the role of nursing homes internationally.
- View various approaches to death in modern society.
- Survey the network of community services available and international and national social activism on behalf of the aged.

CONCEPT OF AGING

Aging begins before we are born and continues throughout our lives; the only cure for it is death (Greer, 1991). The biopsychosocial model provides a framework for the study of the aging process. *Biologically,* aging encompasses all the chronological changes that occur over a lifetime—increase in height throughout childhood, onset and cessation of menstruation, changes in the muscular and sensory systems, and shaping of the young adult and middle-aged body.

The pace of biological aging differs among individuals, but its course is inevitable. The morbid side of growing old — illness, infirmity, and looming death — often is underplayed in the literature. Biologists use the word *senescence* to refer to the process of aging for all life forms. The process involves deterioration over time, during which viability decreases and vulnerability increases (Mann, 1995). The process is not uniform but occurs jerkily, as Greer suggests.

Aldous Huxley's *Brave New World* (1969; orig. 1932) depicted a future that contained death but not aging; through the miracle of chemistry the old did not physically age and therefore died young. In the real world, however, only through death can we stave off the effects of the ravages of time. The inevitability of growing old is accompanied by an obvious physical decline. Four out of five people over age sixty-five have at least one chronic condition; among the most common are arthritis, hearing impairments, various forms of cardiovascular diseases, and cancer (Dunkle and Norgard, 1995). However, the exact relationship between chronological age and the decrease in capabilities has yet to be satisfactorily determined.

Because it affects all of one's dealings with people, hearing impairment is crucial in its consequences (Beaver and Miller, 1992). Among characteristics of the aging process is the marked inability to hear clearly in such crowded places as restaurants and theaters or where there is background noise from appliances, air conditioning, TV sets, or radios. Much of sound, such as music, becomes irritating in later life. Other age-related changes — in vision, muscular strength, and reaction time — lead to a sense of vulnerability and fear in strange and unusual surroundings.

Physical limitations such as ambulatory disabilities coupled with lack of adequate transportation limit the aged in their ability to shop, obtain legal counsel, or much needed medical care. Fourteen percent of the elderly people in the United States are classified as disabled; five percent of the elderly population are institutionalized (Olson, 1994). With the rapid increase in the number of people over age eighty-five, Alzheimer's disease and other forms of dementia are much more frequent occurrences than in the past. Half of persons over this age are thought to be affected (Miranda and Morales, 1995).

Psychological aging is related to biological aging in the way the mind is very closely linked to the body. The psychological dimension refers to changes in personality or ways of processing information accompanying the aging process. Factors of health, idleness, loss of contemporaries, reduced income, and many other social variables shape the psychological reality experienced by older adults.

PART 2: CARE THROUGH THE LIFE CYCLE

With the vastness of the future no longer before them and the typical empti-
ness of the present, the past assumes an ever-increasing importance. Through
the medium of poetry, Wordsworth captures the essence of psychological survival:

> Though nothing can bring back the hour
> Of splendour in the grass, of glory in the flower;
> We will grieve not, rather find
> Strength in what remains behind
> —*Ode: Intimations of Immortality IX,* 1803–1806

In a youth-oriented, fast-paced industrialized society, the process of aging
begins to acquire a negative meaning as we move past early adulthood. The
middle-aged and elderly often suffer from internalized ageism, seeing themselves as failing to meet prevailing ideals of beauty and health and therefore
as substandard in some way. A sense of worthlessness and depression may result,
not from the aging process itself, but from the perception of ourselves as embarking on a downward spiral, as being "over the hill." Such a perception may set
in as early as the late twenties.

The *social* side of aging refers to the cultural expectations for people at
various stages of their lives. Socially constructed definitions are important because
they ultimately are translated into public policies (Gonyea, 1994). To the extent
that the elderly are expected to continue making an active contribution to their
families and to society, or conversely, to disengage from responsibility in deference to the younger generation, has profound—and perhaps unsettling—
implications for one's social adjustment to growing old. The extent to which
older citizens are seen as privileged and well-taken care of by the state—as a
tax burden in other words—public policies will be shaped accordingly (Gonyea,
1994). (Sadly, the word *burden* permeates the literature on care for the aged.)

Race and ethnicity as social class status are significant determinants of
an individual's experience with aging. Membership in an extended family is a
primary buffer against the losses associated with advancing age. About twice
as many African and Hispanic Americans live in extended family situations
as do European Americans (Dunkle and Norgard, 1995). In the upper-upper
class, the elderly occupy a position of honor due to their link to an illustrious
and perhaps more prosperous past. Older people with higher incomes report
their health as being much better than that of those with lower incomes (Dunkle and Norgard, 1995). Regardless of background, economic factors are

instrumental, having ramifications for the biological (health related) and psychological dimensions of aging as well as for the social (status) dimension.

While the three aspects of aging discussed in this section—the biological, psychological, and social—overlap to a large extent, the focus of this chapter will be primarily on the social side of aging. Emphasis will be placed on caretaking, or how society provides for the care of the frail elderly.

AGING AROUND THE WORLD

The United States

Quite apart from chronological and physiological considerations, old age is a social category of roles, relationships, and life-styles. The traditional example of the elderly Asian or African elder cared for solicitously and respectfully by younger family or tribal members (described by Sandhu, 1974) is a far cry from the ambivalent response to older citizens in most Western and Westernized nations.

In his detailed study, *The Old Ones of New Mexico,* Robert Coles provides character portraits of aged residents of a Spanish American settlement where family members achieve a true dignity with age, where there is a sense of *growth* with the years rather than *decline* (1974). Although other conclaves of tradition abound in the United States' ethnically pluralistic society, generally the final stage of life is one accompanied by predominantly negative perceptions about growing old. These perceptions transcend geographical boundaries; they hold true in Great Britain, Sweden, Greece, Japan, Puerto Rico, and the United States (Katz, 1978). Consistent with the economic and social demands of modern industrialism and rapid technological change has been the gradual decline in stable, extended kinship systems. Because of the work/productivity and future orientation of the industrialized, urban society, ageism is most prevalent in the United States. According to an extensive Harris (1975) survey taken decades ago, the image of old people in America is that of "senile, lonely, used-up bodies, rotting away and waiting to die," an image which is, if anything, truer today than formerly. In a survey of college students, Barrow (1989) used a word-association technique to study stereotypes about the aging. Students paid the most attention to the changing physical and mental capabilities of the elderly.

The attitude toward the aged as measured in an open-ended questionnaire, however, was generally compassionate although closer to pity than admiration for older people.

Interestingly, in early American history, the elderly were viewed in a generally positive light. Many older people continued to work and carry out useful family functions. However, as Popple and Leighninger (1993) indicate in their review of the history of aging in America, attitudes began to shift by the mid-1800s, and by World War I, many Americans had come to equate old age with ugliness, disease, and uselessness. These dramatic shifts seem to have come more from cultural and intellectual teachings, such as social Darwinism which stressed survival of the fittest and the newfound stress on science and efficiency, than from any occupational or demographic trends. The negativism was further entrenched as numbers of the poor elderly migrated to the cities where they were perceived as a social problem. The first retirement programs inadvertently reinforced the idea that the elderly were incapable of useful work. By 1910, poorhouses had been transformed into old age homes. Meanwhile, the numbers of the aged in the population continued to increase. Only after the social turmoil associated with the Great Depression did the idea of social security catch on as a means of providing social insurance for workers and their families—insurance against loss of a parent, disabilities, and old age.

The policies of today are linked to the orientations and solutions of yesterday. Two developments from the eighteenth and nineteenth centuries are germane to our treatment of the elderly at the present time—a lack of coordination in a federally-operated system that developed in an ad hoc fashion, and a tendency to favor the young. Actually, McDaniel and Gee (1993) singled out these particular characteristics in their study of the Canadian system of elder care. Policy concerning the aged and caregiving is integrally linked to federalism, the peculiar relationship that evolved over time between the federal government and the states (provinces in Canada). State responsibility for the health and welfare of the people operates under the restraint of federal allotment of the finances to make the care possible. For provision of health care today, the federal government does not have the "right"; the state government does not have the resources (McDaniel and Gee, 1993). Differences among the states in service availability and quality of care provided complicate the system further and hinder sweeping social change. In European countries, in contrast, operations under one government are less complex and less fraught with power imbalances and irregularities in providing services.

CHAPTER 9: CARE FOR THE AGED

Historically, medical care was instituted to treat the *young,* to deal with war wounds, industrial accidents, childbirth, and children's diseases. Consequently, as McDaniel and Gee further indicate, the medical, physician-oriented, and cure-based nature of health care is unsuited to the needs of older persons, who typically have chronic conditions with social dimensions. The use of advanced technologies on the aged who may finish out their lives on a respirator in intensive care results in unnecessary pain for the old, guilty feelings for family members, and great expense for the society. This process further creates a convenient scapegoat—the elderly themselves—for rising health care costs.

Our country, the demographic changes notwithstanding, is still a youthoriented society, and the risk is that the older adults, in their expanding numbers, will be regarded as a drain. As Zastrow (1996) asserts, we glorify the body beautiful and knowledge which is new and of practical value. These views, unwittingly, shortchange the elderly. Older persons are viewed as "out of touch" and "behind the times." They are dispensable, because we have already dispensed with them, or as Sidel (1992) phrases it, they are extraneous. The avoidance of older adults stems, in part, from our feelings or "hang-ups" about death. In avoiding the problems of old age, we attempt to avoid our old age; in turning our backs on the sick and dying, we attempt to turn our backs on our own inevitable deterioration and death (Sidel, 1992).

One fifth of the elderly in the United States have incomes close to or below the poverty line. In a materialistic society, the old are devalued because they are poor, and they are poor because they are devalued. In this, as in other matters, the economic and social are intertwined. The poverty of older adults clearly reveals the order of priorities in our society. Social security benefits are well below the official poverty level. While other Western nations divert a substantial portion of their national wealth into old-age supplements, in the United States getting older generally means getting poorer. Lack of money, lack of adequate transportation, the high cost of health care in spite of Medicare and other programs, the mandatory loss of occupational role: these all combine to produce a social situation described by de Beauvoir (1973) in her monumental work on aging as "downright criminal."

Much of the literature and mass media today, however, are decidedly unsympathetic to the needs of the aged. Often older adults' needs are pitted against the needs of the very young who, it is said, lack voting power (unlike the elderly) and are therefore neglected (Gonyea, 1994; Jones, 1995). According to most public officials, the demands of the elderly are consuming a disproportionate share of the national budget (Olson, 1994; Gonyea, 1994). Following a barrage of press reports, in effect, blaming the needs of the elderly for the current fiscal crisis, resentment by the general public is mounting. Viewed as politically powerful and selfishly pursuing their own interests, the aged are justified in suspecting that they have become the sacrificial lambs of the country's austerity policies. "Why should the young be saddled with high taxes to support retired people?" is a question commonly asked. A retrenchment in Medicaid and Medicare and other programs serving the elderly is underway.

An Overview of Aging Worldwide

By the year 2000, the world will have half a billion people older than sixty-five (Stamets, 1993). Not only is population aging universal, but it is also unprecedented historically (Olson, 1994a). By 2025, the proportion of elderly in Japan will leap to 25 percent or higher, far above the 18 percent level America faces when its mammoth corps of baby boomers retires (Dentzer, 1991).

While the challenge of caring for progressively larger numbers of elderly persons is the same the world over, the way in which this challenge is met varies greatly from country to country. The major distinction is regarding who assumes responsibility for the care of an elder parent or parents. Is it the family, the state, or a combination of both? What are the cultural norms concerning family life, in general, and obligations to the older generation in particular?

The phenomenon of mass aging is being experienced virtually everywhere. An obvious exception is in sub-Sahara Africa where the birthrates and death-rates are still incredibly high. In all these other countries, the mass aging phenomenon is so relatively new that coping mechanisms and social institutions have yet to be developed. On the other hand, the fact that the numbers of aged have not yet reached the point of crisis allows countries a period of time to plan for their support and absorption—if they act soon enough (Sennott-Miller, 1994).

In her book, *The Graying of the World: Who Will Care for the Frail Elderly?*, Olson (1994) examines the demographic changes occurring across the globe. A key issue is how various countries are accommodating these changes. What is the availability of adequate health care and social services? Is there reliance on institutional or on home-based care? To what extent is there dependence on women family members to provide care for aging relatives? Olson's findings concerning these basic questions will be summarized briefly by topic.

The essence of successful long-term care for the frail elderly is in the kind of health care and social services available in the wider society. Nations with collectivist approaches assume that frailty among the aged is a social problem engendering social solutions. Sweden, Finland, Israel, and France provide services universally and with dignity for those in need of aid. In Sweden and Finland as in the rest of Scandinavia, pensions and housing allowances are viewed as essential components of elder care. Britain and Canada, in contrast, despite an entitlement approach to health care, place the responsibility on the family to provide long-term care; programs are developed only to fill gaps when emergency care is needed. The promotion of greater privatization in both countries is threatening to create a greater gap between the "haves" and "have-nots." In the United States, the continued emphasis on individualism and self-reliance fosters a tradition of privately provided support including support by family members.

A second aspect of elder care is the degree to which the aged are institutionalized. Many of the countries studied by Olson have similar institutionalization rates, usually around 5 percent, with a high of 7.5 percent in Canada and a low of 2 percent in Japan. In both the United States and Britain there have been nursing home scandals of abuse, lack of proper hygiene, fire hazards, and other problems. Nursing homes in many of the countries studied, however, provide normal, homelike atmospheres as opposed to medical environments. Due to both economic and humanitarian considerations, there is a thrust toward state funding for home and community-based services. Service apartments in Scandinavia provide a wide range of supportive services for the elderly including prepared meals. Israel, which has provided extensive care for the large influx of elderly immigrants, is shifting to a focus on community-based services including daycare. Germany, similarly, offers a variety of services but still fails to meet the needs of all the frail elderly, especially of those who are poor.

Finally, Olson considers the role of the immediate family in caring for the aged. In all the nations studied, informal care remains in the women's domain. In Israel, where few of the elderly are living alone and with a strong Jewish tradition of honoring one's parents, the family plays a major role in caregiving. In Japan, likewise, over 60 percent of people aged sixty-five and over and nearly 80 percent of those aged eighty and over, live with their adult children. And in China, familism based on the Confucian concept of filial piety promotes cooperation and obligation among the generations. The daughters-in-law provide the actual care; if they work, they often must take a leave of absence from their jobs.

Regardless of political economy, the common theme in every country with extended life expectancies is the struggle with varying political, social, economic, and psychological issues associated with caring for growing older populations. Furthermore, the steady increase in the number of mentally impaired older people tends to be a worldwide issue: currently 5 to 7 percent of the elderly have some form of dementia. Suicide is another problem; actually it is the tragic solution to a host of problems, including loneliness and depression. In the United States, elderly men are more likely to commit suicide than is any other age group—eight out of ten of the suicides involve use of firearms (Kaplan, Adamek, and Johnson, 1994). In Japan, similarly, suicide rates are higher in the elderly than in the younger age groups and apt to be associated with health problems (Tatai and Tatai, 1991).

Shah (1992) traveled across the world to report on care for the aged in nations already dealing with population shifts toward the upper end of the age spectrum. What she found can be summarized briefly. Balking from the high cost of health and social spending, Sweden has seen fit to trim many other programs. China's government, meanwhile, is promising support to its citizens in their old age as a means of keeping the birthrate down; resources are lacking, however. In workaholic Japan, retired persons, especially men, have much difficulty with leisure time so the government is organizing activities at neighborhood centers. And India, where care is provided through the extended family, is unprepared for the explosion of old people as it still struggles to feed the young.

Throughout the world, care of an elderly parent is often regarded by the children as an unwanted burden. In a thoughtful comparison of two works of literature, Donow (1990) reveals how two cultures—the American and Japanese—approach a similar family crisis involving the need to care for an elderly father or father-in-law. Anderson's play, *I Never Sang for My Father* (1968) later made into a movie starring Gene Hackman and Melvyn Douglas, is a deeply moving drama depicting the agony experienced by the children of an 80-year-old autocratic father who descends suddenly upon them. "My responsibility is to my husband and my children," declares the anguished daughter (p. 95). The son, somewhat more sensitively, reveals his pain in these words: "I can't tell you what it does to me as a man . . . to see someone like that . . . a man who was distinguished, remarkable . . . just become a nuisance" (p. 94).

In the American play, the adult children wrestle with their guilty feelings, and issues which they are never able to resolve so much as to endure.

The Japanese novel *Kokotsu no hito (The Twilight Years)* by Ariyoshi (1972) is told from the perspective of Akiko who faces the crisis of caring for her father-in-law, an egocentric and difficult man suffering from dementia. Unlike its American counterpart, in this story the central character, though nearly overwhelmed by the burden of her father-in-law's illness, emerges richer for the experience as does her father-in-law. As Donow concludes from his comparative study of these culturally distinct, but circumstantially similar texts, both works leave us with some troubling questions about family relations and what role other social institutions ought to play in the care of an elderly parent.

With an average life expectancy about four years longer than that of Americans and a plunging birthrate, Japan's aging society, according to an article in the *U.S. News and World Report* (Dentzer, 1991) is creating a near hysteria within Japan. Unlike America's policymakers who have largely ducked the issue (until recently), Japan's planners have settled upon a target stated in terms of a "national burden"—the sum of all taxes, plus all other payments workers make to fund Japan's universal health insurance and pension systems. The national burden is headed to 60 percent or higher by 2020 driven by the expense of care for the elderly. One change that is inevitable is a reduction in hospital care. The average length of a hospital stay for a person over seventy years of age in Japan is ninety-five days (Dentzer, 1991). Actions that Japan can take are to raise the retirement age from sixty to sixty-five, increase the number of public home helpers, build more nursing homes, and recruit volunteers from "the young-old" to help in the care of "the old-old." According to Campbell (1995), Japan is shaping innovative policy and at the forefront in establishing a long-term care insurance system to establish the kinds of services that are now becoming necessary. Japan's moves, as Campbell argues, contrast starkly with those of the United States which is in the process of dismantling its already inadequate provisions for long-term care.

THE ELDERIZATION OF POVERTY

Paralleling the feminization of poverty which refers to the social and economic structures and processes that increasingly locked women in poverty (Hartman,

PART 2: CARE THROUGH THE LIFE CYCLE

1990), I am introducing the term the *elderization of poverty* or alternatively, the *povertization of the elderly* to refer to a trend that goes beyond the census data statistics. This trend relates to the quality of life that awaits a large percentage of the rapidly growing group of older people who can expect to live in poverty, many in abject poverty. Specifically, elderly women have a far higher rate of poverty than do elderly men (Sidel, 1992). Older women's incomes are on average only 58 percent of the incomes of older men. This seems to be the case for the following reasons: because much of women's work has been unpaid and thus without retirement benefits (even the majority of working women are not covered by private pension plans); because of the great likelihood that women will take care of their spouses and then be left alone (over age eighty-five, 50 percent of the men are married compared to only 8 percent of the women); and because so many women live to an advanced age (Sidel, 1992). Thus women's greatest blessing — longevity — turns into their greatest woe, and the feminization of poverty and the elderization of poverty become one.

When ethnic and racial characteristics are factored in, the situation becomes ever more dismal. The poverty rate of Hispanic women over sixty-five is 25 percent while 38 percent of African American women are in poverty. For older women living alone, nearly one in four lives below the poverty level. For women of color over eighty-five and living alone, 73 percent are poor. Lower income for people of color is evident in the elderly of both genders. Just over 10.7 percent of elderly whites, 28 percent of elderly African Americans, and 28 percent of elderly Hispanic Americans lived below the poverty level in 1993. While only 10 percent of the elderly population are people of color, this figure is expected to double by 2030 (Bellos and Ruffolo, 1995).

A distinction should be made between two segments of the older population — the young-old (age sixty-five to seventy-five) and the old-old (age seventy-five and up). Newly retired people, compared to other age groups in the United States, are doing quite well. Their health is good; marriages and relationships boost their income and reduce expenses; and their retirement benefits have not yet been eaten up by inflation. After age seventy-five, the numbers of the living are depleted. For those still living, their income declines significantly while expenses climb. The oldest-old (eighty-five years and over) experience a poverty rate twice that of people age sixty-five to seventy-five (Dunkle and Norgard, 1995). We can conceive then of slowly but surely escalating elderization of poverty. Only those with vast accumulations of wealth are invulnerable past a certain age.

Much is made of the fact that, due to social security and Supplemental Security Income, poverty has been reduced in the overall elderly population to nearly the average for the population as a whole. In fact, however, in the belief that they need less income, the Census Bureau applies a different poverty standard to elders than to those below age sixty-five. For example, in 1993, the poverty level for individuals under age sixty-five was $7,518 while older people were not considered impoverished until their income dropped below $6,930. The fastest growing segment of the population in industrialized societies, the elderly, is a population at risk. Inflation eats up retirement income; and health care costs mount because of age-related illnesses. Medicare beneficiaries typically spend more than $2,000 each year for out-of-pocket health care expenses, including some $500 for part B premiums which covers medical insurance other than hospital care (covered in part A) and $1,200 for other supplementary policies (Lieberman, 1995).

In light of extremely high health care expenses, especially for medication, the elderly very often have to choose between filling a prescription and buying food. A frail elderly woman, typically, may have to find a way to obtain long-term health care for an ailing spouse when she no longer can physically provide the care herself. But with expenses for institutionalized health care skyrocketing, even the most scrupulous handling of finances over decades of retirement cannot protect a formerly middle income family from ruination in the end. Housing deteriorates over time, and many of the homes of elderly people require renovation to make them handicapped-accessible. About 30 percent of the elderly live in substandard housing that does not meet their needs; many reside in crime-ridden neighborhoods and are easy prey for thieves and muggers. Tragically, in Chicago during the heat wave of 1995, 529 people died of the heat; the majority were old people who lived alone. Their burglar-proof homes prevented adequate ventilation, pushing indoor temperatures to dangerously high levels (*Facts on File*, 1995). When pronouncements are made about how well the elderly are doing, it is important to be aware of the stark realities of being old in America.

U.S. GOVERNMENT PROGRAMS

The Social Security Act of 1935, discussed in chapter 2, is the cornerstone of legislation for older people. Never intended to be the main source of income for the elderly, but rather as a supplement to assets, the social security system has become the sole support for many persons (Zastrow, 1996). In the 1960s, before a reorganization of government programs, one-third of all elderly had incomes below the poverty line. Due to improvements in the standard of living and social security and pension benefits, the poverty rate was cut in half between 1966 and 1974 (Dunkle and Norgard, 1995). This is when Medicare and Medicaid were signed into law by President Johnson; Medicare provides health care to people sixty-five and over and to the disabled; Medicaid provides health care to poor and older Americans as well as long-term care to individuals of all ages. Today people sixty-five and older account for more than one-third of the nation's personal health care expenditures (U.S. Senate, 1992).

The coverage Medicaid provides aids not only the eligible poor but also middle class nursing home residents who have exhausted their savings in paying the nearly prohibitive nursing home fees. Medicare and Medicaid have provided important health care benefits. There are deficiencies, however: long-term care provision is limited, many costs are not adequately covered, and home health care provisions are insufficient. Current health care reform proposals may alter the nature of these programs, not in the direction of benefiting the elderly, however, but by curbing spending, reducing mandated benefits that the states have to offer, and shifting more of the responsibility to the financing of Medicaid over to the states. One thing is certain: in the short run, as federal funding will be cut, the elderly will be forced to move over to privately run managed care programs. But what will happen in the long run?

We can predict with some certainty the cohort known as the baby boom generation or "boomers" who did so much to change the meaning of education, marriage, and the family will not stand idly by when it comes to public policies pertaining to the elderly. The political clout of people over sixty-five likely will grow as their numbers double over the next century (Torres-Gil and Puccinelli, 1995). But in the meantime, services for the elderly are under great strain. As the government relinquishes control over all forms of health care, private providers are rapidly moving in to claim the territory.

An additional government funded program that is more promise than reality is the array of human and social services for the elderly offered under the rubric of the Older Americans Act. Enacted in 1965, with the ambitious goal of assuring the well-being of the elderly, this program operated under a budget of approximately one billion dollars in 1994 (Torres-Gil and Puccinelli, 1995). Popular community programs and informational services are funded for all those over age sixty.

POLICY CONSIDERATIONS

A World View

Despite the many flaws in the system, such as those mentioned above, in industrialized societies retired people enjoy some sense of economic security due to pensions, social security provisions, access to health services, and possession of some political clout (Rao, 1992). In other parts of the world, older persons continue to function in multigenerational contexts until the time of their death. Under both sets of circumstances, however, changing age and social structures, in conjunction with economic adjustments, are rendering the "ideal" situations remnants of the past.

In industrialized nations, older persons increasingly are being marginalized through forced early retirements and decreased social spending by the state on retirement, pension, and medical arrangements. Without accumulated assets and non-work related income, the poor elderly suffer the most in a climate of economic restructuring and erosion of previously available safety net schemes. As cost saving measures, and to decrease the national debt, nations are shifting the responsibility for the care of the elderly from the state back to the family and to private agencies for those with the necessary financial resources. In most of the industrialized countries, however, the middle-aged women who are expected to assume the caregiving functions have chosen, for economic and personal reasons, to enter the work force. This turn of events places women as the designated caregivers in positions of extreme personal conflict. In England, for example, as Walker (1993) informs us, the rhetoric promoting community care is played out as care by female kin and provided without the necessary support services for caregivers. Privatization supposedly increases choice in an expanded economy of mixed welfare offerings. In reality, however, choice is restricted due to strict admissions criteria on the basis of health and financial status of the applicant. The choice is in the hands of the private homes, not the needy elderly. Walker refers to the present arrangement as a mockery of supermarket style consumerism. In the field of social care many older people are mentally disabled, frail, and vulnerable; they are not in a position to shop around, and once admitted into private care have no realistic prospect of exiting it. In the context of chronic underfunding of government services for the elderly, an overreliance on unpaid female labor, and a constant search for cheaper alternatives, the likely outcome of the changes taking place in the United Kingdom will be a reduction of the quantity and quality of support available to the elderly and their families.

What about care in non-industrialized parts of the world? According to Rao's (1992) analysis of aging policies and programs, the "ideal" situation for the traditional societies has weakened also. The same global economy that is having a negative impact on the most industrialized of nations also is promoting individualism and materialism elsewhere. Increasing materialism has been at the expense of the traditional family values of respect and care for the elderly and familial interdependence. The communications revolution promoting modern and Western commercialism has continued to undermine the traditional foundations of family roles and function.

In her participant observation study, *Understanding Older Chicanas*, Facio (1996) explores the meaning of old age to Mexican American women. During their childhood, grandparents were a vital part of the family (p. 15):

> Older Chicanas . . . were socialized with certain ideas about old age: that it would bring harmony, status, respect, and solace. However, the reality of their present lives (poverty, family structural changes, differential life expectancies, longevity) calls for the aged to reassess their expectations and thus redefine their old age. Older Chicanas, in particular, must also deal with traditions that reinforce a gender hierarchy.

In China, too, the old ways are weakening under the influence of capitalism and world trade. Still, traditional Chinese society venerates its elders and emphasizes filial duty as mentioned earlier. Generally, the family is expected to take care of any of its members who are old, frail, sick, or disabled. It is an offense, punishable by a fine, to neglect elderly members of the family (Webb, 1992). If there is no family to help, the state will step in. Pensions are provided to ex-government workers (workers at state-owned factories also qualify). Others, however, get no pension.

NURSING HOME CARE

By way of introduction to some of the cruelties of present day nursing home care, let us look back to the world of Jane Addams. During her visit to old women confined in the Cook County Infirmary, Addams (1910: 156) comments:

To take away from an old woman whose life has been spent in household cares all the foolish little belongings to which her affections cling and to which her very fingers have become accustomed, is to take away her last incentive to activity, almost to life itself. To give an old woman only a chair and a bed, to leave her no cupboard in which her treasures may be stowed, not only that she may take them out when she desires occupation, but that her mind may dwell upon them in moments of revery, is to reduce living almost beyond the limit of human endurance.

Similarly, today a forced move from home to a nursing facility can be traumatic. And as surprising as it is, even elderly prison inmates can find this transition severely disturbing. Some inmates even commit attempted "escapes" in order to circumvent release plans. The position that aged persons may actually receive better treatment and are less vulnerable to the effects of the aging process behind bars than are their counterparts in nursing homes, is less absurd than it would appear on the surface. Reed and Glamser (1979) found older prisoners to be significantly less depressed when compared to similar residents of nursing homes. Moreover, they had a quality of agelessness about them, and in interviews acknowledged that they felt much younger than those of the same age living on the outside.

Some years ago when I was doing research in the Alabama prison for women I was struck by the sense of contentment among older inmates housed together with a few younger convicts in "the old folks' cell." One very sweet eighty-year-old, "Granny," imprisoned for poisoning her son-in-law who had made her a virtual slave in her own home, described her love for prison life, "All of my people are here; I never want to leave this place." Indeed, she did not; she died happily several years later, surrounded by her loved ones, her "girls."

"What have we got to lose?" This question (that is more of a comment) is raised by George Burns in the satirical and very funny 1979 film, *Going in Style,* as he and two elderly peers set out to rob a Manhattan bank. In light of the reduced living circumstances and physical health of these old friends, there is very little that they have not lost already. In prison, in the final scene, the nonrepentant hero (played by Burns) remarks that his life on the outside had become a prison anyway. Although some of the crime sequences are not terribly convincing, this poignant film, considered a Gray Power film at the time, is a sad commentary on the social world of the very old. This brings us to a discussion of nursing home care.

The term *nursing home* generally is applied to residential facilities in which 50 percent or more of the residents receive nursing services. Secondly, facilities that receive Medicare and Medicaid reimbursement are certified by the federal government as skilled or intermediate care facilities (Beaver and Miller, 1992). There is a third level of care—custodial care. Custodial residents, who may be blind, or in various stages of Alzheimer's or Parkinson's disease, need assistance in daily living; the cost is covered by Medicaid for those poor enough to qualify.

Although only 5 percent of the elderly are currently in a nursing home, nearly one in three of those who are age eighty-five and over eventually will end up there (Zastrow, 1996). These personal care facilities range enormously in price, quality, size, and services offered. Nursing homes are a billion dollar industry; there are more patient beds in nursing homes, in fact, than in hospitals. Nursing homes, moreover, have become the repositories for mentally ill elderly people. As hospitals close or severely shorten the length of stays as a part of government-enforced cost containment measures, nursing homes are picking up the slack. Registered nurses, now being laid off as a result of hospital downsizing, increasingly are employed in nursing care facilities. Unfortunately, pay levels are much lower than the pay for hospital work, and incredibly, health benefits often are not provided to the workers in these facilities.

Costs per resident average thousands of dollars per month. Medicare provides only for limited convalescence coverage. Medicaid covers the rest, but only for persons whose life savings have been exhausted, a fact creating an enormous psychological toll on the elderly who may have skimped and saved in early years for themselves and their descendants. Now, as mentioned previously, they are forced to unload their assets, transfer them to a surviving spouse, or to pay it all out for nursing care. Meanwhile, there is a national outcry against the escalating costs of health care, with attention directed toward Medicaid: Sixty nine cents of every Medicaid dollar goes to nursing home care (Mann, 1995).

In 1995, while the federal government contemplated deregulating nursing homes and reducing enforcement of standards for nursing home care, scandals were prevalent. Zastrow (1996) lists the following recent cases:

- In Houston an elderly woman was ignored to the point that her death was not discovered until rigor mortis had set in.
- A nursing home resident was hospitalized due to rat bites.
- Doctors have been charged with giving needless injections to patients to raise their fees.

- Patients are often restrained in beds for long periods of time; heavy doses of tranquilizers may also be given.
- Investigators have reported finding patients lying in their own feces or urine.

Scandals in Britain have occurred as well; these have been widely documented in the mass media (Walker and Warren, 1994). Most of the complaints have come from the private homes. Residents find their rapidly shrinking social security benefits from the state inadequate to keep up with increases in residential and nursing home charges. Lack of resources makes the elderly extremely vulnerable to abuse — financial, emotional, and physical. Care in the public sector is generally considered to be of a higher standard. The primacy of government economics, however, is superseding social considerations.

The need for long-term care, however, is growing rapidly. Most of this care is provided by families already. But sometimes there is no family who can help; often the "children" are elderly themselves. The average nursing home patient is cognitively impaired, mostly with Alzheimer's. Two-thirds are incontinent; half have no relatives nearby (Goodman, 1995). Under new proposals Medicaid will be cut drastically and the impact will be felt by the 1.5 million elderly Americans who require institutionalized care.

Much more can be done to help families keep their elderly and disabled members at home, such as providing tax breaks for informal caretakers or better yet, paying them for their care. Homemaker services, visiting nurse services, "meals on wheels," adult foster care, day care, and group home care are among the offerings that can prevent the need for nursing home care. An innovative program in Wisconsin offers a host of alternative services such as homemaker services, home-delivered meals, adult foster care, and group home care. The program is cost-effective and preferred by clients over institutionalized care (Zastrow, 1996). It is only for the indigent, however.

Oregon, similarly, offers a mix of foster home care, group homes for the healthy, and assisted living, a new style of private apartment housing for frail elderly people who don't have serious medical problems (Mann, 1995). The assisted living complex provides housekeeping, meals, laundry, transportation, nurse visits, and social activities. Perhaps one of the most encouraging experiments is the very practical Senior Companion Program in Missoula, Montana, which trains low-income senior citizens to provide home care to the frail elderly. Seniors get a yearly stipend which helps them as they help others in need of their services (Cook, 1993).

A major fallacy in the present system is the either/or approach to elder care: either the institution or total home care. Distinctly absent is a middle ground of offerings for people who have a range of health and social service needs (Neysmith, 1994). Humanistic policy supports deinstitutionalization and keeping elderly people in the community. Community care without an extensive support system, however, pushes more and more family members, many of whom may be resentful, into taking responsibility (Hartman, 1990). Caregiving by "families," a euphemism for *women* as Canadian sociologists McDaniel and Gee (1993) remind us, is so taken for granted that the dwindling numbers of women available for work, and the lack of support they face, is invisible to social policies on caregiving. In the rhetoric endorsing community and home care, the risk is that future policies in Canada (and the United States) will encourage the unpaid labor of women at home to care for elders as a substitute for formal or social services. Proof of the government's sincerity will come in its willingness to invest in back-up services and extensive, professional home health care and other maintenance services to enable the elderly to enjoy the final years of their lives in the comfort of home or at least in a homelike atmosphere near the sources of social support.

ELDER ABUSE

However, sometimes home is not the best place for the aged. Affection and closeness actually can dissipate under the real strains of caregiving and such strains can contribute to elder abuse, as Olson (1994) suggests.

Like child abuse, elder abuse is much more widespread than is commonly realized. Probably hundreds of thousands of the nation's elderly are victimized each year, yet this is one of the most hidden and neglected of social problems (Tatara, 1995). There are many reasons why the aged who are abused would hesitate to report it; a sense of shame is primary, but also there is the fear if caregivers are involved that removal to a nursing home might be a worse fate than remaining where they are. Knowing the true incidence of elder abuse is therefore extremely difficult. A nationally representative sample of over two thousand elderly people revealed a domestic elder abuse rate of 3.2 percent (Pillemer and Finkelhor, 1988). Elder or parent abuse, as Zastrow (1996) indicates, occurs most often when the parents live with their children or are dependent on them.

The term *abuse* tends to be used variously in the literature on the aged. Sometimes it refers to neglect such as dumping off the elderly person in a public place or leaving him or her to freeze to death in the cold. Physical attacks are often involved. Finally, the abuse may be financial maltreatment as relatives, through extortion, spend the money and resources of a helpless dependent.

While the perpetrators in domestic elder abuse are more likely to be men, the victims are more likely to be women. More than 30 percent of abusers are adult children of the victims. They are people who tend to have emotional problems; substance abuse is commonly involved (Tatara, 1995). Only a fraction of the incidents that take place are ever reported. Some states have mandatory reporting laws for certain professionals such as physicians and social workers, but there is rarely much follow-through after an incident is reported.

In Alberta, Canada, a $500,000 study conducted by the Kerby Centre provided an in-depth profile of seniors who were suffering some form of abuse. The need for special shelters and continuation of a twenty-four-hour telephone crisis line were identified (Editorial, *Calgary Herald,* 1995). Home care is the order of the day, according to the editorial, while seniors are discharged earlier than ever before from hospitals. For elderly women who are abused, there are few avenues of escape as cuts to social services for seniors get underway. Is there time for yet another highly expensive study, the editorial asks, or is it time for politicians to do something about elder abuse?

All abuse of the elderly is not domestic. Just as in the United Kingdom where there have been problems in some of the private, profit-making homes for the elderly, so there have been reports of institutional abuse in the unlicensed and unregulated care provided in American board and care homes. As Olson (1994) writes, many of the homes offer squalid conditions, and their residents are often subjected to various forms of abuse including theft, control through drugs, and violence.

The problem of elder abuse will only grow in the future as increasing numbers of the population reach into the advanced age group. Neglect of the needs of this age by the society will make its members more vulnerable to attack by those on whom they are physically and psychologically dependent.

FACING DEATH

Death is the inevitable outcome of life and clearly a preoccupation of the aged. The lucky ones who live into old age bury their contemporary friends and relatives and hope for a death of dignity for themselves. In modern societies where one lives in the present and invests in the future, old age and death are commonly denied. The painful paradox of death in life is addressed with rare eloquence in Becker's classic, *The Denial of Death* (1973: 268):

> We saw that there really was no way to overcome the *real* dilemma of existence, the one of the mortal animal who at the same time is conscious of his mortality. A person spends years coming into his own, developing his talent, his unique gifts, perfecting his discriminations about the world, broadening and sharpening his appetite, learning to bear the disappointments of life, becoming mature, seasoned—finally a unique creature in nature, standing with some dignity and nobility and transcending the animal condition, no longer a complete reflex, not stamped out of any mold. And then the real tragedy, as André Malraux wrote in *The Human Condition*: that it takes sixty years of incredible suffering and effort to make such an individual, and then he is good only for dying.

When I was working for a brief period at a community home health care and hospice in Washington state, I pondered the remarkable resilience of the staff in dealing with death and dying every day. I began to study the various styles of coping by staff and family alike. By the time I left the hospice, I had drawn up a list of coping devices, all normal reactions to the psychological demands of work with the bereaved and the dying (van Wormer, 1990). From the literature on death and dying and my work, I filtered out five ideologies, all different but all united by the theme of denial, the denial of the reality of death. All were escape mechanisms, but under conditions in which escape is not necessarily an unhealthy response.

Blaming the victim, the first theme, is a way we can divorce ourselves from the sense of injustice of death, especially of premature death. This ideology is manifested in blaming the patient for lifestyle activities that destroyed his or her health and also blaming patients for not following specific medical orders and even for their failure to recover.

Denial of death, the second defense mechanism, is consistent with the American creed that stresses youth, optimism, and progress. Denying death involves maintaining the patient past the point when trying to get well makes any sense. "Now we will try radiation treatments," the doctor may say to one who may only have weeks left to live. The battle is against death as the final enemy. The healthy side of denial is that people (the patient or friends and relatives) can go on, they can delay coping with cruel realities until they are ready.

The weaknesses, however, are summed up brilliantly in the following widely quoted passage from Tolstoy (1960: 131; orig. 1881):

> What tormented Ivan Ilych most was the deception, the lie, which for some reason they all accepted, that he was not dying but was simply ill, and that he only need keep quiet and undergo a treatment and then something very good would result. He, however, knew that, do what they would nothing would come of it, only still more agonizing suffering and death. This deception tortured him—their not wishing to admit what they all knew and what he knew, but wanting to lie to him concerning his terrible condition and wishing and forcing him to participate in that lie. Those lies—lies enacted over him on the eve of his death and destined to degrade this awful, solemn act to the level of their visitings, their curtains, their sturgeon for dinner— were a terrible agony for Ivan Ilych.

Escape through medical jargon is a strategy widely used among health care professionals. Physicians are trained to treat diseases, not people, so an escape into technology is consistent with a medical education oriented toward cure rather than care. Placing our focus on machines helps remove us from the personal suffering (Kubler-Ross, 1975). It may do more for us than the patient.

Escape through social death is an interesting social psychological defense against the dying itself rather than death. We simply bury the person prematurely and say good-bye. Avoidance of the dying person and of very old people is a phenomenon the terminally ill are well aware of. In his penetrating participant observation study of the hospital, Sudnow (1967) provides numerous examples of the too-early burial of some unsuspecting victim. In one case, a woman found a replacement for her husband when to everyone's shock, he recovered!

Lastly, *escape through redefinition* is introduced as the solution to the problem of denial. Yet this, the modern approach to death and dying, creates some problems of its own. One writer sarcastically referred to this phenomenon as "the happy death movement." Our society seems to swing to extremes in its attempt to deal with the anxieties surrounding death, notes Wasow (1984). The focus here, under this conceptualization, is on the stages of awareness of dying. Although a great deal of good has come from this movement, when taken to extremes, the overly-positive focus overlooks the patient's reality or reduces the reality to a mere passage through inevitable states—of denial, anger, bargaining, and so on.

Fortunately, there are many excellent hospice-connected programs which are set up to provide quality of life to the terminal patient and to assist the patient at home or in a home-like setting. Pain relief is encouraged to keep the person as comfortable as possible (Zastrow, 1996). Hospice workers, often social workers, also assist families throughout the bereavement process.

CONFRONTING AGEISM

A society that equates beauty with youth, denies aging and death, and lacks valued rituals for passages through all the stages of life is a society that practices ageism. *Ageism* refers to discrimination and prejudice against people simply because they are old (Zastrow, 1996). Examples of ageism are: devaluing older workers because they are regarded as slow and as having skills that are outmoded; using the word *old* in an intolerant and pejorative way; avoiding dining in restaurants frequented by seniors; using the word *burden* in reference to care for the old but not for care for the young; derogatory mass media portrayals of old persons such as comedy routines making fun of aging bodies; refusing to let those age sixty-five and over rent cars (common European policy); and politically attacking social welfare programs that make life tolerable for the older population (prevalent in the United States and Canada).

Internalized ageism occurs as the elderly devalue themselves as worthless, useless, ugly, and inferior to the young. The extent to which old people accept the treatment they receive will determine if ageism will win out. If they externalize injustice and fight for their rights, persons who have reached the final quartile of life will be able to see that their interests are represented. The elderly, in fact, are rapidly becoming one of the most politically organized and influential groups in the United States. High voting rates, much higher than for other age groups, and high rates of membership in political organizations such as the American Association of Retired Persons (AARP) open to anyone over age fifty, provide political clout to upcoming generations.

The activism of the Gray Panthers, an organization founded in 1970 inspired by the Civil Rights era to fight discrimination against the aged, has done much to refute the negative image of the elderly. Such social activism was instrumental in promoting enforcement of the Age Discrimination in Employment Act in 1967. This act provides some protection against blatant age bias in the workplace, but cannot protect people from discrimination in its subtler forms. The Gray Panthers are credited with banning mandatory retirement laws. Although the United Nations has not taken the keen interest in mistreatment of the aged that they have against other groups, they did produce an International Plan of Action at the World Congress on Aging in 1982 which put the spotlight on programs for the aged. Continued or renewed militance will go a long way to confront ageism and its manifestations. Perhaps advocacy for such exemplary programs as the following will some day bring about favorable results:

- Pay to family members for caregiving (available in northern Europe and Nova Scotia, Canada).
- Hiring of retired persons to clean for and care for the frail elderly in their own homes (available in a few areas of the United States).
- Passage of a long-term care act providing the right to nursing care for all older people in need of such care (as legislated in Israel).
- Extensive home help services, day care centers and communal-owned old people's homes (as offered in Finland).
- Guaranteed pensions whether one was a wage-earner or not and service apartments for semi-independent living (as in Sweden).

CONCLUSION AND SUMMARY

This chapter completes part II which has addressed social welfare needs across the life span, from childhood through old age. Taking these four chapters or four intervals of life as a whole, one theme that emerges is that those who are born poor are apt to die poor. This fact is true within the United States and cross-culturally. Events along the way ensure this outcome. Children at risk for poverty, ill health, and maltreatment enter the working world, if they enter it at all, with a tremendous liability, both educationally and socially. Lack of access to the essential preventive health care and healthy living conditions including proper nutrition and housing compounds any existing problems and in many societies may lead to homelessness or economic migration. Then, for the lucky ones who achieve old age, "the last scene of all," as Shakespeare refers to the final stage of life, may recapitulate the first scene, as the deficiencies early in life are played out at the end. Conversely, the privileges of a favorable upbringing leading in to a successful career set the stage, to continue the dramaturgical metaphor, for health, wealth, and happiness or at least security, later on.

In short, we can say, and this is especially true for women, that the infantilization of poverty breeds the elderization of poverty. Several facts of life create the conditions of impoverishment for older women, among them, employment discrimination, the sacrifice of self for the caretaking role of both children and parents, and the frequency of single parenting, divorce, and widowhood. Moreover, the life span for women in the industrialized nations is very long; and as we have seen, the poverty rate for persons over age eighty-five is substantial.

The extent to which gender was stressed in this chapter is because persons who survive to the oldest and poorest age groups are overwhelmingly women. In the economic and social well-being of aging women, we see the interaction of ageism, sexism, and racism (Hartman, 1990). But there is also classism. The conditions of poverty in old age, although related to gender, transcend gender when class enters the picture. Men over age eighty-five and especially men of color are apt to be poor. With so many men suffering loss of job security and generous pensions, the postretirement years may be expected to bring extreme economic hardship. The high suicide rate for elderly men is a statistic that requires no comment. Inflated medical expenses including nursing home care affect everyone of advanced age and in need of professional care. The plight of the elderly who finish their lives in a nursing home is the plight of those who so often have outlived their health, their husbands, wives, and siblings, and who face exhausting their savings as well. Under a means-tested welfare system such as exists in the United States, the very poor sometimes fare better than the working class and middle class. The increasing subordination of social policy to economic policy, and questionable economic policy at best, is taking a heavy toll on programs affecting the elderly. The retrenchment of federal funding for housing, health care, and financial aid is pitting the interests of children against the interests of senior citizens. What is needed is not an array of piecemeal policies providing benefits to one group at the expense of another but a unified agenda ensuring economic security, health care, and adequate housing across the life span. A government's investment in its children is, in a real sense, an investment in their old age. Such an investment may even determine whether or not an individual reaches old age.

In summary, this chapter has considered the following trends pertaining to the elderly:

- People age sixty-five and over now comprise over 12 percent of the U.S. population; by 2000, one in ten will be over age eighty.

- The diversity of the younger U.S. population will be reflected in the statistics into the twenty-first century.
- The U.S. elderly are not a homogenous group; those living below the poverty line are apt to be people of color, women, the old-old, and persons living alone.
- People age sixty-five and older consume more than one-third of the nation's health care expenditures; their own out-of-pocket medical expenses often reduce them to a poverty level not reflected in the income statistics.
- The high suicide rate for elderly males, higher than for any other age group, is daunting.
- Domestic elder abuse is estimated to affect 3.2 percent of the U.S. elderly.
- The aging of America is a small part of the aging of the world; the populations in Japan and Sweden are aging more rapidly than the United States; only in sub-Sahara Africa does the total population remain disproportionately young; the decimation of social programs uniquely affecting the aged is occurring universally.
- The U.S., unlike most of Europe, however, has no comprehensive long-term health care policy.
- Only a small percentage of the elderly finish out their lives in nursing homes in any country, yet a need for good nursing home care and comprehensive alternative services for the elderly persists.

Policy recommendations from the literature on the aging reviewed in this chapter are the assurance of minimal income levels to protect the many who are without adequate pensions, the provision of universal health care covering prescription drugs, effective housing and transportation assistance, comprehensive homemaker and home health care programs, and the availability and affordability of home-like nursing homes for persons in need of round-the-clock assistance. In short, the best prevention of an *elderization of poverty* (a term introduced to depict a reality that transcends the statistics) is a social welfare system guaranteeing the right to health, housing, and quality of life throughout the life span. In this way, the child who learns to trust (as in Erikson's first stage) can achieve integrity (as in Erikson's final stage). In the words of Erik Erikson (1963: 269) who paraphrased the relation of adult integrity and infantile trust, "Children will not fear life if their elders have integrity enough not to fear death."

REVIEW QUESTIONS

1. What does the phrase, the graying of America mean?
2. How does the biopsychosocial model provide a framework for the study of the aging process? Relate each aspect of this model to facts on aging.

3. What is the image of old age in the United States? How has old age been viewed historically?
4. There is a controversy concerning whether or not many of the elderly in America can be considered poor. Take a stand on this issue and present the facts.
5. Discuss demographic changes across the world pertaining to the elderly.
6. Describe the service apartments in Scandinavia and the types of services they provide.
7. How are Sweden and Japan handling the demographic shift they are presently experiencing?
8. Compare the Japanese and American works of literature on care for an aging parent that are presented in this chapter. How are they alike and different?
9. Discuss the concept of the *elderization of poverty.*
10. Distinguish between young-old and the old-old.
11. Discuss the benefits offered under the Social Security Act of 1935, Medicaid, Medicare, and the Older Americans Act.
12. How are the old ways weakening for older Chicanas and elderly Chinese?
13. Discuss the need for safety regulations for nursing home care.
14. Describe how nursing home care is financed by the average citizen.
15. What are the facts concerning elder abuse? Contrast domestic and institutional elder abuse.
16. Describe each of the five escape mechanisms used by people to cope with death. How is the denial of death consistent with the American creed?
17. How can ageism be confronted? What has social activism achieved to date?
18. Summarize the recent trends in the United States and the world pertaining to the elderly population.

REFERENCES

Addams, J. (1910). *Twenty Years at Hull-House.* New York: Macmillan.

Anderson, R. (1980; orig. 1968). I Never Sang for My Father. In R. Lyell, ed. *Middle Age, Old Age: Short Stories, Poems, Plays and Essays on Aging.* New York: Harcourt Brace Jovanovich.

Ariyoshi, S. (1984; orig. 1972). *The Twilight Years.* (M. Thahara, Trans.) London: Peter Owen.

Barrow, G. (1989). *Aging, the Individual, and Society,* 4th ed. St. Paul, MN: West Publishing Co.

Beaver, M. and D. Miller. (1992). *Clinical Social Work Practice with the Elderly,* 2d ed. Belmont, CA: Wadsworth.

Becker, E. (1973). *The Denial of Death.* New York: Free Press.

Bellos, N. and C. Ruffolo. (1995). Aging: Services. In the *Encyclopedia of Social Work,* 19th ed.: (165–173). Washington, DC: NASW Press.

Campbell, J. (1995, August). Is there a Japanese-Style Welfare State? *Social Science Japan* 4: 22.

Coles, R. (1974). *The Old Ones of New Mexico.* Albuquerque: University of New Mexico Press.

Cook, A. (1993, Summer). Missoula's Senior Companions Help Create a Community that Cares. *Aging*: 32.

de Beauvoir, S. (1973). *The Coming of Age.* New York: Warner Books.

Dentzer, S. (1991, September 20). The Graying of Japan. *US News and World Report*: 65–73.

Donow, H. (1990). Two Approaches to the Care of an Elder Parent: A Study of Robert Anderson's *I Never Sang for My Father* and Sawako Aryoshi's *Kokotsu no hito. Gerontologist* 30(4): 486–490.

Dunkle, R. and T. Norgard. (1995). Aging Overview. In the *Encyclopedia of Social Work,* 19th ed.: (142–152). Washington, DC: NASW Press.

Editorial. (1995, July 31). Hollow Homilies. *Calgary Herald*: A2.

Erikson, E. (1963). *Childhood and Society.* New York: W.W. Norton.

Facio, E. (1996). *Understanding Older Chicanas.* Thousand Oaks, CA: SAGE.

Facts on File. (1995). Heat Wave Kills 100s: Chicago Hit Hard. *Facts on File: World News Digest* 55(2852): 540–541.

Gonyea, J. (1994). The Paradox of the Advantaged Elder and the Feminization of Poverty. *Social Work* 39(1): 35–41.

Goodman, E. (1995, October 29). Look at the Horrors Ahead for Nursing Home Patrons. *Waterloo/Cedar Falls Courier*: F2.

Greer, G. (1991). *The Change: Women, Aging and the Menopause.* New York: Fawcett Columbine.

Harris, L. and Associates. (1975). *The Myth and Reality of Aging in America.* Washington, DC: The National Council on Aging, Inc.

Hartman, A. (1990). Aging as a Feminist Issue. *Social Work* 35(5): 387–388.

Huxley, A. (1969; orig. 1932). *Brave New World.* New York: Harper and Row.

Jones, R. (1995). The Price of Welfare Dependency: Children Pay. *Social Work* 40(4): 496–505.

Kaplan, M., M. Adamek, and S. Johnson. (1994). Trends in Firearms Suicide among Older American Males: 1979–1988. *Gerontologist* 34(1): 59–65.

Katz, S. (1978). Anthropological Perspectives in Aging. *Annals: Planning for the Elderly* 438: 1–12.

Kubler-Ross, E. (1975). *Death, the Final Stage of Growth.* Englewood Cliffs, NJ: Prentice-Hall.

Lieberman, T. (1995, November 6). How the G.O.P. Made "Mediscare." *The Nation*: 536–540.

McDaniel, S. and E. Gee. (1993). Social Policies Regarding Caregiving to Elders: Canadian Contradictions. In S. Bass and R. Morris, eds. *International Perspectives on State and Family Support for the Elderly*:(57–72). New York: Haworth.

Mann, J. (1995). Aging and Social Work. In W. Johnson, ed. *The Social Services: An Introduction*: (223–239). Itasca, IL: Peacock.

Miranda, M. and A. Morales. (1995). Social Work Practice with the Elderly. In A. Morales and B. Sheafor, eds. *Social Work: A Profession of Many Faces,* 7th ed. (369–400). Boston: Allyn and Bacon.

Neysmith, S. (1994). Canadian Long-Term Care: Its Escalating Costs for Women. In L. Olson, ed. *The Graying of the World: Who Will Care for the Frail Elderly?* (163–188). New York: The Haworth Press.

Olson, L. (1994). Introduction. In L. Olson, ed. *The Graying of the World: Who Will Care for the Elderly?* (1–23). New York: The Haworth Press.

Pillemer, K. and D. Finkelhor. (1988). The Prevalence of Elder Abuse: A Random Sample Survey. *The Gerontologist* 28: 51–57.

Popple, P. and L. Leighninger. (1993). *Social Work, Social Welfare, and American Society,* 2d ed. Boston: Allyn and Bacon.

Rao, M. (1992, December). Aging Policies and Programs: New Century—New Hopes—New Challenges. *Journal of International Federation on Aging*: 1–27.

Reed, M. and F. Glamser. (1979). Aging in a Total Institution: The Case of Older Prisoners. *The Gerontologist* 19(4): 354–360.

Sandhu, H. (1974). *Modern Corrections: The Offenders, Therapies, and Community Re-integration.* Springfield, IL: Thomas and Sons.

Schenck-Yglesias, C. (1995, September). A Frail Mom Is a Full-Time Job. *American Demographics* 17: 14.

Sennott-Miller, L. (1994). Research on Aging in Latin America: Present States and Future Directions. *Journal of Cross-Cultural Gerontology* 9: 87–97.

Shah, R. (1992, August 2). Aging around the World. *St. Petersburg Times*: 1A+.

Shakespeare, W. (1600). *As You Like It* II, VII: 139.

Sidel, R. (1992). *Women and Children Last.* New York: Penguin.

Stamets, R. (1993, March 7). Aging around the World. St. Petersburg Times: 1A+.

Sudnow, D. (1967). *Passing On.* Englewood Cliffs, NJ: Prentice-Hall.

Tatai, K. and K. Tatai. (1991). Suicide in the Elderly: A Report from Japan. *Crisis* 12(2): 40–43.

Tatara, T. (1995). Elder Abuse. In the *Encyclopedia of Social Work,* 19th ed. (834–842). Washington, DC: NASW Press.

Tolstoy, L. (1960) *The Death of Ivan Ilych and Other Stories.* (131–150). New York: American Library of World Literature.

Torres-Gil, F. and M. Puccinelli. (1995). Aging: Public Policy Issues and Trends. In the *Encyclopedia of Social Work,* 19th ed. (159–164). Washington, DC: NASW Press.

U.S. Senate, Special Committee on Aging. (1992). *Development in Aging: 1992* (vol. 1). 103rd Congress 1st Session Report No. 103-140. Washington, DC: U.S. Government Printing Office.

van Wormer, K. (1990). Private Practice with the Terminally Ill. *Journal of Independent Social Work* 5(1): 23–37.

Walker, A. (1993). Under New Management: The Changing Role of the State in the Care of Older People in the United Kingdom. In S. Bass and R. Morris, eds. *International Perspectives on State and Family Support for the Elderly*: (127–154). New York: Haworth.

Walker, A. and L. Warren. (1994). The Care of Frail Older People in Britain: Current Policies and Future Prospects. In L. Olson, ed. *The Graying of the World: Who Will Care for the Frail Elderly?* (129–162). New York: The Haworth Press.

Wasow, M. (1984). Get out of my Potato Patch: A Biased View of Death and Dying. *Health and Social Work* 9(4): 261–267.

Webb, S. (1992). Child Checkers. *Social Work Today* 23(17): 20.

Wordsworth, W. (1806). *Ode: Intimations of Immortality IX*: st. 10.

Zastrow, C. (1996). *Introduction to Social Work and Social Welfare,* 6th ed. Pacific Grove, CA: Brooks/Cole.

PART III

WORLD POLICY ISSUES

10

MARGINALIZED POPULATIONS:
A STUDY IN OPPRESSION

Injustice anywhere is a threat to justice everywhere.—Martin Luther King

We in South Africa here learnt through bitter experience that security for a few is in fact insecurity for all.—Nelson Mandela

Why put women, Northern Irish Catholics, European Gypsies, Australian aborigines, African and Hispanic Americans, and gays, lesbians, and bisexuals all in one chapter? What is the common thread? Are these groups the victims of their own lives or are they society's victims? Or neither? Or both? And are they merely survivors or are they the heroes in their struggle for liberation?

Instead of offering the usual multicultural description of America's minority groups, the aim of this chapter is much more complicated. Its purpose is to study the phenomenon of *marginalization,* the process by which a people (or category of people) are held down in terms of their socioeconomic position in society. A commonly used term in Argentina, marginalization means "being pushed to the fringes of society" (Miller, 1992). In Argentina, poor people are marginalized, young people are marginalized, and so are gays and lesbians.

We are going to deal here not with ethnic groups but with ethnocentrism, not with race but with racism, not with gender but with sexism, not with religion but with sectarianism, and not with sexual orientation but with homophobia. Because these processes are universal, the perspective is international.

Thus the discussion will address such varied topics as extremist race hatred in the United States and Canada, dowry deaths in India, genital mutilation in Africa, and death squads against gays and lesbians in Latin America. The focus of the discussion is consistent with the Council on Social Work Education's mandate, revised in 1992, to promote special attention to the oppression experienced by minority groups.

PREJUDICE AND HATE CRIMES

The basic starting point for oppression is prejudice, an unjustified negative attitude. Prejudice and discrimination will be viewed interactively: not only does prejudice lead to discrimination or activated prejudice, discrimination leads to prejudice as individuals seek to justify their bad behavior. Some of the marginalized groups chosen for consideration in this chapter have been persecuted simply because they were different, some because of their possessions — jobs, land, or resources that outsiders wanted — and others were oppressed as a means of social control. Several groups such as the Australian aborigines have been attacked for the aforementioned, traditional reasons, and as scapegoats of people who were themselves persecuted, such as the convict laborers who settled Australia. (The next chapter continues the theme of oppression as we consider human rights abuses through war and economic bondage or slavery.)

Except for discrimination against gays and lesbians, which is probably largely tied in with attitudes (and "hang-ups") related to sexuality and procreation, economic interests underlie much of the mistreatment of subjugated groups. Yet in regard to heterosexism, as well as racism, sexism, and sectarianism, those who control the wealth in the society can force people to behave in certain ways in order to survive. The power balance is skewed. The major tactic of the dominant class, according to Pharr (1988), is to arrange for inadequately compensated labor through limiting educational and training opportunities such as for women and people of color. Then blaming the economic victim (for lack of achievement) both lowers the victim's self-esteem and provides a rationale for perpetuating the system. The threat of violence against women (and gays and lesbians) who oppose the status quo is a strategy used the world over by the oppressor group to maintain power and control of jobs and other resources. Generally, as Morales and Sheafor (1995) indicate, those reaping the benefits will fight very hard to maintain their advantaged, superior position.

In her analysis of the dynamics of oppression, Canadian author Bishop (1994) describes one of the processes by which the favored group solidifies its political and economic base—namely, through *ideological* power—the power of belief. If people can be made to believe that the injustice and inequality are right or at least inevitable, they will not try to change their society. However, involvement in social reform can expose the source of exploitation and release people from their docility into action.

Hate crimes or hate violence crimes are criminal acts stemming from prejudice based on race, religion, sexual orientation, disability, or ethnicity. Directed against persons, families, groups, or organizations, these crimes include arson of homes and businesses, harassment, destruction of religious property, cross burnings, personal assaults, and homicides (Barnes and Ephross, 1994). Often associated with a sense of powerlessness or *anomie* among young males and a new visibility in society among vulnerable populations, hate crimes are apparently on the rise throughout the world. For example:

- An upsurge in burning of black churches in the U.S. South leads to a national investigation.
- A gay priest's murder in Montreal becomes the latest in a long string of homosexual murders.
- Three members of the U.S. Marine Corps beat a gay man in reaction to President Clinton's earlier plan to lift the ban on gay and lesbian military personnel.
- In Germany, authorities arrest neo-Nazi suspects in a fire bombing of a house occupied by Turks.
- In Los Angeles, a group of skinheads are arrested for plotting to murder black leaders and destroy black churches.
- Anti-Semitic graffiti and the desecration of tombstones in Billings, Montana, unites the community against hate crime.
- Skinheads in Houston are blamed for the stomping of a Vietnamese immigrant, causing his death.
- Five Algerian women are killed in one day in 1995 by religious militants who are targeting women for "immorality."

In one of the horror stories of the decade, *Eight Bullets: One Woman's Story of Surviving Anti-Gay Violence,* Claudia Brenner (1995) argues that hate violence is bred when intolerance is socially endorsed. Brenner's survival of anti-lesbian gunfire in which her partner was killed, described in her book, is of a piece with killings at abortion clinics, the rape, impregnation, and torture of Muslim women in Bosnia, and bride burnings in India. All these are examples of the rhetoric of prejudice and hatred gaining expression in individual acts of terrorism.

An explosion of hate violence on U.S. college campuses has caused many universities to adopt campus speech codes to protect students from displays of intolerance. Civil libertarians and political conservatives alike, however, have criticized colleges for trying to enforce a narrow, politically correct point of view on issues involving race, ethnicity, and sexuality (Jost, 1993). At universities in Britain, the term *politically correct* has come to denote an outrageous suppression of free speech.

By now all but a few states in the United States have enacted laws increasing penalties against hate crimes. Under the Hate Crime Statistics Act of 1990, the FBI has been directed to publish annual reports on the number of crimes committed each year that manifest prejudice based on race, religion, sexual orientation, or ethnicity. In 1994, there was a total of 2,064 incidents of anti-gay harassment alone. The majority of incidents, 62 percent of them, however, were race related.

Due to an upsurge of hate crime activity in Canada, much of it stirred up by white supremacists who exploit public resentment toward immigrants in tough economic times, new legislation has been passed. The legislation directs judges to impose stiffer sentences when there is evidence that a crime is motivated by hatred of a victim's race, religion, ethnic origin, or sexual orientation (Corelli, 1995). Statistics now being gathered city by city indicate, as in the United States, that most of the hate crimes are race related, directed against Haitians in Montreal, blacks in Nova Scotia, and natives across the country. Religious related attacks have been directed at mosques and synagogues.

Theory of Hate Violence

In times of uncertainty, many people are attracted to a leader with a simple message, a demagogue perhaps, over an emotionally mature leader who does not seem to have all the answers. While the mature leader may appear to equivocate on the issues, the demagogue is self-assured, simplistic, and zeroes in on the problem—taxes, national deficit, lazy poor people—and offers magical solutions—return to family values, end welfare, toughen laws (Godwin, 1994). Today, as competition for well-paying and secure jobs in a global economy heats up, dangerous right-wing extremist movements are winning followers throughout the world. In the United States, the pro-life movement has threatened the lives of people involved with abortions while hate groups descendent of the Ku Klux Klan and Nazis form armed militias to prepare for violent insurrection. In Canada, a white supremacist movement is attracting a strong following among angry unemployed white youth; Asians, gays, and Jews are targeted. Popular political parties in Austria, France, and Italy fight to preserve their nations' cultural "purity." These developments along with the success of Vladimir Zhirinovsky's ultranationalist, anti-Semitic appeal in Russia and the "ethnic cleansing" in former Yugoslavia suggest that the extreme right is at a level in Europe unequalled since the end of World War II. Meanwhile, religious fundamentalism in Muslim nations (Islamism) has put women back in the *chador* (a garment which covers the head and most of the body) and has subjected them to brutal humiliations throughout the Middle East. Religious fundamentalism in the United States has been associated with anti-abortion and anti-homosexual movements and harsh treatment of society's underdogs.

SECTARIANISM: IN THE NAME OF RELIGION

Because religious fundamentalism is behind much of the extremist politics in the world today, this discussion will start with a form of oppression (of women, gays, and lesbians among others) that stems from modern religious fanaticism. In late 1994, the Vatican joined Muslim fundamentalists in opposing women's reproductive rights in a joint statement presented at the U.N. Population and Development Conference in Cairo. The Islamic religious revival has been a tremendous set-back for many Islamic women throughout the world who, after a limited period of liberation, have been required to return to wearing the veil.

In another corner of the world, Northern Ireland, religious fundamentalism is more a carryover from historic ethnopolitical rivalry than an attempt to oppress women. In this section we will consider how sectarian violence flourishes against women under Islam and against men and women in Northern

Ireland under Christianity. Themes underpinning religious fundamentalism are: self-identification by members as belonging to a particular religious sect; literalism in interpreting sacred texts such as the Koran or the Bible; exclusion of the heathen who will not be saved; zealotry in pronouncing one's beliefs often associated with war; and a patriarchal authority. Significantly, under religious fundamentalism, there is one way and only one way to the truth. There is no room for dissent or diversity.

Northern Ireland

"Are you a Protestant atheist or a Catholic atheist?" — a typical Northern Irish joke

As a young English teacher in Northern Ireland (1967-1969), I taught at a convent school and a Protestant secondary modern school. I gradually became embroiled in religious controversy and as a civil rights activist was victimized by Protestant extremists (staff and pupils who dominated the Portadown school) on an almost daily basis. The civil unrest and the various political and security responses which collectively became known as the Troubles had begun in the 1920s with the partition of Ireland and were reactivated in the late 1960s. Today, the issue of civil rights for the roughly one-third of the population that is Catholic has been subsumed by a more traditional Irish nationalist campaign for the independence of the whole of Ireland (Sugden and Bairner, 1993). The Irish Republican Army (I.R.A.) and the Ulster Volunteer Force (U.V.F.) are potent paramilitary forces in the province. Whereas Protestants of the six northern countries generally insist that Northern Ireland remain part of the United Kingdom, Irish Catholics look toward unity with the South.

Some memories of Northern Ireland which illustrate the religious conflict include: orange flowers called "Sweet Williams" planted to bloom in conjunction with the North's major holiday on the 12th of July; an interminably long parade of Orange Order members (followers of the Protestant William of Orange) and anti-Catholic "kick the pope" bands; complete segregation of public schools which are either Protestant or Catholic; institutionalized child brutality especially evidenced in the schools; school kids bragging of their venturing into Catholic neighborhoods to beat up the Fenians, members of an organization dedicated to the overthrow of British rule.

As foreigner, social activist, and neophyte teacher, my complaints about child brutality inflicted in the Protestant schools fell on deaf ears. "Americans spoil their children," I was told. "Besides the Christian Brothers (a much-respected Catholic religious order) are worse offenders." My Catholic friends confirmed the latter remark. Gradually, in a year (the first of many) characterized by mounting police killings, I.R.A. terrorism, and Protestant vigilante violence, the link between the violent and verbal abuse by adults of children and children's later propensity to fight, bomb, and kill authority figures in adulthood became all too apparent.

Today, fortunately, because of pressure from the European Union of which the United Kingdom and Ireland are members, corporal punishment in state-run schools is no longer allowed. However, according to a recent article from the British social work magazine, *Community Care* (Francis, 1995), in addition to the politically based violence to which Northern Ireland's children have been constantly exposed, the high rate of severe child abuse has created a child welfare system dominated by child protection services. The violence against children on this religiously-torn territory therefore persists. Abused children, explains Bishop (1994), have learned to hate, particularly their weak, powerless childhood state. Later, as adults, they project these hated parts of themselves back on children or on others less powerful (or more powerful) than themselves. Campbell and Pinkerton (1995) describe in almost humorous terms how if social workers must go into certain neighborhoods to remove a child in danger, they must be accompanied not only by police but by the army as well. The army is there to protect the police who are there to protect the social workers. Such behavior—attacks on the police who symbolize authority—can be explained in terms of Dollard et. al.'s (1939) *frustration-aggression hypothesis*. According to this hypothesis, when people cannot direct their aggression at the actual sources of their rage (parents, teachers, priests), they will seek a substitute target. According to Bishop, we all carry the roles of both oppressor and oppressed very deeply rooted in us.

Jonathan Swift's (1905; orig.1706) memorable words, "We have just enough religion to make us hate, and not enough to love one another" apply today as formerly. As of 1995, only five percent of Catholics go to non-Catholic schools, and virtually no Protestants attend Catholic schools. "Mixed" marriage is a strong taboo. Unemployment is very high; for Catholics the rate is twice that of Protestants.

Between 1969 and 1990 over three thousand people have died and thirty thousand have been injured due to political violence. Political murders, car bombings, internal disciplinary shootings, and "human bombs" have given Northern Ireland the highest levels of *internal* political violence of any member-state of the European Union (O'Leary and McGarry, 1993).

The women of Northern Ireland, under the aegis of their respective churches, have been socially repressed. Catholic women, as a minority within a minority, put the focus on the men and women engaged in the military war. Knowing the extent of anti-Irish prejudice within the United Kingdom, Catholic women put solidarity ahead of such issues as contraception and abortion (Fairweather et al. 1984). Irish Catholic morality, according to Fairweather et al., dictates that women exist primarily as childbearers. On a far deeper level, Catholicism's suspicious and punitive attitude toward female sexuality can undermine women's entire sense of dignity and self-worth.

Sectarianism, a form of prejudice that is religion-based, similarly, has hindered the development of working-class consciousness and the emergence of trade unions. To employers, sectarianism has been a useful tool which could be used to keep the rank and file divided and divert their attention from the politics of industrial exploitation (Sugden and Bairner, 1993).

Social workers in Northern Ireland have worked for years to bridge the gap between religions. Yet discrimination in agencies mirrors the general discrimination in the society. In child welfare, for instance, Catholic agencies cater to Catholic families and Protestant agencies to Protestants (Campbell and Pinkerton, 1995). A new training packet (Sone, 1994), long overdue, is a response to the British accrediting authorities' earlier refusal to take sectarianism as seriously as race and ethnicity in anti-discriminatory practice.

For the first time, due to the collaborative efforts of lawyers and social workers, the Children Order of 1995 for Northern Ireland recognizes the child's needs as paramount. There is no right, however, for the court to exclude from the home a parent or other adult suspected of abusing a child (Francis, 1995). Still, emergency protection orders can be issued by the courts, and a guardian *ad liten* service is available to oversee the interests of the child.

Another positive development is the establishment of the Quaker Cottage Family Centre, a healing center for mothers and their children. Established in 1980, and partly funded by the state, the center has forged an unusual tradition of working with mostly single mothers from all areas of Belfast (both Catholic and Protestant). Childcare is offered as is the teaching of parenting skills to the mothers. Because of the mothers' own lost childhoods, they have to be taught how to play with their children and how to discipline nonviolently. Mothers learn to express their feelings and frustrations in group sessions, and all this is happening across religious lines (Francis, 1995).

Islamism

From the Muslim world, horror tales of crimes against humanity abound. "Islamic Radicals Terrorize Algeria's Working Women" proclaims one headline (Bowers, 1995). Muslims who criticize the fundamentalist version of Islam are often targeted for assassination or forced into exile. The misogynist brutality of modern fundamentalist regimes is chronicled with unforgettable realism in Jan Goodwin's *Price of Honor* (1994). Graphic interviews with persecuted women in Pakistan, Iran, and Egypt and elsewhere get beneath the veil to reveal the dramatic and detrimental changes in the lives of women under the yoke of Islamic fundamentalism or Islamism. Male interpreters of religious texts emphasize Koranic passages that reinforce Islam's patriarchal aspects while overlooking its clear injunctions giving women equality, justice, and education. Veiling the face is an innovation, never an Islamic obligation.

The sense of the sheer terror of absolute powerlessness comes across in stories from country after country—a young woman set on fire in Pakistan because her dowry was too small (the family had demanded a color television and VCR); a fifty-five-year-old Iranian woman is flogged because her head-scarf slipped back revealing her hair; a woman of the United Arab Emirates who loses all her possessions, her home, and her children because her husband divorced her without telling her of the divorce.

To pay for oil, the United States has become the world's largest arms producer, with three-fourths of weapons sales going to Middle Eastern countries whose moral agenda, according to Goodwin, is the complete enslavement of women. Where the extremists are in power, the laws often force women to remain confined in the home or to suffer other indignities. Egyptian law requires a wife to be obedient and requires the police to return an abused wife to her husband. In Egypt genital mutilation of rural women is also common. In Iran, a man may legally kill his wife for infidelity. Rape victims in Pakistan are punished for sexual immorality. Women may be stoned to death in Saudi Arabia for adultery.

Alice Walker and Pratibha Parmar (1993) in *Warrior Marks: Female Genital Mutilation and the Sexual Blinding of Women* have produced one of the most graphic and emotionally moving accounts of genital mutilation of African children in the literature. As Walker (p. 82) shares with us in her diary account:

> I've been crying over the lives of women and children who've been dead, some of them, thousands of years (one estimate is that genital mutilation is at least six thousand years old), as well as mourning the lives of those I've encountered, whose suffering is apparent. I grieve, as well, for all those children whose future holds a day of seizure, of being pinned down by adults known and unknown, and brutally hurt.

Goodwin (1994) supplies the medical details. In Egypt, where the majority of rural women are sexually mutilated in an operation involving removal of the clitoris, the results may be infection, bleeding, damage to the urinary tract, and even death. The reasons given for clitoridectomies in Egypt are "cleanliness" and "so that girls will not run after men." The reasons given by women are as a necessity so that a woman would be marriageable. Today, an estimated one hundred million women have undergone the ritual. Over 90 percent of Sudanese women undergo the most extreme form of mutilation. Known as infibulation, the labia minora and labia majora are removed also. The damage done makes later sexual penetration and childbirth extremely precarious. In the name of religion (Islam), but having nothing to do with religion, such horrors are perpetrated. And, as Goodwin tells us, the oppression and fear engendered by the religious extremists is invariably felt first by women.

Warrior Marks offers a journalistic account of the making of a documentary of the same title on girls and women who have undergone the painful so-called female circumcision ritual in places such as Senegal and Gambia. In Walker's opinion shared in a personal interview, the film shows that the genital mutilation of women is really just a part of the global mutilation of women, of "the terrorization of women, one of the numerous things done to keep them in their place, under the foot of the dominant patriarchal culture" (p. 282). Some women have escaped, often with their daughters, and been granted political asylum in Canada and the United States on this basis.

WORLDWIDE ABUSE OF WOMEN

This section continues the consideration of women as an oppressed, marginalized population subject to physical and economic victimization. Related information is contained in the chapters on poverty, child welfare, work and family welfare, health care and housing, and care for the aged. The following chapter continues the discussion with a focus on human rights violations through war-related rape, enforced prostitution, and sex slavery. Here, an overview of global law, custom, and crimes against women will be given. Such issues as the world's war against women, women and the global economy, missing females in the population, violation of reproductive rights, and the mobilization of the world's women against the systematic violence will be covered.

The World's War against Women

Throughout the world there is an epidemic of violence against women accompanied by a widespread exclusion of half of humanity from institutions of power and governance. According to a conference document of the United Nations Fourth World Conference on Women (Mason, 1995), the cultural origins of this violence are in the historically unequal power relations between men and women. Indeed, the low social and economic status of women can be both a cause and a consequence of violence against women. The dowry bride burnings in India (an illegal custom in which a bride is set on fire by her in-laws if the demands for dowry payment from the bride's family are unmet) which number over five a day, illustrate crass materialism at its extreme. Stone and James (1995) study the phenomenon in terms of recent changes in women's roles and sources of female power. Bride burnings not only reflect women's relative lack of economic power in India but also, given the diminished emphasis on fertility today, a reduced function in producing the next generation. Bride burnings occur most often in cases of arranged marriages and among the urban middle class. As India has shifted to a market cash economy, the new consumerism puts more value on the size of the dowry itself than on the woman. Forever vulnerable to being beaten and killed by disgruntled in-laws, many women in India are rendered powerless to challenge what is happening to them. Thus economic discrimination against women and their vulnerability to violence are intertwined.

In the United States, four to five women are killed by their husbands every day. Every eighteen minutes, a woman in this country is beaten, with only one in a hundred cases of domestic violence ever reported (United Nations, 1991). Every six minutes a woman in the United States is raped, again a low estimate because only a fraction of cases are reported (United Nations, 1991). The greatest risk of violence to women in the United States and Canada is in the home. Such acts of violence against women occur within a social context of male power and female oppression; woman's position in the society is reflected in her treatment within the family. The war on welfare in the United States can be construed as largely a backlash against poor women; their increasing impoverishment makes them prey for mistreatment by men on whom they must rely for financial support and protection. It is estimated that over half of the homeless women living in shelters in the United States are fleeing domestic abuse. Adequate financial assistance is a necessity for battered women attempting to make a transition to an independent life.

The worldwide backlash against women is gruesomely symbolized in the one hundred recorded burnings or stonings of women accused of being witches in South Africa (Drogin, 1994). The killers tend to be friends and neighbors. Village elders convene a tribal court when witchcraft is suspected. Many women accused of casting evil spells who are not killed have been forced to flee their villages while their homes were set afire. Scores of accused witches and their families now live in Witches Hill, a kind of refugee camp for exiles.

Around the globe, death by stoning in Iran, genital mutilation in twenty-eight African nations, witch hunts in South Africa, dowry deaths in India and Pakistan, sexual slavery in Thailand, and wife abuse in all countries are shocking the sensibilities of humanists.

Link to the Global Economy

Penetration of local markets by transnational corporations often has led to sharp declines in the marketability of local products (Prigoff et al. 1994). This, in turn, has resulted in severe loss of income, unemployment, and mass migration. The trickle-down approach, according to Prigoff et. al., has not been effective in raising living standards of the world's women or for their families.

In recent years, for instance, China has opened itself up to private enterprise and capitalism. Although the market-oriented reforms have brought new opportunities for women, China's abandonment of social egalitarianism for a new ethos of competition has been profoundly damaging to women's status (Polumbaum, 1992). While women have been laid off by companies downsizing and forced into sweatshops, many men have gotten started as successful entrepreneurs. The value of sons to their families has increased in recent years. Chinese women, reportedly, are changing their dress styles from pants to high heels and wearing makeup. Prostitution, long ago eliminated, has returned to the coastal cities. Nevertheless, women's rights are protected in progressive laws, and women's attorneys and politicians are organizing to hold the government to its word.

In any society, as anthropologists inform us, status goes to those who control the distribution of valued goods and services outside the family (Friedl, 1994). Equality arises when both sexes work side by side in food production, and the products are evenly distributed among the workers. But, according to Friedl's comprehensive survey, when women (for example, the traditional Eskimos) make less of a tangible contribution to their people's survival than men, they become subordinate.

The conservative *U.S. News and World Report* (MacFarquhar, 1994: 42) acknowledges that what the United Nations said about the burden of inequality: "Women, half the world's population, do two-thirds of the work, earn one-tenth of the income, and own one-hundredth of the world's property," is even more true today. In many places, according to the article, political and economic gains of the past decade have dragged women backward. Women have been victims of capitalistic reform and reduction of benefits in Eastern Europe; victims of freedom where they are thrown out of work; victims of progress where modern technology has led to abortions of female fetuses; and victims of the holy war which has put feminists under death threats. Women will not advance economically until their political power is increased. For a moving account of the struggling women of Bulgaria, see box 10.1.

Women in the United States and Canada earn seventy-one cents for every dollar that men earn; the amount has increased due to reduced wages for blue collar males. Women in the United States make up under 10 percent of the Congress, compared to 41 percent of the Swedish Parliament. Lamentably, the United States is the only major democratic nation that has refused to ratify the International Convention on the Elimination of all Forms of Discrimination against Women. Jimmy Carter (1995) who signed this international treaty for women's equality under his presidency, deplores the lack of decisive action by the U.S. Congress. The United States, notes Carter in an editorial (1995), has fallen far short of ensuring equality of women, particularly in areas of employment, education, and health care.

BOX 10.1

BULGARIAN WOMEN: CENTURIES OF SILENCE

There are so many poets
among women in my land.
The mute whose speech
is suddenly restored
will rend the air
with a moan or a shout—
centuries of silence
crying to come out.

When Blaga Dimitrova, dissident poet and former vice president of Bulgaria, wrote this, the last verse of her poem, "The Women Who Are Poets in My Land," she expressed in a few well-connected words the purpose of my summer's work. As I traveled again, halfway round the world from Iowa to Bulgaria, the most Eastern of East European countries, I felt myself sufficiently prepared for this long anticipated project on Bulgarian women.

What I did not anticipate was that this research would not only put faces upon the facts, but would also change forever the way I feel about my own children, sear the most poignant memories into my mind, and carve wounds upon my soul. Asking a question was like opening a long shut faucet—the fears, the pain, and the longings of mothers poured out like the now familiar floods through a broken levee.

Meet, for example, my friend, Violetta. As she taught me how to bake barutza one afternoon, she told me she had been denied

admission to advanced medical studies abroad. Though she was the top student in her class, she was considered a "fascist bastard" by the chair of the admissions committee. She is a brilliant, 31-year-old physician with little hope of ever practicing medicine in a land where there are far too many physicians. Violetta is expecting her second child this November and is scrambling to assemble enough money to purchase a safe birth for herself and her baby.

Svetla is an unemployed electrical engineer, an anachronism in a country where production has precipitately declined. With her husband, two children, and her husband's parents, Svetla lives in a tiny apartment in the building next to mine. With two old-age pensions and one salary, the key factor in this family's survival is Svetla's garden. The day we went "farming" with her, we were delighted to discover that a favorite hen was nesting with maternal dedication a clutch of 15 eggs! Since wild dogs had killed all but two of her rabbits a few days earlier, these future chicks represent crucial protein for Svetla's children. When I tell her that many Iowa women, including me, preserve vegetables for the sheer enjoyment of the task, she thinks I am joking! Gardening and canning are essential survival strategies in this place.

(Continued on next page)

BOX 10.1 (Continued)

Krasimira is a doctor on the medical faculty, separated for four years and the mother of a five-year-old daughter. Like about 80 percent of the population, her salary of 2000 leva (about $83 a month) places her in the government category, "socially weak," thankfully qualifying her for reduced fees for social services, including her daughter's kindergarten. Krasimira is living with the certainty that her position will be eliminated soon, as the medical college reduces its admissions by 80 percent. With no financial support from an absent husband and little chance of other employment, this family's future is bleak.

We celebrate over lunch the impending birth of Juliana's child. Although she shares that first-time mother's dread of childbirth, she is filled with joy at the prospect of being able to continue this pregnancy, instead of having the much more familiar abortion. Juliana speaks of the heartbreak of her friend who, at the age of 32, has already had 10 abortions and, with two children, will probably have several more.

Perhaps I am most touched by Boryana. She and her husband have been terribly worried about the health of their five-year-old son, who recently contracted hepatitis while hospitalized for blood tests. They suspect he has leukemia, but have been unable to consult with a medical specialist who can make a diagnosis. Regulations required that the child be isolated in a hospi-

tal ward with no visitors during his illness. In an attempt to be near him, Boryana informs us that she drank his urine, in hopes of contracting the disease herself. During our last meeting there is joyful news! Boryana, her husband and son, have made a connection in the states and are leaving for Washington in September! She asks me to recommend a medical facility in America where he can be evaluated.

Galya takes me to spend a weekend in a village with her elderly grandparents. We are the first Americans to visit there and become immediate curiosities. Grandmother, Maria, gave birth to her first child at home in 1944, while her husband was away fighting in Hungary. She asks me if it is true that American men attend the births of their children—she had heard it was so, but could not imagine such a thing.

Like grandmothers everywhere, Maria spends the weekend stuffing our bodies with food, our minds with advice, and our hearts with generosity. We trade recipes as well as stories. She instructs me in the art of creating sarmé (wrapped in grape leaves) and I reciprocate with my mother's cherry pie recipe, including the lattice top on which my family reputation rests). Over numerous glasses of homemade brandy, wine, and a gut-numbing vodka, she instructs me in the ways of women, an experience which provides me with a whole

(Continued on next page)

BOX 10.1 (Continued)

new definition of "cultural immersion." She sings me the melancholy Bulgarian folk story of Dimitrina, whose lover is ashamed of her because her skin is not white enough. I teach her the steps of "Achy Breaky Heart."

With memory piling upon memory, stacks of audio tapes and notebooks growing inevitably, how can one say the best was saved for last? Yet through a fortuitous series of connections (and plenty of chutzpah), it was my privilege to spend my final morning with 72-year-old Blaga Dimitrova, the national poet of Bulgaria, a heroine of the people, respected dissident and, then, the country's vice president.

During our conversation, I made reference to a recent article about her in the American Ms. Magazine and she hastened to assure me that she certainly would not describe herself as a "one-sided feminist." She spoke of the Bulgarian woman as the "rescuer of the family," a "centuries-old tradition established when men were often away fighting in wars or earning money to support the family."

The researcher's tasks of identifying cultural themes, constructing paradigms, and contrasting information with familiar theoretical foundations of conflict resolution and

women's studies will continue for many months. Scholarly articles will be written and papers will be presented. I believe, however, that the most intimate effects of this experience will be with me far longer. Each time I go to the market, I am reminded of Svetla and hope that her chickens have hatched and her rabbits have replaced themselves. When my paycheck arrives, I remember Krasimira, and hope that she still has work. When I bake barutza, I think of Violetta, and hope that her baby is born in safety and health. When I embrace my own strong, healthy, and favored American children, I think of Boryana, and hope that she and her family find a better life. My most fervent hope is that the government of Bulgaria, with appropriate assistance from the West, can survive the winter of its transition and craft a political and economic system which can support and give voice to all citizens, including women.

With the exception of Blaga Dimitrova, a public figure in Bulgaria, all the names used are pseudonyms.

Source: S. J. Koch, *Des Moines Register,* August 29, 1993. Reprinted with permission of the *Des Moines Register.*

Case of the Missing Females

The United Nations report, *The World's Women 1995*, cites the facts concerning infanticide (which occurs in China, India, and certain Arab countries) and the incredibly high female infant and child mortality rates due to the deprivation of food and medical care for girls in countries where a low premium is put on female life. Due to the development of the amniocentesis test which can determine the sex of the unborn child, countries such as India can now get rid of females even before birth. In some Indian states the ratio of women to men is below nine hundred women for every one thousand men. Girls are a financial burden in India due to dowry requirements and the fact that upon adulthood she will belong to her husband's family. The government of India is contemplating payments to poor families for the rearing of females. In the meantime, in China, India, Pakistan, Afghanistan, and Bangladesh, there are about seventy-seven million "missing" females (Courier/Medill News Service, 1993). Females unaccounted for in population statistics are likely aborted before birth or allowed to die due to medical neglect in early childhood.

Violation of Reproductive Rights

Unless women can manage and control their own fertility and sexuality, they cannot manage and control their own lives. The statistics representing unwanted pregnancies are staggering (UNICEF, 1994):

- Fourteen million more girls than boys fail to attend school.
- There are one million child prostitutes in Asia.
- A girl growing up in Africa faces a one in twenty risk of dying during pregnancy and childbirth.
- An estimated 120 million women in the developing world do not want to become pregnant but are not using birth control; one pregnancy in every five, therefore, is unwanted.
- The education of girls is closely correlated with falling family size.

The fierce cultural clash that took place at the International Conference on Population and Development in Cairo in September, 1994, demonstrated the various strongly held beliefs regarding reproductive rights. A conference on population control turned into a battleground for women's equality. Catholic and Muslim clerics alike condemned the secular West for its resolutions advocating that a full range of reproductive and health care services be made available for all (Elliott and Dickey, 1994). While the Vatican accused the United Nations of trying to promote abortion at the expense of families, several Muslim nations boycotted the conference entirely. The forced childbearing advocated by the traditionalists constitutes a severe form of violence that is at once physical (in terms of the toll on the body) and structural (reflective of women's place in the social system).

A patriarchal system, a global economy, and exploitation of female sexuality coalesce into prostitution, especially forced prostitution. The international trafficking of children and women in the sex industry procured through deceptive advertising for employment or marriage, is built on the exploitation of vulnerable girls and women such as refugees and runaways (Wetzel, 1993). The situation in Thailand, where as many as half a million youths provide sex to customers, is the prime example of economic servitude of girls and women. Wherever the military has established bases, prostitution economies have developed around them. Leuchtag (1995) credits the U.S. military and the need of the Thai government for hard currency with the sex tour industry that was established in Thailand during the Vietnam war. Today, slick brothel agents visit the villages where they induce parents to board their daughters out to the brothels in exchange for cash. Once in the brothel, the girl is virtually a slave, unable to ever repay her debt. An illegal enterprise, the sex trade derives its protection from corrupt politicians and policemen who invest in the trade and the enforcement of the debt bondage of the prostitutes. Commercial sex has become a part of everyday life for Thai men (*Economist*, 1992). When the girls finally return home upon adulthood they typically are infected by the virus that causes AIDS. Within a few years the rate of AIDS in the country is expected to reach two million. The fear of AIDS throughout the world is increasing the demand for new child prostitutes, many of whom are kidnapped or sold.

Since the breakup of the Soviet Union, a new population of impoverished girls and women ripe for the mill of international organized prostitution has emerged (Leuchtag, 1995). The new business etiquette in Russia calls for secretaries to serve men's needs "in every capacity." As the gap between rich and poor widens significantly, poor women have a wretched struggle to make ends meet.

Worldwide Social Mobilization

"Women Link up from Austria to Zambia" noted one newspaper headline (Nifong, 1995) and "Consensus on Women's Rights Cleared the Skies in China" proclaimed another (Chesler and Dunlop, 1995). When the women of the world organized globally in record numbers—thirty thousand by some estimates—to tackle problems from sex slavery to employment discrimination at Beijing and Huairou for the United Nations Fourth World Conference on Women, the response exceeded all expectations. Whereas at previous women's conferences, feminists from the Westernized nations were reluctant to even appear to criticize traditions from other parts of the world for fear of being accused of lacking cultural sensitivity, this time women's voices were united on behalf of the many who are unable to speak. At the 1995 conference, the debate on health and reproductive rights was led primarily by delegates who were neither Western nor white. In demanding that women's rights should supersede national traditions, the Beijing accord marked a historic breakthrough (Chesler and Dunlop, 1995). This time at the biggest and most diversified gathering of its kind, the dialogue was constructive, moved forward by persons who were skilled at lobbying, negotiating, and devising challenging strategies for a new era. The pressure is now on governments to change laws and generate economic opportunities for women.

Ultimately, the hallmark of the Fourth World Conference on Women may be in urging the rest of the world to think about where global women's issues intersect our lives. Gender based violence, for instance, can be viewed as a means of intimidating women in every country. Women are beginning to recognize the extent to which the global market exploits women economically, thereby reducing their power on the domestic front. In the final analysis, the following has become clear: The battle for women's rights will have to be fought on the international arena. Influential international organizations such as the World Bank and the United Nations will need to do their part to ensure progress toward a transformation in attitude and behavior toward women's equality, and to provide external funding of grass-roots organizations for educating women about their legal and social rights.

Related to sexism in its requirements for gender conformist behavior and in its intolerance of behavior that falls outside a rigid code of sexuality, is the prejudice against gays, lesbians, and bisexuals.

HOMOPHOBIA: A WORLDWIDE PHENOMENON

A gay, Turkish seventeen-year-old, beaten and raped by the police in Istanbul, flees to the United States. Gay Cubans are pushed out of their country in boatloads. A lesbian in Costa Rica is raped by police "to show her what it is like to be a woman." In places as far distant as Romania and Chile, gay males are still stashed away in labor camps and prisons. In Colombia, hundreds of killings occur of "social undesirables" including homosexuals. Sodomy is punished in Iran by execution. In Oklahoma, a gay law student detained in jail on a driving-while-intoxicated charge is repeatedly raped by inmates. In India, a new 1995 law makes homosexual sex punishable by ten years imprisonment. In Virginia, a lesbian mother lost custody of her child due to her "immoral conduct" and the grandmother was awarded custody.

A study of 151 hate crime slayings of homosexuals concluded that 60 percent involved extraordinary and gruesome violence, according to the New York City Gay and Lesbian Anti-Violence Project. Whereas guns are used in the large majority of murders in the United States, in these slayings, knives, baseball bats, clubs, and hammers were the weapons of choice (Associated Press, 1994). Where did this hostility directed against gays and lesbians originate?

Homosexuality was accepted in early Scandinavian, Celtic, Greek, and Asian civilizations and in some North American Indian communities with ritualized roles—for example, "the berdache" whereby feminine men and masculine women were assigned to a special status in the community (O'Neill and Naidoo, 1990). The form of homophobia that we know today is a modern phenomenon. Investigators explain the modern vehemence as a counter-reaction to gay and lesbian unity which emerged following World War II and has gained momentum ever since (Miller, 1992), and more immediately, to men's anxieties as their work roles have become more circumscribed and less male-specific (Rotundo, 1993). The backlash probably also echoes the general punitive social climate as well.

Any attempt at a worldwide perspective has to take into account vast differences in Western and Eastern approaches to sexual orientation. While the contemporary, Western model dichotomizes people as straight and gay or lesbian, in countries such as Egypt, China, Japan, and Thailand, men can have sex with other men as a sexual outlet devoid of connotations of identity or lifestyle. Lesbianism, seemingly, is unrecognized. Miller (1992), in his survey of homosexuality around the world, makes the interesting observation that countries that were once colonized by Britain had a heightened awareness of homosexuality; anti-sodomy laws are still on the books in many of the former colonies today. However, the role of the West has changed today; Europe and North America are now the world's leading exporters of the ideas of gay and women's liberation. Countries cut off from this influence—for example, China, Cuba, and Iran—regard homosexuality with great hostility. What is changing the picture today, according to Miller, is the international organization to combat AIDS. From the AIDS awareness movement has sprung a sense of bonding and community. International AIDS activism is having unanticipated social consequences. Whether a counter-reaction in the form of intensified gay-bashing will set in, remains to be seen. Let us turn to the social psychology of homophobia.

The Nature of Homophobia

A universal occurrence, homosexuality is a characteristic of all cultures and social groups. Its manifestations would be of no more than passing interest were it not for the heated response it engenders. To the extent that there is a problem, it is a heterosexual, not a homosexual, problem. This problem is rooted in society's intolerance for nonnormative, gender-specific behavior—the name for this problem is homophobia.

Homophobia is the irrational fear of homosexuals or of homosexuality (Barker, 1995). Originally introduced by Weinberg (1972), the term *homophobia* encompasses a range of behaviors from mild derision to lethal assault and battery. *Internalized homophobia* refers to the tendency for gays and lesbians to absorb the fears and prejudices of the society and to turn these fears and prejudices within. Weinberg's (1972: 133) definition of homophobia is consistent with the notion of interactionism:

> Homophobia is the revulsion toward homosexuals and often the desire to inflict punishment as retribution . . . and in the case of homosexuals themselves, self-loathing.

Heterosexism can be distinguished from homophobia in that heterosexism is a viewing of the world through heterosexual eyes, often with obliviousness to the concerns of gays and lesbians. In its dictionary meaning of prejudicial attitudes or discrimination practices against homosexuals (*Random House*, 1987:

898), *heterosexism* is more general and inclusive than the word *homophobia*. Yet both words refer to negative treatment of the gay and lesbian minority. Heterosexism is more often used to refer to the society as a whole and homophobia to the individuals and reference groups within the society. That the heterosexist society encourages homophobia in its citizens is a premise worthy of consideration.

Studies on homophobia indicate: its high prevalence among young white males (Comstock, 1991); a correlation between homophobia, and sexist, traditional attitudes (Weinberg, 1972); a relationship between homophobia and negative self-concept (Cummerton, 1982); and a worsening of heterosexism related to New Right ideology (Logan and Kershaw, 1994).

Homophobia can be viewed as the fundamentalist urge to purge in an age of uncertainty. In fact, as the historian Rotundo (1993) indicates, the ban on gays and lesbians in the military is only half a century old. The significance of this fact is that it suggests, according to Rotundo, that the ban derives from the fears of recent generations of men. At the turn of the century, a new scorn for men who had feminine traits began to emerge; the term "sissy" from sister took on dreaded connotations. In the same manner, a repugnance was directed toward mannish women.

Conduct Unbecoming: Gays and Lesbianism in the U.S. Military by Shilts (1993) chronicles the formal and informal harassment in an organization in which eighteen thousand gays have been driven out over the past decade. The victimization has resulted in casualties by violence and suicide. On college campuses with strict nondiscrimination policies, the presence of military science programs has been a source of controversy pending an end to the military ban on open gay and lesbian recruits.

In Western society, the single-sex environment seemingly is prone to an approach avoidance conflict concerning homoerotic contact. Thus girls' schools, boys' schools, military establishments, and correctional facilities are apt to be plagued by harsh sanctioning relating to atypical sex-role behavior. Under the hostile environment that arises, any same-sex pairing is apt to be ridiculed.

In the socially isolated prison community, sexual activity may take place under the guise of heterosexuality. Prison homophobia, ironically, is expressed through homosexual rape of weaker men by strong, heterosexual males. Victims are "made into women" and in every sense of the word, enslaved (Irwin, 1980). In women's prisons, likewise, homophobia is expressed in a shunning by inmates of women who are homosexually linked. Women prisoners often express physical love for each other by forming pseudo families and relating to each other as mother and sister. Any other closeness, however, is suspect (van Wormer, 1987). Some women are recruited by the prison population to play butch roles. Referred to by the masculine pronoun, these inmates, for a time, become pseudo-men.

Social workers doing counseling within same-sex environments such as on a military base or in a prison, need to be aware of the formidable presence of homophobia both expressed and experienced by their clients. An understanding of the functions and dysfunctions of homophobia can aid in its eradication.

Functions of Homophobia

We will remember from chapter 3 the tremendous fury that was unleashed in the aftermath of the slaughter of the Black Death of 1348, how a frantic populace began to attack scapegoats with a vengeance—Jews, women, the disabled, and homosexuals, among them. Interestingly, Germany, following the cruel defeat of World War I and financial hardship in the decades that followed, sought out virtually the same groups to exterminate.

Homophobia, like other forms of hatred, distracts individual citizens from focusing on economic and political problems in society. Displaced aggression against gays and lesbians can be conceived as the ultimate distraction by a people who are economically and socially insecure. Conservative politicians can capitalize on this persecution of out-groups to galvanize support. In Iowa, for example, in the early 1990s a state Equal Rights Amendment was defeated through the work of a well-financed fundamentalist lobby which publicly equated equal rights with gay and lesbian marriages. A similar strategy paid off earlier in Vermont.

Homophobia leads to group solidarity within certain circles of people as the group unites to fight deviants. Young, apparently heterosexual males capitalize on homophobia to confirm their masculine identity. In this way, they prove themselves not in terms of *who* they are but of *what* they are. Young females may establish their "normalcy" and femininity, likewise, by ridiculing and teasing tomboyish or lesbian schoolgirls. This solidarity, in fact, also characterizes the bonding of gay and lesbian political and support groups.

Above all, homophobia is a highly effective means of social control. It provides incentives for boys to pursue super-masculine outlets such as playing football or studying military science. It encourages girls to pursue cheerleading or popularity with boys. Indirectly, homophobia encourages courtship and sexual experimentation with the opposite sex. Males may court their conquests as badges of masculine honor. Reproduction undoubtedly is enhanced thereby.

Finally, all the problems of being gay in a puritanical society produce work for practitioners such as mental health professionals who work with the depressed and worried recipients of society's wrath.

Dysfunctions of Homophobia

Suicide, alcoholism, broken lives, brutal victimization: these are only a few of the dysfunctions of the irrational fear of homosexuality in society. A lesser toll is taken in punitive laws, denial of marriage and other legal rights to gay and lesbian partners, loss of children in custody battles, and stifled love relationships between same-sex heterosexual friends. Even the father and son relationship suffers from homophobic restrictions on the love expressed.

The pressure on children and youths to conform to society's rigid sex-role expectations produces intense conflict in those who cannot do so. The recent report of the Secretary's Task Force on Youth Suicide by the U.S. Department of Health and Human Services (1989) concluded that lesbian and gay male youth were several times more likely to attempt and commit suicide than were their nongay peers. The report, which originally was suppressed, is strongly critical of mental health professionals for their denial of the clients' homosexuality. Workers, uncomfortable in addressing the issue, are unable to "help the client where the client is." Remafedi, a researcher on gay and lesbian suicide (cited by Bull, 1994: 40) sums up the results as follows, "The findings of the studies indicating a high incidence of suicide among gay youth are a break from traditional thought because the researchers are looking for a psychological diagnosis where there is none . . . it's homophobia that's killing these kids." School-sanctioned homophobia is widespread and a major contributor to the medical and psychosocial problems of adolescent youth (Uribe and Harbeck, 1992).

Homophobia combined with puritanical attitudes results in the elimination of any discussion of non-mainstream life-styles and sexuality in school-based sex education programs. Such a lack of information can be fatal in the age of AIDS (Blumenfeld, 1992). At all levels of the school system, those who depart from traditional sex-role stereotypes are silenced. People perceived as gay or lesbian, whether they are or not, often receive harsh treatment for their sex-role nonconformity. As long as gay and lesbian teachers are closeted out of deference to a homophobic community, there will be a lack of positive role models for gay and lesbian children to emulate (Dempsey, 1994). A significant portion of the boys in the Uribe and Harbeck interview samples reported early same-sex experiences that parallel the "date rape" experiences of many young women. Yet because of the stigma of homosexual involvement, these students felt they could tell no one. The involvement in alcohol and other substance abuse of this sample was startlingly high.

Early diagnosis and treatment of depression and substance abuse in homosexual men may prevent extreme acts of self-destruction. Psychiatrists Flavin, Franklin, and Frances (1986) report in the *American Journal of Psychiatry* of three alcohol-dependent gay men who consciously attempted to contract the acquired immune deficiency syndrome (AIDS) virus as a means of committing suicide. One man acknowledged having intercourse with over six hundred men in the year before he was examined. This patient wanted to kill himself but could not get up the nerve to do it directly.

The rate of alcoholism among gays and lesbians, although possibly exaggerated in the literature due to sampling bias, is substantial. Kus (1988) in a *Journal of Homosexuality* article cites estimates that 31 percent of gays and lesbians in a Los Angeles study and 29 percent of gay men in a Michigan sample were alcoholic. Saghir and Robins (1973) found 35 percent of the lesbians surveyed had severe drinking problems compared to 5 percent of heterosexual women. Skinner and Otis (1996), however, found high drinking rates but a reduced rate of about 10 percent alcoholism in a southern sample of over 1,000. Marijuana and nicotine use, however, were found to be disproportionately high. More research is needed to determine the actual alcoholism rates of the lesbian, gay, and bisexual populations.

Lewis and Jordan (1989) probe the link between self-loathing due to internalized homophobia, and suicidal thoughts and alcoholism. High alcoholism rates among gays and lesbians, to the extent that they exist, would seem to be the end result of society's hostility toward gay people as reflected in low self-esteem and guilt feelings over sexuality. The act of drinking lowers inhibitions and increases risk-taking behavior. Thus alcohol abuse may prove fatal to high-risk populations for whom safe-sex practices are essential.

While lesbians and gays press for equity, the resistance, anger, and hatred remind us of the depth, intensity, and pervasiveness of homophobia (Hartman, 1993). For every social revolution there is backlash: Society's hostility toward gay men and lesbians is expressed today in rampant victimization. The book, *Violence Against Lesbians and Gay Men* (Comstock, 1991), gives statistical information on victims and their perpetrators. Physical assaults against this minority group have become quite common, a fact that, as the author suggests, probably reflects the backlash accompanying publicity over gay rights. A college first year class surveyed by Comstock (1991) reported that 16 percent of males had attacked gays. In this same sample, 30 percent of the physical violence against gay males was committed by family members—most often by fathers and step-fathers. Ninety-four percent of the perpetrators of attacks on both homosexual males and females are male. Heterosexual females attack lesbians but not gay men. Eighty-five percent of lesbians who were physically attacked, however, were attacked by men; sometimes the attack included rape.

Lesbians suffer doubly from homophobia because of its link with sexism. A woman who steps outside the rules of patriarchy and threatens its authority expects to be hated and feared by men and by heterosexual women who seek social change but fear the lesbian label (Pharr, 1988). The effect on the women's movement—as women are divided from women by the male power structure—has been devastating.

Living at the margins without a clear-cut identity as either gay or straight, *bisexuals* have been the pariahs in whichever circles they choose to move. "To a social order based on monogamy," writes Leland (1995: 47), "bisexuality looms as a potent threat . . . as a rupture in the social structure, conjuring up fears of promiscuity, secret lives, and instability." With the threat of AIDS today, many are horrified when a person identifies himself or herself as "bi." In reality, bisexuals need not be involved with members of both sexes simultaneously; they simply have a flexibility that is an anomaly in a world that thinks in terms of polarities and clear-cut labels.

Homosexuality is outlawed in many parts of the world including Zimbabwe, Nigeria, Ghana, India, and Nicaragua. Having such laws in the books makes gays and lesbians particularly susceptible to violence. Incidents of robbery and violence cannot be reported to the police under the circumstances, and the attackers know this (Jost, 1993).

In short, societies' persecution of gays and lesbians deprives a sizeable segment of the population of the help and support they need. Alienation from the traditional church's teachings, lack of awareness of counseling services, the living of a life-style that is taboo in most circles, and abuse inflicted by peers and family members all combine to close the avenues to much needed social support. The results are a loss not only to gays and lesbians but to the society which deprives itself of the gay and lesbian contribution.

Legal Rights

Reflecting the homophobia that is embedded in the fabric of Western society, laws and social norms have punished same-sex forms of sexual behavior. For centuries in the Middle Ages, under church law, men and women suspected of homosexual behavior were tortured, mutilated, or burned at the stake. After a return to secular law in the twelfth century, antihomosexual attitudes became a cultural value supported by the developing science of medicine (Longres, 1995). Homosexual behavior was classified as a mental disorder by the American Psychiatric Association until 1974 when this category was officially removed from consideration.

Only nine states in the United States have passed legislation prohibiting discrimination based on sexual orientation in employment, housing, public accommodations, and credit. Some cities, moreover, such as Berkeley, California, and Madison, Wisconsin, have introduced ordinances providing protection on the basis of sexual orientation. In most states, however, gays, lesbians, and bisexuals can be discriminated against with impunity. Teachers regularly are fired from their jobs on this basis; ministers are forced to resign; and housing may be restricted on the basis of living arrangements. Although Hawaii is considering the matter, same-sex marriage is not legally recognized anywhere in the United States or Canada.

In Texas and twenty-one other states, sodomy between consenting adults is illegal (Amnesty International, 1994). Such state laws have been upheld by the U.S. Supreme Court. Similar laws exist throughout much of the world. There is a trend in Europe, however, toward moderation. In recent years, several former Soviet republics including Russia have decriminalized consensual homosexual activity between adults in private. Today, homosexual conduct is legal in most of Australia and nearly all the Western European countries including most recently, Ireland. In Sweden, Canada, and the United States, lesbian and gay organizations have assisted gay and lesbian refugees in their quest for political asylum from places such as the Middle East, Asia, and Latin America where gays and lesbians are in peril. When in 1995, U.S. government policy declared that lesbians and gays could be a "social group" for the purposes of political asylum, this marked a giant reversal, considering that up until 1990, gay and lesbian immigrants could be denied entry into the country (Dorf, 1995). This is a life and death matter for many people at risk from "death squads" in such places as Mexico, Ecuador, Colombia, and Brazil (Amnesty International, 1994). In Iran, execution is the official punishment for sodomy; hundreds have been put to death in recent years. In Costa Rica, officials sexually abuse lesbians and gay males as a means of torture.

Miller (1992) who interviewed gays and lesbians from all over the world, concluded that four preconditions were necessary for a modern-style gay and lesbian social identity and community to emerge in a given society: a modicum of personal freedom and social tolerance; a level of economic development that offers independence and private living space (not available in much of Latin America); a relatively high status for women (in the non-Western world lesbianism is completely invisible except in Japan where women are gaining ground); and a decline in the power of family and religious institutions.

Positive Developments

As mentioned earlier, gays and lesbians are organizing internationally to combat the spread of AIDS and advocate for human rights. A newly formed interracial gay and lesbian community in South Africa had its first pride march in 1990 with eight hundred blacks and whites participating. Then later that same year, in the new bill of rights drafted by the African National Congress, discrimination was barred on the grounds of sexual orientation.

In Denmark, Norway, and Sweden, countries which pride themselves on tolerance, same-sex partnerships have been legalized, an act providing the crucial benefits that spouses enjoy such as rights to inheritance and decision-making in dire health care situations. Some rights such as the right to adopt children, however, have still not been granted. The Netherlands is currently considering providing full marriage rights to same-sex couples. Recently, Hungary legalized common law gay marriage, although the right to civil marriage was not granted.

In 1993 the United Nations accepted for roster status the International Lesbian and Gay Association. This gives this organization the right to present information on human rights abuses on the basis of sexual orientation. The data collecting efforts of such nongovernmental organizations as Amnesty International are helping to publicize human rights violations of this kind.

In the United States, cities and organizations such as universities and treatment centers are including persons of the same-sex orientation as a designated group to be protected from discrimination. Such clauses are less essential in states, such as New York, which provide such protection. Canada is giving serious consideration to including sexual orientation in its federal Human Rights Act. Until this happens, however, gay and lesbian couples in Canada are not provided the rights (such as child custody, pension, and health benefits) of their heterosexual counterparts (Fisher, 1995). In 1996, Canada's human rights tribunal ruled that the federal government must extend health benefits to same-sex partners of government workers. Meanwhile, schools of social work in Canada are under scrutiny by the Canadian Association of Schools of Social Work (CASSW) to provide attention to homophobia and other injustices in their course curricula (Callahan, 1994). And in the United Kingdom, the Central Council for Education and Training in Social Work (CCETSW) states that social work students should be prepared to combat discrimination based on sexual orientation (Logan and Kershaw, 1994).

Homophobia prevention efforts are an important means of curbing violence against gays and lesbians; such educational efforts help individuals, especially children, develop self-awareness about their own sexuality. Quietly, school systems across the United States, as a part of suicide-prevention efforts and safe-sex education, have begun to include consideration of homosexual as well as heterosexual youth in their programming. The state of Massachusetts, for instance, mandates that sexual diversity be included in teacher education and school programming. A comprehensive counseling program for gay, lesbian, and bisexual youth, and educational programs for all youth have been implemented throughout the Los Angeles school district following excellent results in reducing prejudice in a demonstration project (Uribe and Harbeck, 1992). A follow-up survey of the general student body revealed the importance of exposure to openly gay and lesbian teachers in shaping positive attitudes toward homosexuality. The most glaring fact emerging from the study is the need for intensive education about safe-sex practices among teenage male homosexuals. New York City has an exclusively gay and lesbian school, the

Harvey Milk School, while Toronto has the Triangle Program which provides gay and lesbian students with their own educational experience. In Calgary, Alberta, the Board of Education has a strict nondiscrimination policy to protect gay and lesbian youth from harassment.

To summarize, regardless of the different varieties of homosexuality around the world, the existence of hate crimes against gays and lesbians is a near-universal reality. Because gays, lesbians, and bisexuals are different, and because their difference bears on sexuality, they are ready targets for ridicule and hatred. Social groups, including families and peers, may set up what they consider "perversions" as negative examples to reinforce gender role expectations. Many individuals conform their behavior accordingly, sometimes with tragic consequences.

From the societal and personal point of view, the dysfunctions of homophobia far outweigh the functions. The fear and hatred entailed in homophobia destroy those who practice gay-bashing as well as those who receive this kind of treatment. Although in certain religious quarters the gay male's susceptibility to AIDS is viewed as just punishment for their life-style and provides a reason for discrimination against gay males as carriers of a disease, internationally, AIDS prevention work is playing an important role in forging a gay and lesbian community. A great deal of work remains to be done in shaping civil rights protection laws and safe-sex educational programs, and in creating a world where people can be accepted for what they are.

ETHNOCENTRISM

As defined in chapter 1, *ethnocentrism* is the tendency to view another culture through the lens of one's own culture; the belief in one's own cultural superiority is ingrained in this outlook and perhaps inevitable. The world today has been reintroduced to the notion of ethnic cleansing as the Serbs have tortured, raped, impregnated, and killed members of minority Muslim groups and the Croats have taunted fleeing Serbian refugees. In an earlier war, World War II, Serbs were the victims of ethnic cleansing at the hands of Croats who collaborated with the Nazis.

Other recent examples of ethnic cleansing are Kuwaitis expelling persons of different ethnic heritage many of whom had been born in Kuwait; Estonians encouraging Russians to leave; Japanese denying full citizenship to third generation residents of Korean ancestry; and Israel's acceptance of foreign Jews over native Palestinians. Apart from racist groups such as the Ku Klux Klan and militia groups, Americans and Canadians have been more prone to stress inclusion (learn to live like us and act like us) than exclusion (Smith and Stuart, 1982). The point is debatable, however, especially in light of Jim Crow laws in the Old South and laws against miscegenation in many states.

American Indians

In any case, European Americans upon "discovering" America unmistakably practiced ethnic cleansing with regard to the native population with whom they were in fierce competition over land and resources. Much of the worst devastation occurred in the earliest years of contact, when previously unexposed populations lacked acquired immunities to European diseases and were especially vulnerable (Wood, 1992). Through deliberate policies of exclusion and extermination not to mention the illnesses, firearms, and alcohol, the Indian population went from an estimated three to seven million to 240,000 by 1920 (Green, 1995). Today, their numbers have risen to approximately two million, still fewer than 1 percent of the total U.S. population, however.

Native Americans, like many Mexican Americans, did not choose to become part of the United States; they are a conquered people, in fact, defeated after several battles with the U.S. Army. American Indians and many of the Mexican Americans are different from other minority groups in that they did not arrive here from other lands. Lewis (1995), a member of the Cherokee Nation and a professor of social work, turns to the socioeconomic theories of colonialism to describe the relationship between conqueror and the conquered.

Lewis defines *colonialism* as a situation in which the destiny of a nation or an identifiable group within a state is controlled by external authorities and their agencies. Under the colonial relationship, the dominant partner extracts benefits from the subordinate partner. Two types of colonialism singled out by Lewis are structural and cultural.

With regard to American Indians, *structural* colonialism is illustrated by the political controls which resulted in the seizure of lands through battle, treaties, and the passage of federal acts calling for the placement of Indians onto barren lands in the West. Thousands of Cherokees perished on the forced march westward to Oklahoma, often referred to as "the Trail of Tears." Decision making for Indians by non-Indian governmental agencies, such as the Bureau of Indian Affairs formed in 1849, has gone hand in hand with economic dependence on the authorities.

Cultural colonialism has been evidenced in the settlers' sense of religious superiority over persons considered barbarians and heathens. Tribal religious traditions and ceremonies were outlawed; by 1930 the majority of Native Americans professed a Christian affiliation (Longres, 1995). Children were removed from reservations to attend boarding schools hundreds of miles away where they could become acculturated. The speaking of Indian languages was strictly forbidden.

Although the Indians in Canada suffered a similar loss of culture and autonomy when the white settlers moved westward, there are some major differences in the Canadian government's handling of the situation. An incident in Canadian history, the Cypress Hills Massacre of 1873 reported by Martys (1995), graphically captures the contrast in the two countries' treatment of Indians. American freetraders escaping the U.S. marshall in Montana set up four whiskey forts in the Cypress Hills area north of the border. Along with the whiskey came smallpox and much misery for the Plains Indians. Of those who did not succumb to disease, scores died in drunken fights. Citizens in eastern Canada were alarmed; they did not wish the American frontier mentality to extend into Canada. Then a drunken dispute over stolen horses (both the white traders and Indians were drunk) led to a massacre of an estimated twenty to fifty Indians. When word of the massacre broke, the Canadian government created a mounted police force to preserve the peace and counter American influence. The Cypress Hills massacre, according to Martys, remains an anomaly in Western Canadian history. That there was discrimination against the Indians in Canada, however, will become apparent under the section on indigenous populations.

Today in the United States about one-third of the American Indians live permanently on reservations, one-third in urban areas, and one-third moving back and forth. The statistics for income, education, mental health, and crime present a bleak picture. Almost 31 percent of all Native Americans have incomes below the poverty level. The major health problem facing the American Indians (like the Australian aborigines) is alcoholism.

During the past decades, thanks to political activism from the 1960s to the present, an expanded recognition of the role of tribal self-government has taken place. The Indian Civil Rights Act of 1968 prohibited the states from acquiring jurisdiction over Indian reservations without the consent of the tribes living there. The passage of the Indian Child Welfare Act in 1978 was an effort to prevent the adoption of Indian children in non-Indian homes. The act gave Indian tribes jurisdiction over Indian children. The restoration of social justice between Native Americans and the U.S. government is still being played out in the courtroom (Lum, 1992).

RACISM

The dominant culture's disparaging views of persons of different racial stock tends to be pervasive and institutionalized. In Britain, the origins of racism can be traced to the development of colonialism which brought about the slave trade (Christodoulou, 1991). The colonial powers' dilemma of how to be Christian and slave traders at the same time was resolved in favor of exploitation. Some groups were meant to rule, it was argued, and others to serve; some groups were morally and culturally superior to others. Not only were racist ideas recycled into "scientific" theories but these ideas were embraced in the dominant race's culture, songs, nursery rhymes, pictures, news stories, and textbooks, according to Christodoulou (1991).

Racism in American Life

Racism is perhaps the "original sin" in U.S. history, the curse upon the land which could never be expunged. Chao (1995) briefly summarizes racist practices starting with the Constitution and the Bill of Rights which did not include African Americans or the native people. The passage of the Chinese Exclusion Act and the herding of 100,000 innocent Japanese Americans into internment camps are often overlooked examples of racism involving Asian-American and Asian people. Such measures were adopted both in the United States and Canada.

Angela Davis, a black Communist activist accused of a conspiracy to aid convicts in an escape attempt, recounts an autobiographical experience (1974) in a jail cell: The woman next door is in the throes of some type of mental collapse. Hearing her pour forth a tirade of racist obscenities, Davis reflects on the pitiful inadequacy of psychiatrists to treat her.

How could she be cured Davis asks (p. 37) without an awareness "of the way in which racism, like an ancient plague, infects every joint, muscle and tissue of social life in this country?" For it was from the society that such a woman had so perfectly learned to hate black people.

Racism, being a complex system of beliefs, attitudes, and practices permeates every aspect of society (Christodoulou, 1991). Phenomena associated with racism range from what Maya Angelou (1989) terms "the little murders and petty humiliations" to "the grand executions" which are life-threatening. The constant barrage of negative remarks, looks, and threats take their toll in terms of generalized stress and internalized racism.

The Ku Klux Klan, which preached fanatical racial hatred after World War I and the lynchings which punished "uppity" black males by the thousands in the years before World War I, are examples of unofficially sanctioned racism, lawlessness, and violence of a gruesome sort. (The National Association for the Advancement of Colored People—NAACP—began in 1909 in response to a lynching in Illinois; it is still a major civil rights organization today). In modern times, there are the all-white militias, organizing as a paramilitary force to "protect" the country from perceived threats to the status quo. This antigovernment ideology focuses on federal gun control, taxes, and perceived attacks on constitutional liberties. White supremacist states' rights arguments and other theories rooted in racial bigotry also pervade the militia movement (Berlet and Lyons, 1995).

Internalized racism involves picking up the prejudices of the dominant culture and turning them within—onto the self. Feelings related to low self-esteem, powerlessness, and rejection of blackness may play an indirect role in high school dropout rates, drug use, high homicide and suicide rates, and teenage pregnancy. The reduced availability of young African American males compared to African American females is associated directly and indirectly with racism. The death rate (often through shootings) and incarceration rate of young black males is high enough to create a severe sex ratio imbalance in the population (Morales and Sheafor, 1995). Due both to perceived danger and racism, police homicides perpetrated against young black males are disporportionately high.

Violence leads to violence and racism to racism. The already overfamiliar and numbing picture of white police officers standing idly by while two of their number savagely beat a helpless black man, Rodney King, is now history. The shocking aftermath of hordes of rioting people—young, male, and black or Hispanic—beating innocent bystanders, trashing Korean stores, and setting a section of Los Angeles aflame demonstrates the racial tension present in the United States.

But racism is not confined to the police or to a small, underprivileged segment of the population. For despite the progress of the 1960s, the tremendous network of civil rights legislation in the last decade, and the half-hearted and sincere affirmative action steps which followed, the legacy of racism and oppression continues to define the existence of African Americans in the land where there is "liberty and justice for all."

Whites are rarely aware of the extent to which racism permeates American life. Even social workers, on the whole, often have taken a color-blind attitude toward the issue of race (Christodoulou, 1991). Stokely Carmichael coined the term, *institutional racism,* to describe this indirect and often unwitting mistreatment of minority groups in modern America. The tendency to overlook the black contribution to American history and to history in general, is an example of something that is more than an oversight. Institutional racism expands the parameters of racist behavior beyond the person-to-person realm of deliberate, individual acts to a relatively constant pattern of prejudice and discrimination between one party who is favored and another who is not (Greene, 1995).

African American History

When slavery in the United States finally ended, African Americans believed they were free. What they did not expect was the cruel legacy of slavery—in the laws, attitudes, and habits that were capable of existing for years. Habits of thought nurtured over centuries passed down from one generation to another are not easily eliminated. What Martin Luther King, Jr., called "a strange indecisiveness and ambivalence toward the Negro" is the characteristic white response. James Baldwin described the problem concerning white people in *The Fire Next Time* (1963: 22–23):

> They are, in effect, still trapped in a history which they do not understand, and until they understand it, they cannot be released from it. They have had to believe for many years, and for innumerable reasons, that black men are inferior to white men.

As children of two cultures—African and American—black people are the only immigrant group to have been brought to America in chains. The involuntary removal of millions of Africans from their homeland and the harsh journey to America is one of the most tragic events in the history of humankind (Leashore, 1995). Under laws known as the Black Codes, the slaves were considered property, not people. The slavery practiced in North America was the cruelest form of slavery because it split up families. Slavery was maintained by violence, something black Americans learned only on this continent. For most of their history, in fact, African Americans were the victims, not the instigators of violence (Silberman, 1978).

The indomitable shades of plantation life are with us still. In his posthumously published book, *Where Do We Go From Here: Chaos or Community?* (1968), Martin Luther King, Jr., presents this appreciation of his historical origins (p. 62):

> Who are we? We are the descendants of slaves. We are the offspring of noble men and women who were kidnapped from their native land and chained in ships like beasts. We are the heirs of a great and exploited continent known as Africa. We are the heirs of a past of rope, fire, and murder. I for one am not ashamed of this past.

In Louisiana, like Latin America, conversely, the French-Spanish Roman Catholic heritage produced an entirely different set of racial concepts from those found in Anglo-Saxon Protestant realms. Free people of color enjoyed many of the same economic and legal privileges as white persons. This little-known yet remarkable Louisiana history which culminated in a clash of Creole custom with American law is recorded by Mills' *The Forgotten People: Cane River's Creoles of Color* (1977). That there was a uniqueness in racial history and custom in southern Louisiana is evidenced in the varied pigmentation among all racial groups in the land of the bayous.

Internalized Oppression

As Pinkney once suggested in his document, *Black Americans* (1975), after nearly three and a half centuries, white Americans continue to react to Afro-Americans with a mass irrationality which precludes the complete entrance of blacks into the larger society. The oppression of blacks by whites has understandably left a residue of self-hatred and suspicion. The effect works its cancer in ways that crush the spirit of many young people. Bishop (1994) observes the same phenomenon among all oppressed groups in the United States and Canada today.

Following the race riots that flared up in the late sixties, two African American psychiatrists analyzed what they defined as the "black rage" which they had observed in their patients but which they saw as rooted in a sickness in the society at large. Grier and Cobbs (1991) located the reflection of the past in the seeming aberrations of the present. The past of the black man and woman, they wrote, was evidenced in their daily lives. "It is revealed," they said, "in character structure and child-rearing. It can be heard on a Sunday morning in a Baptist church. It reveals itself in the temper of the ghetto and in the emerging rage now threatening to shatter this nation, a nation that black Americans helped to build. A few black people may hide their scars, but most harbor the wounds of yesterday" (Grier and Cobbs, 1971: 18). The scars of oppression linger in those reared in an abusive society (Bishop, 1994).

In a newspaper editorial entitled, "Given Blacks' Experiences, Why Should We Think Much of Whites?" Betty Jean Furgerson (1995: 2c) describes the daily burden of living in a world where the hostility is often disturbingly subtle:

> We as African Americans are often forced to operate from a defensive posture called social paranoia, which has become absolutely necessary for our survival and, beyond survival, for maintaining our sanity and self-respect.

"Aggression against one's own group" is the phrase provided by Allport to depict a characteristic of people who have been victimized (1954: 148). One has only to check into inner-city hospitals on Saturday night to see the evidence of injury inflicted by blacks on other blacks. Moreover, the availability of guns and other lethal weapons in conjunction with the relentless media coverage of violence in various forms, can cause emulation of aggression by those who live in an already harsh environment (Allen-Meares and Burman, 1995).

Nevertheless, to overemphasize historical abuse and yesterday's racism as causes of today's social problems may be to fail to acknowledge the very real structural influences stemming from intense global competition and technological change. As the U.S. economy faces the challenges of competition, according to a lead article in *Business Week* (1992), there has been a sharp increase in wages for those with specialized education and skills, while wages and jobs for less skilled have dropped sharply. Meanwhile poorly funded education and eviscerated public programs are the rule. The direct and indirect costs of tolerating a so-called underclass of urban poor, according to *Business Week*'s calculations, is at least $230 billion annually and mounting. The long-term consequences in terms of family breakdown, criminality, violence, and substance abuse are even more compelling.

Telling Statistics

Although Leashore (1995) applauds the improvements African Americans (who constitute 12.5 percent of the U.S. population) have managed to make in their lives against considerable odds, he lists the disparities in socioeconomic indicators between blacks and their white counterparts. Among these disparities, African Americans compared to whites experience the following:

- A net wealth that is only one-tenth as much.
- An infant mortality rate twice as high.
- A significantly lower marriage rate.
- A college-completion rate about half that of whites (the reduction in financial aid is probably involved in this figure which reflects a decline for blacks).
- Death rates among children ages five to fourteen which are 30 to 50 percent higher than those for white children.
- Nearly twice the rate of teenage motherhood.
- A homicide rate for young men seven times that of whites.
- A life expectancy of six years less for women and eight years less for men.
- An imprisonment rate that is 46 percent of all prisoners and a death sentence representation that is 40 percent of the total of those sentenced to death.

Such grim statistics both reflect the institutionalized racism in the society and the reaction of an oppressed group to the existence of such hostility.

African Cultural Survival

In a significant addition to the literature, Daly et al. (1995) discuss the Africentric orientation to coping and resolving externally caused racial problems through interpersonal processes. The Africentric paradigm proposes that in African culture, humanity is viewed in collectivist rather than individualist terms; system maintenance is sought for the group rather than individual achievement; and materialism and competition are supplanted by spiritual awareness and by cooperation with others. The African American community, therefore, has served as a buffer between African Americans and the dominant European American society. Whereas European American women when abused by their spouses are likely to use the perspective of sexual oppression and turn to mental health services for help, African American women are more likely to view their physical abuse from the perspective of racial oppression. The extended family is an important support system in alleviating such violence. As Daly et al. conclude, this group-derived ego strength can then mediate against assaults on the self from the wider society. Moreover, Daly et al. state (p. 245):

> These values have provided the community with the resilience to make effective responses against the violence and oppression of slavery and legalized segregation. Thus, the family cannot be underestimated as a mechanism of survival in the African American community.

In many cities of varying sizes there is a community movement underway to control drugs, crime, and legal marketing of harmful products by means of neighborhood action programs. In Waterloo, Iowa, for instance, midnight basketball leagues, the introduction of community patrols to combat drug dealing, and an active cultural-specific substance abuse outreach program have combined to produce favorable results. If these kinds of grass-roots programs can be combined with a national agenda to save the cities through expansion of such programs as Head Start, the Job Corps, and child nutrition, much would have been done to offer a real "economic restructuring" to help offset the post-industrial realities which have taken such a toll upon the inner-city poor.

Canada

The fact that slavery once existed in Canada is little known. The predominant emphasis on the fur trade rather than agriculture, however, made large-scale slavery unprofitable in colonial Canada (Christensen, 1995). Under French rule, a small number of slaves provided labor mainly for French-speaking Canadians. After the American Revolution, British loyalists moved to Canada with their slaves. A second influx, according to Christensen, occurred during the War of 1812 when blacks who had deserted their masters to join the British often were offered freedom. These were the ancestors of most of Nova Scotia's present black or African Canadian population. Schools were legally segregated in Ontario and Nova Scotia until the 1960s (Christensen, 1995).

There is a long history in Halifax, Nova Scotia, of black people not being allowed to enter public bars. This problem finally led to a violent disruption on the streets of the city in 1991 (Bishop, 1994). Today the total number of blacks in Canada is approximately three million. The overwhelming majority of these are immigrants, however—Haitians reside in the French-speaking areas, and others from the Caribbean and Africa live in major cities such as Toronto where blacks comprise the largest visible minority group. (Christensen, 1995).

Europe

The resurgence of racism in many European countries is being encouraged by demagogic politicians taking advantage of declining economic and social conditions which create a climate in which racism can flourish (Christodoulou, 1991). Black immigrants from the British Commonwealth who were once welcomed into Britain due to a labor shortage were expected to assimilate in the 1960s and 1970s. When this failed to happen, a racist backlash ensued. An article in *World Press Review* (1994), in fact, reports that racial harassment of ethnic minorities, who now represent 6 percent of the total population in Britain, has grown so vehement that black citizens are planning to emigrate in unprecedented numbers.

Racism in Europe, argues Lorenz (1994), has to be seen in the context of the prevailing political climate in the 1990s and in the way policies both reflect and reinforce ultranationalist sentiments. An overwhelming influx of migrants and refugees from Eastern Europe and elsewhere has created a hostile environment at a time when national economic priorities have begun to shift in the direction of greater competitiveness. Subtle racism evidenced in immigration policies favoring persons who can "integrate smoothly" into European countries is overshadowed by overt racism by organized, neo-fascist groups. In France,

Germany, and other European countries, systematic violence against foreigners and minorities has been reported. In France reports describe the mistreatment of Moroccan and Algerian detainees awaiting deportation. For instance, a guard was charged with raping an Algerian transvestite, and a Moroccan was badly beaten by fellow inmates (*Prison Legal News*, 1995). In Italy, France, Norway, and Sweden, for instance, the influence of extremely anti-immigrant, right-wing, political parties has led to restrictive political asylum policies. Within the E.U., legislation explicitly prohibiting racial discrimination and racism exists only in Belgium, France, Ireland, Portugal, and the United Kingdom. Greece and the Netherlands rely on general antidiscrimination legislation. In southern European countries, opposition to black migrants is striking. The most systematic opposition to racism in Europe, according to Lorenz, has come from the churches who have offered both shelter and services to illegal immigrants.

Social workers, especially youth workers, are directing attention to skinheads and hooligans, the perpetrators of racial violence. Because social control measures would further isolate them from society, social workers focus on addressing their feelings of powerlessness while working for political changes concerning opportunity. In the United States, similarly, judges commonly sentence youths who have engaged in such practices as vandalism against synagogues and erecting Ku Klux Klan crosses to participation in intensive interracial, consciousness raising programs.

Very closely related to racism and sometimes indistinguishable from it, yet more socially acceptable somehow, is the outcry against those from foreign lands — the anti-immigrant sentiment

ANTI-IMMIGRANT SENTIMENT

Europeans express their anti-immigrant prejudices in terms of the need to preserve the homogeneity of the society (Lorenz, 1994). Americans and Canadians, of course, have no homogeneity to preserve. Right-wing politicians speak instead in terms of economics — costs in jobs and costs in welfare. In the United States and Canada restricting the tide of immigration is a major concern; yet, ironically both nations are known as "nations of immigrants." U.S. history books refer to this country as "the great melting pot" or crucible, a blending of old world nationalities into a new American alloy. The comparable Canadian concept is of "a mosaic of people," a concept which stresses the retention of unique cultural identity.

Population migration is perceived as a problem in most industrialized nations and in many non-industrialized nations as well. The United States, Canada, Australia, and Israel are the only countries that willingly accept large numbers of immigrants. These countries like to regard themselves as lands of freedom and opportunity, and yet a backlash against foreigners has been occurring everywhere. Competition over scarce jobs, resentment over costs to taxpayers, and racism seem to be behind the populist outcry to close the borders. While California has voted to cut off nearly all public social services to undocumented immigrants, and Florida has started denying their children foster care, Canada, where immigration is carefully controlled, has reduced current immigration levels to about 1 percent of total population (*Los Angeles Times,* 1994). A little known fact is that American taxpayers spent nearly two hundred million dollars in 1994 on immigration detention. For the eighty-two thousand immigrants who were imprisoned, often because of lack of proper documentation, prison conditions are deliberately abominable to discourage refugees (Solomon, 1995). Because of the civil nature of the cases, detainees have no constitutional protection against cruel and unusual punishment. The Immigration and Nationalization Service facilities have been condemned by the American Civil Liberties Union, the U.N. High Commission for Refugees, and Amnesty International, among others. In the United Kingdom, similarly, illegal immigrants and asylum seekers alike are held in specially designated centers run by the private sector; many are also detained in local prisons (Ryan and Sim, 1995).

While immigration into the western United States has boosted the population growth to startlingly high levels, other countries are taking serious measures against such an influx. Taking aim at illegal immigration in Britain is a part of the conservative agenda (*The Economist,* 1995). India is building the world's largest fence to block immigrants from Bangladesh, and many European countries are rewriting their policies to restrict those who seek political asylum. War refugee problems are creating havoc in parts of Africa, Asia, and Europe; these are addressed in chapter 8 under the section on war.

Anti-Immigrant Sentiment in North America

The dominant settlement group to populate a region establishes its language, culture, religion, and customs as the norm. Even if the settlers were debtors, illiterates, ne'er-do-wells, their descendants acquire high status and may join exclusive clubs such as the Daughters of the American Revolution, the Mayflower Maidens, or the Colonial Dames of Maryland. In Canada, similarly, there is still the prevailing colonial mindset that "real Canadians" are only those who descended from British and French stock (*Los Angeles Times,* 1994). Recently arrived immigrants have to fight to make a way for themselves; their hope is that their children will become successful and then be socially acceptable. Often the assimilated groups look down on the later arrivals (for example, the descendants of early Mexican-American settlers often wish to dissociate themselves from the newcomers; this is true of Cubans and Vietnamese also). Regardless of how long the immigrants or their ancestors have resided in a country, the visibility of their physical characteristics may set them apart and subject them to prejudice and victimization. The United States prides itself on being a "great melting pot," yet this concept refers only to those of mainly European roots. Persons of other racial ancestry were excluded.

Like African Americans, Asian Americans have been the victims of pervasive institutional discrimination, often punctuated by violence for much of American history (Jost, 1993). After Chinese immigration was disallowed after 1882, anti-Asian sentiment was directed against Japanese and Filipino residents. Discriminatory state laws were passed. In more recent years, Japanese persons have been attacked and blamed for loss of jobs in the auto industry. Vietnamese fishermen in Texas have been victimized for working too hard and catching too many fish, thereby upsetting the established balance.

In Canada, similarly, much anti-Asian discrimination has been recorded. Following a smallpox epidemic of 1892, for which Chinese immigrants were blamed, the level of violence against them was so high in Alberta that the Royal Canadian Mounted Police had to be called upon regularly to prevent lynchings (Christensen, 1995). In both Canada and the United States today, despite the prejudice to which they have been exposed, Asian immigrants and their descendants have achieved above average levels of education and family income. Does education bring full acceptance however? Asian-Canadian feminist therapist Nayyar Javed (1995: 17) in her chapter in *Racism in the Lives of Women* speaks from the pain of personal experience:

> Our devaluation by the society remains invisible when our men talk about racism. So-called multicultural policies do not take racism into account, and racialized men ignore the gender issues. Male critics have brought racism out of obscurity, but make no mention of sexism in their analysis.

Similarly, feminist analysis of oppression has not included our realities. Our feminist sisters tend not to challenge many social assumptions about us. They find us "smelly" and "submissive" and see our cultures as male-dominated and "barbaric." We do not deny the presence of male dominance in our cultures, but we are also aware of the extent of patriarchy in Canada. We experience it every moment of our lives. Racialized and alone, most of us endure our oppression silently. In the countries we left behind, we were at least equal to other women, and we had access to mechanisms compensating for our subordination to men. Yet many well-meaning individuals tell us to be thankful for "the freedom and equality in Canada." What equality are they talking about? Their own?

More than a million immigrants, most with official permission, enter the United States each year. In Canada it is over two hundred thousand per year. Compared to Europe, countries on this side of the ocean keep their doors relatively open. Yet a growing intolerance of immigrants is being felt as outsiders are being made scapegoats for the failings of the U.S. economy. Such sentiment is especially pronounced along the U.S./Mexican border. The job insecurities related to the low-wage, low-skill economy and 27 percent poverty rate of El Paso, Texas, provide fertile ground for anti-immigrant hostility, for instance. An *NASW News* (Hiratsuka, 1995) account interviews social workers in border states who are experiencing the effects of state laws such as Proposition 187 denying services, including health care and education, to undocumented aliens. Such restrictions, according to the article, can exacerbate public health and safety problems, including crime and outbreaks of tuberculosis and sexually transmitted diseases. Furthermore such measures, which require the reporting of persons suspected to lack proper documentation, present an ethical dilemma for social workers committed to nondiscrimination, provision of access to services, putting the clients' interests first, and client confidentiality. Many California social workers, accordingly, have signed a pledge of noncompliance with the dictates of Proposition 187. As a solution for the high immigrant health care and educational costs borne by a few states, many urge the federal government to pay a larger share. Otherwise, the official and unofficial backlash will be considerable. Sometimes the backlash emerges in the issue over language.

"Now get this straight," a Texas judge lectured the mother in a child custody case. "You start speaking English to this child otherwise," he told her, "you're abusing that child and you're relegating her to the position of a housemaid" (reported in *Progressive*, 1995). Bigotry against Mexican Americans is underscored in this judicial reprimand as well as in the "English only" movement that is sweeping across the United States.

Hispanics in the United States

The U.S. Census Bureau projects that by 2010, Hispanics will become the largest minority in the land (Cose, 1995). As the numbers climb, and the Hispanic presence is felt across the United States, prejudice against the newcomers is mounting. The national assault on affirmative action and welfare is directed as much against Hispanics as it is against women and blacks (Morcate, 1995). Their ethnic, cultural, and linguistic diversity make this group's pluralisms most important agents, declares Morcate. "Hispanicization" of America is as significant a phenomenon as is the "Americanization" of Hispanics. When the *Des Moines Register* ran a series on Hispanic workers in Iowa which provided a personal and largely favorable portrait of the newcomers, some readers were less than charitable. Marshall (1995: 6C) comments:

> I think your "Hispanics in Iowa" series was disgusting. Please tell the readers what is "invisible" about them. Why not mention how many jobs they have taken away from American citizens?
>
> Mexico's population explosion has wrecked that country and left no job opportunities for its people, so now they want to slip into our country and take it over.

And from Drew (1995) of Urbandale, Iowa, we hear:

> From your last two articles in the "Hispanics In Iowa" series it is apparent that you live in a bubble. I feel very sorry for those people in Iowa who believe your "poor abused Mexican" articles, because in ten years' time, everyone in Iowa will be paying for the browning of America.
>
> How about painting a more complete picture?
>
> Let's tell the people of Iowa that illegal means they should not be in Iowa, not to mention America, and they have no rights as Americans. Let's tell

the people of Iowa what bilingual classes are really like and how they affect our children's education.

And while you are at it, let's tell Iowa what "bilingual" will cost because we have to have translators in our government agencies and every document sent home from school, driver's tests, voting ballots, etc. will be written in Spanish on one side and English on the other. And let's not forget to tell our Iowa business community what kind of additional cost it will incur.

Mexicans do not only take the jobs Americans don't want. They take construction jobs, manufacturing jobs, technical jobs and they take our children's summer jobs.

I would suggest that you talk to Governor Pete Wilson of California to get a clear picture of what the real issues are because in ten years, if the trend continues, the people of Iowa will be trying to pass a Proposition 187 like the people of California have passed.

Two other writers applauded the series for the informative, multicultural focus.

Who are the people designated as Hispanic and how did they happen to be in the United States? According to the U.S. Bureau of Census (1994), more than twenty-seven million people are classified under the designation *Hispanic* (undocumented aliens are not included in these figures); this is 9 percent of the total U.S. population. This figure represents an almost doubling in numbers over the past decade. Of the total, about 63 percent are of Mexican origin, 13 percent Puerto Rican, 13 percent from Central or South American countries, and 5 percent Cuban. The importance of a common language and strong family ties that span the generations are solidifying forces (Longres, 1995).

The history of the relationship between Hispanic Americans and Anglos began in 1848 with the Treaty of Guadalupe Hidalgo which formally ended the Mexican-American War, an adventure in American expansionism. Under this treaty, Mexico ceded Texas, New Mexico, Arizona, and California to the United States; the war had resulted from Mexico's refusal to sell the southwest territories. Despite the treaty's granting of certain rights to the Mexicans remaining on the now conquered land, these residents became second-class citizens, deprived of land and social status (Lum, 1992). Traditionally, Mexico has provided a source of cheap labor for agriculture and industry, and typically, these settlers have been scapegoated when conditions got bad. When the Great Depression of the 1930s hit, many Americans including Mexican Americans drew public assistance. In the Southwest where there was pressure to reduce the welfare rolls, massive deportations (of approximately 500,000 people) known as "repatriations" occurred. It is estimated that half of those removed were U.S. citizens (Curiel, 1995). Again, during the 1950s over two million Mexicans in the United States were rounded up and sent back across the border. In the 1960s, under the leadership of Cesar Chavez, farmworkers were organized and the consciousness of the American people was raised to the many injustices suffered by Mexican Americans. Today, nevertheless, Mexican Americans suffer the effects of poverty to a much greater extent than the general population, and among Hispanic subgroups in the United States, Mexican Americans have the highest percentage of people with only primary school education (Curiel, 1995).

Not immigrants but migrants, because citizens of Puerto Rico have been granted U.S. citizenship since 1917, Puerto Ricans have similarly been subject to discrimination and associated poverty and unemployment. Since Puerto Rico is a true blend of Spanish, African, and traces of Native American, racially the Puerto Rican community covers the color spectrum (Campos, 1995). Puerto Ricans have been subject to the same kinds of racial prejudice on the mainland as African Americans have. Concentrated in low-paying jobs and as in the memorable lines from *West Side Story*, Puerto Ricans complain that they are "free to be anything you chose, free to wait tables and shine shoes."

Increasing numbers of households headed by single women, high school drop-out rate, high infant mortality, drug abuse, and AIDS contraction rate are consistent with a high poverty rate. In the territory of Puerto Rico itself, 59 percent of the people live below the federal poverty line (Campos, 1995).

Despite the educational, socioeconomic, and political achievements of Cuban Americans, as a group their incomes are still below the national average (Jimenez-Vazquez, 1995). Following Castro's revolution, the exodus of 10 percent of the Cuban population is reflected in the ethnic composition of Dade County, Florida, which is largely Cuban. Whereas the first wave of refugees were predominantly of the well-educated middle and upper classes, the sixth wave which followed the Mariel boatlift of 1981 was a "gift" to the United States of Cuba's "social outcasts." Mental institutions and prisons were emptied, and gays and lesbians were sent on the journey to Key West, Florida. Darker complected than many of the Cuban refugees who preceded them, Mariel Cubans complain that the others discriminate against them (Longres, 1995). Cuban Americans, in short, are a highly diverse group.

The anti-immigrant fervor in Florida has been demonstrated in demands that the federal government provide economic assistance, and in controversy over bilingual educational programs. Since, according to this argument, federal government policies are bankrupting the state's social and correctional services, adequate assistance should be provided for what amounts to an international social welfare program (McNeece, 1995).

TREATMENT OF INDIGENOUS POPULATIONS

Historically, indigenous people are the opposite of immigrants. While immigrants arrive after a country is settled, indigenous people are the ones who got there first. Indigenous peoples, the nations within nations, are often overlooked in the field of international social welfare. Who are the indigenous people and what distinguishes these diverse groups from the dominant culture in present-day societies? The difficulty of definition is compounded by inconsistencies in word usage in the literature. The word *indigenous* is used in various ways—in the dictionary sense, to connote originating in a particular region or country, and in social work, to denote a member of a community as in "indigenous worker" (Barker, 1995). For our purposes, the word *indigenous* will be used as in indigenous or native populations, as a relative term to differentiate the original inhabitants of a certain region and their descendants from invaders and colonists who later laid claim to the territory devising various schemes of conquest. *Indigenous* is also used to describe native tribes who have been forced into migration from the original homeland. Unique to this word usage is the comparative aspect—groups are considered indigenous only in relation to dominant groups who subordinate them in some way. The Hutu and Tutsi, for example, are distinct tribal groups spread out over Burundi, Rwanda, and Uganda. The Hawaiians are considered indigenous in reference to the descendants of the latecomers who migrated there.

Groups chosen for in-depth coverage under the rubric of indigenous peoples are the Australian and Canadian aboriginal populations. Briefer descriptions will be provided of the Indians in Chiapas, Mexico, the Rom (Gypsies) in Europe, and the Sami (Lapps) in Scandinavia. These particular groups were chosen in light of their dynamic and colorful history, the availability of an extensive and accessible literature, and geographical and cultural diversity. In reading their histories, I was searching for patterns that transcended the differences. Apart from the aboriginal Australians, the various cultural groups extend across national boundaries that were often carved out by invading or colonial powers at various points in history. The historical process is denoted in the United Nations working definition of *indigenous peoples* (1987):

> Indigenous communities, peoples and nations are those which, having a historical continuity with pre-invasion and pre-colonial societies that developed on their territories, consider themselves distinct from other sectors of the societies now prevailing in those territories, or parts of them. They form at present non-dominant sectors of society and are determined to preserve, develop and transmit to future generations their ancestral territories, and their ethnic identity, as the basis of their continued existence as peoples, in accordance with their own cultural patterns, social institutions and legal systems.

Defining characteristics of historically indigenous communities delineated in the U.N. study include one or more of the following: occupation of ancestral lands; common ancestry with the original occupants of these lands; and common culture of language and residence.

Numbering 300 million by United Nations' estimates, the globe's indigenous people have ancient ties to the land, water, and wildlife of their ancestral domains. These ties have been threatened, often through colonization and conquest by foreign invaders. Typically, the processes of exclusion, relocation, and land confiscation accompanied the spread of dread diseases, and have not only led to dependency and demoralization, but also to an awakening of sorts to a mobilization for the return of rights and, in a less palpable sense, pride.

The definitive study on the world's indigenous peoples is provided by Franke Wilmer (1993) in her book, *The Indigenous Voice in World Politics*. In a surprisingly optimistic account (in light of mass sufferings still inflicted on "those who got there first"), Wilmer reveals the unprecedented effectiveness of united, international, indigenous activism and the profound political implications of this collective action for the structure of the state. *Self-determination* as a principle of international law has emerged in relation to former colonized peoples. Before we consider "the indigenous voice in world politics," let us look at the commonality of experience among marginalized groups who were variously dominated, subjugated, terrorized, polluted, and dehumanized, a process extending even beyond the mere seizure of land and/or resources. And let us consider the social psychology of economic exploitation.

Theoretical Framework

As a basic principle of human psychology, the dehumanization of a people dehumanizes the conqueror as well as the conquered. Oftentimes mistreatment leads to more mistreatment, and initial persecution leads to blanket extermination. The key to understanding the process of this ever-escalating brutality can be found in the social psychology of guilt. Severy et al. (1976) summarize relevant findings from small group experiments with guilt inducing situations: if the guilty person cannot repay the victim fully, or if the "cost" of repaying is an inhibiting factor, the guilt-ridden person might react in various predictable ways. Devaluing victims by believing that they deserved the mistreatment is psychologically satisfying for the violater in letting him or her "off the hook." Minimization of the harm done ("nomads don't belong to the land, anyway") is a second common defense strategy. Finally, justification of victimization for some higher purpose ("we must remove the children for their own good" or "for the good of the nation") further diminishes the sense of individual guilt. The findings of such research reinforce the notion that guilt feelings are unpleasant, and that humans will act to assuage them in one way or another. Eric Hoffer (1951) in his classic, *The True Believer*, ingeniously described the intimate connection between hatred and a guilty conscience; people will go to about any lengths to keep from feeling bad about themselves. According to this logic, people hate those they wronged even more than those who have wronged them. On the collective scale, not only does prejudice breed discrimination but the act of discrimination breeds prejudice.

The basic human motivation toward guilt reduction offers a partial explanation for the imposed suffering by a dominant group on subjugated populations — the namecalling, the contempt, the forced migrations, and genocide. Removal of the source of the guilt is a very effective maneuver psychologically. This is represented by Indian reservations, concentration camps, mass deportations, apartheid programs, and the like. And certainly with regard to those tribal groups once referred to by the National Geographic Society (1968) as "the vanishing peoples of the earth" — for example, the Sami of Scandinavia, African Bush peoples, Inuit (Eskimo), Ainu in Japan, Asmet in New Guinea, Australian aborigines, Nilgiri of India, Central Brazilian Indians, and Hopis in the United States — there was no small residue of bad behavior on the part of their conquerors.

The sixteenth and seventeenth centuries, according to Bishop (1994) a Canadian community development worker and analyst of the social psychology of oppression, have given us a legacy of property, gender, and class relations that persist into modern times. And universal processes come into play whenever people with competitive, hierarchical, separation-based values come into contact with people who practice a more connected, cooperative way of life. The end result, observes Bishop, is that the core cooperative group eventually is forced to absorb and live by the competitive values. This phenomenon is especially evident with the colonized groups whose histories will be recalled in the body of this discussion.

Over the past four centuries, indigenous peoples have been subjected to every conceivable kind of coercion and humiliation, often in the name of modernization and progress. Without exception, in nations that are rich or poor, the poorest of the poor are the original inhabitants. Invariably, with regard to their poverty, the official response is justification, minimization of the pain, and racism. According to the rhetoric of modernization, people living on the periphery of the industrialized state are primitive and backward (Wilmer, 1993). To experience modernization from the native viewpoint, we will first turn to Australia.

Australian Aborigines

Often used to denote native populations, the word *aborigine* is derived from Latin *ab origine,* meaning from the beginning. This is an appropriate appellation for the natives of the Australian continent. When the Europeans first came to Australia in the eighteenth and nineteenth centuries (the first settlement was a penal colony for British convicts), they found a world which had been home to aboriginal peoples for over twenty thousand years. The attitudes of the colonists toward the Australian natives paralleled the European attitudes toward Indians in North America; a sense of moral and intellectual superiority prevailed. Aborigines were regarded as primitive, devoid of culture, uncivilized, and lacking the inventions of a written language, the wheel, or developed agricultural methods. They, in turn, not unlike the American Indians, were appalled at the way in which Europeans squandered the resources they themselves used so sparingly. In their missionary Christian zeal to convert the aborigines, the whites destroyed their social order and value notions.

Because the newcomers to Australia were mainly convicts and were brutally treated as assigned slave laborers (the floggings were some of the worst

in human history), they seemed to take a special delight in degrading the "blacks."
Robert Hughes (1987), in his landmark study, *The Fatal Shore: The Epic of
Australia's Founding*, makes this argument (p. 281): "The more opportunistic
the settlers were, the more their sense of being poor white trash demanded relief,
the more they spoke of civilization and racial superiority, reflecting that even
their diseases facilitated destiny's plan for the blacks."

When social systems and cultures are destroyed, Wilmer (1993) reminds
us, people are destroyed. First the white people took the land. During the economic depression of the 1890s, increased pressures to make the fertile Poonin-
die land available to unemployed whites resulted in the displacement of a coastal
tribe into the desert interior. Throughout the rest of Australia, even the
humanitarians, according to Hughes, could salve their consciences by reflecting that the aborigines were, after all, nomads—hunter-gatherers who did not
belong to the land. Eventually, when friction arose, the colonists went after the
tribes. Two contradictory policies with regard to the aborigines, in fact, existed
side by side. The first, that of the early governors, was to convert the natives
to Christianity and farming so that they could be absorbed into the lower classes
of the colony. The second, and much more popular policy, involved undeclared
war against various threatening tribes. The fact that aborigines had been paid
by jailers to round up escaped convicts endeared them to no one. Convicts did
not stop despising and fearing aborigines after they served out their sentences.
Settling near the tribal areas, the ex-convicts answered the pattern of sporadic
aborigine attacks with retaliation and murder. Sometimes ill from epidemic diseases, natives would come to the settlement to beg for medicine. Settlers would
trick them with lethal dosages of veterinary medicine "as befitted their animal
status." To get money, the aborigines sold their women as prostitutes, a fact
which led to catastrophic outbreaks of venereal disease as well as to the birth
of a whole generation of half-castes. The worst treatment took place on the
island of Tasmania. Here virtually the entire population of Aborigines was hunted
down and exterminated.

Brock (1993) chronicles the response of the state in "protecting" aborigines,
a process that entailed their removal from the sight and awareness of the general
Australian population, restraining them within carefully defined lands, and maintaining them as unproductive, dependent communities which could serve as labor
pools when needed. Under the Acts of 1897 and 1911, all half-caste children
could be removed from their wandering families and put under the control of the
State Children's Department. Adults could be removed to reserves or institutions.

This policy of essentially kidnapping light skinned children away from dark families continued until the 1960s. Today bitter aborigines, who grew up in church-run orphanages and white adoptive homes, are suing the government for "stolen childhoods" (Shenon, 1995). The torment of the so-called stolen generation continues with thousands of aborigines struggling to track down family members they never knew. Alcoholism, the most serious health problem faced by Australia's natives, is pronounced among members of the stolen generation (Shenon, 1995).

Coinciding with the child snatching, the 1930s saw a shift in policy from segregation and control toward assimilation of people of mixed descent into the general population. Over the next twenty years, the release of aboriginal people into the community without arrangements for housing, education, and financial assistance forced them to live in camps on the edges of towns. During the 1960s, the Australian government granted the aborigines the basic citizenship rights of which they had been deprived formerly. In 1976 the aborigines in the Northern Territory gained the right to collectively own land in the form of reserves. The population has continued to grow and is today estimated to be up to 150,000, one-half of the original number but double the low point of the 1930s. Living standards on the reserves are pitifully low, writes Schneider (1992) whose observations are largely negative. Unemployed and fully dependent on welfare, the inhabitants have given up their hunting and food gathering, according to Schneider. Education for children is rejected as a foreign institution; school attendance is for the minimal period of time required. Tribal initiation ceremonies including male circumcision rituals are widely practiced; teachers resent the educational disruption from these ceremonies that can last for months.

Schneider (1992) contrasts the historically peaceful, well-organized, and stable society in which family clans moved from waterhole to waterhole and lived in ecological harmony with their environment (the men were the hunters of game and women and children were the gatherers of edible plants) with the ennui and hopelessness characteristic of life on the reserves today. The old ways of doing things have been lost, and new ways not adopted. Urbanized aborigines, however, are taking advantage of available opportunities for decent housing and education for their children. Financial assistance available for higher education is actively being taken advantage of. Due to the relatively recent introduction of alcohol to the aboriginal people, and the manner of its introduction by hard-drinking colonists, however, the cultural resistance to strong liquor was and is extremely low. In the past, the Europeans alternatively forbade natives from drinking alcohol and offered alcohol as a bribe to get them to sign away rights (Brock, 1993). High crime and jail-suicide rates reveal the toll of widespread alcohol abuse. While constituting slightly over 1 percent of the Australian population, aborigines make up about 30 percent of the total prison population (Schneider, 1992). Aborigines are disproportionately represented in the juvenile justice system as well.

At the International Social Welfare in a Changing World Conference at the University of Calgary, Australian social work educator Janet George (1995) summarized the public health issues pertinent to the native population. Having a life expectancy twenty years less than the rest of the population, the aborigines are the poorest, sickest, and the worst housed in Australia. Tuberculosis and sexually transmitted diseases are major health problems. Reliance on indigenous health workers who can offer a holistic, culturally specific approach will be far more effective, advises George, than looking to external medical experts to solve massive structural problems.

Native people throughout the world, aborigines included, are pursuing the primary goal of self-determination or control over their own affairs. Pursuing land claims through appeals to national and international law is a part of the empowerment process. Until recently, Australian law assumed that the territory was unoccupied until the white settlers came. Then, in 1993, a high court judgment awarded a few square miles of land to the descendants of aborigines who once lived there. The decision has given tremendous encouragement to aborigine rights groups.

Canadian First Nations Peoples

There is a new indigenous community activism, likewise, among Canada's aboriginal people, collectively known as First Nations people or First People. Joining representatives of native groups from Australia, Scandinavia, and Latin America among others, Canadian tribal activists are addressing concerns through the U.N. Commission on Human Rights, a commission which through its working group on indigenous peoples serves as a forum for handling grievances against national governments. Locally, indigenous community activists work to rebuild functioning Indian communities and to offset what Wilmer (1993) terms the *ethnostress* caused by four centuries of ethnocultural degradation at the hands of European colonizers.

The story of Canadian aboriginal history is a story of barter, conquest, territorial disputes, and culture clash. In contrast with the Australian aborigine campaigns, which were infinitely bloodier, and with the brutality that characterized the U.S. Indian experience, less outright genocide was practiced in these northern territories. Admittedly, the Beothuk of Newfoundland were treated as wild animals and exterminated. Generally, however, when European settlers, mainly Frenchmen, first arrived, they relied upon the natives for their survival, and peaceful relations based on fair exchange were established. Because the European pioneers had a great deal to learn from the inhabitants of these lands, they owed them considerable respect and emulated them. Modes of transportation — canoes for summer and toboggans and snowshoes for winter — were adopted appropriate to the harsh climate of the new land. The Indians' knowledge of farming within the limits of the terrain made survival possible for the early settlers: maize, beans, pumpkins, and squash were indigenous to the Americas. Serving as guides and hunters, Indians were respected for their keen know-how and survival skills. The French, historically not averse to racial intermixture, intermarried with the native population (Jenness, 1977).

Throughout the 1700s, an influx of settlers arrived and migrated westward. For a spell, both aboriginal people and the newcomers were self-sufficient. The fur trade suited the needs of the parties involved; in exchange for pelts, the Europeans offered weapons, ornaments, and utensils. In the interests of commercialization — to procure status-bearing items — the Indians' engagement in overhunting exhausted the supply of a wide range of species heretofore plentiful. At the same time, the Indians fell victim to the demands of an external market on which they were increasingly dependent. To meet ever increasing needs, Indians unwittingly were impelled to alter their precarious ecological relationship with their world. Whether the tribes cooperated with the invasion or resisted it, however, according to Jenness, they all ended up paying the same heavy price for their contact with European civilization. The First Nations' susceptibility to smallpox, tuberculosis, yellow fever, typhus, and flu decimated the population. The epidemics disrupted most of the networks of kinship and authority that had previously organized Indian communities. Then there was the widely reported weakness for alcohol which wreaked havoc socially, economically, and spiritually. Prejudices and stereotypes were aggravated by economic conditions and the desire by the whites to acquire more and more Indian land (*Canadian Encyclopedia,* 1988).

Gradually, pushing deeper and deeper into the continent, the explorers and settlers discovered the tremendous diversity in subsistence lifestyle, language, customs, and political structures among the inhabitants. Historically, six Indian culture areas have been identified in Canada; most extend into the United States (Bissonnette, 1993). Over fifty separate languages have been identified. From nomadic hunters such as the Plains Indians who followed migrating herds of game to the more sedentary existence of the Iroquois of the east who were farmers to the fishermen of the Pacific coast, the lifestyle differences of the various tribal groups or bands were pronounced. That most advanced political systems developed among the more settled and prosperous tribes of the southeast and southwest, as opposed to those of the north where the struggle for survival was paramount, is among Bissonnette's (1993) observations.

Jenness (1977), in a similar vein, draws an interesting conclusion related not so much to geography as to time. Between the early trappers and explorers and the natives, according to this argument, the cultural gap was far less extreme than that between the later colonists and the Indian tribes. "For the Europeans who took possession of the Pacific coast," reasons Jenness (p. 35), "were farther advanced in civilization than the primitive farmers and fur trappers who had settled in the east. Machinery and rapid transportation were ushering in a new age that the Indians could not comprehend and in which they had no place." White people's laws outlawing such customs as slavery and the potlatch in conjunction with the removal of the Indians onto reserves destroyed the structure of a complicated social organization, as Jenness further notes. Cultural genocide ensued.

By the middle or late nineteenth century, relations between Indians and Europeans had entered a new phase as hundreds of thousands of immigrants settled in the Maritimes and the plains. The new dominant economy of agriculture pushed the Indians to the sidelines and backwaters of social and economic life (*Canadian Encyclopedia*, 1988). Under the auspices of the Royal Proclamation, a series of land surrender treaties confined Indians to restricted areas within which they had exclusive hunting and settlement rights. Because of the attention to native rights in this document, contemporary Indian leaders regard this proclamation as pivotal. In 1876 the Indian Act was passed, and then revised in 1951. Under this act, the federal government increased its control over the cultural-educational, social, and political activities of Indians. The Indian Act did not apply to the Inuit (Eskimos) or the Métis, however, who were not registered as Indian people.

To prepare them for full assimilation into the general society, the bands (tribes) were assigned to reserve lands (reservations). Stringent qualifications had to be met before the First Peoples were allowed to vote. Subjected to the indignities of residential schools, children were told to forget their language, culture, and spiritual beliefs. Such practices were justified by Euro-Westerners of the day in the ethnocentric belief that aboriginal people were inherently inferior to Europeans (Mawhiney, 1995). Many restrictive provisions, in short, were associated with successively more controlling and punitive legislation passed over the years, known collectively as the Indian Acts. Drawing on native women's sources, Emberly (1993) provides a pointed feminist perspective on these acts: Written by men in the Euro-Canadian patriarchal tradition, the acts ensured that native women, like non-native women, were subject to controls over marriage, sexuality, and reproduction. Their very claim to being Indian was provided through their marriage and husband. Not until 1985, after much heated controversy, were the gender discriminatory provisions of the acts amended.

Unique to Canadian history is the recognition, as reinforced in the Canadian constitution, of three distinct groups of aboriginal people—the Indians, Inuit, and Métis. These groups are culturally and even racially distinct. A population of approximately one million altogether (out of a total Canadian population of over twenty-nine million), the Indians make up over 70 percent of the indigenous total. The largest concentrations are found in the four western provinces and in Ontario.

Unlike the Indians who have inhabited the land called Canada for over twenty thousand years, the Inuit (formerly called Eskimos) have occupied the northernmost regions for around five thousand years. This distinct group of people, noted for their extraordinary survival skills and hospitality, occupy the northern area of Alaska, Greenland, and Siberia as well as Canada.

Descendants of dual Indian and European ancestry, the Métis live in the three prairie provinces where they enjoy a unique culture and lifestyle based on the traditions of their mixed ancestry (Bissonnette, 1993). Due to their mixed heritage, however, they have been denied any special privileges (such as hunting rights), an issue requiring resolution in the future.

As in Australia and elsewhere, the Canadian social welfare system of today is wrestling with the commissions and omissions of a bygone era. Poverty, unemployment, family violence, alcohol abuse, and high crime rates are among the areas of greatest concern. The statistics underscore the extent of the problem. For instance, the tuberculosis rate among Indians is forty-three times higher than among the nonaboriginal Canadians (Maclean's, 1994). More than half of aboriginal children live in poverty. The infant mortality rate is double that of other Canadians, and the rate of death due to injuries for Indian children is six times the national average (Bissonnette, 1993). The suicide rate is nearly three times that of the general population. Deaths of Indians under age forty-five are caused mainly by violence—motor vehicle accidents, suicides, burns and fire, firearms, and drowning (*Canadian Encyclopedia*, 1988). Crime rates are several times that of the general population. The crimes, like the accidents, are often related to substance abuse. Prison rates are extremely high on the prairies and in the North (where over 40 percent of inmates are native Canadians). On reserves the rate of family violence is also exceedingly high.

To combat such problems, the federal government has funded extensive Brighter Futures projects aimed at the needs of Indian and Inuit children. Prevention, intervention, and treatment services devised and delivered by Indian communities are being directed at Indians on reserves. A family violence school prevention curriculum is being developed, and thousands of health and social services personnel are being trained to deal with family violence in the home.

A major undertaking in the Ojibwa community at Hollow Water in Manitoba is serving as a model program for aboriginal people living in a climate of rampant alcohol-related sexual abuse against children. In recognition of a problem of overwhelming proportions in which the majority of the community had been victims and many residents were victimizers, the community embarked on an intensive native healing program to help abusers and the abused alike. Close cooperation between social workers and the criminal justice system has been crucial. In exchange for guilty pleas in court, the offender receives a term of probation and a mandated treatment plan. Anger management, feeling work, sweat lodges, and community service are active parts of the program. Alcoholism treatment has been highly successful, with the alcoholism rate having plummeted from around 80 to 20 percent, according to a report in *The Globe and Mail* (Moon, 1995). The Community Holistic Circle Healing program for sexual assault and domestic violence is just one of the many new initiatives underway to help restore native traditions and pride. The availability of generous financial aid enables aboriginal Canadians to enroll in postsecondary education. Many programs are culturally specific and emphasize native studies. Accordingly, the number of Indians and Inuit enrolled in college has surged in recent years and continues to grow (Ratelle, 1995). Part of the impetus, no doubt, for the attention to indigenous Canadian needs has sprung from the political activism of the past several decades.

At both the provincial and national levels, First Nations people have banded together to fight for political and territorial rights. They have been impressively successful. Recently, an Arctic ambassador was appointed to work for environmental protection in the far north where the Inuit culture is threatened by pollution from the Russian Arctic (Fennell, 1995). Meanwhile, in the west of Canada, treaty agreements are underway in British Columbia to settle historic land disputes. The turning over of non-native owned land to native Canadians who dwelled there, however, is highly unlikely (Wood, 1995). More successful has been the creation of a new territory, Nunavut, out of 135,000 square miles in the Northwest Territories. De facto self-government for the Inuit will be established by 1999 (Bissonnette, 1993). Other land claims are currently being settled in the interests of the aboriginal people as well. There are few such positive developments, however, for the Chiapas Indians of southern Mexico, the next group for study.

Chiapas Indians

A visitor to almost any Indian village in Chiapas, as in other Mexican Indian villages, will see the effects of malnutrition, alcoholism, illiteracy, and dire poverty in a community cut off from modern society because of lack of roads, electricity, or telephone service (Oster, 1989). In the face of near feudal poverty and governmental military repression, indigenous peasants engaged in an armed uprising. On January 1, 1994, the day the North American Free Trade agreement went into effect, the Zapatista National Liberation Army, consisting mainly of indigenous peasants, seized four towns and declared war on Mexico. The Mexican army, in retaliation, terrorized the civilian populations as the Zapatistas fled. Why was there this trouble in Chiapas?

Stephen (1994) hazards an intelligent guess in her survey of a conflict which goes back five hundred years to the struggle against slavery and then against the Spanish colonizers, to the resisting of North American expansion efforts into Latin America, and finally, to the opposition to the imperialism of the French. Historically, Chiapas belonged to Guatemala but later broke away. Due to political unrest in Guatemala, refugees have flocked into the area in large numbers; the Mexican army guards this border region carefully, much to the distress of the local population. At the heart of the Chiapas rebellion is the repressive political system, according to Stephen.

Today, two million residents of Chiapas live in a world of serfs and land-lords. At least 27 percent of persons who live in the state of Chiapas speak an indigenous language. Most of the ethnic groups in the state are descendants of Mayan civilization, a once flourishing agricultural people noted for their scientific and artistic achievements unequalled in the Americas or even in Europe for centuries. Left out of the land redistribution carried out after the Mexican Revolution, most indigenous people in Chiapas continued to lose land to encroaching raiders, loggers, and miners. The destruction of tropical forests for pasture involved the seizure of peasant land and the strengthening of already powerful ranchers. The trend toward privatization today as Mexico moves toward a globally dictated economy is putting an end to earlier efforts to redistribute land to peasants. Meanwhile, the Zapatistas, under strong influence of the Catholic liberation theologist movement, continue to fight for indigenous rights of self-determination. A little publicized aspect of this grass-roots activity, described by Stephen (1994), is the issuance by militant women of the Revolutionary Law of Women, a nondiscriminatory declaration of women's rights in the areas of work, family planning, and protection from domestic violence.

Romany People (Gypsies)

Quite unlike the Chiapas who have become heroes in a Robin-Hood like revolt, the people known to the world as Gypsies are universally reviled. Also in contrast to most indigenous groups, they are without a homeland or a fixed seat of government. According to *The Economist* (1993), two-thirds of Europe's eight million Gypsies live in Central and Eastern Europe. Largely illiterate, often unemployed, the Romany people have families more than twice the European average, and live in dwellings without running water. Today Germany is paying Romania to forcibly repatriate thousands of Romany people who fled Communist terror earlier (Cargas, 1992). Yet the reason for the mass exodus from Romania is the threat of violence against them as Romanians blame the gypsies for a failing economy. This treatment is a continuation of a pattern of forced exile spanning the centuries.

Probably originating in northern India (as revealed in linguistics research), the Romany people or the Rom have roamed the earth for a thousand years. As Yoors (1967: 5) who grew up among the Rom describes them, "They are in constant motion, like the waving branches or the flowing of water. Their social organization is forever fluid, yet has an internal vitality." Strong family ties, according to Yoors, provide stability and social control.

The travellers in Ireland, sometimes called Gypsies, live similar traveling life-styles and, in company with other Gypsies, are labeled as thieves and illiterates. Ethnically, however, they are not related to the Romany people. Nor do they bear any physical resemblance to persons whose ancestors came from the East. Yet because of remarkably similar lifestyles and the challenges these wanderers present to the members of the European Union, the Commission of the European Communities (Liégeois, 1987) treats the needs of the Gypsies and travellers jointly. The focus of their study (authored by Liégeois) is the discriminatory legislation and unofficial attacks by the various European countries against these historically persecuted peoples. Notes the report (p. 28): "The image of strangeness, reconstructed in each new era, is a mirror of the preoccupations of the time, evoking the uncertainties and phobias of the wider society."

The E.U. report singles out three policies that have dominated in European history with regard to the gypsies. These are exclusion, inclusion, and assimilation. *Exclusionary* policies taken to the extent of extermination policies were the dominant theme in Europe in the fourteenth and fifteenth centuries. As homeless nomads arrived, strange in clothing, language, and lifestyles, mistrust, fear, and mistreatment were inspired. In Germany, accused of witchcraft and child abduction, the Rom could be killed with impunity. Gypsy hunters operated to eliminate them. Banishment was the law in Sweden and Norway.

Then, in the most systematic persecution of all, in the twentieth century Nazi Germany killed between half a million to a million Gypsies in Hitler's gas chambers. Little was known until recently about the Gypsy holocaust (Leith, 1995). Even now, new evidence of atrocities that took place at the Lety camps in the Czech Republic is being uncovered. According to the E.U. report, the extermination of all Gypsies in Nazi-occupied countries was nearly complete. Today, the Holocaust Museum in Washington, D.C. provides graphic material chronicling the mass slaughter of the Romany people.

Inclusion is a form of socially enclosing the group so that members are under tight control. In Romania, from the fourteenth century until 1856, the Rom (this word is not derived from Romania) were slaves of the state, church, and nobility and sold at public auctions. Spain tried to imprison the bulk of the Gypsy population, an effort that was to no avail and ultimately abandoned. Austria looked to forced integration in the 1700s; peculiar costumes, languages, and trades were forbidden, and Romany children were adopted out. Due to an incredible Gypsy resistance to relinquish their cultural identity, all these strategies failed.

Assimilation or absorption is the modern counterpart of the state's effort to deal with their nomadic citizens. Forcing the children to attend school to enhance their socialization, controlling members of the group through the allotment of welfare benefits, and the refusal to recognize cultural distinctions are themes of the assimilation approach. The result of assimilation policies is not integration but marginalization, according to Liégeois (1987). The fact that the profusion of regulations enacted against Gypsies and travellers are contrary to international law is the conclusion of the E.U. report.

Today in Eastern Europe, the economic restructuring means people lash out at visible targets. The nomadic and often criminal life-style of some Gypsy communities makes them easy prey for scapegoating, according to *U.S. News and World Report* (1992). While not denying their economic adaptability, Sway (1988), in her ethnographic study, attributes the Romany belief in ghosts for this group's absolute reluctance to engage in violence that could lead to murder. Wife beatings, fights, and child abuse, accordingly, are rare as Sway suggests.

Because the Rom, in their justified paranoia, do not declare themselves to have any special ethnic identity, they rarely figure in government statistics. What is known is that the unemployment rate is very high as is their arrest rate for petty theft. Because the children rarely attend school, official or otherwise, illiteracy is a given. "No Gypsies allowed" is a sign commonly seen in shops in Europe. In the Czech Republic, the citizenship law of 1993 makes citizenship difficult for the Romany population. Mob violence in Romania has been so extensive that, according to human rights report, "lynch law" or vigilante justice prevails (Neier, 1995). People in Finland hate Gypsies to whom they refer with a derogatory term for dark skinned people (*Christian Science Monitor*, 1995). Meanwhile Slovakia, where the prejudice against the Rom (who are 10 percent of the population) is a major problem, is taking active measures to help combat this. Architects and educators are working together to help preserve the Rom's rich cultural heritage.

Hope for the Romany people lies in the acknowledgment of their existence and championing of their cause by international figures such as Pope John Paul II and the European Union. The Gypsies, as a truly transnational people, can show the way to a future Europe without borders. A growing number of scholars are studying Gypsy folklore and their astonishing resilience against over-whelming maltreatment (Bollag, 1994).

Sami in Norway

Another ethnic group whose members span national boundaries are the Sami of Norway, Sweden, Finland, and Russia who live well above the Arctic circle. The native Sami—also called Lapps or Laplanders which they resent—have inhabited the northern uplands for at least two thousand years. Originally the Sami were nomadic hunters and fishermen. When the stock of wild reindeer declined about four hundred years ago, they began to herd reindeer. Only about 10 percent still engage in reindeer herding as a means of subsistence; many are now employed in industry. Today there are about forty thousand Sami overall, about twenty thousand of whom live in Norway. Although Sami origins are obscure, the language is related to Finnish and Hungarian; physically, the Sami are shorter and darker than other Norwegians (Selbyg, 1987).

When the Finns entered Finland around the year 100 A.D., the Sami were pushed northward as they were in Norway and Sweden (*Encyclopaedia Britannica,* 1993). As their grazing land was overtaken, the nomadic Sami had difficulty maintaining their traditional migratory routes (Selbyg, 1987). When the border to Russia closed after the revolution of 1917, they were further restricted in movement.

Sami drawings and paintings date back to 250 A.D. Equality for women is a very old tradition; women and men always had an equal political voice. Newly married men lived with the wife's parents, and children often took the name of the mother's family (Jones, 1982).

While most of the Sami today are relatively poor, many have entered the professions (farming for men and nursing for the women), the arts (government support of the arts is extremely generous), and the academic world. In contrast to other indigenous people of the world, the Sami never suffered enslavement or other atrocities. They were granted ordinary rights as Norwegian citizens from the early days, in fact. The Nordic nations did try to "civilize" them, however, and their religious practices were suppressed. The sudden introduction of alcohol also was associated with all the predictable problems (Poikolainen et al. 1992). Although discrimination against the Sami is illegal today, because of the national tradition of prejudice and contempt—much diminished in recent decades—the Sami have tended to conceal their identity and language (Jones, 1982). Many have settled in large cities such as Oslo. Quite in contrast to the Gypsies who seem to be universally despised, the Sami are a source of cultural pride and enrichment for the nations, such as Norway, where they live. While subjected to the ravages of modernization which has threatened traditional forms of livelihood, the Sami are also protected, as are the Scandinavians, by their citizenship in some of the world's most favored welfare states. Mass media reports concerning the Sami are highly positive. Through assimilation, the apparent number of self-identified Sami population has been reduced. Correspondence with a college professor who teaches social work in the far north of Norway and who asked that her name not be used, confirms the reality of the assimilation process in 1995:

> The situation is that the Sami live integrated in our society, and we do not know who is Sami and who is not. Example: My partner thinks he has some Sami blood, but nobody can tell him if it is true. That is the typical situation in Norway. Many Sami people realized after the struggle about Alta river (described below) that they are Sami, and they spoke out to the press. One example is Mari Boine, a famous Norwegian singer.

The biggest threat to the Sami today comes in terms of the assault to their physical environment. The deforestation, mining, traffic congestion (which often kills reindeer), and pollution from eastern Europe (most recently nuclear contamination from Chernobyl) are forms of encroachment that threaten the Sami culture and the remaining reindeer herders who are esteemed representatives of that culture. The Sami and their many supporters, however, are resisting these encroachments.

To assert influence in both the national and international arena, the Sami in alliance with other indigenous peoples have organized and mobilized world opinion to their causes. In 1956 the Scandinavian Sami formed the regional Nordic Sami Council. Organizing globally with other indigenous groups was the next step. The World Council of Indigenous Peoples, mentioned previously, is an important vehicle for the mobilization of international solidarity.

Tactics of passive resistance included hunger strikes and civil disobedience on behalf of the pastoral Sami when their traditional reindeer-herding economy was threatened by the government's plans to build a dam on the Alta River. The confrontation over the Alta river hydroelectric power project, 1979–1981, brought international attention to the concerns of the indigenous people of Norway (Wilmer, 1993). The project was stopped temporarily. Although the Supreme Court of Norway eventually ruled against the Sami's claims, the Sami were awarded monetary compensation.

From the solidarity that emerged over the Alta protest movement, the Sami Rights Committee was born. In cooperation with the Norwegian government, the committee drew up a formal request for the establishment of a national advisory body, a Sami parliament or *Samithing*. Sami representatives are elected from all across Norway; their major function is to propose legislation affecting the Sami people (Henriksen, 1987). A second milestone took place when the Norwegian Parliament amended its constitution to ensure the right of the Sami to preserve their own culture and language. The issue of rights to land and water has not been resolved.

Impact of the Global Economy and Other Themes

An underlying theme affecting the indigenous groups discussed here and of others merely alluded to is the "new world order," a multinational phenomenon ruled by the dictates of the global economy and corporate interests. Financial development has become antithetical to social development. Central to an understanding of the forces operating to the disregard of a nation's most vulnerable people, is an awareness of the significance of the current debt crisis. Most of the international debt accumulated by the poor countries has come from the purchase of sophisticated weapon systems and other technologies by the state. Under pressure from the International Monetary Fund to improve the balance of payments and reduce the national debt before receiving more loans, the industrializing countries have been forced to reduce government welfare spending and to encourage exploitation of economic resources. A legacy of destruction is seen in ecologically damaging projects such as the construction of roads through rain forests and clearing land for pasture. Overdependence on the growth of cash crops for export to other nations in exchange for hard currencies has been associated with unrestricted use of pesticides and the displacement of indigenous peoples who have gotten in the way of "progress." Ranchers in Chiapas, for example, with the support of the government, have taken away the peasants' land and armed themselves in case of confrontation. The significance of the global market is that external economic forces dictate internal policies to the detriment of those on the periphery of the power structure. The free market economy approach considers direct attention to the preservation of the physical environment and to people's needs as a wasteful and unnecessary diversion of resources. A focus on sustainable development, on the other hand, is concerned when balancing energy needs, agriculture, and food security with ecological considerations to ensure a habitable earth (Healy, 1992).

Indigenous nations then, often considered people of "The Fourth World" (Wilmer, 1993), are arguably the most marginalized populations in the world system. As we have seen in the discussion of several nations within nations, indigenous people generally share the following history: centuries of communal living in tune with the natural rhythms of the ecosystem; openness to foreigners who eventually would wrest power away from them; loss of land which in their culture could not be owned; loss of life through exposure to alien bacteria and viruses; treatment from dominant groups and missionaries as uncivilized beings of a lower order; patterns of forced isolation and/or assimilation; and finally, impoverishment (mentally and physically) due to forces of modernization and industrialization and international monetary and trade agreements. In recent times, indigenous people generally share the following characteristics: a reluctance to accept European-derived values of individualism and ambition; the development of health, social, and economic problems; an experience of worsening of the situation due to indirect pressures from the global market; and finally, a compelling mobilization of energies to pursue demands for autonomy, self-determination, and compensation for earlier losses.

These common themes, which transcend the particulars of individual groups and circumstances, form the basis for a model that social workers can use for an understanding of the context of individual behavior patterns which otherwise would seem incomprehensible. A global perspective that extends beyond the individual case is paramount. For example, the native Hawaiians who were virtually eliminated after contact with Western sailors, found their world view undermined by the work of missionaries, and their land lost steadily over the years to foreign speculators (Mokuau and Matsuoka, 1995). Social work researchers in Hawaii have been instrumental in providing social support for community initiatives.

A starting hypothesis of this section was that, inasmuch as people do not like to conceive of themselves as cruel, they will condemn those they violate (a guilt reduction strategy) and strive to exclude them from the territory (out-of-sight, out-of-mind mentality). Certainly, the history of the particular groups in question reveals a steady escalation in exploitation and violence over time up until the present day. The pattern includes mistreatment plus denigration. And yet we would do the individual groups a disservice not to acknowledge the differences among them.

Whereas some indigenous people found their homelands threatened through the redrawing of national borders—for example, the Chiapas got stranded across from their native Guatemala, and the Sami and Native Canadians got divided across nation-state lines, others were colonized by foreign governments—for example, the Indians in the Americas and the aborigines in Australia. Still another group, the Romany people are unique in their seeming destiny to roam the earth, to belong everywhere and nowhere, and to defy the ordinary channels of social control for centuries. Viewed in totality, the degree of mistreatment varied significantly across nations. The range was from land confiscation and neglect to outright genocide. And now there are vast group differences also. While land claims are being substantiated for Canada's first people, for instance, and to some extent for Scandinavian and Australian peoples, the Romany are subjected to mob violence and banishment and the rebel Chiapas Indians are subjected to brutal military repression.

In a world often plagued by the politics of ethnic domination and narrow scapegoatism, the indigenous voice is critical: From the aborigines of Australia to the Chiapas of Mexico to the Sami of Norway, indigenous peoples worldwide are voicing their despair and demanding the right to have a say in their own future. Because the world is ever-shrinking due to unprecedented economic interdependence and competition among nations, the exploitation of natural resources—of the forests, wildlife, air, and water—native economies are dwindling. Existing in direct and balanced dependence on nature, indigenous peoples who have resisted being uprooted are the first to suffer when nature is poisoned, degraded, or exhausted. ("Landless nations" such as the Romany have survived culturally by their very refusal to lay down roots and be absorbed by any community.)

All the indigenous peoples described in this section of the chapter have been, in one way or another, survivors. For the better part of four centuries they have fought—against conquest, enslavement, plagues, and attempts at physical and cultural annihilation—to preserve their cultural identities and life-styles. And today, the pursuit of international activism, as Wilmer (1993) suggests, may simply be a continuation of these efforts.

Through unprecedented global organizing and the close attention paid to the rights of indigenous peoples by the United Nations, the Inter-American Conference on Human Rights, and the European Union, allegations concerning specific violations are being heard at the highest levels of international law. What the world is witnessing today is the empowerment of its indigenous peoples who have united in a recognition of their common status as internal colonies within their various nation states. Their claim is simply for control over their own existence. In isolation in their own countries they are often powerless, but collectively, indigenous people can galvanize world public opinion, a strategy which has brought striking results. Significantly, the target of mounting virulent criticism for its policies of economic exploitation, the World Bank itself, in 1982 issued guidelines providing for the consideration of indigenous peoples affected by bank-financed projects.

Implications for Social Work

Historically, while individual social workers have helped members of dispossessed communities receive welfare benefits from the state, provided grass-roots activities in Latin America and elsewhere, and worked in every country with indigenous clients, international social work has failed to single out indigenous populations as a focus of collective political attention. One exception, a project with much promise for the future, is the international networking of aboriginal social work educators organized by the Saskatchewan Indians Federated College; the Aboriginal Social Research Center has recently been established in Saskatoon. Nevertheless, in the new voluminous *Encyclopedia of Social Work* (1995), the word *indigenous* is not indexed nor is there any specific attention even in articles on international social work to the needs of indigenous populations. There also isn't a section on environmental degradation and the human cost of such destruction. The article on social development does present an all-encompassing concept appropriate for addressing the needs of previously colonized people who have lost their sense of purpose. Yet again, there is no reference to indigenous folk. NASW's recent and expanded edition of the *Dictionary of Social Work* (Barker, 1995), similarly, does not include indigenous populations as a category. Yet social work education has a moral and professional obligation to heed the voices of activated indigenous peoples for reasons that bear not only on their lives but on our lives. For to protect the indigenous homelands and preservation of ancient cultures is to protect biological and cultural diversity as well.

AFFIRMATIVE ACTION REMEDIES

To offset the impenetrability of racism and sexism, to keep people from being locked out of the opportunity structure by reason of birth or race, the programs of the New Frontier and the Great Society in the United States sought to provide hope to those previously excluded from life in the mainstream. *Affirmative action* (the term was introduced by President Kennedy in 1961) programs are strategies both for alleviating prejudice through encouraging equal status contact among people who are different and for compensating for what prejudice is ingrained in the society. Affirmative action programs provide for preferential hiring and admission requirements (for example, admission to graduate school) for minority applicants, including women.

Passed by the U.S. Congress in 1964, the Civil Rights Act was hailed as a triumph in the history of race relations. Discrimination on grounds of race, color, religion, national origin, or sex was forbidden. Racial segregation as ingrained in the law was dead. An Equal Opportunity Commission was established to enforce the provision. The balance of racial power did not shift, however, and for the most part African Americans continued to be economically and politically deprived (Karger and Stoesz, 1990). Affirmative action strategies were conceived as a necessary pro-active stance that went beyond simple nondiscrimination policies. Rigorously enforced affirmative action policies by educational institutions have done much to increase racial and ethnic diversity among faculty and students alike. African, Hispanic, and Asian Americans have been able to move into the middle class professions through enhanced educational opportunities. For African Americans, indeed, one of the cruel ironies of the upward mobility of so many is that the plight of the poorest blacks has worsened thereby. The mass exodus of the middle class from the inner cities has depleted these neighborhoods of leadership and a strong financial base. Role models today, in some areas, are likely to be those who live outside the law—pimps and drug dealers—who achieve material wealth and social clout. In some circles, a training school or prison record has become a badge of honor.

Affirmative action has benefited women tremendously. When the professional doors were closed to them, and the place of middle-class white women was thought to be in the home, professional schools were reluctant to admit women. "A waste of resources," they said, "to admit coeds." Although sex discrimination still exists, female doctors, lawyers, police officers, and professors are so plentiful, it is hard for the younger generation to realize they were once regarded as freaks. An interesting sidelight buried in history is that the word *sex* was originally included in the Civil Rights Act as a diversionary tactic by a hostile southern senator who wished to defeat the bill. Without any fanfare, however, it passed. For years, not until the early 1970s when women's liberation got underway, was the inclusion of gender even noticed. Once the Equal Opportunity Commission decided to enforce the law in the area of gender discrimination as well as race discrimination, women were able to assert their claims with regard to equality. As with African Americans, however, many women have been unable to escape society's impoverishment of them inherent in the social structure. As with all minorities, a backlash against affirmative action has set in, a backlash fueled by conservative, angry ideology. Before delving into the extent of this backlash, let us look at efforts to remedy discrimination against one additional vulnerable group—the disabled.

Protection for Disability

Negativism toward those with physical blemishes harks way back to ancient history when imperfect infants were eliminated. Much later "defective persons" were thrown in concentration camps in Nazi Germany for experimentation and extermination. In the present day, persons who are handicapped, especially those who are mentally retarded or extremely obese are the butt of endless jokes and ridicule. Disabled persons, in short, still face discrimination, restrictions, and resentment.

Spurred by the civil rights movement in the 1950s and 1960s, a consciousness of injustice awakened persons with physical and mental disabilities (Zastrow, 1993). Disabled persons and their families began speaking out against and seeking legal action to end job discrimination, limited educational opportunities, and architectural barriers. Because of the body beautiful cult in the United States and the documented preference in hiring for those who are tall, slim, and physically fit, persons with disabilities have found it necessary to lobby for protection against job discrimination. In 1973 Congress passed the Vocational Rehabilitation Act, one section of which includes an affirmative action policy wherein employers who receive federal funds must demonstrate efforts to hire persons with disability. The Education for all Handicapped Children Act, enacted in 1975, mandated that education be open to all children. In other words, children with various mental and physical impairments were to be mainstreamed. In 1990 the Americans with Disabilities Act prohibited discrimination in employment or through limiting access to public buildings. Canada, New Zealand, and Australia, similarly, have granted disabled people wide-ranging rights. In Britain, however, despite intensive lobbying from pressure groups, resistance over the high cost of making buildings and mass transit accessible has stalled appropriate legislation on this matter (*Economist,* 1995).

Due to wars, birth defects, and poor health care, disability is an ongoing problem worldwide. As a result of United Nations leadership, more useful information and statistical data have been collected since the early 1980s. In general, according to Seipel (1994), disabled persons in the poorest regions of the world are over-represented in the illiterate and minimal education categories. Moreover, employment opportunities are extremely limited; even in the industrialized nations disabled persons are more often directed to welfare systems than to labor markets. Japan, Egypt, and Sweden, however, reserve a certain number of public sector jobs for disabled persons who are unemployed. These and other countries use shelter workshops to provide rehabilitation and employment for the severely disabled. Activities inspired, in part, by the U.N.'s Decade of Disabled Persons (1983–1992) were geared toward the prevention of disability problems (Seipel, 1994). Worldwide immunization, disease control, and international workshop strategies have been launched on a mass scale.

Norway provides an example of grass-roots activity initiated at the level of the marginalized group itself and ultimately adopted by the government despite a storm of resistance from those who would preserve the status quo. Ingstad (1995) describes how the situation came about. In 1965, the journalist father of a mentally retarded child took the other parents of disabled children and social workers in institutions to task the institutions' neglect of disabled children who were kept hidden away. From the first step, the movement kept growing and an association called Justice for the Handicapped was formed. Today an umbrella organization represents all forms of disability and is in direct dialogue with the government. The key themes of the new discourse are integration, normalization, and decentralization (community control). All state institutions and special schools recently were closed down. Community and home care have been generously funded.

Affirmative Action in Various Countries

While use of quotas in the United States has fallen out of favor, Sweden, the United Kingdom, and Bangladesh impose quotas unabashedly to ensure female representation. Through this system, Sweden is now the one country in the world where the government consists of 50 percent women. This accomplishment was achieved when the political parties required some men to step down from re-election so that women could run for office in their place. Norway uses a gender quota system in employment. In the United Kingdom, the Labour Party provided leadership in affirmative action for women by declaring that one quarter of Labour's representatives will be women. This policy recently has been discontinued, however, due to a male political backlash. Bangladesh imposes a small female quota of at least 10 percent for high level civil service jobs, while Pakistan reserves 5 percent of all government jobs for women.

Since 1971, the multiculturalism policy has been the Canadian federal government's response to the call for increasing racial and ethnic diversity (Christensen, 1995). Since the 1980s, in fact, Canadian demographics have changed dramatically as a result of immigration from non-European countries. This, at a time when the government has had to respond to calls from various ethnic groups and native peoples to shift the focus from French and English cultures to cultural diversity. Accordingly, there is now a separate Department of Multiculturalism and Citizenship with a minister to implement policies ensuring equal employment and advancement. The equality clause of the Canadian Constitution's Charter of Rights and Freedoms, enacted in 1982, provides for affirmative action programs for amelioration of conditions of disadvantage including race, ethnic origin, color, sex, religion, and physical disability. According to Christensen, women have been the chief beneficiaries of affirmative action legislation. Equality rights for persons who are disabled are included in the Constitution's Federal Charter also. Provincial governments generally have enacted legislation to reinforce the intentions of the charter (Basbaum, 1995). Various vocational rehabilitation programs have been in effect for some time. As in other countries, the public mood and job crisis have led to consistent calls for reductions in government spending and criticism of programs geared toward the disadvantaged.

In Japan, where the male/female wage gap is extremely high compared to other advanced economies and where research on the role of women in labor is in its infancy, affirmative action policies are beginning, very slowly, to make inroads. The passage of the Japanese Equal Employment Opportunity Law in 1986 brought promising results at first, but then when recession hit after 1990, female workers found they lacked adequate protection to ensure their full work force participation (MiSook, 1994).

In India, affirmative action programs have been in place since the country's independence in 1947 to protect members of the scheduled castes ("untouchables") and aboriginal tribes. Under a stringent quota system, which is the most extensive in the world, more than half of all government and educational jobs are permanently reserved for caste minorities. For decades, such groups have been guaranteed special places in government and educational employment. Today a controversial effort is underway to extend benefits to other lower castes. Such a proposal would weaken the priority given to the present protected classes. Opposition from powerful upper-caste members is creating a rash of protests, some involving public suicides by self-immolation (Blank, 1995).

While enthusiasm for affirmative action is waning worldwide, to use an understatement, the new government in South Africa is taking action to remedy a situation in which people of color are stuck in low-wage, low-skilled jobs following years of apartheid. The policy, according to a spokesperson on a National Public Radio broadcast (1995), is "not retribution but restitution, a positive discrimination." While white workers no doubt feel threatened and the mining industry has shown resistance, other industries welcome the opportunity to attract a diversified labor force.

Race relations have been a primary concern in Britain following the influx of immigrants from the Commonwealth beginning in the 1960s and drastically changing the racial composition of the country from that time on. At first, in fact, the British government denied there was a problem, but then in 1976 the Race Relations Act authorized local authority departments, such as social services, to work to eliminate discrimination and to promote equality of opportunity. A series of riots in black communities (the British use the term *black* to refer to persons of Asian as well as African ancestry) intensified the government's concern that remedies to racism be found. Consistent with the state's belated recognition that racism is endemic in British society, social work departments have devised anti-racist and anti-discriminatory course curricula (Bhatti-Sinclair, 1994). Often issues of gender, race, disability, and sexual orientation are taught together under the rubric, Issues of Discrimination, as for example, at the Universities of Southampton and Sheffield. Paradoxically, however, due to shifting allegiances at the highest levels, the providers of such course content are under government pressure to beware of "ideologically loaded" offerings (Dominelli, 1994).

Backlash

The backlash against immigrants (those who take jobs away) and persons on "welfare" (those who "refuse" to take jobs) is often voiced as a disenchantment with affirmative action. "You have to be black, female, in a wheelchair, and bilingual to get a job these days," or so goes the typical American complaint by the dominant group. In Britain it is said, "You become so politically correct in trying to achieve equality that you become stupid with it." In India, Hindu mobs killed two dozen Muslims to protest a ten minute news broadcast in the language spoken by Muslims (Black, 1995). And Indian university campuses are in turmoil over the government's efforts to expand affirmative action (Dube, 1995).

The assault on affirmative action worldwide is gathering strength from a slow-growth economy, stagnant middle-class incomes, and corporate downsizing, all of which make the question of who gets hired or fired an issue close to home (Roberts, 1995). The stress on work and merit is ingrained in Anglo-American culture. Consistent with this tradition, conservative columnist Samuelson (1995: 51) explains the unpopularity of mandatory policies of affirmative action as revealed in a national survey of whites: "It is wildly unpopular because it offends most Americans' belief that individual effort and reward should be connected." In fact, argues Samuelson, mandatory policies establishing racial and gender preferences are already being slowly dismantled by court order and state policies. The suspension of affirmative action student admissions policies in the California university system is a case in point.

The widely publicized argument of Herrnstein and Murray's *The Bell Curve* (1994) that blacks as a group are intellectually inferior to whites and Asians plays into public anxieties over so-called preferential hiring. The message of this controversial book is that a dream of a truly integrated society is just that—a dream—and policies to lift the poor out of poverty are futile. Affirmative action, according to this view, poisons race relations by promoting unqualified blacks. The preferential policies of the "old boys' club" are not acknowledged. Whether the supporters or opponents of affirmative action will win out or whether, as

Roberts (1995) suggests, a possible compromise will be reached focusing eligibility on class instead of on race or gender remains to be seen. Whether the society will lean toward policies of equality or privilege may depend on which faction has the loudest voice.

HEALING, EMPOWERMENT, AND BECOMING AN ALLY

We as humans are both oppressor and oppressed incarnate. We carry around inside of us the guilt (collective or individual) of those who hurt or have hurt others and the pain of being despised by reason of group membership. The form that oppression takes is affected greatly by the particular history of the group in question; sometimes different histories make enemies of people experiencing different forms of oppression (Bishop, 1994). Thus African Americans may attack Koreans or Jews and Canadian First Nations people may refuse to unite with blacks against racism, while visible minorities may envy those whose differences are less visible (persons with some forms of disability and gays/lesbians/bisexuals). The divisions between people can be used by supporters of the status quo to prevent the marginalized groups from coming together for empowerment.

When society's blaming of the downtrodden, voiced at the individual and media levels, becomes thoroughly internalized, the oppressed are rendered ineffectual. For example, middle-class women from the fifties "towed the line" or conformed to narrowly defined standards of femininity so as not to be thought masculine or "castrating." The journey from victim to survivor to activist is a journey of many miles. Bishop (1994: 79) describes the process:

> The oppression cycle makes it very difficult to organize the kind of social justice actions required to build a co-operative society. What makes justice possible is the amazing ability of human beings to grow in consciousness and to heal.

Healing requires self-awareness and location of the causes of pain and the learning of new ways of thinking and feeling. One-on-one work with a therapist as guide may help objectify one's personal experience and prepare the oppressed person to *externalize* anger which may have been turned within. With the ultimate goal of therapy as liberation, personal and political, the multiculturally-oriented therapist works with the client in realizing the connection between personal disempowerment—as a woman, as a person of color, as a foreigner—and society's institutionalized prejudice. Wilson and Anderson (1995) have developed a social work practice model incorporating five dimensions of empowerment: personal, social, educational, economic, and political. The attainment of social justice and equality for all groups in a society is the goal of the political dimension of empowered social work practice, according to this model. The process involves consciousness raising activities in which participants mutually enhance their ability to comprehend their "situation as an historical reality susceptible of transformation" (Friere, 1993: 66). Mutually reinforcing and supportive gatherings working toward tangible social change link the personal and political and help overcome the internalized oppression that is characteristic of marginalized people.

Approaching cultural heritage as a kind of sacred realm, family therapists in Greater Wellington, New Zealand, allow only Maori staff to work with Maori clients (the Maori are a native people originally from Polynesia), and European staff with European clients (Markowitz, 1994). According to their approach, therapy and community building are synonymous. As a result of the family centre's work, clients have created tenants' unions and unemployed people's unions; they have fought for better housing and welfare laws. The team insists, according to Markowitz, that there is no healing in isolation and that the root of the clients' problems is in their disconnection from a vitalizing sense of belonging and meaning. Similar ways of healing are being employed in North America where First Nations people are developing their own traditionally-based, ritualized programs. In Canada, the principle of self-determination is interpreted to mean that the indigenous people alone can reaffirm their traditional beliefs and customs and educate their own people in their own schools of social work for this purpose. They are also educating non-Natives who can learn from aboriginal folk knowledge about the art of healing (Mawhiney, 1995).

In her work in breaking the cycle of oppression, Bishop (1994) finds that anger, sharing grief, and above all, friendship are sources of power. People linked in a joint struggle, according to Bishop, lose their sense of society-induced shame. They are able through consciousness and healing to move beyond oppression and become allies to other oppressed groups. For a relevant description of one social worker's powerful transformative experience, see box 10.2.

BOX 10.2

CONSCIOUSNESS RAISING AGAINST OPPRESSION

The following empowerment exercise was presented at the feminist social workers Fem School Gathering in Bowling Green, Kentucky, 1994. The purpose of the exercise is to raise awareness of the existence of oppression in our society and of ways that a negative event can be a turning point toward a transformation or new beginning. The results of the exercise, when shared, make participants aware of ways that oppressive processes can be stopped and of strengths in the community.

Participants pair off; each with a partner who will read back to the group the other's response. Each participant fills in the blanks of this exercise with regard to an instance of oppression as follows:

I heard: _____

I saw: _____

I smelled: _____

I tasted: _____

I felt: _____

This to me was: _____

One participant provided the following compelling response which was recorded and read out by her partner. It demonstrates the spiraling effect of saying no.

Opinion

I *heard* a group of people talking, I heard shuffling of chains. A man's voice. A psychiatrist's voice — white psychiatrist — saying everyone should close the doors. Everyone should lock this child out if she leaves my session. I *saw* two adult men carrying an overweight thirteen-year-old African American girl who was screaming out of her dorm room. I saw frightened children. I saw panicked faces, angry faces. I *smelled* heat, sweat, grass. I *tasted* my saliva — salty saliva. I *felt* tension in my hands. Pressure. Rapid heart beat. Pressure in my ears, my head. Probably fear. Anger. *This to me* was racism, sexism . . . oppression. And it was social work.

I said *no*. I will never close the door. This is not the social work I will do. I resisted. I took a risk. I sought support from my supervisor and co-workers. My supervisor was scared but took a stand. We both went on to be life-long activists working to transform the world — and social work along the way. To me this was resistance, taking risks and building alliances. It was *solidarity*.

CONCLUSION AND SUMMARY

This is a chapter of isms—sectarianism, sexism, heterosexism, ethnocentrism, and racism, all forms of oppression and disempowerment. Although the focus was on the process of marginalization, a process that differs only in degree from one part of the globe to another, suppression of the weak by the strong, of those who have not by those who have, and of those who are just somehow different, seemingly is universal. But so also is empathy, appreciation, and a desire to help. Today, while nations are torn internally and political repression is widespread, there is a global awareness of sorts. The United Nations sponsored world conferences on social development, poverty, and women are bolstering this awareness. If liberation for the world's oppressed peoples comes, it will come only through international solidarity (thinking globally) in combination with grass-roots organization (acting locally).

Some of the greatest headway is being made, as we have seen, by one of creation's ancient and least powerful groups, the indigenous peoples of the world. Devoid of military might, political power, or wealth, somehow through persistence and international unity, these people—for example the North American natives, the Australian aborigines, the Sami of Scandinavia—have spoken before the councils of the world. They have gained many allies and aroused the conscience of nations. Preservation of aboriginal cultures is now viewed as an important goal which has aroused the conscience of nations. The world's women, likewise, have come to realize that in order to break the chains of religious fundamentalism they must bury their ethnic and political differences and seek common ground.

Common ground among women and their allies is found in the United States in Wisconsin and California where political attack has been launched against single welfare mothers; in Sudan where prepubescent girls are genitally mutilated because the men require it; in Delhi, India, where young brides are burned on a regular basis; in China where female children are vanishing from the population; and universally where women of the world are coming together to demand their human rights.

Commonality exists also among gays and lesbians who are subject to horrible hate crimes in New York City; in Colombia where death squads put homosexuals at grave risk; in Iran where execution is the official punishment for sodomy, and in Costa Rica where officials sexually abuse lesbians and gay males in custody. Gays and lesbians of the world who have also united over the AIDS issue are now belatedly taking their concerns to the world.

Those who are oppressed, as we know from social psychology, tend to turn on themselves and each other. Each way of "taking it out" is a form of displaced aggression (see chapter 1). Thus in the jail suicides of intoxicated aborigines in Sydney, Australia, and Vancouver, Canada, there is common ground. Likewise with aggression: we can see this in the gang fights among immigrant youth in Toronto, Canada, and in the wife beatings by migrant workers in rural Texas.

One area where commonality exists but where it is barely recognized is in the impact of global market. With regard to cutthroat international competition there is common ground: in Waverly, Iowa, where family farmers struggle for a fair price for their products; in the jungles of Brazil where the rain forests are removed for cash crop farming with dire consequences for the indigenous population; in Bucharest, Romania, where the economic crisis of the free market leads to vicious attacks on the Romany people; in Mexico City, Mexico, where small businesses are folding due to their inability to compete against the cheap mass produced items coming in from abroad.

Conversely, when people come together, there is hope. Sharing power to shape society and shaping society to share power are more than distant ideals for the world's minorities; they are matters of survival. Two general conclusions emerge from this study of disparate marginalized groups around the world: the importance of self-determination and community empowerment so that the people can determine their own needs and how to meet them, and the momentum of global awareness inspired by the international standards of the United Nations and nongovernmental human rights organizations. If there is any hope for improvement in the living standards for marginalized people, the chances are it will come through some form of collective activity reinforced by external pressure.

In the next chapter we will take a closer look at human rights and human rights violations as recognized in international law. Subjects such as treatment of criminals, enforced labor, prostitution, and war crimes will be addressed.

REVIEW QUESTIONS

1. Discuss the term marginalization and various groups that fit under this rubric.
2. Give some examples of hate crimes. What are the United States and Canada doing to try to stop them?

3. Discuss religious fundamentalism as a force in world politics.
4. Explore and explain the link between child abuse and political violence with reference to events in Northern Ireland.
5. Compare the themes of *Price of Honor* and *Warrior Marks*.
6. Is there a worldwide backlash against women? Discuss.
7. What does box 10.1 tell us about the women of Bulgaria?
8. What is "the case of the missing females"?
9. How can the Fourth World Conference on Women be considered historic?
10. Illustrate instances of homophobia in various parts of the world.
11. "There is a heterosexual, not a homosexual problem." Discuss.
12. What are some functions and dysfunctions of homophobia?
13. Discuss the legal status of gays and lesbians and some positive developments.
14. Differentiate structural and cultural colonialism in terms of American Indians.
15. "The shades of the plantation are with us still." Discuss.
16. Explore the process of internalized oppression.
17. Discuss the resilience of the African American family.
18. Describe the European experience with racism.
19. Account for the spread of anti-immigrant sentiment across a number of countries.
20. Recall the history of Hispanics in the United States.
21. Who are the indigenous populations of the world? What are some common themes?
22. How is the story of Australia's aborigines unique?
23. Who are Canada's First Nations peoples?
24. What is the background of the Chiapas Indian uprising?
25. Who are the Romany people? How have they been mistreated?
26. Who are the Sami, and what is the biggest threat to them today?
27. Discuss how the global economy affects all indigenous people.
28. Discuss affirmative action programs in the United States and in various parts of the world.
29. What is the healing process as explored by Bishop?

REFERENCES

Allen-Meares, P. and S. Burman. (1995). The Endangerment of African American Men: An Appeal for Social Work Action. *Social Work* 40(20): 268–274.

Allport, G. (1954). *The Nature of Prejudice*. Reading, MA: Addison-Wesley Publishing Co.

Amnesty International. (1994). *Breaking the Silence: Human Rights Violations Based on Sexual Orientation*. New York: Amnesty International.

Angelou, M. (1989, June 6). (Interview). *The Oprah Winfrey Show.* Chicago, IL: American Broadcasting Company.

Associated Press. (1994, December 21). Group Says Study Shows Gay Killings More Brutal. *Courier Journal*: A3.

Baldwin, J. (1963). *The Fire Next Time.* New York: Dial.

Barker, R. (1995). *Social Work Dictionary,* 3d ed. Washington, DC: NASW.

Barnes, A. and P. Ephross. (1994). The Impact of Hate Violence on Victims: Emotional and Behavioral Responses to Attacks. *Social Work* 39(3): 247–251.

Basbaum, M. (1995). Programs for the Physically Disabled. In J. Turner and F. Turner, eds. *Canadian Social Welfare,* 3d ed.: 381–390. Scarborough, Ontario: Allyn and Bacon.

Berlet, C. and M. Lyons. (1995). Militia Nation. *The Progressive* 59(6): 22–25.

Bhatti-Sinclair, K. (1994, July 10–15). *Developing an Anti-Racist Social Work Curriculum.* Paper presented at the 27th Congress for the International Schools of Social Work, Amsterdam.

Bishop, A. (1994). *Becoming an Ally: Breaking the Cycle of Oppression.* Halifax, Nova Scotia: Fernwood.

Bissonnette, J. (1993). Aboriginal Canadians: Past, Present, and Future. *Canada Today* 23(1): 3–14.

Black, J. (1995, March 27). Quotas that are Cast in Stone. *U.S. News & World Report*: 38–41.

Blumenfeld, W., ed. (1992). *Homophobia: How We All Pay the Price.* (Introduction). Boston: Beacon Press.

Bollag, B. (1994, August 3). Gypsy Studies on the Move. *Chronicle of Higher Education*: A37–38.

Bowers, F. (1995, June 28). Islamists Strike at Women in Algeria War. *Christian Science Monitor*: 7.

Brenner, C. (1995). *Eight Bullets: One Woman's Story of Surviving Anti-Gay Violence.* Ithaca, New York: Firebrand Books.

Brock, P. (1993). *A History of Aboriginal Institutionalization and Survival.* Cambridge, England: Cambridge University Press.

Bull, C. (1994, April 5). Suicidal Tendencies: Is Anguish over Sexual Orientation Causing Gay and Lesbian Teens to Kill Themselves? *The Advocate*: 35–42.

Business Week. (1992, May 18). The Economic Crisis of Urban America. *Business Week*: 38–48.

Callahan, M. (1994). Editorial. *Canadian Social Work Review* 11(1): 5–7.

Campbell, J. and J. Pinkerton. (1995, July 29–August 1). *Social Work and Social Conflict in Northern Ireland: Lessons from the Past and Hopes for the Future.* Paper presented at the International Social Welfare in a Changing World Conference: Calgary, Alberta, Canada.

Campos, A. (1995). Hispanics: Puerto Ricans. In the *Encyclopedia of Social Work*: 1245–1252. Washington, DC: NASW Press.

Canadian Encyclopedia. (1988). *Native People. The Canadian Encyclopedia*, 2d ed. Edmonton, Alberta: Hurtig Publishers.

Cargas, J. (1992, November 13). Gypsies in Terror as European Fascism Grows. *National Catholic Reporter* 29: 24.

Carter, J. (1995, March 8). Rights? Not for Women. *USA Today*: 9A.

Chao, C. (1995). A Bridge over Troubled Waters. In J. Adleman and G. Enguidanos, eds. *Racism in the Lives of Women: Testimony, Theory, and Guides to Antiracist Practice*: 33–43. New York: Harrington.

Chesler, E. and J. Dunlop. (1995, September 29). Consensus on Women's Rights Cleared the Skies in China. *Christian Science Monitor*: 18.

Christensen, C. (1995). Immigrant Minorities in Canada. In J. Turner and F. Turner, eds. *Canadian Social Welfare*: 179–212. Scarborough, Ontario: Allyn and Bacon.

Christian Science Monitor. (1995, June 14). After Four Centuries Gypsies Still Live on the Fringe. *Christian Science Monitor*: 11.

Christodoulou, C. (1991). Racism—A Challenge to Social Work Education and Practice: The British Experience. *Journal of Multicultural Social Work* 1(2): 99–106.

Comstock, G. (1991). *Violence Against Lesbians and Gay Men*. New York: Columbia University Press.

Corelli, R. (1995). A Tolerant Nation's Hidden Shame. *Maclean's* 108(33): 40–43.

Cose, E. (1995, February 13). One Drop of Bloody History. *Newsweek*: 70.

Courier/Medill News Service. (1993, October 1). Documents Show Extent of Abuse Against Women. *Waterloo Courier*: 1.

Cummerton, J. (1982). Homophobia and Social Work Practice with Lesbians. In A. Weick, and S. Vandiver, eds. *Women, Power and Change*: 114–124. Washington, DC: NASW Press.

Curiel, H. (1995). Hispanics: Mexican Americans. In the *Encyclopedia of Social Work*: 1233–1244). Washington, DC: NASW Press.

Daly, A., J. Jennings, J. Beckette, and B. Leashore. (1995). Effective Coping Strategies of African Americans. *Social Work* 40(2): 240–248.

Davis, A. (1974). *With My Mind on Freedom: An Autobiography*. New York: Bantam Books.

Dempsey, C. (1994). Health and Social Issues of Gay, Lesbian, and Bisexual Adolescents. *Families in Society* 75: 160–167.

Dollard, J. et al. (1939). *Frustration and Aggression*. New Haven: Yale University Press.

Dorf, J. (1995, January/February). Border Patrol. *10 Percent*: 24–26.

Drew, D. (1995, July 16). [Letter to the Editor]. *Des Moines Register*: 66.

Drogin, B. (1994, December 29). Witch Hunts Making a Comeback in South Africa. *Courier Journal*: A12.

Dube, S. (1995). India's Bitter Divide. *The Chronicle of Higher Education* 41(39): A38.

Economist. (1995, August 13). Disablement: The Price of Rights. *Economist*: 51- 52.

_____. (1995, June 15). Excessive Use of Force. *Economist*: 39–40.

_____. (1993, May 15). Gypsy Kings. *Economist*: 62.

_____. (1992, February 8). Thailand: Sense about Sex. *Economist*: 32–33.

Elliott, M. and C. Dickey. (1994, September 12). Body Politics: Population Wars. *Newsweek*: 22–26.

Emberly, J. (1993). *Thresholds of Difference: Feminist Critique, Native Women's Reference Writings, Postcolonial Theory.* Toronto: University of Toronto Press.

Encyclopaedia Britannica. (1993). Lapp. In *The New Encyclopaedia Britannica,* 15th ed. Chicago: University of Chicago Press.

Encyclopedia of Social Work. (1995). In the *Encyclopedia of Social Work,* 19th ed. Washington, DC: NASW Press.

Fairweather, E., R. McDonough, and M. McFadyear. (1984). *Only the Rivers Run Free.* London: Pluto Press.

Fennell, T. (1995). The Arctic Advocate. *Maclean's* 108(6): 23–25.

Fisher, J. (1995, January/February). Index on Same-Sex Rights. *Canadian Forum*: 48.

Flavin, D., J. Franklin, and R. Frances. (1986). The Acquired Immune Deficiency Syndrome (AIDS) and Suicidal Behavior in Alcohol-Dependent Homosexual Men. *American Journal of Psychiatry* 143(11): 1441–1442.

Francis, J. (1995, May 25–31). Order of Merit-Children: Northern Ireland. *Community Care*: 16–18.

Friedl, E. (1994). Society and Sex Roles. In A. Podolefsky and P. Brown, eds. *Applied Cultural Anthropology,* 2d ed.: 152–157. Mountain View, CA: Mayfield.

Friere, P. (1993). *Pedagogy of the Oppressed.* New York: Continuum.

Furgerson, B. (1995, November 19). Given Blacks' Experiences, Why Should We Think Much of Whites? *Des Moines Register*: 2C

George, J. (1995, July 29–August 1). *Social Development and Social Welfare: Principles and Policy.* Paper presented at the International Social Welfare in a Changing World Conference: University of Calgary: Canada.

Goodwin, J. (1994). *Price of Honor: Muslim Women Lift the Veil of Silence on the Islamic World.* New York: Little, Brown and Co.

Godwin, R. (1994). On the Function of Enemies: The Articulation and Containment of the Unthought Self. *Journal of Psychohistory* 22(1): 79–102.

Green, J. (1995). *Cultural Awareness in the Human Services: A Multi-Ethnic Approach,* 2d edition. Englewood Cliffs, NJ: Prentice-Hall.

Greene, B. (1995). Institutional Racism in the Mental Health Profession. In J. Adleman and G. Enguidanos, eds. *Racism in the Lives of Women: Testimony, Theory, and Guides to Antiracist Practice*: 113–125. New York: Harrington.

Grier, W. and P. Cobbs. (1971). *Black Rage*. New York: Bantam Books.

Hartman, A. (1993). Out of the Closet: Revolution and Backlash. *Social Work* 38: 245–246, 360.

Healy, L. (1992). *Introducing International Development in Social Work Curriculum*. Washington, DC: NASW Press.

Henriksen, G. (1987). Introduction. In IWGIA, *Self Determination and Indigenous Peoples*: (1-11). Copenhagen, Denmark: International Work Group for Indigenous Affairs.

Herrnstein, R. and C. Murray. (1994). *The Bell Curve: Intelligence and Class Structure in an American Life*. New York: The Free Press.

Hiratsuka, J. (1995). Immigration Cost, Compassion Collide. *NASW News* 40(1): 3.

Hoffer, E. (1951). *The True Believer*. New York: Harper & Row.

Hughes, R. (1987). *The Fatal Shore: The Epic of Australia's Founding*. New York: Alfred A. Knopf.

Ingstad, B. and S. Whyte. (1995). Public Discourses on Rehabilitation: From Norway to Botswana. In B. Ingstad and S. Whyte, eds. *Disability and Culture*: 174–195. Berkeley: University of California Press.

Irwin, J.C. (1980). *Prisons in Turmoil*. Boston: Little, Brown.

Javed, N. (1995). Salience of Loss and Marginality: Life Themes of "Immigrant Women of Color" in Canada. In J. Adkman and G. Enguidanos, eds. *Racism in the Lives of Women*: (13–22). New York: Harrington Park Press.

Jenness, D. (1977). *The Indians of Canada*, 7th ed. Toronto: University of Toronto Press.

Jimenez-Vazquez. (1995). Hispanics: Cubans. In the *Encyclopedia of Social Work*: (1223–1232). Washington, DC: NASW Press.

Jones, J. (1982). *The Sami of Lapland*. London: Minority Rights Group Ltd.

Jost, K. (1993, January 8). Hate Crimes. *CQ Researcher* 3(1): 3–14.

Karger, H. and D. Stoesz. (1990). *American Social Welfare Policy: A Structural Approach*. New York: Longman.

King, M. (168). *Where Do We Go From Here: Chaos or Community?* New York: Bantam Books.

Kus, R. (1988). Alcoholism and Non-Acceptance of Gay Self: The Critical Link. *Journal of Homosexuality* 15: 24–41.

Leashore, B. (1995). African Americans Overview. In the *Encyclopedia for Social Work*: (101–115). Washington, DC: NASW Press.

Leith, S. (1995, June 18). Uncovering Atrocities: Researcher Finds Details of WW II Gypsy Camp. *Waterloo Courier*: A1, A6.

Leland, J. (1995, July 17). Bisexuality. *Newsweek*: 44–50.

Leuchtag, A. (1995). Merchants of Flesh: International Prostitution and the War on Women's Rights. *The Humanist* 55(2): 11–16.

Lewis, G. and S. Jordan. (1989). Treatment of the Gay or Lesbian Alcoholic. In G. Lawson and A. Lawson, eds. *Alcoholism and Substance Abuse in Special Populations*: 165–203. Rockville, MD: Aspen.

Lewis, R. (1995). American Indians. In the *Encyclopedia of Social Work*: 216–225. Washington, DC: NASW Press.

Liégeois, J. (1987). *School Provision for Gypsy and Traveller Children: A Synthesis Report.* Luxembourg: Office for Official Publications of the European Community.

Logan, J. and S. Kershaw. (1994). Heterosexism and Social Work Education: The Invisible Challenge. *Social Work Education* 13(3): 61–80.

Longres, J. (1995). Hispanics Overview. In the *Encyclopedia of Social Work*: 1214–1222. Washington, DC: NASW Press.

Longres, J. (1995). *Human Behavior on the Social Environment,* 2d ed. Itasca, IL: F.E. Peacock.

Lorenz, W. (1994). *Social Work in a Changing Europe.* London: Routledge.

Los Angeles Times. (1995, February 23). Blacks Fall Behind in Family Income. *Waterloo Courier.*

Lum, D. (1992). *Social Work Practice and People of Color: A Process-Stage Approach,* 2d ed. Pacific Grove, CA: Brooks/Cole.

MacFarquhar, E. (1994). The War Against Women. *U.S. News and World Report* 116(12): 42–48.

Maclean's. (1994). A Staggering Statistic. *Maclean's* 107(50): 27.

McNeese, A. (1995, July 29–August 1). *The Impact of Legal and Illegal Immigration on Human Services in Florida.* Paper presented at the International Social Welfare in a Changing World Conference: Calgary, Alberta, Canada.

Mari, O. (1994). The Gender Revolution in Social Science. *Social Science Japan* 2: 24.

Markowitz, L. (1994, July/August). The Cross-Currents of Multiculturalism. *The Family Therapy Networker*: 18–69.

Marshall, L. (1995, July 16). Letter to the Editor. *Des Moines Register*: 6C.

Martys, S. (1995). Prairie Oasis. *Canadian Geographic* 115(7): 46–59.

Mason, R. (1995, June 1–4). An Agenda for Women's Empowerment. *Quaker United Nations Office Briefing Paper.*

Mawhiney, A. (1995). The First Nations in Canada. In J. Turner and F. Turner, eds. *Canadian Social Welfare,* 3d ed.: 213–230. Scarborough, Ontario: Allyn and Bacon.

Miller, N. (1992). *Out in the World: Gay and Lesbian Life from Buenos Aires to Bangkok.* New York: Random House.

Mills, G. (1977). *The Forgotten People: Cane River's Creoles of Color.* Baton Rouge: Louisiana State University Press.

MiSook, K. (1994). Empty Exhortation: Japan's Equal Employment Legislation. *Social Science Japan* 2: 17.

Mokuau, N. and J. Matsuoka. (1995). Turbulence among a Native People: Social Work Practice with Hawaiians. *Social Work* 40(4): 465–472

Moon, P. (1995, April 8). Nature Healing Program Helps Abusers. *The Globe and Mail*: A1, A5.

Morales, A. and B. Sheafor. (1995). *Social Work: A Profession of Many Faces*, 7th ed. Boston: Allyn and Bacon.

Morcate, D. (1995, August 10). Understanding "Hispanicization" of America. *Waterloo/Cedar Falls Courier*: D5.

National Geographic Society (1968). *Vanishing Peoples of the Earth*. Washington, DC: National Geographic Society.

National Public Radio. (1995, August 24). National Public Radio. *The Morning Edition*.

Neier, A. (1995). Watching Rights. *The Nation* 260(17): 587.

Nifong, C. (1995, April 19). Women Link up from Austria to Zambia. *Christian Science Monitor* 1: 10–11.

O'Leary, B. and J. McGarry. (1993). *The Politics of Antagonism: Understanding Northern Ireland*. London: The Athlone Press.

O'Neill, B. and J. Naidoo. (1990). Social Services of Gay Men in Ontario. *Social Worker* 58(3): 101–104.

Oster, P. (1989). *The Mexicans: A Personal Portrait of a People*. New York: Harper & Row.

Pharr, S. (1988). *Homophobia: A Weapon of Sexism*. Little Rock, AR: Chardon Press.

Pinkney, A. (1975). *Black Americans*. Englewood Cliffs, NJ: Prentice Hall.

Poikolainen, K., S. Nayha, and J. Hassi. (1992). Alcohol Consumption among Male Reindeer Herders of Lappish and Finnish Origin. *Social Science and Medicine* 35(5): 735–738.

Polumbaum, J. (1992). China: Confucian Tradition Meets the Market Economy. *MS* 3(2): 12–13.

Prigoff, A., C. Abrahams, and C. Adeyeri. (1994). Introduction to Gender and Social Development: Working Toward Social Justice on a Global Level. *Social Development Issues* 16(1): 1–2.

Prison Legal News. (1995). News in Brief. *Prison Legal News* 6(7): 18–19.

Progressive. (1995, October). Prejudice in the Court. *The Progressive*: 10.

Random House. (1987). *The Random House Dictionary of the English Language*, 2d ed. unabridged: 898. New York: Random House.

Ratelle, L. (1995, January 20). Gains for Indians and Inuit. *The Chronicle of Higher Education*: A45–46.

Roberts, S. (1995). Affirmative Action on the Edge. *U.S. News & World Report* 118(6), 32–38.

Rotundo, E.A. (1993, March 31). Where the Military's Antipathy to Homosexuals Came From. *The Chronicle of Higher Education*: B1–B2.

Ryan, M. and J. Sim. (1995). The Penal System in England and Wales. In V. Ruggiero, M. Ryan, and J. Sim, eds. *Western European Penal System: A Critical Anatomy*: 93–128. London: SAGE

Saghir, M.T. and E. Robins. (1973). *Male and Female Homosexuality*. Baltimore, MD: Williams & Wilkins.

Samuelson, R. (1995, August 14). Affirmative Action as Theater. *Newsweek*: 51.

Schneider, H. (1992). Life in a Societal No-Man's Land: Aboriginal Crime in Central Australia. *International Journal of Offender Therapy and Comparative Criminology* 36(1): 5–19.

Seipel, M. (1994). Disability: An Emerging Global Challenge. *International Social Work* 37: 165–178.

Selbyg, A. (1987). *Norway Today: An Introduction to Modern Norwegian Society*. Oslo: Norwegian University Press.

Severy, L., J. Brigham, and B. Schlenken. (1976). *A Contemporary Introduction to Social Psychology*. New York: McGraw Hill.

Shenon, P. (1995, July 20). Bitter Aborigines Are Suing for Stolen Childhoods. *New York Times*: A4.

Shilts, R. (1993). *Conduct Unbecoming: Gays and Lesbians in the U.S. Military*. New York: St. Martin's Press.

Silberman, C. (1978). *Criminal Violence, Criminal Justice*. New York: Random House.

Skinner, W. and Otis, M. (1996). Drug and Alcohol Use among Lesbian and Gay People in a Southern U.S. Sample. *Journal of Homosexuality* 30(3): 59–117.

Smith, F. and P. Stuart. (1982). Integrating Ethnic and Minority Group History into Social Welfare Policy and History Courses. *Journal of Education for Social Work* 18(3): 101–107.

Solomon, A. (1995, August 8). Yearning to Breathe Free. *Village Voice*: 30.

Sone, K. (1994, November 24–30). Line Drawing. *Community Care*: 28.

Stephen, L. (1994). The Chiapas Rebellion. *Radical America* 28(2): 7–17.

Stone, L. and C. James. (1995). Dowry, Bride-Burning, and Female Power in India. *Women's Studies International Forum* 18(2): 125–134.

Sugden, J. and A. Bairner. (1993). *Sport, Sectarianism and Society in a Divided Ireland*. Leicester, London: Leicester University Press.

Sway, M.(1988). *Gypsy Life in America*. Urbana: University of Illinois Press.

Swift, J.(1905; orig. 1706). Thoughts on Various Subjects. In T. Scott, ed. *The Prose Works of Jonathan Swift*: Vol. 1, 273. London: George Bell and Sons.

Tuller, D. (1993). Political Asylum for Gays? *The Nation* 256: 520.

UNICEF. (1994). *The Progress of Nations*. New York: United Nations Children's Fund.

United Nations. (1987). *Study of the Problem of Discrimination against Indigenous Populations*. New York: United Nations.

_____. (1991). *Women: Challenges to the Year 2000*. New York: United Nations.

_____. (1995). *The World's Women 1995: Trends and Statistics*. New York: United Nations.

U.S. Bureau of the Census. (1994). *Hispanic Americans Today*. Washington, DC: U.S. Government Printing Office.

U.S. Department of Health and Human Services. (1989). *Prevention and Interventions in Youth Suicide* (Report of the Secretary's Task Force on Youth Suicide, Vol. 3). Rockville, MD: Author.

U.S. News & World Report. (1992). The Nomads of Eastern Europe. *U.S. News & World Report* 113(16): 31.

Uribe, V. and K. Harbeck. (1992). Addressing the Needs of Lesbian, Gay and Bisexual Youth: The Origins of PROJECT 10 and School-Based Intervention. *Journal of Homosexuality* 22: 9–27.

van Wormer, K. (1987). Female Prison Families: How are they Dysfunctional? *International Journal of Comparative and Applied Criminal Justice* 11: 263–272.

Walker, A. and P. Parman. (1993). *Warrior Marks: Female Genital Mutilation and the Sexual Blinding of Women*. New York: Harcourt Brace & Co.

Weinberg, G. (1972). *Society and the Healthy Homosexual*. Garden City, NY: Double-day Anchor Books.

Wetzel, J. (1993). *The World of Women*. London: Macmillan.

Wilmer, F. (1993). *The Indigenous Voice in World Politics*. Newbury Park, London: SAGE.

Wilson, M. and S. Anderson. (1995, July 29–August 1). *Internationalizing American Social Work: Looking to Social Welfare in a Changing World for Answers*. Paper presented at the International Social Welfare in a Changing World Conference: Calgary, Alberta, Canada.

Wood, C. (1995). Populist Backlash. *Maclean's* 108(10): 18–19.

Wood, P. (1992, Fall). Re-Viewing the Map: America's "Empty Wilderness." *Cultural Survival Quarterly*: 59–62.

World Press Review. (1994). In Britain, A Black Exodus. *World Press Review* 4(2): 12.

Yoors, J. (1967). *The Gypsies*. New York: Simon & Schuster.

Zastrow, C. (1993). *Introduction to Social Work and Social Welfare*. Pacific Grove, CA: Brooks/Cole.

11

HUMAN RIGHTS
AND SOCIAL JUSTICE

The degree of civilization in a society can be judged
by entering its prisons.—Dostoevski

I n the preceding chapter, we reviewed the histories and contemporary circumstances of some of the world's most severely disadvantaged populations. We saw that whether or not these groups enjoyed legal rights within their own countries, there was a higher body to which they or their representatives could appeal. Such approaches are based on the principle, as embodied in international law, of human rights.

Throughout this volume, human rights (and the denial thereof) has been a major theme. Populations whose rights have been violated—women, children, indigenous people, immigrants, gays and lesbians—by their society or by its representatives are populations at high risk of experiencing other abuses jeopardizing their general welfare. The interaction between human rights and social welfare is complicated. To illustrate the connection on a mass scale, we can consider an indigenous group of people whose land and therefore livelihood is taken away out of a kind of vendetta or on the individual level of a child sold into slave-prostitution and doomed ultimately to contract the AIDS virus.

The principal concern of this chapter is the domestic side of human rights and of human rights policy. Because the topic is so broad, a mere chapter can

591

at best provide only an overview of the international scene regarding the pressing political issue of human rights.

Passed by the General Assembly in 1948, without a dissenting vote, the United Nations Universal Declaration of Human Rights provides an appropriate organizing framework for a chapter focusing on criminal and social justice. Some may ask why criminal justice is also included. First, criminal justice is about social control of deviance through legal channels. It is also about protection from those who violate the most highly valued of society's norms. This protection, however, must be weighed against the rights of the individual accused of a crime. To learn of the criminal justice process, therefore, and of the laws which guide it, is to learn of the basics of power, privilege, and punishment in a given society. But there is still a second reason for a focus on criminal justice, and this is, admittedly, the inherent fascination of the topic.

The key aspects of criminal justice—the crime, courts, and corrections—are part of the fabric of American society, indeed, of virtually any society. The idea that criminal justice systems are organic and rooted in society is an underlying assumption of this volume. In the pages ahead we will look at the criminal justice process with special emphasis on one undeniable dimension in the United States—racism—racism embodied in the law, and in the sanctions imposed by the law. The "ultimate sanction," the death penalty, will be examined against a human rights backdrop. Infused with ideology and emotion, the U.S. criminal justice labyrinth does not offer a pretty picture, but rather one marred by the public's seemingly insatiable appetite for vengeance.

From a global standpoint, crime and punishment will be addressed briefly for comparative purposes. Then we will turn our attention to state-sanctioned violence against a person, violence of the most brutal sort resulting in maiming and death and systematically practiced in many parts of the globe. Topics for special consideration are the human rights violations of slavery and mass rape as weapons of war. Finally, the work of Amnesty International and other nongovernmental organizations in exposing human rights violations throughout the world will be described.

HUMAN RIGHTS: AN OVERVIEW

If anything good can be said to have come from the Holocaust, it was the boost to the development of international human rights norms, and action designed to ensure that the Holocaust would never happen again. In truth, the human rights record of the Allies of World War II was hardly exemplary. As Donnelly (1993) summarized historical events, the world watched and essentially turned a blind eye to the genocidal massacre of six million Jews, a half million Romany people, and tens of thousands of Communists, homosexuals, and others. Some who were able to flee were denied refuge; no internationally based rescue missions were conducted. The Nuremberg war crimes trials which followed the war, prosecuted leading Nazis under the novel charge of crimes against humanity. Although perhaps setting a dangerous precedent for victors judging losers, the Nuremberg trials marked an important moment in human rights history. From that point onward, human rights moved to the forefront in international discourse. Two years after the trials, marking a milestone in human relations, the General Assembly of the United Nations unanimously adopted the *Universal Declaration of Human Rights*. (See box 11.1 to review the document). This remarkably progressive and concise document spells out in thirty brief articles, principles affirming the human dignity and equal rights of men and women to be protected under international law.

Three categories of rights are provided in the declaration: economic and cultural rights; protection against discrimination based on race, color, sex, language, religion, and political opinion; and civil and political rights against the arbitrary powers of the state. This chapter is concerned with the latter category, the civil and political rights provided in the U.S. Constitution and in many other constitutions of world governments. Those articles of the declaration concerned with economic, social, and cultural rights range from the less urgent rights of "rest, leisure, and reasonable limitation of working hours and periodic holidays with pay" (Article 24) to the more fundamental rights of food, housing, health care, work, and social security (Article 25). The fact that these rights are included nowhere in the U.S. Constitution (but in many European constitutions) has hindered the American people in their claims to basic social and economic benefits. Wronka (1991) argues convincingly that the United States abide by its international commitment and incorporate in its constitutions the principles of the universal declaration. D'Souza (1993) urges the profession of social work to include these values in addition to a peace and environmental platform in its NASW Code of Ethics.

The definition of human rights that will guide our discussion is provided by Donnelly (1993). *Human rights*, according to Donnelly, is a concept that refers to the ways in which a state treats its citizens. Thus police hostility and

BOX 11.1

UNITED NATIONS UNIVERSAL DECLARATION OF HUMAN RIGHTS

General Assembly Resolution 217A (III), 10 December 1948.

Whereas recognition of the inherent dignity and of the equal and inalienable rights of all members of the human family is the foundation of freedom, justice and peace in the world,

Whereas disregard and contempt for human rights have resulted in barbarous acts which have outraged the conscience of mankind, and the advent of a world in which human beings shall enjoy freedom of speech and belief and freedom from fear and want has been proclaimed as the highest aspiration of the common people,

Whereas it is essential, if man is not to be compelled to have recourse, as a last resort, to rebellion against tyranny and oppression, that human rights should be protected by the rule of law,

Whereas it is essential to promote the development of friendly relations between nations,

Whereas the peoples of the United Nations have in the Charter reaffirmed their faith in fundamental human rights, in the dignity and worth of the human person and in the equal rights of men and women and have determined to promote social progress and better standards of life in larger freedom,

Whereas Member States have pledged themselves to achieve, in co-operation with the United Nations, the promotion of universal respect for and observance of human rights and fundamental freedoms,

Whereas a common understanding of these rights and freedoms is of the greatest importance for the full realization of this pledge,

Now, therefore,

The General Assembly

Proclaims this Universal Declaration of Human Rights as a common standard of achievement for all peoples and all nations, to the end that every individual and every organ of society, keeping this Declaration constantly in mind, shall strive by teaching and education to promote respect for these rights and freedoms and by progressive measures, national and international, to secure their universal and effective recognition and observance, both among the peoples of Member States themselves and among the peoples of territories under their jurisdiction.

Article 1. All human beings are born free and equal in dignity and rights. They are endowed with reason and conscience and should act towards one another in a spirit of brotherhood.

(Continued on next page)

BOX 11.1 (Continued)

Article 2. Everyone is entitled to all the rights and freedoms set forth in this Declaration, without distinction of any kind, such as race, colour, sex, language, religion, political or other opinion, national or social origin, property, birth or other status.

Furthermore, no distinction shall be made on the basis of the political, jurisdictional or international status of the country or territory to which a person belongs, whether it be independent, trust, non-selfgoverning or under any other limitation of sovereignty.

Article 3. Everyone has the right to life, liberty and the security of person.

Article 4. No one shall be held in slavery or servitude; slavery and the slave trade shall be prohibited in all their forms.

Article 5. No one shall be subjected to torture or to cruel, inhuman or degrading treatment or punishment.

Article 6. Everyone has the right to recognition everywhere as a person before the law.

Article 7. All are equal before the law and are entitled without any discrimination to equal protection of the law. All are entitled to equal protection against any discrimination in violation of this Declaration and against any incitement to such discrimination.

Article 8. Everyone has the right to an effective remedy by the competent national tribunals for acts violating the fundamental rights granted him by the constitution or by law.

Article 9. No one shall be subjected to arbitrary arrest, detention or exile.

Article 10. Everyone is entitled to full equality to a fair and public hearing by an independent and impartial tribunal, in the determination of his rights and obligations and of any criminal charge against him.

Article 11.—1. Everyone charged with a penal offence has the right to be presumed innocent until proved guilty according to law in a public trial at which he has had all the guarantees necessary for his defence.

2. No one shall be held guilty of any penal offence on account of any act or omission which did not constitute a penal offence, under national or international law, at the time when it was committed. Nor shall a heavier penalty be imposed than the one that was applicable at the time the penal offence was committed.

Article 12. No one shall be subjected to arbitrary interference with his privacy, family, home or correspondence, nor to attacks upon his honour and reputation. Everyone has the right to the protection of the law against such interference or attacks.

Article 13.—1. Everyone has the right to freedom of movement and residence within the borders of each state.

(Continued on next page)

BOX 11.1 (Continued)

2. Everyone has the right to leave any country, including his own, and to return to his country.

*Article 14.—1.*Everyone has the right to seek and to enjoy in other countries asylum from persecution.

2. This right may not be invoked in the case of prosecutions genuinely arising from non-political crimes or from acts contrary to the purposes and principles of the United Nations.

Article 15.—1. Everyone has the right to a nationality.

2. No one shall be arbitrarily deprived of his nationality nor denied the right to change his nationality.

Article 16.—1. Men and women of full age, without any limitation due to race, nationality or religion, have the right to marry and to found a family. They are entitled to equal rights as to marriage, during marriage and at its dissolution.

2. Marriage shall be entered into only with the free and full consent of the intending spouses.

3. The family is the natural and fundamental group unit of society and is entitled to protection by society and the State.

Article 17.—1. Everyone has the right to own property alone as well as in association with others.

2. No one shall be arbitrarily deprived of his property.

Article 18. Everyone has the right to freedom of thought, conscience and religion; this right includes freedom to change his religion or belief, and freedom, either alone or in community with others and in public or private, to manifest his religion or belief in teaching, practice, worship and observance.

Article 19. Everyone has the right to freedom of opinion and expression; this right includes freedom to hold opinions without interference and to seek, receive and impart information and ideas through any media and regardless of frontiers.

Article 20.—1. Everyone has the right to freedom of peaceful assembly and association.

2. No one may be compelled to belong to an association.

Article 21.—1. Everyone has the right to take part in the Government of his country, directly or through freely chosen representatives.

2. Everyone has the right of equal access to public service in his country.

3. The will of the people shall be the basis of the authority of government; this will shall be expressed in periodic and genuine elections which shall be by universal and equal suffrage and shall be held by secret vote or by equivalent free voting procedures.

(Continued on next page)

BOX 11.1 (Continued)

Article 22. Everyone, as a member of society, has the right to social security and is entitled to realization through national effort and international co-operation and in accordance with the organization and resources of each State, of the economic, social and cultural rights indispensable for his dignity and the free development of his personality.

Article 23.—1. Everyone has the right to work, to free choice of employment, to just and favourable conditions of work and to protection against unemployment.

2. Everyone, without any discrimination, has the right to equal pay for equal work.

3. Everyone who works has the right to just and favourable remuneration insuring for himself and his family an existence worthy of human dignity, and supplemented, if necessary, by other means of social protection.

4. Everyone has the right to form and to join trade unions for the protection of his interests.

Article 24. Everyone has the right to rest and leisure, including reasonable limitation of working hours and periodic holidays with pay.

Article 25.—1. Everyone has the right to a standard of living adequate for the health and well-being of himself and of his family, including food, clothing, housing and medical care and necessary social services, and the right to security in the event of unemployment, sickness, disability, widowhood, old age or other lack of livelihood in circumstances beyond his control.

2. Motherhood and childhood are entitled to special care and assistance. All children, whether born in or out of wedlock, shall enjoy the same social protection.

Article 26.—1. Everyone has the right to education. Education shall be free, at least in the elementary and fundamental stages. Elementary education shall be compulsory. Technical and professional education shall be made generally available and higher education shall be equally accessible to all on the basis of merit.

2. Education shall be directed to the full development of the human personality and to the strengthening of respect for human rights and fundamental freedoms. It shall promote understanding, tolerance and friendship among all nations, racial or religious groups, and shall further the activities of the United Nations for the maintenance of peace.

3. Parents have a prior right to choose the kind of education that shall be given to their children.

Article 27.—1. Everyone has the right freely to participate in the cultural life of the community, to enjoy the arts and to share in scientific advancement and its benefits.

(Continued on next page)

BOX 11.1 (Continued)

2. Everyone has the right to the protection of the moral and material interests resulting from any scientific, literary or artistic production of which he is the author.

Article 28. Everyone is entitled to a social and international order in which the rights and freedoms set forth in this Declaration can be fully realized.

Article 29.—1. Everyone has duties to the community in which alone the free and full development of his personality is possible.

2. In the exercise of his rights and freedoms, everyone shall be subject only to such limitations as are determined by law solely for the purpose of securing due recognition and respect for the rights and freedoms of others and of meeting the just requirements of morality, public order and the general welfare in a democratic society.

3. These rights and freedoms may in no case be exercised contrary to the purposes and principles of the United Nations.

Article 30. Nothing in this Declaration may be interpreted as implying for any State, group or person any right to engage in any activity or to perform any act aimed at the destruction of any of the rights and freedoms set forth herein.

Source: United Nations, Resolution 217A (III). Passed by General Assembly, December 1948.

---

torture are considered human rights violations in contrast to street muggings and private assault. The boundaries between state-sanctioned and private forms of violence, however, are not always clearly drawn especially with regard to acts of war. Whereas the U.S. government has seemingly abandoned its focus on international human rights violations following the end of the Cold War against communism, well respected nongovernmental organizations (NGOs) such as Amnesty International and Britain's Anti-Slavery International continue to inform the world of systematic abuses. Extensive documentation of abuses is provided at regular intervals and preserved in public sources of information. For a long time—forty-five years, in fact—women's rights were not included in the panorama of human rights. Conceived as a largely cultural matter, violence against women and the denial of women's political and civil rights were not addressed. Then, in the Declaration of the 1993 World Conference on Human Rights, governments finally acknowledged that women's rights are human rights and should be protected as such (Amnesty Intentional, 1995).

U.S. CRIME AND CRIMINAL JUSTICE: AN OVERVIEW

The verdict was in. O.J. Simpson, a former U.S. sports hero charged with the stabbing deaths of his wife and her friend, was going home. The nation was stunned and cruelly, inexorably divided. "The trial of the century" had dragged on for nine months, played out in mind numbing detail in America's living rooms. And then, only three hours of jury deliberation decided it all. O.J. Simpson was a free man.

As the nation alternatively cried and cheered, the national polls continued to show that approximately 70 percent of whites believed Simpson was guilty while the same number of African Americans believed he was innocent. The jury's verdict (the jury consisted of nine African Americans, one Hispanic, and two whites) of not guilty did not mean the jury members necessarily believed Simpson did not commit the crimes; the not guilty verdict meant, as always, that the proof was not convincing beyond a reasonable doubt. In any case, with the use of hindsight, one can see that a combination of huge expenditures on the defendant's side with a team of "the best and the brightest" lawyers, tainted evidence on the prosecution's side, where the key witness was a proven racist and perjurer, plus a passioned summing up argument by a defense attorney likening the case against Simpson to "genocidal racism," convinced the jury. Proof given of the escalation of violence by the defendant against his estranged ex-wife and DNA evidence did not.

In the long run, whether O.J. Simpson committed the crime or whether he was framed by a racist police department, or both, is not significant. The significance lay not in the verdict itself, but in the reaction it unleashed, because the trial did not so much polarize a nation as bring a nation's attention to the racial divide which was there all along. White feminists were stunned: How could there be a near-hero worship of a man earlier convicted of wife-battery and very possibly guilty now of double homicide? How could other women be celebrating the verdict in the streets?

In an article entitled "Two Nations, Divisible," the British Journal, the *Economist* (1995a: 18) provides perspective:

> Nowhere is the difference between white and black America sharper than in their experiences of justice and the police. The travesty of justice that many whites see in the Simpson verdict has its foundation in the less public travesties many blacks see up and down the land.

Racism infests both sides. An instance of white racism displayed to the world occurred in 1992 when a jury that did not include any African Americans found the police officers who savagely beat black motorist Rodney King almost to death not guilty of charges of using excessive force (the incident had been recorded on videotape). Following this verdict came the worst civil unrest in this country in decades as Los Angeles exploded in burnings, lootings, and attacks on motorists (Zastrow, 1996).

We will get back to the racial factor in criminal justice, hopefully in a way that will make sense of at least some of what happened in Los Angeles and the nation following the Rodney King and O.J. Simpson verdicts. First, let us look at crime and at the system which has evolved to handle it.

Violent Crime in America

In studying criminal justice, the best place to start is with crime. Controlling crime, after all, is the main reason for having a criminal justice system. And the kind of crime people most want to control is violent crime.

American crime is an outgrowth of the greatest strengths and virtues of American society—its openness, its ethos of equality, its heterogeneity—as well as its greatest vices, such as the long heritage of racial hatred and oppression (Silberman, 1980). The premium placed on winning often leads to achievement of success but with a disregard for the means of getting there. Although the impact of white collar or corporate crime in the United States is so vast as to be incalculable in its cost (the savings and loan scandal of the eighties carried a price tag in the billions; the tobacco companies' manipulations of nicotine levels in cigarettes has taken a huge toll in human lives) our concern here is with crimes of personal violence, the crimes that are prosecuted through the criminal justice system. Fear of this type of crime, a fear perhaps generated more by the mass media than by the actual statistics, is debasing the quality of relationships in many communities, breaking the sense of trust, and leading to a fortress mentality. This fortress mentality is debasing the quality of American political life as well, at least from a social welfare point of view. Politicians who take a punitive stance are likely to punish "welfare mothers" at least economically along with the criminals who are punished more honestly.

Before considering the current crime figures, let us put criminal violence into historical perspective. Homicide rates were extraordinarily high in Europe during the Middle Ages and in the United States during the early nineteenth century. During the first half of the nineteenth century, all cities were dangerous. In the second half of the century, European cities were bringing crime and disorder under control while American cities were not (Silberman, 1980). In the United States violent traditions required violent solutions: Recall the mass slaughter kindled by the Civil War and its aftermath; the evil of slavery; the genocidal wars against the Indians; the vigilante violence against former slaves; race riots by white and black; frontier feuds; and massacres of labor organizers (Fairchild, 1993). Much white racial violence followed World War I, and criminal violence associated with bootlegging and organized crime during Prohibition made the 1920s memorable and set the stage for political corruption to follow. Except for a low-point in crime and violence in the 1950s, violence can be said to be endemic in American society.

The American culture of violence, as Schachter and Seinfeld (1994) contend, is reflected in the history, attitudes, belief systems, and coping styles of the population in dealing with conflicts, frustration, and the quest of wealth and power. The culture of violence legitimizes and rationalizes stepping on others who are weak and defenseless. Discussing a link between the culture of violence and personal violence, Shachter and Seinfeld (p. 349) note:

> When U.S. culture idealizes violent solutions in dealing with small and weak countries such as Panama, Grenada, Libya, Cuba, Nicaragua, and Iraq should we be surprised when people in our cities respond to their personal, immediate problems with violent solutions?

The homicide rates have fallen to some extent—from 10.5 homicides per 100,000 people in 1993 to 9.7 in 1994, according to nationally collected statistics (*Washington Post,* 1995). Arrest for females for murder and other violent crimes also declined (male homicides outnumbered the female rate by a ratio of nine to one). This marks the third straight year that homicide rates have dropped. Even the new rate, however, is three to four times the Canadian rate and nearly double that of Spain, which has the next highest rate in the industrialized world. In addition, the United States leads these other countries in the commission of rape, robbery, and aggravated assault (Fraser, 1995). The honors for the highest homicide rate in the world, however, go to Colombia, home of the cocaine cartel and a kidnapping-for-ransom scheme that is a major business (Associated Press, 1994). In Russia where the mafia controls the economic life of the country, the crime rate has escalated to the extent that the murder toll per day—eighty-four—is double the U.S. rate (Viviano, 1995). Prominent among those killed are bankers.

The nature of homicide in the United States has changed dramatically with frightening implications for the population as a whole. According to Justice Department crime data, since 1991, for the first time ever, more than half of the nation's murders were committed by strangers or in scenarios in which the relationship between the victim and offender could not be determined. In Canada, in contrast, where the murder rate is at the lowest point in twenty-five years, only 13 percent of homicides were committed by a stranger (Canadian Press, 1995). The best measure of violence in a society is the murder rate; unlike other crimes most homicide is known to the police. In the United States, offenders and their victims are likely to be youths as much of the shootings are drug related. The rate of solving homicides, accordingly, has dropped drastically.

Missing from the national debate on crime is attention to the crime that poses the greatest danger for women, and this is aggravated assault or murder by a current or former boyfriend or husband (Jones, 1994) About two-thirds of all acts of violence against women are committed by family members or acquaintances, according to government collected data (Bachman, 1994). Women at greatest risk for violence tend to be African American or Hispanic, young, residents of central city areas, single, and at low-education and income levels. Battering is now the leading cause of injury to women between the ages of fifteen and forty-four and is driving women to emergency rooms and onto the streets. More than twice as many American women are shot and killed by their husbands and lovers as by strangers. Women may go into hiding for protection. If they continue to go to work, however, they may be at grave risk of being murdered while on the job.

Despite the overall drop in the U.S. homicide rate, the increase in the rate of serious crimes committed by youths portends ill for the future. Victims tend to be gang members and strangers. Prosecutors and criminologists interviewed for a *Washington Post* article attributed the rise in these times of violence to three factors: a proliferation of firearms especially among the young who are apt to be more trigger happy than their elders, an exploding drug trade, and demographic changes in the population. The demographic change with ominous implications is the large number of small children in poverty today; these are the teenagers of tomorrow. Significantly, the population increase is the greatest among those living in areas with the highest crime rates (Gest and Friedman,

1994). Guns plus drugs plus youth plus declining social and economic conditions add up to increased crime rates. Teens in drug rings arm themselves, and neighbors pack pistols in self-defense, spreading firearms through the community as the report by Gest and Friedman suggests. Handguns are used in over half of all homicides, a proportion that is steadily rising. In 1990, handguns were used to murder ten people in Australia, thirteen in Sweden, twenty-two in Great Britain, sixty-eight in Canada, eighty-seven in Japan, and 10,567 in the United States (Frankel, 1993). The National Rifle Association spends millions each year through political action committees lobbying members of Congress to prevent restrictions on gun ownership. And the suicide rate by firearm deaths is somewhat higher than the homicide rate. With over 200 million guns in circulation, perhaps the wonder is that the death toll is not higher.

In Canada too, a wave of teenage crime is threatening the character of some of the major cities (Fulton, 1992). Experts blame the surge in youth violence on a number of social forces, including the high number of single-parent homes, economic pressures, gang membership often organized across racial lines, and movie and television violence. In the United Kingdom, an alarm has been sounded and a new Criminal Justice and Public Order Act has been passed for the purpose of bringing twelve- to fourteen-year-olds into the criminal justice system. Yet there has been no increase as such in crime among youth (Bell, 1994).

A less tangible impact on violent crime in the United States is the influence of the mass media. By the time children reach grade school, they have viewed eight thousand acts of murder on television (Mauro and Stone, 1995). There is no clear cause and effect impact, however, apart from imitative children's play on the playground and occasional crimes reported in the news as copycat crimes inspired by TV drama or graphic news reports. Most studies indicate that heavy viewers of violence are more accepting of aggressive attitudes and behavior than are nonviewers. Children who watch television violence regularly are significantly less likely than those who do not to stop other children from hurting one another (Morales, 1995). The heavy diet of violence to which American children are exposed is now a worldwide phenomenon through the international access to multiple television channels and to videotapes.

The Adversary System

In the United States, the overwhelming number of criminal cases never reach trial; they are settled through the process of negotiation between prosecutor and defense attorney known as plea bargaining. The right to trial by a jury of one's peers is virtually the only protection defendants have against abuse of power by prosecutors. This is the right to be heard if desired, but also the right to stand mute inasmuch as the burden of proof rests solely with the prosecution. Jury trials are vital for another reason: for the society, trials play a vital symbolic role as evidence that justice is being done, as Silberman (1980) indicates. Trials of major crimes provide the contemporary equivalent of the medieval morality play.

In light of the millions spent by the defense to bring in a string of internationally prominent expert witnesses and in their luck not only to have a racist, perjured police officer on the other side, but to be able to prove it, the O.J. Simpson case was hardly typical. No, the prolonged, sensationalized trial of this celebrity defendant was by no means ordinary. The process, however—the presentation of evidence and the final decision making which was revealed to the world with the aid of the mass media—is the basic means for determination of guilt that we have in this country. This is the process known to the world as the adversary system.

One of the most taken-for-granted and sacrosanct institutions in Anglo-Saxon society, the adversary system is rarely analyzed. The rationale for our Anglo-American adversary legal approach is found in its history. The history is one of the ancient customs of judicial ordeal based on magical dogma. In the Middle Ages in England, the ordeal of fire, food, and poison required the accused to demonstrate the solicitude of some all-powerful spirit. With William the Conqueror, trial by battle was brought to the island. Eventually, no dispute existed that might not be submitted to the decision of the sword or club. Hired champions represented the interests of involved parties. According to Ann Strick (1978) whose book, tellingly entitled *Injustice for All,* provides the preceding historical information, trial by ordeal is alive and functioning in the United States; the judicial ordeal is now called the "adversary system" (1978: 37).

Central to Anglo-American law is the concept of *due process*. In criminal justice, the notion of due process relates to fairness; the scales of justice must not tilt too much toward government (Friedman, 1993). Arrests must be based on evidence; trials must be a presentation of evidence. The opposite of due process is found in a police state where the accused is presumed guilty and the burden of proof is on the accused. There has been a long, dynamic process of evolution in the meaning and practice of due process, as Friedman indicates. In the American colonial period, already as early as 1641, torture was forbidden as a means of gaining confession, interestingly, except in capital cases and then it must not be "barbarous and inhumane." Colonial justice was not corrupt; judges and magistrates were respected citizens of their day. While trials in England were relying on judges, not lawyers, to look after the rights of the defendant, trials in the colonies were also lawyerless until the eighteenth century. The right of counsel ultimately was written into the American Bill of Rights. Of course, the system could never be truly equalized; criminal justice invariably would serve as an arm of the state, as a part of the social control apparatus bearing down heavily on the poor, deviant, and unattached. Friedman (1993: 462) contrasts the ideal with the real in this absorbing passage:

> Our criminal justice system—maybe *every* criminal justice system—includes an aspect that is downright oppressive. Criminal justice is, literally, state power. It is police, guns, prisons, the electric chair. Power corrupts; and power also has an itch to suppress. A strain of suppression runs through the whole of our story. The sufferers—burnt witches, whipped and brutalized slaves, helpless drunks thrown into fetid country jails, victims of lynch mobs—cry out to us across the centuries.

The adversary model attempts to resolve differences through the formalized presentation of diametrically opposing arguments; the ultimate aim of cross-examination is to arrive at the truth (Gardner, 1982: 22). Yet if we are to believe Bailey (F. Lee) and Rothblatt (1974), at every trial there is perjury (often on both sides). Moreover, in the United States, the whole truth (such as a prior criminal record of the defendant or evidence gathered illegally) is often kept out of the purview of the jury. In the Middle Ages, interestingly, when the institution of the jury first was established, persons were chosen for jury duty who knew the *most* about the crime—eye witnesses, for instance. In modern times, in stark contrast, the persons who are selected know the least about a particular crime. In the O.J. Simpson case, accordingly, the judge eliminated jurors who had read the news or watched news broadcasts over the past year. Later, critics wondered if this was the best way to select individuals for a case involving complicated DNA testimony. The goal of the court, however, was to eliminate individuals who might have been biased by preliminary news reports. To protect the Simpson jury further from influence generated by news accounts, the jurors were sequestered and guarded by court personnel. In Canada, on the other hand, where due process is emphasized over freedom of speech, the media are not allowed to print evidence of which the jury was unaware. And jurors are forbidden from speaking to the press under penalty of law (Corelli, 1995). So there is no need to sequester the jury; you might say the press is sequestered instead. In the British trial, where the formality is much more pronounced (barristers and judges wear gowns and wigs), the judge is more decisive as he or she instructs the jury as to how they should decide the case. The jury, however, is free to reach its own decision. This is in sharp contrast to the first juries whose members faced execution if the king did not appreciate the verdict.

Consistent with its trial-by-combat origins, the adversary system is built on dueling as opposed to negotiation and compromise. The winner, in a very real sense, takes all. In civil cases in the United States, the person who sues stands to gain substantially in economic terms paid by the defendant if the defendant loses. The plaintiff's lawyers, paid on a contingency basis, share up to one-third to one-half of the winnings. But from the European perspective, oddly, if the plaintiff loses he or she pays nothing and no one, not even the attorney. In both civil and criminal matters, the legal system is built on dichotomous or black-and-white reasoning. The kind of logic applied in social work resolution of conflict is markedly different; the contrast between law and social work is between legalism and holism (Polansky et al., 1981). Table 11.1 juxtaposes the legal approach with the social work *modus operandi* for heuristic purposes.

Race and Crime

While the O.J. Simpson verdict was barely hot off the presses, an equally compelling revelation also hit the news though with considerably less fanfare. The Sentencing Project, a Washington-based group, released the report that one in three African American men in their twenties is behind bars or on probation and parole (Gest, 1994). In 1990, the then shocking figure was one out of four.

As approximately 12 percent of the population, blacks' share of arrests is over 57 percent for murder, 62 percent for robbery, and 39 percent for drug offenses. Of those who go to prison for drug offenses, significantly, blacks account for 74 percent of the total. The discrepancy in these figures underscores a sentence disparity which provides harsher penalties for crack cocaine, a cheaper form of powder cocaine popular in the black community, than for powder cocaine which is used more frequently by whites and Hispanics. Otherwise, drug use is no more prevalent among blacks than among whites. Proponents of the

TABLE 11.1
Contradictory Professional Attitudes

Law	Social Work
Historical origins of the profession in combat. Use of power on behalf of client, paternalistic relationship.	Historical origins in "doing good," charity. Encourages self-determination, helps client to help him/herself.
Serious concern with civil rights of client.	Serious concern with treatment and long-term outcome for client.
De-emphasis on bad behavior of client and shift of responsibility to other forces (temporary insanity, other people).	Stress on individual responsibility for acts.
Knowledge of the field from tradition and legal precedents.	Knowledge of the field from research findings and highly developed theory (much borrowed from psychology and sociology).
Attacks individual on opposing side. System built on dichotomous reasoning.	Stress on individual worth of all parties, not viewing reality in terms of right and wrong.
Emphasis on winning, and on the end not the means	Emphasis on help for future outcomes, stress on both means and the ends.
Use of "tricks of the trade" in court.	Straightforward by nature, growing recognition the less said on the stand the better.
Attorneys usually represent clients, not agencies.	Social workers are agency representatives, hired by agencies.
Resolution emerges out of battle.	Resolution out of negotiation and consensus.
Members of male dominated field with all the privileges accorded thereby, member of very old, elitist profession.	Members of female dominated field with all the stigma accorded thereby, members of relatively new, generally underpaid profession.

tougher sentencing say tougher state and federal penalties for crack are justified because this variety of cocaine is more addictive and spurs more violence than others as smoking a substance brings its effects directly to the brain. Opponents need only utter one word to make their case, however — *racism.* How else could one explain how a sale of as little as a five grams of crack, barely a teaspoon, gets violators a minimum of five years in prison? It takes one hundred times that amount of the more expensive powder to produce a comparable sentence (Isikoff, 1995).

Substance abuse in the inner city, as explained in a new book, *In Search of Respect: Selling Crack in El Barrio* by Bourgois (1995) is merely a symptom — and vivid symbol — of deeper dynamics of marginalization and alienation, a brutal fact shaping daily life on the street. Why should these young men and women, asks Bourgois, take the subway to work minimum wage jobs in downtown offices when they can usually earn more selling drugs on the street corner and can preserve their personal dignity as well? And as Irwin and Austin (1994) remind us, don't overlook the thrill factor in this kind of work. Under the circumstances, in fact, Bourgois is amazed that so many residents of the Barrio do work legally in the subsistence wage economy.

African Americans and Hispanics who get caught trafficking drugs forfeit their future. Many nonviolent offenders and a majority of men of color acquire criminal records as a result of minimal drug involvement. A national outcry of sorts has been unleashed against the racial disparity in sentencing for drug crimes. This mass media exposure to the sentencing discrepancy has prompted some Congresspersons not to contemplate *lowering* the penalties for one specific form of cocaine but *raising* all the penalties to same inordinately high level. In this way they can be both fair and punitive at once. Before examining America's controversial war on drugs, let us turn to a comparative view of criminal justice.

COMPARATIVE CRIMINAL JUSTICE SYSTEMS

From a global and historical standpoint, often it is not the intensity or severity of punishment that determines its meaning but rather the meaning that determines its effectiveness. In a simple or closed society, unofficial sanctions carry the same weight as the most severe act of public discipline in a modern, industrialized state. As Nathaniel Hawthorne (*The Scarlet Letter,* 1960: 52/1850) so eloquently put it, "A penalty which, in our days, would infer a degree of mocking infamy and ridicule, might be invested with almost as stern a dignity as the punishment of death itself." Similarly, Durkheim in *The Rules of Sociological Method* (1938: 67/1858) envisioned a society of saints where "faults which appear venial to the layman" will create the same scandal that the ordinary offense does in ordinary circumstances."

Insofar as today's prison system is an outgrowth of society's earlier formal and informal methods of punishment, the many debates on this issue are on the ethics of social control. Culturally, criminal justice is the official apparatus of the society for enforcing the norms and preserving the boundaries between what is tolerated and what is not. George Herbert Mead in "The Psychology of Punitive Justice" (1918) speaks of the revulsions against criminality that reveal themselves in a sense of solidarity with the group.

In modern society, the majesty of the law represents the dominance of group sanctions over the individual. The paraphernalia and ritualism of criminal law serve not only to exile the rebellious individual from the group, but also to awaken in law-abiding members of society the inhibitions which make rebellion impossible to them. Prosecuting the criminal has the advantage, according to Mead, of uniting the public sentiment against a common enemy. Attitudes of retribution, repression, and exclusion have the unique attribute of drawing together all members of the community in the emotional solidarity of aggression (1918: 589).

The punishment process itself—imprisonment—is analyzed by Goffman (1961) in his social psychological treatise on "total institutions." Whether one is residing in a convent, military academy, mental hospital, or prison, the process is the same—socialization into absolute, unquestioning conformity. Locked away from the world, the inmate is no longer a part of the world. A series of abasements, degradations, and mortifications of the self assure a clean and swift break with the past. One day a person is in control of his or her own life, and the next day that same person is stripped of all personal possessions and forced into humiliating acts of deference toward authorities. To be sentenced to serve time in prison, therefore, is to be sentenced to relinquish an important part of one's social identity or, in Goffman's terms, "to embark on a new moral career." Now we will view crime and its control cross-culturally.

Despite the very high density of population in Japan, the crime rate is phenomenally low. Japanese culture, as we have seen in previous chapters, stresses group conformity over individualism, and deviant behavior is controlled through internalization of group norms coupled with an aversion to bringing shame on oneself or one's family. The low crime rate also undoubtedly reflects the small income inequality between rich and poor and the lack of a severely deprived class trapped at the bottom of the social structure. A third factor in controlling Japanese crime is the close surveillance over the population exercised by the police who are situated in the community and who enjoy the trust of the community. As Fairchild (1993), in her comparative study of criminal justice in five model nations, indicates, the low crime rates in Japan cannot be attributed to punitiveness. In Japan, only hard-core criminals are sent to prison, and sentences are far shorter than those meted out in Western countries. Japan still does have the death penalty, however.

Even though sentencing in Japan is moderate by American standards, a human rights group is checking into violations in international standards concerning prisoner treatment (Hirakawa, 1995). Prisoners' rights to exercise, use the telephone, and communicate with each other are not honored, according to a report by the New York-based Human Rights Watch. The most striking feature of Japanese prisons is said to be the silence. The major recommendation of the report is that the prison system be open to external inspection to ensure that prisoner rights are protected.

Notably, both Japan and Germany, as conquered nations after the second world war, adopted constitutions modeled on the American Constitution and including the process of judicial review. Due process in criminal procedure is provided in the Japanese constitution. Japan does not have a jury system, however (Champion, 1992). In Japan, Germany, and France, court proceedings are inquisitional rather than adversarial as they are in the Anglo-Saxon countries.

Fairchild also considers Saudi Arabia, another low-crime rate country. The Saudis themselves attribute their success in curbing crime on their use of corporal punishment as an effective deterrent—for example, amputation of the hand for theft and flogging for use of alcohol. (Nigeria has similar penalties.) A second reason given for the low-crime rate in the Middle East is the religious orthodoxy; the laws and precise penalties for each offense are even spelled out in scripture.

Mexico, like a lot of other countries in Latin America, has no predictable, functioning judicial system. According to an article in the *Wall Street Journal* (Carroll, 1994), companies doing business south of the border should be prepared for killer highways, telephone connection problems, disastrous railroads, and a justice system that operates on the basis of who you know. Business people involved in disputes may be thrown in jail for long periods if they offend the wrong person. President Zedillo commented in the article that reviving the economy, though hard as it is, will be easier than establishing a clear, consistent judicial system.

Human rights violations throughout most of Latin America are rampant, especially pertaining to what are considered political crimes of dissidence. For most of the twentieth century up to the present time, ruling military dictatorships and governments used terror and torture to suppress opposition (Luft and Goering, 1995). In almost every country, dissidents have vanished in the night, never to be found again. All told, more than 100,000 people have disappeared in this manner since the 1960s. Organizations supporting human rights such as Human Rights Watch/Americas continue to exhume atrocities from the past. As summarized in Luft and Goering's article, the following information has come to light:

- In Colombia, the government acknowledged responsibility for wiping out an entire village in the late 1980s.
- In Chile, retired secret police officials were on trial for murdering a foreign minister in 1976.
- One hundred people disappeared in Bolivia in a military coup supported by drug traffickers.
- Thirty prisoners were thrown out of airplanes in Argentina in the 1970s.
- In Brazil, nearly 2000 dissidents were tortured during the 1964–1985 military rule.

Much of the killings today in Latin America are drug related. The U.S. demand for cocaine can be supplied from ninety-six square miles of Latin America (Will, 1993). For a nation with a two thousand mile open border (and skies) to try to put a stop to a $100 billion demand for drugs north of the border could be likened in futility to Don Quixote's delusionary "tilting at windmills" (Cervantes, 1949). America's war on drugs is fought with a zeal that many observers find incongruous (Fairchild, 1993). Enforcement of this policy has important implications for criminal justice and for the human rights of citizens.

Both Canada and the United Kingdom are beginning to adopt a hard line toward offenders as well. Canada in some provinces is suspending prisoners' rights to such things as conjugal visits and color television, while the United Kingdom is imposing harsh sentencing on women for crimes such as shoplifting and failure to pay the television license fee (*Economist*, 1995b). One thing

Britain is good at, as Ryan and Sim (1995) note sarcastically, is locking people up. Both Canada and the United Kingdom are contemplating "get-tough" measures for young offenders including the introduction of military style boot camps, a popular idea in the United States. These countries want to center the training camps around a rehabilitative ideal, however.

Germany's approach is to consider crime seriously but to seek solutions outside the sphere of prolonged incarceration. The emphasis is placed on prevention and rehabilitation. Even murderers usually are paroled after fifteen years (Burke, 1994). Differences in societal structures help explain differences in attitude, according to Burke. The fact that the Americans have no answer for the poverty question inclines them toward a "more cops, more prisons" agenda. An opposing view, however, is offered by Messner and Ruggiero (1995) who believe the pendulum in Germany may be swinging back again to a harsher model. The German prison population is rising, most likely fueled by a backlash against reunification, immigration, and drug-related crime.

In Sweden, the rehabilitative ideal is very strong as is the sense of human rights. By law, custodial correctional care must be designed to promote the resocialization of the inmate to the outside world and to counteract any deleterious effect of incarceration (Leander, 1995). Many convicted offenders who serve time in correctional institutions are entitled to four-week paid vacations each year as private citizens (Champion, 1992). Moreover, frequent weekend furloughs are available to preserve family ties. Work in prison is of a kind that is an aid to seeking employment on the outside.

AMERICA'S WAR ON DRUGS

Declared by President Ronald Reagan in 1982 and aggressively pursued ever since, America's war on drugs is in a sense a replay of Prohibition, the Eighteenth Amendment that preoccupied law enforcement efforts from 1920 to 1933. The following description of this short but stormy era is adapted from my textbook, *Alcoholism Treatment: A Social Work Perspective* (van Wormer, 1995).

Of attempts throughout history to control the use of alcohol, the most resounding failure was that of the United States from 1920 to 1933 (*Encyclopaedia Britannica,* 1993). The American experiment with prohibition—the "noble experiment"—gave drinking the allure of the forbidden and led to the burgeoning and glamorizing of crime, the growth of organized crime, the corruption of the police and politicians, and the criminalizing of ordinary citizens.

The brother of Mafia godfather Sam Giancana gives, in *Double Cross* (1992), a graphic account of what began in Chicago during the years of prohibition—the Mafia/Hollywood/Las Vegas/Washington, D.C., connection that continues to the present day (Giancana and Giancana, 1992: 227):

> (Joseph) Kennedy's ties to the underworld intersected a hundred points. Besides making a fortune in bootlegging, Kennedy had made a financial killing in Hollywood in the twenties—with the help of behind-the-scenes persuasion with New York and Chicago muscle. When Prohibition came to a close, as part of a national agreement between the various bootleggers, Kennedy held on to three of the most lucrative booze distributorships in the country—Gordon's gin, Dewar's, and Haig & Haig—through his company, Somerset Imports.

If the attempt was noble, the end result was sad. Although the quantity of alcohol consumed did go down as did the cirrhosis of the liver rate, the overall social consequences were devastating. As Thornton (1992) argues, the potency of the alcohol that was manufactured increased about 150 percent or higher compared to what was produced before or after Prohibition. Those products also were likely to contain dangerous adulterants. The death rate from poisoned liquor was appallingly high at this time. Homicide rates in large cities increased by 78 percent over the pre-Prohibition figures. As Thornton notes, the lessons of Prohibition remain important today. They apply not only to the debate over the war on drugs but also to such issues as censorship and bans on insider trading, abortion, and gambling.

Economic interests played a role in the impetus to repeal, as they had in the impetus to criminalize. Corporate moguls such as John D. Rockefeller believed that a repeal would lower income taxes by substituting taxes on alcohol (Helzer and Canino, 1992). The widespread disrespect for the law that had developed made people realize that the cure had become worse than the original problem. Moreover, the Depression created a desperate demand for more jobs and government revenue, and a hope that perhaps the reestablishment of the liquor industry could help in this regard. Besides, the new immigration quotas stemmed the tide of immigration and the public had associated drinking with immigration. In 1933, the Eighteenth Amendment was repealed.

Today, the legacy of Prohibition prevails. Age-restrictive laws have been instituted against use of tobacco and alcohol. In the South, dry counties and townships still outlaw the sale of alcohol, while Sunday sales of alcohol are illegal in many places.

Then there is the war on drugs. Like its predecessor, the war on drugs is a desperate attempt to curb the unstoppable. The focus is placed on punishment rather than on treatment—more Americans are imprisoned for drug offenses than for property crimes (Will, 1993), 70 percent of the federal government's expenditure on the drug problem goes to law enforcement agencies, and just 30 percent for prevention and treatment (Mauer, 1995). Criminalizing the use of a highly pleasurable (to some) and addictive substance (to others) raises the rate of crimes committed to procure the substance. Putting drug dealers in jail boosts the price of drugs thus making the selling of them more lucrative. A high percentage of murders among the young in urban areas is over this business. (During Prohibition, similarly, the murder rate soared.)

Drug offenders now make up more than half of all the inmates in federal prisons; violent criminals are released early to make room for nonviolent drug offenders who are incarcerated on mandatory-length prison terms. Moreover, as law professor Wisotsky (1993) argues, public safety is sacrificed when law enforcement efforts are diverted from more serious crimes to crimes such as possession of marijuana. Higher taxes are raised to pay for this all-out effort and for the new jails and prisons being built to hold all those arrested and convicted.

Relevant to the human rights theme of this chapter, Wisotsky laments the substantial erosion of constitutional protections that have resulted from the drug-use crack-down. The war on drugs, he states, is a war on the rights of all of us, directed not against the drugs themselves but against the people. With virtually everyone a suspect, all citizens must be observed, checked, screened, and tested continually. Law enforcement officials joined by U.S. military forces have the power to canine sniff and search almost at will as the laws on search and seizure are interpreted broadly in favor of local police and federal drug agents. And punishments for drug possession have become draconian.

In the United Kingdom, similarly, although the punishments seem amazingly lenient by American standards, a package of tough anticrime measures gives police and the courts far more power than previously. When suspects refuse to answer questions asked by authorities, this refusal may be used against them in court (Schmidt, 1994). The attitude toward illegal drug use, however, is far more medical than punitive. Needle exchange programs in Britain and Australia have been quite successful in reducing the spread of AIDS. But then, these countries take a pragmatic rather than moralistic approach to prevention of HIV infection.

COMPARATIVE CRIME SOLUTIONS

While the United Kingdom and the United States, generally speaking, have sought to contain crime by stiffening laws and punishments, and countries such as Iraq, Singapore, and Malaysia resort to executing people for involvement in drug trafficking, other countries have looked elsewhere for solutions. In the Netherlands, instead of enforcing laws against drug use, rehabilitation and treatment are stressed (Fairchild, 1993). This policy cuts down on drug-related crime and is the most progressive drug policy in the world.

British social work professor, John Pitts (1995), praises Germany and France for containing crime through policies which strive to minimize unemployment and ameliorate its effects. According to the philosophy of the French social prevention initiative, the citizenship of the majority is cheapened if the benefits are not extended to those on the social and economic margins. The Canadian government, in opposition to the gun lobby but with the support of the people, is toughening up gun registration laws even further. In 1993, there were 1,400 firearm deaths in Canada, 1,100 of them were suicides (Clayton, 1994).

PRISONS

The Santa Fe prison riot has been called the most savage and bloodiest slaughter in U.S. penal history. For thirty-six hours in February, 1980, inmates were hanging, torching, disemboweling, beheading, and raping prison snitches first, personal enemies next, and then everyone else was fair game. In all, thirty-three inmates were dead, their bodies mutilated almost beyond recognition. And the New Mexico State Penitentiary was virtually destroyed.

The conditions that sparked this insurrection were at once unique and typical, the tragedy of one prison and every prison. The prison population was

12 percent black, 58 percent Mexican American, and 30 percent white. The slaughter was largely Chicano against Chicano. Yet apart from the ethnic composition, the facts that shaped the Santa Fe riot are universally common to most institutional life—brutality, overcrowding, incompetence, and idleness. In institutions all across the country, inmates' lives are in the hands of other inmates; beatings, rape, and stabbings are commonplace.

For one brief moment, events of the Santa Fe bloodbath loomed large in the news. Explanations were faltering and the facts leading to the riot were unsensational, complicated, and in many cases, downright unpalatable. The promise was of more explanations to come but they never did. In the end, the bloody stories which at first had so dominated the news were quickly forgotten. As a consequence, few law-abiding citizens recognize what goes on behind prison walls.

Compared to the New Mexico bloodbath, the more recent riots of 1993 and 1995 would not be so impressive. Both sets of riots took place at federal prisons, three in 1993 and four in 1995. The most recent riots led to the injury of about a dozen guards and caused millions of dollars in damage. Compared to their predecessor, the 1990s riots were more politically based and unique to American correctional history since they took place in federal, not state institutions. The issue in these riots was the federal crack cocaine law which has resulted in thousands of young black and Hispanic males serving long sentences, often twenty or thirty years without hope of parole. The longer the sentences, the less control prison authorities can exert over inmates who are apt to feel they have very little to lose by expressing their anger. This has meant more violence; in 1994 there were over one hundred assaults on staff in federal prisons.

In 1995, the number of men and women entering federal and state prisons soared for the first time to over one million. Combined with the almost half a million in jail, the number climbs to 1.5 million behind bars. This increase in 1994–1995 was the greatest ever for one year. The new figures gave the United States the edge on Russia for the highest incarceration rate in the world (Myers, 1995). The U.S. figure has tripled since 1980. Several factors, according to Irwin and Austin (1994), have fueled the imprisonment binge. Among these are the public's perception that crime and drug problems have accelerated, the war on drugs, and uncertainty about the economic future. One of the major booming industries in the United States, in fact, is the $31 billion incarceration business (Meddis and Sharp, 1994). State spending in corrections is the fastest category of all state spending categories; for counties building jails it is their major expense, likewise. California now spends more on prisons than it does on higher education (Pens, 1995). The nation's huge appetite for prisons is paying off in corporate revenue and corrections jobs. Driven by a decade's worth of "get tough" rhetoric enacted in laws, massive prison growth has been paralleled by cuts in social services and welfare. What we are witnessing, in the words of criminal justice reformer Jerome Miller (1995: 659), is "the replacement of the social safety net with the dragnet."

Human Rights Issues

The prison represents the ultimate power the modern democratic state exercises over its citizens. *Corrections,* the handling and processing of serious criminals, whether in prisons, jails, training schools, or by probation and parole offices, is that aspect of criminal justice with which the public is the least familiar. Yet the study of corrections is a study of the American system of justice. It is the study of how society treats the most deviant and unruly members.

The penitentiary was introduced to American society and the world by the Quakers who saw it as a moral advance over physical punishments. The original model consisted of separate cells where inmates could read the Bible and repent. Historically, there were three fundamental goals of imprisonment: incapacitation, reform, and punishment. The focus today is on incapacitation of the criminal to protect society and on punishment for the sake of punishment. In practice, however, there always has been and always will be overlap among these various frameworks.

In March, 1995, the United Nations conducted its first ever review of the human rights situation in the United States (*Progressive,* 1995). The United States is in violation of the terms of the International Covenant on Civil and Political Rights which includes a ban on the execution of juveniles. U.S. law permits the execution of persons whose crimes were committed when they were under the age of eighteen. Article 5 of the U.N. Universal Declaration of Human Rights states: No one shall be subjected to torture or to cruel, inhuman, or degrading treatment or punishment. The treatment of prisoners—extreme overcrowding and limited physical activity—the death penalty, and Native American rights are among the human rights issues that are under international scrutiny for the first time. The use of chain gangs as forms of involuntary, unpaid labor could be challenged under Article 4's prohibition of slavery. The U.S. Constitution, in fact, does not prohibit slavery entirely. It prohibits slavery and involuntary servitude "except as a punishment for crime whereof the party should have been duly convicted" (the Thirteenth Amendment to the Constitution).

Past national investigations of violations of the civil rights of inmates have led to changes in every aspect of life within prison—hiring practices of workers in the institutions, practices of punishment, and matters of freedom of speech and religion. The fact that these correctional facilities and their quality-of-life programs resulted from thirty years of litigation and the establishment of civil rights for incarcerated persons merely whets the appetite for returning these "new generation correction centers" back to punitive environments (Maghan, 1995). A backlash of dread proportions is now upon us. In more recent times, the deprivation that prisoners face has more to do with a withdrawal of resources (even including frequency of family visits) than with denial of first amendment issues.

"Back to the Chain Gang" is the headline of an article in *Newsweek* (Reibstein, 1994). The article chronicles the latest in a series of get-tough on criminal measures taking place from Albany to Sacramento. Lawmakers have banned telephones, TV, weight-lifting, educational grants for college courses, and basketball in various prisons. The chain gang and punishment is back while rehabilitation is out. Ex-convict Stratton (1994: 89) offers this plea for the nation's prisoners:

> I did eight years in federal prison for smuggling marijuana. I was punished, I was demeaned, and I was scared. I waded through sewage backed up from toilets. I lived in overcrowded cells. I saw men brutally beaten. It could have been worse: it could have been pointless. I wasn't condemned to idleness. I wasn't denied a place to exercise, a television to watch, an education to embrace. By the time I left prison, I had earned a bachelor's degree, written a novel, and mastered enough law to get out early. Now I have a wife, two sons, a job, and a message: don't make prisons more miserable than they already are.

The Prisoner Experience

Who are the prisoners today? A national survey from the Bureau of Justice Statistics (reported by Hall and Watson, 1993) reveals that those under the control of correctional authority do not represent a cross section of the nation's population. African Americans, who comprise 12.5 percent of the nation's population now account for 46 percent of prisoners; Hispanics who make up 9 percent of the U.S. population account for 17 percent, and women account for 6 percent of prisoners. Almost half are young—age twenty-five to thirty-four; most earned under $10,000 in legal jobs before their sentencing; and nearly half were under the influence of alcohol or drugs when the crime was committed. While women are incarcerated most frequently for drug offenses, men are typically incarcerated for violent crime. Nearly half of the women were sexually or physically abused in the past. In Europe, foreign born residents make up a disproportionately high percentage of inmates while women are a tiny fraction of the whole (Ruggiero et al., 1995).

Few law-abiding citizens recognize what goes on behind prison walls or the link between prison and society. There is not only the impact of prison on the culture (the return of hardened, criminalized citizens) but the impact of the culture on prison, the cultural baggage that today's inmates carry into prison with them. Any attempt to comprehend the social organization of the prison must address the contemporary prisoner experience in light of the politicization and gang activity of inmates today. Every level of the social system and the broad criminal justice process leaves its imprint indelibly on the later stages. Thus inequities in the society, in the law, and in law enforcement affect court processing and ultimately, institutional composition. And racial tensions in the community lay the groundwork for the "race wars" behind bars. A classic useful definition of a prison is that of a wall built around problems. Contemporary prisons are in turmoil, politically and racially. The path from the food riots of the now distant past to the "expressive mutinies" of the present day can be conceived as an outgrowth of collective internal dynamics in combination with external politics.

Racial hatred, which often leads to violence, is characteristic of the modern prison. In men's prisons, gangs attempt to control prison riots, pursue vendettas against their enemies, and earn prestige as tough convicts by menacing all other prisoners (Irwin and Austin, 1994). Faced with the daily evidence of societal rejection and condemnation and with daily blows to their personhood and sense of self, inmates have no choice but to seek their own sources of dignity and pride, their ways of investing their lives with meaning (Silberman, 1980). For men, since manhood cannot be demonstrated through heterosexual prowess, there is an exaggerated sense of toughness behind prison walls. Assaults and homicides in most high-security penitentiaries have become so common that the possibility of being attacked or killed has loomed as the major concern of new inmates. Non-streetwise whites are in particular danger.

Essentially the prison society is a world of predators and the preyed upon. Few talk about it and it is unrecognized in the national crime and victimization statistics, but in men's prisons (and more so in jails) rape is rampant. Rape (or the threat of rape) is the form of peer group social control exerted by the aggressors and leaders in confinement. It is the rapist who wields the power and respect, and it is the victim who is shamed. The aggressor during the sexual act is considered the heterosexual, the submissive prisoner is considered the homosexual or "woman." Once victimized, a prisoner is marked as a target for sexual exploitation and repeatedly subjected to gang rapes; one escape avenue is to become more or less a prostitute to one "protector." This same pattern prevailed among the convict laborers in colonial Australia and is described in graphic detail by Hughes (1987) in his epic history, *The Fatal Shore*.

After he was gang-raped fifty times in a Washington, DC jail, Stephen Donaldson, a Quaker and Vietnam war protester, declared a war of his own (Getlin, 1991). Today, Donaldson is president of Stop Prison Rape, an organization which collects data and advocates on behalf of victims. Based on several decades of study, Donaldson's organization estimates that 250,000 sexual assaults on inmates take place each year in U.S. correctional facilities.

In the first comprehensive survey to look at an entire state, Professor Struckman-Johnson tabulated the results of over five hundred questionnaires filled out by Nebraska inmates (*Prison Legal News,* 1995). Findings stated that 22.3 percent of the males indicated they had been pressured or forced to have sexual contact against their will. The figure in the women's prison was 7.7 percent. Consistent with other reports, most of the victims were heterosexual, white, were repeatedly victimized, and reported bad effects from the attacks, but no one informed authorities about it. Due to the small number of women prisoners, it is hard to generalize but three of the thirty-nine surveyed reported sexual victimization. "Genital touching" was reported in two cases and attempted touching in the third. Males who were attacked experienced rape and forced fellatio and half the incidents involved multiple attackers.

Rape in prison, as in society, is about power. Behind bars, the ultimate triumph is to destroy another man's manhood, to make him feel totally and often permanently degraded. And when the wolf (aggressor) is black and the punk (victim) is white which is the usual arrangement, the wolf's demonstration of power is infinitely sweeter. Sexual exploitation becomes a political statement, a symbolic reversal of racial roles (Silberman, 1980).

The catastrophic experience of violent penetration, unimaginably devastating to the typical victim, tends to transform the survivor into a capsule of pent-up rage, seeking to somehow regain his manhood by whatever means (Donaldson, 1995). Not only is one's psychological survival at stake but due to the risk of infection with HIV in an environment in which AIDS is prevalent and growing, one's physical survival is now at stake also. As Donaldson writes (42):

> The situation is getting worse, not better. Every year, increasing numbers of nonviolent offenders are being locked up and subjected to rape. As a result of ever-lengthening prison terms, convicts who used to think they could forego sex for a few years now feel that, with womanless decades ahead them, they might as well give high priority to finding themselves a punk. The widespread association of AIDS with homosexuals has put a premium on heterosexual anal virgins as preferred sex objects and these can be obtained through rape.

For a solution, Donaldson urges breaking the silence in society and bringing the issue to public light. Instead of denying the reality of sex in prison, administrative policy might permit the distribution of condoms (still contraband in most prison systems). This is a life and death public health issue, yet it tends to be treated moralistically. One encouraging development was the Supreme Court's 1994 decision in *Farmer v. Brennan* reinstating a prisoner's claim for money damages from prison officials for failure to protect him from prison rape. A concurring opinion called the system of institutionalized rape nothing less than torture.

Black Muslims

Whereas criminology and corrections textbooks tend to pay little heed to the development apart from the legal dimensions, the role of the Muslim faith in reforming criminals is worthy of mention. From the 1950s onward, Elijah Muhammad's teaching that "the white man is the devil" spread rapidly among the black prisoner population. Black Muslims had to fight many court battles before winning the right to practice their religion and dietary rules freely behind prison bars (Smith, 1993). Although the black separatist theme was repugnant at first to administrators, the disciplined life-style, the stress on education, self-improvement, and healthy living has turned many lives around. Following a period of dormancy, the Black Muslim movement is today a force for rehabilitation and hope deserving of our attention.

Women in Prison

In sharp contrast with the male prison society organized around power, women prisoners, at least in the United States, organize themselves in pseudo-family groups. "Married" couples may head such families and include a father figure, although this is somewhat rare. Prison "mammas" keep their "children" in line and provide emotional support (see Giallombardo, 1966; van Wormer, 1987). Homosexual involvement (often interracial) as opposed to forced contact provides a certain emotional intensity to the female prison scene.

Most women prisoners, about 75 percent, are serving time for nonviolent offenses because of mandatory drug-sentencing laws. Over half of all female prison inmates are women of color. Most, 70 to 80 percent, are mothers, many having been the primary caretaker for several children. When a mother is imprisoned, often merely held in a jail awaiting trial, the separation from her children can be traumatic for both of them. Prisons, and especially women's prisons, generally are located in remote, rural areas far away from home and community. Family ties, over time, are broken. Yet prisoners' family relationships are very important not only for mental health considerations but also in terms of post-release success (Hairston, 1995). Yet, as Hairston indicates, traditional public policies have provided minimal support for the maintenance of family relationships for individuals involved in the criminal justice system.

As a result of major advocacy efforts, visitation between women prisoners and their families is being humanized to some extent in some places. Prison nurseries in New York State, for example, allow parents to keep their infants with them until the child is about one year old. In many European countries, however, children can remain with their incarcerated mothers for much longer periods.

Two other areas of major concern to women in prison are substance abuse and sexual assault. Drug abuse programs are crucial in lowering recidivism rates of women sentenced for crimes related to alcohol or other drug involvement. Since much of these women's susceptibility to substance abuse stems from early childhood sexual abuse and is associated with a general pattern of self-destructive behavior, therapy for sexual abuse can help break the cycle (van Wormer, 1995). In a women's prison in Australia, extensive workshops are being conducted focusing on the women's experience of sexual assault (Pinnuck and Kay, 1994). A secondary focus is on ways to protect their children from sexual victimization.

Work with Juveniles

Prevention and rehabilitation must start with juveniles. With facilities throughout San Francisco, the grant-funded Walden House serves the substance abuse treatment needs of over one thousand people every day including people who are difficult to reach such as the homeless, emotionally disturbed, and abused adolescents (Lanza, 1995). Job skills training and educational opportunities are provided. While the public clamors for more punishment, however, finding the resources to save young lives from ruin is not easy.

Massachusetts has long led the way in juvenile justice reform. Few delinquent youth are held in custody. There are no large prison-like facilities in the state; fifteen-bed facilities with a teacher-to-student ratio of one to four are used instead. As a result of this approach, few juveniles are incarcerated as repeat offenders. For youths convicted of gun-related charges, however, a tough new mandatory-sentencing law requires a six-month term in custody. In Baltimore at the University of Maryland Choice Program, caseworkers visit each of 650 troubled kids three to five times *daily* in their homes. A follow-up study showed most of the youngsters stayed out of trouble—a record better than traditional corrections programs (Gest and Friedman, 1994).

In the first extensive research study to compare crime prevention progress to incarceration on the basis of cost effectiveness, RAND, a non-profit, non-partisan research institute found that dollar for dollar, prevention efforts aimed at high-risk youths are highly effective (Montgomery, 1996). Programs that encourage youths to finish school and avoid trouble prevent five times as many crimes as stiff penalties imposed on repeat offenders with so-called three-strikes-and-you're-out laws. Programs that teach better parenting skills to families of aggressive children prevent almost three times as many serious crimes for every dollar spent as harsh treatment does. RAND's findings confirm the key role of the family and the school in producing law-abiding citizens.

Unique in the United Kingdom for its emphasis on alternatives to the use of prison, Scotland relies strongly on social workers who operate within the criminal justice system. Family based and community based work are seen as going "hand in glove" with criminal justice services (Mitchell, 1994).

RACE AND THE DEATH PENALTY

The opposite of rehabilitation is execution; rehabilitation is to execution as life is to death. In 1995, in the United States, there were over three thousand inmates on death row and a record number of executions — fifty-six — since capital punishment was reinstated in 1977 (*USA Today,* 1995). As with other aspects of the criminal justice system, imposition of the death penalty has been shown to be fraught with racial bias (Mauer, 1995). These are the facts according to a summary presented in *U.S. News and World Report* (Gest, 1994):

- Killers of whites seem more likely to be executed than killers of blacks. Since 1976, 245 convicts have been executed; 84 percent of their victims were white. Only 35 percent of all murder victims are white.
- Overall, about 40 percent of convicts put to death since 1977 have been black, a bit less than blacks' share of arrests for murder.

In 1994, there were thirty-one executions in the United States, the same as in Egypt. Singapore had 32, Iran, 139, and Nigeria, 100, according to data collected by Amnesty International. In all, 95 countries retain the death penalty. Most countries either declare execution illegal or do not practice it according to the report (Ribbans, 1995).

When in 1989, a German citizen, facing extradition to the United States on murder charges, appealed to the European court of human rights in Strasbourg, the decision marked an important step toward banning extradition to countries with the death penalty. In its ruling, the European court took the view that condemning criminals to languish for years on death row is "inhuman and degrading" (Forum, 1994). Extradition was therefore opposed. Then in 1994, the Council of Europe's Parliamentary Assembly voted to recommend abolition of capital punishment and therefore end the debate once and for all.

Arguments in favor of the death penalty are: deterrence of the individual who will be incapacitated from further crime; deterrence of others who learn of the punishment; cost—theoretically it should be cheaper to exterminate rather than incarcerate; retribution—an eye for an eye; and a valuing for human life. Although there was a time in the seventies when capital punishment was considered primitive and "cruel and unusual punishment," most Americans today favor the use of this severe sanction.

Arguments against the death penalty are along the same lines as the arguments in favor, except the focus on gruesomeness here is on the act of killing by the state. Proponents of the death penalty focus on the gruesomeness of the crime. Those who oppose the death penalty are rarely impressed by the deterrence argument. Statistics do not seem to bear out the argument that persons are deterred from murder because they might be executed. There is some evidence, in fact, that some morbid types of people may be attracted to the idea of being "put out of their misery" and in such a public manner at that. On a statistical basis, the homicide rates in death penalty states are significantly higher than in states without this form of punishment. On the practical side, the cost factor is the reverse of what many would think: Current estimates are an additional $1 million to $2 million for each execution. The counties bear most of the expense since much of the money comes from local property taxes. Accordingly, some states such as Iowa have been scared away from legalizing this form of punishment. (A united effort by all mainstream churches was highly influential.) Other arguments made by opponents of the death penalty are the discriminatory factor (race and class), the likelihood of executing an innocent person, and belief in the possibility of redemption. Most of the mainline churches have issued statements condemning the taking of human life as punishment.

Controversies surrounding the imposition of the death penalty—in its modern sanitized form of lethal injection—are played out with rare realism in the haunting, award-winning Hollywood drama *Dead Man Walking*. Based on Sister Helen Prejean's (1994) unsentimental account of her ministry to condemned death row inmates and the families of the inmates' victims, the film presents the complex human dimension of capital punishment.

Underlying the whole death penalty debate is the question of just how rational people really are, especially those prone to murder. In Denmark in 1767, because the death penalty was attracting so many killings by certain "melancholy and dismal persons" who were seeking to end their own lives, a law was passed forbidding its use in such cases. Apparently, there is a type of person who is both psychopathic and suicidal. This type of personality, oblivious to the suffering of others and unable to get the nerve to kill himself (or herself) will go to great efforts to get the state to do it for him or her. Sometimes such individuals try to get the police to do the job quickly in a shoot-out. Or they may even commit some horrible act first, such as shooting family members or strangers, in this way, compelling themselves to do what they want and fear most — take their own lives. How do you make sense of such horror? Read box 11.2 to learn more about how the death penalty may actually invite murder in some individual cases.

WAR AND RAPE

Wars and terrorism often have dramatic effects on the systems of law and justice in a country. In the U.S. Civil War, President Lincoln curtailed many of the citizens' constitutional rights, an act for which he was greatly criticized. Restrictions on freedom of the press have characterized more recent military operations. In the national interest, many of the traditional civil liberties are suspended. Britain, for example, has responded to the Irish Republican Army's (IRA) bombing attacks with repressive measures that have resulted in claims of human rights violations (Fairchild, 1993). Imprisonment of suspected terrorists without trial, searches and seizures without warrants, and suspension of the right to remain silent under questioning are examples. Amnesty International (1995) has published several reports detailing allegations of ill-treatment bordering on torture in Britain by police officers and private security guards. This human rights organization has also published a report on political killings of IRA suspects by government officials in Northern Ireland.

Even more than in fighting terrorism, the standards of ordinary law-abiding conduct give way under the exigencies of war. Horrible crimes against humanity are sometimes tolerated in the interests of defeat of the enemy or in wreaking revenge for atrocities inflicted by the other side. In wartime, normal inhibitions against violence are loosened, and in a general climate of killing and bloodshed, women are likely to be subjected to horrific abuses. A central component of military strategy, such as we have seen in Bosnia and Rwanda, is the deliberate violation of the human rights of women (Amnesty International, 1995). The scope of rape in these countries was so widespread and so systemically carried

BOX 11.2

THOSE WHO SEEK EXECUTION: CAPITAL PUNISHMENT AS A FORM OF SUICIDE

Crime continues to lead in polls that gauge prioritizing of the most serious issues facing the United States. An outcry for harsher punishment, including the death penalty, is reflected in legislation at the state and Federal levels. Politicians' platforms calling for the death penalty echo the public rage against the violent criminal.

What is the impact of the death penalty on the homicide rate? Can victimization be prevented by letting the public know that killers will face death themselves? To address these questions, it is imperative to understand what goes on in the minds of some killers, especially those who attack not out of passion, but in cold blood, often claiming multiple victims.

Public execution has been an established means of punishment since the founding of America. From 1967 to 1977, however, use of the death penalty ceased, partly due to Supreme Court decisions that the penalty, as then applied, was unconstitutional. In 1976, as states revised their guidelines for execution, the practice was resumed. In 1977, Gary Gilmore was the first person in a decade to be executed. He had killed strangers ruthlessly — a crime which, on the surface, made no sense.

Upon examining the life of Gilmore, a key theme that emerges is the self-hatred and utter self-contempt of a man apparently bent on his own destruction. Criminologist G. Richard Strafer and author Norman Mailer each have singled out Gilmore as the prototype of one who plotted his own dramatic end. After being paroled from Marion Federal Penitentiary, he (consciously or unconsciously) was attracted to Utah, where execution was by firing squad, rather than his home in Oregon, then a non-death penalty jurisdiction. After fighting his attorney for the right to be killed and receiving extensive public attention, Gilmore managed to be immortalized in death as he could not be in life.

The implications of Gilmore's actions are staggering. Innocent persons were gunned down at a gas station, it seems, so a criminal could have himself executed. Utah's death penalty therefore may have *attracted,* rather than repelled, crime, at least in this case. Are there others?

Sociologist Thorsten Sellin, author of *Capital Punishment,* reports on an unnamed prisoner at Leavenworth who committed

(Continued on next page)

BOX 11.2 (Continued)

murder in order to exchange his life sentence for a death sentence. Numerous psychiatric reports attest to the phenomenon. Psychiatrist George Solomon in 1975 wrote about two cases involving capital punishment used as suicide. In the first, a Vietnam veteran, hardened to killing, chose to end it all by engaging in murder for hire. He knew that, in his state, the death penalty was mandatory for murder-for-hire killings. He told his sister, "I'm too much of a coward to commit suicide." The inability to take one's own life is a theme seen throughout such suicidal killings.

In Solomon's second case, a twenty-year-old baby-sitter suffocated two children. In her words: "I killed my girls; I killed two pieces of me. They were like my sisters and I miss them so much. . . . I had to kill them. . . . Yeah, they would kill me in the electric chair probably. I remember somebody telling me they were trying to get rid of capital punishment, and like I asked the sergeant if like they still had capital punishment and he said yes, so I was pretty happy about it."

Both parties described by Solomon thought about being executed prior to committing their acts. In each case, the state gave them prison terms instead of killing them.

In 1959, at the California governor's request, psychiatrist Bernard Diamond examined a man immediately before his execution. The convict confessed to Diamond that he had committed three rape-murders and had attempted a fourth. His mission was suicide. When asked what he would have done had California not had a death penalty, he replied, "I would have had to go to another state where they did have capital punishment and do it there." Diamond concluded from this case and his confirmation from other forensic psychiatrists that the threat of the death penalty can act as an instigation to crime, rather than a deterrent.

Capital punishment, with its dramatic rituals and ceremonies (even today, when executions no longer are public), is the perfect fantasized death, a glorified crucifixion, for certain sick minds, according to Diamond. The perpetrator of the crime is not afraid of death. What he or she fears is life.

These observations are confirmed in the work of psychiatrist Louis J. West, who described the case of a Texas farmer, "tired of living," who shot and killed a total stranger in a cafe. West also mentioned the case of an already convicted Oklahoma murderer, Howard Otis Lowery, who killed a second time in order to make sure he would get the electric chair.

On the basis of these cases, West speculated that the prospect of execution is extremely attractive to some individuals who crave a violent means of committing suicide. West even cited the case of a person who

(Continued on next page)

BOX 11.2 (Continued)

confessed to a murder done by another so he could get himself put to death in this manner. West further speculated that death penalty states have higher homicide rates than non-death penalty states because of the attractiveness of the prospect of execution to certain sick minds.

The mass slaughter of eight nurses by Richard Speck in Illinois was included by West as a possible example of a psychopath's attraction to death penalty crimes in a death penalty state. This was supported by the fact that Speck previously had moved from Michigan, which did not have capital punishment. West's "guess" has not been confirmed by other evidence.

In 1980, in Warren County, Ky., I interviewed Sherril Harston, who faced the death penalty. Harston had killed his lover and her three-year-old child. Ironically, both the defendant and the prosecutor were pleading for the maximum penalty. Harston tried again and again to fire his attorney, who was trying to save the defendant's life.

While in jail, Harston composed a song that expressed his sentiments: "Now my life is doomed to be / Face to face with the magistrate — / For my final destiny, / For all eternity, / The Electrical Hanging Tree." When given a life sentence instead, he successfully fired his attorney and filed an appeal for a new trial. In prison, he threatened to kill again if he did not get his way.

Although Harston never did get his wish and refrained from further murder — today, he is working toward a college degree — his case is reminiscent of the earlier case of James French, who was more successful in achieving his ends. In 1958, French was convicted of murdering a motorist. He testified at his trial that he hoped to be executed, but his pleas for the death penalty were to no avail. Sentenced to life in prison, he strangled his cellmate and, when tried on the new murder charge, reiterated his desire to be electrocuted. The state executed him in 1966. French admitted that he always had "chickened out" at the last minute on several suicide attempts.

Sometimes, the urge to be killed may be so strong that the convict may turn on the jury. In 1980, rape-murderer Steven Judy threatened his jury with: "You had better put me to death, because next time it might be one of you or your daughter."

In 1992, the Louisville *Courier-Journal* quoted an interview with a seventeen-year-old Indiana prisoner. The youth told police and others that, when he was fifteen, he wanted to die, but was afraid to commit suicide, so he killed his friend, thinking the state would execute him. The state declined to do so.

Days before Lloyd Wayne Hampton was to die by lethal injection in Illinois, he

(Continued on next page)

BOX 11.2 (Continued)

spoke bluntly about the fact that he had murdered in 1990 in order to get the death penalty. In a telephone interview with a *Courier-Journal* reporter, Hampton stated: "I either had to put myself in a position of being killed by somebody else or committing suicide. [A]t that point I had strong beliefs about not killing myself. . . . So I put myself in a position to have the state kill me."

Charlie Brown and Charles Kelley committed murders in Minnesota in 1962, then came to Iowa to commit another, particularly horrible killing. They asked to be tried in Iowa because it had a death penalty, while Minnesota did not. Brown said, "I want to die for what I did. I don't want to spend the rest of my life in jail." The state of Iowa accommodated his request and executed both men. Former Iowa Gov. Robert Ray often has cited their case as an example of murder attracted by capital punishment. Iowa abolished the death sentence in the mid 1960s.

Aberrations or a Troubling Pattern?

Extensive media coverage is given to criminals facing execution. While some of the residents of death row proclaim their innocence and others claim repentance, still others seem to welcome their demise. These latter cases raise important policy questions. Are they aberrations or part of a consistent and troubling pattern? Are innocent persons — the victims — put at risk in death penalty states?

In 1993, Westley Allan Dodd was hanged in the prison at Walla Walla, Wash. He stalked and murdered two young boys, strangled a third, and then was arrested while trying to abduct a six-year-old boy from a movie theater. He readily confessed to the killings, showed pictures of the victims to the police, and insisted on execution by hanging. Several witnesses claimed that he had a religious conversion in his final hour.

Also in 1993, a headline in *The Chicago Tribune* declared: "AIDS Patient Charged in Attack with Syringe." Trannie Blue had attacked a nurse at the University of Chicago Hospital with a syringe filled with his HIV-infected blood. According to the Cook County state attorney, Blue told investigators he had done so because he wanted to receive the death penalty and end his suffering.

In *The Execution Protocol*, Stephen Trombley reports on a story from the Missouri State Penitentiary. Two prisoners became lovers; one ended up on death row after killing two inmates. In order to join him, the other one strangled his cellmate. They now are together on death row.

Thomas Grasso, serving a life sentence in New York, requested to be transferred to Oklahoma on a previous murder charge. He would rather be executed than grow old in prison, he said. Then-New York Gov. Mario

(Continued on next page)

BOX 11.2 (Continued)

Cuomo refused to extradite Grasso, but his successor, George Pataki, had Grasso returned to Oklahoma soon after Pataki took office in January, 1995.

A small minority of sick and suicidal individuals find the prospect of highly publicized punishment intriguing. Such people are sufficiently irrational to wreak havoc upon themselves and others, yet rational enough to plot out this destructive course to its bitter and gruesome end.

Those most prone to carry out execution-inspired homicides are young white males with a history of unsuccessful suicide attempts. Restrictions on the scope of capital punishment are not a barrier to them. If the death penalty is limited to the death of police officers or Federal marshals, then a police officer or a Federal marshal will become the target. The same holds true with prison murders, crimes of an especially heinous nature, murder for hire, etc. that call for the death penalty. For each group targeted in that state, there is an increased risk for the commission of those designated crimes. The notoriety generated through the mass media to those scheduled for execution provides additional attraction to the Richard Specks who say they are "born to raise hell" and to the Sherril Harstons who beg for death by "the electrical hanging tree."

When cases such as those described above are examined individually, each seems to be one of a kind, a bizarre product of a sick mind. When all are considered together, though, a pattern emerges. There is a method in such seemingly senseless murders. "I couldn't do it myself," the killers say. "I needed the state to do it for me."

In this pattern of calculated, externally inflicted suicide, there is a danger in even just having the death penalty on the statute book in a state. For every person who verbalized this wish of execution, there probably are many others who failed to reveal their innermost motives. Death by lethal injection would seem to offer an especially easy way out to one desirous of this form of state-sponsored euthanasia.

Source: USA Today Magazine, March, 1995, pp. 92–93. Reprinted with permission of the Society for the Advancement of Education.

out as a weapon of ethnic cleansing as to defy the imagination. It is a repeat of what happened in Bangladesh in 1971 when 200,000 to 400,000 Bengali women were raped as Bangladesh sought independence from West Pakistan. According to the Amnesty International report (4):

> Rape is not an accident of war or an incidental part of armed conflict. Its widespread use in times of conflict reflects the special terror it holds for women, the special contempt it displays for its victims. It also reflects the inequalities and discrimination women face in their everyday lives in peacetime.

Rape of the enemy's women is so much a part of war and its aftermath that under conditions of military occupation, it is more remarkable in its absence than in its presence. The rape that accompanies war involves both a tremendous act of aggression and humiliation against a conquered people and a reward to soldiers who are encouraged by their officers to loot a village and rape the women at will. Rape is the act of patriotism, misogyny, and lust rolled into one. In the name of victory and the power of the gun, war provides men with a tacit license to rape (Brownmiller, 1975). In her analysis of rape in warfare, Brownmiller (1993: 37) does not equivocate:

> Sexual sadism arises with astonishing rapidity in ground warfare, when the penis becomes justified as a weapon in a logistical reality of unarmed non-combatants, encircled and trapped. Rape of a doubly dehumanized object — as woman, as enemy — carries its own terrible logic. In one act of aggression, the collective spirit of women *and* of the nation is broken, leaving a reminder long after the troops depart. And if she survives the assault, what does the victim of wartime rape become to her people? Evidence of the enemy's bestiality. Symbol of her nation's defeat. A pariah. Damaged property. A pawn in the subtle wars of international propaganda.

Notably, in the battles of ancient Greece, the Crusades, the U.S. Civil War, World Wars I and II, and Vietnam, rape was utilized as a physical and psychological weapon of war (Wing, 1993). So in this context, it may be heartrending, but not surprising, to hear of mass rapes by all factions in the Bosnian and Rwandan conflicts. In Haiti, too, military rapists targeted women in terrorism preceding the recent government overthrow. Compounding the injury to the victims, the husbands often transfer their feelings of revulsion from the enemy to their victimized wives. Such rejection of women as defiled beings is consistent with traditional patriarchal ideology that universally demands that women should not allow more than one man to have access to their bodies (Wetzel, 1993).

Law professor Adrien Wing, herself a descendant of Confederate General Beauregard and of one of his slave-mistresses, draws a gripping parallel between the ethnic cleansing and forced impregnation in Bosnia and the history of rape and miscegenation in the American South (Wing and Merchan, 1993). On six key attributes related to what Wing and Merchan call "spirit injury" or "the slow death of the psyche, of the soul, and of the identity of the individual" (p. 2) and of the group, the early American South and Bosnia share a common ground. These traits are: rape as defilement not only of the individual woman but of a whole culture; rape as silence as the women internalize their experience of oppression rendering them more vulnerable to males within their own group; rape as sexuality with raped women seen as promiscuous and impure; rape as emasculation of men due to their sense of helplessness to protect their wives and daughters; rape as trespass on the "property" rights of men most pronounced under slavery where the women were the property of their white masters as were the racially mixed offspring as well; and rape as pollution of the victim and of her children born as a result of nonconsensual sex.

Rape as an instrument of war is clearly a violation of international law and its proscriptions against war crimes, taking of hostages, torture, and violation of human dignity (Wing and Merchan, 1993). Deplorably, although torture has been prosecuted as a war crime, only recently was war-rape considered anything more than an inevitable byproduct of war (Goodman, 1993; Mahoney, 1995). Now, at last, however, women's rights are seen as human rights. And justice and accountability for past abuses increasingly are seen as bedrock issues for human rights organizations everywhere, and a vital protection against future abuses. Under the auspices of the U.N. Security Council, the International Criminal Tribunal will prosecute rape and other war crimes in the former Yugoslavia. Another major recognition of women's rights comes with recognition of the U.S. Immigration and Naturalization Service of rape and other systematic forms of violence against women as grounds for political asylum (*Progressive*, 1995b). Because of the law's transformative potential or potential to transform values, these recent developments carry a major significance (Mahoney, 1995).

Slavery

As stated by Article 4 of the U.N. Universal Declaration of Human Rights, "No one shall be held in slavery or servitude." Yet human bondage or slavery is alive today throughout the world. According to Britain's Anti-Slavery International, the world's oldest human rights organization, more than 100 million people around the world still suffer as slaves—a figure that includes an estimate for child labor (Associated Press, 1995). Mauritania in Northwestern Africa still practices traditional slavery. Most common is the slavery of debt bondage, forcing whole families to work in vain efforts to pay off loans. In Pakistan, for instance, parents and their children work in this manner, generation to generation making bricks. In Pakistan, India, and some parts of Latin America too, the basic formula is the same: give an illiterate, desperate worker a job, then pay less than it takes to survive on. The facts ring true throughout the world. According to an article in the *Christian Science Monitor,* slavery has survived in Brazil as forced labor on plantations. Laborers, lured from the impoverished northeast, work under armed guards as they struggle to pay off their incurred debts (Epstein, 1995). In Peru, similarly, debt bondage is used in mines and forestry.

It wasn't until 1992 that Korean "comfort women" overcame their shame sufficiently to tell of their unwilling role in World War II as sexual conscripts for the Japanese army (Brownmiller, 1993). As we have seen in chapter 10, sexual slavery is practiced in Thailand and Burma today. Girls are sold by the parents to sex tourism procurers who promise good wages in the cities (Wetzel, 1993).

A WORD ON AMNESTY INTERNATIONAL

Much of the documentation provided in this chapter concerning human rights abuses comes directly or indirectly from Amnesty International sources. Founded in 1961, this nongovernmental organization has an international membership of more than one million people and publishes an extensive annual report documenting human rights abuses in each country where substantiated abuses have occurred (137 nations including Canada, the United States, and the United Kingdom are listed for 1995). Representatives of this organization testify before national legislatures and submit reports to the United Nations and other intergovernmental organizations (Donnelly, 1993). According to the 1995 flyer distributed by Amnesty International, this organization, best known for its letter-writing campaigns on behalf of individual prisoners of conscience, works specifically for:

- the release of prisoners of conscience — men, women, and children imprisoned for their beliefs, color, sex, ethnic origin, language, or religion, provided they have neither used nor advocated violence.
- Fair and prompt trials for all political prisoners.
- An end to torture, executions, political killings and "disappearances."

Amnesty International also has actively campaigned against the death penalty throughout the world; members in one country work to help people in countries other than their own. The basic strategy is to show that people from around the world are watching and that they care. Their presence on behalf of the women in China was made known to the world in a public demonstration at the United Nations Fourth World Conference on Women at Beijing.

CONCLUSION AND SUMMARY

Social welfare, in the sense of the well-being of a people, and human rights are inextricably linked. People cannot enjoy a sense of security and well-being if their rights are systematically violated by the very state representatives from whom they would seek protection. Nor can they enjoy the benefits of human rights such as exists in a democracy if their social welfare needs for such things as food, shelter, and clothing are not met. Hence the reason for a chapter in this textbook on human rights issues. Inclusion of such a chapter is consistent with the NASW policy statement on Peace and Social Justice which strongly endorses implementation of the Universal Declaration of Human Rights (National Association of Social Workers, 1994).

The point of departure for this penultimate chapter has been the United Nations' Declaration. Written in 1948 by world leaders shattered by their own lack of action against the horror known to the world as the Holocaust, the declaration constructed the framework for a greater and more specific recognition of human dignity and freedom. Included in this concise but comprehensive document are three categories of human rights: the right to meet one's physical and social needs, protection from state-sanctioned discrimination, and civil rights against the awesome powers of the state. This chapter has been concerned with the latter two categories which are highly interrelated (for example racism and the rights to a fair trial, sexism and the right against being sold into sexual bondage).

Throughout the world, the U.N. Declaration standards, though without authoritative legal status, have gained acceptance as "customary international law" and are substantively shaping the course of jurisprudence in the United States and elsewhere (Wronka, 1995). As Wronka summarizes it, the document outlaws torture, genocide, slavery, murder, the causing of disappearances, arbitrary detention, systematic racial discrimination, and consistent patterns of gross violations of human rights. These are standards that know no frontiers.

A major challenge for any nation is the treatment accorded those who offend against the nation's cardinal values as codified into law. Will mob justice prevail or will there be a process to protect the rights of the accused? Anglo-Saxon law and the Napoleonic Code have done much to civilize, or at least formalize, the criminal justice process throughout the world. Criminal justice does not exist in a social vacuum. This chapter has traced its evolution from trial by physical combat in medieval times to the present. A history of the Anglo-American adversary system of adjudication through the presentation of evidence by two opposing sides was provided. Reference to the O.J. Simpson case highlighted the adversarial nature of dispute as well as the racial divide affecting the institution of justice in the contemporary United States. The O.J. Simpson verdict, and the polarized reaction it generated, raises the difficult question of why have so many American citizens lost faith in their system of justice. The facts reviewed in this chapter—racism in the law and law enforcement, racism in the courts, and racism in the prisons—provide a partial answer. Those who were sickened at the celebratory response of so many blacks to the acquittal of a man who seemed so guilty would do well to see the celebration in the context of a criminal justice system which has sent so many African Americans unnecessarily, often unjustly, off to prison. Astonishingly, one in three of young African American males are in prison or on probation or parole.

The uniqueness of the U.S. system of justice—not in its process, but in tradition—is revealed in several major respects: in the tolerance for guns, fervor for the "war against drugs," and in the popularity of the death penalty (in theory if not in the practice of carrying it out). The nature of American criminality was viewed in this chapter in international perspective. Criminal justice systems were viewed comparatively as well.

The theme of gender emerged once again in this volume in the discussion of women in crime and women in confinement (women comprise 6 percent of the total inmate population) and of female victimization under conditions of war. Unlike incarcerated men engaged in endless power struggles, women in prison seem more interested in reproducing family-type ties. The section on war and rape described specific human rights violations suffered by women universally in war-torn areas. This chapter has viewed the deliberate violation of women as a deliberate component of military strategy. The role of rape or sexual bondage in altering the ethnic and racial composition of a people has been seen historically in American slavery and more recently in the ethnic conflicts in Bosnia and Rwanda.

Related to mass rape is the continuation of slavery in many places where it is officially outlawed. Girls are sold by their poverty-stricken families into prostitution in places like Thailand and India while debt bondage involving whole families proliferates in Southeast Asia and Latin America. The form of slavery practiced in Mauritania is more of the classic master-slave variety. International documentation by nongovernmental organizations reveals the extent to which the world's impoverished see their rights to life and liberty threatened daily. Girls and women are often the most vulnerable of all.

A controversial issue in the United States is the reintroduction of the chain gangs of forced prison laborers. Although involuntary servitude of this sort is clearly outlawed by the Universal Declaration of Human Rights, the U.S. Constitution allows involuntary servitude as a condition of punishment. The return to chain gangs and boot camps is a part of a disturbing trend toward ever-more punitive responses to society's socially-generated problems. This chapter concludes on a note of hope in the work of the vibrant human rights organization, Amnesty International, which has done so much to let the world know that human rights abuses anywhere are a threat to us all.

REVIEW QUESTIONS

1. Trace the history of the growth of international human rights norms. What was the precedent at Nuremberg?
2. Study box 11.1, the Universal Declaration of Human Rights. What progressive elements strike you as significant? Is the United States in compliance with the articles of this document? Why or why not?

3. Define human rights.
4. Discuss the significance, if any, of "the trial of the century." What was the racial divide?
5. "The fortress mentality is debasing the quality of American political life." Discuss.
6. What is the history of crime in the United States?
7. Discuss several reasons for the rise in homicide rates among the young. Compare handgun murder rates in various countries.
8. Review the history of the adversary system. What are the basic principles? Consult table 11.1 and compare legal and social work approaches to resolving conflict.
9. What is the link between race and crime? How is the criminal justice system racist? Discuss prosecution for drug offenses.
10. Compare criminal justice systems in the United States, Japan, Saudi Arabia, and Mexico.
11. Relate America's war on drugs to Prohibition.
12. Discuss prison riots and precipitating factors.
13. What does the U.S. Constitution say about slavery? What is the significance today?
14. Relate the U.S. prisoner experience to human rights issues. Discuss the facts pertaining to prison rape.
15. Characterize the prison scene for women behind bars.
16. Argue in favor or against the reinstitution of the death penalty. Discuss the implications of the murder-suicide phenomenon described in box 11.2.
17. Provide a historical description of rape as a war crime.
18. Human bondage is alive today throughout the world. Explain.
19. Describe the work of Amnesty International.

REFERENCES

Amnesty International. (1995). *Amnesty International Report.* New York: Amnesty International U.S.A.

Associated Press. (1994, November 10). Security Is Big Business in Terrorist-Ridden Colombia. *Waterloo/Cedar Falls Courier.* B6.

_____. (1995, September 19). Report: Millions of Child Slaves Sweat, Suffer for Pennies a Day. *Des Moines Register.* 8A.

Bachman, R. (1994). *Violence Against Women.* Washington, DC: U.S. Government Printing Office.

Bailey, F. and H. Rothblatt. (1974). *Fundamentals of Criminal Advocacy.* Rochester, NY: The Lawyers Co-operative Publishing Co.

Bell, C. (1994). Silent Right. *Community Care* 1045: 1–7.

Bourgois, P. (1995). *In Search of Respect: Selling Crack in El Barrio.* New York: Cambridge University Press.

Brownmiller, S. (1975). *Against Our Will: Men, Women and Rape.* New York: Bantam.

———. (1993, January 4). Making Female Bodies the Battlefield. *Newsweek*: 37.

Burke, J. (1994, December 21). Germans Spare the Rod to Reform the Criminal. *Christian Science Monitor*: 2.

Canadian Press. (1995, August 2). Canadian Murder Rate Lowest in 25 Years, Report Says. *Calgary Herald*: 2.

Carroll, P. (1994, October 28). Companies Are Often Unprepared for Just How Different Mexico Is. *Wall Street Journal*: R6.

Cervantes, M. (1994/1605). *Don Quixote.* New York: Modern Library.

Champion, D. (1992). *The Juvenile Justice System.* New York: Macmillan.

Clayton, M. (1994, December 2). Canadians Take Aim at Registering All Guns. *Christian Science Monitor*: 7.

Corelli, R. (1995). North Versus South. *Maclean's* 108(22): 18–20.

Donaldson, S. (1995, May). Can We Put an End to Inmate Rape? *USA Today (Magazine)* 123: 41–42.

Donnelly, J. (1993). *International Human Rights.* Boulder, CO: Westview Press.

D'Souza, H. (1993). Preventing War: Need for an Internationalist Perspective on Social Work Values. *Journal of International and Comparative Social Welfare* 9(1 & 2): 33–45.

Durkheim, E. (1938/1858). *The Rules of Sociological Method.* Chicago: University of Chicago Press.

Economist. (1995b, July 15). Jailbirds. *Economist*: 40.

———. (1995a, October 7). Two Nations, Divisible. *Economist*: 18.

Encyclopaedia Britannica. (1993). Alcohol Drug Consumption. Chicago: Encyclopaedia Britannica, Inc.

Epstein, J. (1995, July 24). Slavery Nags Brazil as It Moves Ahead. *Christian Science Monitor*: 7–8.

Fairchild, E. (1993). *Comparative Criminal Justice Systems.* Belmont, CA: Wadsworth.

Forum. (1994, December). *Human Rights*: 12–15.

Frankel, B. (1993, December 29). USA in Its Own League When It Comes to Firearms. *USA Today*: 6A.

Fraser, M. (1995). Violence Overview. In *Encyclopedia of Social Work*, 19th ed.: 2453–2460). Washington, DC: NASW Press.

Friedman, L. (1993). *Crime and Punishment in American History.* New York: Basic Books.

Fulton, E. (1992, May 18). The Young Offenders. *Maclean's*: 34–35.

Gardner, R. (1982). *Family Evaluation in Child Custody Litigation.* Cresskill, NJ: Creative Therapeutics.

Getlin, J. (1991, May 23). Prison Rape Victims Crusade Against Attacks Behind Bars. *Waterloo Courier*: A1, A3.

Gest, T. (1994). Crime's Bias Problem. *US News and World Report* 117(4): 31–32.

Gest, T. and D. Friedman. (1994). The New Crime Wave. *US News and World Report* 117: 26–28.

Giallombardo, R. (1966). *Society of Women: A Study of a Woman's Prison*. New York: Wiley.

Giancana, S. and C. Giancana. (1992). *Double Cross*. New York: Warner.

Goffman, E. (1961). *Asylums: Essays on the Social Situation of Mental Patients and Other Inmates*. Garden City, NY: Doubleday.

Goodman, E. (1993, March 6). Women Activists in a Hundred Countries. *The Washington Post*.

Hairston, C. (1995). Family Views in Correctional Programs. In *Encyclopedia of Social Work*, 19th ed.: 991–996. Washington, DC: NASW Press.

Hall, M. and T. Watson. (1993, May 20). Typical Inmate: Abused, Abuser, Repeater. *USA Today*: 8A.

Hawthorne, N. (1960/1850). *The Scarlet Letter*. Cambridge, MA: The Riverside Press.

Helzer, J. and G. Canino. (1992). *Alcohol in North America, Europe and Asia*. New York: Oxford University Press.

Hirakawa, N. (1995, March 20–26). Human Rights Group Urges Impartial Prison Inspections. *The Japan Times Weekly*: 4.

Hughes, R. (1987). *The Fatal Shore: The Epic of Australia's Founding*. New York: Alfred A. Knopf.

Irwin, J. and J. Austin. (1994). *It's About Time: America's Imprisonment Binge*. Belmont, CA: Wadsworth.

Isikoff, M. (1995). Crack, Coke, and Race. *Newsweek*: 77.

Jones, A. (1994, May/June). Living with Guns, Playing with Fire. *MS*: 38–44.

Lanza, K. (1995). Walden House Provides Alternative to Incarceration. *Substance Abuse and Mental Health Services Administration News* 3(2): 16–18.

Leander, K. (1995). The Normalization of Swedish Prisons. In V. Ruggiero, M. Ryan, and J. Sim, eds. *Western European Penal Systems: A Critical Anatomy*: 169–193. London: SAGE.

Luft, K. and L. Goering. (1995, March 22). Awareness Growing of Latin America's Violent Past. *Waterloo/Cedar Falls Courier*: A1.

Maghan, J. (1995, May 2). Why U.S. Prisons Should Keep the Barbells and TV. *Christian Science Monitor*: 19.

Mahoney, K. (1995, July 29–August 1). *Theoretical and Practical Suggestions to Implement Equality Rights and Overcome Gender Bias in the Courts*. Paper presented at the International Social Welfare in a Changing World Conference: Calgary, Alberta.

Mauer, M. (1995). Sentencing of Criminal Offenders. In *Encyclopedia of Social Work*, 19th ed.: 2123–2129. Washington, DC: NASW.

Mauro, T. and A. Stone. (1995, June 6). Violence in the Media: Picture Unlikely to Change. *USA Today*: 4A.

Mead, G. (1918, March). The Psychology of Punitive Justice. *American Journal of Sociology*: 585–592.

Meddis, S. (1994, December 13). Success of Expansion a Matter of Debate. *USA Today*: 10A.

Meddis, S. and D. Sharp. (1994, December 13). Prison Business is a Blockbuster. *USA Today*: 10A.

Messner, C. and V. Ruggiero. (1995). Germany: The Penal System Between Past and Future. In V. Ruggiero, M. Ryan, and J. Sim, eds. *Western European Penal Systems: A Critical Anatomy*: 128–148. London: SAGE.

Miller, J. (1995). Criminal Justice: Social Work Roles. In *Encyclopedia of Social Work,* 19th ed.: 653–659. Washington, DC: NASW Press.

Mitchell, D. (1994). Young Defender. *Community Care* 1043: 18.

Montgomery, L. (1996, June 20). Prevention Plans Most Successful at Fighting Crime. *Des Moines Register:* IA.

Morales, A. (1995). Homicide. In *Encyclopedia of Social Work,* 19th edition: 1347–1358. Washington, DC: NASW Press.

Myers, L. (1995, December 4). Prison Population is Soaring in U.S. *Chicago Tribune*: A5.

National Association of Social Workers. (1994). Peace and Social Justice. In *Social Work Speaks: NASW Policy Statements*, 3d ed.: 200–205. Washington, DC: NASW Press.

Pens, D. (1995). CA Prison Guards. *Prison Legal News* 6(3): 1–3.

Pinnuck, F. and J. Kay. (1994). Yes We Are Survivors of Prison and Child Sexual Abuse. *Australian Social Work* 47(1): 43–47.

Pitts, J. (1995). Youth Crime. *Community Care* 1066: ii–viii.

Polansky, N. et al. (1981). *Damaged Parents: An Anatomy of Child Neglect.* Chicago: University of Chicago Press.

Prejean, Sister H. (1994). *Dead Man Walking.* New York: Vintage Books.

Prison Legal News. (1995). New Statewide Data Show Prison Rape a Widespread Problem. *Prison Legal News* 6(11): 17.

Progressive. (1995). Human Rights in the USA. *Progressive* 59(5): 15.

———. (1995b). Refuge for Women. *Progressive* 59(7): 9.

Reibstein, L. (1994, October 17). Back to the Chain Gang? *Newsweek*: 87–89.

Ribbans, L. (1995, September 24). Executed by the State. *The Observer*: 25.

Ruggiero, V., M. Ryan, and J. Sim. (1995). *Western European Penal Systems: A Critical Anatomy.* London: SAGE.

Ryan, M. and J. Sim. (1995). The Penal System in England and Wales: Round up the Usual Suspects. In V. Ruggiero, M. Ryan, and J. Sim, eds. *Western European Penal Systems: A Critical Anatomy*: (93–127). London: SAGE.

Schacter, B. and J. Seinfeld. (1994). Personal Violence and the Culture of Violence. *Social Work* 39(4): 347–350.

Schmidt, W. (1994, December 19). What Britons Don't Say May Now Be Used Against Them in Court. *Courier Journal*: A4.

Silberman, C. (1980). *Criminal Violence, Criminal Justice.* New York: Vintage Books.

Smith, C. (1993). Black Muslims and the Development of Prisoners' Rights. *Journal of Black Studies* 24(2): 131–146.

Stratton, R. (1994). Even Prisoners Must Have Hope. *Newsweek*: 89.

Strick, A. (1978). *Injustice for all: How Our Adversary System of Law Victimizes Us and Subverts True Justice.* London: Penguin.

Thornton, M. (1992, March). Prohibition's Failure: Lessons for Today. *USA Today Magazine*: 70–73.

USA Today. (1995, December 29). Record Year for Executions. *USA Today*: 3A.

van Wormer, K. (1987). Female Prison Families: How Are They Dysfunctional? *International Journal of Comparative and Applied Criminal Justice* 11(2): 263–271.

———. (1995). *Alcoholism Treatment: A Social Work Perspective.* Chicago: Nelson-Hall.

Viviano, F. (1995, May/June). The New Mafia Order. *Mother Jones*: 44–55.

Washington Post. (1995, October 23). The Changing Face of Homicide. *Waterloo/Cedar Falls Courier*: A1, 5.

Wetzel, J. (1993). *The World of Women: In Pursuit of Human Rights.* London: Macmillan.

Will, G. (1993, June 27). Our Harmful Drug Policy. The Washington Post: C7.

Wing, A. and S. Merchan. (1993). Rape, Ethnicity, and Culture: Spirit Injury from Bosnia to Black America. *Columbia Human Rights Law Review* 25(1): 1–46.

Wisotsky, S. (1993). The War on Drugs and Civil Liberties. *USA Today* 122: 17–21.

Wronka, J. (1991, June). *An Analysis of Human Rights Principles, as Defined by the U.N. Universal Declaration of Human Rights.* Unpublished doctoral dissertation, Brandeis University: Waltham, MA.

———. (1995). Human Rights. In *Encyclopedia of Social Work*, 19th ed.: 1405–1416. Washington, DC: NASW Press.

12

SUSTAINABLE DEVELOPMENT

But ask now the beasts, and they shall teach thee;
and the fowls of the air, and they shall tell thee;
Or speak to the earth, and it shall teach thee. —Job 12:7–8

Don't it always seem to go
That you don't know what you've got
Til it's gone
They paved paradise
And put up a parking lot. —Joni Mitchell, 1969

This final chapter is about the environment. The theoretical framework is consistent with the person-in-the-environment emphasis of social work except that here the reference is to the physical environment, and to the convergence of social and environmental problems so often neglected in the social work literature (Hoff and Polack, 1993; Weick, 1981). As we approach the next millennium, environmental conditions promise to be the major force determining human survival and social development. The interconnection between social welfare and the environment is underscored in the social importance of arable land, sanitary water, and clean air and in the balance between the population and natural resources. We are talking in this chapter about nature's limits — limits in the yield of oceanic and inland water fisheries in fresh water, in the amount of fertilizer soil can use, and in the population the earth can sustain — that are beginning to impose themselves on the human agenda. The depletion of natural capital — of forests, rangeland, topsoil, underground aquifers, and fish stocks — and the pollution of air and water have reached the point in many countries where the economic effects are becoming highly visible, including a loss of output, of jobs, and of exports (Brown, 1995). The loss of animal and human life are the indirect consequences. At some point severe ecological stresses begin to manifest themselves on a scale of desperate proportions: Ethnic conflict is exacerbated, and once war breaks out all normal constraints, all concerns for tomorrow, give way and havoc is wreaked on the already overtaxed environment. War depletes habitats and species, the shortage of which in turn, creates new tensions and re-ignites old ones. Mass migration of people fleeing death and destruction further burdens the resources and upsets the ecological balance.

As the title of this chapter indicates, sustainable development, or the meeting of the needs of the present generation without compromising future needs, is crucial to the stabilization of life on planet earth. Recognizing that interaction with the environment impacts all levels of social development, and that environmental and human welfare are intrinsically linked, this chapter will:

- Examine the scope of the environmental crisis.
- Define what is meant by sustainable development.
- Explore the interrelationship between ecological imbalance and social and political concerns.
- Review the facts on overpopulation and efforts to curtail the world's population growth.
- Demonstrate that recent agricultural trends are geared to short-term benefits with serious long-term consequences for the human and physical environment.
- Consider the impact of war on the environment and of environmental depletion as a factor leading to war.
- Discuss the discriminatory effects of environmental degradation with consequences borne by the poor and ethnic minorities.
- Explore policy solutions to protect both people and the physical environment.

SCOPE OF THE ENVIRONMENTAL CRISIS

For those who read of the expanding global economy in the business section of the newspaper, the impression is of unlimited economic growth and infinite developmental possibilities. In calculating a nation's economic performance, the gross national product (GNP) takes into account economic activity and profits but not loss of topsoil, water reservoirs, or forests involved in reaping the profits. On paper then, the destruction of resources is good economics. Paradoxically, loss becomes registered as growth. This is no small matter: countries with solid GNP measures qualify for extensive loans from international banks to finance more "growth." Yet to read the popular or academic scientific journals is to get a totally different impression: these depict "growth" as resources being steadily exhausted. To the extent that there is expansion, it is an expansion of desert land, population, and pollution in the atmosphere. Brown et al. (1993) explain the differences in viewpoint as follows:

> From an economist's perspective, ecological concerns are but a minor sub-discipline of economics—to be "internalized" in economic models and dealt with at the margins of economic planning. But to an ecologist, the economy is a narrow subset of the global ecosystem.

In truth, the health of the planet is deteriorating at a rapid pace. Not too long ago economic growth was hailed as the way to improve people's lives, both within nations and internationally as it was thought the benefits would trickle down through the classes. Better circumstances for the few were created but often at the expense of the many. Even as early as the late 1960s, according to the NASW report on internationalizing the curriculum (Healy, 1992), evidence that benefits did not trickle down from the capitalists to the masses emerged. In fact, measures of the gross national product of a country are not necessarily linked to improved survival rates and quality of life for the majority. Economic development, very often in fact, is the reverse of social development. Pressure from international monetary lending sources to increase the capital available for business investment has mandated sacrifice of health, nutritional, and other programs for the people.

A second myth is the equally optimistic belief that a green revolution through the wonder of fertilizers and pesticides could feed the world. The problem is that after a few years of treating (mistreating) the soil in this way, the increased yields taper off and soil erosion and water pollution hinder further food production.

Today, due to agricultural and industrial pollution and evaporation probably related to global warming, at least a billion people lack access to clean water. The clearing of forests is proceeding at the rate of over seventeen million hectares a year. One hectare is roughly two and a half acres. Deforestation on a massive scale has happened in Brazil, Indonesia, and western Canada and is associated with a decline in rainfall. Since more water is stored in the plants of the earth than its lakes, the loss of plants means a serious decline in the amount of water vapor released into the atmosphere (Gore, 1992). The clearing of forests is also associated with soil erosion as well as flooding and mud-slides as mud flows down to the river banks. Replanting, if it is done at all, usually involves only one or two tree species. Because they are all of the same age and size, the new plants often even fail to regenerate, and the biodiversity of the region is lost permanently. In Europe, the forests are threatened by air pollution, often from industrial fumes hundreds of miles away. But the raging monster upon the land is population growth (Wilson, 1992). Land is being lost through urban sprawl and industrialization. Population migrations into cities result from recent agricultural trends pushing small farmers off the land, other economic pressures, and ethnic tensions.

As most environmentalists are painfully aware, human activities — burning fossil fuels, emitting pollutants from industry, and clearing forests that are the habitats for plant and animal species — now match or even surpass natural processes as agents of change. In the first comprehensive study of the issue by the world's scientists, the Global Biodiversity Assessment, a U.N. report, estimates that more than thirty thousand plant and animal species now face possible extinction (Associated Press, 1995). Since 1810 nearly three times as many bird and animal species have disappeared as in the previous two centuries. This report decries the loss of genes, habitats, and ecosystems. Hoff and McNutt (1994: 4–5) decry the loss of something else as well — the loss of beauty:

> Perhaps the most dramatic way to express this interdependency, this imbed-dedness in nature, is to say that, if we destroy our environment we destroy ourselves — our irreplacable source of sheer physical sustenance, as well as the source of our imaginative capacities for experiencing the penultimate realities of the good, the true, and the beautiful.

Human activities are transforming the global environment in ways that are only beginning to be realized. People in richer, highly industrialized countries, with only one quarter of the world's population, consume most of the world's energies. Most of the gases and chemicals emitted into the atmosphere are from these countries. Yet people in the rest of the world, where three-fourths of the population reside, are also contributing to resource depletion. The poor, by virtue of their pressing short-term needs have few incentives to manage resources for the long haul (Lusk, 1994). In order to survive, the desperately poor and hungry are driven to tear down every living thing (Silver, 1990). Improved standards of living, however, can break the cycle of rapid population growth and the environmental hazards it engenders.

Sometimes the environment is intentionally despoiled by humans. Zastrow (1996) reminds us of the tragic events in Kuwait, 1991, when during the Gulf War, Saddam Hussein of Iraq ordered his military forces to set six hundred oil wells in Kuwait on fire. Skies were blackened for months and the quality of human and lower-level animal life suffered greatly thereafter.

Then there are the environmental accidents. The Exxon oil spill in 1989 in Valdez, Alaska, resulted in the deaths of millions of birds, animals, fish, and plants. Although many critics focus on capitalism as a primary culprit, the Communist approach to rapid industrialization also has contributed to ecological crises. The nuclear power plant explosion in Chernobyl, Ukraine, placed the lives of tens of thousands of persons in eastern and western Europe in extreme jeopardy. The much publicized birth defects and deaths by cancer have alerted the rest of the world to the dangers of nuclear energy and to the interconnectedness of environmental problems.

THE WAR AGAINST NATURE

The predominant paradigm of the Industrial Revolution was that science was king and that the forces of nature could be subdued or controlled. "Man against nature" is a notion that permeates Western thought. Historically, the progress of civilization has been conceived in terms of the struggle with and overcoming the natural elements, and in embarking on a journey marked by indefinite and inevitable progress (Glacken, 1971). The emphasis was on the dichotomy, on two distinct worlds—that of humankind and that of nature. Bateson (1972: 492) summarized the dominant beliefs promulgated in his day as:

- It's us *against* the environment.
- It's us *against* others.

- It's the individual (or the individual company, or the individual nation) that matters.
- We *can* have unilateral control over the environment and must strive for that control.
- We live within an infinitely expanding "frontier."
- Economic determinism is common sense.
- Technology will do it for us.

Anthropologist and systems theorist Gregory Bateson was already concerned with ecological stability in the 1970s, long before many others had given these matters a second thought. One thing that concerned Bateson especially was the population explosion that arose when we began to tamper with the death rate by controlling major diseases without limiting the birth rate. In any living system, notes Bateson, every increasing imbalance will generate its own limiting factors as side effects. And overpopulation was an imbalance of dire proportions. The wake-up call to humankind is uttered in these signs of imbalance—smog, pollution, poisoning, industrial wastes, famine, atomic fallout, and war itself. Because we can see, smell, and experience these effects, environmental awareness, just in its infancy in Bateson's time, is now almost mainstream. A whole generation of school children, in fact, has been brought up to be aware of the earth, to recycle, and "to save the environment." Many have transmitted this education to their parents.

Hoff and Polack (1993) look toward Native American and feminist sources for the concepts and values to enrich an expanded ecological model of social welfare. American Indian tribes valued their resources and did not waste them. They saw themselves as one with the earth and its creatures (Cronon, 1983). Ecofeminists, similarly, see the earth as mother and deplore aspects of the modern male ethic stressing disconnectedness, hierarchy, and power over the world (Berger and Kelly, 1993). This notion of oneness with the universe is congruent also with the Darwinian notion of the interrelatedness of species in a "web of life." Presently, as we face imminent ecological collapse and the social disintegration which accompanies it, we—many of us, at least—are seeing ourselves not in opposition to nature but holistically, as a part of nature. Now that our relationship to earth has changed so utterly, we have to acknowledge the change and understand its implications (Gore, 1992). Instead of being startled into immediate and effective action, however, the images of death and destruction seem to have produced instead, as Gore observes, a kind of paralysis. In our fascination with parts of nature, we neglect to see the whole picture.

The ecological model of science emphasizes that human beings are organic and embedded in the larger ecosystem, and that life is evolutionary, dynamic, and adaptive (Hoff and Polack, 1993). However, as Berger and Kelly (1993) indicate, although knowledge of the natural world abounds, wisdom does not. Our moral development has not caught up with our technological accomplishments.

The environmental crisis is global and multidimensional in its impact; the economic, political, and social components are integrally linked. Lester Brown (1995) of the Worldwatch Institute, an environmental research organization, describes the ricocheting effect of unsustainable practices. First, the ecological symptoms include shrinking forests, thinning soils, contaminated and falling aquifers, collapsing fisheries, expanding deserts, and rising global temperatures. Next the economic consequences include falling incomes, rising unemployment, and grinding poverty. Then the political and social ramifications include hunger and malnutrition, starvation, environmental and economic refugees, and ethnic, tribal, and religious wars. As stresses mount, governments weaken and what results is an extreme imbalance that affects every level of the social and economic structure. A strain in one part of the ecosystem (e.g., use of pesticides) is met by a counterforce in another part (pests becoming resistant) which is met by a counter-reaction (intensified pesticide use) and so on. Aggressive measures often bring forth unexpected consequences such as human health suffering and depleted resources. To the example of excessive pesticide use, we can add poor irrigation wrecking the water supply, the impact of overpopulation on a region, and of air pollution and deforestation on the world. Regional excesses become magnified by feedback loops into serious global matters. Answers to the global ecological crisis, to the state of disequilibrium that now plagues us, are found not in fleeing from science, but in redirecting science and economics to an ecologically sustainable model (Hoff and Polack, 1993).

SUSTAINABILITY

With the publication of the Brundtland report (U.N. World Commission, 1987), the need for a new development paradigm to satisfy the material needs of the present generation without mortgaging the future, was given formal recognition. Adapted and popularized under the leadership of Gro Harlem Brundtland, the Prime Minister of Norway, the much heralded report, *Our Common Future,* linked the once separated issues of environment and economic development. Even before the United Nations report was published, however, the U.N. had already declared its attempt to halt the cycle of poverty that existed in the world's least developed countries a failure (Estes, 1993). In these countries, the combination of high debt to international banks, devastating environmental practices, and inability to compete in the global marketplaces, it was now realized, had raised rather than lowered the profound levels of human suffering.

The concept of *sustainable development* (which promotes an appropriate balance between the physical and material environment) has succeeded, claims Estes, in uniting widely divergent theoretical and ideological perspectives into a single conceptual framework. Defined specifically in an ecological context, sustainable development creates a process that ensures that natural resources are replenished, and that future generations continue to have the resources they need to meet their own needs (Midgley, 1995). Sustainability entails an economic and political order that is in harmony with the biological resource base of society. Although Midgley credits the sustainable development approach with successfully harmonizing economic and social perspectives, he believes that claims of a new development paradigm are premature.

Nevertheless, numerous international gatherings have been held to address the question of what can be done to protect societies from depletion of resources which provide life and livelihood for people. In 1992, the Rio de Janeiro Earth Summit, also known as the United Nations Conference on Environment and Development, laid down the founding principle of sustainable development in a five hundred page document. The idea is that any development worth promoting should respect social justice, nature, and economic efficiency (Sachs, 1995). Significantly, the conference pointed to the need for a global partnership in order for sustainable development to be achieved (French, 1995).

Then in 1994, the International Conference on Population and Development in Cairo put the spotlight on the desperate need to curb overpopulation. Solutions were seen in expanding access to family planning, and improving women's and children's health and literacy. Protecting the environment, slowing population growth, and preventing poverty were now recognized as interlinked priorities. At the Population Conference and later at the World Summit for Social Development held in Copenhagen, 1995, the terms of the discourse shifted. At this juncture, the link between women's issues and sustainability was recognized: Not only were women on the agenda, women helped set the agenda (United Nations, 1995).

The well-publicized involvement of the world's citizenry at each recent international forum has bolstered the understanding of the human dimension of the environmental crisis. In Rio, for example, twenty thousand concerned citizens and environmental activists from around the world outnumbered official representatives by at least two to one. The same at Cairo and most strikingly at the Women's Conference at Beijing. At these conferences, members of non-governmental organizations (NGOs), rather then official delegates, captured the imagination of the world. Many of the organizations represented, for example, Greenpeace, Amnesty International, International Planned Parenthood, and Friends of the Earth, are themselves international. And according to French (1995), the participation of the world scientific community also has been crucial in providing the data to inform the world of the need for renewable energy sources, a very important development to counterbalance the lobbying efforts of oil and coal companies.

Over the past two or three decades, the world community has responded to the environmental challenge through the signing of innumerable treaties protecting the oceans, the land (from desertification), the air (from pollution in Europe and in polar regions), and endangered species of wild flora and fauna. Yet for all the advances in helping reduce carbon emissions here, in helping protect water loss there, the reality remains: the relentless pace of global ecological decline shows no signs of abating. Income inequality continues to rise; pressures from the global market still benefit the rich at the expense of the poor; and much of the world is in a continual state of warfare. There is recognition of pending environmental disaster, in other words, but no remedy is, as yet, in sight.

In summary, our societies are paying a high price for having followed policies of economic development that operate at the expense of social development and the protection of nonrenewable resources. The smog of Eastern Europe, eroded hillsides of Nepal, toxic waste sites of Russia, and denuded forests of Brazil and the Pacific West Coast testify to the massive destruction. Yet today, fortified by United Nations summits and much grass-roots energy surrounding these international events, a new paradigm may lead to a re-appraisal of the traditional focus on growth, progress, and "modernization" as ends in themselves. The notion of sustainable development is here to stay.

OVERPOPULATION

Lester Brown of the Worldwatch Institute is referred to as a "doomsayer" because of his widely publicized projections that the coming population boom is expected to outstrip the world food supply (Begley, 1994). In a *Newsweek* article that investigates the behind the scenes action of the Cairo Population Conference, Begley contrasts doomsaying biologists with sanguine economists. Viewing the world as a finite system of limited resources, biologists warn that the ten billion people (who the United Nations projects will live on the planet in 2050) will exhaust the water, soil, and other resources, causing horrific environmental damage and global misery. Some economists counter that free markets will help stimulate the search for substitutes and provide technological remedies through the green revolution. The U.N. Food and Agriculture Organization agrees that growth in the food supply will continue at high rates (Lekic, 1994).

From all current indications, the United Nations is leaning more in the direction of the scientists. The World Population Plan of Action is a response to the urgency that unless population growth can be slowed quickly, the resulting scarcity will intensify pressure on all other systems. The environmental, economic, and social consequences will be great. The World Population Plan, accordingly, calls for intensified family planning programs to prevent unwanted pregnancy.

Executing the plan, however, may be more complicated than it would appear on the surface. The U.N. conference itself was upstaged by religious attacks. A strongly-worded attack by the Vatican and its newfound Islamic allies on what they considered an agenda for immorality and permissiveness marred the proceedings (MacFarquhar, 1994). This time, however, unlike at the last population conference in Mexico City when the Reagan administration led an anti-abortion challenge, the United States was strongly supportive of international action backing family planning. One anticipated benefit of satisfying the demand for contraception is that the number of maternal deaths per year would be significantly cut as about half of them are caused by unsafe abortions.

The United Nations report, *The World's Women 1995,* presents and interprets statistics on women and men in the light of issues and objectives raised in global forums organized by the U.N. Two chapters in the report are devoted to population issues. The facts revealed are these:

- Fifty-seven percent of men and women live in the developing countries of Asia and the Pacific, with 22 percent in the developed regions of the world—North America, Europe, Japan, and Oceania, 13 percent in Africa, and 8 percent in the Caribbean.
- Europe's population is declining but Africa's is increasing rapidly.

- Urban populations are growing quickly in the poorest countries.
- There are more men than women in the world. In a few Asian countries the ratio of boys to girls is increasing.
- Women's roles in the rural areas—cooking and gathering fuelwood and carrying water—are affected by environmental degradation.

Throughout Africa, which has had a 34 percent annual growth in population over the past decade, the food supply decreased by 5 percent. Overpopulation is now recognized, according to Gore (1992) and Zastrow (1996), as one of the most severe threats to the preservation of the quality of human life. Economic progress tends to be canceled out by increased population. With large numbers of children in the population, many will be malnourished and uneducated. Conditions are ripe, as Zastrow suggests, for political unrest and international terrorism. The environmental problems discussed below—relevant to water, air, and the soil—are all compounded by excessive human use.

WATER

When Lord Byron composed the following words: "Man marks the earth with ruin, his control stops with the shore" (*Childe Harold's Pilgrimage*, Stanza 179) little could he have imagined that humankind's relentless assault one day would extend to the oceans as well. An article aptly entitled "The Rape of the Oceans" (Satchell, 1992: 64) describes "America's last frontier" as seriously overfished, badly polluted, poorly managed, and in deepening trouble. A chief concern is the destructively effective harvesting technology as practiced by fishing fleets from Japan and the United States.

By choosing to concentrate its swelling population along the coasts, humanity is locating the ecological damage of its activities precisely where the world's most productive ecosystems are concentrated (Weber, 1994). Pollution from coastal populations and industry is affecting the aquatic food chain as toxic compounds are commonly found in coastal organisms. Oil and even hypodermic needles washing up along beaches are familiar images thanks to extensive press coverage of these disturbing events. Human waste is also a major contributor to water pollution (Zastrow, 1996). The sewage from New York City alone produces five million cubic yards of sludge a year, which is dumped into the ocean and now covers over fifteen square miles of ocean bottom (Kornblum and Julian, 1992). The Rio Grande which divides the United States and Mexico is sometimes referred to as an "open toxic sewer."

In the United States, the Clean Water Act of 1972 has reduced pollution levels markedly (Gore, 1992). Once the Cuyahoga River in Cleveland became so polluted with industrial chemicals that it caught fire. Today, it has been cleaned up considerably. In Ukraine, however, in recent years, the river Noren exploded when a farmworker threw his cigarette butt in the water (Gore, 1992).

Equally alarming in its immediate impact, is the fact that vast underground reserves of water deposited over thousands of years are being seriously and rapidly depleted. More and more cities and farms overdraw aquifers to keep expanding economies afloat and to quench the thirst of growing populations (Gardner, 1995). The earth's water is 97 percent saline; most of the rest is snow and ice. Fresh water is a small percentage therefore, of the water that falls as rain. One-quarter of the water that irrigates, powers, and bathes the United States is taken from an ancient network of underground aquifers. The use of pesticides by the world's farmers spreads pollution in creeks, streams, lakes, and ground water. Acid rain is an additional source of contamination formed from emissions of cars, trucks, and industrial plants that combine with rain as it falls back upon the land and water. The Chinese people's increasing burning of coal as their primary energy source is causing crop and forest damage in scores of countries (Lenssen, 1995).

In many parts of the world, in urban areas especially, the drinking water is contaminated with human waste. In Latin America, serious communicable diseases are on the rise. Unknown there until 1991, cholera arrived in Peru apparently in water dumped from an Asian ship (Goering, 1995). Nine thousand people have died. With tuberculosis and malaria also making comebacks, the death toll is expected to be in the millions. Strategies are desperately required to build and maintain sewers for the growing populations of the non-industrialized world.

AIR

In satisfying the energy needs of burgeoning human population, humans are likely affecting the climate of the entire planet. The facts are still not known, so the debate over global warming and its consequences continues. Most scientists agree that so-called greenhouse gases such as carbon dioxide and methane are depleting the ozone layer of the atmosphere. The amount of carbon pumped into the air by fossil fuel burning rose slightly in 1994 while deforestation added billions of additional tons of carbon into the atmosphere. The emissions released in the atmosphere surpass the rate at which the world's oceans and forests can absorb the chemical (Roodman, 1995). Trees and other plants counter the carbon dioxide in the atmosphere and replace it with oxygen. Destruction of the earth's vegetation is thus extremely damaging to life on earth, affecting the very air we breathe. As more pollution enters the atmosphere, sun rays become more penetrating. The recent rise in skin cancer rates may be related to this fact (Brown et al., 1993).

Air pollution in Eastern Europe is so shockingly high that trees and grass are stained with soot. In some areas of Poland children are taken down in mines periodically to escape the buildup of gases in the air. Mexico City suffers some of the worst air pollution of any city in the world. In the United States, Canada, and Western Europe, a great deal has been done to prevent the kind of "killer smogs" that paralyzed cities in the 1950s. Air pollution, however, reaches every place on earth, and one country's neglect is paid for, in one way or another, by the entire world.

SOIL

In *A Thousand Acres* by Jane Smiley (1991: 131–132), the narrator depicts her love affair with the Iowa wetlands teeming with life—"sunfish, minnows, nothing special, but millions or billions of them: I liked to imagine them because they were the soil, and the soil was the treasure, thicker, richer, more alive with a past and future abundance of life than any soil anywhere."

Poet and environmentalist Wendell Berry (1977), in his classic work on agriculture, *The Unsettling of America,* states that if we regard plants as machines, we wind up with huge monocultures (corn and soybeans) and if the soil is regarded as a machine, then its life, its involvement in living systems and cycles, must perforce be ignored. If, like the strip miners and the "agribusiness" interest groups, we look on all the world as fuel or as extractable energy, we can do nothing but destroy it. And ultimately, what we turn against, turns against us. Vice President Al Gore (1992: 144) voices a similar sentiment, "We are, in effect, bulldozing the Gardens of Eden," he writes.

Soil is the source of life. Food chains are the living channels which conduct energy upward; death and decay return it to the soil (Leopold, 1966). In his collection of essays called *A Sand Country Almanac* originally published in 1949, Aldo Leopold defined fertility as the ability of the soil to receive, store, and release energy. Agriculture, by overdrafts on the soil, or by too radical a substitution of domestic for native species in the superstructure, explains Leopold, may derange the channels of flow or deplete storage. Soils depleted of their storage or of the organic matter anchors it, wash away faster than they form. This is erosion.

Berry (1993) goes further and talks of *land abuse.* Any form of land abuse—a clearcut, a strip mine, an overplowed or overgrazed field—is a dire threat to the earth's ecosystem. Land abuse goes back to early American history. In *Grassland,* Richard Manning (1995) offers a critique of modern agricultural practices that began with procedures done to the rich prairies of early America. European Americans transformed a land that supported fifty million bison into one that supports about forty-five million cattle. As for the soil, the cattle ate plants right to the dirt, killing saplings that could have controlled erosion. Whereas bison migrated with the seasons allowing the plant life to be replenished, the cattle stayed permanently on the land. Plowing, too, took its toll, turning long-evolved plant communities into a system of monocrop farming.

In *Broken Heartland*, Osha Davidson (1990) surveys the modern scene: our system of agriculture doesn't just mine water (groundwater mining for irrigation), the soil itself is rapidly disappearing. Iowa, home of some of the world's most fertile soil, for example, has taken a little over one hundred years to use up half of its topsoil. Not only is farm land lost; but by reducing river and reservoir capacity, the migrating soil also increases the likelihood and severity of floods.

To force some life out of the depleted soil, farmers use an incredible amount of chemicals—many of them highly toxic—which seep into the rural waterways, drinking water, soil, and air. The threat to human health and to the health of other animals, earlier documented so graphically in Rachel Carson's (1962) *Silent Spring,* still persists in the United States today. In Iowa, pesticides are showing up in one-third of the state's wells; in Nebraska one-half of the state's municipal water systems are similarly tainted (Davidson, 1990). It's not just farmers, however, who are responsible. According to state officials, home owners in Iowa apply three times more pesticides on lawns, per acre, than farmers do on cropland (Beeman, 1994). Then there are golf courses which represent the most artificially managed acreage in existence.

The most damaging pesticide, DDT, was banned in the United States years ago, but this and other highly lethal chemicals are applied by human hands all across Latin America and elsewhere throughout the world. According to the World Health Organization (WHO) ten thousand people die each year from accidental pesticide poisoning (Lambrecht, 1993). Many crops sent back to the United States are contaminated in this manner with residues of dangerous chemicals. The manufacturers, however, point to the benefits of pesticides in helping satisfy the world's demand for food. Meanwhile, the soil and food chain are heavily contaminated with DDT residues throughout Africa, Asia, Central and South America, and the South Pacific, with alarming levels of this chemical showing up in mothers' milk (Agena, 1994). Meanwhile, Rachel Carson's prediction regarding insects—that their predators would be weeded out and weaker insects eliminated until only the most resistant insects would survive—has come to pass with a vengeance.

The ancient Greeks had a concept of *hubris* or overweening pride to explain the occurrence of tragedy. Wes Jackson (1993) described as "a guru of sustainability," and the founder and director of the Land Institute in Salina, Kansas, refers to this concept to depict the present situation. Hubris entails introducing a human-made pattern into the world, one that disrupts a larger pattern. What we must understand, argues Jackson, is that the larger pattern is not of our making, and we must accept that we depend on it. This determination to disrupt natural processes for short-term pay-offs brings us to the farm crisis.

THE FARM CRISIS

Responsibility for pesticide use lies not only with Latin American growers but with U.S. agribusiness partners as well. When the interests of local communities and their economies are relentlessly subordinated to the interests of transnational corporations, the demise of the traditional farm communities becomes understandable.

The term *farm crisis* is often used to refer to a lengthy period of major economic depression in large agricultural areas of the United States and Canada which came to a head in the late 1970s when a series of international and domestic events and policy decisions contributed to long-term economic problems in the agricultural sector (van Hook, 1990). The exodus from the farm has been

PART 3: WORLD POLICY ISSUES

almost continuous. And the loss of a farm is not the same as a loss of a job; it is the loss of a way of life, a self-identity, a community.

Contrary to popular belief, the farm crisis did not originate in the recession of the late 1970s and '80s, but actually started several decades earlier (Pins, 1994). Seven million people left farming during the 1940s followed by nearly ten million more in the 1950s. Forty percent of Americans who were farming when the fifties began were still farming when the fifties ended. Unlike today, however, then it was not so much push as pull: the pull of good job opportunities. According to the U.S. Census Bureau, the number of U.S. farms in 1992 was smaller than at any time since before the Civil War (Slakey, 1994). While the number of farms shrank, overall farm production expanded.

The little noted disappearance of the black farmer has serious implications for urban America (Davidson, 1990). These farmers are leaving the land today, both through foreclosure and because a majority are too old to continue farming. Few African Americans now, as formerly, are able to obtain the financing necessary to make farming a profitable enterprise. They, like other farmers, are collapsing under modernization pressures to get big or get out.

Large farms, with more land in production and more crops to sell, are in a position to benefit from subsidies (Swander, 1995). While they deplete the soil with monocropping, overproduction, and heavy use of chemicals, the large farmers produce at a lower cost, eventually driving traditional farmers out of business. And when the family farm goes, so does the local hardware store, the farm equipment store, the local school, and the café. Food prices are kept artificially low by the government; today U.S. farmers sell their products for low prices in a market glutted with food. They operate an intensified farming system that requires capital that must be borrowed at high interest rates (Barlett and Brown, 1994). Families forced off the farm often end up in factory work or domestic labor.

Karger and Stoesz (1990) go beyond the statistics to the human side of the farm crisis. For the farm family, the connection to the land is often a legacy from parent or grandparents, a family heritage that links family members to the wider community. Financial failure therefore, leaves farmers with a sense of personal failure and public shame. The 1984 movie, *Country,* depicts the tragedy befalling an Iowa farm family after the banks foreclose and the father suffers a breakdown.

The biggest beneficiaries of modern agricultural policies, as Davidson asserts, are not the large growers but the distributors of chemicals such as pesticides, and the food processing industry. These giant corporations do well even when a farm recession is underway. One reason government policies consistently benefit these industries over family-sized farmers, according to Davidson, is that the U.S. government and these industries are intertwined. Corporate political action committees (PACs) outspend environmentalists eighteen to one in contributing to the political campaigns of congressional candidates and members of agricultural committees. Although food in the United States is cheap, American taxpayers, as Davidson further argues, pay for the cheap food through diminished quality of the environment, federal farm programs farming conglomerates, drought disaster aid, and agricultural research. The kind of research being done is destructive to the society in the long term. Researchers develop a genetically uniform strain of wheat or tomatoes to maximize some simple characteristic and then arrange for the planting of unvaried acres of that crop, a crop that could potentially be wiped out by a single plague (Bateson, 1990). See box 12.1 for a commentary on Iowa farming.

What is happening in the United States is being replicated around the world. In Australia pressures on farmers to stay afloat give them little choice but to pursue short-term efficiency at the expense of sound ecological policy (Cheers, 1995). In Europe the standardization demanded by modern agricultural methods is diminishing the number of species and varieties grown (Vellvé, 1993). In Asia rural villages are dying as cities become overpopulated due to developing agricultural technology, and rural values and support systems are eroding as well (Critchfield, 1994).

In short, the cost of progress in agriculture is high and the global implications are considerable. Some day we will have to address the long-term cultural and political forces that have created a system of food and agriculture that has lost its biological and economic resilience and has become extremely vulnerable to short-term weather events and international politics (Enshayan, 1993). And some day we may have to address the psychological toll in farm families forced off the land.

WAR AND THE ENVIRONMENT

Throughout history, the environment has been one of the war's worst casualties: Romans spread salt of the fields of Carthage; Sherman's troops marched

BOX 12.1

IOWA: LIVING IN THE THIRD WORLD

When I moved to rural Iowa, almost three years ago, I did not know the troubles it faced. I had heard of rural flight, but as an urban dweller, not facing the daily reality of rural life, I had ignored the rural crisis.

I moved here, to northeast Iowa, because I wanted to live in beauty and relative solitude, because I thought it might be possible to have a culturally rich life in rural America. I know now that I was overly optimistic and naive. I had, in fact, very little idea of what it would mean to live on an isolated farm ten miles from either of the nearest towns, trying to earn a living as a writer and publisher.

When I moved here I believed what possibly many others believe: that rural America is a place where people still gather in community, sure in themselves and their friends. I believed the land and water were pure and uncontaminated, even though I had read and heard otherwise. I believed that the best of modern technology had been absorbed, the worst rejected. I believed all these things because I did not live in rural America.

Perhaps I had been affected by the television commercials which try to sell products by identifying them with farms and country towns. I believe that many of us still associate rural America with what is uncontaminated and cleanest in ourselves. It is a myth which helps sustain us. Like the ever-shrinking wilderness, we must have it, at least in our fantasies, a land or town where it is still possible to escape from an ever-more frantic and directionless society.

But that, as I said, turns out to have been extremely optimistic and naive. The fact is that rural America is dying.

There is little energy and self-confidence here. And little work. The farmers are leaving their lands for low-skilled jobs in the cities. What few jobs small towns do offer pay mostly minimum wage. The young people, those who can, leave as soon as the high school diploma is in their hands.

I live in the *Third World,* in Iowa, not far from the Mississippi River. Oh yes, Iowa is part of the *Third World.* If you need convincing, just look at what third world countries do, then look at Iowa.

Typically a third world country has natural resources and human labor that it's willing to sell for a pittance, resources and labor that developed countries want, especially at bargain prices.

Does that fit Iowa? You bet. Iowa exports its produce and livestock, and in exchange receives a pittance. That is, the family farmer does. The profits from the small farmer's produce, stock, and hard work go to someone else, usually out of state. On

(Continued on next page)

BOX 12.1 (Continued)

the other hand, the corporate farmer makes good money because he's farming in volume. But the corporate farmer, more than likely, doesn't live in Iowa, but in some large metropolitan center like Chicago or Dallas. Thus the profits made from family and corporate Iowa farms flow across its borders.

The condition of the third world country worsens as its resources are gobbled up and its workers and farmers become more and more destitute. We see that happening here. Corn, Iowa's biggest crop, takes an enormous toll on one of Iowa's greatest natural resources, its soil. But federal subsidies for corn growers encourages this loss. And, of course, Iowa farmers, thanks to the present agricultural system, remain poor and continue leaving the land in a steady stream.

This situation occurs in third world countries when the industry and agricultural methods of developed countries — the colonizers — disrupt the traditional way of life in the colonies. It lures peasants from their land and villages for jobs in factories, mines, and deforestation crews.

Likewise Iowans continue to leave Iowa for opportunity elsewhere. Iowa's most valuable export, more important than its grain and livestock, is its high school and college graduates. They can't afford to stay.

The colonizer's economy takes away the native's self-sufficiency in a local economy and replaces it with dependence on the colonizer's economy. Control of their own lives is no longer in the hands of the locals.

That's Iowa's situation, and the situation of every other rural area in this nation, where local and regional economies have been destroyed, first under development of the national economy, later under pressure from an ever-growing international economy.

Meanwhile no one in Washington seems particularly concerned about the state of the third world within the United States' own borders.

Source: Robert Wolf, "Iowa: Living in the Third World," *Des Moines Register,* July 16, 1995. Reprinted with permission of the *Des Moines Register.*

through Georgia; the United States defoliated Vietnam's jungles; and Hussein set fire to the oilfields in Kuwait. Long after the wars are over, major unanticipated effects may occur. Fischer (1993) reminds us of the "Just Cause" invasion of Panama in 1989 which, along with imposed U.S. sanctions, broke the economy causing the people to turn to the land and take the forests. Just as war leads to environmental decimation, so does depleting the environment produce ethnic and territorial conflict. Waves of refugees fleeing war zones further ravage environmental resources (Hoff, 1995).

The techno-industrial military of the approaching twenty-first century is responsible for massive environmental pollution resulting from the development of biological, chemical, and nuclear weapons (Zeman, 1994). Hanford Reservation in Washington state, which produces weapons-grade plutonium used in the manufacture of nuclear bombs, constitutes a vast toxic waste legacy. Preparation for war and military operations in modern times is among the primary destroyers of the earth. In her annual statistics drawn from United Nations and government sources, Ruth Sivard (1993) estimates that, in the United States alone, environmental restoration will cost $100 billion over a twenty year period. In the former USSR, the cleanup of toxic residues is even more monumental.

The general trend toward increased militarism in our society is reflected in the fact that fifty cents of every federal tax dollar is spent on the military, while two cents is spent on the environment (Verschelden, 1993). Moreover, the United States has solidified its position as the world's leading weapons-trafficking nation, selling more than $36 billion worth of military equipment last year alone, according to a senior researcher at the World Policy Institute (Hartung, 1994). Weapons sold now generally end up being used against the United States later; this has happened in Panama, Iraq, and Somalia. U.S. government subsidies for weapons exports increase the weapon outflow.

Yet, as Boulding (1994) observes, the seeds of peace are here too, evidenced in the two thousand plus intergovernmental bodies created to deal with interstate problems such as acid rain, currency flows, and people flows. The seeds of peace are being sown in international treaties, global nongovernmental organizations, and the United Nations system itself. Mary and Morris (1994) urge social workers to look to their peers worldwide for solutions to problems, to make the connection "between the private violence of child abuse and the public violence of war, the individual's futile denial of drug addiction, and the international denial of nuclear and military addiction and the destruction of the earth's natural resources" (99).

ENVIRONMENTAL RACISM

Do we all live downstream and experience environmental toxicity equally or do some people bear the consequences disproportionately? This is the question that a loose coalition of church, civil rights, and community groups led by people of color is trying to get answered. In fact, we all know the answers. The incinerators and toxic-waste dumps, and the contaminated air, drinking water, and rivers are located disproportionately in African American neighborhoods and on Indian reservations. Enforcement of environmental laws, significantly, is far less vigorous in communities of color than in white communities. Because American Indian lands are self-governed, many of the states' waste management laws can be ignored by commercial waste operations. Tribes are offered financial incentives to allow their land to be used as toxic dumping ground (Rogge, 1994). In his collection of essays on environmental racism, sociologist Robert Bullard (1994) documents the glaring disparities in who pays the price of the nation's extravagant use of energy. Contained in his book, *Unequal Protection*, is the story of Louisiana's "Cancer Alley." Here in the lower Mississippi River valley where more than a quarter of the nation's chemicals are produced, incredibly high cancer rates are found. Activists organized to expose this fact have revealed to the world the severe health problems of children living near the industrial sites. In 1989 in a victory of sorts, Louisiana passed its first air quality act (Gore, 1992). Built from the grass roots up, the environmental justice movement is an effort with long-term implications for changing national policies.

CONCLUSION AND SUMMARY

Before he became known to the world as a best-selling novelist (for his book *Bridges of Madison County*), Robert Waller was known to Iowa as a professor of business management and an environmentalist. His environmental book, *Iowa: Perspectives on Today and Tomorrow* (1991), spoke with passion about farmers confronting poisoned wells, city dwellers building systems to remove nitrates from their water, and surplus crops steadily destroying the environment. Everywhere, concludes Waller, there is a lack of vision. And as we face inevitable scarcity—scarcity of potable water, fertile soil, and of compassion and caring as well—there is an almost total lack of imagination in finding ways of living more in harmony with the environment. We have to find ways to get beyond the old and limiting concepts and promote sustainable agriculture, a sustainable environment, and sustainable social welfare. This means not living beyond our own resources and not trampling on the rights of other people—as by toxic dumping, for instance. The dictates of the mass consumer culture, prodded by relentless marketing of luxury products, must be replaced with new models fostering the care of the earth and its people.

Erik Erikson's (1963) seventh life stage development crisis is *generativity versus stagnation* and has important implications for humans' relationship to the environment and its resources. As enunciated by Erikson, generativity involves what the older generation imparts to the young and what it leaves behind — the legacy of life from generation to generation. Protection of the environment is an active part of this legacy. In its absence, the opposite of generativity — stagnation — prevails. Although the statistics are fairly bleak concerning environmental havoc across the globe, there are many signs of hope. Consider these examples:

- Cuba is one place in the world where organic farming is being practiced on a large scale. Accordingly, this country is relatively independent of other countries and of transnational corporations. Oxen are being bred; they have a major advantage over tractors in that they don't compact the soil. The Amish point this out also.
- In New South Wales, Australia's most populous state, the wood-chipping industry is facing extinction due to environmentalist pressure to spare the forest (Rohde, 1995).
- Despite dire poverty and a horrendous AIDS outbreak, Kenya has made laudable progress in organizing family planning in decentralized programs reaching all areas (Chege, 1995).
- In Copenhagen, Denmark's prosperous capital, car ownership has dropped steadily over the years: the key to this success is the popularity of the bicycle enhanced by a network of cycle lanes (Knight, 1994).
- Twelve European countries agreed on a $76 billion proposal to link major cities by high-speed rail; two tracks of rail can carry as many people in an hour as sixteen lanes of highway — with far less energy and pollution (Lowe, 1994).

The gravest threat to our social welfare — habitat destruction — is a problem for which we have solutions as indicated above. One thing is for certain: countries of the world cannot go on doing what they are doing now. Environmentally, the world is interconnected; industrial fumes in one part of the earth travel over to pollute another part. With regard to contamination of the air, forests, and water, there are no national boundaries. As we have seen in this chapter, economic development and social development are not synonymous and very often gross business profits take place at the expense of natural resources. Governmental and world monetary policies that are penny-wise and pound-foolish have helped create some of the following situations worldwide:

- Shrinking arable land area due to development and population spread.
- Depletion of the world's fisheries due to overfishing.
- Most rapid population growth in the poorest regions of the world, much of it due to inadequate family planning efforts.
- Fossil fuel resources (oil, coal, and natural gas) are rapidly being depleted.
- Industrial air pollution killing trees within a radius of many hundreds of miles; loss of trees and pollutants in the air causing global warming.
- Soil erosion resulting from wasteful agricultural practices; ground water disappearing due to irrigation for farming of arid land and demands from urban development.
- Today our rivers, streams, oceans, and soils are laced with chemicals, and so are our bodies; in some parts of the world pesticides kill more people than do major diseases.

Many of the above problems could be alleviated through an emphasis on sustainable development. If the World Bank is to promote such development, economic success must be judged not by standard financial indicators but must be measured against the depreciation of natural assets such as forests and fisheries. In fact, there is evidence that, under pressure, the World Bank gradually is moving in this direction. Encouragingly, there is a growing movement worldwide to create sustainable cities and communities. Grass-roots organizations are beginning to make their influence felt in international forums. The time of making a distinction between economy on one hand and ecology on the other is over. Any ecological disaster is an economic disaster and vice versa. The world's military spending and preparation for war are destructive for both realms — for the environment and the economy. Yet this military spending could be, must be, redirected toward reclaiming the earth's resources. Replacing competition with creative and peaceful interdependence and mobilizing the world's nations toward global solutions are the challenges facing our species today. The social welfare professions, in coming to conceptualize the person-in-the-physical (as well as social) environment, have an important role to play in promoting human survival.

REVIEW QUESTIONS

1. What does chapter 12 add to the person-in-the-environment configuration of social work theory?
2. How could calculation of the GNP be changed to more accurately reflect economic reality?

3. What is the theory of the "green revolution"?
4. How has the environment been intentionally and accidentally despoiled by humans?
5. Discuss the idea of "man against nature." Contrast with progressive thinking today.
6. Define sustainability and the goals of sustainable development. What is happening through the United Nations?
7. Discuss the impact on the environment of overpopulation. What are the two contrasting views on this problem?
8. Discuss disturbing facts revealed in the UN report, *The World's Women 1995*.
9. Challenge Lord Byron's thoughts on the ocean. What is happening with regard to beaches and the sea?
10. What has been the impact of the Clean Water Act of 1972? How is water purity threatened worldwide?
11. What is the connection between the earth's vegetation and the atmosphere?
12. "What we turn against, turns against us." Discuss with relation to the soil.
13. Describe the risks to the environment of modern agricultural practices. What is the human price?
14. How is Rachel Carson's 1962 work *Silent Spring* relevant today?
15. Discuss the concept of the farm crisis. What has been the lot of the African American farmer?
16. List the various ways that warfare, directly and indirectly, is destructive of the environment.
17. What is environmental racism? Cite the facts.
18. Relate Erik Erikson's stage of generativity to facts revealed in this chapter.

REFERENCES

Agena, K. (1994, November 29). DDT Use Threatens Sustainable Agriculture. *Christian Science Monitor*: 19.

Associated Press. (1995, November 14). U.N. Report Tabulates Human Destruction. *Waterloo/Cedar Falls Courier*: A6.

Barlett, P. and P. Brown. (1994). Agricultural Development. In A. Podolefsky and P. Brown, eds. *Applied Cultural Anthropology*, 2d ed.: 109-116. Mountain View, CA: Mayfield.

Bateson, G. (1972). *Steps to an Ecology of Mind: Collected Essays in Anthropology, Psychiatry, Evolution, and Epistemology*. San Francisco: Chandler Pub. Co.

Bateson, M. (1990). *Composing a Life*. New York: Penguin.

Beeman, P. (1994, March 20). Earthly Issues Await Action. *Des Moines Register*: B1.

Begley, S. (1994, September 12). Can More=Better? *Newsweek*: 27.

Berger, R. and J. Kelly. (1993). Social Work in the Ecological Crisis. *Social Work* 38(5): 521–526.

Berry, W. (1993, March/April). Decolonizing Rural America. *Audubon*: 100–105.

———. (1977). *The Unsettling of America: Culture and Agriculture*. San Francisco: Sierra Club Books.

Boulding, E. (1994). The Dialectics of Peace. In E. and K. Boulding, eds. *The Future: Images and Processes*: 196–205). Thousand Oaks, CA: SAGE.

Brown, L. (1995). Nature's Limits. In L. Brown et al., eds. *State of the World 1995*: 3–20. New York: W.W. Norton and Company.

Brown, L., C. Flavin, and S. Postel. (1993). A Planet in Jeopardy. In J. Allen, ed. *Environment 93/94*, 12th ed.: 6–8. Guilford, CT: Dushkin.

Bullard, R. (1994). *Unequal Protection: Environmental Justice and Communities of Color*. San Francisco: Sierra Club Books.

Byron, Lord G. (1812). *Childe Harold's Pilgrimage*, st. 179. In J. Bartlett (1968). *Familiar Quotations,* 14th ed. Boston: Little, Brown and Company: 557.

Carson, R. (1962). *Silent Spring*. Boston: Houghton Mifflin Co.

Cheers, B. (1995, July 29–August 1). *Social Care in a Changing Rural World*. Paper presented at the International Social Welfare in a Changing World Conference: Calgary, Alberta.

Chege, N. (1995). Kenya's Plans for Its Children. *World Watch* 8(1): 20–22.

Corwin, J. (1994, September 12). Easing Gridlock, European-Style. *U.S. News and World Report*: 82–83.

Critchfield, R. (1994). *The Villages: Changed Values, Altered Lives: The Closing of the Rural-Urban Gap*. New York: Anchor/Doubleday.

Cronon, W. (1983). *Changes in the Land: Indians, Colonists, and the Ecology of New England*. New York: Hill and Wang.

Davidson, O. (1990). *Broken Heartland: The Rise of America's Rural Ghetto*. New York: Doubleday.

Enshayan, K. (1993, December 5). Iowa's Farm Woes Are a Chronic Illness. *Des Moines Sunday Register*: 5C.

Erikson, E. (1963). *Childhood and Society,* 2d ed. New York: Norton.

Estes, R. (1993). Toward Sustainable Development: From Theory to Praxis. *Social Development Issues* 15(3): 1–22.

Fischer, E. (1993). War and the Environment. In J. Allen, ed. *Environment 93/94*, 12th ed.: 73–38. Guilford, CT: Dushkin.

French, H. (1995, May). Forging a New Global Partnership to Save the Earth. *USA Today (Magazine)*: 76–80.

Gardner, G. (1995). Water Tables Falling. In L. Brown, N. Lenssen, and H. Kane, *Vital Signs 1995*: 122–123. New York: W.W. Norton and Company.

Glacken, C. (1971). Man Against Nature: An Outmoded Concept. In E. Penchef, ed. *Four Horsemen: Pollution, Poverty, Famine, Violence*: 16–27. San Francisco: Canfield Press.

..

Goering, L. (1995, November 26). Old, New Plagues a Latin Scourge. *Chicago Tribune*: A3.

Gore, A. (1992). *Earth in the Balance: Ecology and the Human Spirit.* Boston: Houghten Mifflen Co.

Hartung, W. (1994, June 27). Arms Control? U.S. Is Worst Offender. *USA Today*: 13A.

Healy, L. (1992). *Introducing International Development Context in Social Work Curriculum.* Washington, DC: NASW Press.

Hoff, M. (1995, July 29–August 1). *Physical Environmental Decline and Violent Conflict: An Exploration of the Linkage to Economic and Social Development.* Paper presented at the International Social Welfare in a Changing World: Calgary, Alberta.

Hoff, M. and J. McNutt. (1994) Introduction. In M. Hoff and J. McNutt, eds. *The Global Environmental Crisis: Implications for Social Welfare and Social Work*: 1–11. . Aldershot, England: Avebury.

Hoff, M. and R. Polack. (1993). Social Dimensions of the Environmental Crisis: Challenges for Social Work. *Social Work* 38: 204–211.

Jackson, W. (1993). Listen to the Land. *Amicus Journal* 15: 32–34.

Karger, H. and D. Stoesz. (1990). *American Social Welfare Policy: A Structural Approach.* New York: Longman.

Knight, R. (1994, September 12). Easing Gridlock, European Style. *U.S. News and World Report*: 82–83.

Kornblum, W. and J. Julian. (1992). *Social Problems*, 7th ed. Englewood Cliffs, NJ: Prentice-Hall.

Lambrecht, B. (1993, November 14). Pesticides Abuse Goes from Latin America to Your Table. *Waterloo/Cedar Falls Courier*: A1, 10.

Lekic, S. (1994, August 14). Population Boom Expected to Outstrip World Food Supply. *Courier Journal*: A10.

Lenssen, N. (1995). Coal Use Remains Flat. In L. Brown, N. Lenssen, and H. Kane, eds. *Vital Signs 1995*: 50. New York: W.W. Norton and Company.

Leopold, A. (1966). *A Sand Country Almanac.* New York: A Sierra Club/Ballantine Book.

Lowe, M. (1994, November/December). Back on Track. *Utne Reader*: 48–52.

Lusk, M. (1994). Foreward. In M. Hoff and J. McNutt, eds. *The Global Environmental Crisis: Implications for Social Welfare and Social Work:* xv–xvii. Aldershot, England: Avebury

MacFarquhar, E. (1994). Population Wars. *US News and World Report* 117(10): 54–57.

Manning, R. (1995). *Grassland.* New York: Viking Penguin.

Mary, N. and T. Morris. (1994). The Future and Social Work: A Global Perspective. *Journal of Multicultural Social Work* 3(4): 89–101.

Midgley, J. (1995). *Social Development: The Development Perspective in Social Welfare.* London: SAGE.

Pins, K. (1994, March 20). Agriculture Weighs Cost of Progress. *Des Moines Register*: J1, 2.

Rogge, M. (1994). Environmental Injustice: Social Welfare and Toxic Waste. In M. Hoff and J. McNutt, eds. *The Global Environmental Crisis: Implication for Social Welfare and Social Work*: 53–74. Aldershot, England: Avebury.

Rohde, D. (1995, June 27). In Australia, Environment Wins Over Jobs. *Christian Science Monitor*: 10–11.

Roodman, D. (1995). Carbon Emissions Resume Rise. In L. Brown, N. Lenssen, and H. Kane, eds. *Vital Signs 1995*: 66. New York: W.W. Norton and Company.

Sachs, I. (1995, March). Dismantling the Mechanism of Exclusion. *UNESCO Courier*: 9–13.

Satchell, M. (1992, June 22). The Rape of the Oceans. *U.S. News and World Report*: 64–68, 70–71, 75.

Silver, C. (1990). *One Earth: One Future*. Washington, DC: National Academy Press.

Sivard, R. (1993). *World Military and Social Expenditures 1993*. Washington, DC: World Priorities.

Slakey, B. (1994, November 10). Census Shows Number of U.S. Farms Down to Pre-Civil War Counts. *Waterloo/Cedar Falls Courier*: B6.

Smiley, J. (1991). *A Thousand Acres*. New York: Knopf.

Swander, M. (1995, March 21). A Farmer's Tale. *USA Today*: 9A.

United Nations. (1995). *The World's Women 1995*. New York: United Nations.

United Nations World Commission on Environment and Development. (1987). *Our Common Future*. Oxford: Oxford University Press.

van Hook, M. (1990). Family Response to the Farm Crisis: A Study in Coping. *Social Work* 35(5): 425–431.

Vellvé, R. (1993, March/April). The Decline of Diversity in European Agriculture. *Ecologist*: 64–69.

Verschelden, C. (1993). Social Work Values and Pacifism: Opposition to Wars as a Professional Responsibility. *Social Work* 38(6): 765–769.

Waller, R. (1991). *Iowa: Perspectives on Today and Tomorrow*. Ames: Iowa State.

Weber, P. (1994). Failing Coasts. *World Watch* 7(2): 20–29.

Weick, A. (1981). Reframing the Person-in-Environment Perspective. *Social Work* 26: 140–145.

Wilson, E. (1992). *The Diversity of Life*. New York: W.W. Norton and Company.

Zastrow, C. (1996). *Introduction to Social Work and Social Welfare*, 6th ed. Pacific Grove, CA: Brooks/Cole.

Zeman, C. (1994). Militarization, Misogyny, and Environmental Destruction. *The SEACer* 1(2): 1, 2.

EPILOGUE

Over the past decade or so and even during the writing of this book, the world economy has been changing at a rate that has never before been greater or faster. All of us are heirs to opportunities, knowledge access, and possibilities scarcely imaginable to our grandparents. At the same time, in the name of progress and to spur the global market, rainforests have been leveled, the atmosphere polluted, and people relocated by the millions. In our ever-shrinking universe, our global village, national economies increasingly are interdependent. Decisions that affect all of us are made on Wall Street, by the World Bank, and transnational corporations. Across continents, aided by the tools of computer technology, the flow of capital and ideas is happening at the speed of light. As international corporations have grown into transnational corporations whose interests transcend the interests of any one state or enterprise, the national thrust to be commercially competitive becomes all-encompassing. Accordingly, the trend in one country—privatization, industrial automation, downsizing, cost-efficiency—is the trend in every country. Clearly, one could say the global market calls the shots. Or does it?

The capitalists are united globally and therefore the world's people are united in a global awareness. A crisis in one region of the world has a ripple effect at the other end of the globe. Common crises often lead to common solutions, and common solutions often lead to common crises. The workers of the world may not be united but the women of the world are coming together under United Nations auspices in ways never before imagined, as are the world's indigenous populations, gays, lesbians and bisexuals, environmentalists, and the advocates for children. Nongovernmental organizations such as the Red Cross, Save the

Children, Amnesty International, and World Watch gather the facts and present them before world bodies and the world media.

International business, international activism — what does all this have to do with social welfare? World developments, as we have seen throughout the chapters of this volume, have profound implications for the needs of a nation's people (for example, the availability of jobs, health care, etc.) and for the way these needs are addressed.

An international perspective is invaluable for knowing how other nations resolve the age-old tension between people's rights as proclaimed in international law — the right to meet one's physical and social needs, protection from discrimination and against arbitrary powers of the state — and the demands of the market. Put simply, the universal paradox of welfare is how to achieve a balance between people's entitlements and conflicting economic demands. The paradox of welfare is the central theme of this book. A comparative perspective was adopted to provide a context within which the uniqueness of American individualism, strident work ethic, and ambivalent approach to the social welfare state could be understood. A comparative perspective was adopted, furthermore, to reveal the possibilities and innovations not only from Canada and Europe, but from further afield. So many places in the world are facing the same issues — rethinking the boundaries for social care between the family and the state, reckoning with the aging of the population, and bearing responsibility toward marginalized groups including the aged, women, and ethnically diverse. We are all more or less in the same boat, in other words. But because of cultural distinctions, the solutions to common problems may be decidedly different. (For example, in the face of mass unemployment, one country may require the few to work harder and lay off the rest; another country may strive to spread the work around.)

SCOPE OF THE BOOK

International insights inform the several major divisions of this text. The scope of the book was daunting: first, the topic of social welfare, referring to the well-being of a people and a state's efforts toward this end, is extremely broad in itself; second, to span the globe on so many separate issues compounded the original task. But a major difficulty, as mentioned previously, was in keeping abreast of the changes. Relative to the United States, for instance, during the writing of this book, the government went from a plan to expand health care to all the people to proposals to shrink the offerings while military expenditures moved in the opposite direction—from agreed-upon retraction to unexpected expansion. On a more immediate note, somewhere between the writing of chapters 2 through 10, O.J. Simpson went from indictment to acquittal in the double homicide case that seized the attention of the media. While media attention focused on what was billed as "the trial of the century," right-wing generated attacks against so-called government handouts for the poor and disabled carried the day. In the absence of any formidable opposition, a hatchet was taken to programs involving persons with little political clout and proposal after proposal for "adjustments" became an inevitability. These kinds of adjustments were made not only in the United States, but in virtually every country studied, to the extent that exemplary programs that could be singled out for emulation when I began the writing of the text no longer seemed so exemplary at its end. It was hard to write new material for the constant necessity of going back and updating sections that once had seemed over and done with. Visits to both England and Canada during the period of the writing led to even greater awareness of a revolution of sorts and confirmed my sense that what is happening here is happening there and vice versa.

A second major difficulty in shaping a text of this sort pertains to the nature of the subject matter itself—controversial, emotionally laden, and at times, jarring to the senses. A few examples of the kind of material dealt with: loyal workers tossed to the winds as profitable companies downsize; women throughout the world dying in childbirth and illegal abortion due to lack of proper medical care; genital mutilation of young females; girls starving as their brothers thrive; small boys recruited as soldiers and deliberately brutalized; executions, hate crimes, and atrocities of war. The challenge was to be objective but not dispassionate. For verification of facts that seemed somewhat astonishing or even possibly exaggerated, I drew upon multiple sources, relying heavily on *The Wall Street Journal* and *Business Week* for economic developments, and on the United Nations and other reputable international sources for statistics and trends from data. News reports from around the world and from the *Christian Science Monitor* which stations reporters across the globe and covers world events faithfully, were helpful in providing human interest accounts of current happenings. Social work literature furnished a holistic, humanistic perspective that helped me place disparate facts in theoretical context, to see the interplay, for example, of sexism, ageism, classism, and racism.

Part I was constructed to lay out the theoretical context, to offer the framework for later discussion and more specifically, the framework for the social welfare systems for Canada, Japan, Mexico, Sweden, and Great Britain as well. Although economics tempers the scope of social welfare offerings, what emerges as paramount is the cultural value system of a given country. A nation that stresses cooperation and equality above competition, for instance, will have different kinds of social policies than a society stressing individual achievement over sharing the wealth. Because culture and history are so intertwined, two chapters were devoted to an examination of cultural themes and ideologies which varied with the times. Social work, the profession most closely associated with social welfare, was viewed historically and internationally. The key question whether or not social work has lost its mission was answered in the negative. Geared toward both the personal and the political, social work offers therapy and other forms of intervention to help individuals heal and ideally to increase their political awareness. Unique to this profession is its orientation toward community and political action to alleviate oppression. Strikingly, the social work profession itself is composed of many individuals who themselves are members of oppressed groups or who have known and overcome oppression. Working both within the system as the representatives of the social order, and on the periphery of the system to effect social change, social workers have often had to improvise, discover new ways of doing things, and chart new courses. Historically, they have battled bigotry, rigidity, and the pettiness of "red tape." Many, of course, have succumbed along the way, burning out and/or bending whichever way the political wind blows. Many others, happily, have managed to acquire some vestige of what I call the *social work imagination.*

The quest for the *social work imagination* reaches back to the world of our inheritance, to our foremothers—Addams, Konopka, and Reynolds—and forward to a burgeoning New Age of ecological awareness. By ecological awareness, I mean a sense of the synthesis, connectedness of things. Everything is connected: future to the past, the parts to the whole, the biological to the social, the inner to the outer (body, mind, etc.), personal to political, the local to the global. The future of potential social work lies in our grasping the essence of this awareness, this almost spiritual sense of beingness and relatedness. Perhaps, in this way, we can recapture some of the psychic and creative energies that have gone into making the field of social work what it is today.

The social work imagination begins by examining the person in the environment and the environment in the person; it proceeds by drawing on the human qualities of empathy, critical thinking, consciousness raising and altruism, and concludes by reconciling differences whether between individuals, groups, or ideas. Against the tyranny of economic constraints, the social work imagination allows for a nurturance of the deeper questions such as: How can we end violence? Do we start with the family or the world or both? How do we promote the central social work values of self-determination, human rights, and social equity when human resources are drained to finance a war economy? Finally, what is the role of social work in all of this?

Our struggle is about creating sustainable lives in a sustainable universe; our mission is to promote peace and justice globally through working to eradicate racism, poverty, sexism, homophobia, and other forms of oppression worldwide. At the professional level, our call is to educate ourselves and others toward a world view, to further internationalize social work for an active leadership role in the twenty-first century, a century which promises to be at once dangerously and excitingly global.

Part II, I conceived ambitiously, almost masochistically, as a means of taking social welfare with its world view through the life span from birth to death. My underlying rationale was this: Just as the way a society treats its children reveals much about family, gender, and work and government and how they interconnect, so does protection of workers—from stress, unemployment, illness, retirement—and so does care provided to the elderly. A truth that emerged through this section of the book was that inequities and maltreatment practiced against one age group, the young, are carried forward into a later period of development. Thus children born in poverty are likely to suffer in their work histories and die in old age or prematurely in a situation of extreme dependency on others. There was much that was gripping but also horrendous in this part of the book—the brutalization of children throughout the world; the tragedies of workers retired prematurely in Western countries into nothingness and worked to death in conditions of debt bondage elsewhere; the prevalence of elder abuse in institutions and the home.

Delving into human rights issues, part III covered the gamut from marginalized populations, to social justice, criminal justice, and through exploitation of the physical environment. From what would be an otherwise grim account of the persecution of the world's peoples through such tactics as hate crimes and "ethnic cleansing," hope shines through in the momentum of community empowerment and international activism. The appeal of human rights violations before the United Nations is bringing about results, at least in nations concerned with world opinion. Many countries are endeavoring to follow the principles of international law. This volume concludes with an appeal for a sustainable environment to be transmitted by present generations to our children and our children's children. Chapter 12, although last, is not an afterthought or addendum to the book; rather, it is a culmination of what has gone before. Nowhere is the global village concept as relevant as in our management of our physical resources — contamination of the water and earth in one country may produce a drought or flood somewhere else; human and environmental health are closely interlinked as well. How much the global environment is of a piece, interconnected, I did not fully realize until I had almost put my pen to the final sections of this book. This was when facts that once had seemed somehow discrete began to come together in interesting and meaningful ways. Consider the fact that today there is unprecedented human migration across the earth. The migration is both cause and effect, a cause of ecological damage as refugees exploit the earth in their struggle to survive, and the effect of ecological devastation which creates large numbers of rootless people. War, overpopulation, and ecological problems keep people on the move which, in turn, produces situations ripe for conflict and war.

THEMES OF THE BOOK

Interactionism, a guiding motif of social work theory, is one theme of this text. This nonlinear, nondichotomous approach to human behavior is concerned with the dimensions of interconnectedness. Two chapter titles reflected this theme in combining mixed elements: work and family welfare (chapter 7) and health care and housing (chapter 8). Work problems threaten the family survival and family problems threaten the work environment. Poor health care can lead to loss of housing and vice versa. The variables in chapters 7 and 8 are interrelated with each other. The collapse of a clear-cut relationship between economic growth and increasing prosperity for the average family is an important political event with ramifications that are only beginning to be realized. Thriving industries now reduce their work force, asking fewer people to do more work. Ultimately, however, what goes around will come around. With prosperity declining, who will be able to buy the new cars and endless gadgets that sophisticated technology produces? Who among the overworked workers will have the leisure time to use them?

Another theme interwoven throughout this book is the importance of *prevention*, prevention in contradistinction to treatment. The challenge for social work at the dawn of the millenium will be to promote national and international efforts in health care toward care rather than cure as in child rearing and criminal justice. Prevention of disease, bloodshed, and family break-up requires collective efforts directed against environmental contamination; the dumping of dangerous pesticides from one country to another; the accumulation of wealth in the hands of a few at the expense of the many; the sale of arms to poor nations where military spending exceeds the spending on education or health, firearm availability; wars, poverty, corporal and capital punishment; and the exploitation of children as prostitutes and bonded-out laborers. In rich countries such as in the United States and Canada, there is no question about our ability to feed and clothe and house everyone; it is a question of national priorities and values and weighing of short-term over long-term goals. Social policies, if they are just, will prevent homelessness, poverty, overpopulation, mass unemployment, mass imprisonment, and preventable disease. Far better to invest money at the front end rather than paying for expensive emergency treatment to correct a condition which could have been prevented in the first place. By rechanneling the energy investment, in fact, many social welfare programs offering special aid to various needy groups could be done away with entirely.

The challenge to social work and to our social work imagination involves taking the meaning of social welfare to a higher plane—a plane of political consciousness such as the world never before has seen. Only through alliances across national borders can the power of the transnational corporations be checked, and the focus of international financial institutions such as the World Bank be redirected toward social as opposed to mere economic development. The globalization of the economy must be matched by the globalization of environmental standards, health regulations, and labor rights. Otherwise industry, as now, will gravitate toward the lowest common denominator—the lowest bid for the work and the weakest environmental standards.

In truth there can be no dichotomy between international social welfare and domestic welfare, or between economic interests and the people's interests. The short-term benefits may vary, but in the long term, the advantage to one is the advantage to all. For what use is money without resources—clean air, water, and land? Of what use is the profitable manufacturing of splendid goods if there is no market to purchase them? Of what use is military might (or arms-sales) if it risks the lives of us all? In the end, there is a common ground between the economy and the people. Hopefully, the renewed internationalization of social work and of social work education combined with a heightened appreciation of the personal as political, and of the local as global, will facilitate the kind of sustainable development that ultimately is and must be everyone's goal.

INDEX

INDEX